613.2
G 369c

Geriatric Nutrition

The Health Professional's Handbook

Edited by

Ronni Chernoff, PhD, RD

Associate Director
Geriatric Research Education and Clinical Center
John L. McClellan Memorial Veterans' Hospital

Professor
Dietetics and Nutrition
College of Health Related Professions
University of Arkansas for Medical Sciences
Little Rock, Arkansas

AN ASPEN PUBLICATION®
Aspen Publishers, Inc.
Gaithersburg, Maryland
1991

Library of Congress Cataloging-in-Publication Data

Geriatric nutrition : the health professional's handbook / edited by Ronni Chernoff.
p. cm.
Includes bibliographical references and index.
ISBN: 0-8342-0228-X
1. Aged—Nutrition. I. Chernoff, Ronni.
[DNLM: 1. Aging—physiology—handbooks. 2. Nutrition—in old age—handbooks.
QU 39 G369]
RC952.5.G44342 1991
612'.084'6—dc20
DNLM/DLC
for Library of Congress
91-17210
CIP

Aspen Publishers, Inc., is not affiliated with the American Society
of Parenteral and Enteral Nutrition

The authors have made every effort to ensure the accuracy of the information herein, particularly with regard to drug selection and dose. However, appropriate information sources should be consulted, especially for new or unfamiliar drugs or procedures. It is the responsibility of every practitioner to evaluate the appropriateness of a particular opinion in the context of actual clinical situations and with due consideration to new developments. Authors, editors, and the publisher cannot be held responsible for any typographical or other errors found in the book.

Editorial Services: Ruth Bloom

Library of Congress Catalog Card Number: 91-17210
ISBN: 0-8342-0228-X

Printed in the United States of America

1 2 3 4 5

This book is dedicated to
my father Samuel
Who taught me how to dance, how to dream,
and how to joust with windmills
With love

Table of Contents

Contributors . . . .   **xi**

Forewords . . . .   **xv**

Preface . . . .   **xix**

Chapter   1—Demographics of Aging **1**
            Ronni Chernoff

            Demographic Trends   2
            Impact on the Health Care System   5
            Quality of Life and Health Status   5
            Health Care Costs   6
            Conclusion   8

Chapter   2—Macronutrient Requirements for Elderly Persons **11**
            William J. Carter

            Protein Metabolism and Requirements   11
            Age and Energy Requirement   15
            Water Intake in Elderly Persons   17
            Desirable Fat Intake in Elderly Persons   18
            Dietary Restrictions and Longevity   21
            Conclusion   21

Chapter 3—Vitamin Requirements **25**
Paolo M. Suter

Vitamin A 26
Vitamin D 28
Vitamin E 30
Vitamin K 32
Vitamin C 33
Vitamin B_1 35
Vitamin B_2 36
Niacin 37
Vitamin B_6 37
Folate 39
Vitamin B_{12} 40
Biotin 42
Pantothenic Acid 42
Conclusion 42

Chapter 4—Mineral Requirements **53**
Robert D. Lindeman and Amanda A. Beck

Sodium 53
Potassium 60
Calcium 66
Phosphorus 72
Magnesium 72
Conclusion 74

Chapter 5—Trace Metal Requirements **77**
Gary J. Fosmire

Zinc 78
Copper 84
Chromium 88
Selenium 91
Aluminum 93
Molybdenum 95
Manganese 96
Nickel 98
Iodine 99
Conclusion 100

Chapter 6—Oral Health in the Elderly **107**
Wendy E. Martin

Review of Anatomy and Functions of the Oral Cavity ... 107
Oral Health Status and Needs in the Elderly 111
Changes in Oral and Circumoral Structures
    with Aging 113
Changes in Oral and Circumoral Structures
    with Disease 119
Systemic Diseases and Medications Affecting
    Oral Health 137
Impact of Nutritional Status on Oral Health 149
Impact of Oral Health on Nutritional Status 155
Conclusion 164

Chapter 7—The Aging Gut **183**
Michael D. Cashman

Aging and the Gastrointestinal System 183
Esophagus 184
Stomach/Duodenum 192
Pancreas 193
Small Intestine 198
Intestinal Disorders 201
Liver.. 207
Colon 215
Conclusion 218

Chapter 8—Aging and the Cardiovascular System **229**
Jeanne P. Goldberg

The Disease Processes 230
Risk Factors and Their Modification in Elderly
    Subjects 234
Conclusion 247

Chapter 9—The Aging Renal System **253**
Robert D. Lindeman

Changes in Renal Morphology with Age 253
Changes in Renal Function with Age 255

Age-Related Changes in Renal Response to
Environmental Alterations   261
Pathophysiology of Age-Related Decline in Renal
Function   262
Compensatory Renal Hypertrophy   263
Role of Hyperperfusion, Hyperfiltration, and Renal
Reserve   263
Conclusion   266

Chapter 10—Impact of Nutrition on the Age-Related Declines in
Hematopoiesis **271**
David A. Lipschitz

Effect of Age on the Hematopoietic System   271
Does Anemia Occur As a Consequence of
Normal Aging?   273
Hematologic Manifestations of Protein Energy
Malnutrition in the Elderly   276
Iron Deficiency Anemia   280
Folic Acid   283
Conclusion   285

Chapter 11—Skeletal Aging **289**
Christine Snow-Harter and Robert Marcus

Organization of the Skeleton   289
Measurement of Bone Mineral Density   290
Role of Bone Remodeling   293
Changes in Bone Mass with Age   293
Onset of Bone Loss   295
Changes at Menopause   299
Peak Bone Density   300
Loss in Bone Mass and Bone Strength   301
Mechanisms of Bone Mass Regulation   302
Conclusion   306

Chapter 12—Endocrine Aspects of Nutrition and Aging **311**
John E. Morley and Zvi Glick

Nutritional Aspects of Diabetes Mellitus   311
Thyroid Function   317
Adrenal Cortex   320

Water Metabolism 321
Growth Hormone and Insulin Growth Factors 322
Male Hypogonadism 322
Calcium Metabolism 323
Hormonal Regulation of Energy Balance 324
Conclusion 329

Chapter 13—Pharmacology, Nutrition, and the Elderly:
   Interactions and Implications **337**
Jeffrey B. Blumberg and Paolo Suter

Extent and Patterns of Drug Use by the Elderly 337
Age-Related Pharmacokinetic Changes 339
Age-Related Pharmacodynamic Changes 342
Food Choice and Nutritional Status of the Elderly 344
Drug Effects on Nutritional Status 345
Food Effects on Drug Therapy 350
Effect of Nutrient Supplements on Drug Therapy 352
Implications for Aging 354
Conclusion 355

Chapter 14—Nutritional Assessment of the Elderly **363**
Carol O. Mitchell and Ronni Chernoff

Clinical Assessment 364
Anthropometric Assessment 369
Biochemical Measures 383
Immunologic Measures 386
Hematologic Measures 387
Dietary Assessment 387
Conclusion 389

Chapter 15—Nutritional Support in the Elderly **397**
Ronni Chernoff

Indications for Nutritional Support 397
— Oral Supplements 399
Enteral Feeding 401
Parenteral Nutrition 408
Home Nutritional Support 410
Conclusion 411

Chapter 16—Nutrition Services for Older Americans **415**
Barbara Millen Posner and Elyse Levine

Health and Nutritional Status 416
Public Policy Statements 417
Nutritional Excesses 419
Nutrient Deficiencies 422
Risk of Malnutrition in the Elderly 422
Providing Nutrition Services to Older Persons 425
Community-Based Programs for Older Adults 431
Nutrition Services Payment Systems 436
Medicare 437
Medicaid 441
Blue Cross/Blue Shield and Other Commercial
    Carriers 441
Department of Veterans Affairs System 442
Conclusion 442

Chapter 17—Health Promotion and Disease Prevention in the
                Elderly **449**
Ann Sorenson, Nancy Chapman, and David N. Sundwall

Types of Prevention 450
General Considerations for Successful Health Promotion
    and Disease Prevention 451
Health Promotion and Disease Prevention for
    Older Adults 452
Aging versus Pathology 455
Strategies for Disease Prevention and Health Promotion
    in Old Age 458
Training of Health Professionals 474
Conclusion 475

Index **485**

Contributors

Amanda A. Beck, MD, PhD
Medical Director, Nursing Home Care Unit
Albuquerque Veterans Medical Center
Assistant Professor of Medicine
Department of Medicine
University of New Mexico School of Medicine
Albuquerque, New Mexico

Jeffrey B. Blumberg, PhD, FACN
Associate Director and Professor
Chief, Antioxidants Research Laboratory
USDA Human Nutrition Research Center on
  Aging
Tufts University
Boston, Massachusetts

William J. Carter, MD
Chief, Geriatrics
Little Rock VA Medical Center
Professor of Medicine
University of Arkansas for Medical Sciences
Little Rock, Arkansas

**Michael D. Cashman, MD, FACP,
  FACG**
Clinical Associate Professor of Medicine
University of Illinois College of Medicine at
  Peoria
Chairman, Department of Medicine
Methodist Medical Center of Illinois
Peoria, Illinois

Nancy Chapman, RD, MPH
President
Chapman Associates, Inc.
Washington, DC

Ronni Chernoff, PhD, RD
Associate Director
Geriatric Research Education and Clinical
  Center
John L. McClellan Memorial Veterans'
  Hospital
Professor
Dietetics and Nutrition
College of Health and Related Professions
University of Arkansas for Medical Sciences
Little Rock, Arkansas

Gary J. Fosmire, PhD
Associate Professor of Nutrition Science
Department of Nutrition
The Pennsylvania State University
University Park, Pennsylvania

Zvi Glick, PhD
Professor of Medicine
University of California, Los Angeles
Associate Chief of Education
Sepulveda VA Medical Center
Sepulveda, California

Jeanne P. Goldberg, PhD, RD
Assistant Professor
School of Nutrition
Tufts University
Medford, Massachusetts

Elyse Levine, MS, RD
Consultant
Health and Medical Communication
Northport, Alabama

Robert D. Lindeman, MD
Associate Chief of Staff for Geriatrics/Extended
  Care
Albuquerque VA Medical Center
Chief, Division of Geriatric Medicine
Department of Medicine
University of New Mexico School of Medicine
Albuquerque, New Mexico

David A. Lipschitz, MD, PhD
Professor of Medicine
University of Arkansas for Medical Sciences
Director, Geriatric Research Education and
  Clinical Center
John L. McClellan Memorial Veterans'
  Hospital
Head, Division on Aging
University of Arkansas for Medical Sciences
Little Rock, Arkansas

Robert Marcus, MD
Professor of Medicine
Stanford University
Director, Aging Study Unit
Geriatrics Research Education and Clinical
  Center
VA Medical Center
Palo Alto, California

Wendy E. Martin, DDS, MPH
Staff Gerodontist
Dental Service
John L. McClellan Memorial Veterans'
  Hospital
Little Rock, Arkansas

Carol O. Mitchell, PhD, RD
Assistant Professor
Nutrition Graduate Program
Department of Home Economics
Memphis State University
Memphis, Tennessee

John E. Morley, MB, BCh
Dammert Professor of Gerontology
St. Louis University School of Medicine
Director, Geriatric Research Education and
  Clinical Center
St. Louis VA Medical Center
St. Louis, Missouri

Barbara Millen Posner, DrPH, RD
Assistant Director for Research
Boston University
School of Public Health
Director, Nutrition Research
The Framingham Study
Boston, Massachusetts

Irwin H. Rosenberg, MD
Professor and Director
USDA Human Nutrition Research Center on
  Aging
Tufts University
Boston, Massachusetts

Maurice E. Shils, MD, ScD
Department of Public Health Sciences
The Bowman Gray School of Medicine
Wake Forest University
Winston-Salem, North Carolina

Christine Snow-Harter, PhD
Assistant Professor
Department of Exercise and Sport Science
Oregon State University
Corvallis, Oregon

Ann Sorenson, PhD
Director, Nutrition and Aging Office
Biology of Aging Program
National Institute on Aging
National Institutes of Health
Bethesda, Maryland

David N. Sundwall, MD
Vice President and Medical Director
AMHS Institute
Washington, DC

Paolo M. Suter, MD
Institute of Physiology
Medical Faculty
University of Lausanne
Lausanne, Switzerland

Forewords

Just as the numbers of the elderly are increasing dramatically throughout the world, so also are concepts of the aging process undergoing dramatic change. Indeed, the fastest growing segment of the population of most industrialized nations is that group over the age of 85. Presently, nearly 1 in 10 of the American population is over the age of 65 and that number will double in the early years of the 21st century. The magnitude of this demographic shift can only be appreciated if one observes that at the beginning of this century, only 1 in 25 of the population was over the age of 65. There is perhaps no greater long-term challenge to our social and health care systems than that imposed by this growing population which tends to consume such a large amount of the total health care and long-term care resources.

Until recently the declining physical and cognitive function that has been associated with the aging process has been considered to be an inevitable consequence of aging. Only in the last few decades, however, has the process of aging come under much more detailed scrutiny and only in the past 1 or 2 decades has there been close attention to those environmental and behavioral factors that might influence the aging process. Among the most important of these factors is diet and nutrition and only now are we beginning to understand the differences in the older patient in respect to physiological handling of food, diet, and nutrients and the manner in which these processes affect nutritional requirements. As we learn more about these age-related changes, we also learn that the declining functions associated with aging are not inevitable consequences of aging or age-related degenerative diseases. Indeed, we learn that diet is important both for its effect on the risk of certain degenerative conditions such as heart disease, diabetes, osteoporosis, and also for the way in which dietary and nutritional factors may influence the aging process.

A book such as *Geriatric Nutrition: The Health Professional's Handbook* is important therefore, not only because it provides guidance based on current information of how best to meet the dietary and nutritional requirements of the growing older population, but also because much of this information addresses appropriately the pregeriatric or middle age years when many of the processes and habits that determine future health and independence are established.

By addressing the changes in individual organ systems with aging, this book provides a basis for approaching the prevention of degenerative conditions as well as providing guidelines for their most effective nutritional and dietary management. Translating the results of contemporary research into practical approaches to dietary and nutritional management, this text will contribute to a much more comprehensive approach to the care of older persons in hospitals, nursing homes, as well as at home. Nothing short of such comprehensive care will meet the challenge that we face to maintain the highest quality of life throughout the span of years.

Irwin H. Rosenberg, MD
Professor and Director
USDA Human Nutrition Research Center on Aging
Tufts University
Boston, Massachusetts

As we view the very wide spectrum of health and disease problems of elderly men and women, it becomes clear that the emphasis on prevention must extend over the lifetime of the individual. The goal is a continuum of physical and mental well-being for as long as possible. The rapid and massive increase of our elderly population makes the issue of prevention not only an individual matter, but also a national issue of profound social, economic, and political importance. Adequate prevention initiatives must include continuing health surveillance, health care, and health promotion through effective systems for all citizens.

There is much more to be learned about the amelioration, retardation, and prevention of the chronic diseases affecting so many elderly persons. Nevertheless, biomedical research has given us clear evidence that early detection and prevention measures are effective in cardiovascular disease, osteoporosis, type II diabetes, and hypertension. Diet and nutrition are key in the prevention and management of each. Our knowledge about the roles of diet and nutrition in cancer prevention and control remains rudimentary with a poor scientific base; however, recent advances in the understanding of the molecular biology of cancer initiation, promotion, and progression give great promise that the roles of diet and nutrition in other chronic diseases will be given more objective substance and direction for application. Meanwhile general recommendations for a prudent diet emphasizing fruits and vegetables appear warranted.

The contributions in this volume review our current knowledge about the effects of aging on nutrient needs and problems that still require answers. Another area of nutrition that may prove to be of practical importance relates to the potential enhancement of immunologic and other physiologic defenses by an increased provision of food substances that we have considered to be either nonessential in adult life or needed in much smaller amounts to prevent deficiency symptoms and signs. For example, arginine is not considered to be an essential beyond the period of active growth; it is, therefore, of great interest to learn that, in a normal individual, relatively large supplements of arginine significantly enhance lymphocyte cytotoxicity.[1] This confirms prior laboratory animal research. Wattenberg and others have convincingly demonstrated that non-nutrient components of certain foods can block or suppress certain carcinogens.[2] Provisions of alpha linolenic acid, or its higher homologs, in amounts appreciably higher than needed to prevent essential fatty acid deficiency, are associated with important metabolic effects in immune and lymphokine reactions, blood clotting, and experimental cancer therapies.

To help meet the need for widespread and effective prevention measures, there is need for improved education, not only for the public, but also health care professionals at all levels. The cooperation of many groups and many disciplines in the recently organized effort of the Nutrition Screening Initiative is a much needed, and potentially effective, effort on behalf of the elderly. A much more vigorous effort is essential in the field of medical education at undergraduate, graduate, and postgraduate levels concerning the importance of nutrition and diet in prevention of chronic illnesses as part of medical care of all adults. This type of education needs to be included in all aspects of medical education, i.e., all lectures, case presentations, and bedside teaching must incorporate a view of preventive aspects as well as disease management. In the area of dietitian/ nutritionist education and practice, increased attention needs to be given to effective skills and experience in prevention. There is the need for increasing subspecialty training and practice for clinical dietitians in hospital settings and as well as for teaching faculty in clinical departments. It is obvious that we still have much to learn and to do, and the discipline of nutritional science is alive and well despite its increasing age.

1. Park KGM, Hayes PD Garlic PJ, et al. Stimulation of lymphocyte natural cytotoxicity by arginine. *Lancet.* 1991;337:645–646.

2. Wattenberg LW. Inhibition of carcinogenesis by minor constituents of the diet. *Proc Nut Soc (UK).* 1990;49:173–183.

Maurice E. Shils, MD, ScD
Department of Public Health Sciences
The Bowman Gray School of Medicine
Wake Forest University
Winston-Salem, North Carolina

Preface

Until recently, geriatric nutrition was thought of in terms of modifying the textures of food. Recognition of the relationships that exist among physiologic aging, chronic and acute disease conditions, and nutrition have taken some time; these relationships are difficult to define and even more difficult to classify. This is due to the lifelong interactions between nutrition and health, and the experiences that are unique to each individual which impact on the rate and manner in which people age. There are so many uncontrolled variables that impact on the human condition that it is difficult to isolate any of them and assign a degree of responsibility for health or disabling conditions.

The purpose of this book is to examine the impact of physiologic aging on nutritional requirements, to review some of the effects of illness, to discuss health promotion strategies, and to consider intervention methods. The contributing authors are renowned experts in their field who have conducted research in their areas of interest. They have written state-of-the-art chapters that will provide the health professional with a text that explores geriatric nutrition more thoroughly and with a perspective not previously seen in books that focus on this topic.

The first chapter addresses some of the issues facing our society due to the demographic shifts in the population and the effect this change will have on the future of the American health care system. The next four chapters deal with nutrient requirements in healthy elderly people, including macronutrient (protein, fat, carbohydrate, water), vitamin, mineral, and trace metal requirements. These chapters reflect current information on specific nutrient requirements for older adults.

The next chapters review the manner in which aging affects most of the organ systems. The gastrointestinal tract is divided into two chapters because of the importance of oral health on nutritional intake and nutritional status in elderly persons. The first of the two chapters discusses oral health and its relationship to general health status, the impact of disease on oral health, and the influence of oral health on nutritional status as well as other oral health-related issues. The following chapter focuses on the aging gut from the esophagus to the colon. This chapter examines the mechanical, digestive, and absorptive activities of the gastrointestinal tract, including liver, gall bladder, and pancreatic functions.

The circulatory, renal, hematologic, skeletal, and endocrine systems are discussed in some detail in the next chapters. These chapters contribute to a greater understanding of physiologic aging and the role that nutrition plays in chronic illness and as an interventional factor. Some interesting aspects of aging and nutrition are discussed in these chapters; the hope is that these discussions contribute to a broader understanding of human aging and the various roles of nutrition in the process.

One of the insidious problems that is frequently experienced by older people is polypharmacy; for this reason, an entire chapter has been devoted to pharmacology, nutrition, and aging. Elderly people use more prescription medications, and probably more over-the-counter drugs, than do younger people. The interactions between drugs and nutrition may have serious consequences on the health and maintenance of homeostasis in elderly people.

The impact of aging on the parameters that are commonly used to assess nutritional status is discussed in the following chapter. The various components of a comprehensive nutritional assessment must be carefully considered and applied appropriately to provide an accurate picture of an individual's nutritional status. This is an important activity to undertake so that appropriate nutritional interventions can be selected and successfully administered to elderly patients in a variety of care settings. The next chapter describes indications and techniques for nutritional support for use in elderly patients.

Nutritional support may require more than an adequate knowledge of intervention techniques. Many free-living elderly people can avoid the consequences of malnutrition and avoid institutionalization due to deteriorating health status if intervention is early and effective. Nutrition services for older Americans are available and successful. One of the problems associated with nutrition services is related to a lack of awareness of available programs and eligibility requirements. The next chapter describes the services and programs that are available for elderly Americans.

Last, but certainly not least, is the topic of health promotion and disease prevention. Whereas this chapter has been written with a focus on aging, much of the advice provided, and interventions described, are applicable to younger individuals. I hope that the reader of any age will benefit from the discussion of these authors.

All of us who contributed to this book recognize that it is not the perfect text, and it will always be incomplete because of all we have learned since it was written, but we think that it approaches geriatric nutrition in a rationale and unique way. The hope is that it will contribute to a greater understanding of aging and nutrition. Perhaps it will contribute to the reader's successful aging and will support efforts to enhance aging in others.

Ronni Chernoff, PhD, RD

Chapter 1

Demographics of Aging

Ronni Chernoff

Aging is a process experienced by all living creatures as they approach their predestined life spans. It has been described as "intrinsic, deleterious, universal, progressive and irreversible."[1] Most likely, it begins when growth and development cease, and it is a uniquely individual experience that is affected by many factors over which individuals have no control; even geriatrics experts do not possess the ability to predict how aging will occur in any particular individual. In fact, society and tradition have provided an arbitrary age—65 years—as a demarcation between middle age and old age that has no basis in the study of human aging processes. Biologic aging occurs on a continuum that varies among individuals. The arbitrary age of 65 years was established in the 1880s by Bismarck as the dividing line beyond which people became eligible for retirement pensions.[1]

Factors that may affect individual aging include such diverse occurrences as genetic inheritance, food supply, social circumstances, political events, exposure to disease, climate and natural disasters, and other environmental events. The impact of these factors and that of other life events are impossible to quantitate and are hard to interpret, especially since it is very difficult and expensive to conduct prospective aging studies for the entire life span of a group of people large enough to permit conclusions that make any sense. In fact, the premier study on aging that exists in the United States is the Baltimore Longitudinal Study of Aging, which has been going on prospectively since 1958. The most valuable information collected about human aging must be gathered prospectively so that events that occur throughout life can be linked to physiologic, physical, and psychologic changes experienced by aging individuals. It is certainly easier to conduct cross-sectional studies, in which groups of people of varying ages are examined and differences among them at one point in time are measured or described; but such a study tells us nothing about the events that preceded that point in time or which factors contributed to the differences measured.

1

This area of study is further complicated by the fact that humans are subject to an uncontrolled genetic pool; medical knowledge that changes from one generation to the next; advances in science that affect the quality of life, such as an improved food supply, refrigeration, transportation systems, availability of medicines, and environmental control; and the lack of biologic markers that indicate true physiologic age. Although this is an area that is demanding attention and research resources, little progress has been made in our ability to identify individual life expectancies or to quantify the impact of disease on life span.

It is notable that the human life span has been estimated at approximately 112 to 114 years, and that estimate has not changed in more than 200 years. Noteworthy, however, is the significant change that has occurred in human life expectancy. In fact, just in this century, life expectancy has increased by more than 25 years.[2] Demographic trends, advances in medicine, and eradication of some diseases indicate that this increase in life expectancy will continue well into the next century.

DEMOGRAPHIC TRENDS

Until research provides us with a better definition of old age, people who have reached the age of 65 years or over will remain the reference group when the elderly population is discussed. Between 1950 and 1980, the population of those over age 65 more than doubled. What is truly significant about this increase is not the total size of this group but rather that the greatest increase occurred in the group over age 85 years. During this period of time the percentage of people over age 85 years increased by 281%[3] (Figure 1-1).

Death rates have been declining or remaining constant throughout the 20th century; however, declines in mortality rates vary by age, race, and sex. Women have had a consistently greater decline in mortality rate, making the proportion of women larger, the older the age group. The ratio of males to females declines with advancing age. Actually, more boys than girls are born, but since there is a higher death rate for males and an improvement in mortality rate for women, this ratio changes quickly. In 1980, there were 44 males to every 100 females over age 85 years; this ratio is expected to fall to 36 males for every 100 females by 2020.[3] The result will be an increasingly large group of women in the very old age group, and this is not expected to change (Figure 1-2).

There are also differences in population demographics by race, in addition to those that occur by age and sex. There are many more elderly white people than there are elderly black people, despite a proportionately higher birth rate among blacks. This discrepancy is due to a higher mortality rate at younger ages for blacks. Although the mortality rate for blacks is expected to decrease, it is not projected to compensate for the gap between races in the near future.

Projected Numbers of Elderly People
1960-2040

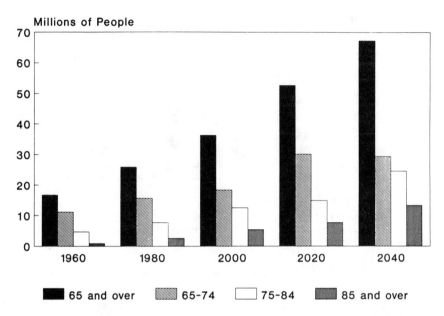

Figure 1-1 Population projections for various age groups from 1960 to 2040, based on Social Security Administration data.

The income of today's elderly populace is greater than that of similarly aged cohorts of previous generations. Social Security benefits represent the largest source of income for this group, followed by earnings and income from property, pensions, and investments. Although the current group of elderly people is less educated than are Americans of younger age groups, the gap between generations is closing and is expected to change by the end of the century. This fact will have an impact on income levels of future groups of older people, most likely making them more sophisticated with greater expectations of social care systems and medical care options.[3] This may lead to greater expenditures for health care services. These factors will probably contribute to more of the elderly population's owning their own homes in the future and wanting to stay in them for as long as they can manage.

Another demographic factor that distinguishes the present cohort of elderly people from future generations of older people is their mobility. Older people tend to move geographically less often, and less far, than do younger people; they tend to settle in the geographic region where they were born and raised or where they settled when they married.[3] As population demographics shift, population pro-

Population Growth by Age and Sex
1960-2040

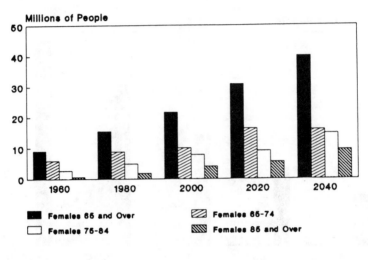

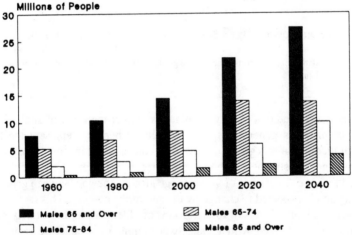

Figure 1-2 Comparison of population growth by age and sex for men and women in the United States, based on Social Security Administration data.

jections by the Bureau of the Census predict significant differences in rates of change in different regions of the United States. The regions that are expected to grow the fastest are the South and the West, while the north-central region of the country will lose population.[4] These factors will influence the need for, and accessibility to, health care resources in the future.

IMPACT ON THE HEALTH CARE SYSTEM

One of the natural occurrences that accompanies aging is an increase in the prevalence of disabilities and diseases. The incidence of concurrent illnesses and multiple disabilities rises sharply with age and is greatest in the very old segment of the population, those over age 85 years.[2] When an acute episode occurs, the consumption of health care resources is greater in this group of patients because of the multiple chronic problems they may have that must be attended to along with their acute illnesses. Unfortunately, the health care system in the United States is becoming increasingly focused on the delivery of acute health care for brief time spans, allowing expensive and limited technologies to be used for the maximal number of patients. Complex, frail, very old patients require these expensive, life-saving technologies; but concurrently they also require extended periods of skilled care for adequate recuperation and rehabilitation. This increasingly large portion of the population will soon strain the resources in the existing health care system.

Based on relatively recent statistics, the population segment over age 65 years—approximately 12% of the total population—uses approximately 40% of the acute care hospital bed days, buys 25% of all the prescription drugs, spends 30% of the health care dollars spent in the United States (about $53 billion), and accounts for more than 50% of the federal health budget (about $20 billion).[2,5] There is no doubt that health care managers must assess the growth of the older segment of the population carefully and plan accordingly. For example, although only 5% of elderly people are in nursing homes at any one time, 85% of those residing in nursing homes are over age 65 years, making the availability of nursing home beds and services an increasingly important part of planning for and allocating health care resources in the future. It is projected that the nursing home population will increase from 1,511,000 in 1980 to 5,227,000 in 2040. When the "baby boomers" come of age, between 2020 and 2040, the largest demands for services will occur[5] (Figure 1-2).

QUALITY OF LIFE AND HEALTH STATUS

It is well known that older people have more health problems than do younger individuals. However, it is often overlooked that a large percentage of the population over age 65 years is relatively healthy and vigorous. Needless to say, good health status contributes to vitality and quality of life.

Quality of life is a difficult term to define well. When objective indicators are used to define quality of life, there is only a weak relationship to individuals' perceptions of quality of life.[6] There are many subjective factors that contribute to quality of life, of which health status is only one. For example, general health and functional status represent one dimension of perceived quality of life, along with socioeconomic status, general life satisfaction, and self-esteem.[7] Of interest is that subjective estimates of health status by the individual do not correlate closely with objective assessment of health status as measured by laboratory tests and physical examination.[6] However, the dimension that appears to correlate better when perceptions are compared with objective measures is functional status. Functional status is defined as the ability to perform activities related to self-care and daily living and can be measured by several instruments.[3] Frequently, poor health status and physical disability have an impact on functional ability; it is difficult to separate the two dimensions.

Quality of life takes on different meanings when applied to institutionalized elderly people. Since their health status is questionable—or they would not need institutional care—factors that contribute to their perceptions of quality of life are more circumspect, focusing on their immediate environment. The quality of their food; the ability to make choices and control some parts of their lives; participation in events in the institution, such as self-feeding or exercise programs; and the attitudes of the care providers and other residents all contribute to the quality of life for chronically ill, elderly people cared for in institutions.[8] Certainly, satisfaction with one's life and surroundings contributes to perception of the overall quality of life. A positive outlook can contribute to better cooperation and compliance with health care regimens and perhaps help to maintain health status for a greater part of the latter years of life. All of these factors contribute to successful aging.

HEALTH CARE COSTS

As the elderly portion of the population expands, the consumption of health care resources may grow beyond their present availability. Efforts to curb expenditures have focused on acute care resources and have had an impact primarily on elderly, poor, and underprivileged patients. Many factors contribute to the large amounts of money spent on health care in the United States. Certainly, advances in medical technology, resulting in expensive equipment needed to perform diagnostic tests and to provide technical treatment modalities, have contributed to rising costs. Another important contributing factor is that a large proportion of the population is living longer since the management of chronic disease has become easier, and technologic advances have made the diagnosis and treatment of serious illnesses more effective. Data from the National Center for Health Statistics support the proposal that one of the reasons the elderly segment of the population is getting larger is that their death rates are decreasing.[9] Because older people tend to have more disabilities and more chronic conditions, they require—and use—more health care resources. There is no doubt that people over age 65 years require more acute care hospital days than do younger people, and this need increases in even older groups: individuals over age 85 years use 8300 days of acute care hospital resources per 1000 persons[5]; for chronic care resources, individuals over age 85 years use 86,400 days per year per 1000 persons.[5]

The need for quality long-term care is beginning to attract the attention of policy makers. There are few demographic data to describe residents of long-term care facilities because they are often missed or overlooked in censuses or household surveys. However, as the population of frail elderly people increases, interest in payment sources for their care becomes greater. Currently, public or private insurance to help defray the costs of long-term care is limited. Skilled nursing services are expensive, and it is likely that in most cases public funds such as Medicare or Medicaid will not cover the costs of care. Proprietary nursing homes are reluctant to accept patients who require skilled care; facilities that may accept this type of patient may have staff inadequately skilled to care for ill patients. This limitation often creates a difficult situation when services are needed but are not affordable or available.[3]

Alternatives to nursing home care are being explored through experimental or demonstration projects. Home health care services are one option that may prove to be a viable alternative to nursing home care. There are limitations to home care services, particularly the need for caregiver support required to make it work. In one model, a large portion of the care provided (about 72%) is delivered by family members, particularly if the patients' disabilities are not great. Costs for home services increase with the level of patient disability.[10]

Some physicians do not favor the home health care concept because they are concerned with malpractice issues, quality-of-care issues, loss of control over patient care, and loss of reimbursement, since the home health agencies take over managerial responsibilities.[4] Physicians have a limited role in the delivery of health care when the home care agencies become the primary providers. The physician is involved only in approving forms that allow home care professionals to be reimbursed, or in providing telephone consultations to the primary care provider. In order to be paid for patients' home health care, physicians must see the patients in the office or visit them in their homes; these activities are very time-consuming and not very cost effective.[11]

Hospitals are becoming involved in developing home health services because they are a viable option for extending services and marketing other hospital programs, which have become prime objectives since hospital reimbursement systems have limited income in many facilities.[4] In fact, hospital-based home health care programs have grown much faster than independent home health care agencies.[12]

Another model of home care has been developed by the Department of Veterans Affairs. For frail, but medically stable, elderly individuals who have able care givers, the hospital-based home care program is a successful alternative. The hospital-based staff members make home visits within a 50-mile radius of their base, and skilled health care professionals (social workers, pharmacists, dietitians, nurses, and physicians) track patients on a regular schedule and assess their home situations. This program provides continuity of care, an important dimension of caring for frail elderly people. There is regular contact by telephone so that problems can be dealt with early and hospitalization arranged efficiently when needed.

Another program alternative that may be a feasible solution to the problems of providing health care to elderly patients is adult day health care.[13] Access to appropriate adult day health care facilities may be a factor that enables frail elderly people to remain in their home surroundings and maintain a relatively familiar life style. There are different types of adult day care models. The most common model is the social model. Social day care programs are designed to meet the needs of clients who may be disabled but are medically stable. The primary purpose of these programs is to maintain social and physical capacities through recreational and other social programs and to prevent or delay institutionalization.[4]

Medical model day care programs are designed to provide rehabilitative and support services, with the goal being the restoration of physical and functional abilities. One type of medical model adult day care has been under study through a multicenter health services research grant provided by the Department of Veterans Affairs. In this program, elderly people can remain in their own homes yet receive health care through a day care center that provides therapeutic services. Family members, friends, or other support providers must arrange for transportation to the sites, or the program must provide transportation. Patients can be enrolled in the program if they require rehabilitative care, such as physical or occupational therapy, medical treatment, or respite care. Patients can attend the center as needed, but usually patients visit two or three times per week. They are brought in in the morning and are picked up in the late afternoon, making it possible for care providers, spouses, or adult children to continue to participate in other activities, such as work or household or child care responsibilities.

Although there may not be ready-made answers to the problems of providing health care to elderly people in the future, there are certainly options being explored.[14] It is obvious that something must be done to provide quality health care for this segment of the populace, but in order to develop the services and find the resources to pay for them, a great deal must be learned about aging, diseases that are common in old age, and the maintenance of health in aging people.

CONCLUSION

There is no doubt that the expansion of the population segment over age 65 years will force health care providers to face problems associated with an aging society sooner than they might have liked. Many creative options have been proposed to provide appropriate quality health care to elderly people; but they need to be tested and evaluated before solutions can be found to the problems inherent in health care delivery to a large, distinct population of patients who have different income levels, unique medical problems, and diverse life experiences.

Within this context, health care providers must understand the role of nutrition in the maintenance of health, the management of chronic conditions, and the treatment of serious disease. The remainder of this text addresses the interrelations among physiologic aging, nutrition, and disease. Comprehension of these important associations and the application of this knowledge will contribute to more effective health promotion, disease prevention, and disease management in elderly persons.

REFERENCES

1. Haynes SG, Feinleib M. *Second Conference on the Epidemiology of Aging.* Washington, DC: US Public Health Service; 1980. US Dept. of Health and Human Services publication NIH 80-969.

2. Besdine RW. The data base of geriatric medicine. In: Rowe JW, Besdine RW, eds. *Health and Disease in Old Age.* Boston, Mass: Little, Brown & Co; 1982.

3. Gilford DM, ed. *The Aging Population in the Twenty-First Century: Statistics for Health Policy.* Washington, DC: National Academy Press; 1988.

4. Taeuber C. America in transition: an aging society. In: *Current Population Reports.* Washington, DC: Bureau of the Census; 1983. US Dept of Commerce special studies series P-23, No. 128.

5. Pegels CC. *Health Care and the Older Citizen.* Gaithersburg, Md: Aspen Publishers Inc; 1988.

6. Vinokur A, Cannell CF, Eraker SA, et al. *The Role of Survey Research in the Assessment of Health and the Quality-of-Life Outcomes of Pharmaceutical Interventions.* Ann Arbor, Mich: Institute for Social Research, University of Michigan. Cost-Effectiveness of Pharmaceuticals Report Series; 1983:6.

7. George L, Bearon L. *Quality of Life in Older Persons: Meaning and Measurement.* New York, NY: Human Sciences Press; 1980.

8. Institute of Medicine Committee on Nursing Home Regulations. *Improving the Quality of Care in Nursing Homes.* Washington, DC: National Academy Press; 1986.

9. *Vital Health Statistics: Health Statistics on Older Persons, U.S., 1986.* 3rd series, No. 25. Washington, DC: US Government Printing Office; 1987.

10. Liu K, Manton KG, Liu BM. Home care expenses for the disabled elderly. *Health Care Financ Rev.* 1985;7(2):51–58.

11. Alper PR. Count me out of the home care boom. *Med Econ.* April 15, 1985:90–92.

12. Kaye HM, Hitchcock KA. Home healthcare: the hospitals' target. *Caring.* 1984;3:37–39.

13. Hedrick SC, Rothman ML, Chapko M, et al. Adult day health care: evaluation study methodology and implementation. *Health Serv Res.* In press.

14. Rivlin AM, Wiener JM. *Caring for the Disabled Elderly: Who Will Pay?* Washington, DC: The Brookings Institution; 1988.

Chapter 2

Macronutrient Requirements for Elderly Persons

William J. Carter

It is important to modify environmental factors to minimize or postpone deleterious processes associated with aging. An optimal intake of macronutrients and proper exercise appear to be important in maintaining health and function in old age. Optimal intake of protein and energy, coupled with adequate exercise, will minimize the loss of skeletal muscle. Similarly, an appropriate energy intake supplied by a proper balance of fat, carbohydrate, and protein is likely to retard the progression of atherosclerosis and keep vascular disease below the clinical horizon as long as possible.

PROTEIN METABOLISM AND REQUIREMENTS

Age-Related Changes in Body Protein Content, Distribution, and Turnover

Age-related changes in body protein content, distribution, and turnover make consideration of protein intake particularly important in older persons. There is a decline in lean body mass with age that is manifested by a decrease in total body potassium, nitrogen, and water content.[1] The age-related decline in body potassium content is greater than the decline in nitrogen content.[2] This occurs because potassium is more concentrated in muscle tissue than in nonmuscle lean tissue, and the decline in muscle mass accounts for essentially all the age-related reduction in lean body mass[2] (Table 2-1). In contrast, nonmuscle lean tissue mass does not decrease with age.

Direct measurement of muscle weight at autopsy demonstrates a substantial loss of muscle mass with age.[3] Skeletal muscle accounts for about 45% of body weight during young adulthood, but its contribution declines to about 27% at age 70 years.[3] Uauy and associates[4] have shown that skeletal muscle makes a smaller

Table 2-1 Effect of Age on Body Composition in Normal Men

Age (y)	Nonmuscle Mass (kg)	Muscle Mass (kg)	Total Body Fat (kg)
20–29	37	24	15
40–49	38	20	19
60–69	37	17	23
70–79	38	13	25

Source: Adapted with permission from *American Journal of Physiology* (1980;239:E524), Copyright © 1980, American Physiological Society.

---

contribution to total body protein metabolism with advancing age. In young adulthood, skeletal muscle accounts for about 30% of whole-body protein turnover, which decreases to 20% or less in old age. In addition to decreased strength, postural stability, and mobility, the decreased skeletal muscle reservoir may provide a supply of amino acids inadequate to make the new proteins needed for physiologic responses to illness or other stress.[4] Dietary protein intake by older persons should be high enough to minimize the age-related loss of skeletal muscle. It is clear that an inadequate protein intake may accelerate this loss.

Measurement of Dietary Protein Requirement

Most estimates of adult protein requirements have been made in young and middle-aged individuals. Two general methods have been used to estimate dietary protein requirements.[5] The factorial method measures all losses of nitrogen compounds in individuals adapted to a protein-free diet and assumes that the dietary protein requirement is equal to the amount of protein necessary to replace these losses. The second method determines directly the minimal amount of dietary protein needed for nitrogen equilibrium in adults and optimal growth in infants and children. Based on these methods, the adult daily requirement for protein of average quality appears to be approximately 0.8 g/kg.[5] Variation in energy intake reduces the accuracy of this estimate. At high energy intakes, less protein is required to achieve nitrogen balance than at low energy intakes.[5] In nitrogen balance studies, energy intake often has been increased beyond the basal requirement to prevent weight loss on low-protein diets.[5] This approach tends to produce estimates of protein requirements that are too low when applied to individuals with borderline or low energy intakes.

Daily Protein Requirement for Elderly Persons

Although earlier studies suggested that the protein requirement of elderly subjects was less than that of young adults, more recent studies indicate that the protein requirement per kilogram of body weight does not decline with age.[1] In fact, a recent, carefully performed nitrogen balance study showed that a daily allowance of 0.8 g of high-quality egg protein was not sufficient to maintain nitrogen balance in half of the elderly men and women studied for 30 days.[6] Since the digestibility of dietary protein is about 90%, and mixed animal and plant protein is likely to have lower quality (ie, reduced proportion of essential amino acids) than egg protein, a minimal daily allowance of 1 g of mixed protein per kilogram of body weight appears reasonable for elderly subjects.[1] A number of stresses may increase protein requirements well above this level, as indicated below. A recent dietary survey of 239 men and 452 women aged 60 to 95 years strongly suggests that 1 g of protein per kilogram of body weight is an adequate daily allowance.[7] Persons with debilitating diseases were excluded from this study, which focused on overtly healthy, free-living men and women in an urban environment. Nutrient intake was estimated from a diary listing all foods, beverages, and nutrient supplements consumed over a 3-day period. Protein intake was correlated with indices of protein nutrition, including serum albumin, prealbumin, transferrin, ceruloplasmin, retinol-binding protein, and upper arm muscle mass. Dietary protein intake averaged 1.02 to 1.06 g/kg of body weight. In the 12% to 15% of the group with protein intakes below 0.8 g/kg, there was no relationship between protein intake and plasma concentrations of albumin, prealbumin, or transferrin or upper arm muscle mass.[7] Therefore, the intake of 1.0 g of protein per kilogram appeared to be adequate in this healthy elderly population.

Requirements for Essential Amino Acids

It is important to ensure that the daily protein allowance provides an appropriate proportion of the essential amino acids that must be ingested in the diet. Since there is no information about essential amino acid requirements in elderly persons, it is assumed that the requirements in old age are similar to requirements during young adulthood.[1] The 1985 Food and Agriculture Organization of the United Nations (FAO)/World Health Organization (WHO)/United Nations University (UNU) Expert Group concluded that essential amino acid requirements per unit of body weight were substantially less in young adults than in children 2 to 5 years old.[8] This conclusion was based on nitrogen balance studies, which may have underestimated nitrogen losses.[1] Recent studies of the metabolism of leucine, valine, lysine, and threonine given in graded doses to young adults suggest that essential amino acid requirements are much greater than those estimated by the 1985 FAO/WHO/UNU Expert Group.[9–12] The rate of oxidation and plasma levels of these amino acids were clearly related to the intake level. At daily intake levels below 20 mg/kg for leucine, 16 mg/kg for valine, 20 mg/kg for lysine, and 20 mg/kg for threonine, estimated rates of oxidation exceeded intake, implying a negative balance of these essential amino acids.[9–12] These estimates significantly exceed the 1985 FAO/WHO/UNU recommended daily allowance of 14 mg/kg for leucine, 10 mg/kg for valine, 12 mg/kg for lysine, and 7 mg/kg for threonine.[8] These recent studies suggest that approximately 30% of dietary protein should provide an appropriate mixture of essential amino acids.[1]

Quality of Dietary Protein

An ideal protein provides all essential amino acids in optimal concentrations to meet requirements when consumed in adequate amounts.[5] Although the amino acid content is a useful means to describe the nutritional potential of dietary protein, it is not ideal. The ability of a test protein to support growth in infants and nitrogen balance in adults can be used as another index of protein quality.[5] Most animal proteins contain a satisfactory mixture of essential amino acids and can be considered to be of high quality. On the other hand, many plant proteins have a lower nutritional value because they contain too little of one or more essential amino acids, causing inefficient utilization and the need for a larger protein intake to maintain nitrogen equilibrium. Nevertheless, adequate protein nutrition can be obtained by using predominantly or exclusively plant proteins provided that complementary groups of plant proteins (such as proteins of the cereal and legume families) are consumed during the course of a day in the same or separate meals.[1]

Factors Affecting Protein Requirement in Elderly Persons

Aging is accompanied by an increasing frequency of acute and chronic diseases. Enhanced protein catabolism in response to stresses such as surgery, infection, fractures, and other trauma can greatly increase protein requirements.[13] These catabolic responses are mediated by increased levels of cortisol, glucagon, and catecholamines, and cause loss of lean body mass, especially muscle tissue.[13] Although adequate protein intake during the first week following these stresses does not prevent increased proteolysis, it minimizes the negative nitrogen balance that ensues.[13] Protein intake should be increased 1.5- to 2-fold as soon as tolerated and continued until lean body mass is restored.[13] If the patient is malnourished at the onset of the illness or if enteral intake is delayed for more than 7 days, parenteral nutrition should be considered[13] (Chapter 15).

Effect of Protein Intake on Age-Related Decline in Renal Function

Brenner and associates[14] have suggested that the high and continuous protein intake common in current Western societies increases renal blood flow, glomerular filtration rate, and the transcapillary pressure gradient in the glomerulus. They further suggest that these changes contribute to age-related glomerular sclerosis. [14] In support of this hypothesis, over half of the glomeruli are sclerotic in senescent rats fed a high-protein diet ad libitum, [15] and development of these lesions is delayed by feeding a low-protein diet. [16] Although the 30% reduction in functioning glomeruli seen in humans between the fourth and eighth decades does not cause significant renal insufficiency by itself, it may be very important when combined with intrinsic renal disease. [14] However, recent studies do not support a relationship between protein intake and the age-related decrease in renal function. [17,18] When healthy individuals on a high-protein diet were compared with vegetarians on a long-term, low-protein diet, no difference in the age-related deterioration in creatinine clearance was noted. [17] Furthermore, an analysis of male subjects in the Baltimore Longitudinal Study of Aging failed to show a relationship between high protein intake and impairment of creatinine clearance. [18] At present, there is little basis for reducing protein intake to spare renal function.

Recommended Protein Allowance for Elderly Persons

Energy expenditure declines with age, whereas protein requirement per unit of body weight does not change. Therefore, the dietary protein intake should represent a greater proportion of total energy intake as age advances. [1] A daily protein intake of approximately 1 g/kg of body weight, or 12% to 14% of total energy intake, is recommended. [1,7] When necessary, protein intake must be increased to satisfy the demand of specific diseases and to replenish protein stores in malnourished subjects.

AGE AND ENERGY REQUIREMENT

Effect of Age on Energy Requirement

There is evidence that energy intake declines progressively with age. In a cross-sectional survey, the total energy intake of men enrolled in the Baltimore Longitudinal Study of Aging declined from 2700 kcal at age 30 years to 2100 kcal at age 80 years. [19] About one third of this decrement can be attributed to a declining basal metabolic rate (BMR) and the remainder to decreased physical activity. [19] A subsequent longitudinal analysis of this study population over 15 years confirmed the reduction in energy intake with age. [20] The decline in energy intake appeared to be a pure effect of age, with no confounding cohort or time effects. Reduced fat consumption by elderly subjects accounted for the decreased energy intake. [20] In addition, other cross-sectional studies, such as the Health and Nutrition Examination Survey[21] (HANES) and the Framingham Diet Study,[22] have shown declining energy intake with age. In the HANES survey, energy intake in men decreased from 2700 kcal in the 23- to 34-year-old age group to 1800 kcal in the 65- to 74-year-old age group.[21] Although a declining BMR has been cited as contributing to the reduced energy requirement of older individuals,[19] Owen and associates[23] found little effect of age on the resting metabolic rate (RMR) in healthy men. In their study, RMR was measured by indirect calorimetry in 60 men, only 4 of whom were aged 65 years or older. Increasing age was associated with a small, statistically insignificant reduction in RMR. The small number of elderly subjects in this study reduces the impact of the authors' conclusion that age has an insignificant effect on RMR in healthy subjects.[23]

Estimation of the Energy Requirement of Elderly Persons

The BMR is determined by body size, body composition, and age.[8] Within a given sex and age range, weight is the most useful and practical index for predicting BMR.[8] The FAO/WHO/UNU Expert Group has calculated regression equations relating BMR to body weight that can be used to estimate the BMR of adults.[8] The adult category has been divided into three age ranges: 18 to 30 years, 30 to 60 years, and over 60 years. Regression equations are presented in Table 2-2 for men and women in each age range. Inadequate data have precluded dividing the large age spectrum over age 60 years into smaller divisions.[8]

Total energy requirement can be estimated by multiplying the BMR by factors accounting for the energy costs of physical activity, maintenance of muscle tone, and the thermic effect of food.[8] The energy costs of various levels of physical activity expressed as multiples of the BMR are presented in Table 2-3. The energy requirement per 24 hours can be estimated by summing the energy costs for different levels of activity that occur throughout the day.[8] The energy required for

---

Table 2-2 Estimate of BMR (kcal) According to Age and Sex

Age Range	Men	Women
18–30	15.3 W* + 679	14.7 W + 496
30–60	11.6 W + 879	8.7 W + 829
60+	13.5 W + 487	10.5 W + 596

*W = body weight in kilograms.

Source: Adapted from Technical Report Series No. 724 (p 71) with permission of the World Health Organization, © 1985.

Table 2-3 Energy Costs of Physical Activity Expressed as Multiples of the BMR

Level of Activity	Men	Women
Light work	1.7	1.7
Moderate work	2.7	2.2
Heavy work	3.8	2.8
Residual time (no activity, but awake)	1.4	1.4
Sleeping	1.0	1.0

Source: Adapted from *Technical Report Series No. 724* (p 76) with permission of the World Health Organization, © 1985.

Table 2-4 Estimated Energy Requirement of a Man Aged 75 Years, Weight 60 kg, with an Estimated BMR of 54 kcal/h

Level of Activity	Time at Level (h)	Energy Need (kcal)
In bed at 1.0 × BMR	8.0	430
Social activities at 3.3 × BMR	2.0	355
Household tasks at 2.7 × BMR	1.0	145
Cardiovascular fitness exercise at 3.8 × BMR	0.3	70
Residual time energy needs at 1.4 × BMR	12.7	960
Total	24.0	1960

Source: Adapted from *Technical Report Series No. 724* (p 77) with permission of the World Health Organization, © 1985.

each level of activity is estimated by multiplying the rate of energy expenditure in kilocalories per hour times the number of hours spent at that level of activity. Table 2-4 presents the daily energy requirement of a healthy retiree estimated as indicated above.[8]

WATER INTAKE IN ELDERLY PERSONS

Although required water intake is not substantially different in young and old adults, elderly individuals are prone to an inadequate water intake. In fact, dehydration is the most common fluid and electrolyte disturbance in elderly people.[24] In many instances, diseases that cause mental or physical incapacity also reduce the ability to recognize thirst, create an inability to express thirst, or decrease access to water.[25] In addition to the effects of acquired diseases, healthy elderly individuals appear to have reduced thirst in response to fluid deprivation.[24] Healthy elderly men (aged 67 to 75 years) and young men (aged 20 to 31 years) were deprived of all fluid intake for 24 hours, followed by free access to water for

60 minutes. In spite of a higher serum osmolality in the elderly group following dehydration, they were less thirsty and consumed only half as much water during the 60-minute rehydration period as did the young subjects.[24] Furthermore, young subjects fully corrected elevated serum osmolalities during the rehydration period, whereas elderly subjects did not.[24] In addition to reduced thirst, elderly subjects produced moderately less concentrated urine following fluid deprivation.[24] Since elderly subjects had higher serum vasopressin levels in response to dehydration, the decreased capacity to concentrate the urine appears to be at the renal level.[24] (Chapter 9) As this study indicates, healthy as well as ill elderly subjects are less able to respond to dehydration. In most instances, elderly subjects should be encouraged to consume approximately 2 L of fluid per day, or more if indicated by specific losses,[25] or 1 mL of fluid per kilocalorie ingested to approximate at least 1500 mL/d. If severe hypodipsia occurs like that described following cerebrovascular accidents, fluid intake must be rigidly prescribed to prevent repeated episodes of dehydration.[25]

DESIRABLE FAT INTAKE IN ELDERLY PERSONS

Dietary Fat Requirement

The desirable fat intake for elderly individuals does not differ from that of younger adults.[26] Fats and carbohydrates are the major sources of dietary energy, providing 85% to 90% of the total intake. Fats are by far the most efficient energy source, with twice the energy content per gram as carbohydrate and protein. At least 10% of the total energy intake should be fat, to allow an adequate intake of fat-soluble vitamins and the essential fatty acids, linoleic and arachidonic acid.[26] Essential fatty acids are required for the synthesis of prostaglandins and cell membrane phospholipids.[27] The fat content of the average American diet, approximately 40% of the total energy intake, is too high and contains a higher proportion of saturated fat and cholesterol than is desirable for the optimal health of adults.[28] To retard atherogenesis, the American Heart Association recommends that the total fat intake be limited to 30% or less of the total energy intake, the saturated fat intake be limited to 10% to 15% of total energy intake with substitution of unsaturated fatty acids for saturated ones, and the cholesterol intake be limited to 300 mg/d or less[29] (Chapter 8).

Serum Cholesterol and Coronary Heart Disease

Serum cholesterol is a powerful risk factor for coronary heart disease until approximately age 55 years, but its impact wanes with increasing age.[30–32] Serum cholesterol does not predict the incidence of coronary heart disease past age 70 years in men, but it retains a weaker predictive effect in elderly women.[30,31] On the other hand, its atherogenic component, low-density lipoprotein (LDL) cholesterol, and its protective component, high-density lipoprotein (HDL) cholesterol, as well as the LDL-HDL ratio continue to be related to the incidence and mortality of coronary heart disease in elderly men and women.[30,31]

Dietary Treatment of Hypercholesterolemia

Diet may greatly influence serum cholesterol and its atherogenic LDL component. Total and LDL cholesterol are increased by excess dietary intake of energy, saturated fats, and cholesterol.[33] They can be lowered by reduced intake of energy and of total fat and by substitution of unsaturated fats for saturated fats.[33] By eliminating smoking and reducing the intake of saturated fat and cholesterol in normotensive middle-aged men, the Oslo Study Group reduced coronary heart disease morbidity and mortality by 47%; 60% of the benefit derived from a 13% reduction in serum cholesterol.[34] In the Lipid Research Clinics Coronary Primary Prevention Trial, cholesterol reduction by diet and drugs decreased the coronary heart disease mortality rate by 24% and the incidence by 19%.[35] There have been no dietary intervention studies of elderly populations to demonstrate directly whether lowering cholesterol reduces the morbidity and mortality of coronary heart disease when instituted at advanced age.[31] In the absence of direct evidence, indirect evidence has been cited that reduction of risk factors in older populations may lower mortality rates for coronary heart disease.[36,37] Since 1968, the death rate for coronary heart disease in persons aged 75 to 84 has declined 14.5%; in persons over age 84, it has declined 18.7%. These reduced death rates are probably due in part to better acute and chronic care. They may also be related to reduced risk factors, such as decreased fat and cholesterol intake, decreased smoking, and better control of hypertension that occurred beyond middle age.[31]

Dietary Control of Hypercholesterolemia

It is not clear which elderly hypercholesterolemic patients are likely to benefit from extensive dietary intervention to reduce cholesterol levels.[38] For relatively healthy individuals below age 70 years, adherence to the American Heart Association recommendations may be appropriate.[39] This includes reducing dietary cholesterol to 250 mg per day or less, total fat to 25% to 30% of energy intake, and saturated fat to 8% to 10% of energy intake. On the other hand, such dietary intervention may not be indicated in individuals over age 70 years who have limited economic resources, limited activity and quality of life due to advanced disease, or relatively poor dietary intake. In such patients, the stress and potential complications of changing diets are probably not justified by the small potential gains.[38]

Carbohydrate and Fiber Intake in Elderly Persons

Dietary Carbohydrate Requirement

The major function of dietary carbohydrate is to provide energy. Glucose can be used by all body tissues and is required for energy production in brain and red blood cells.[40] In the absence of dietary carbohydrate, fatty acids are incompletely oxidized, leading to ketosis, which may cause lethargy and depression.[40] To prevent ketosis, a minimum of 50 g of dietary glucose or complex carbohydrate equivalent is required per day.[40] Although sufficient carbohydrate to prevent ketosis is the minimal desirable intake, no ideal level of consumption has been defined. When the protein requirement and desirable fat intake have been defined, the remaining dietary energy needs should be met by prescribing the appropriate amount of carbohydrate. If the protein requirement is 10% to 15% of dietary energy and the desirable fat intake is 30% as indicated above,[28] the carbohydrate intake should be 55% to 60% of dietary energy.

Benefits of Dietary Fiber

Excessive refining of foods with removal of indigestible dietary fiber may contribute to disorders such as constipation, diverticular disease of the colon, diabetes, and hyperlipidemia, which are particularly prevalent in the elderly.[41] Dietary fiber is derived from structural components of plant cell walls and consists of plant polysaccharides and lignin, which are resistant to digestive enzymes in man.[41] Water-holding particulate fiber with high pentosan content, such as wheat bran, increases fecal bulk and decreases gut transit time and intraluminal pressure within the colon.[42] These effects are helpful in reducing constipation and the formation of colonic diverticuli. On the other hand, soluble fibers, such as gums and pectins, increase the viscosity of intestinal contents, increase gut transit time, and decrease the rate of small intestinal absorption.[41] Increased consumption of fibers such as guar, pectin, and tragacanth reduced insulin secretion after a test meal in normal subjects and increased carbohydrate tolerance in diabetics.[43,44] The mechanism of the beneficial effect appears to be delayed gastric emptying and reduced rate of absorption of carbohydrate in the small intestine. As a consequence of these effects, the American, Canadian, and British Diabetes Associations have recommended increased consumption of high-fiber, carbohydrate-containing foods.[41] Although less well established, purified fibers such as guar, pectin, and oat bran, and high-fiber foods such as cereals, starchy vegetables, and beans have been reported to lower serum lipids.[45] Decreases in total cholesterol, LDL cholesterol, and triglycerides without change in HDL cholesterol were observed.[45] Again, the mechanism appears to be decreased gastric emptying and reduced intestinal absorption of cholesterol and triglyceride. For the above reasons, a fiber intake of 25 to 35 g/d appears prudent. Fiber from a variety of sources such as fresh fruits, vegetables, legumes, and whole-grain products is recommended.[44]

DIETARY RESTRICTIONS AND LONGEVITY

There has been much speculation that nutrition is a modifiable factor in longevity; however, evaluating its role in human subjects is not a viable option for many reasons. Therefore, investigations involving dietary restrictions and longevity have been conducted in rodents.[46] The experimental guidelines are that malnutrition be avoided and that calorie restriction, to be valid, be at least 20% less than the animals would eat ad libitum.[46] Food restriction is often referred to as calorie restriction, probably because many studies that have demonstrated that food restriction after weaning extends life span have used different food sources.[46] Restriction of protein, fats, and minerals appears to have no influence on longevity without calorie restriction. In animal studies, food or calorie restriction after weaning increases life expectancy and life span, retards many of the age-associated physiologic changes, and delays or prevents some age-associated diseases.[46] Mechanisms for the process that contributes these results have not yet been defined. In addition, it is difficult to extrapolate data from animal studies, particularly with the complexity of factors that are involved in human life.[47] Limiting caloric intake while maintaining adequate levels of other essential nutrients is difficult, may not have the same effect in humans as it does in rodents, and may have negative consequences in young people.[47]

CONCLUSION

Macronutrient intake has a major influence on health and function in old age. Although energy requirements decline substantially with age, protein requirements do not. A daily protein intake of 1 g/kg of body weight, or 12% to 14% of total energy intake, is recommended. Optimal protein and energy intake, together with appropriate exercise, will minimize age-related loss of skeletal muscle mass. Elderly persons are prone to inadequate water intake because of diseases causing mental and physical incapacity and reduced thirst in response to fluid deprivation. For this reason, elderly persons should be encouraged to consume 1.5 to 2 L of fluid per day, or more if indicated by specific losses. Although there is no direct evidence that lowering cholesterol reduces the morbidity and mortality of coronary heart disease in elderly persons, it appears prudent to limit fat intake to 30% of total energy in relatively healthy older persons. In addition, saturated fat intake should be limited to 10% to 15% of total energy intake by substituting unsaturated fatty acids for saturated fatty acids, and cholesterol should be limited to 300 mg/d.

On the other hand, limiting fat intake may be counterproductive in debilitated elderly individuals with poor intake and limited quality of life due to advanced disease. The major function of dietary carbohydrate is to provide energy. If fat intake is limited to 30% of dietary energy and protein intake supplies 10% to 15%, then the carbohydrate intake should be 55% to 60% of dietary energy. The recommended fiber intake of 25 to 35 g/d appears to reduce constipation, improve carbohydrate tolerance, and lower serum lipids. Although reduced calorie intake is the most potent experimental manipulation for increasing life span in rodents, there is no current evidence that this applies to longer-lived, larger species, including man.

REFERENCES

1. Fukagawa NK, Young VR. Protein and amino acid metabolism and requirements in older persons. *Clin Geriatr Med.* 1987;3:329–341.

2. Cohn SH, Vartsky D, Yasumura S, et al. Compartmental body composition based on total-body nitrogen, potassium and calcium. *Am J Physiol.* 1980;239:E524–E580.

3. Korenchevsky V. Major involution of organs and tissues with ageing. In: Bourne GH, ed. *Physiological and Pathological Ageing.* New York, NY: Hafner Publishing Co Inc; 1961.

4. Uauy R, Winterer JC, Bilmazes C, et al. The changing pattern of whole body protein metabolism in aging humans. *J Gerontol.* 1978;33:663–671.

5. Munro HN, Crim MC. The proteins and amino acids. In: Shils ME, Young VR, eds. *Modern Nutrition in Health and Disease.* 7th ed. Philadelphia, Pa: Lea & Febiger; 1988.

6. Gersovitz M, Motil K, Munro HN, et al. Human protein requirements: assessment of the adequacy of the current recommended allowance for dietary protein in elderly men and women. *Am J Clin Nutr.* 1982;35:6–14.

7. Munro HN, McGandy RB, Hartz SC, et al. Protein nutriture of a group of free-living elderly. *Am J Clin Nutr.* 1987;46:586–592.

8. FAO/WHO/UNU. Energy and protein requirements. *Technical Report Series No. 724.* Geneva, Switzerland: World Health Organization; 1985.

9. Meguid MM, Matthews DE, Bier DM, et al. Leucine kinetics at graded leucine intakes in young men. *Am J Clin Nutr.* 1986;43:770–780.

10. Meguid MM, Matthews DE, Bier DM, et al. Valine kinetics at graded valine intakes in young men. *Am J Clin Nutr.* 1986;43:781–786.

11. Meredith CN, Wen ZM, Bier DM, et al. Lysine kinetics at graded lysine intakes in young men. *Am J Clin Nutr.* 1986;43:787–794.

12. Zhao ZH, Wen ZM, Meredith CN, et al. Threonine kinetics at graded threonine intakes in young men. *Am J Clin Nutr.* 1986;43:795–802.

13. Souba WW, Wilmore DW. Diet and nutrition in the care of the patient with surgery, trauma, and sepsis. In: Shils ME, Young VR, eds. *Modern Nutrition in Health and Disease.* 7th ed. Philadelphia, Pa: Lea & Febiger; 1988.

14. Brenner BM, Meyer TW, Hostetter TH. Dietary protein intake and the progressive nature of the kidney disease: the role of hemodynamically mediated glomerular injury in the pathogenesis of progressive glomerular sclerosis in aging, renal ablation, and intrinsic renal disease. *N Engl J Med.* 1982;307:652–659.

15. Elema JD, Arends A. Focal and segmental glomerular hyalinosis and sclerosis in the rat. *Lab Invest.* 1975;33:554–561.

16. Yu BP, Masoro EJ, Murata I, et al. Life span study of SPF Fischer 344 male rats fed ad libitum or restricted diets: longevity, growth, lean body mass and disease. *J Gerontol.* 1982;37:130–141.

17. Blum M, Averbach M, Wolman Y, et al. Protein intake and kidney function in humans: its effect on "normal aging." *Arch Intern Med.* 1989;149:211–212.

18. Tobin J. Nutrition and organ function in a cohort of aging men. In: Hutchinson M, Munro HN, eds. *Nutrition and Aging: 5th Annual Bristol-Meyers Symposium on Nutritional Research.* New York, NY: Academic Press Inc; 1986.

19. McGandy RB, Barrows CH, Spanias A, et al. Nutrient intakes and energy expenditure in men of different ages. *J Gerontol.* 1966;21:581–587.

20. Elahi VK, Elahi D, Andres R, et al. A longitudinal study of nutritional intake in men. *J Gerontol.* 1983:38·162–180.

21. *Health and Nutrition Examination Survey No. 2.* Hyattsville, Md: Division of Health Statistics, US Public Health Service; 1981.

22. Kannel WB, Gordon T. *The Framingham Diet Study: An Epidemiological Investigation of Cardiovascular Disease.* Washington, DC: Section 24, Public Health Service; 1970. US Dept of Health, Education, and Welfare.

23. Owen OE, Holup JL, D'Alessio DA, et al. A reappraisal of the caloric requirements of men. *Am J Clin Nutr.* 1987;46:875–885.

24. Phillips PA, Rolls BJ, Ledingham JGG, et al. Reduced thirst after water deprivation in healthy elderly men. *N Engl J Med.* 1984;311:753–759.

25. Miller PD, Krebs RA, Neal BJ, et al. Hypodipsia in geriatric patients. *Am J Med.* 1982;73:354–356.

26. Lowenstein FW. Nutritional requirements of the elderly. In: Young EA, ed. *Nutrition, Aging and Health.* New York, NY: Alan R Liss Inc; 1986.

27. Linscheer WG, Vergroesen AJ. Lipids. In: Shils ME, Young VR, eds. *Modern Nutrition in Health and Disease.* 7th ed. Philadelphia, Pa: Lea & Febiger; 1988.

28. Kannel WB. Cholesterol and risk of coronary heart disease and mortality in men. *Clin Chem.* 1988;34:B53–B59.

29. American Heart Association. *Dietary Guidelines for Healthy American Adults: A Statement for Physicians and Health Professionals by the Nutrition Committee.* Dallas, Tx: American Heart Association; 1986.

30. Garber AM, Sox HC Jr, Littenberg B. Screening asymptomatic adults for cardiac risk factors: the serum cholesterol level. *Ann Intern Med.* 1989;110:622–639.

31. Kannel WB. Nutritional contributors to cardiovascular disease in the elderly. *J Am Geriatr Soc.* 1986;34:27–36.

32. Mariotti S, Capocuccia R, Farchi G, et al. Age, period, cohort and geographical area effects on the relationship between risk factors and coronary disease mortality. *J Chron Dis.* 1986;39:229–242.

33. Grundy SM. Cholesterol and coronary heart disease. *JAMA.* 1986;256:2849–2858.

34. Hjermann I, Velve Byre K, Holme I, et al. Effect of diet and smoking intervention on the incidence of coronary heart disease: report on the Oslo Study Group of a randomised trial in healthy men. *Lancet.* 1981;2:1303–1310.

35. Lipid Research Clinics Program. The Lipid Research Clinics Coronary Primary Prevention Trial results, I: reduction in the incidence of coronary heart disease. *JAMA.* 1984;251:351–364.

36. Stout RW. Cardiovascular disease, atherosclerosis and ischaemic heart disease. In: Exton-Smith AN, Weksler ME, eds. *Practical Geriatric Medicine*. New York, NY: Churchill Livingstone Inc; 1985.

37. Thom TJ, Kannel WB. Downward trend in cardiovascular mortality. *Annu Rev Med*. 1981;32:427.

38. Myrianthopoulos M. Dietary treatment of hyperlipidemia in the elderly. *Clin Geriatr Med*. 1987;3:343–359.

39. Nutrition Committee and the Council of Arteriosclerosis of the American Heart Association. Recommendations for treatment of hyperlipidemia in adults. *Circulation*. 1984;69:1064A–1090A.

40. MacDonald I. Carbohydrates, A: general. In: Shils ME, Young VR, eds. *Modern Nutrition in Health and Disease*. 7th ed. Philadelphia, Pa: Lea & Febiger; 1988.

41. Jenkins DJA. Carbohydrates, B: dietary fiber. In: Shils ME, Young VR, eds. *Modern Nutrition in Health and Disease*. 7th ed. Philadelphia, Pa: Lea & Febiger; 1988.

42. Cummings JH, Branch W, Jenkins DJA, et al. Colonic response to dietary fibre from carrot, cabbage, apple, bran and guar gum. *Lancet*. 1978;1:5–9.

43. Jenkins DJA, Wolever TMS, Leeds AR, et al. Dietary fibres, fibre analogues, and glucose tolerance: importance of viscosity. *Br Med J*. 1978;1:1392–1394.

44. Vinik AI, Jenkins DJA. Dietary fiber in management of diabetes. *Diabetes Care*. 1988; 11:160–173.

45. Jenkins DJA, Reynolds D, Slavin B, et al. Dietary fiber and blood lipids: treatment of hypercholesterolemia with guar crispbread. *Am J Clin Nutr*. 1980;33:575–581.

46. Masoro EJ. Food restriction in rodents: an evaluation of its role in the study of aging. *J Gerontol Biol Sci*. 1988;43(3):B59–B64. Minireview.

47. Morrison SD. Nutrition and longevity. *Nutr Rev*. 1983;41(5):133–142.

Chapter 3

Vitamin Requirements

Paolo M. Suter

In the United States and all other Western countries, the elderly segment of the population is rapidly increasing in age and number (Chapter 1). In 1984 about 28 million (almost 12%) of the population of the United States were age 65 years or older. This population group has been identified as the fastest growing segment of the population of the United States.[1] Although most of the increasing life expectancy is due to declining death rates among the elderly, this does not necessarily imply better health. More than 80% of all older Americans have at least one chronic health condition, and they use health care services at a significantly higher rate than does the rest of the population[2] (Chapter 1).

Old age is a period of life with increased psychologic and disease-related stress events and diminished capacity to cope with these multiple challenges.[3] Aging implies physiologic changes in the gastrointestinal tract (Chapter 7) and metabolism.[4,5] Knowledge of the potential impact of these alterations on human nutritional requirements is rather scanty, and the information presently available seems to be insufficient for practical implementation.[6] The current (1989) recommended dietary allowances (RDAs)[7] attempt to define the level of nutrient intake that will maintain good health in most of the individuals of a population. The 1989 RDA offers recommendations for everyone aged 51 years or older; however, evidence suggests that generalizations about the nutritional requirements of elderly people should be made only with great caution. There is no rational basis to warrant grouping together all elderly people in one category over age 51 years.[1] It has been suggested that recommendations be made for the older population by grouping them in two age groups, 51 to 69 years (mature adults) and 70 years and older (older adults).[1,8]

In this chapter, present knowledge of vitamin nutriture in the elderly (ie, subjects aged 65 years and older) in relation to the 1989 RDAs for the group over age 51 years is discussed. Important information regarding vitamin-drug interactions is discussed in Chapter 13.

VITAMIN A

Vitamin A (retinol) plays an important role in growth and cell differentiation, vision, and maintenance of immune function.[9,10] There is growing interest in the vitamin A/carotenoid nutriture of individuals and populations because of epidemiologic evidence suggesting a potential anticarcinogenic effect of vitamin A and carotenoids.[11–14] Vitamin A activity in the human diet can be obtained either from preformed vitamin A (primarily vitamin A esters and retinol) or provitamin A compounds (primarily β-carotene). The current RDA for the group over age 51 years is 1000 mg of retinol equivalents (RE) for men and 800 mg of RE for women.[7]

The richest dietary sources of preformed vitamin A are liver and the liver oils of marine fish; other good dietary sources are milk products and whole eggs. Carotenoids are found in large amounts mainly in carrots and dark-green, leafy vegetables. Vitamin A intakes vary widely, and up to 65% of elderly people, depending on their income, sex, and race, have been shown to have vitamin A intakes less than two-thirds of the RDA (Table 3-1). Because of the wide variability of the vitamin A content in food and the technical difficulties in analyzing the vitamin A content of foods, data on vitamin intake must be interpreted with caution. An expert panel on vitamin A nutriture concluded that serum vitamin A levels <20 μg/dL (0.70 μmol/L) in individuals up to age 74 years represent an increased likelihood of physiologic impairment.[17] Plasma retinol levels about 20 μg/dL appear to be essential, while plasma levels above 30 μg/dL appear to ensure modest body stores of vitamin A.[7] Different studies[15,16,18–21] clearly show that most of the elderly maintain a normal vitamin A status (determined by serum/plasma vitamin A levels) despite low intakes relative to the RDA. Surprisingly, hardly anyone in the group of elderly surveyed (Table 3-1) showed vitamin A serum/plasma levels below the threshold level.

Table 3-1 Dietary Vitamin A Intakes and Biochemical Status in the Elderly

Author	Population Characteristics (Dietary Recall)	Intakes Men	Intakes Women	Plasma Levels Men	Plasma Levels Women
HANES I[15]	Nationwide, 60–74 y, free-living (24-h recall)	47–65*	42–51*	0–0.3	
		<⅔ RDA			
Garry et al[16]	New Mexico, free-living, healthy, 60–93 y (3-day food records; 4-y follow-up)	6†	5†	0	0
		<¾ RDA			

*Depending on sex, race, and income.
†Averaged dietary intakes for three separate collections spanning 4 years; percentage less than three fourths of RDA.

Circulating plasma/serum vitamin A levels reflect only the immediate availability of vitamin A for cellular metabolism. Vitamin A plasma/serum levels do not reflect adequate vitamin A nutriture, since normal plasma levels are maintained as long as liver stores are maintained.[22,23] Present evidence suggests that liver stores of vitamin A are not affected by age per se in humans,[24] but in animals the liver retinoid stores have been shown to increase with age.[25]

Vitamin A absorption increases with age in animals. In humans the few available data are conflicting; evidence from one study using vitamin A tolerance curves showed higher peak levels in elderly subjects than those in a young control group after physiologic doses. The reported increased absorption of vitamin A with age in animals and humans might be due to age-related changes in the character of the unstirred water layer.[26]

Vitamin A has considerable toxicity.[9,23] In view of the widespread vitamin A supplement used by the elderly,[16,18,19] it has been suggested that the increased absorption of vitamin A with age could contribute to toxicity in elderly individuals who have high vitamin A intakes from dietary supplementation.[26]

Chronic diseases that occur mainly in aging people may influence vitamin A nutriture negatively by affecting vitamin A absorption, recycling and conservation, tissue utilization, and storage. Lipid malabsorption syndromes (mainly pancreatic insufficiency and hepatic insufficiency) reduce vitamin A absorption by causing inadequate lipolysis and poor capacity for micelle formation.[9] Of major importance in elderly people are chronic liver diseases, often related to the chronic ingestion of alcohol, which impairs the storage of vitamin A in the liver as well as the ability of the liver to synthesize retinol-binding protein.[23,27,28] In normal aging, defined as occurring in the absence of any disease, however, the liver hardly senesces, and constitutive liver functions are maintained, suggesting no alterations in vitamin A metabolism. It is important to note that several drugs (eg, phenobarbital and ethanol) are capable of affecting the metabolism by accelerating hepatic retinol breakdown.[29]

There are two forms of hypervitaminosis A: acute and chronic.[30] Acute hypervitaminosis A is rare in elderly people, whereas chronic hypervitaminosis A can be seen in this group.[31,32] Chronic toxicity is more often due to overdoses or overuse of vitamin A supplements rather than consumption of vitamin A-rich foods. Because of the availability of over-the-counter vitamin A capsules containing up to 25,000 IU of vitamin A, the potential for hypervitaminosis A is high.[33] Recently it was shown that supplemental vitamin A intake is associated with greater levels of circulating retinyl esters in fasting blood (plasma retinol levels are unrelated to vitamin A intake), and high levels of plasma retinyl esters may be an indicator of liver damage or toxicity.[32] It has been suggested that the margin of safety for vitamin A intake in elderly people may be decreased because of the predisposition of this population group to hypervitaminosis A. Several factors and diseases may predispose for vitamin A toxicity, such as age, high vitamin E intake,[32] protein malnutrition, kidney disease, and liver disease.[31] In animal studies, large doses of vitamin E increased vitamin A uptake and hepatic storage, therefore predisposing to potential toxicity; however, vitamin E has also been shown to protect biomembranes from disruption due to high vitamin A intake.

Patients with alcoholic liver disease show low levels of hepatic vitamin A, although blood vitamin levels are normal.[34] In view of the evidence for potential liver damage due to hepatic vitamin A depletion in animals, supplementation with vitamin A may be indicated. However, there is evidence that the amounts of vitamin A considered to be safe under normal conditions (ie, in the absence of chronic alcoholism) may show considerable hepatotoxicity in alcoholics.[35]

Because of the well-controlled regulation of the conversion of carotene to retinol, hypervitaminosis A does not occur with higher intakes of carotenoids.[31] At the present time no statement about the optimal intake of carotene can be made. However, in view of the potentially important roles of carotenoids (chiefly β-carotene) in the prevention of different diseases, and the nontoxicity of even high intakes of carotenoids, high *dietary* intake can be recommended and should be encouraged.[36–39]

Healthy elderly persons are able to maintain adequate body stores of vitamin A and normal vitamin A plasma/serum levels despite intakes well below the actual RDAs. It can be concluded that the vitamin A status of healthy elderly individuals does not require special attention, and the 1989 RDAs seem to be more than adequate.[8,9] However, one part of the total vitamin A is ingested in the form of carotenoids and they may supply important antioxidant capacity by quenching singlet oxygen, thus being theoretically involved in the potential prevention of "free radical diseases" (ie, the major diseases associated with aging).[11,12,40] Further research addressing this important—and thus far only theoretical—issue is needed. With the exception of defined subgroups, such as chronic alcoholics, vitamin A nutriture appears to be adequate in most healthy elderly people.

VITAMIN D

Vitamin D, or the vitamin D endocrine system, is involved not only in the regulation of bone and mineral metabolism but also in the modulation of several fundamental cellular processes.[41,42] The current RDA for vitamin D for elderly people, ie, aged 51 and older, is 5 μg/d (200 IU), ie, half of the RDA for vitamin D recommended during growth (400 IU).[7] Vitamin D can be obtained either from dietary sources or by synthesis in the skin on exposure to the sun; however, it is controversial which of the two possible sources is more important for the maintenance of adequate vitamin D nutriture.[42–44]

It has been shown that 60% to 74% of the free-living elderly have intakes of vitamin D that are less than two-thirds of the RDA.[19,21,44,45] Plasma and serum levels of 25-hydroxyvitamin D_3 (25(OH)D_3), which are good markers of vitamin D nutriture, have been reported to decline with age; plasma levels in elderly subjects are decreased by more than 50% as compared with younger controls.[21,44,46–48] Blood levels of 25(OH)D_3 below 10 ng/mL have been reported in 2% to 40% of free-living elderly people and in 70% to 90% of homebound elderly. In addition to low dietary vitamin D intakes, there are several mechanisms leading to low or decreased plasma 25(OH)D_3 levels (Table 3-2). Exposure to sunlight decreases with age, and a decreased capacity of the skin to synthesize vitamin D has been reported. Therefore, elderly individuals show a decreased 7-dehydrocholesterol (provitamin D_3) content in the skin, and the conversion of the provitamin after exposure to ultraviolet light decreases in the skin of elderly people, leading to a suboptimal endogenous vitamin D synthesis.[49] This is reflected in less marked seasonal variations of 25(OH)D_3 plasma levels.

Plasma levels of 1,25-dihydroxyvitamin D_3 (1-25(OH)$_2D_3$) decrease by up to 40% with age.[46–48] The cause for this change is an age-related decline in renal 1α-hydroxylase activity,[48] probably due to decreased responsiveness of this enzyme to parathyroid hormone over time. Present evidence for vitamin D malabsorption in the elderly is controversial[44] and probably is not a factor in these metabolic changes.

Calcium absorption does decrease with age and, with aging, there is a failure to adjust (ie, increase) the rate of absorption to low levels of calcium intake[50] (Chapter 4). The mechanism of this age-related decline in calcium absorption is not exactly known; however, the failure to synthesize adequate amounts of 1,25(OH)$_2D_3$ might be at least partly responsible.

There is evidence that age-related bone loss is caused in part by the alterations in vitamin D metabolism.[48] Vitamin D supplementation might be of therapeutic value for patients with osteoporosis; however, the smallest dosage that will increase calcium absorption should be used, and serum and urine calcium concentrations should be monitored to prevent hypercalcemia and hypercalciuria.[51]

Table 3-2 Age-Related Changes in the Vitamin D Endocrine System

- low vitamin D intake
- decreased vitamin D absorption*
- decreased synthesis in the skin
- decreased 25(OH)D_3 hydroxylation in the liver*
- decreased 1-hydroxylation in the kidney
- decreased plasma binding capacity for different vitamin D metabolites
- increased risk for vitamin D drug interactions
- decreased sun exposure in the aged

*Indicates evidence is weak and controversial

Because of the central role of the liver in vitamin D metabolism, any malfunction of the liver will interfere with the absorption, transport, and metabolism of vitamin D. For example, reduced synthesis of vitamin D-binding protein will occur with cirrhosis of the liver. Alcohol-related liver disease, in particular, will impair vitamin D nutriture; this is reflected in decreased plasma 25(OH)D₃ levels in alcoholics.[27,42] Of greater relevance to aging is the decline in renal function with functionally impaired 1 α-hydroxylase as discussed above. Self-supplementation of vitamin D by elderly people without biochemical monitoring should be discouraged under any circumstances.[51]

The 1,25(OH)₂D₃ receptors are found in many different body tissues other than the classic target tissues (bone, kidney, and intestine), therefore suggesting that the active form of this vitamin may have a wider biologic role than in the regulation of mineral and bone metabolism.[52,53] Interactions of vitamin D with the hematopoietic system have been reported.[52,54] The discovery of vitamin D receptor expression in hematopoietic cells and the finding that these receptors are induced in activated lymphocytes[55] suggest that this vitamin may play an important role in the immune response.[56,57]

Besides other functions, 1-25(OH)₂D₃ has been shown to inhibit the growth-promoting lymphokine interleukin-2, thus inhibiting the proliferation of mitogen-activated lymphocytes.[58] Furthermore, the production of immunologically active lymphokines, such as interferon-γ may be suppressed through the action of the active form of vitamin D.[52,59] In addition, immunoglobulin production by activated peripheral blood mononuclear cells is suppressed by vitamin D₃. It has been suggested that 1-25(OH)₂D₃ is able to regulate macrophages, and it has been shown that different vitamin D metabolites promote and are needed for the natural resistance to tuberculosis.[59] There is growing evidence that the active metabolite of vitamin D may play an important role in immunoregulation.[52,53] However, further research of these interesting and potentially clinically relevant aspects of vitamin D on the immune system is needed.

In summary, there are several different age-related changes in vitamin D metabolism that have great potential to interfere negatively with vitamin D status (Table 3-2). Presently there is not yet adequate evidence to suggest an alteration in the RDA for vitamin D. In view of the different age-related changes, an increase in exposure to sunlight whenever possible, in combination with biochemically controlled low-dose vitamin D supplementation (10 μg/d, or 400 IU), especially for housebound elderly persons, should be considered.

VITAMIN E

Because of the potential involvement of antioxidants in aging,[60,61] interest in vitamin E metabolism and nutriture is growing. The present daily RDA for vitamin E for the group over age 51 years is 8 mg of α-tocopherol equivalents for women and 10 mg for men.[7] There are 8 tocopherol isomers; however, the α-tocopherol form has the highest biologic activity. In general, polyunsaturated fatty acid-rich foods are good sources of vitamin E.[62]

Up to 40% of elderly persons have been reported to have vitamin E intakes less than three-fourths of the RDA[19,63,64]; however, intake of vitamin E supplements in elderly people in the United States is rather common.[18,19]

In recent reviews, Kelleher and Losowsky[65] and Ledvina[63] reported an age-related increase in plasma vitamin E levels in most of the populations they studied. This age-related increase in plasma tocopherol levels is probably related to an increase in the lipoprotein carriers, as well as increased tissue stores of this lipid-soluble vitamin with advancing age.[21] Others have reported a decrease in plasma vitamin E levels after age 60 years, paralleling the observed decline in plasma lipid levels in some segments of the elderly population; plasma lipid levels may seem to decrease after age 60 years because of the increased premature mortality rates of persons with hyperlipidemias. Different trends in the concentrations of vitamin E isomers have been reported by Vatassery and colleagues.[66] The concentrations of α-tocopherol and total tocopherol in plasma did not significantly change with age; however, the plasma γ-tocopherol and the platelet α- and γ-tocopherol and total tocopherol concentrations decreased significantly with age. These changes have been related to increased platelet aggregation and enhanced lipid peroxidation in platelets from aged individuals.[67]

By the erythrocyte hemolysis test, up to 38% of hospitalized, acutely ill patients aged 65 and older had low serum tocopherol levels (ie, 4.5 μg/mL).[65] There was an age-related increase in the vitamin E requirements in animals using the erythrocyte hemolysis or bioassay procedures (fertility assay);[68] similarly, lipid peroxidation was reported to increase with age in animal liver tissue.[69] Others, however, reported no change in the prevalence of vitamin E deficiency, detected by the erythrocyte hemolysis test, with advanced age.[70] Evidence for lower requirements with age comes from finding that in older rats, compared with younger animals, depletion of body stores of vitamin E was more difficult.[71]

There is no clear evidence for an age-related alteration in vitamin E absorption.[63,65] Similarly, the findings on vitamin E tissue concentrations in subjects of advanced age are controversial and vary according to the technique used as well as the population studied.[21,63]

Free radical damage, and thus antioxidation, may play an important role in different diseases[67,72,73] as well as in immunologic status[74]; epidemiologic[75] and experimental evidence offers potential therapeutic or preventive applications for vitamin E. It is well known that vitamin E aids in the stabilization of biologic membranes. One of the primary roles of vitamin E is the protection of lipids from peroxidation by aggressive oxygen forms such as molecular oxygen, superoxide anion, hydroperoxy radical, or singlet oxygen. The formation of the different oxygen forms in a free radical chain reaction induces direct cellular damage.[76] This cellular damage leads to other changes, such as an increase in the cytosolic concentration of calcium ions, causing further cell damage and leading to some of the well-known clinical conditions.[72]

Vitamin E is a major free radical chain-interrupting antioxidant in the lipid phases of biologic systems.[77] Of the different vitamin E isomers, α-tocopherol has the highest biologic activity. Oxygen radicals may play an important role in certain diseases and clinical conditions, such as inflammatory immune injury; ischemic conditions; alcohol-induced organ damage, eg, alcoholic cardiomyopathy; immune deficiency conditions such as immune deficiency of advanced age; certain cancers; Parkinson disease; and atherosclerosis.[72,76,77]

A correlation between vitamin E status and ischemic heart disease has been reported.[75] Gey and associates[75] found higher vitamin E levels in plasma in areas with low to medium coronary mortality, compared with areas with a high coronary mortality. Therefore, a potential preventive effect of vitamin E on ischemic heart disease has been suggested. No intake recommendations can be given at present, however, since vitamin E requirements depend on the dietary intake of polyunsaturated fatty acids. These epidemiologic data are supported by the findings that plasma low-density lipoprotein (LDL) is subject to free radical attack. Oxidized LDL particles show different functional changes leading to improved recognition by the scavenger receptor on macrophages, thus potentially enhancing atherogenesis.[78,79] It is not known what specific role vitamin E may have in the pathogenesis of different diseases, since data are conflicting.

Presently there is no evidence for altered vitamin E requirements with aging, and the present RDAs seem to be adequate. To clarify the confusing issue of requirements, more reseach is greatly needed.

VITAMIN K

The most important role of vitamin K is to support the post-translational carboxylation of glutamate residues, which are involved in the formation of the modified amino acid γ-carboxyglutamate, necessary for normal blood coagulation.[80]

Despite recent discoveries in the fast-moving field of vitamin K metabolism, only incomplete information is available on vitamin K requirements. In the 1989 RDA, a recommendation for vitamin K is given for the first time. Although the recommendation is based on only a few studies, it appears that a dietary intake of 1 μg/kg of body weight per day should be sufficient for the maintenance of normal blood clotting in adults.[7] Therefore, the RDA for a 79-kg man is 80 μg/d; for a 63-kg woman, it is 65 μg/d.[7] However, it is not known whether more vitamin K is needed for optimal function of other vitamin K-dependent proteins that contain γ-carboxyglutamyl residues.

Diet and the bacterial flora in the jejunum and ileum are sources of vitamin K.[7,81] Diet-induced vitamin K deficiency occurs only rarely.[82] Very few data exist on vitamin K nutriture in the elderly. A prolongation of prothrombin time is indicative of vitamin K deficiency; it is usually corrected easily with vitamin K administration. By use of a test depending on all four vitamin K-dependent clotting factors, it was shown that more than 50% of surveyed elderly patients (randomly selected, aged 56 to 100 years) had an impaired vitamin K status,[83] suggesting a subclinical vitamin K deficiency. However, many of the subjects surveyed by Hazell and Baloch[83] suffered a variety of diseases, such as cerebral thrombosis, bronchopneumonia, myocardial infarction, and diabetes mellitus, and therefore were not a representative sample of healthy elderly subjects. Experimental vitamin K deficiency is achieved more easily in older animals than in younger animals;[84] however, it is not clear whether this is due to specific age-related changes in vitamin K metabolism or simply increased vitamin K intake per unit of body weight in the younger adults.

Regarding drug interactions, there is great interest in vitamin K and anticoagulation therapy. Despite no significant age-related changes in warfarin pharmacokinetics, healthy elderly persons without liver disease have an increased sensitivity to warfarin.[85]

In view of the popularity of vitamin supplementation,[18,19] the potentially important interaction of vitamin E with vitamin K should be mentioned. High intakes of vitamin E, and also of vitamin A, can produce a vitamin K-responsive hemorrhagic condition in persons treated with anticoagulant drugs.[7,81] The anticoagulant potential of the tocopherols in physiologic amounts is probably of no clinical significance in healthy adults, and it has been shown that daily vitamin E intake of no more than 400 IU of tocopherol seems to be safe in normal elderly persons as well as in persons treated with anticoagulants.[86] Any higher intake of vitamin E, especially in the elderly, should be discouraged to minimize potentially lethal bleeding. No statement regarding the adequacy of the RDA of vitamin K for elderly people can be made, and, because of the lack of studies, it is not known whether older healthy people have altered vitamin K requirements.

VITAMIN C

The vitamin C deficiency disease, scurvy, is very rare in Western society; however, it might occur in certain subjects who ingest an inadequate diet.[87] To prevent scurvy, approximately 10 mg of ascorbic acid is needed daily. The present RDA for vitamin C is 60 mg/d for both sexes.[7] Despite the abundance of vitamin C in food, vitamin C intakes in elderly people vary widely, and up to 60% of the elderly have been shown to have intakes below 30 mg/d.[15,19–21,45,88–92] Dietary ascorbic acid intake decreases with age. In the Health and Nutrition Examination Survey I (HANES I),[15] 23% to 42% of the elderly, depending on income and race, have been shown to have intakes below 30 mg/d. Other studies, however, report dietary ascorbic acid intakes as high as 100 mg/d.[88] Furthermore, ascorbic acid supplements are widely used, even among the elderly population.[18,19,88]

With increasing age there is a decrease in ascorbic acid levels in whole blood, serum/plasma, and leukocytes.[93–95] Some studies have failed to show an age-related decline in serum ascorbic acid levels. Some of the controversy might be caused by the strong seasonal variation of vitamin C intakes, contributing to the availability of vitamin C-containing foods, and social differences in the populations studied. In general, institutionalization affects vitamin C status adversely.

Elderly individuals have lower blood/plasma/serum ascorbic acid levels compared with younger controls, and up to 43% of the aged have been shown to have low ascorbic acid levels (less than 0.2 mg/dL).[21,95] Most studies show lower ascorbic acid levels in elderly men than in elderly women; it has been suggested that the sex difference in plasma ascorbic acid concentration is due to lower tubular reabsorption of the vitamin in elderly men.[96] However, other factors, such as increased debilitation in men, have also been suggested as a possible explanation.[93] Results concerning changes in ascorbic acid tissue levels with age are controversial.[97,98] To date, there is no clear evidence for age-related changes in vitamin C absorption.[21]

Low levels of vitamin C in the blood of healthy elderly people can be corrected easily by the administration of oral ascorbic acid supplements; however, withdrawal of the supplement leads to a rapid decrease.[99] These findings suggest that low blood levels of vitamin C can be attributed only to low intakes and not to an age-related physiologic defect such as decreased absorption. Since the reported low ascorbic acid levels usually are not associated with obvious clinical symptoms, it has been concluded that there is no need to raise levels in the blood through supplementation. However, the health consequences of chronic marginal vitamin C deficiency and its pathophysiologic role in the development of diseases is not known.[100]

Several conditions, such as stress and smoking, increase vitamin C requirements.[7] Some evidence suggests an inverse relation between certain diseases and vitamin C nutriture; vitamin C may play a role in prevention of cancer[12,101,102] and atherosclerosis.[103–105] Considering the high use of drugs by elderly people and the importance of vitamin C in xenobiotic metabolism—and thus drug metabolism—an adequate intake of vitamin C might be desirable for them[106] (Chapter 13).

In summary, present evidence suggests that the actual RDA for vitamin C of 60 mg/d seems to be adequate for elderly people in our society. So far there are no known age-related changes in vitamin C metabolism, and impairment of vitamin C nutriture is caused mainly by inadequate dietary intakes. Regarding the potential role of vitamin C in the development of different important diseases of the aged, it seems appropriate to encourage adequate intake of this vitamin.

VITAMIN B₁

The classic vitamin B_1 (thiamine hydrochloride) deficiency syndrome of beriberi is seen rarely in Western populations, except in alcoholics.[107–109] Because of the important role of thiamine in carbohydrate metabolism, the RDA for vitamin B_1 is directly linked to total carbohydrate and overall energy intake. The 1989 RDA for thiamine is 1.2 mg/d for men and 1.0 mg/d for women.[7] The minimal requirement appears to be between 0.20 and 0.23 mg/1000 kcal; to have a large enough factor of safety, an intake of 0.5 mg/1000 kcal is recommended.[7] For elderly people, a maintenance intake of 1 mg/d is recommended, even if their consumption is less than 2000 kcal/d.[7] Recently, this recommendation has been criticized as being too generous when consideration is given to the fact that, in young subjects with an intake of 0.3 mg/1000 kcal, no biochemical deficiency could be detected.[8,108]

Up to 50% of the elderly, depending on income and race, have been reported to have intakes below two-thirds of the 1989 RDA.[15,18,21,45,108–110] Although 18% to 46% of the elderly surveyed in HANES I had thiamine intakes less than two-thirds of the RDA, the calorie-corrected intake was 0.77 mg/1000 kcal.[108] In HANES II, the calorie-corrected thiamine intake was 0.76 mg/1000 kcal.[108]

Baker and colleagues[111] reported a thiamine hypovitaminemia, measured by microbiologic assay, in 11% of the free-living elderly aged 60 to 102 years. The physiologic or functional significance of the age-related decrease in the mean red blood cell transketolase, a thiamine pyrophosphate-requiring enzyme, is not known.[112] Abnormal erythrocyte transketolase activation coefficients (ie, the enzyme response to thiamine pyrophosphate) were reported in 15% or less of the free-living elderly and in 7% to 23% of geriatric patients. Based on urinary thiamine excretion, an inadequate thiamine nutriture was found in up to 20% of free-living elderly and up to 50% of institutionalized elderly.[108,109]

There is no conclusive evidence that age alone changes vitamin B_1 absorption, and no specific age-related changes in vitamin B_1 metabolism are known.[107,108,113] Aside from low dietary intake, the most important factor affecting thiamine nutriture is alcoholism.[107,109] Alcohol interference with thiamine nutriture may occur in three ways: first, inadequate intake; second, decreased absorption by blockage of egress of thiamine from mucosal cells; and third, decreased utilization.[107]

In summary, inadequate thiamine nutriture in the elderly seems to be mainly due to low intakes or disease, or both. Despite diminished calorie intake with age, the calorie-corrected thiamine intake seems to be appropriate for most of the free-living, nonalcoholic elderly.

VITAMIN B$_2$

Vitamin B$_2$ (riboflavin) acts with its coenzymes flavin mononucleotide and flavin adenine dinucleotide in many electron transfer reactions.[114] The 1989 RDA for the group aged 51 years and over is 1.4 mg/d for men and 1.2 mg/d for women.[7] For practical reasons, the riboflavin allowance in the 1989 RDA has been computed as 0.6 mg/1000 kcal for people of all ages, and 0.5 mg/1000 kcal is considered to be the minimal requirement for adults.[7]

Depending on race and income, 12% to 36% of the elderly surveyed in HANES I had intakes less than two-thirds of the 1974 RDA[13]; 19% to 27% of the surveyed elderly in the Ten State Nutrition Survey were also below this limit.[110] In contrast, less than 6% of the healthy, free-living, middle-class elderly, aged 63 to 93 years, surveyed by Garry and associates[115] in New Mexico had vitamin B$_2$ intakes less than three-fourths of the 1989 RDA. Other studies reported adequate intakes compared with the present RDA in most of the elderly people studied.[116]

Assessment of riboflavin nutriture by either the urinary riboflavin excretion test[116,117] or the erythrocyte glutathione reductase activity coefficient (EGR-AC)[21,118] showed that 27% or less of the surveyed elderly were deficient in this nutrient. The mean ERG-AC has been shown to decrease with advancing age independent of riboflavin intakes, even in supplement users.[115] At present there is no conclusive evidence for an age-related change in vitamin B$_2$ absorption,[119] and there are no changes in tissue vitamin B$_2$ levels with age.[120]

Population subgroups with increased risk for riboflavin deficiency are persons with hypothyroidism (thyroxine regulates the flavokinase that catalyzes the conversion of riboflavin to flavin mononucleotide), diabetes mellitus (there is evidence of increased urinary losses and lower intakes due to therapeutic calorie restrictions), or chronic stress situations.[114]

Milk and milk products are the best sources of dietary riboflavin in the United States.[114] Riboflavin deficiency may therefore be a problem in populations with limited milk consumption, particularly in the elderly, probably because of lactose intolerance.

In summary, at present there is no evidence that aging affects riboflavin metabolism. The high variation in riboflavin nutriture in healthy elderly people is principally due to low intakes and is thus easily corrected.

NIACIN

Niacin plays an important role as a coenzyme component in nicotinamide adenine dinucleotide and nicotinamide adenine dinucleotide phosphate.[121] Since the amino acid tryptophan can be converted to niacin, niacin requirements are expressed as niacin equivalents (NE). Thus the 1989 RDA is 15 mg of NE per day for men and 13 mg of NE per day for women.[7] The classic niacin deficiency disease, pellagra, is uncommon in Western societies, except in association with chronic alcoholism.[121,122]

Biochemical procedures for the assessment of niacin nutriture are uncertain and only of limited practical value, leading to a lack of data regarding niacin nutriture in the elderly. Niacin intakes in elderly people vary widely depending on income and race. In HANES I, 53% of the surveyed black elderly with incomes below the poverty level had intakes below two-thirds of the RDA.[15] However, only 6% of the healthy, free-living, middle-income elderly surveyed by Garry and colleagues[19] had intakes less than three-fourths of the 1989 RDA.

By measuring the urinary excretion of *N*-methyl nicotinamide, 1% to 50% of the surveyed elderly have been shown to be niacin-deficient, depending on social status, presence of disease, or institutionalization.[123–125] Niacin absorption is not influenced by age alone.[126] Despite the paucity of data regarding niacin nutriture in elderly people, the actual recommendations seem to be adequate.

VITAMIN B$_6$

The 1989 RDA for the group aged 51 years and over is 2.0 mg of vitamin B$_6$ daily for men and 1.6 mg daily for women.[7] High protein intakes increase the need for vitamin B$_6$, and an intake of 0.02 mg of vitamin B$_6$ per gram of protein eaten is recommended.[7]

Intakes below the 1980 RDA[19,45,127–130] have been shown in 50% to 90% of elderly people. In a study by Garry and colleagues,[19] 61% of the women consumed less than 1 mg of vitamin B$_6$ per day (ie, less than 62% of the 1989 RDA); 54% of the surveyed men consumed less than 1.1 mg (less than 55% of the 1989 RDA). In approximately half of the institutionalized elderly subjects (aged 60 to 98 years) surveyed by Guilland and associates,[129] vitamin B$_6$ intakes were below 1 mg/d.

Serum and plasma vitamin B$_6$ levels are subject to large variations, depending on recent food intake, and thus do not reflect the long-term vitamin B$_6$ nutritional status. Several studies have shown a decline in serum and plasma levels of pyridoxal phosphate (PLP) (the most active form of vitamin B$_6$) with age[130–132]; the decrease in plasma PLP is approximately 0.90 ng/mL,[131] leading to an increased prevalence of low plasma levels of PLP (less than 5 ng/mL) from about 3% in healthy individuals younger than age 40 years to about 12% in individuals aged 80 years or older. An age-related increase in the enzyme alkaline phosphatase, suggested to be principally responsible for PLP degradation, combined with low dietary intakes, recently was proposed to be the reason for the age-related decline in plasma/serum levels of PLP.[133] However, animal experiments suggest an age-related alteration in the capacity to form PLP.[134] Little evidence for an alteration in pyridoxine phosphorylation with age comes from a few clinical case reports of primary sideroblastic anemia; the anemia did not respond to pyridoxine treatment, but it did respond to treatment with pyridoxal-5-phosphate.[135]

By using the tryptophan loading test as an index of vitamin B₆ nutriture, an age-related increase in abnormal loading tests was found.[130,132,136] Vitamin B₆ status, evaluated on the basis of measurements of serum or erythrocyte transaminase levels, showed an inadequacy in up to 40% of free-living elderly and up to 70% of institutionalized elderly.[21,127,129,130] Usually these abnormalities were corrected by oral vitamin B₆ supplementation[124,125]; however, in several studies the enzyme abnormalities were not corrected in up to 20% of the surveyed elderly.[127,128,137] Based on these observations, the possibility of age-related changes in vitamin B₆ metabolism and thus increased requirements with age have been suggested.[137,138]

Because most of the vitamin B₆ in food is bound to protein, normal gastric function (ie, gastric acid production, pepsin output) is crucial in the absorption of dietary vitamin B₆. Atrophic gastritis, a condition characterized by decreased acid output, is commonly found in the elderly (see also the discussions of folate and vitamin B₁₂). Recently it was shown that there is no evidence of impaired vitamin B₆ status as measured by red blood cell glutamic oxaloacetic transaminase activity coefficients in elderly subjects with atrophic gastritis.[139] It was suggested that there might be malabsorption of vitamin B₆ due to impaired hydrolysis and absorption of dietary vitamin B₆; however, this malabsorption of dietary PLP in atrophic gastritis could be compensated for by increased synthesis of vitamin B₆ by bacteria from overgrowth in the upper gastrointestinal tract due to an increased intraluminal pH.[132]

Excessive alcohol consumption and liver diseases in general are of great importance in the etiology of vitamin B₆ deficiency. Low dietary intakes, promotion of PLP degradation through the ethanol metabolite acetaldehyde, decreased storage capacity of tissues, and impaired ability of the liver to synthesize PLP lead to vitamin B₆ deficiency in most alcoholics.[140]

✳   Low dietary intakes are considered to be the main reason for the impairment of vitamin B₆ nutriture in the elderly. However, in human and animal studies, age-related alterations in vitamin B₆ metabolism have been found, suggesting the need for increased vitamin B₆ requirements with age. It is hoped that further research will soon clarify the present inconclusive data.

FOLATE

The main function of folate is the transport of single carbon atoms in intermediary metabolic processes.[141] The present RDA for the group over age 51 years is 200 µg/d for men and 180 µg/d for women.[7] Mean folate intakes in subjects up to age 65 years have been reported to vary between 149 and 205 µg/d without clinical evidence for impaired folate nutriture.[142] Jagerstad and Westesson[143] surveyed the folate intakes and blood levels of free-living elderly people, aged 60 to 67 years, over a 6-year period and reported a mean intake between 100 and 200 µg of folate per day. Surprisingly, normal folate blood levels were detected in all but five of the surveyed group. Accordingly, Bates and associates[144] reported that in a group of free-living elderly persons consuming a diet containing approximately 135 µg of folate per day, red blood cell folate was greater than 100 ng/mL and no hematologic abnormalities were detected. In general, folate intakes in elderly people vary widely; 37% of the male and 43% of the female elderly subjects surveyed by Garry and associates[19] had intakes below the 1989 RDA. However, only approximately 5% had red blood cell folate levels less than 140 ng/mL. Similarly, as recently reviewed, only 12% or less of free-living elderly were found to have low plasma/serum folate levels (ie, less than 3 µg/mL).[145] The dietary folate intake correlates with the red blood cell folate level, and 5% to 60% of elderly people, depending on their health status, socioeconomic status, and institutionalization, had red blood cell folate levels below 140 ng/mL.[145]

Folate is widely distributed in food, where it is mainly found in the form of polyglutamates. Prior to absorption, polyglutamates must be deconjugated by an intestinal folate conjugase (pteroylpolyglytamyl hydrolase) present in the brush border and intracellular fraction of the jejunal mucosa.[141] Whether the activity of this enzyme is subject to age-related alterations is controversial; however, present evidence suggests that folic acid absorption is not influenced by age.[20,146] The activity of the folate conjugase, and thus the folate absorption, is highly pH-dependent.[141] Russell and associates[146] reported diminished folic acid absorption in elderly subjects with atrophic gastritis, which is characterized by diminished gastric acid output, and thus a higher proximal small intestinal pH, leading to bacterial overgrowth of the upper gastrointestinal tract. This malabsorption may be due to a high intraluminal pH that negatively influences the pH-sensitive active uptake of folic acid by small intestinal epithelial cells. In the study by Russell and associates,[146] the folic acid malabsorption in subjects with atrophic gastritis was completely corrected (ie, normalized) by the administration of 0.1 N hydrochloric acid. Despite this folate malabsorption in atrophic gastritis, these individuals had normal serum folate levels, which might have been due to folate synthesis by bacteria that were overgrowing the upper intestinal tract.[146]

A high intake of alcohol in combination with an inadequate diet is one of the most important factors contributing to a clinical folate deficiency.[141,147] Alcohol has the potential to block several metabolic pathways of folic acid. Therefore, folic acid deficiency is widely found among chronic alcoholics.[148] Chronic alcohol intake leads to a reduced intake of folate[149] and interferes with intestinal absorption,[150] folate transport to tissues, and folate storage and release from the liver.[148,151] Furthermore, alcohol ingestion leads to an enhanced urinary excretion of folic acid.[152] The increase in urinary folate excretion produced by ethanol ingestion has been shown to be dose-related.[153] There is additional evidence of increased intestinal folate losses caused by an alcohol-related block in the enterohepatic circulation of folate, leading to a decreased concentration and redistribution of tissue folate. Because of these multilevel interactions of ethanol with folate metabolism, folate deficiency, as reflected by low serum folate levels, can be found in 20% to 80% of recently drinking alcoholics.[152]

Alcohol ingestion has a very fast and dramatic effect on serum folate levels, leading to a decrease in serum folate of more than 50% within 48 to 75 hours after ingestion.[148] These toxic effects of ethanol occur in the presence of adequate liver folate stores.[148,149] However, as soon as alcohol is cleared from the body, folate metabolism normalizes. Because of the latter circumstances, dietary supplementation of folate in chronic alcoholics may, in part, prevent some of the folate-related clinical abnormalities (eg, megaloblastic erythropoiesis) seen in these individuals. However, abstinence from ethanol nevertheless should remain the primary therapeutic goal. Folate deficiency and the toxic effect of ethanol synergistically suppress small bowel function to lead to malabsorption of other essential nutrients. Therefore, in alcoholics, a multinutrient deficiency often is found.

Present evidence suggests that there are no specific age-related changes in folate metabolism, and elderly people are capable of maintaining an adequate folate status despite low intakes. Elderly adults seem to have the same folate needs as do younger adults, and therefore the 1989 RDA of 200 μg of folate per day can be regarded as adequate.[142,143]

VITAMIN B$_{12}$

The 1989 RDA for vitamin B$_{12}$ is 2 μg/d for both men and women; the primary dietary sources of this micronutrient are animal products.[7] Nutritional vitamin B$_{12}$ deficiency from inadequate dietary intake is rare but can occur in strict vegetarians.[154] Vitamin B$_{12}$ intakes in free-living elderly may vary widely, and approximately 40% have been shown to consume less than the 1989 RDA.[19,21,45,52,155,156] Altogether, 24% of the male and 39% of the female elderly subjects in the study by Garry and associates[19] had vitamin B$_{12}$ intakes below the 1989 RDA; up to 15% had intakes below 75% of the recommended intake for vitamin B$_{12}$. Most elderly individuals, however, are capable of maintaining normal vitamin B_{12} levels despite low intakes.[156] In various surveys it has been shown that serum/plasma levels of vitamin B_{12} decline with age; however, they remain within the suggested normal range. The occurrence of low vitamin B_{12} levels (less than 150 pg/mL) increases with age.[21,157–160] It has been suggested that this age-related decline in plasma/serum vitamin B_{12} levels might be related to the increased occurrence of atrophic gastritis with increasing age.[159,160] The prevalence of atrophic gastritis in subjects aged 60 to 69 years was 24%, increasing to almost 40% in the group over age 80 years. It has been shown that atrophic gastritis decreases the bioavailability of dietary vitamin B_{12}.[161] Several mechanisms lead to the malabsorption of protein-bound vitamin B_{12} in atrophic gastritis. Because of the diminished or completely lacking gastric acid production, protein digestion is impaired and vitamin B_{12} cannot be released from its bound protein.[161] Additionally, bacteria that may overgrow the upper gastrointestinal tract may bind vitamin B_{12} or convert it to analogues, rendering the vitamin B_{12} unavailable; some of the analogues may even inhibit vitamin B_{12} absorption.[162,163] The decreased output of intrinsic factor in atrophic gastritis is probably of no clinical significance, because usually the degree of parietal cell destruction is only partial. It is not yet fully established which of the possible mechanisms is of greater importance.

The factor of age per se (ie, the absence of age-related physiologic factors such as atrophic gastritis) does not influence vitamin B_{12} absorption.[164] Recently it has been shown that vitamin B_{12} deficiency, diagnosed by measurements of serum methylmalonic acid and total homocysteine, might be present even in the absence of hematologic abnormalities, normal Schilling tests, and normal or only minimally depressed serum/plasma cobalamin levels.[165] These findings suggest that vitamin B_{12} deficiency could be a major undetected problem in apparently healthy elderly; therefore, the importance of vitamin B_{12} assessment in periodic metabolic screening of elderly subjects (especially if atrophic gastritis is present) should be emphasized.

In view of the lack of specific age-related changes in vitamin B_{12} metabolism in healthy elderly persons and the absence of apparent clinical symptoms,[154] the recommended daily intake has been lowered to 2 μg/d in the present RDA.[7] However, in view of the newer findings of Lindenbaum and associates,[165] the suggested decrease in the recommended vitamin B_{12} intake for elderly people should be interpreted and implemented with caution. Further research regarding the importance of subclinical vitamin B_{12} deficiency is needed, and newer methods for the assessment of vitamin B_{12} nutriture should be used in survey and clinical studies.

In summary, in the presence of atrophic gastritis, the bioavailability of vitamin B_{12} decreases with age in certain segments of the elderly population. Despite the different age-related changes, at present there is no conclusive evi-

dence for altered vitamin B_{12} requirements with advancing age. Elderly subjects
who may be at risk for deficiency, especially those who have atrophic gastritis,
should be monitored regularly.[7]

BIOTIN

Biotin deficiency seems to occur rarely, but it has been reported in persons who
have been on long-term total parenteral nutrition, who have ingested raw eggs
excessively, or who have certain inborn errors of metabolism.[166] There is no RDA
for biotin; however, the estimated safe and adequate daily dietary intake for biotin
is 100 to 200 µg of biotin per day, with a suggested ratio of 50 µg/1000 kcal.[7]

One study reported significantly lower biotin plasma levels in a small group of
elderly as compared with young athletes[166,167]; others reported normal values of
biotin in elderly subjects.[111] Achlorhydria has been reported to affect biotin
nutriture negatively.[168] The currently available data regarding biotin nutriture in
elderly people are very scarce and contradictory; therefore, no definitive conclusion can be reached.

PANTOTHENIC ACID

There is no RDA for pantothenic acid; however, the estimated safe and adequate
daily intake is 4 to 7 mg/d for both men and women.[7] The mean daily pantothenic
acid intake, excluding that from beverages, in a nursing home diet was 3.75 mg/d,
or 2.22 mg of the vitamin per 1000 kcal, which is less than the suggested
intake[169]; however, others reported intakes within the recommended allowance
for institutionalized and noninstitutionalized elderly.[170] In humans[171] and in
animals,[172] a decrease in protein-bound pantothenic acid in blood has been
reported; other investigators failed to show any age-related decline. Data using
urinary excretion as an index of pantothenic acid nutriture in elderly people are
contradictory; therefore, no conclusions can be drawn.

CONCLUSION

Present evidence suggests that, for most of the vitamins, the actual recommendations seem to be adequate for older people, and reported biochemical deficiencies of these vitamins are mainly due to low dietary intakes. There is evidence that
current recommendations for vitamin A are more than adequate; however,
because of the importance of vitamin A compounds in tissue differentiation and
their potential anticancer effects, a reduction in the recommendations is unwise.

Table 3-3 Adequacy of the 1989 RDA for the Elderly Population

Evidence Too Low	Evidence Too High	Evidence Adequate or No Data*
Vitamin D	Vitamin A	Riboflavin
Vitamin B_6		Folate
		Thiamine
		Vitamin C
		Niacin*
		Biotin*
		Pantothenic acid*
		Vitamin E
		Vitamin B_{12}
		Vitamin K*

*Conflicting or only little evidence.

There is some evidence to suggest higher requirements for vitamins B_{12} and B_6 in certain subgroups of the elderly population; however, further research is needed. In view of the different age-related changes in vitamin D metabolism and the importance of the vitamin in the pathogenesis of osteoporosis, increased intake might be advantageous. Very recent research suggests that vitamin E has a special role as an important membrane-bound antioxidant and, theoretically, the potential to interfere with different aging processes and diseases. Further research is needed, and at present there is no conclusive evidence for altered vitamin E requirements in the aged. Table 3-3 summarizes the evidence as discussed in this chapter. As noted above, there is still much controversy regarding vitamin nutriture and vitamin requirements in the elderly.

In view of these conflicting findings, suggestions, and recommendations, it is probably best to follow the 1989 RDA, because there is probably no harm associated with the ingestion of vitamin amounts in the recommended ranges, and a healthy individual can maintain adequate intakes for all of the vitamins from food alone. It is hoped that ongoing research will clarify some of the existing controversies.

REFERENCES

1. McGinnis JM. The Tithonus syndrome: health and aging in America. In: Chernoff R, Lipschitz DA, eds. *Health Promotion and Disease Prevention in the Elderly*. New York, NY: Raven Press; 1988.

2. Pepper C. Health care for the elderly: the "emergency response" approach. *Mt Sinai J Med (NY)*. 1987;54:2–4.

3. Sussman N. Stress and medical illness in the elderly. *Mt Sinai J Med (NY)*. 1987;54:41–46.

4. Shock NW, Greulich R, Andres R, et al. *Normal Human Aging: The Baltimore Longitudinal Study*. Washington, DC: US Government Printing Office; 1984. NIH publication No. 84-2450.

5. Bianchi L, Holt P, James OFW, et al, eds. *Aging in Liver and Gastro-intestinal Tract*. Lancaster, England: MTP Press Ltd; 1988.

6. Schneider EL, Vining EM, Hadley EC, et al. Recommended dietary allowances and the health of the elderly. *N Engl J Med*. 1986;314:157–160.

7. Food and Nutrition Board, National Research Council. *Recommended Dietary Allowances*. 10th ed. Washington, DC: National Academy Press; 1989.

8. Rosenberg IH. Nutritional needs of the elderly. In: Bianchi L, Holt P, James OFW, et al, eds. *Aging in Liver and Gastro-intestinal Tract*. Lancaster, England: MTP Press Ltd; 1988.

9. Olson JA. Vitamin A. In: Machlin LJ, ed. *Handbook of Vitamins: Nutritional, Biochemical and Clinical Aspects*. New York, NY: Marcel Dekker Inc; 1984.

10. Chandra RK, Au B. Single nutrient deficiency and cell mediated immune responses, III: vitamin A. *Nutr Res*. 1981;1:181–185.

11. Burton GW, Ingold KU. Beta-carotene: an unusual type of lipid antioxidant. *Science*. 1984;224:569–573.

12. *Diet, Nutrition and Cancer*. Washington, DC: National Academy of Sciences Press; 1982.

13. Diplock AT. Antioxidant nutrients and disease prevention: an overview. *Am J Clin Nutr*. 1991;53:189S–193S.

14. Garewal HS. Potential role of beta-carotene in prevention of oral cancer. *Am J Clin Nutr*. 1991;53:294S–297S.

15. Bowman BB, Rosenberg IH. Assessment of nutritional status of the elderly. *Am J Clin Nutr*. 1982;35:1142–1151.

16. Garry PJ, Hunt WC, Bandrofchak JL, et al. Vitamin A intake and plasma retinol levels in healthy elderly men and women. *Am J Clin Nutr*. 1987;46:989–994.

17. Pilch S, ed. *Assessment of the Vitamin A Nutritional Status of the U.S. Population Based on Data Collected in the Health and Nutrition Examination Surveys*. Bethesda, Md: Federation of the American Societies for Experimental Biology; 1985.

18. Gray GE, Paganini-Hill A, Ross RK. Dietary intake and nutrient supplement use in a Southern California retirement community. *Am J Clin Nutr*. 1983;38:122–128.

19. Garry PJ, Goodwin JS, Hunt WC, et al. Nutritional status in a healthy elderly population: dietary and supplemental intakes. *Am J Clin Nutr*. 1982;36:319–331.

20. Yearik ES, Wang MSL, Pisias SJ. Nutritional status of the elderly: dietary and biochemical findings. *J Gerontol*. 1980;5:663–671.

21. Suter PM, Russell RM. Vitamin requirements of the elderly. *Am J Clin Nutr*. 1987; 45:501–512.

22. Olson JA. Serum levels of vitamin A and carotenoids as reflectors of nutritional status. *J Natl Cancer Inst*. 1984;73:1439–1444.

23. Olson JA. Recommended dietary intakes (RDI) of vitamin A in humans. *Am J Clin Nutr*. 1987;45:704–716.

24. Hoppner K, Phillips WEJ, Murray TK, et al. Survey of liver vitamin A stores of Canadians. *Can Med Assoc J*. 1968;99:983–986.

25. Hendriks HFJ, Blaner WS, Brouwer A, et al. Age related changes in retinoid status and some parameters of retinoid metabolism. In: Bianchi L, Holt P, James OFW, et al, eds. *Aging in Liver and Gastro-intestinal Tract*. Lancaster, England: MTP Press Ltd; 1988.

26. Russell RM. Malabsorption and aging. In: Bianchi L, Holt P, James OFW, et al, eds. *Aging in Liver and Gastro-intestinal Tract*. Lancaster, England: MTP Press Ltd; 1988.

27. Green PHR. Alcohol, nutrition and malabsorption. *Clin Gastroenterol*. 1983;12:563–574.

28. Leo MA, Lieber CS. Hepatic fibrosis after long administration of ethanol and moderate vitamin A supplementation in the rat. *Hepatology*. 1983;3:1–11.

29. Leo MA, Lowe N, Lieber CS. Decreased hepatic vitamin A after drug administration in men and rats. *Hepatology*. 1982;5:679. Abstract.

30. Kamm JJ, Ashenfelter KO, Ehmann CW. Preclinical and clinical toxicology of selected retinoids. In: Sporn MB, Roberts AB, Goodmann DS, eds. *The Retinoids*. New York, NY: Academic Press; 1984;2.

31. Bendich A, Langseth L. Safety of vitamin A. *Am J Clin Nutr*. 1989;49:358–371.

32. Krasinski SD, Russell RM, Otradovec CL, et al. Relationship of vitamin A and vitamin E to fasting plasma retinol, retinol-binding protein, retinyl esters, carotene, α-tocopherol, and cholesterol among elderly people and young adults: increased plasma retinyl esters among the vitamin A supplement users. *Am J Clin Nutr*. 1989;49:112–120.

33. Herbert V. Toxicity of 25,000 IU vitamin A supplements in "health" food users. *Am J Clin Nutr*. 1982;36:185–186.

34. Leo MA, Lieber CS. Interaction of ethanol with vitamin A. *Alcohol Clin Exp Res*. 1983;7:15–21.

35. Leo MA, Lieber CS. Hypervitaminosis A: a liver lover's lament. *Hepatology*. 1988; 8:412–417.

36. Krinsky NI. The evidence for the role of carotenes in preventive health. *Clin Nutr*. 1988;7:107–112.

37. Lachance P. Dietary intake of carotene and the carotene gap. *Clin Nutr*. 1988;7:118–122.

38. Block G. Dietary guidelines and the result of food consumption surveys. *Am J Clin Nutr*. 1991;53:356S–357S.

39. Ziegler RG. Vegetables, fruits, and carotenoids and the risk of cancer. *Am J Clin Nutr*. 1991;53:251S–259S.

40. Harman D. The free-radical theory of aging. In: Warner HR, Butler RN, Sprott RL, et al, eds. *Modern Biological Theories of Aging*. New York, NY: Raven Press; 1987.

41. Anonymous. Vitamin D: new perspectives. *Lancet*. 1987;1:1122–1123.

42. Miller BE, Norman AW. Vitamin D. In: Machlin LJ, ed. *Handbook of Vitamins: Nutritional, Biochemical and Clinical Aspects*. New York, NY: Marcel Dekker Inc; 1984.

43. Holick MF. The photobiology of vitamin D3 in man. In: Kumar R, ed. *Vitamin D*. Boston, Mass: Martinus Nijhoff Publishing; 1984.

44. Parfitt AM, Gallagher JC, Heaney RP, et al. Vitamin D and bone health in the elderly. *Am J Clin Nutr*. 1982;36:1014–1031.

45. McGandy RB, Russell RM, Hartz SC, et al. Nutritional status survey of healthy non-institutionalized elderly: energy and nutrient intakes from three-day diet records and nutrient supplements. *Nutr Res*. 1986;6:785–798.

46. Baker MR, Peacock M, Nordin BEC. The decline in vitamin D status with age. *Age Ageing*. 1980;9:249–252.

47. Egsmose C, Lund B, McNair P, et al. Low serum levels of 25-hydroxyvitamin D and 1,25-dihydroxy-vitamin D in institutionalized old people: influence of solar exposure and vitamin D supplementation. *Age Ageing*. 1987;16:35–40.

48. Eastell R, Heath H, Kumar R, et al. Hormonal factors: PTH, vitamin D, and calcitonin. In: Riggs BL, Melton LJ III, eds. *Osteoporosis: Etiology, Diagnosis, and Management*. New York, NY: Raven Press; 1988.

49. McLaughlin J, Holick MF. Aging decreases the capacity of human skin to produce vitamin D$_3$. *J Clin Invest*. 1985;76:1536–1538.

50. Armbrecht HJ. Changes in calcium and vitamin D metabolism with age. In: Armbrecht HJ, Prendergast JM, Coe RM. *Nutritional Intervention in the Aging Process*. St. Louis, Mo: Springer-Verlag; 1984.

51. Riggs BL. Practical management of the patient with osteoporosis. In: Riggs BL, Melton LJ III, eds. *Osteoporosis: Etiology, Diagnosis, and Management*. New York, NY: Raven Press; 1988.

52. Reichel H, Koeffler HP, Norman AW. The role of the vitamin D endocrine system in health and disease. *N Engl J Med*. 1989;320:980–991.

53. Tobler A. Vitamin D as immuno-hematopoietic hormone: new perspectives for a long known substance. *Schweiz Med Wochenschr*. 1988;118:1436–1467.

54. Koeffler HP, Norman AW. Interaction between the hematopoietic system and the vitamin D endocrine system. In: Norman AW, Schaefer K, Grigoleit HG, et al, eds. *Vitamin D: Molecular, Cellular and Clinical Endocrinology*. New York, NY: Walter de Gruyter & Co.; 1988.

55. Lemire JM, Adams JS, Kermani-Arab V, et al. 1,25-Dihydroxyvitamin D$_3$ suppresses human T-helper/inducer lymphocyte activity in vitro. *J Immunol*. 1985;134:3032–3035.

56. Rigby WFC. Vitamin D: a steroid hormone of the immune system, by the immune system, for the immune system. In: Norman AW, Schaefer K, Grigoleit HG, et al, eds. *Vitamin D: Molecular, Cellular and Clinical Endocrinology*. New York, NY: Walter de Gruyter & Co; 1988.

57. Manolagas SC. Immunoregulatory properties of 1,25(OH)$_2$D$_3$: cellular requirements and mechanisms. In: Norman AW, Schaefer K, Grigoleit HG, et al, eds. *Vitamin D: Molecular, Cellular and Clinical Endocrinology*. New York, NY: Walter de Gruyter & Co; 1988.

58. Tsoukas CD, Provvedini DM, Manolagas SC. 1,25-Dihydroxyvitamin D$_3$: a novel immunoregulatory hormone. *Science*. 1984;224:1438–1440.

59. Crowle AJ, Ross EJ, May MH. Vitamin D and human antituberculosis immunity. In: Norman AW, Schaefer K, Grigoleit HG, et al, eds. *Vitamin D: Molecular, Cellular and Clinical Endocrinology*. New York, NY: Walter de Gruyter & Co; 1988.

60. Warner HR, Butler RN, Sprott RL, et al, eds. *Modern Biological Theories of Aging*. New York, NY: Raven Press; 1988.

61. Cutler RG. Antioxidants and aging. *Am J Clin Nutr*. 1991;53:373S–379S.

62. Machlin LJ. Vitamin E. In: Machlin LJ, ed. *Handbook of Vitamins: Nutritional, Biochemical and Clinical Aspects*, New York, NY: Marcel Dekker Inc.; 1984.

63. Ledvina M. Vitamin E in the aged. In: Watson RR, ed. *Handbook of Nutrition in the Aged*. Boca Raton, Fla: CRC Press; 1985.

64. Leichter J, Angel JF, Lee M. Nutritional status of a select group of free-living elderly people in Vancouver. *Can Med Assoc J*. 1978;118:40–43.

65. Kelleher J, Losowsky MS. Vitamin E in the elderly. In: DeDuve C, Hayaishi O, eds. *Tocopherol, Oxygen and Biomembranes*. Amsterdam, Holland: Elsevier/North Holland Biomedical Press; 1978.

66. Vatassery GT, Johnson GJ, Krezowski AM. Changes in vitamin E concentration in human plasma and platelets with age. *J Am Coll Nutr*. 1983;4:369–375.

67. Bieri JG, Corash L, van Hubbard S. Medical uses of vitamin E. *N Engl J Med*. 1983;308:1063–1070.

68. Ames SR. Age, parity, and vitamin A supplementation and the vitamin E requirement of female rats. *Am J Clin Nutr*. 1974;27:1017–1025.

69. Chen LH. The effect of age and dietary vitamin E on the tissue lipid peroxidation of mice. *Nutr Rep Int*. 1974;10:339–344.

70. Tulloch JA, Sood NK. Vitamin E deficiency in Uganda. *Am J Clin Nutr.* 1967;20:884–887.

71. Grinna LS. Effect of dietary alpha-tocopherol on liver microsomes and mitochrondria of aging rats. *J Nutr.* 1976;106:918–929.

72. Cross CE, mod. Davis conference: oxygen radicals and human disease. *Ann Intern Med.* 1987;107:526–545.

73. Knekt P, Aromaa A, Maatela J, et al. Vitamin E and cancer prevention. *Am J Clin Nutr.* 1991;53:283S–286S.

74. Carpenter MP. Effects of vitamin E on the immune system. In: Meyskens FL, Prasad KN, eds. *Vitamins and Micronutrients.* Clifton, NJ: Humana Press; 1985.

75. Gey KF, Brubacher GB, Stähelin HB. Plasma levels of antioxidant vitamins in relation to ischemic heart disease and cancer. *Am J Clin Nutr.* 1987;45:1368–1377.

76. Gardner H. Oxygen radical chemistry of polyunsaturated fatty acids. *Free Radic Biol Med.* 1989;7:65–86.

77. Niki E. Antioxidants in relation to lipid peroxidation. *Chem Phys Lipids.* 1987;44:227–253.

78. Juergens G, Hoff HF, Chisolm GM, et al. Modifications of human serum low density lipoprotein by oxidation: characterization and pathophysiological implications. *Chem Phys Lipids.* 1987;45:315–336.

79. Heinecke JW. Free radical modification of low density lipoprotein: mechanisms and biological consequences. *Free Radic Biol Med.* 1987;3:65–73.

80. Friedman PA, Przysiecki CT. Vitamin K dependent carboxylation. *Int J Biochem.* 1987; 19:1–7.

81. Olson JA. Recommended dietary intakes (RDI) of vitamin K in humans. *Am J Clin Nutr.* 1987;45:687–692.

82. Colvin BT, Lloyd MJ. Severe coagulation defect due to a dietary deficiency of vitamin K. *J Clin Pathol.* 1977;30:1147–1148.

83. Hazell K, Baloch KH. Vitamin K deficiency in the elderly. *Gerontol Clin.* 1970;12:10–17.

84. Doisy EA Jr. Nutritional hypoprothrombinemia and metabolism of vitamin K. *Fed Proc.* 1961;20:989–994.

85. Shepherd AMM, Hewick DS, Moreland TA, et al. Age as a determinant of sensitivity to warfarin. *Br J Clin Pharmacol.* 1977;4:315–320.

86. Corrigan JJ Jr, Ulfers LL. Effect of vitamin E on prothrombin levels in warfarin-induced vitamin K deficiency. *Am J Clin Nutr.* 1981;34:1701–1705.

87. Connelly TJ, Becker A, McDonald JW. Bachelor scurvy. *Int J Dermatol.* 1982;21:209–211.

88. Garry PJ, Goodwin JS, Hunt WC, et al. Nutritional status in a healthy elderly population: vitamin C. *Am J Clin Nutr.* 1982;36:332–339.

89. O'Sullivan DJ, Callaghan N, Ferriss JB, et al. Ascorbic acid deficiency in the elderly. *Ir J Med Sci.* 1968;1:151–156.

90. Roine P, Koivula L, Pekkarinen M, et al. Vitamin C intake and plasma level among aged people in Finland. *Int J Vitam Nutr Res.* 1974;44:95–106.

91. Milne JS, Lonergan ME, Williamson J, et al. Leucocyte ascorbic acid levels and vitamin C intake in older people. *Br Med J.* 1971;2:383–386.

92. Olson JA, Hodges RE. Recommended dietary intakes (RDI) of vitamin C in humans. *Am J Clin Nutr.* 1987;45:693–703.

93. Kirk JE, Chieffi M. Vitamin studies in middle-aged and old individuals, XI: the concentration of total ascorbic acid in whole blood. *J Gerontol.* 1953;8:301–304.

94. Loh HS. The relationship between dietary ascorbic acid intake and buffy coat and plasma ascorbic acid concentration at different ages. *Int J Vitam Nutr Res*. 1972;42:80–85.

95. Cheng L, Cohen M, Bhagaven HN. Vitamin C and the elderly. In: Watson RR, ed. *Handbook of Nutrition in the Aged*. Boca Raton, Fla: CRC Press; 1985.

96. Garry PJ, Vanderjagt DJ, Hunt WC. Ascorbic acid intakes and plasma levels in healthy elderly. *Ann NY Acad Sci*. 1987;498:90–99.

97. Schaus R. The ascorbic acid content of pituitary, cerebral cortex, heart and skeletal muscle and its relation to age. *Am J Clin Nutr*. 1957;5:39–42.

98. Yavorsky M, Almaden P, King CG. The vitamin C content of human tissues. *J Biol Chem*. 1934;106:525–529.

99. Kirk JE, Chieffi M. Vitamin studies in middle-aged and old individuals, XII: hypovitaminemia C: effect of ascorbic acid administration on the blood ascorbic acid concentration. *J Gerontol*. 1953;8:305–311.

100. Ginter E. Chronic marginal vitamin C deficiency: biochemistry and pathophysiology. *World Rev Nutr Diet*. 1979;33:104–141.

101. Kyrtopoulos SA. Ascorbic acid and the formation of N-nitroso compounds: possible role of ascorbic acid in cancer prevention. *Am J Clin Nutr*. 1987;45:1344–1350.

102. Block G. Vitamin C and cancer prevention: the epidemiologic evidence. *Am J Clin Nutr*. 1991;53:270S–282S.

103. Gey KF, Brubacher GB, Stähelin HB. Plasma levels of antioxidant vitamins in relation to ischemic heart disease and cancer. *Am J Clin Nutr*. 1987;45:1368–1377.

104. Gey KF, Stähelin HB, Puska P, et al. Relationship of plasma level of vitamin C to mortality from ischemic heart disease. *Ann NY Acad Sci*. 1987;498:110–123.

105. Jacques PF, Hartz SC, McGandy RB, et al. Vitamin C and blood lipoproteins in an elderly population. *Ann NY Acad Sci*. 1987;498:100–110.

106. Holloway DE, Peterson FJ. Ascorbic acid in drug metabolism. In: Roe DA, Campbell TC, eds. *Drug and Nutrients: The Interactive Effects*. New York, NY: Marcel Dekker Inc; 1984.

107. Gubler CJ. Thiamine. In: Machlin LJ, ed. *Handbook of Vitamins: Nutritional, Biochemical and Clinical Aspects*. New York, NY: Marcel Dekker Inc; 1984.

108. Iber FL, Blass JP, Brin M, et al. Thiamin in the elderly: relation to alcoholism and to neurological degenerative disease. *Am J Clin Nutr*. 1982;36:1067–1082.

109. Baum RA, Iber FL. Thiamin: the interaction of aging, alcoholism and malabsorption in various populations. *World Rev Nutr Diet*. 1984;44:85–116.

110. Beauchenne RE, Davis TA. The nutritional status of the aged in the USA. *Age*. 1979;2:23–28.

111. Baker H, Frank O, Thind IS, et al. Vitamin profiles in elderly persons living at home or in nursing homes, versus profile in healthy subjects. *J Am Geriatr Soc*. 1979;27:444–450.

112. Markkanen T, Heikinheimo R, Dahl M. Transketolase activity of red blood cells from infancy to old age. *Acta Haematol (Basel)*. 1969;42:148–153.

113. Thomson AD. Thiamine absorption in old age. *Gerontol Clin*. 1966;8:354–361.

114. Cooperman JM, Lopez R. Riboflavin. In: Machlin LJ, ed. *Handbook of Vitamins: Nutritional, Biochemical and Clinical Aspects*. New York, NY: Marcel Dekker Inc; 1984.

115. Garry PJ, Goodwin JS, Hunt WC. Nutritional status in a healthy elderly population: riboflavin. *Am J Clin Nutr*. 1982;36:902–909.

116. Alexander M, Emanuel G, Golin T, et al. Relation of riboflavin nutriture in healthy elderly to intake of calcium and vitamin supplements: evidence against riboflavin supplementation. *Am J Clin Nutr*. 1984;39:540–546.

117. Lowenstein FW. Nutritional status of the elderly in the United States of America, 1971–1974. *J Am Coll Nutr.* 1982;1:165–177.

118. Chen LH, Fan Chiang WL. Biochemical evaluation of riboflavin and vitamin B_6 status of institutionalized and noninstitutionalized elderly in central Kentucky. *Int J Vitam Nutr Res.* 1981;51:232–238.

119. Said HM, Hollander D. Does aging affect the intestinal transport of riboflavin? *Life Sci.* 1985;36:69–73.

120. Schaus R, Kirk JE. The riboflavin concentration of brain, heart, and skeletal muscle in individuals of various ages. *J Gerontol.* 1957;11:147–150.

121. Hankes LV. Nicotinic acid and nicotinamide. In: Machlin LJ, ed. *Handbook of Vitamins: Nutritional, Biochemical and Clinical Aspects.* New York, NY: Marcel Dekker Inc; 1984.

122. Leevy CM, Baker H, Hove W, et al. B-complex vitamins in liver disease of the alcoholic. *Am J Clin Nutr.* 1965;16:339–346.

123. Morgan AG, Kelleher J, Walker BE, et al. A nutritional survey in the elderly: blood and urine vitamin levels. *Int J Vitam Nutr Res.* 1975;45:448–462.

124. Bonati B, Nani S, Rancati GB, Eliminazione urinaria di vitamine del complesso B nei vecchi. *Acta Vitaminol.* 1956;10:241–244.

125. Harrill I, Cervone V. Vitamin status of older women. *Am J Clin Nutr.* 1977;30:431–440.

126. Fleming BB, Barrows CH. The influence of aging on intestinal absorption of vitamin B_{12} and niacin in rats. *Exp Gerontol.* 1982;17:121–126.

127. Vir SC, Love AHG. Vitamin B_6 status of institutionalized aged. *Int J Vitam Nutr Res.* 1977;47:364–372.

128. Vir SC, Love AHG. Vitamin B_6 status of the hospitalization aged. *Am J Clin Nutr.* 1978;31:1383–1391.

129. Guilland JC, Bereksi-Reguig B, Lequeu B, et al. Evaluation of pyridoxine intake and pyridoxine status among aged institutionalized people. *Int J Vitam Nutr Res.* 1984;54:185–193.

130. Driskell JA. The vitamin B_6 status of the elderly. In: *Human Vitamin B_6 Requirements.* Washington, DC: National Academy of Sciences; 1978.

131. Rose CS, Gyorgy P, Butler M, et al. Age difference in vitamin B_6 status of 617 men. *Am J Clin Nutr.* 1976;29:847–853.

132. Hamfelt A. Age variation of vitamin B_6 metabolism in men. *Clin Chim Acta.* 1964;10:48–54.

133. Reynolds RD, Moser-Veillon PB, Kant AK. Effect of age on status and metabolism of vitamin B_6 in man. In: Leklem JE, Reynolds RE, eds. *Current Topics in Nutrition and Disease: Clinical and Physiological Applications of Vitamin B_6.* New York, NY: Alan R Liss Inc; 1988;19.

134. Fonda ML, Eggers DK. Vitamin B_6 metabolism in the blood of young adult and senescent mice. *Exp Gerontol.* 1980;15:465–472.

135. Mason DY, Emerson PM. Primary acquired sideroblastic anemia: response to treatment with pyridoxal-5-phosphate. *Br Med J.* 1973;1:389–390.

136. Ranke E. Tauber SA, Horonick A, et al. Vitamin B_6 deficiency in the aged. *J Gerontol.* 1960;15:41–44.

137. Hoorn RKJ, Flikweert JP, Westerink D. Vitamin B_1, B_2 and B_6 deficiencies in geriatric patients, measured by coenzyme stimulation of enzyme activities. *Clin Chim Acta.* 1975;61:151–162.

138. György P. Development leading to the metabolic role of vitamin B_6. *Am J Clin Nutr.* 1971;24:1250–1256.

139. Ribaya-Mercado JD, Otradovec CL, Russell RM, et al. Atrophic gastritis does not impair vitamin B_6 status in the elderly. *Gastroenterology.* 1987;93:222.

140. Driskell JA. Vitamin B$_6$. In: Machlin LJ, ed. *Handbook of Vitamins: Nutritional, Biochemical and Clinical Aspects*. New York, NY: Marcel Dekker Inc; 1984.

141. Davis RE, Nichol DJ. Folic acid. *Int J Biochem*. 1988;20:133–139.

142. Herbert V. Recommended dietary intakes (RDI) of folate in humans. *Am J Clin Nutr*. 1987;45:661–670.

143. Jagerstad M, Westesson AK. Folate. *Scand J Gastroenterol*. 1979;14(suppl 52):196–202.

144. Bates CJ, Fleming M, Paul AA, et al. Folate status and its relation to vitamin C in healthy elderly men and women. *Hum Nutr Appl Nutr*. 1982;36:422–429.

145. Rosenberg IH, Bowman BB, Cooper BA, et al. Folate nutrition in the elderly. *Am J Clin Nutr*. 1982;36:1060–1066.

146. Russell RM, Krasinski SD, Samloff IM, et al. Folic acid malabsorption in atrophic gastritis. *Gastroenterology*. 1987;91:1476–1482.

147. Halsted CH. Folate deficiency in alcoholism. *Am J Clin Nutr*. 1980;33:2736–2740.

148. Hillaman RS, Steinberg SE. The effect of alcohol on folate metabolism. *Annu Rev Med*. 1982;33:345–354.

149. Lindenbaum J. Folate and vitamin B$_{12}$ deficiencies in alcoholism. *Semin Hematol*. 1980;17:119–129.

150. Halsted CH, Robles EA, Mezey E. Intestinal malabsorption of folate deficient alcoholics. *Gastroenterology*. 1973;64:526–532.

151. Wilkinson JA, Shane B. Folate metabolism in ethanol fed rats. *J Nutr*. 1982;112:604–609.

152. Russell RM, Rosenberg IH, Wilson PD, et al. Increased urinary excretion and prolonged turnover time of folic acid during ethanol ingestion. *Am J Clin Nutr*. 1983;38:64–70.

153. McMartin KE, Collins TD, Shiao CQ, et al. Study of dose-dependence and urinary folate excretion produced by ethanol in humans and rats. *Alcohol Clin Exp Res*. 1986;10:419–424.

154. Herbert V. Recommended dietary intakes (RDI) of vitamin B$_{12}$ in humans. *Am J Clin Nutr*. 1987;45:671–678.

155. Garry PJ, Goodwin JS, Hunt WC. Folate and vitamin B$_{12}$ status in a healthy elderly population. *J Am Geriatr Soc*. 1984;32:719–726.

156. Prothro J, Mickles M, Tolbert B. Nutritional status of a population sample in Macon County, Alabama. *Am J Clin Nutr*. 1976;29:94–104.

157. Tauber S, Goodhart RS, Hsu JM, et al. Vitamin B$_{12}$ deficiency in the aged. *Geriatrics*. 1957;12:368–374.

158. Dawson AA, Donald D. The serum vitamin B$_{12}$ in the elderly. *Gerontol Clin*. 1966; 8:220–225.

159. Elsborg L, Lund V, Bastrup-Madsen P. Serum vitamin B$_{12}$ levels in the aged. *Acta Med Scand*. 1976;200:309–314.

160. Doscherholmen A, Ripley D, Chang S, et al. Influence of age and stomach function on serum vitamin B$_{12}$ concentration. *Scand J Gastroenterol*. 1977;12:313–319.

161. King CE, Leibach J, Toskes PP. Clinically significant vitamin B$_{12}$ deficiency secondary to malabsorption of protein-bound vitamin B$_{12}$. *Dig Dis Sci*. 1979;24:397–402.

162. Welkos SE, Toskes PP, Baer H, et al. Importance of anaerobic bacteria in the cobalamin malabsorption in the experimental blind loop syndrome. *Gastroenterology*. 1981;80:313–320.

163. Herbert V, Drivas G, Manusselis C, et al. Are colon bacteria a major source of cobalamin analogues in human tissues? *Trans Assoc Am Physicians*. 1984;97:161–171.

164. McEnvoy AW, Fenwick JB, Boddy K, et al. Vitamin B$_{12}$ absorption from the gut does not decline with age in normal elderly humans. *Age Ageing*. 1982;11:180–183.

165. Lindenbaum J, Healton EB, Savage DG, et al. Neuropsychiatric disorders caused by cobalamin deficiency in the absence of anemia or macrocytosis. *N Engl J Med*. 1988;318:1720–1728.

166. Bonjour JP. Biotin. In: Machlin LJ, ed. *Handbook of Vitamins: Nutritional, Biochemical and Clinical Aspects*. New York, NY: Marcel Dekker Inc; 1984.

167. Bonjour JP. Biotin in man's nutrition and therapy: a review. *Int J Vitam Nutr Res*. 1977; 47:107–118.

168. Markkanen T, Mustakallio E. Absorption and excretion of biotin after feeding minced liver in achlorhydria and after partial gastrectomy. *Scand J Clin Lab Invest*. 1963;15:57–61.

169. Walsh JH, Wyse BW, Hansen RG. Pantothenic acid content of a nursing home diet. *Ann Nutr Metab*. 1981;25:178–181.

170. Srinivasan V, Christensen N, Wyse BW, et al. Pantothenic acid nutritional status in the elderly: institutionalized and noninstitutionalized. *Am J Clin Nutr*. 1981;34:1736–1742.

171. Ishiguro K. Aging effect of blood pantothenic acid content in females. *Tohoku J Exp Med*. 1972;107:367–372.

172. Sugarman B, Munro HN. [C-14]-Pantothenate accumulation by isolated adipocytes from adult rats of different ages. *J Nutr*. 1980;110:2297–2301.

Chapter 4

Mineral Requirements

Robert D. Lindeman and Amanda A. Beck

Establishing requirements for minerals in humans is difficult, and although some of them are known to be essential to human life, specific recommendations regarding necessary intake are not available. There are no Recommended Dietary Allowances (RDAs) for sodium or potassium, although they are required for physiologic function; there are recommendations for calcium and magnesium. However, with the development of accurate, inexpensive techniques for quantifying sodium, potassium, calcium, and magnesium concentrations in biologic fluids, a vast literature has been generated documenting that deficits and excesses of these minerals create many clinical challenges for practitioners. The ability of elderly people to maintain concentrations within normal ranges is often impaired by the frequently observed decrease in renal function (Chapter 9) and by aberrations in other homeostatic mechanisms designed to conserve minerals. Certainly for some of the minerals, calcium and magnesium in particular, what is of concern is the failure to consume amounts adequate to meet known nutritional needs.

SODIUM

Sodium is an essential component in human nutrition and in the maintenance of fluid and electrolyte homeostasis. Serum sodium concentration is an accurate, precise, routinely performed laboratory measure that is useful in classifying sodium balance into hyponatremic, hypernatremic, and normal categories. Water balance status is judged by the clinical assessment of extracellular fluid volume (ECFV), which is much more subjective than the measurement of serum sodium concentration. Figure 4-1 demonstrates the relationships of sodium and water in various deficit or excess states.

Dehydration means a decrease in total body water, but the pathophysiology of its development may focus on either primary water loss or salt loss with obligated

53

SALT and WATER IMBALANCES

		DEHYDRATION	PSEUDOHYPONATREMIA	DILUTIONAL HYPONATREMIA
SERUM SODIUM CONCENTRATION	LOW	DEHYDRATION (Primary Salt Loss) Na^+ Loss > H_2O Loss	Hyperglycemia Hyperlipemia Hyperproteinemia SYNDROME OF INAPPROPRIATE ADH WATER INTOXICATION	H_2O Retention > Na^+ Retention
	NORMAL	DEHYDRATION Na^+ Loss = H_2O Loss	NORMAL	UNCOMPLICATED EDEMA H_2O Retention = Na^+ Retention
	HIGH	DEHYDRATION (Primary Water Loss) H_2O Loss > Na^+ Loss	HYPERALDOSTERONISM HYPERCORTISONISM	STEROID EXCESS SALT INTOXICATION Na^+ Retention > H_2O Retention
		LOW	NORMAL	HIGH
		EXTRACELLULAR FLUID VOLUME		

Figure 4-1 Salt and water imbalances. ADH = antidiuretic hormone.

water. Water depletion, which occurs when there is water loss without proportionate sodium loss, is reflected by an increased serum sodium concentration, ie, hypernatremia. Normally, with free access to water, normal thirst mechanisms ensure that the individual maintains an adequate fluid intake. Patients who have primary salt depletion become volume-depleted (dehydrated), and they maintain normal serum sodium concentrations and osmolalities until the volume depletion becomes sufficient to stimulate release of antidiuretic hormone (ADH). If fluid then is replaced, water is retained, and hyponatremia begins to develop.

The excessive retention of body fluids (overhydration) may result from primary salt retention with its osmotically obligated water (simple edema) or from retention of water in excess of salt (dilutional hyponatremia). Simple edema may be local or generalized. Generalized edema occurs with increasing frequency with age because those disease states, specifically congestive heart failure, renal insufficiency, cirrhosis, nephrotic syndrome, and hypoalbuminemia, that are associated with edema are more common in elderly people.

Hyponatremia

A low serum sodium concentration may result from (1) a loss of sodium in excess of osmotically obligated water (primary salt depletion), (2) a retention of water in excess of sodium (dilutional hyponatremia), or (3) a combination of both

Table 4-1 Hyponatremic Syndromes

I. Hyponatremia with contracted ECFV
   A. Urinary sodium <10 mmol/L
      1. Inadequate intake
      2. Excessive sweating
      3. Excessive gastrointestinal loss
         (a) Diarrhea
         (b) Fistulous tracts (bowel, biliary)
   B. Urinary sodium >10 mmol/L
      1. Severe metabolic alkalosis due to vomiting (bicarbonaturia)
      2. Excessive urinary losses
         (a) Adrenal insufficiency (Addison disease, hypoaldosteronism)
         (b) Renal salt wasting (renal tubular acidosis, interstitial nephritis, end-stage renal disease)
         (c) Diuretic induced

II. Hyponatremia with normal ECFV
   A. Displacement syndromes
      1. Hyperglycemia
      2. Hyperlipemia
      3. Hyperglobulinemia
   B. SIADH
      1. Malignancies (eg, of lung, pancreas)
      2. Pulmonary diseases, including treatment with positive pressure breathing
      3. Cerebral conditions (eg, trauma, infection, tumor, cerebrovascular accident)
      4. Drugs (eg, sulfonylureas, thiazides, antitumor agents)
      5. Myxedema
      6. Porphyria
      7. Idiopathic
   C. Water intoxication

III. Hyponatremia with expanded ECFV
   A. Dilutional hyponatremia (low solute excretion)
      1. Congestive heart failure
      2. Cirrhosis
      3. Nephrotic syndrome
      4. Renal insufficiency
      5. Hypoalbuminemia

(syndrome of inappropriate ADH [SIADH]) (Table 4-1). Hyponatremia also may result from a displacement of plasma water with large-molecular-weight solute (eg, protein, lipids) or from the addition of an uncharged solute (eg, glucose) to the ECFV.

A reduction in serum sodium concentration to less than 125 mmol/L, regardless of etiology, may produce symptoms ranging from mild, nonspecific complaints, such as malaise, irritability, muscle weakness, and change in personality, to marked functional central nervous system impairment. Serious central nervous system impairment occurs when the shift of fluid from the hypo-osmotic extracellular fluid into isotonic brain cells increases brain volume and intracranial pressure significantly. Depending on the severity of hyponatremia and the state of hydration, a spectrum of alterations of consciousness, ranging from confusion to coma, may appear. Seizures are frequent manifestations of these conditions also.

Hyponatremia with Contracted ECFV (Primary Salt Depletion)

Early in primary salt depletion, salt and water are lost at comparable rates, so that serum sodium concentrations and osmolality remain normal. After volume depletion becomes evident, ADH release is stimulated, resulting in water retention while salt loss continues. If the urinary sodium concentration is less than 10 mmol/L, suspected etiologies include decreased salt intake, excessive sweating with only water provided to replace losses, or gastrointestinal salt losses. If urinary sodium concentration is greater than 10 mmol/L, inappropriate renal losses of sodium and water may be due to excessive use of diuretics, adrenal or pituitary insufficiency, or intrinsic renal disease (ie, salt-losing nephritis, renal insufficiency, or renal tubular acidosis). In severe vomiting with metabolic alkalosis and bicarbonate wasting, urinary sodium concentrations also may be elevated despite hypovolemia and hyponatremia. Elderly subjects may be more prone to hyponatremia while developing these disorders. Epstein and Hollenberg[1] have shown that there is a modest reduction in the capacity of the kidney to conserve sodium in normal elderly subjects when subjected to salt depletion (Chapter 9). Treatment generally is accomplished with isotonic saline, although in severe cases hypertonic saline may be used initially. When it remains unclear whether the etiology is primary salt depletion or SIADH, one can place a central venous pressure (CVP) catheter and infuse normal saline until the CVP climbs, unless the patient has left ventricular failure or pulmonary hypertension and thereby requires a Swan-Ganz catheter. An important clue to making the differential diagnosis may be the blood urea nitrogen concentration, as this is elevated in primary salt depletion and is usually subnormal in SIADH.

Hyponatremia with Expanded ECFV (Dilutional Hyponatremia)

Impairment in water excretion occurs commonly in conditions in which salt excretion also is severely impaired. Patients with advanced cardiac, hepatic, and renal disease and generalized edema often are placed on diets that sharply restrict salt intake without placing limitations on fluid intake. Once hyponatremia begins to develop, restriction of water intake may become necessary. Although total ECFV in such patients often is increased, the blood volume in the arterial vascular system tends to be decreased, stimulating baroreceptors in the arterial system to initiate retention of salt and water. A decrease in glomerular filtration rate or an increase in sodium reabsorption in the proximal tubule limits water excretion by decreasing delivery of tubular salt and water to the distal diluting segment of the nephron. If little salt and water reach the distal nephron, the individual becomes unable to dilute his or her urine much below isotonic levels. Since normally the relative intakes of salt and water constitute a hypotonic solution, this results in the development of hyponatremia. Decreases in intra-arterial or left atrial pressure or volume, which are potent stimuli to ADH release, also have a role in the pathogenesis of hyponatremia. Treatment consists of diuretic administration and fluid restriction in addition to treatment of the underlying etiology. Diuretics active in the loop of Henle, such as furosemide, that promote excretion of hypotonic to isotonic urine even in the presence of ADH are the diuretics of choice.

Hyponatremia with Normal ECFV (SIADH)

A diagnosis of SIADH can be made only when other causes of hyponatremia have been excluded. The following criteria must be met: (1) the extracellular fluid osmolality and sodium concentration must be decreased; (2) the urine must be hypertonic to serum; (3) urinary sodium excretion exceeds 10 mmol/L; (4) adrenal, renal, cardiac, and hepatic functions are normal; and (5) the hyponatremia can be corrected by water restriction. Persistence of circulating ADH is considered inappropriate when neither serum hyperosmolality nor volume depletion is present. Inability to excrete water normally leads to volume expansion, which, by several mechanisms, promotes urinary salt loss. SIADH is seen most frequently in patients with pulmonary neoplasms, most notably oat cell carcinomas, but it may also be seen in numerous other conditions as listed in Table 4-1. Usually, the etiology for SIADH is impaired blood flow through pulmonary circulation, resulting in impaired filling of the left atrium, which stimulates ADH release. Any person treated with positive pressure breathing has the potential for a similar consequence.

Hyponatremia in the Elderly

Surveys of older persons in both acute and chronic care facilities show a high prevalence of hyponatremia. Kleinfeld and colleagues[2] reported that 36 of 160 chronically ill patients (23%) had serum sodium concentrations below 132 mmol/L (mean 120 mmol/L). In most patients, low serum sodium concentrations were not readily explained except by the presence of debilitating diseases and old age.

In another nursing home study,[3] over half the patients had been hyponatremic on at least one occasion over the last year; over one third of these were chronically hyponatremic. The chronically hyponatremic patients, after administration of a water load, were able to achieve a mean minimal urine osmolality of only 237 mmol/kg, compared with 84 mmol/kg in a healthy population. In the chronically hyponatremic patients, the mean excretion of the water load over a 5-hour period was only 57% of that of normal controls. The patients with intermittent hyponatremia also had a less severe, but abnormal, response to the water load.

Anderson and colleagues[4] prospectively evaluated the prevalence, cause, and outcome of hyponatremia in an acute care facility. The prevalence was 2.5%, with two thirds being iatrogenic. The mean age of these subjects was nearly 60 years. The most frequent cause was SIADH (normovolemic hyponatremia), accounting for 34% of cases; hypovolemia, hypervolemia, and hyperglycemia each accounted for 16% to 19% of cases; and renal failure (overhydration) and error accounted for the remainder. Anderson and colleagues demonstrated that non-osmotic (baroreceptor) stimulation of vasopressin release was a major factor in this electrolyte disorder regardless of cause. Other evidence suggests that elderly persons may be more susceptible to the development of hyponatremia similar to that seen in patients with SIADH than are their younger counterparts. Antidiuresis and hyponatremia have been observed postoperatively, primarily in elderly patients.[5] Sulfonylureas create SIADH almost exclusively in older persons.[6] Diuretic-induced hyponatremia is an entity occurring primarily in older patients.[7,8]

A number of studies suggest increasing ADH activity in the serum or plasma of elderly persons. For example, in subjects who were water-deprived overnight, Rondeau and associates[9] found a significant relationship between age and serum arginine vasopressin (AVP) levels, measured by radioimmunoassay of samples obtained in the morning from supine individuals. The regression of these values predicts a baseline serum ADH level of 2.37 pg/mL with an increase of 0.03 pg/mL per year of age.

Observations reported by Helderman and associates[10] may help to explain the increased susceptibility of older patients to the development of hyponatremia. In older subjects, serum AVP concentrations showed a greater increase (twofold) after a standardized hypertonic saline infusion designed to raise serum osmolality to 306 mmol/L than did those of younger subjects despite comparable baseline AVP concentrations. In contrast, ethanol infusion, known to inhibit ADH secretion, produced a more prolonged depression in serum AVP concentrations in young than in old subjects. These two observations suggest an increasing osmoreceptor sensitivity with age with a greater release of AVP and, therefore, more water retention in response to any given stimulus or balance state.

Rowe and associates[11] subsequently reported studies designed to determine whether this phenomenon represented a consistent, age-related increase in vasopressin responsiveness or whether it was specific for osmotic stimuli. Older subjects, after 8 minutes of quiet standing, failed to increase their serum AVP concentrations as much as did younger subjects. Furthermore, Rowe and associates could divide their subjects into those who released AVP (responders) and those who failed to release AVP (nonresponders) in response to orthostasis. Whereas less than 10% of the young subjects were nonresponders, nearly half of the older subjects failed to release AVP in response to orthostasis. Because these subjects had an intact norepinephrine response to orthostasis, the authors felt that the age-related defect was distal to the vasomotor center in the afferent limb of the baroreceptor reflex arc. They further suggested that the altered vasopressin response to osmolar and volume-pressure stimuli in some elderly subjects might be related primarily to impaired baroreceptor input to the supraoptic nucleus. Secondarily, there would be an impaired responsiveness to osmotic stimuli.

It is most difficult for a normal person to ingest sufficient water to become symptomatically hyponatremic. Some patients with schizophrenic illnesses, how-ever, have been reported to be capable of ingesting sufficient fluids without vomiting to become symptomatically hyponatremic.

A decrease in serum sodium concentration does not always indicate a decrease in the osmolality of body fluids. With hyperglycemia, the cause of hyponatremia is the glucose-related increase in the osmolality of extracellular fluid, which results in a movement of water from the intracellular to extracellular fluid compartments. Expansion of the extracellular fluid space triggers a diuresis of excess fluid along with sodium.

The serum sodium concentration in hyperlipemia and hyperproteinemia is decreased because of the volume occupied by lipids or proteins, respectively. If lipids or proteins are removed from the plasma, the sodium concentration in the remaining plasma water is normal.

Hypernatremia

An increase in serum sodium concentration is a result of loss of body water in excess of salt loss, although it also can result from ingestion or administration of salt without sufficient water to provide an isotonic solution. Among elderly patients, hypernatremia is most common in those who are bedfast and not provided sufficient water to satisfy their thirst, or in those whose thirst sensation is diminished by impaired central nervous system function. A net deficit of water also can be associated with vomiting and diarrhea, diabetes insipidus, an osmotic diuresis such as is seen with hyperosmolar nonketotic diabetic acidosis, and hyperpyrexia (excessive sweating).

In general, older patients appear to be predisposed to the development of hypernatremia. Snyder and associates[12] reported that more than 1% of their hospital admissions were patients over age 60 years who developed hyper-natremia (serum sodium concentration greater than 148 mmol/L). Over half of these patients developed hypernatremia while in the hospital. Surgery, febrile illnesses, infirmity, and diabetes mellitus accounted for two thirds of the diagnoses of these cases. Hypernatremia is a marker for severe associated illness, and the mortality rate in this group of patients was 42%. In these patients, rapid fluid replacement contributed to increased mortality rates.

Lavizzo-Mourey and colleagues,[13] in a systematic evaluation of the factors leading to dehydration in hospitalized nursing home residents, found a constellation of important risk factors that included advanced age, female sex, several chronic diseases, number of medications (especially laxatives), and decreased functional status. Alterations in thirst perception in healthy young and old persons were studied by Phillips and colleagues.[14] All subjects were deprived of water for 24 hours, after which free access to water was allowed. The older individuals drank less water even though they lost more fluid during the period of water deprivation and ended with higher plasma sodium concentrations and osmolalities, suggesting an impaired thirst responsiveness in older subjects. Furthermore, the decline in renal concentrating ability commonly observed with age (Chapter 9) might increase the potential for hypernatremia by augmenting urinary losses of water.

Hypernatremia reflects an increase in serum osmolality, which results in a shift of water from the intracellular to extracellular spaces. One consequence of this phenomenon is a shrinkage of brain cells, causing intracranial injury to blood vessels, which may lead to hemorrhage, venous thrombosis, or infarction.

The earliest manifestation of hypernatremia is thirst, followed by confusion and lethargy and, ultimately, delirium, stupor, and coma. Because intravascular volume is preserved at the expense of cell water, changes in blood pressure, pulse rate, and skin turgor are not prominent features of hypernatremia.

Once life-threatening hypernatremia has occurred, parenteral restoration of fluid and electrolyte balance usually is necessary. The amount of water (or dextrose and water, if given parenterally) needed can be estimated by multiplying the percentage increase in sodium concentration over normal by the total body water (60% of body weight). To prevent a recurrence, a fluid prescription establishing the quantity of fluid to be ingested daily may be an important part of treatment.

POTASSIUM

Potassium is the primary intracellular cation, with less than 2% of total body potassium contained in the extracellular fluid compartment. Therefore, the serum concentration of potassium may not reflect accurately total body potassium stores. A potassium flux into the cells occurs with cell growth, intracellular nitrogen and glycogen deposition, and increases in extracellular pH; potassium leaves the cell with cell destruction, glucose utilization, and decreases in extracellular pH. When interpreting serum potassium concentrations, those factors that affect the ratio of intracellular to extracellular concentration must be considered, since normally a steep concentration gradient is maintained. For example, the patient with diabetic ketoacidosis has a high serum potassium concentration, but rehydration, correction of the acidosis with bicarbonate, and treatment of the hyperglycemia with insulin combine to produce a dramatic decrease in plasma potassium concentration as the cation moves intracellularly. Age alone does not appear to affect the ability to maintain this concentration gradient. Isotopic dilution studies and muscle biopsies, however, have been used to demonstrate that intracellular stores of potassium can be decreased in a variety of clinical conditions commonly seen in elderly patients, eg, metabolic and respiratory acidosis, congestive heart failure, cirrhosis, and uremia, with serum potassium concentrations remaining within normal limits.

Hypokalemia

The causes of hypokalemia are listed in Table 4-2.[15] The most frequent cause of hypokalemia in elderly people is diuretic therapy used for treatment of edematous and hypertensive conditions. Probably the most frequently overlooked cause of hypokalemia in elderly people is excessive use of enemas and purgatives, behavior which should be suspected whenever unexplained hypokalemic alkalosis occurs in older persons.

Multiple pathophysiologic mechanisms occur in many, if not most, cases to explain the development of hypokalemia. For example, the patient who vomits not only has a reduction in potassium intake and some loss of potassium in the vomitus, but loses hydrogen ions, producing a metabolic alkalosis that in turn shifts potassium intracellularly and augments urinary potassium losses. The contracted intravascular volume increases proximal tubular sodium and bicarbonate reabsorption, which further enhances the metabolic alkalosis and induces a secondary hyperaldosteronism that increases urinary potassium losses.

Although the normal kidney is not as effective in conserving potassium as it is in conserving sodium, it can reduce excretions below 15 mmol/d even in the presence of acidosis or alkalosis. Since little potassium normally is lost through the gastrointestinal tract, it takes 2 to 3 weeks on a virtually potassium-free intake for a person to reduce his or her serum potassium concentration to 3.0 mmol/L, providing all organ systems are functioning normally. A reasonable criterion for establishing a diagnosis of potassium wasting when the serum potassium concentration falls below 3.5 mmol/L would be the daily excretion of more than 20 mmol of potassium per day. The etiologies of excessive urinary potassium loss have been separated into four categories: (1) pituitary-adrenal disturbances, (2) renal defects, (3) drug-induced losses, and (4) idiopathic and miscellaneous causes.[15]

Table 4-2 Causes of Hypokalemia

I. Inadequate intake

II. Excessive sweating

III. Dilution of extracellular fluid volume

IV. Shift of potassium intracellularly
   A. Increase in blood pH (alkalosis)
   B. Glucose and insulin
   C. Familial hypokalemia periodic paralysis

V. Excessive gastrointestinal losses
   A. Vomiting
   B. Biliary, pancreatic, and intestinal drainage from fistulas and ostomies
   C. Diarrhea
      1. Chronic infections and inflammatory lesions
      2. Malabsorption
      3. Villous adenomas of colon and rectum
      4. Catechol-secreting neural tumors
      5. Abdominal lymphomas
      6. Non-alpha, non-beta islet cell tumors of pancreas
      7. Excessive use of enemas and purgatives
   D. Ureterosigmoidostomy

VI. Increased urinary losses
   A. Pituitary-adrenal disturbances
      1. Primary aldosteronism
      2. Secondary aldosteronism (renal artery stenosis, accelerated hypertension, volume depletion)
      3. Cushing syndrome (adrenal adenomas, carcinomas, and hyperplasia, pituitary corticotropin hypersecretion, ectopic corticotropin secretion secondary to tumor)
   B. Renal disorders
      1. Distal or proximal renal tubular acidosis
      2. Renin-secreting renal tumor
      3. Salt-losing nephritis
      4. Diuretic phase of acute tubular necrosis
      5. Postoperative diuresis
   C. Drug induced
      1. Diuretics (thiazides, loop diuretics)
      2. Licorice extracts (glycyrrhizic acid)
      3. Large, nonabsorbable anions, eg, carbenicillin
      4. Acetylsalicylic acid (respiratory alkalosis)
   D. Idiopathic and other pathologies
      1. Bartter syndrome
      2. Hypomagnesemia
      3. Thyrotoxicosis
      4. Idiopathic or familial

The structural and functional defects associated with potassium deficiency are shown in Table 4-3. These involve the kidney, the myocardium and cardiovascular system, the neuromuscular and central nervous system, and the gastrointestinal tract. Potassium deficiency also contributes to an impairment in carbohydrate metabolism and protein synthesis.

Since alkalosis (chloride depletion) usually accompanies hypokalemia, replacement therapy should be instituted with potassium chloride rather than with the alkaline salts of potassium. Foods rich in potassium (citrus and tomato juices, bananas, meats, and vegetables) provide the safest way to administer potassium. When additional oral replacement is needed, commercial supplements may be considered. Most commercial preparations contain 20 mmol/15 mL; this amount can be given 2 to 4 times daily in a glass of water. Intravenous potassium repletion may be necessary but can be hazardous, especially if infusion rates exceed 20 mmol/h or concentrations of infusate exceed 40 mmol/L. Adequate urine

---

Table 4-3 Manifestations of Hypokalemia

I. Myocardial and cardiovascular
   A. Focal myocardial necrosis
   B. Electrocardiographic changes (Figure 4-2)
      1. Depressed ST segment, inversion of T waves
      2. Accentuated U waves
   C. Arrhythmias
   D. Potentiation of digitalis toxicity
   E. Salt retention
   F. Hypotension

II. Neuromuscular and psychiatric
   A. Muscle weakness to flaccid paralysis
   B. Muscle pain and tenderness secondary to muscle necrosis
   C. Depressive reaction (anorexia, constipation, weakness, lethargy, apathy, fatigue, depressed mood)
   D. Acute brain syndrome (memory impairment, disorientation, confusion)

III. Renal
   A. Defect in urine-concentrating ability with polyuria
   B. Paradoxical aciduria
   C. Sodium retention

IV. Gastrointestinal
   A. Decreased motility and propulsive activity of intestine
   B. Paralytic ileus

V. Metabolic
   A. Carbohydrate intolerance (delayed release of insulin)
   B. Growth failure due to impaired protein synthesis

output should be demonstrated and electrocardiographic monitoring should be done before potassium infusions are pushed above these levels.

The need for replacement potassium therapy in edematous and hypertensive patients receiving diuretic therapy is questionable. In hypokalemic patients receiving diuretics, intracellular potassium concentrations are decreased more in patients with edematous or acidotic conditions than they are in hypertensive patients, making it appear necessary to give supplements to patients with edema and acidosis more often than to hypertensive patients. In fact, several studies have shown that hypertensive patients receiving diuretics, even though they may develop mild hypokalemia, maintain normal intracellular potassium concentrations; supplements do little to change these levels.

A great deal of concern and discussion has been generated suggesting that hypokalemia may precipitate cardiac arrhythmias and sudden death in patients made hypokalemic with diuretics, especially patients receiving digitalis for cardiac disorders or patients with acute myocardial infarction.[16] Controlled trials with patients either receiving supplements or not receiving supplements suggest that treatment with potassium supplementation fails to affect outcome. A significant incidence of life-threatening hyperkalemia in patients receiving supplements suggests that the potential benefits of supplemental therapy be weighed against the risks.

Hyperkalemia

The causes of hyperkalemia are outlined in Table 4-4. Most cases of hyperkalemia are observed in patients with impaired renal function. However, most patients with chronic renal failure who maintain good flow rates do not develop significant hyperkalemia until the azotemia becomes life-threatening. Because the distal nephron has such a large capacity for secreting potassium, even in advanced renal failure, hyperkalemia develops only when there is some associated factor, such as (1) oliguria, eg, acute renal failure; (2) excessive potassium load (tissue catabolism, potassium supplementation, or administration of excess potassium in some other form such as potassium penicillin G); (3) severe acidosis; (4) spironolactone or triamterene diuretic therapy; or (5) a deficiency of endogenous steroid (aldosterone, cortisol). Poorly monitored potassium supplementation in patients receiving diuretic therapy leads to potentially lethal hyperkalemia with frightening frequency, especially in older patients who have some level of renal impairment.

In the Boston Collaborative Drug Surveillance Program,[17] more than 16,000 consecutive patients were monitored for adverse reactions to medications they were taking. In this group, 31% received potassium chloride as a supplement for diuretic therapy. There were 7 deaths directly attributable to hyperkalemia and 21 lives threatened by significant hyperkalemia. Two significant risk factors were

Table 4-4 Causes of Hyperkalemia

I. Hyperkalemia caused by
  A. Decreased urinary excretion of potassium
  B. Increased exogenous or endogenous potassium
  C. Both

II. Decreased urinary excretion
  A. Renal insufficiency
  B. Potassium-retaining diuretics (spironolactone, triamterene)
  C. Adrenal hypofunction (Addison disease, hyporeninemic hypoaldosteronism)

III. Increased exogenous or endogenous load
  A. Supplemental potassium (with diuretics)
  B. Potassium-containing drugs (eg, penicillin)
  C. Tissue catabolism (starvation, crush injury)
  D. Metabolic acidosis

---

identified. Azotemia as a risk factor was predictable, but the second risk factor—age—was not. Only 0.8% of 1404 patients under age 50 years who received potassium supplements developed hyperkalemia. In contrast, the frequency of hyperkalemia in groups over age 50 years increased from 4.2% to 6.0% with advancing age. To explain this observation, reports have shown that elderly subjects on both restricted and unrestricted salt intakes, both upright and supine, have much lower plasma renin activities and urinary aldosterone excretion than do comparable young subjects.[18,19] This failure of the renin-aldosterone system in older patients produces an appearance of type IV renal tubular acidosis in the more severe cases.

The clinical manifestations of hyperkalemia often are subtle and may occur only shortly before death occurs from cardiac arrhythmia. Anxiety, restlessness, apprehension, weakness, stupor, and hyporeflexia should alert the clinician to the potential existence of this imbalance in patients at risk. Characteristic electrocardiographic changes are peaking of T waves followed by widening and then loss of P waves, and widening of the QRS complex (Figure 4-2).

Therapy should be started when the serum potassium concentration exceeds 5.5 mmol/L; a true medical emergency exists when it exceeds 7.0 mmol/L. Acute treatment is with glucose, insulin, and sodium bicarbonate to shift potassium intracellularly, and with calcium and sodium salts, which act as physiologic antagonists. Sodium polystyrene sulfonate (Kayexalate) resins are used to remove excess potassium from the body and can be given orally or in enema form. To avoid constipation and fecal impaction with oral administration of these resins, sorbitol can be given as necessary, titrating the dose. When hyperkalemia is due to a mineralocorticoid deficiency, 9-fluorohydrocortisone (Florinef) can be given. If all else fails, hemodialysis can be used to remove excess potassium.

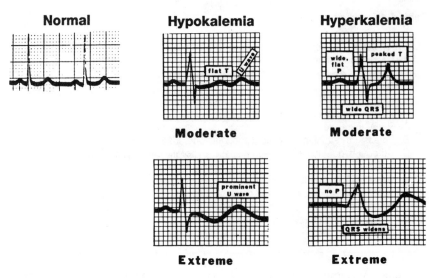

Figure 4-2 Impact of moderate and severe hypokalemia and hyperkalemia on the electrocardiogram.

One last observation that deserves further investigation is that, in hypertensive laboratory animals, a high potassium intake protected against the development of cerebrovascular accidents. In the only study in humans,[20] a cohort of Southern Californians followed for 10 years showed a 40% decrease in the risk of stroke mortality for every 10 mEq/d increase in potassium intake. If these observations can be corroborated by further study, supplemental potassium may become a rational prophylactic therapy in high-risk persons.

CALCIUM

A finely tuned endocrine system exists to maintain serum ionized calcium concentrations within a narrow normal range by controlling intestinal absorption, bone exchange, and renal excretion of calcium (Chapter 13). Whenever serum ionized calcium concentrations decrease, parathyroid hormone (PTH) secretion increases, resulting in mobilization of calcium from bone, decreased renal tubular phosphate resorption with resultant decreased serum phosphate concentration (this facilitates bone resorption of calcium), increased renal tubular calcium resorption, and increased intestinal calcium resorption, either directly or by enhancing the effect of vitamin D. Vitamin D is converted by the liver to the carrier metabolite, 25-hydroxycholecalciferol $(25(OH)D_3)$, and by the kidney to the active metabolite, 1,25-dihydroxycholecalciferol $(1,25(OH)_2 D_3)$. The conversion in the kidney acts primarily to increase calcium absorption in the intestine, but it also increases bone resorption of calcium and decreases urinary calcium and phosphate excretion. PTH appears to produce its effects on the intestine by accelerating the conversion of $25(OH)D_3$ to $1,25(OH)_2D_3$. When serum calcium concentrations increase, serum thyrocalcitonin concentrations increase, producing effects counter to those of PTH.

Serum calcium exists in both the ionized and bound states, but only ionized calcium is physiologically active. The un-ionized calcium is either bound to serum proteins, primarily albumin, or is bound in a complex with various anions, eg, citrate. The binding is dependent on the concentration of serum protein (albumin) and the blood pH, with calcium binding increasing as the pH increases. Since most laboratories report only serum total calcium concentrations, these factors must be recognized in evaluating a specific serum calcium concentration.

Both hypocalcemia and hypercalcemia occur with increasing frequency in elderly individuals, primarily because specific disease entities causing these imbalances are more common in elderly persons. Of more importance in the elderly, however, is the inevitable age-related loss of bone calcium that occurs in both sexes but is more severe in women; this loss leads to the development of osteoporosis, with increased risk of fractures (Chapter 11). Since this entity is also discussed elsewhere, this narrative covers primarily the problems encountered in evaluating severity and progression or improvement of osteoporosis and the calcium requirement known to prevent its development and progression.

Osteoporosis

Riggs and Melton,[21] in reviewing involutional osteoporosis, have postulated that at least two distinct clinical entities exist, specifically, type I (postmenopausal osteoporosis) and type II (senile osteoporosis). The distinctions between these two types of osteoporosis are based on different clinical features, densitometric and hormonal changes, and relation of disease patterns to menopause and age. In women, the impact may be additive. Among the different mechanisms involved in bone loss, dietary factors appear to play an important role in both entities. In older persons, calcium intake is generally low and is associated with reduced calcium absorption.[22,23] In addition, hypovitaminosis D is frequently associated with increased age through mechanisms of avoidance of dairy products, intestinal malabsorption of fat-soluble vitamin D, decreased exposure to sunlight, and a decreased ability of the skin to produce previtamin D[23–25] (Chapter 3). As vitamin D is a major regulator of calcium absorption, the cumulative response of a deficit of calcium intake and an inadequate intake of vitamin D is a negative calcium balance, which stimulates parathyroid hormone secretion. This secondary hyperparathyroidism increases bone calcium resorption and the risk of fractures with its subsequent morbidity and mortality.[21]

The requirement for calcium, especially in older persons, continues to be a very controversial subject. Calcium deficiency is difficult to define and hard to measure, and uncertainty remains about its impact. These problems arise from the slow turnover of bone tissue, which makes the monitoring of both breakdown and repair a long-term procedure since bone status monitoring techniques are still relatively crude.

The requirements and recommended daily allowances of most nutrients are derived from experimental and clinical evidence of the effects of a deficiency and the amount of nutrient that is needed to prevent these effects from occurring. After the deficiency syndrome is characterized, the amount of the nutrient required to prevent or cure it is determined, and an allowance is decided on. With most nutrients, the deficiency develops relatively rapidly and the effect of the intervention is manifested rapidly also. Calcium differs from most other minerals in that the plasma calcium concentration is not a guide to the individual's calcium nutriture. The regulation of plasma calcium levels is so fine that intraindividual variation is not much greater than the technical error in its measurement, and interindividual variation is not much larger. This fine regulation is mediated by the parathyroid glands. Because there are 1200 g of calcium in the skeleton and only 1 g in extracellular fluid, serum calcium concentration does not reflect calcium economy in the body. Calcium deficiency has been shown to lower the plasma calcium concentration by 0.15 mg/dL when large numbers of subjects are studied by paired observations.[26] It is not possible to discriminate between individuals in positive and negative calcium balance by means of serum calcium concentration alone.

Since serum calcium concentrations cannot be used to gauge calcium balance, measurement of the blood level of PTH, which increases in response to calcium deficiency, and plasma $1,25(OH)_2D_3$ level, which also increases in response to calcium deprivation, might be used as indicators of calcium nutritional status. However, the assay for PTH is still too imprecise, and there are many other regulators of plasma $1,25(OH)_2D_3$ levels (eg, phosphorus intake, growth hormone, prolactin), precluding its use as a reliable indicator of calcium nutriture.

The quantification of bone density itself also might provide a criterion of nutritional calcium status. However, the wide individual variation in bone density ($\pm 10\%$) and the many hormonal and other factors that affect bone density, along with the relatively severe depletion that must occur before bone deficiency can be detected, preclude this end-point, even if it were agreed that osteoporosis is the clinical end-point of calcium deficiency. When everything is considered, the only practical definition of calcium requirement is the amount of calcium required to maintain calcium balance, and the only way to determine it is by balance techniques.

If calcium requirement is defined as the amount required to maintain calcium balance, then it can be determined by calculating from calcium balances the mean intake at which intake and output are equal. In healthy young adults, this is estimated to be around 500 mg/d.[27] From available data, an RDA of 800 mg/d was proposed for the United States, recognizing that pregnant and lactating women and postmenopausal women have higher requirements. These recommendations were not changed in the 1989 revisions made by the Food and Nutrition Board of the National Academy of Sciences–National Research Council.[28] Nordin et al[29] and Heaney et al[30] found that the requirements in postmenopausal women were 900 and 1500 mg/d, respectively. Older persons generally do not attain these levels of intake. One study[31] reported that 62% of the subjects studied had an intake less than 500 mg/d and 21% less than 300 mg/d.

There is no evidence of bone loss in premenopausal women on a normal diet; bone loss starts abruptly at menopause. Women 1 year after the start of menopause have significantly higher serum concentrations and urinary excretions of calcium, serum alkaline phosphatase activity (evidence of new bone formation or osteoblastic activity), and urinary hydroxyproline excretions (evidence of bone resorption or osteoclastic activity)[32] (Table 4-5) (Chapter 11). Several theories have been proposed to define the pathophysiology of the change at menopause. First, the loss of estrogen activity may cause a small increase in plasma calcium concentration (perhaps due to a change in the PTH set-point), which increases urinary calcium excretion, bone resorption, and bone re-formation. The other possibility is that increased bone resorption is the primary event, resulting in an increase in plasma and urine calcium levels. Under normal circumstances, the efficiency of intestinal calcium absorption is regulated to meet the body's need for calcium. In elderly persons, the adaptive response to a low calcium intake is reduced. The negative calcium balance is due not only to a low intake but also to the reduced vitamin D level, which impairs intestinal absorption. The vitamin D status is influenced significantly by length of exposure to sunlight. Ambulatory elderly persons had much higher plasma $25(OH)D_3$ levels than did long-term hospitalized patients who did not go outdoors.[31] The same risk exists for institutionalized elderly patients.

Table 4-5 Immediate Biochemical Effects of Menopause*

Variable	Premenopausal Women	Women 1 y after Menopause	P
Plasma calcium (mmol/L)	2.38 ± 0.016	2.42 ± 0.015	<.05
Calcium:creatinine (mmol/mmol)	0.18 ± 0.026	0.26 ± 0.033	<.05
Alkaline phosphatase (U/L)	62.1 ± 3.0	77.6 ± 4.3	<.005
Hydroxyproline:creatinine (mmol/μmol)	14.2 ± 0.83	22.0 ± 1.7	<.001

*Mean values ± standard error; n = 22. From reference 31.

Supplements of calcium (1000 mg/d) and ergocalciferol (20 mg/d) induced a significant increase in serum calcium and $25(OH)D_3$ concentrations and a decrease in serum PTH concentrations in 65 elderly patients.[31] These data provide evidence that bone resorption can be retarded by adequate intakes of calcium and vitamin D.

Hypocalcemia

In contrast to most other electrolyte disturbances, hypocalcemia is not much more common in elderly persons than in young persons. The causes of hypocalcemia are listed in Table 4-6. In patients with unexplained hypocalcemia or hypokalemia, or both, clinicians should be aware that hypomagnesemia may be the underlying etiology; hypomagnesemia causes a peripheral resistance to PTH and decreases the release of PTH in response to the hypocalcemic stimulus.

The symptomatology associated with hypocalcemia primarily is related to increased neuromuscular excitability, as manifested by tetany. Long-term manifestations include cataracts; abnormalities of the nails, skin, and teeth; and mental and growth retardation.

Acute correction of symptomatic hypocalcemia can be accomplished with parenteral calcium gluconate. Oral calcium salts (carbonate, gluconate, or lactate) can be used to treat mild or latent hypocalcemia. Vitamin D and its metabolites increase serum calcium concentrations by increasing intestinal absorption and bone resorption of calcium.

Table 4-6 Causes of Hypocalcemia

   I. Malignancies, especially with osteoblastic metastases (prostate)

   II. Renal insufficiency

   III. Hypoparathyroidism; pseudohypoparathyroidism

   IV. Gastrointestinal disorders (malabsorption)

   V. Vitamin D deficiency or resistance

   VI. Acute pancreatitis

   VII. Calcitonin-producing tumors (medullary carcinoma of thyroid)

   VIII. Hypomagnesemia or hyperphosphatemia, or both

   Note: Patients in categories II and III have high serum phosphorus concentrations; phosphorus concentrations tend to be normal in others.

Hypercalcemia

The most frequent cause of hypercalcemia in elderly patients is malignant disease. A number of mechanisms operate, both with and without bony metastases.[33] Primary hyperparathyroidism has an increased prevalence among older women and is often asymptomatic in its early stages.[34] Other causes of hypercalcemia are listed in Table 4-7. Early symptoms are vague and nonspecific and include anorexia, nausea, vomiting, constipation, fatigue, somnolence, muscle weakness, pruritus, and psychiatric disturbances. Ultimately, polyuria with dehydration and azotemia with cardiac arrhythmias, especially in digitalized patients, are likely to occur. Nephrolithiasis and nephrocalcinosis are manifestations of chronic hypercalcemia.

The initial therapy for patients with hypercalcemia is rehydration with normal saline. This decreases the serum calcium concentration by hemodilution and increases urinary calcium excretion. Loop diuretics (furosemide) also greatly increase urinary calcium excretion, whereas thiazide diuretics decrease urinary calcium excretion and may potentiate hypercalcemia. Oral phosphate and diphosphonate (etidronate [Didronel]) salts are effective and well tolerated, except for gastrointestinal disturbances and diarrhea. Prednisone in high doses is effective when the mechanism of the hypercalcemia is increased vitamin D-mediated calcium absorption from the intestine (sarcoid, multiple myeloma, vitamin D intoxication) but is less effective in malignancies with metastatic bone disease and hyperparathyroidism. Mithramycin appears to be the drug of choice in the treatment of hypercalcemia associated with malignancy that is unresponsive to steroids or other therapies. This antitumor agent acts by inhibiting bone resorption and blocking vitamin D action. Its application is limited by the necessity of intra-

---

Table 4-7 Causes of Hypercalcemia

I. Malignancies
   A. With osteolytic metastases (enhanced bone resorption)
   B. Without osteolytic metastases
      1. Ectopic hyperparathyroidism
      2. Increased urinary cyclic adenosine monophosphate
      3. Osteolytic activating factor (myeloma, lymphoma)

II. Hyperparathyroidism

III. Thiazide administration

IV. Immobilization

V. Miscellaneous (vitamin A or D intoxication, tuberculosis, sarcoidosis, hyperthyroidism, Addison disease, milk alkali syndrome, acute renal failure)

venous administration. Transient nausea and vomiting and bone marrow suppression are the major adverse effects. Injections of calcitonin decrease the skeletal release of calcium, phosphorus, and hydroxyproline. The most impressive results are seen in conditions in which a high rate of bone turnover occurs, such as in immobilization, thyrotoxicosis, and vitamin D intoxication. Nonsteroidal anti-inflammatory agents may be helpful in reducing the hypercalcemia in some malignancies, such as renal cell carcinoma, in which prostaglandin E appears to be the mediator of excessive bone breakdown without evidence of bony metastases. If all else fails, hemodialysis is effective in acutely lowering serum calcium concentrations.

PHOSPHORUS

Selective phosphorus deficiency induced in normal subjects by an inadequate diet or by ingestion of large quantities of phosphate-binding antacids leads to a distinctive clinical syndrome characterized by anorexia, weakness, and bone pain. Symptoms appear primarily when the serum phosphorus concentration falls below 0.32 mmol/L, and clinical improvement occurs rapidly when dietary phosphorus is restored. Severe hypophosphatemia has been documented in association with alcohol withdrawal, diabetes mellitus, excessive antacid ingestion, recovery from burns, unsupplemented hyperalimentation, nutritional recovery syndrome, and severe respiratory alkalosis.[35] Patients with severe hypophosphatemia may develop a metabolic encephalopathy (irritability, muscular weakness, hypoesthesias and parethesias, dysarthria, confusion, seizures, and coma), rhabdomyolysis, hemolysis, leukocyte dysfunction (abnormal phagocytic, chemotactic, and bacteriocidal activities of granulocytes), and platelet dysfunction. Milk is the best dietary source of phosphorus; oral or intravenous phosphorous salts can be used as a supplement in individuals with severe deficits.

The 1989 RDA for adults is 800 mg/d; 1200 mg/d is recommended during pregnancy and lactation. A one-to-one ratio of calcium to phosphorus provides sufficient phosphorus and, since there is more phosphorus than calcium in most diets, phosphorus deficiency generally does not occur until calcium intake also is deficient.[28]

MAGNESIUM

Magnesium is the second most important intracellular cation; about 60% of body magnesium is located in bone, 40% is in the intracellular space (half of this in skeletal muscle), and only 1% exists extracellularly. The normal serum magnesium concentration is remarkably constant (0.7 to 1.1 mmol/L) and correlates poorly with intracellular magnesium. About 30% of serum magnesium is protein-bound, with most of the remainder in ionized form, making it ultrafilterable through the kidney. Most of the intracellular magnesium also is bound to protein and energy-rich phosphates. Magnesium is important in over 300 different enzyme systems, being indispensable to the metabolism of adenosine triphosphate, and therefore it affects glucose utilization; synthesis of fat, protein, and nucleic acids; muscle contraction; and several membrane transport systems.

The National Research Council, utilizing available balance data, has established an RDA of 350 mg/d for adult men and 280 mg/d for adult women, with slightly higher values for pregnant and lactating women. These recommendations were not changed in the 1989 revisions made by the Food and Nutrition Board of the National Academy of Sciences–National Research Council.[28] Studies by Pao and Mickle[36] on 37,000 healthy adults showed that the mean intakes for men and women were 266 and 228 mg/d, respectively. Furthermore, Schroeder and colleagues[37] reported that the usual hospital diet contains a mean of 200 mg of magnesium per day. For elderly persons with chronic conditions that might affect gastrointestinal absorption or urinary excretion of magnesium, a deficiency of magnesium becomes a very real concern.

Magnesium Deficiency

The causes of magnesium deficiency are listed in Table 4-8; the first two factors are the most commonly encountered. Hypomagnesemia produces neuromuscular and psychiatric disturbances, including neuromuscular hyperirritability, tetany, hyperacusis, seizures, muscle weakness, vertigo, gross tremors, and mental

---

Table 4-8 Causes of Hypomagnesemia

I. Gastrointestinal disorders with malabsorption

II. Chronic alcoholism

III. Endocrine disorders
   A. Hyperaldosteronism
   B. Hyperparathyroidism
   C. Diabetic ketoacidosis

IV. Acute pancreatitis

V. Renal magnesium loss
   A. Diuretic therapy
   B. SIADH
   C. Sodium, calcium, or magnesium wasting
   D. Renal tubular acidosis

VI. Protein-calorie malnutrition

changes (eg, irritability and aggressiveness). Individuals with hypomagnesemia also may develop polyuria and other electrolyte disturbances (hypocalcemia, hypokalemia, hypophosphatemia).

There is no evidence that older patients have a higher incidence of magnesium depletion than do younger people, and no decrease in serum magnesium concentration is observed with advancing age. Significant depletion of intracellular magnesium can occur, however, before the serum magnesium concentration falls below the normal range.[38] The concern then arises of how best to measure intracellular magnesium; most methods are invasive, requiring tissue (muscle) biopsy, which is not practical for human studies. One method for quantifying a magnesium deficit is to determine the amount of magnesium retained, or excreted, in a 24-hour urine sample after infusion of a standardized quantity of magnesium.[39] This procedure has been useful in patients with suspected symptomatology of magnesium depletion despite normal serum magnesium concentrations, but it has not been used specifically in comparing young and old subjects. Whether magnesium supplementation is warranted in conditions such as hypokalemia associated with diuretic therapy in elderly people remains speculative.

Hypermagnesemia

The earliest manifestations of hypermagnesemia are somnolence and hypotension, and an electrocardiogram may show prolongation of the PR interval and QRS duration with peaking of the T waves. Later, respiratory depression or paralysis and cardiac arrest can be terminal events. Such hypermagnesemia is usually seen only in patients with renal insufficiency who also are taking magnesium-containing antacids or cathartics.

CONCLUSION

Elderly patients are more susceptible to the development of both hyponatremia and hypernatremia. There appears to be an increasing osmoreceptor responsiveness and a decreasing baroreceptor responsiveness in elderly people, which make them prone to the development of SIADH. Elderly individuals also develop a defect in their thirst mechanisms, especially when associated with cerebral disease, making them more prone to develop hypernatremia resulting from dehydration secondary to primary water depletion.

Hypokalemia and hyperkalemia are more common in elderly people. Hypokalemia frequently occurs in the elderly because of their increased use of medications (eg, diuretics, purgatives, and enemas). Hyperkalemia is related to the lower renin-aldosterone levels seen in older persons under comparable conditions, making it more difficult to clear any excess potassium via the kidneys.

Osteoporosis is a major problem in elderly individuals, but a finely tuned endocrine system tends to ensure that serum calcium concentrations are maintained within a narrow normal range. Calcium and vitamin D intakes often are inadequate to prevent a negative calcium balance and bone demineralization. Hypercalcemia occurs more frequently in elderly persons primarily because the malignancies that cause hypercalcemia are more frequent.

Disorders of magnesium balance, even though they are not more common in elderly subjects, must be recognized for the well-being of the patient.

REFERENCES

1. Epstein M, Hollenberg N. Age as a determinant of renal sodium conservation in normal man. *J Lab Clin Med*. 1976;87:411–417.

2. Kleinfeld M, Casimir M, Borra S. Hyponatremia as observed in a chronic disease facility. *J Am Geriatr Soc*. 1979;27:156–161.

3. Miller M, Morley, JE, Rubenstein LZ, et al. Hyponatremia in a nursing home population. *Gerontologist*. 1985;25:118. Abstract.

4. Anderson RJ, Chung HM, Kluge R, et al. Hyponatremia: a prospective analysis of its epidemiology and the pathogenetic role of vasopressin. *Ann Intern Med*. 1985;102:164–168.

5. Deutsch S, Goldberg M, Dripps RD. Postoperative hyponatremia with the inappropriate release of antidiuretic hormone. *Anesthesia*. 1966;27:250–256.

6. Weisman PH, Shenkman L, Gregerman R. Chlorpropamide hyponatremia: drug induced inappropriate antidiuretic hormone activity. *N Engl J Med*. 1971;284:65–71.

7. Fichman MP, Vorherr H, Kleeman CR, et al. Diuretic-induced hyponatremia. *Ann Intern Med*. 1971;75:853–863.

8. Ashouri OS. Severe diuretic-induced hyponatremia in the elderly. *Arch Intern Med*. 1986;146: 1355–1357.

9. Rondeau E, de Lima J, Caillens H, et al. High plasma antidiuretic hormone in patients with cardiac failure: influence of age. *Miner Electrolyte Metab*. 1982;8:267–274.

10. Helderman JH, Vestal RE, Rowe JW, et al. The response of arginine vasopressin to intravenous ethanol in man: the impact of aging. *J Gerontol*. 1978;33:39–47.

11. Rowe JW, Minaker KL, Sparrow D, et al. Age related failure of volume-pressure mediated vasopressin release. *J Clin Endocrinol Metab*. 1982;54:661–664.

12. Snyder NA, Feigal DW, Arieff AI. Hypernatremia in elderly patients: a heterogenous, morbid, and iatrogenic entity. *Ann Intern Med*. 1987;107:309–319.

13. Lavizzo-Mourey R, Johnson J, Stolley P. Risk factors for dehydration among elderly nursing home residents. *J Am Geriatr Soc*. 1988;36:213–218.

14. Phillips PA, Rolls BJ, Ledingham JJG, et al. Reduced thirst after water deprivation in healthy elderly men. *N Engl J Med*. 1984;311:753–759.

15. Lindeman RD. Hypokalemia: causes, consequences, and correction. *Am J Med Sci*. 1976; 272:5–17.

16. Fries ED. Diuretic induced hypokalemia: the debate over its relationship to cardiac arrhythmias. *Postgrad Med*. 1987;81:123–129.

17. Lawson DH. Adverse reactions to potassium chloride. *Q J Med*. 1974;171:433–440.

18. Weideman P, DeMyttenaeu-Bursztein S, Maxwell MH, et al. Effect of aging on plasma renin and aldosterone in normal man. *Kidney Int*. 1975;8:325–333.

19. Crane MG, Harris JJ. Effect of aging on renin activity and aldosterone excretion. *J Lab Clin Med*. 1976;87:947–959.

20. Khan KT, Barrett-Conner E. Dietary potassium and stroke associated with mortality. *N Engl J Med*. 1987;316:235–240.

21. Riggs BL, Melton LJ III. Involutional osteoporosis. *N Engl J Med*. 1986;314:1676–1684.

22. Bullamore JR, Gallagher JC, Wilkinson R, et al. Effect of age on calcium absorption. *Lancet*. 1970;2:535–537.

23. Gallagher JC, Riggs BL, Eisman J, et al. Intestinal calcium absorption and serum vitamin D metabolites in normal subjects and osteoporotic patients: effect of age and dietary calcium. *J Clin Invest*. 1979;64:729–736.

24. Tsai KS, Heath H III, Kumar R, et al. Impaired vitamin D metabolism with aging in women: possible role in pathogenesis of senile osteoporosis. *J Clin Invest*. 1984;73:1668–1672.

25. MacLaughlin J, Holick MF. Aging decreases the capacity of skin to produce vitamin D_3. *J Clin Invest*. 1985;76:1536–1538.

26. McFadyen IM, Nordin BEC, Smith DA, et al. Effect of variation in dietary calcium. *Br Med J*. 1985;1:161–164.

27. Food and Nutrition Board, National Research Council. *Recommended Dietary Allowances*. 8th rev ed. Washington, DC: National Academy Press; 1980.

28. Food and Nutrition Board, National Research Council. *Recommended Dietary Allowances*. 10th ed. Washington, DC: National Academy Press; 1989.

29. Nordin BEC, Horsman A, Marshall DM, et al. Calcium requirement and calcium therapy. *Clin Orthop*. 1979;140:216–246.

30. Heaney RP, Recker RR, Saville P. Menopausal changes in calcium balance performance. *J Lab Clin Med*. 1978;94:953–963.

31. Chapuy MC, Chapuy P, Meunier PJ. Calcium and vitamin D supplements: effects of calcium metabolism in elderly people. *Am J Clin Nutr*. 1987;46:324–328.

32. Nordin BEC, Pollen KJ, Need AG, et al. The problem of calcium transport. *Am J Clin Nutr*. 1987;45:1296–1304.

33. Sherwood LM. The multiple causes of hypercalcemia in malignant disease. *N Engl J Med*. 1980;303:1412–1413.

34. Kochersberger GG, Lyles KW. Osteoporosis followed by primary hyperparathyroidism: a reason for continued vigilance. *J Am Geriatr Soc*. 1987;35:61–65.

35. Knochel JP. The pathophysiology and clinical characteristics of severe hypophosphatemia. *Arch Intern Med*. 1977;137:203–220.

36. Pao EM, Mickle SJ. Problem nutrients in the United States. *Food Technol*. 1981;35:58–69.

37. Schroeder HA, Nason AP, Tipton IH. Essential metals in man: magnesium. *J Chron Dis*. 1969; 21:815–841.

38. Reinhart RA. Magnesium metabolism: a review with special reference to the relationship between intracellular content and serum levels. *Arch Intern Med*. 1988;148:2415–2420.

39. Sheehan JP, Sissam D, Shumacher OP. Clinically significant magnesium deficiency of dietary origin. *J Am Coll Nutr*. 1984;3:245.

Chapter 5

Trace Metal Requirements

Gary J. Fosmire

Within the general domain of nutrition, there is growing concern for the nutritional needs and status of the elderly, with increasing attention focused on various trace metals. Studies of dietary intake and status, both generally and in response to various disease states, have revealed that elderly people may be particularly vulnerable to developing deficiencies of one or more of the trace metals. The reasons for this increased vulnerability include decreased energy intake without an increased density of trace metals in the diet, changes in food intake patterns, age-related physiologic changes that impair absorption or retention, and various chronic and acute diseases and the medications used to treat them. For several of the essential trace metals (zinc, copper, chromium, and selenium), there is a sufficient body of published literature to allow some estimation of the effects of aging on their metabolism, some evaluation of the consequences of a deficient state, and, in some cases, an estimation of the prevalence of deficiency in various population groups. Each of the trace metals is considered separately, although there are considerable interactions among trace metals; these are discussed where the interactions are potentially important.

Several physiologic changes associated with aging[1] might be expected to affect the metabolism of most trace minerals and, perhaps, increase or decrease the requirements of these essential nutrients. Changes in body composition, including a decline in lean body mass and a relative increase in body fat, can be expected to alter body pool sizes of, or requirements for, most of the trace metals since they tend to be associated primarily with non-adipose tissues. The decline in basal metabolic rate associated with advancing age is usually accompanied by a decrease in energy intake, exacerbating problems of insufficient density of trace minerals in the diet. The impairment in kidney function observed with aging may result in less efficient elimination with a concomitant retention of certain minerals, or less efficient reabsorption with resultant increased losses (Chapter 9). The relative hypochlorhydria associated with aging adversely affects the solubility of

77

the minerals and results in a decreased bioavailability or decreased absorption of various trace metals. The senescent changes in the intestine (Chapter 7) result in a decreased mucosal surface area and decreased motility, potentially contributing to an impaired absorption of trace metals; such impairment with aging has not been a consistent finding, however, suggesting that, in the absence of disease, there is sufficient capacity for appropriate absorption.[2] The greater prevalence of disease states among the elderly may adversely affect nutritional status as a result of the disease processes or through drug-nutrient interactions (Chapter 13).

Changes in dietary choices may also influence trace metal status. Certainly, selection of foods that do not contain substantial quantities of a particular trace mineral can result in a deficient state; but, in addition, the incorporation of large amounts of fiber or foods containing phytate (*myo*-inositolhexaphosphate), found in whole grains and legumes, can decrease the bioavailability of the minerals present in the diet and may also serve to reduce body levels of those minerals, such as zinc, that are secreted into the lumen of the small intestine.[3] In the absence of a complexing agent, such as fiber or phytate, the mineral might be reabsorbed, but with the incorporation of large amounts of fiber or phytate, this reabsorption may be impaired. Thus, it is apparent that these senescent changes in the physiology of the aged, coupled with changes in dietary patterns, the presence of disease, or frequent medication usage, may lead to a disproportionate frequency of suboptimal trace metal nutriture among elderly people.

ZINC

Zinc was demonstrated to be an essential nutrient more than half a century ago, and its importance to human health has been recognized for the last 25 years. Zinc is a component of more than 80 metalloenzymes and proteins, where it may have catalytic or structural functions. It is an important factor in the synthesis of deoxyribonucleic acid, ribonucleic acid, and protein, and is thought to stabilize cell membranes. It is essential for growth and cell division, reproduction, taste acuity, wound healing, and normal immune function. Given the important physiologic roles that zinc has, and the likelihood that these may be disrupted in some manner by a deficient state, it is important to consider the dietary adequacy of zinc and other factors that may influence requirements for zinc.

Among the factors affecting zinc status is the amount in the diet. A review of 10 studies of elderly people revealed that mean intakes ranged between 7 and 10 mg/d,[4–6] or approximately 50% to 67% of the recommended dietary allowance (RDA) of 15 mg established for both men and women over age 51 years[7]; there are no more specific recommendations for older or much older individuals. The RDAs have recently been revised to reduce zinc intake to 12 mg for women while retaining the 15-mg/d level for men.[8] Published comparisons have used the 15-

mg/d value for both men and women. An intake of less than two thirds of the RDA in most reported cases is at least, in part, a reflection of the density of zinc in the diet and the lower energy intake associated with aging. Solomons[9] has introduced an interesting way of viewing this relationship. He defines "critical nutrient density" as the amount of a given micronutrient contained in 1000 kcal of a given individual's diet that will provide the RDA when an individual meets his or her daily energy needs with the minimal caloric intake compatible with the maintenance of health. For individuals over age 74 years, the critical nutrient density values obtained for zinc were 9.1 mg/1000 kcal for men and 12.5 mg/1000 kcal for women. Actual densities of zinc in the dietary intake of elderly individuals are much less than these levels. Usual densities range between 4.0 and 6.0 mg/1000 kcal. For example, Fosmire and colleagues[6] found the density of zinc in the diet of a rural elderly population to be 6.0 mg/1000 kcal for men and 5.8 mg/1000 kcal for women. Other studies using younger populations have reported densities of 4.7[10] and 4.2 mg/1000 kcal.[11] It is evident that, without being particularly careful to choose foods rich in zinc, the RDA is unlikely to be met. If elderly people consume proportionately less of the foods that are richer in zinc (ie, meats, fish, and poultry), the density of zinc in their diets will decline further, exacerbating problems of obtaining sufficient zinc from dietary sources. The zinc content of selected foods is given in Table 5-1. In addition, differences in bioavailability of zinc from various dietary sources may influence dietary adequacy. It is clear from a number of studies that zinc is generally less available for intestinal absorption from foods of vegetable origin than from foods of animal origin, probably because of the presence of phytate (*myo*-inositolhexaphosphate) and fiber when these are present in substantial amounts in foods of vegetable origin.[3]

Despite significant research efforts directed toward elucidating the mechanisms of zinc absorption and maintenance of zinc homeostasis by the body, a clear understanding of these processes remains elusive. The absorption of zinc appears to occur via two processes, a saturable process that is stimulated by zinc depletion and a nonsaturable process that is not affected by zinc status.[12] At lower levels of intake, absorption is achieved primarily by the saturable process; above a certain level of intake, the capacity of the saturable process is exceeded.[13] Although it is clear that zinc is not absorbed from the stomach and colon, the relative importance of different portions of the small intestine remains uncertain. Most of the research data implicate the duodenum as the primary site of zinc absorption based on considerations of the luminal pH and that this segment of the small bowel has the first opportunity for absorption.[14] As part of the maintenance of zinc homeostasis, gastrointestinal secretion of zinc occurs. This endogenous zinc excretion may occur via desquamation of intestinal cells or through intestinal secretions, such as pancreatic fluid, bile, or the succus entericus. Zinc homeostasis is accomplished primarily by modulation of the rate of absorption and the rate of endogenous secretion; conditions that interfere with these processes can adversely affect maintenance of appropriate levels of zinc in the body.

Table 5-1 Zinc Content of Selected Foods

Food, Portion Size	Zinc Content (mg)
Beverages	
Carbonated, nonalcoholic, 12 fl oz	(0.2–0.4g)
Coffee, 1 cup	Trace
Tea, 1 cup	0.1
Wine, 4 fl oz	0.1
Beer, 12 fl oz	0.1
Bread, 1 slice	
White	0.2
Mixed grain	0.5
Rye	0.4
Whole wheat	0.6
Dairy products	
Milk, 1 cup	0.9–1.0
Cheese, 1 oz	0.9
Cottage cheese, 1 cup	0.7–1.0
Eggs, 1 each	0.6
Fish, 3½ oz	
Bass	0.5
Cod	0.8
Swordfish	1.1
Tuna	0.9
Fruits, fresh, 1 each	
Apple	Trace
Peach	0.1
Pear	0.2
Plum	0.1
Orange	0.1
Legumes, 1 cup cooked	
Kidney beans	2.0
Soybeans	2.1
Black-eyed peas	1.3
Dried peas	1.9
Meat	
Beef, cooked, 3 oz	5.1
Pork roast, 3 oz	2.2
Chicken, 1 cup	2.9
Beef liver, 3 oz	5.2
Chicken liver, 3 oz	3.6

Table 5-1 continued

Food, Portion Size	Zinc Content (mg)
Nuts, 1 cup	
Almonds	4.2
Cashews	7.7
Filberts	2.8
Peanuts	4.8
Pecans	6.5
Walnuts	3.3
Shellfish	
Oysters, eastern, 3½ oz	62.0
Oysters, western, 3½ oz	48.0
Clams, 3½ oz	2.7
Vegetables	
Green beans, 1 cup	0.5
Beets, ½ cup	0.2
Carrots, 1 each	0.1
Corn, 1 ear	0.4
Green peas, 1 cup	1.8
Potato, baked without skin, 1 each	0.5
Cabbage, raw, 1 cup	0.1

Source: Values from *Nutrition for Living* (pp A12–A37) by JL Christian and JL Greger, Benjamin Cummings Publishing Company, 1988.

A number of other factors, called "conditioning factors" by Sandstead and colleagues,[5] that impair the absorption or increase the excretion of zinc (or both) from endogenous pools may influence requirements or lead to a deficient state. Chronic malabsorption syndromes, such as gluten-sensitive enteropathy or Crohn's disease, can result in decreased zinc absorption and an impaired ability to control zinc homeostasis, as the gut is the apparent major point of control. Any physiologic stress that results in substantially increased urinary zinc losses will increase requirements. Stresses, such as physical trauma, wounds (including surgery), thermal burns, and muscle-wasting diseases all result in dramatic increases in urinary zinc losses. The consumption of alcohol results in increased urinary losses of zinc due to alcohol consumption per se. If consumption has been sufficiently prolonged to cause alcohol-induced cirrhosis, urinary losses of zinc will be high and the zinc content of the liver abnormally low. Many of the medications (both those sold over the counter and by prescription) used by elderly people can affect zinc status. Diuretics, chelating agents, antacids, laxatives, and iron supplements all may decrease absorption or increase excretion from the body.

Given the apparently poor intakes and the likelihood of having one or more of the conditioning factors, what is the evidence that elderly individuals have poor zinc status? The data are meager and clearly insufficient to allow a confident estimate of deficiency among all elderly people, but there have been a number of smaller studies that report variable estimates of deficiency. Data from a number of studies reviewed by Greger[4] as well as several other studies[6,15–20] have evaluated zinc nutriture among elderly people. Prevalence of deficient status, defined somewhat arbitrarily as plasma or serum zinc concentrations below 10.7 μmol/L, ranged between 0% and 61%. As the studies examined quite different populations of varying age ranges, socioeconomic classes, and health status, such variability in prevalence is not unexpected. Studies that examined larger population groups, such as a subset of the Health and Nutrition Examination Survey (HANES II) sample[21] on apparently healthy elderly,[19,20] have reported that approximately 12% had zinc plasma or serum values below 10.1 μmol/L. There is apparently a considerable number of elderly people who demonstrate biochemical evidence of zinc deficiency; prevalence rates appear strikingly higher among those with poor health or low socioeconomic status. Table 5-2 lists a number of clinical conditions that may predispose an individual to developing a deficient state.

Table 5-2 Conditions That Predispose to Zinc Deficiency

Inadequate dietary intake or use
  Protein calorie malnutrition
  Vegetarianism
  Restricted protein diets

Maldigestion and malabsorption of zinc
  Celiac disease and other enteropathies
  Chronic inflammatory bowel disease
  Intestinal resection
  Exocrine pancreatic insufficiency
  Hepatic disease

Increased zinc losses
  Starvation, burns, diabetes mellitus
  Diuretic therapy, proteinuria
  Intravascular hemolysis, porphyria
  Chelating agent therapy
  Chronic blood loss, dialysis
  Exfoliative dermatitis, excessive sweating
  Protein-losing enteropathies

Intravenous feeding

Source: Adapted from *Zinc in Human Biology* (p 266) by CF Mills (Ed) with permission of Springer-Verlag, © 1989.

Consequences of zinc deficiency may be serious and varied, depending in part on the severity of the deficiency. Manifestations of the deficiency have been reviewed by Prasad[22] and may include growth retardation, impaired sexual development and performance, various manifestations of dermatitis, delayed wound healing, anorexia, depressed taste acuity, and impaired immune function. A number of these symptoms arise as a result of a severely deficient state, but even moderate or mild deficiency may adversely affect the health of an individual. A number of the deficiency symptoms resemble problems commonly observed in elderly individuals, and attempts have been made to relate zinc status to the occurrence of several of these symptoms in the aged. Most attention has focused on taste acuity, wound healing, dermatitis, and immune function. The questions posed are whether the specific symptomatology can be related to impaired zinc status and, more important, whether normalization of the depressed status results in amelioration of the symptoms.

Taste acuity is reported to decline with aging,[23] but it is unclear to what extent this can be attributed to zinc deficiency. It has been clearly shown that severe zinc deficiency will result in hypogeusia[24]; it is less clear that a less severe deficiency will result in hypogeusia. Several studies have examined the interaction between zinc and taste acuity. Most studies of elderly subjects who did not have medical conditions that led to a severely deficient state have failed to observe such a relationship or to see a positive change, ie, lower thresholds for the different tastes in response to zinc supplementation.[24-28] The demonstration of improved taste acuity with zinc supplementation among patients rendered severely zinc deficient[29,30] shows the efficacy of such therapy and the possibility of losing taste acuity if the deficiency is acute enough.

An essential role for zinc in wound healing is now well established.[31] It is apparent, however, that an increased rate of wound healing in response to zinc supplementation will occur only if the individual is in suboptimal zinc status; ie, there is not an additional benefit obtained by supplementation once the deficiency has been corrected.[32] Initial poor status, due to insufficient intake or losses associated with surgery or physical trauma, could limit the amount of zinc available for tissue repair and diminish the effectiveness of the healing process.

Zinc deficiency in experimental and domestic farm animals results in parakeratotic skin lesions.[33] Severe zinc deficiency in humans may manifest as bullous pustular dermatitis of the extremities and in the oral, anal, and genital areas.[22] The hypothesis that a portion of the dermatitis seen in elderly people is due to zinc deficiency has not been tested extensively. Weismann and colleagues[34] identified a number of individuals in an institution for elderly people who had skin problems similar to those described in zinc deficiency. A number of these subjects had subnormal plasma zinc concentrations; however, supplementation with zinc for 4 weeks did not result in improvement in their skin lesions.

The hypothesis that zinc nutriture is related to the immune response in elderly people has attracted considerable attention. Elderly individuals are more susceptible to some infectious diseases, and the consequences of infection that they experience may be more severe.[35] Data in humans indicate that the defect is in the delayed immune mechanisms, expressed as deficits in delayed dermal hypersensitivity and a failure of T lymphocytes to respond to stimulation.[36] It is known that severe zinc deficiency markedly impairs cellular immunity,[37–39] but the effects of a less severe deficiency are not as well documented. Two studies have reported beneficial effects of zinc supplementation on cellular immunity in elderly subjects,[40,41] although neither study was conducted in a double-blind research design and the numbers of individuals examined were small. A double-blind zinc intervention trial was begun in 1987. Baseline data revealed that responses to seven skin test antigens were significantly associated with plasma zinc concentrations, and that in vitro lymphocyte proliferative responses to various mitogens were related to various measures of cellular zinc levels. This study, with double-blind intervention at both physiologic (15 mg/d) and pharmacologic (100 mg/d) doses of zinc given for 1 year, will provide much needed data about the relationship between zinc status and immune competence.

It seems prudent to recommend that all elderly people routinely take a small supplement of zinc, given that dietary intakes are generally less than the RDA and given the potential beneficial effects of normalizing suboptimal zinc status. It should be pointed out, however, that excessive use of zinc supplements can result in alterations in copper balance and may affect lipoprotein profiles by reducing high-density lipoprotein cholesterol levels. Use of pharmacologic dosages of zinc for prolonged periods can result in frank copper deficiency and impaired immune responses.[42]

COPPER

Of the various trace minerals, copper was one of the first to be identified as an essential nutrient. Milk contains very low concentrations of copper; therefore, feeding a milk-based diet to rats resulted in a severe hypochromic, microcytic anemia unresponsive to iron.[43] Further research identified many of the biologic roles of copper, primarily as a component of various copper-containing enzymes (Table 5-3) and assisting, in an as yet unidentified way, in disulfide bond formation in keratin.[44] Copper deficiency has been generated in a number of species of experimental animals and has been found in livestock under certain conditions. Symptoms of copper deficiency are somewhat species-specific, but they may be manifested as anemia and neutropenia, osteoporosis, myocardial disease, neurologic effects, and arterial disease. Consequences of a severe copper deficiency

Table 5-3 Copper-Containing Enzymes

Common Name	Functional Role	Known or Potential Consequences of Deficiency
Ceruloplasmin	Ferroxidase, amine oxidase, copper transport	Anemia, deficient supply of copper to other tissues
Cytochrome *c* oxidase	Electron transport chain	Muscle weakness, cardiomyopathy, brain degeneration
Dopamine β-hydroxylase	Catecholamine production	Neurologic effects
Lysyl oxidase	Cross-linking of collagen and elastin	Vascular rupture, loose skin and joints, osteoporosis, emphysema, bladder diverticula
Superoxide dismutase	Free radical detoxification	Membrane damage, other free radical damage
Tyrosinase	Melanin production	Failure of pigmentation

Source: Adapted with permission from *Annual Review of Nutrition* (1988;8:235–257), Copyright © 1988, Annual Reviews, Inc.

can be largely explained by diminished or absent activity of various copper metalloenzymes.

Although copper has been identified as an essential trace metal for more than 60 years, there is substantial uncertainty about the requirements for humans. Copper deficiency has been observed in humans and its essentiality thus proven, but an RDA is not yet established. The data are limited and the Committee on Dietary Allowances, Food and Nutrition Board, National Academy of Sciences, chose in 1980 to list copper in the estimated "safe and adequate daily dietary intake" (SADDI) category at a level of 2 to 3 mg/d for adults.[7] In the most recent recommendations of the Committee on Dietary Allowances, this has been modified to 1.5 to 3.0 mg/d for adults.[8] This presumably represents the best estimate of adequate dietary intake levels for adults; however, it is likely that many population groups do not consume this much copper on a daily basis. A summary of the copper content of various diets indicated that many provided less than 2 mg/d and that intakes of less than 1 mg/d were not rare.[4,45]

Although the dietary requirement for copper is not firmly established and is known to be affected by other dietary variables such as protein and zinc, requirements for young men seem to be in the range of 1 to 2 mg/d.[45] There are relatively few studies of copper balance in elderly people. With mean intakes of 3.2 mg/d, copper balance was close to zero for elderly men in two studies conducted by Turnlund and colleagues.[46,47] Burke and colleagues[48] found that eight of ten elderly subjects were in positive copper balance at 2.33 mg/d. Healthy elderly subjects studied by Bunker and colleagues[16] were not able to maintain balance at intakes of 1.28 mg/d. For housebound elderly,[17] intakes of 0.87 mg/d resulted in substantial negative copper balance. It would appear that requirements for copper do not decline with age and that they are likely in the range of 1.5 to 3 mg/d, although more research is needed to define this requirement more fully.

There have been relatively few studies designed to assess copper intakes of elderly people directly. Gibson and colleagues[49] reported that in vegetarian women (mean age 69 years), copper intake was 2.1 mg/d. More recently, Gibson and colleagues,[15] using duplicate diet composite analysis, reported that the mean intake for elderly Canadian women was 1.2 mg/d. The mean copper intake of 24 healthy elderly people in England was determined to be 1.28 mg/d.[16] For housebound, elderly individuals, because of their lower energy intakes, the copper consumption was 0.87 mg/d.[17] A recent survey of individuals aged 60 to 65 years showed mean daily intakes of 0.86 mg for women and 1.18 mg for men.[50] Thus, it would appear that many elderly people do not consume sufficient copper to meet the SADDI of 1.5 to 3 mg/d. Solomons[51] has estimated the critical nutrient density for copper to be 1.2 mg/1000 kcal for elderly men and 1.7 mg/1000 kcal for elderly women. Bunker and colleagues[17] obtained nutrient densities of 0.63 mg/1000 kcal for men and 0.7 mg/1000 kcal for women in their study of housebound elderly; these values were similar to values for healthy elderly subjects obtained in an earlier study.[16] Similar concentrations of copper in the diet (approximately 0.75 mg/1000 kcal) can be estimated from a study conducted by Gibson and colleagues.[15] Thus, given the energy intake of elderly people, it would seem unlikely that they could obtain diets containing sufficient density of copper to prevent a mildly deficient state without inclusion of some concentrated sources of copper such as liver, whole grains, nuts, legumes, or shellfish. Copper is least abundant in muscle meats, dairy products, and non–whole-grain cereals and baked goods.

Several factors may affect the adequacy of copper in the diet, in addition to food choices that influence density. Among these are dietary components that may increase or impair the absorption of copper.[45] The absorption of copper in humans appears to occur primarily across the gastric and duodenal surfaces. This absorption is regulated by the nutritional status of the individual, but it is influenced by the chemical form in which the element is present and by a substantial number of interactions with other dietary factors that affect bioavailability.[52] Copper appears to be absorbed by two mechanisms, one saturable and the other unsaturable, suggesting active transport for the former and simple diffusion for the latter; lower concentrations of dietary copper are absorbed by the saturable, active pathway.[53] Among the factors that facilitate copper absorption are protein, L-amino acids, citrate, phosphate, and gluconate. Factors that decrease the bioavailability of copper include zinc, cadmium, phytate, fiber, unabsorbed fat, bile, and vitamin C. Individuals who supplement their diets with large quantities of zinc or vitamin C have an added risk of copper deficiency.

The essentiality of copper for humans is well established. Severe deficiencies have been reported in premature infants, in children with severe malnutrition, in patients who have severe malabsorption syndromes, and among individuals receiving parenteral nutrition without adequate copper supplementation. The deficiency is usually manifested by severe anemia, neutropenia, and osteoporosis, and, if uncorrected, may result in death. Such severe copper deficiency is relatively rare and does not usually occur in the absence of other medical problems that impair absorption or increase the rate of copper lost from the body. The most common state, although the prevalence rate cannot be accurately established, is probably that of a mild, chronic copper deficiency. The question of whether mild copper deficiency is a significant nutritional problem in humans was addressed recently by Danks.[44] Some possible features of chronic copper deficiency include anemia and neutropenia refractory to other treatments, osteoporosis, arthritis, arterial disease, loss of pigmentation, myocardial disease, and neurologic effects.

Although none of the above features are proven consequences of a mild, chronic copper deficiency, each has a biochemical or observational rationale that supports its inclusion in this list of suspected outcomes. For example, the anemia seen in copper deficiency has been related to decreased levels of ceruloplasmin, a copper-containing protein in plasma with ferroxidase activity; ceruloplasmin appears to be required for the oxidation of iron from the ferrous to ferric state so that it can be released from enterocytes in the small intestine or parenchymal cells in the liver, to be bound to transferrin for utilization in erythropoiesis.

Copper's essential role in proper bone metabolism and the prevention of skeletal abnormalities is primarily related to the maintenance of activity of lysyl oxidase. This copper-containing enzyme is required for establishing cross-linkages of collagen essential for structural integrity of bone. There is a long history of empirical observations consistent with an anti-inflammatory role for copper, perhaps related to its moderating effects in autoimmune diseases such as some forms of arthritis. The role of copper in arterial and myocardial diseases is partially related to its function in lysyl oxidase. The formation of the cross-linkages of desmosine and isodesmosine in elastin requires lysyl oxidase; failure to form these cross-linkages results in less elasticity and weakening of the major blood vessels.

Copper deficiency has also been shown to result in hypercholesterolemia, glucose intolerance, and hypertension—all risk factors for cardiovascular disease. The loss of pigmentation seen in copper deficiency is due to a decrease in the activity of the enzyme tyrosinase, a copper-containing enzyme required for the first step in the conversion of tyrosine to melanin.

The most severe neurologic manifestation of copper deficiency is neonatal ataxia. Necrosis and degeneration of neurons in the brain stem and spinal cord, as well as myelin aplasia, are thought to be due to a deficiency of cytochrome oxidase, the copper-containing terminal respiratory enzyme, in motor neurons, leading to a depression of aerobic metabolism and phospholipid synthesis. Copper also plays roles in the synthesis and control of neurotransmitters and neuropeptides, in part through its action as a component of monoamine oxidase enzymes.[53]

Since many of the problems observed with substantial frequency in elderly individuals are similar to those listed as possible features of chronic copper deficiency, it seems important to obtain better estimates of the prevalence of suboptimal copper intake and status in this group. This is made more difficult by the absence of an unambiguous indicator of copper status, by the lack of clear dietary recommendations or requirements for copper, and by the uncertainty of reported dietary concentrations of copper in food composition tables.

CHROMIUM

The essential need for chromium for mammals was discovered in 1959 by Schwarz and Mertz,[54] who observed an impaired glucose tolerance in rats fed various diets; glucose tolerance was corrected by supplementation with chromium. Observations with other species, including humans, have confirmed this alteration in glucose metabolism in chromium deficiency, and chromium is now thought to play a role in facilitating the function of insulin in some manner, perhaps by influencing the binding of insulin to cell receptors or by taking part in the interaction of insulin and its target cells. Despite its acceptance as an essential trace mineral, information about the biologic function of chromium is limited, perhaps because of the many technologic difficulties in chromium analysis and uncertainty about the validity of much of the early work.[55] It is clear, however, that chromium deficiency appears to manifest with many of the symptoms of diabetes, especially those of impaired glucose tolerance, altered plasma lipid profiles, and peripheral neuropathy.[56]

A number of factors can impair the chromium status of an individual. The first is the amount of chromium in the diet. The data describing the distribution of chromium in the United States' food supply are quite limited, but studies from Finland have shown a similar distribution among fruit, vegetables, dairy products, beverages, and meats, and lesser amounts from cereals[56]; there were negligible amounts from seafoods and drinking water (Table 5-4). Foods believed to be particularly rich in chromium include mushrooms, brewer's yeast, prunes, raisins, nuts, asparagus, and wine.[56] Obviously, dietary choices can affect chromium status.

Actual intakes of chromium have been determined in a few studies in which the methodology is adequate to trust the validity of the data. Intakes are estimated at 50 to 100 μg/d in the 1980 edition of the RDA, and the SADDI is 50 to 200 μg/d.[7] More recent studies suggest that dietary chromium intakes in England, Finland,

Table 5-4 Daily Intake of Chromium from Various Food Groups

Food Group	Average Daily Intake (µg)	Comment
Cereal products	3.7	55% from wheat
Meats	5.2	55% from pork
Fish/seafoods	0.6	
Fruits, vegetables, nuts, mushrooms	6.8	70% from fruits and berries
Dairy products, eggs, margarine	6.2	85% from milk
Beverages, confectioneries, sugar condiments	6.6	45% from beer, wine, soft drinks
Total	29.1	

Source: Adapted from *Handbook of Nutrition in the Aged*, (p 140) by RR Watson (Ed) with permission of CRC Press, © 1985.

Canada, and the United States are less than 50 µg/d. For example, Anderson and Kozlovsky,[57] using analysis of duplicate daily composites of all food and beverages, reported mean intakes of 28 ± 1 µg/d for both men and women (aged 25 to 65 years); intakes for men were somewhat greater (33 ± 3 µg/d) than they were for women (25 ± 1 µg/d). Analysis of diets of two different groups of elderly subjects revealed intakes of 37 µg/d[58] and 25 µg/d.[59] Expressed per 1000 kcal, chromium in the diets of most of the subjects was between 20 and 25 µg/1000 kcal,[60] although critical nutrient density would need to be 30 µg/1000 kcal for men and 41 µg/1000 kcal for women.[51] From a study by Bunker and colleagues,[59] intakes of 25 µg/d resulted in an estimated slightly negative balance if dermal and miscellaneous losses were considered. These data suggest that chromium intakes among the general population, and elderly people in particular, may be insufficient to provide optimal status.

In addition to insufficient dietary intakes, several other factors can influence chromium requirements. One of these factors is the body's ability, through presently unknown mechanisms, to improve the percentage absorption to compensate for low intakes. Anderson and Kozlovsky[57] showed that the percentage absorption from diets of varying intake is inversely related to chromium intake (Figure 5-1). It is important to note that all the percentages are low (ie, from less than 0.3% to 1.9%), although they reflect more than a sixfold improvement in absorption efficiency with quite low intakes. A second factor that affects chromium requirements is the increase in urinary chromium excretion with consumption of a diet high in refined carbohydrates or simple sugars.[61] Other effects, such as enhanced absorption of chromium when complexed with organic compounds; the so-called "glucose tolerance factor"; and improved absorption in the presence of proteins or amino acids, oxalates, and vitamin C, await confirmation in carefully controlled human studies.[55]

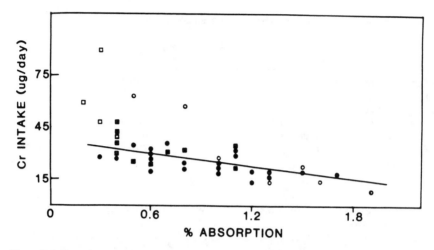

Figure 5-1 Chromium absorption of adult subjects at varying chromium intakes. Solid symbols denote 7-day average values; open symbols, daily values; (■,□) men; (●,○) women. The line was drawn using only the 7-day average values. *Source*: Reprinted with permission from *American Journal of Clinical Nutrition* (1985;41:1177–1183), Copyright © 1985, American Society for Clinical Nutrition, Inc.

Proven, relatively severe, chromium deficiency has been demonstrated. A patient receiving total parenteral nutrition without chromium for 3 years developed hyperglycemia, weight loss, ataxia, and peripheral neuropathy. Symptoms did not respond to insulin, but the addition of chromium resulted in normal glucose tolerance and neurologic function.[62] Similar findings of diabetic-like symptoms refractory to insulin, but reversed by supplemental chromium, have also been reported.[63] Because of the difficulty of establishing a chromium-deficient state, most studies of chromium status are conducted as above; ie, a chromium supplement is given to population groups thought to be at risk, and the effects are monitored before and after supplementation. Putative evidence of deficiency has been observed in malnourished children from a chromium-poor area and among diabetics, elderly people, and individuals with hyper- and hypoglycemia.[55] Because some of these studies have yielded questionable data, particularly regarding the assessment of chromium status, and since investigators have given different amounts and forms of chromium, it is difficult to compare studies. However, there does appear to be an improvement in glucose tolerance and blood lipid profiles if individuals were chromium deficient prior to treatment. This latter point, ie, that normalizing an individual's chromium status will likely improve glucose, insulin, and lipid levels, is important. Certainly as important is the fact that not all impaired glucose tolerance, hyperinsulinemia, or hyperlipidemia states are due to chromium deficiency; further benefits of giving chromium supplements to individuals in good chromium status should not be expected.

Several studies have examined chromium status in elderly people. Levine and colleagues[64] gave 10 elderly individuals who had impaired glucose tolerance a supplement of 150 μg of trivalent chromium for 1 to 4 months; 4 of the 10 responded with improved glucose tolerance tests. Liu and Morris[65] studied 27 women, aged 40 to 75 years, who were given 5 g of brewer's yeast (4 μg of chromium per day) for 3 months. Among those subjects who were hyperglycemic on entry to the study, there was a decrease in fasting glucose levels, a decrease in insulin levels, and a decrease in cholesterol concentrations. In a study by Offenbacher and Pi-Sunyer,[66] 24 individuals, aged 63 to 93 years, responded to 9 g of brewer's yeast per day for 8 weeks with improved glucose tolerance and reduced serum cholesterol levels. In contrast, in a subsequent study by Offenbacher and associates,[58] there was no effect of either 5 g of brewer's yeast or 200 μg of trivalent chromium on glucose tolerance, insulin levels, or cholesterol or triglyceride concentrations. The authors noted, however, that this second sample appeared to be in better nutritional status than did the first group studied. Improved glucose tolerance was seen in about half of the elderly subjects at risk for chromium deficiency in a study conducted by Martinez and others.[67]

It would seem that some elderly people, as well as those in younger age groups, have marginal or suboptimal chromium status. If so, these individuals appear to respond to supplementation by normalized insulin levels, improved glucose tolerance tests, and altered plasma lipid levels, ie, normalized cholesterol levels or increased levels of high-density lipoprotein cholesterol, or both. Because of the great difficulty in collecting and handling samples to prevent contamination; the scarcity of institutions in which determinations can be performed correctly, given the specific equipment requirements; and the apparent failure of any method used on any particular tissue that adequately represents the chromium status of the sample donor,[55] there is currently no practical method to assess chromium status on a routine basis. The only practical way to identify individuals who are in poor chromium status it to try a course of supplementation at levels near the SADDI and see whether symptoms of hyperinsulinemia, hyperglycemia, and hyperlipoproteinemia improve.

SELENIUM

An essential role for selenium has been proven conclusively in a number of species, including humans.[68] A number of diseases are caused by simultaneous deficiencies of selenium and vitamin E. Liver necrosis in rats, exudative diathesis in chicks, mulberry heart in swine, and some forms of muscular dystrophy in lambs and calves can be prevented or cured by supplementation with either selenium or vitamin E. These examples demonstrate the known, and interacting, biochemical roles of selenium as a component of glutathione peroxidase and vitamin E in the detoxification of peroxides and free radicals that have their most damaging effects on cell membranes in blood, liver, and other tissues.

Roles for selenium independent of vitamin E status have also been demonstrated. Pancreatic degeneration occurs in chicks if they are selenium deficient, even if vitamin E intake is adequate. Pure selenium deficiency resulting in growth retardation, cataract formation, lack of spermatogenesis, and dystrophic and necrotic symptoms have been observed in experimental animals.[69] Selenium deficiency resulting in Keshan disease (a cardiomyopathy primarily affecting children in the Keshan region of China), Kashin-Beck disease (an osteoarthropathy with disturbances of endochondral ossification and deformity of the affected joints observed in people living in some regions of China where there are low levels of selenium in the soil), and muscle pain and tenderness in a child receiving total parenteral nutrition have been reported; all syndromes responded to selenium supplementation. It is likely, however, that most of these diseases or symptoms are multifactorial in nature, perhaps having a viral component, but selenium deficiency appears to be a major contributory cause.[70,71]

A role for selenium as an anticancer agent seems well established in animal experiments.[72] Epidemiologists have linked lower selenium intakes with higher incidences of cancers of the colon, rectum, prostate, breast, and leukocytes.[73] Several studies of humans suggest that selenium status does have a role in protecting against the development of several cancers,[74,75] particularly if the levels of other antioxidants (ie, vitamin E and carotenoids) are low.[76] These data seem to suggest that selenium, through its function as an antioxidant, has a role in cancer prevention, although definitive proof of this in humans is still not available. It has also been suggested that selenium may have a role in slowing some of the changes seen as part of the aging process, especially in the reduction of levels of lipofuscin pigments and peroxidative damage to the cellular membranes and subcellular components.[77]

The data reporting selenium intakes and status in elderly populations are quite limited. Selenium status appears to be generally good with intakes that approximate the newly established RDA of 70 μg/d for men and 55 μg/d for women.[8] Selenium intakes of 77.6 ± 44.5 μg/d were reported for a population of elderly Canadian women; 21% of the women had intakes less than the lower limit of the SADDI established by the 1980 RDA (50 to 200 μg/d).[15] These values were similar to those reported by Thimaya and Ganapathy[78] for adults aged 60 years and older in the United States, and a bit less than intakes for elderly adults reported by Lane and colleagues (94 ± 43 μg/d).[79] At this level of intake, most of the elderly subjects had biochemical indications of sufficient status as assessed by serum selenium concentration (0.115 ± 0.03 μg/mL),[15] in comparison with a reference value of 0.096 μg/mL.[80] Requirements for selenium have been examined in young men by using a balance study with periods of depletion and repletion.[81] Young, North American men apparently require dietary intakes of approximately 70 μg/d to replace losses and maintain stores. There are no comparable data for elderly subjects, but there is no indication that their dietary needs for selenium would be strikingly less than those for younger individuals.

There is little evidence of clear clinical disorders in humans directly attributable to suboptimal selenium status. Relationships to a putative role in cancer prevention and to minimizing peroxidative damage to tissues are discussed above; clear experimental confirmation in humans is not yet available. There is an interesting double-blind study conducted on elderly people in Finland[82] relating vitamin E and selenium supplementation to improvements in depression, anxiety, self-care, mental alertness, emotional lability, motivation and initiative, hostility, interest in the environment, fatigue, and anorexia. The authors hypothesized that the changes reflect known effects of vitamin E and selenium on tissue aging, ie, in reducing peroxidative damage. It is important to note that the levels of supplementation were large (100 times the RDA for vitamin E and approximately 120 times the new RDA for selenium) but that no untoward toxic clinical side effects were observed. The number of subjects studied was rather small (15 were given supplements and 15 were given placebo), and it is not possible to differentiate between effects of vitamin E and effects of selenium. It would be interesting to pursue this mode of therapy with a larger population and perhaps at more modest levels of supplementation. The potential hazards of excessive use of selenium supplements have been described.[7] Intakes of 3200 to 6700 µg/d are associated with symptoms of hair and nail loss, dermatitis, garlic odor in breath, fatigue, and irritability.[83]

ALUMINUM

Aluminum is not known to be required for any natural metabolic process and therefore is not thought to be an essential nutrient.[33] Although aluminum-containing compounds were considered to be essentially nonhazardous for many years, concern about the potentially toxic effects of aluminum as it accumulates in tissues has been increasing during the last two decades.[84] This concern has prompted examinations of dietary intakes of aluminum, of response to pharmaceutical-based exposure, and of manifestations of toxicity.

Dietary exposure to aluminum includes that which is present naturally and that which comes from aluminum-containing food additives; other exposure arises from contact with aluminum used in food containers, cookware, utensils, and food wrapping. Most foods and beverages contain low concentrations of aluminum naturally; exceptions are tea, herbs, and spices.[85] Of the three factors affecting the aluminum content of foods, the aluminum-containing food additives have the greatest effects in increasing aluminum levels. The major food sources of aluminum in daily diets probably are grain products with aluminum additives; processed cheese with aluminum additives; tea, herbs, and spices; and salt with an aluminum additive. Little aluminum is contributed to the diet by meat, poultry, and fish; fruit;

vegetables; fats and oils; or sugar and sweeteners. A distribution of aluminum intakes among various food groups has been calculated for a mixed diet containing 2541-kcal[85] (Table 5-5). Aluminum can be transferred from aluminum food-preparation equipment, particularly if the foods are acidic or exposure is prolonged. For example, the aluminum in tomato sauce increased from 0.1 mg/kg (net weight) to 57.1 mg/kg after cooking the sauce in an aluminum pan.[86] This route is not, however, a major or consistent source of dietary aluminum. Total intakes of aluminum are variable, primarily depending on the inclusion of aluminum-containing food additives in the diet, but they are estimated to be about 9 mg/d for adult women and 12 to 14 mg/d for adult men.[85] Intakes in this range currently are not thought to pose a health risk.

The quantities of aluminum consumed in food and beverages are small when compared with those that can be ingested in pharmaceutical products such as antacids, buffered analgesics, antidiarrheal medications, and certain antiulcer drugs. Lione[87] estimated that daily intakes of aluminum could be 800 to 5000 mg from antacids and 126 to 728 mg from buffered analgesics. Such high levels of intake may have adverse consequences, particularly when there is a pre-existing medical condition such as uremia.

Consequences of aluminum toxicity have been reported for several clinical conditions. Uremic patients undergoing dialysis with aluminum-containing dialysate fluids and patients receiving aluminum-containing parenteral fluids have manifested aluminum toxicity.[88] Clinical signs of toxicity generally include osteodystrophy, encephalopathy, and anemia.[89] The osteodystrophy may be expressed as bone pain, an increased incidence of fractures, and an histologic manifestation with aluminum-containing osteomalacic components. The symp-

Table 5-5 Aluminum Intake in a Diet of 2541 kcal/d

Foods	Aluminum Intake mg/d	%
Milk, yoghurt, cheese	3.69	27.0
Meat, poultry, fish	0.41	3.0
Grains and grain products	4.98	36.5
Vegetables	0.52	3.8
Fruits	0.02	0.1
Mixed dishes	0.69	5.1
Fats, sweets, condiments	0.23	1.7
Beverages	0.83	6.1
Desserts	2.26	16.6
Nuts and seeds	0.02	0.1
Total	13.65	100.0

Source: Values from *Journal of American Dietetic Association* (1989;89:659–664).

toms of encephalopathy include dementia, speech difficulties, and motor abnormalities. The anemia is of the normochromic, normocytic type, most likely related to disturbances in heme synthesis and porphyrin metabolism, although the exact mechanism involved has yet to be identified. These symptoms are sometimes seen in uremic patients, especially children, who have not been exposed to aluminum-contaminated dialysis or intravenous fluids; the source of aluminum appears to be the aluminum-containing binder used to treat hyperphosphatemia.[90]

Most interest in aluminum toxicity as it relates to elderly people who are not on dialysis or parenteral feeding regimens is related to the putative connection between deposition of aluminum in the brain and the development of various senile dementias, including Alzheimer's disease. It has been reported that individuals with Alzheimer's disease and with amyotrophic lateral sclerosis (Lou Gehrig disease) with parkinsonism dementia had increased levels of aluminum in regions of the brain that also contained the neurofibrillary tangles associated with these dementias.[91] Dementia refers here to a progressive loss of cognitive function commonly involving memory, orientation, abstract thinking, and the ability to learn new tasks. The hypothesis that aluminum is part of the etiology of various dementias remains controversial and inconclusive. However, it is clear from experimental studies using animal models that, if aluminum does gain access to the central nervous system, it acts as a potent neurotoxin.[92]

Under normal physiologic conditions, relatively little aluminum is absorbed by the gastrointestinal system after oral exposure and, of the portion absorbed, only a much smaller amount is deposited in the central nervous system. It is therefore likely that, under normal conditions, these natural barriers keep virtually all of the aluminum out of the central nervous system. However, Perl[91] has suggested that, under conditions of advancing age, genetic predisposition, or possibly viral damage, these barriers may become impaired, allowing the element to gain access to the central nervous system, possibly inducing the neurofibrillary tangles. Supporting this hypothesis are reports that aluminum tends to accumulate in brain with age.[93,94] The body's ability to remove aluminum that has been absorbed may be diminished in the older individual. The decline in renal function observed with aging[95] and the fact that the major excretory route for aluminum absorbed into the body is via the urine[96] suggest that aging might promote accumulation of aluminum in the body. There has been very little research on the effects of aging on aluminum metabolism; therefore, much of the concern about the potential hazards of aluminum exposure for older individuals remains unresolved.

MOLYBDENUM

The essentiality of molybdenum has been established for a number of species, including humans. It is thought that molybdenum participates in a variety of enzymatic reactions as an essential cofactor termed molybdopterin, an alkylphosphate-substituted pterin to which molybdenum is coordinated through two sulfur atoms.[97] These molybdenum-containing enzymes are involved in the metabolism of purines, pyrimidines, pteridines, and aldehydes, and in the oxidation of sulfite.[98] Specific enzymes known to contain the molybdenum cofactor include xanthine oxidase/dehydrogenase, aldehyde oxidase, and sulfite oxidase. Demonstration of essentiality for humans has largely been based on studies of inborn errors of metabolism involving deficiencies of one or more of the molybdenum-containing enzymes. Affected individuals experience seizures, severe mental retardation, dislocation of the ocular lenses, and eventually death.[99] There is one report of a nutritional deficiency of molybdenum in a patient undergoing prolonged total parenteral nutrition.[100] Clinical symptoms totally eliminated by supplementation with 300 μg of ammonium molybdate per day included irritability leading to coma, tachycardia, tachypnea, and night blindness. Changes were attributed to a loss of sulfite oxidase activity.

Molybdenum is widely distributed in soils, plants, and animal tissues. The richest sources of the element include legumes, cereal grains (and hence bread and baked products), leafy vegetables, milk, beans, liver, and kidney. Fruits, stem and root vegetables, and muscle meats are among the poorest sources.[99] By chemical analysis of common foods, Tsongas and colleagues[101] have determined that the average intake in the United States is 0.18 mg/d. Intakes were lower for older individuals (men aged 65 to 74 years, 0.16 mg; aged 75+ years, 0.14 mg; women aged 65 to 74 years, 0.12 mg; aged 75+ years, 0.12 mg). These intakes fall within the range of the estimate of safe and adequate intakes of 0.075 to 0.250 mg/d set by the Committee on Dietary Allowances.[8] With intakes of approximately 0.1 to 0.2 mg of molybdenum per day, there are no reports of molybdenum deficiency in human populations. American diets appear to provide such levels of molybdenum intake easily. The use of molybdenum supplements is not advised.[102] In animals, excessive molybdenum intake results in copper deficiency and other deleterious effects unrelated to impaired copper status; in humans, there is some suggestion that elevated levels of molybdenum intake may increase the incidence of gout.[98] Humans exposed to 10 to 15 mg of molybdenum per day displayed abnormally high serum uric acid levels and tissue xanthine oxidase activities, with symptoms of recurrent pain in the knees, interphalangeal joints of the hands, and metatarsal-phalangeal joints of the feet associated with erythema, edema, and joint deformity.[101]

MANGANESE

Manganese is an essential element for many animal species and is assumed to be essential for humans as well. Among various animal species, the main manifestations of manganese deficiency include impaired growth, skeletal abnormalities, disturbed or depressed reproductive function, ataxia of the newborn, and defects in lipid and carbohydrate metabolism.[102] For a single human subject inadvertently rendered manganese deficient during an experimental study, the manifestations included hypocholesterolemia, weight loss, transient dermatitis, occasional nausea and vomiting, changes in hair and beard color, and slow growth of beard and hair.[103]

Manganese can function in the body both as an enzyme activator and as a constituent of metalloenzymes. Arginase, the cytosolic enzyme responsible for urea synthesis; pyruvate carboxylase, a key enzyme in gluconeogenesis required for the synthesis of oxaloacetate from lactate or pyruvate; and mitochondrial manganese-superoxide dismutase, which catalyzes the disproportionation of superoxide to hydrogen peroxide and oxygen, are manganese metalloenzymes. Defects in carbohydrate metabolism and increased lipid peroxidation, especially after exposure to hyperbaric oxygen, ozone, or ethanol, may be related to loss of enzymatic activity subsequent to development of manganese deficiency. Manganese can also activate various enzymes. Of particular importance is the manganese-specific activation of glycosyltransferases.[104] It is believed that the skeletal deformities and neonatal ataxia seen in manganese deficiency are due to impairment of cartilage synthesis as a result of decreased activity of the glycosyltransferases.

Common foods in human diets are highly variable in manganese concentration. In general, the highest manganese levels occur in nuts and whole-grain cereals; variable amounts are found in vegetables; and low concentrations are found in meat, fish, and dairy products. Tea is exceptionally rich in manganese.[102] Only a few studies have evaluated the manganese intake of older persons. A study of Canadian women by Gibson and colleagues[105] revealed that vegetarians (mean age 69 years) had greater dietary intakes (4.4 mg/d) than did nonvegetarian women (mean age 60 years; intake 2.6 mg/d); among the nonvegetarians, 43% had dietary intakes less than the lower end of the 2.5- to 5.0-mg/d range suggested as safe and adequate by the Food and Nutrition Board.[7] In a subsequent study of Canadian women[106] ranging in age from 58 to 89 years with a mean age of 66 years, the average intake was 3.8 mg/d; 27% had intakes of less than 2.5 mg/d. In the United States, Pennington and colleagues [50] have analyzed intakes of manganese in conjunction with the 16 Total Diet Study collections conducted from 1982 to 1986. Mean intakes for women aged 60 to 65 years were 2.2 mg/d; for men aged 60 to 65 years, 2.63 mg/d over the 4-year span. Differences between years were very small and were not significant.

Recommended safe and adequate intakes (2.5 to 5.0 mg/d) have been established by the Food and Nutrition Board[7] based on balance studies involving relatively few subjects and a very limited range of levels of manganese intake. More recent studies have reported that 3.5 mg/d is required to maintain balance in young men,[107] that intakes of 2.43 mg/d result in negative balance in postmenopausal women,[108] and that recalculation of data derived from a number of manganese balance studies in the literature suggest a recommended range of intakes of 3.5 to 7.0 mg/d.[109] Reports that a number of dietary components such as fiber and phytate,[110,111] calcium,[112] iron,[113] and sugar[108] have detrimental effects on either the absorption or retention of manganese lead to speculation that manganese requirements might be higher.

It is not clear why the apparently insufficient dietary intakes of manganese (based on both the published estimated safe and adequate intakes and on the more recent estimates of required intakes as noted above) are not reflected in recognized manganese-deficient states. It may be that more marginal levels of deficiency are not easily recognized. Clearly there is insufficient information or research about which manifestations of manganese deficiency might be observed if the deficiency is less severe. However, the use of balance experiments, although the most commonly used technique to determine manganese requirements, may not be entirely appropriate. Results from a factorial design experiment (one designed to determine obligatory losses) indicate that the minimal requirement is 0.74 mg/d.[114] Reconciliation of these vastly different estimates of manganese requirements requires further work. Particular concerns that older individuals may have for how their bodies handle manganese and whether there are additional needs or larger requirements for this essential element and whether some of the consequences of aging can be related to insufficient manganese status remain to be addressed by nutritionists.

NICKEL

Nickel is likely to be an essential nutrient for man, although this has not been definitely proven on the basis of the development of a deficient state, the presence of consistent deficiency symptoms, or the prevention or cure of a deficient state by provision of physiologic levels of this element. Nickel deficiencies, however, have been produced in a number of animal models (chicks, cows, goats, minipigs, rats, and sheep); the most prominent and consistent symptoms are reduced hematopoiesis, depressed growth, and various metabolic alterations.[115] Despite the recognition of these deficiency signs in animals, there is no firmly established biologic function for nickel in humans or animals. It is thought that nickel likely functions as a cofactor or structural component in specific metalloenzymes (as is the case for a number of plants and microorganisms) or as a bioligand cofactor facilitating the intestinal absorption of the ferric ion.[116]

The great effort that must be made to minimize dietary and environmental contamination in order to generate nickel deficiencies in animals and the failure to observe the deficiency in humans suggest that the requirement for nickel is quite low and easily met by the diets consumed or, in some cases, even by environmental pollution with nickel-containing dust.[115] Both inhalation and ingestion constitute the major routes of nickel intake in humans. Total dietary intakes vary greatly in the amounts and proportions of foods with varying nickel content. Foods that contain generally high concentrations of nickel (more than 0.3 μg/g) include nuts, leguminous seeds, shellfish, cacao products, and hydrogenated shortenings; grains, cured meats, and vegetables are generally intermediate in concentration (0.1 to 0.3 μg/g); and fish, milk, and eggs are generally low (less than 0.1 μg/g).[116] Nickel intake is probably in the range of 150 to 700 μg/d.[115] Such intakes easily meet the needs of the individual. The use of nickel supplements is not advisable. Oral nickel, in not particularly high doses, can adversely affect human health. Nickel dermatitis has been estimated to occur at a prevalence rate of between 3% and 13%. For sensitive individuals, an oral dose of as little as 0.6 mg has been shown to be sufficient to produce a positive reaction.[116]

IODINE

Iodine is an integral part of the thyroid hormones thyroxine and triiodothyronine and, as such, is an essential nutrient for all animal species. A deficiency in iodine can result in endemic goiter and cretinism. Severe deficiencies of iodine remain a serious public health problem, particularly in less economically developed regions of the world. For more industrialized regions of the world, iodine exposure is more than adequate to meet metabolic demands.

Iodine occurs in the food supply from endogenous sources and from the use of iodized salt. In addition, several adventitious sources of iodine contribute to total intake. Iodates are used as dough-conditioning agents in the continuous-vacuum/mix process for making bread, and iodine-containing compounds accumulate in dairy products as a result of the use of iodine-containing disinfectants and iodine-containing additives in animal feeds. Milk and dairy products, as well as bread and bakery products, are the largest sources of iodine in human foods.[117]

The RDA for iodine for both men and women is set at 150 μg/d.[8] It is unlikely that individual intake would fall below this amount. Intakes for persons aged 60 to 65 years recently have been determined to be 270 μg for women and 360 μg for men; these intakes were averaged over the years 1982 to 1986.[50] There has been a decline in the intake of iodine over the last few years, resulting in intakes nearer the recommended allowance. Intakes of up to 2000 μg/d are not thought to present a hazard to adults, although higher levels of intake have been associated with an increased incidence of thyrotoxicosis. It is thought that the present iodine intake in the United States is safe and decreasing toward recommended levels.[8]

CONCLUSION

It is clear that we do not know enough about the requirements for various trace minerals, particularly the needs of older individuals. Many of the physiologic changes that accompany aging probably interfere with optimal absorption, utilization, or retention of these minerals. Changes in dietary practices, both quantitative and qualitative (ie, the decrease in food consumption and alteration in dietary choices) can be expected to affect adversely the trace mineral adequacy of the diet. When these changes are coupled with the effects of various disease processes and medications used to treat these conditions, the potential for deficiency states is increased substantially. Evidence has been presented to indicate that the adequacies of zinc, copper, chromium, and manganese are of greatest concern. Intakes of selenium, molybdenum, nickel, and iodine are unlikely to be deficient in other than very unusual circumstances. Aluminum is of concern only as a toxic mineral; minimization of exposure is appropriate. It is clear that most of the trace minerals discussed are essential for normal health and well-being, and it is very important that optimal status be maintained; however, the theory that some of the deleterious effects of aging can be related to deficiencies in one or more of these essential nutrients remains to be proven.

REFERENCES

1. Timiras PS. *Physiological Basis of Geriatrics*. New York, NY: Macmillan Publishing Co; 1988.

2. Mertz W. Trace elements and the needs of the elderly. In: Hutchinson ML, Munro HH, eds. *Nutrition and Aging*. Orlando, Fla: Academic Press Inc; 1986.

3. Solomons NW. Biological availability of zinc in humans. *Am J Clin Nutr*. 1982;35: 1046–1075.

4. Greger J. Trace minerals. In: Chen LH, ed. *Nutritional Aspects of Aging*. Boca Raton, Fla: CRC Press; 1986.

5. Sandstead HH, Henrikson LH, Greger JL, et al. Zinc nutriture in the elderly in relation to taste acuity, immune response, and wound healing. *Am J Clin Nutr*. 1982;36:1046–1059.

6. Fosmire GJ, Manuel PA, Smiciklas-Wright H. Dietary intakes and zinc status of an elderly rural population. *J Nutr Elderly*. 1984;4:19–30.

7. Food and Nutrition Board, National Research Council. *Recommended Dietary Allowances*. 9th ed. Washington, DC: National Academy Press; 1980.

8. Food and Nutrition Board, National Research Council. *Recommended Dietary Allowances*. 10th ed. Washington, DC: National Academy Press; 1989.

9. Solomons NW. Trace elements in nutrition of the elderly, 1: established RDAs for iron, zinc, and iodine. *Postgrad Med*. 1986;79:231–242.

10. Harland BF, Johnson RD, Blenderman EM, et al. Calcium, phosphorus, iron, iodine, and zinc in the "total diet." *J Am Diet Assoc*. 1980;77:16–20.

11. Holden JM, Wolf WR, Mertz W. Zinc and copper in self-selected diets. *J Am Diet Assoc*. 1979;75:23–28.

12. Hoadley JE, Leinart AS, Cousins RJ. Kinetic analysis of zinc uptake and serosal transfer by vascularly perfused rat intestine. *Am J Physiol.* 1987;252:G825–G831.

13. Coppen DE, Davies NT. Studies on the effects of dietary zinc dose on [65]Zn absorption in vivo and on the effects of zinc status on [65]Zn absorption and body loss in young rats. *Br J Nutr.* 1987;57:35–44.

14. Lönnerdal B. Intestinal absorption of zinc. In: Mills CF, ed. *Zinc in Human Biology.* London, England: Springer-Verlag; 1989.

15. Gibson RS, Martinez OB, MacDonald AC. The zinc, copper, and selenium status of a selected sample of Canadian elderly women. *J Gerontol.* 1985;40:296–302.

16. Bunker VW, Hinks LJ, Lawson MS, et al. Assessment of zinc and copper status of healthy elderly people using metabolic balance studies and measurement of leukocyte concentrations. *Am J Clin Nutr.* 1984;40:1096–1102.

17. Bunker VW, Hinks LJ, Stansfield MF, et al. Metabolic balance studies for zinc and copper in housebound elderly people and the relationship between zinc balance and leukocyte zinc concentrations. *Am J Clin Nutr.* 1987;46:353–359.

18. Patterson PG, Lee E, Christensen DA, et al. Zinc levels of hospitalized elderly. *J Am Diet Assoc.* 1985;85:186–191.

19. Sahyoun NR, Otradovic CL, Hartz SC, et al. Dietary intakes and biochemical indicators of nutritional status in an elderly, institutionalized population. *Am J Clin Nutr.* 1988;47:524–533.

20. Bogden JD, Olesky JM, Munves EM, et al. Zinc and immunocompetence in the elderly: baseline data on zinc nutriture and immunity in unsupplemented subjects. *Am J Clin Nutr.* 1987;46:101–109.

21. Fulwood R, Johnson CL, Bryner JD, et al. *Hematological and Nutritional Biochemistry Reference Data for Persons 6 Months–74 Years of Age: United States 1976–1980.* Washington, DC: Public Health Service; 1982. US Dept of Health and Human Services publication PHS 83-1682.

22. Prasad A. Clinical spectrum and diagnostic aspects of zinc deficiency. In: Prasad A, ed. *Essential and Toxic Trace Elements in Human Health and Disease.* New York, NY: Alan R Liss Inc; 1988.

23. Weiffenbach JM, Baum BJ, Burghauser R. Taste thresholds: quality specific variation with human aging. *J Gerontol.* 1982;37:372–377.

24. Henkin RI, Patten BM, Re PK, et al. Syndrome of acute zinc loss. *Arch Neurol.* 1975; 32:745–751.

25. Greger JL, Geissler AH. Effect of zinc supplementation on taste acuity of the aged. *Am J Clin Nutr.* 1978;31:633–637.

26. Hutton CW, Hayes-Davis RB. Assessment of the zinc nutritional status of selected elderly subjects. *J Am Diet Assoc.* 1983;82:148–153.

27. Greger JL. Dietary intake and nutritional status in regard to zinc of institutionalized aged. *J Gerontol.* 1977;32:549–553.

28. Bales CW, Steinman LC, Freeland-Graves JH, et al. The effect of age on plasma zinc uptake and taste acuity. *Am J Clin Nutr.* 1986;44:664–669.

29. Atkin-Thor E, Goddard BW, O'Nion J, et al. Hypogeusia and zinc depletion in chronic dialysis patients. *Am J Clin Nutr.* 1978;31:1948–1951.

30. Mahajan SK, Prasad AS, Lambujon J, et al. Improvement of uremic hypogeusia by zinc: a double blind study. *Am J Clin Nutr.* 1980;33:1517–1521.

31. Wacker WEC. Biochemistry of zinc: role in wound healing. In: Hambidge KM, Nichols BL, eds. *Zinc and Copper in Clinical Medicine.* New York, NY: Spectrum Publications; 1978.

32. Hallböök T, Hedelin H. Zinc metabolism and surgical trauma. *Br J Surg*. 1977;64:271–273.

33. Underwood E. *Trace Elements in Human and Animal Nutrition*. 4th ed. New York, NY: Academic Press; 1977.

34. Weismann K, Wanscher B, Krakaver R. Oral zinc therapy in geriatric patients with selected skin manifestations and a low plasma zinc level. *Acta Dermatol (Stockh)*. 1978;58:157.

35. Carder ID. The affect of aging on susceptibility to infection. *Rev Infect Dis*. 1980;2:801–810.

36. Fernandes G, West A, Good RA. Nutrition, immunity and cancer: a review, III: effects of diet on the diseases of aging. *Clin Biol*. 1979;9:91–106.

37. Allen JI, Kay NE, McClain CJ. Severe zinc deficiency in humans: association with a reversible T-lymphocyte dysfunction. *Ann Intern Med*. 1981;95:154–157.

38. Oleski JM, Westphal ML, Shore S, et al. Zinc therapy of depressed cellular immunity in acrodermatitis enteropathica. *Am J Dis Child*. 1979;133:915–918.

39. Pekarek RS, Sandstead HH, Jacob RA, et al. Abnormal cellular immune responses during acquired zinc deficiency. *Am J Clin Nutr*. 1979;32:1466–1471.

40. Duchateau J, Delepresse G, Vrigens R, et al. Beneficial effects of oral zinc supplementation on the immune response of old people. *Am J Med*. 1981;70:1001–1004.

41. Wagner PA, Jernigan JA, Bailey LB, et al. Zinc nutriture and cell-mediated immunity in the aged. *Int J Vitam Nutr Res*. 1983;53:94–101.

42. Fosmire G. Zinc toxicity. *FASEB J*. 1988;2:5197.

43. Hart EB, Steenbock H, Waddell J, et al. Iron in nutrition, VII: copper as a supplement to iron for hemoglobin building in the rat. *J Biol Chem*. 1928;77:797–812.

44. Danks DM. Copper deficiency in humans. *Annu Rev Nutr*. 1988;8:235–257.

45. Sandstead HH. Copper bioavailability and requirements. *Am J Clin Nutr*. 1982;35:809–814.

46. Turnlund J, Costa BS, Margen S. Zinc, copper, and iron balance in elderly men. *Am J Clin Nutr*. 1981;34:2641–2647.

47. Turnlund JR, Reager RO, Costa F. Iron and copper absorption in young and elderly men. *Nutr Res*. 1988;8:333–343.

48. Burke DM, DeMicco FJ, Taper LJ, et al. Copper and zinc utilization in elderly adults. *J Gerontol*. 1981;36:558–563.

49. Gibson RS, Anderson BM, Sabry JH. The trace metal status of a group of post-menopausal vegetarians. *J Am Diet Assoc*. 1983;82:246–250.

50. Pennington JAT, Young BE, Wilson DB. Nutritional elements in U.S. diets: results from the total diet study, 1982 and 1986. *J Am Diet Assoc*. 1989;89:659–664.

51. Solomons NW. Trace elements in nutrition of the elderly, 2: SADDIs for copper, manganese, selenium, chromium, molybdenum, and fluoride. *Postgrad Med*. 1986;79:251–263.

52. Cousins RJ. Absorption, transport, and hepatic metabolism of copper and zinc: special reference to metallothionein and ceruloplasmin. *Physiol Rev*. 1985;65:238–309.

53. Davies GK, Mertz W. Copper. In: Mertz W, ed. *Trace Elements in Human and Animal Nutrition*. 5th ed. San Diego, Calif: Academic Press; 1987;1.

54. Schwarz K, Mertz W. Chromium (III) and the glucose tolerance factor. *Arch Biochem Biophys*. 1959;85:292–295.

55. Offenbacher EG, Pi-Sunyer FX. Chromium in human nutrition. *Annu Rev Nutr*. 1980; 8:543–563.

56. Anderson RA. Chromium requirements and needs of the elderly. In: Watson RR, ed. *Handbook of Nutrition in the Aged*. Boca Raton, Fla: CRC Press; 1985.

57. Anderson RA, Kozlovsky AS. Chromium intake, absorption and excretion of subjects consuming self-selected diets. *Am J Clin Nutr.* 1985;41:1177–1183.

58. Offenbacher EG, Rinko CJ, Pi-Sunyer FX. The effects of inorganic chromium and brewer's yeast on glucose tolerance, plasma lipids, and plasma chromium in elderly subjects. *Am J Clin Nutr.* 1985;42:454–461.

59. Bunker W, Lawson MD, Delves HT, et al. The uptake and excretion of chromium by the elderly. *Am J Clin Nutr.* 1984;39:799–802.

60. Kumpulainen JT, Wolf WR, Veillon C, et al. Determination of chromium in selected United States diets. *Agric Food Chem.* 1979;27:490–494.

61. Kozlovsky AS, Moser PB, Reiser S, et al. Effects of diets high in simple sugars on urinary chromium losses. *Metabolism.* 1986;35:515–518.

62. Jeejeebhoy KN, Chu RC, Marliss EB, et al. Chromium deficiency, glucose intolerance and neuropathy reversed by chromium supplementation in a patient receiving long-term parenteral nutrition. *Am J Clin Nutr.* 1977;30:531–538.

63. Freund H, Atamian S, Fischer JE. Chromium deficiency during total parenteral nutrition. *JAMA.* 1979;241:496–498.

64. Levine RA, Streeten DHP, Doisy RJ. Effects of oral chromium supplementation on the glucose tolerance of elderly human subjects. *Metabolism.* 1968;17:114–125.

65. Liu VJK, Morris JS. Relative chromium response as an indicator of chromium status. *Am J Clin Nutr.* 1978;31:972–976.

66. Offenbacher EG, Pi-Sunyer FX. Beneficial effect of Cr-rich yeast on glucose tolerance and blood lipids in elderly subjects. *Diabetes.* 1980;29:919–925.

67. Martinez OB, MacDonald AC, Gibson RS, et al. Dietary chromium and effect of chromium supplementation on glucose tolerance of elderly Canadian women. *Nutr Res.* 1985;5:609–620.

68. Combs GF Jr, Levander DA, Spallholz JE, et al, eds. *Selenium in Biology and Medicine, Parts A and B.* New York, NY: Van Nostrand Reinhold Co; 1987.

69. McCoy KE, Weswig P. Some selenium responses in the rat not related to vitamin E. *J Nutr.* 1969;98:383–389.

70. Cohen HJ, Brown M, Lyons J, et al. Clinical physiology and biochemical consequences of human selenium deficiency. In: Prasad A, ed. *Essential and Toxic Trace Elements in Human Health and Disease.* New York, NY: Alan R Liss Inc; 1988.

71. Diplock AT, Chaudry FA. The relationship of selenium biochemistry to selenium-responsive disease in man. In: Prasad A, ed. *Essential and Toxic Trace Elements in Human Health and Disease.* New York, NY: Alan R Liss Inc; 1988.

72. Milner JA. The effects of selenium on virally induced and transplantable tumor models. *Fed Proc.* 1985;44:2568–2572.

73. Schrauzer GN, White DA, Schneider CJ. Cancer mortality correlation studies, III: statistical associations with dietary selenium intakes. *Bioinorg Chem.* 1977;7:23–24.

74. Lewko WM, McConnell UP. Observations on selenium in human breast cancer. In: Combs GF Jr, Levander DA, Spallholz JE, et al, eds. *Selenium in Biology and Medicine, Parts A and B.* New York, NY: Van Nostrand Reinhold Co; 1987.

75. Saito K, Saito T, Hosokawa T, et al. Blood selenium level and the interaction of copper, zinc, and manganese in stomach cancer. In: Combs GF Jr, Levander DA, Spallholz JE, et al, eds. *Selenium in Biology and Medicine, Parts A and B.* New York, NY: Van Nostrand Reinhold Co; 1987.

76. Clark LC, Turnbull B, Graham G, et al. Nonmelanoma skin cancer and plasma selenium: a prospective cohort study. In: Combs GF Jr, Levander DA, Spallholz JE, et al, eds. *Selenium in Biology and Medicine, Parts A and B.* New York, NY: Van Nostrand Reinhold Co; 1987.

77. Yuncie AA, Hsu JM. Role of selenium in aging. In: Combs GF Jr, Levander DA, Spallholz JE, et al, eds. *Selenium in Biology and Medicine, Parts A and B*. New York, NY: Van Nostrand Reinhold Co; 1987.

78. Thimaya S, Ganapathy SH. Selenium in human hair in relation to age, diet, pathological condition, and serum levels. *Sci Total Environ*. 1982;24:41–49.

79. Lane AW, Warran DC, Taylor BJ, et al. Blood selenium and glutathione peroxidase levels and dietary selenium of free-living and institutionalized elderly subjects. *Proc Soc Exp Biol Med*. 1983; 173:87–95.

80. Iyengar V, Woittiez J. Trace elements in human clinical specimens: evaluations of literature data to identify reference values. *Clin Chem*. 1988;34:474–481.

81. Levander OA, Sutherland B, Morris VC, et al. Selenium balance in young men during selenium depletion and repletion. *Am J Clin Nutr*. 1981;34:2662–2669.

82. Tolonen M, Halme M, Sarna S. Vitamin E and selenium supplementation in geriatric patients. *Biol Trace Element Res*. 1985;7:161–168.

83. Parizek J. Dose-response of selenium in nutritional toxicology. In: Combs GF Jr, Levander DA, Spallholz JE, et al, eds. *Selenium in Biology and Medicine, Parts A and B*. New York, NY: Van Nostrand Reinhold Co; 1987.

84. Greger JL. Aluminum and tin. *World Rev Nutr Diet*. 1987;54:255–285.

85. Pennington JAT. Aluminum content of foods and diets. *Food Addit Contam*. 1988;5:161–232.

86. Greger JL. Aluminum in the diet and mineral metabolism. In: Sigel H, ed. *Metal Ions in Biological Systems*. New York, NY: Marcel Dekker; 1988;24.

87. Lione A. Aluminum intake from non-prescription drugs and sucralfate. *Gen Pharmacol*. 1985;16:223–228.

88. Greger JL. Potential for trace mineral deficiencies and toxicities in the elderly. In: Bales CW, ed. *Mineral Homeostasis in the Elderly*. New York, NY: Alan R Liss Inc; 1989.

89. Wills MR, Savory J. Aluminum toxicity and chronic renal failure. In: Sigel H, ed. *Metal Ions in Biological Systems*. New York, NY: Marcel Dekker; 1988;24.

90. Committee on Nutrition. Aluminum toxicity in infants and children. *Pediatrics*. 1986;78:1150–1154.

91. Perl DP. Aluminum and Alzheimer's disease, methodologic approaches. In: Sigel H, ed. *Metal Ions in Biological Systems*. New York, NY: Marcel Dekker; 1988;24.

92. Kruck TPA, McLachlan DR. Mechanisms of aluminum neurotoxicity: relevance to human disease. In: Sigel H, ed. *Metal Ions in Biological Systems*. New York, NY: Marcel Dekker; 1988;24.

93. McDermott JR, Smith I, Iqbal K, et al. Brain aluminum in aging and Alzheimer disease. *Neurology*. 1979;29:809–814.

94. Markesbery WR, Ehmann WD, Hosain TIM, et al. Instrumental neutron activation analysis of brain aluminum in Alzheimer's disease and aging. *Ann Neurol*. 1981;10:511–516.

95. Epstein M. Effects of aging on the kidney. *Fed Proc*. 1979;38:168–171.

96. Ganrot PO. Metabolism and possible health effects of aluminum. *Environ Health Perspect*. 1986;65:363–441.

97. Kramer SP, Johnson JL, Ribeiro AA, et al. The structure of the molybdenum cofactor. *J Biol Chem*. 1987;262:16357–16363.

98. Mills CF, Davies GK, Molybdenum. In: Mertz W, ed. *Trace Elements in Human and Animal Nutrition*. 5th ed. San Diego, Calif: Academic Press; 1987;1.

99. Rajagopalan KV. Molybdenum: an essential trace element in human nutrition. *Annu Rev Nutr*. 1988;8:401–427.

100. Abumrad NH, Schneider AJ, Steel D, et al. Amino acid intolerance during prolonged total parenteral nutrition reversed by molybdate therapy. *Am J Clin Nutr.* 1981;34:2551–2559.

101. Tsongas TA, Meglen RR, Walravens PA, et al. Molybdenum in the diet: an estimate of average daily intake in the United States. *Am J Clin Nutr.* 1980;33:1103–1107.

102. Hurley LS, Keen CL. Manganese. In: Mertz W, ed. *Trace Elements in Human and Animal Nutrition.* 5th ed. San Diego, Calif: Academic Press; 1987;1.

103. Doisy EA. Micronutrient controls on biosynthesis of clotting proteins and cholesterol. In: Hemphill DD, ed. *Trace Substances in Environmental Health.* Columbia, Mo: University of Missouri Press; 1972;6.

104. Leach RM Jr. Biochemical role of manganese. In: Hoeckstra WG, Suttie JW, Ganther JW, et al, eds. *Trace Element Metabolism in Animals.* Baltimore, Md: University Park Press; 1974;2.

105. Gibson RS, Anderson BM, Sabry JH. The trace metal status of a group of post-menopausal vegetarians. *J Am Diet Assoc.* 1983;82:246–250.

106. Gibson RS, MacDonald AC, Martinez OB. Dietary chromium and manganese intakes of a selected sample of Canadian elderly women. *Hum Nutr Appl Nutr.* 1985;39A:43–52.

107. Freeland-Graves JH, Behmardi F, Bales CW, et al. Metabolic balance in young men consuming diets containing five levels of dietary manganese. *J Nutr.* 1988;118:764–773.

108. Hallfrisch J, Powel A, Carafelli C, et al. Mineral balances of men and women consuming high fiber diets with complex or simple carbohydrates. *J Nutr.* 1987;117:48–55.

109. Freeland-Graves JH, Bales CW, Behmardi FB. Manganese requirements in humans. In: Kies C, ed. *Nutritional Bioavailability of Manganese.* Washington, DC: American Chemical Society; 1987.

110. Schwartz R, Apgar BJ, Wien EM. Apparent absorption and retention of Ca, Cu, Mg, Mn, and Zn from a diet containing bran. *Am J Clin Nutr.* 1986;43:444–455.

111. Bales CW, Freeland-Graves JH, Lin P-H, et al. Plasma uptake of manganese: response to dose and dietary factors. In: Kies C, ed. *Nutritional Bioavailability of Manganese.* Washington, DC: American Chemical Society; 1987.

112. Lin P-H, Freeland-Graves JH. Effects of simultaneous ingestion of calcium and manganese in humans. In: Bales CW, ed. *Mineral Homeostasis in the Elderly.* New York, NY: Alan R Liss Inc; 1989.

113. Dougherty V, Freeland-Graves JH, Behmardi F, et al. Interaction of iron (Fe) and manganese in males fed varying levels of dietary manganese. *Fed Proc.* 1987;46:914.

114. Friedman BJ, Freeland-Graves JH, Bales CW, et al. Manganese balance and clinical observations in young men fed a manganese deficient diet. *J Nutr.* 1987;117:133–143.

115. Nieboer E, Tom RT, Sanford WE. Nickel metabolism in man and animals. In: Sigel H, ed. *Metal Ions in Biological Systems.* New York, NY: Marcel Dekker; 1988;23.

116. Nielsen FH. Nickel. In: Mertz W, ed. *Trace Elements in Human and Animal Nutrition.* 5th ed. San Diego, Calif: Academic Press; 1987;1.

117. Matovinovic J. Iodine. In: Olsen R, ed. *Present Knowledge in Nutrition.* 5th ed. Washington, DC: Nutrition Foundation; 1984.

Chapter 6

Oral Health in the Elderly

Wendy E. Martin

As the first segment of the gastrointestinal system, the oral cavity provides the point of entry for nutrients. The condition of the oral cavity, therefore, can facilitate or undermine nutritional status. If dietary habits are unfavorably influenced by poor oral health, then nutritional status may be compromised. However, nutritional status can also contribute to or exacerbate oral disease. General well-being is interrelated with health and disease states of the oral cavity as well as the rest of the body. An awareness of this interrelationship is essential when working with the older patient, since the incidence of major dental problems and the frequency of chronic illness and pharmacotherapy increase dramatically in older people.

REVIEW OF ANATOMY AND FUNCTIONS OF THE ORAL CAVITY

Anatomy of the Oral Cavity

The major parts of the oral cavity (Figure 6-1) include lips; vestibules; teeth; maxilla and mandible (upper and lower jaws, respectively); alveolar bone (termed residual bone, if there are no teeth); gingivae (gums); hard and soft palates (roof of the mouth); tongue and mucous membranes (floor of the mouth); temporomandibular joint; buccal mucosa (lining of the cheeks); salivary glands; and the muscles of mastication and facial expression (orofacial musculature). Throughout the mouth, there are blood vessels, lymphatics, and nerves to ensure rapid communication between the oral cavity and other major organ systems.

At the lips, the skin of the face is continuous with the mucous membranes of the oral cavity. The bulk of the lips is formed by skeletal muscles and a variety of

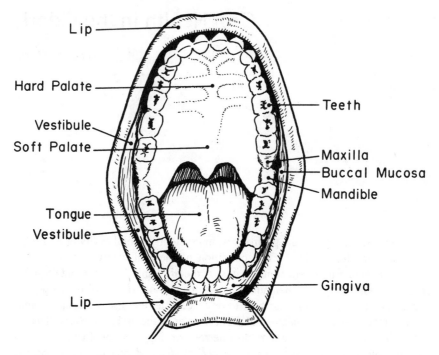

Figure 6-1 Major parts of the oral cavity.

---

sensory receptors that judge the taste and temperature of foods. Their reddish color is due to an abundance of blood vessels near their surface.

The vestibule is the cleft that separates the lips and cheeks from the teeth and gingivae. When the mouth is closed, the vestibule communicates with the rest of the mouth through the space between the last molar teeth and the rami of the mandible.

Thirty-two teeth normally are present in the adult mouth: two incisors, one canine, two premolars, and three molars in each half of the upper and lower jaws. The teeth in the upper jaw are termed maxillary and the teeth in the lower jaw are termed mandibular. The mandible is the movable member of the two jaws, whereas the maxilla is stationary. The components of an individual tooth provide a framework within which to appreciate changes that occur with age (Figure 6-2).

Teeth are highly calcified structures composed of four parts: (1) enamel, the hard, brittle substance covering the outer surface of the crown of the tooth; (2) dentin, a bonelike substance forming the main body of the tooth, surrounding the pulp cavity, and covered by enamel on the crown and cementum on the root; (3) cementum, a bonelike substance that covers the tooth root; and (4) pulp chamber and

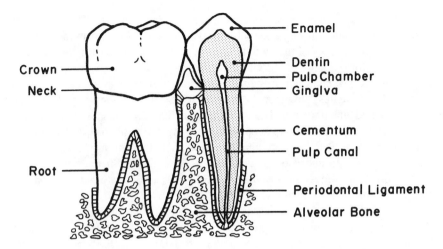

Figure 6-2 Components of a tooth.

canal(s), the soft central parts of the tooth that contain the blood vessels, nerves, and lymphatics. Each tooth in the mouth is surrounded and supported by alveolar bone. The visible portion of the tooth is termed the crown. The portion submerged below the gum line is the root. The region where these portions meet is called the neck of the tooth. The gingiva surrounds the necks of the teeth and covers the alveolar bone. It is composed of dense, fibrous tissue covered by a smooth vascular mucosa. The tooth roots are joined to the alveolar bone by periodontal ligaments.

The hard palate forms the roof of the mouth in the chewing area, and the soft palate lies just posterior to it. The floor of the mouth is formed by the tongue, which nearly fills the oral cavity when the mouth is closed, and mucous membranes. The tongue is a mobile mass of mostly skeletal muscle covered by a mucous membrane with numerous papillae on the surface.

The temporomandibular joint (TMJ), located just anterior to the earlobe, is the only joint needed for chewing. A hingelike movement occurs bilaterally in the TMJ during mouth opening and closing. During chewing, the mandible also exhibits protrusive and lateral movements.

The buccal mucosa forms the side walls of the oral cavity and contains numerous mucous glands. The secretions from these glands mix with food in the mouth to aid in both chewing and swallowing.

There are three major (bilateral) salivary glands, which secrete saliva into the mouth: parotid, submaxillary, and sublingual. The parotid glands are the largest, and their ducts open into the vestibules opposite the upper second molar teeth. The submaxillary (or submandibular) gland ducts open into the floor of the mouth under the tongue from their location in the angles of the mandible. The sublingual glands, the smallest of the major salivary glands, are embedded in the mucous membranes of the floor of the mouth. Their ducts open under the tongue, as well. The major salivary glands contribute about 95% of the total daily volume of saliva; the remaining 5% comes from numerous minor salivary glands in the mucous membranes of the lips, tongue, palates, and cheeks.[1] The primary role of saliva is to protect and maintain oral health.[2,3] In that regard, human saliva contains lubricatory factors (mucins) to keep oral tissues hydrated, pliable, and insulated; contains many antibacterial proteins that regulate colonization of oral bacteria; buffers the acid produced by oral bacteria to maintain tooth integrity; aids in carbohydrate digestion; mediates taste acuity; and is necessary for mastication and preparation of food for swallowing.[4-9]

The orofacial musculature consists of four muscles of mastication: the masseter, the lateral pterygoid, the medial pterygoid, and the temporalis muscles; and almost 20 muscles of facial expression. One of these facial muscles, the buccinator, acts as an accessory muscle of mastication by eliminating the space of the vestibule between the cheek and the jaws during chewing.

Functions of the Oral Cavity

The oral cavity serves in the masticating, tasting, and swallowing of food; as a phonetic box for speech; and as a secondary pathway for breathing. The major and minor salivary glands provide moisture to soften foods as well as supply carbohydrate-digesting enzymes.

Mastication (Chewing)

The teeth are designed for chewing; the anterior teeth provide a strong cutting action and the posterior teeth provide a grinding action. The names of the teeth demarcate their four basic functions. The incisors cut or slice food, the canines tear food, the premolars shred food, and the molars grind food in preparation for swallowing.

Proper chewing is important in the digestion of all foods, especially most fruits and raw vegetables, which contain undigestible cellulose membranes that must be broken down before the food can be used by the body. Also, since digestive enzymes act only on the surfaces of food particles, the rate of digestion is highly dependent on the total surface area of the chewed food that is exposed to intestinal secretions.

The act of chewing has more significance than the mere preparation of food for swallowing. The food is moved around the mouth so that the taste buds are stimulated, and odors are released that stimulate the olfactory receptors. Much of the satisfaction and pleasure of eating depends on these stimuli.

Digestion in the Mouth

Saliva contains the digestive enzyme ptyalin (amylase), which functions to hydrolyze starches into two disaccharides, maltose and isomaltose. This is the first step in the digestion of carbohydrates. However, since food stays in the mouth for such a limited amount of time, only 3% to 5% of the starches that are eaten are hydrolyzed by the time the food is swallowed.[10] Most naturally occurring starches are digested poorly by ptyalin because they are protected by a thin cellulose cover. Cooking destroys these cellulose membranes and facilitates digestion in the mouth.

Swallowing (Deglutination)

In general, swallowing can be divided into three stages: (1) the voluntary stage, which initiates the swallowing process; (2) the pharyngeal stage, which is involuntary and constitutes the muscular contractions for the passage of food through the pharynx to the esophagus; and (3) the esophageal stage, another involuntary phase that promotes the passage of food from the pharynx to the stomach. The oral cavity is involved only with the first (voluntary) stage of swallowing, which takes about 1 second.[11] When the food is ready to be swallowed, pressure from the tongue upward and backward against the palate forces the bolus of food posteriorly into the pharynx. From here on, the process of swallowing becomes automatic and usually cannot be stopped.

Speech

Speech is a complex behavior that integrates the processes of respiration, phonation, oral sensation, resonation, and articulation.[11] The mouth is one of the resonators for speech and other vocalizations. The three major organs of articulation are the lips, tongue, and soft palate. Speech, therefore, relies heavily on the anatomic structures of the oral cavity.

ORAL HEALTH STATUS AND NEEDS IN THE ELDERLY

Oral Health Status

Oral health implies a state that is stable, relatively disease free, and comfortable; and permits adequate functioning for mastication, swallowing, and speech.

Poor oral health may be viewed as an inadequately functioning condition resulting from decayed teeth; periodontal disease; ill-fitting dentures or lack of dentures; neglect of oral hygiene; and the presence of pain, inflammation, or infection in the oral cavity. Although few of these conditions pose mortality risks, they may lead to physical dysfunction, pain, and psychologic anguish in the older patient.

A major criterion of successful aging is how well the individual maintains oral health, the ability to chew, the ability to talk, and personal satisfaction with appearance.[12] Unfortunately, the mouth often becomes one of the first areas of the body to be neglected by people who have chronic diseases and infirmities in old age.

There have been only three national surveys indicating the oral status of the elderly, and the older aged were excluded in two of the studies: the National Health Examination Survey of 1960–1962 excluded participants over age 79 years.[13] The National Health and Nutrition Examination Survey (HANES I) of 1971–1974 included no subjects over age 74 years.[14]

In 1978, the National Institutes of Health (NIH) introduced an oral physiology and aging component to the Baltimore Longitudinal Study of Aging.[15] In Iowa, a longitudinal survey was initiated in 1981 to determine the prevalence and incidence of oral conditions in noninstitutionalized rural elderly Iowans. In 1987, the National Institute of Dental Research (NIDR) published national and regional data on the prevalence of oral conditions in 15,000 working adults and 5600 elderly people who attended multipurpose senior centers.[16] Useful data were obtained from this survey of adult oral health, even though the older participants were not entirely representative of the nation's elderly population. The findings disclosed that Americans are keeping their teeth longer, are going to the dentist more often for preventive checkups, are reducing the number of cavities in their mouths, and have practically eliminated edentulousness in middle age. Serious dental problems, however, still exist among the elderly (Table 6-1).

Table 6-1 Comparison of Oral Health Status of Employed Adults to Older Adults

Oral Status/Treatment Need	% Employed Adults	% Older Adults
Calculus deposits	83.9	88.9
Edentulousness	4.2	41.1
Gingival bleeding (after probing)	43.6	46.9
Gingival recession (1 + mm)	51.1	88.3
Periodontal attachment loss (1 + sites)	76.7	95.1
Retention of all teeth	36.7	2.1
Root caries	21.1	56.9
Visited dentist in past 2 years	79.6	56.4
Perceived need for dental care	50.4	36.0

Source: National Survey of Adult Dental Health, NIDR.[16]

Oral Health Needs

In general, there are many unmet treatment needs affecting a large portion of the noninstitutionalized elderly population. This is true whether the study has been conducted by direct examination of patients or by survey. Data from HANES I indicated that 60% of elderly subjects had at least one dental treatment need.[14] The survey of rural elderly Iowans also found a high level of treatment needed: 40% required at least one restoration, 16% at least one extraction, and 27% some prosthodontic treatment; more than 60% of the dentate subjects needed some periodontal treatment.[17–19]

Many local studies and one statewide survey have documented the large need for dental care among institutionalized residents.[20–25] The results have ranged from 2.3 dental services needed per person, with 3.2 services required for those having remaining natural dentition,[20] to 82.5% of 3247 patients screened in Vermont nursing homes in 1982.[21] In the latter study, examiners found that 37.2% of the residents required immediate attention to eliminate pain, infection, concern of malignancy, or a combination of these symptoms.

CHANGES IN ORAL AND CIRCUMORAL STRUCTURES WITH AGING

Overview

Differentiation of normal aging changes from disease processes in old age is of paramount importance. Not knowing the changes that occur with age might lead to excessive or unnecessary treatment. Similarly, erroneously evaluating a disease process as normal aging may have equally serious consequences. Unfortunately, lack of research in the aging oral cavity has resulted in a number of stereotypes and generalizations.[5,26] Standard graphs, tables, and information in many geriatric medical and dental textbooks delineate inevitable decrements with age. However, these studies included subjects who, although superficially healthy, in fact had some disease or were taking medication that affected oral function.[27] Most of this early information therefore likely reflects oral changes due to disease or its treatment, rather than dysfunctions related directly to increased age.

Hard Tissues

Bone

In the developmental years, bone resorption and deposition occur synchronously in the process of growth and remodeling. Alveolar bone, however, has a remodeling rate greater than that of the other bones of the body.[28] With maturity, bone is notably less active, although there is still some degree of continuing resorption and deposition. After age 35 to 40 years, approximately 1% of bone mass is lost per year in both men and women.[28]

As physical activity diminishes in the later years, so too does the demand for new bone formation. Resorption exceeds deposition, resulting in a net loss of bone. By the time old age is reached, atrophy has resulted from slow resorption with very little remodeling. Not only is there a generalized decline in bone volume,[29] but the composition of bone gradually alters also, resulting in reduced resilience and increased brittleness and fragility[30] (Chapter 11).

Alveolar bone is one of the first bones to be affected by loss of mass. The periosteal and periodontal surfaces of alveolar bone become less resistant to harmful local oral trauma, inflammation, or disease.[31] This is a major factor contributing to periodontal disease, loss of teeth, and, in the edentulous patient, inability to obtain adequate support and stability for dentures.[26,32,33] In both the maxilla and mandible, the amount, extent, and uniformity of the bone loss differs with varying etiologies and health status.[34,35] It is now recognized that alveolar bone or residual ridge resorption is confounded by such factors as age, sex, race, and health status of the patient when the teeth are extracted; the tooth extraction technique; the diet of the patient; the presence of local factors; and the frequency of denture use.[34]

Teeth

It is frequently reported that the teeth themselves undergo changes with age (Table 6-2). Teeth differ from most other parts of the body in that the reparative or regenerative capacity of their constituent tissues is extremely limited. Also, the blood vessels and nerves become less active with age; as a result, the vitality of the average human tooth pulp lasts approximately 70 years.[30]

Attrition. The remaining natural teeth are likely to exhibit some flattening of the chewing surfaces induced by repeated contact with opposing teeth during masticatory movements. To compensate for the natural wear of these surfaces, human teeth erupt with their supporting structures throughout adult life.[36-39]

The patterns of tooth wear vary with each patient and are cumulative, since the enamel is incapable of repair or regeneration. The wear can range from minimal faceting to extreme loss of tooth substance, sometimes extending to the gingiva. However, there is no agreement on the point at which physiologic attrition becomes pathologic or contributes to pathologic conditions.[40] In areas of excessive wear, reparative (or secondary) dentin is deposited on the walls of the pulp chamber and canals for protection. This, as well as reduced innervation, helps to

Table 6-2 Anatomic Changes in the Teeth with Age

Enamel
  Regeneration/repair—incapable
  Permeability—decreased

Dentin
  Permeability—decreased
  Sensitivity—decreased
  Calcification—increased
  Pain conduction—decreased
  Repair—capable with vital tooth pulp

Pulp chamber and canal(s)
  Cellularity—decreased
  Innervation—decreased
  Tooth drainage—decreased
  Vascularity—decreased
  Volume—decreased (due to deposition of reparative dentin)

Apical foramen
  Size—decreased (may cause decreased pulp vascularity and innervation)

Cementum
  Deposition—continuous (major cause of decreased apical foramen size)
  Repair—capable with vital tooth pulp
  Resorption—increased susceptibility

Entire tooth
  Brittleness—increased (predisposing tooth to cracks, fractures, shearing)
  Darkening—increased
  Pain sensitivity—decreased
  Thermal sensitivity—decreased
  Translucency—decreased

---

explain the reduced tooth pain sensitivity and higher pain threshold in elderly people.

Temporomandibular Joint

The TMJ is a complex, disarthrodial joint capable of both swinging (hingelike) and sliding motions in many axes. It undergoes functional remodeling throughout life, usually in response to changes in articulation of the teeth or alterations in the space between the maxilla and mandible. The functional changes in the TMJ are by no means confined to elderly individuals.

Signs of TMJ change include joint clicking, limitation of jaw opening, and deviation of the mandible during function, with the major symptom being pain. Researchers with the Baltimore Longitudinal Study of Aging assessed all of these factors in different age groups and found that limitation of jaw opening was the only change in the joint associated with increasing age.[41] More research into the aging TMJ is needed since these age-related changes may explain some of the masticatory problems in this age group.

Soft Tissues

Mucous Membranes

The stereotypic effect of aging on the oral mucosa is that atrophic changes occur. Clinically, these changes involve the surface epithelium   becoming thinner, drier, less elastic, less vascular, less firmly attached to the underlying connective tissue and bone, and more susceptible to injury from mild stresses.[30,33,42–45] Other changes occur as well with reduction in connective tissue and subcutaneous fat and increased linkage of collagen molecules.[33] Some symptoms have been associated with these alterations, including xerostomia (mouth dryness) and sensations of pain or burning on the tongue, palate, or oral mucosa.[26] These changes, however, must be interpreted with caution. In critical reviews of the literature, Baum[26] and Hill[46] have suggested that no conclusions could be drawn about whether atrophy of the oral mucosa is associated with aging. Other researchers have concluded that specific alterations of the oral tissues may instead be induced by a host of environmental factors, such as tobacco smoking or chronic systemic disease.[47]

Periodontium

Gingiva. The gum tissue of the elderly individual gradually recedes from the tooth, with subsequent exposure of more of the tooth surface and root. The degree that gingival recession progresses is related to age, tooth movement, inflammatory changes due to disease, oral care habits, and heredity.

Periodontal Ligament. The periodontal ligament is not one ligament but a series of short, dense ligaments connecting the cementum of the tooth root to alveolar bone. Since the ligament is made up of connective tissues, aging affects it in the same way it does other connective tissues in the body.[48] The result is a progressive loss of soft-tissue attachment leading to exposure of the root and loosening of the teeth within their bony sockets.

Tongue

The status of the tongue in aging, independent of diseased states and taste acuity, has not been studied in detail. Tongue vascularity changes very little, compared with that of other organs, because there is little tendency in this tissue for arteriosclerosis or obliteration of the capillaries.[47] There is much controversy about whether aging is associated with atrophy of the papillae, increased formation of fissures, and decreasing sensitivity to gustatory stimuli in the tongue.[25,47,49–55]

Circumoral Tissues

Oral Musculature

Changes in aging oral musculature are consistent with those in aging muscle tissue in the body as a whole.[56] In general, there are reductions in muscle tone,[11] in the number and activity of muscle cells,[33] and in the number and size of the muscle fibers. Replacement of the muscle mass by fat or fibrous connective tissue results in generalized atrophy of the musculature attached to the bones in the oral cavity.[57]

Mastication. The muscles of mastication atrophy with age, which decreases the biting force and slows chewing performance.[58–60] The atrophy is probably due in part to disuse, since less muscular effort is required for chewing as a result of failing dentition or a progressively softer diet, or both. In either case, the generalized loss of muscle tissue decreases the biting force and can make chewing difficult.[33]

Deglutination. Aging does not significantly affect the transit of the prepared food bolus through the mouth and pharynx.[61] However, the impact of decreased muscle mass and tone can make swallowing difficult[33] and can alter the ability to form and prepare a bolus in the oral stage of swallowing.[11] Several studies[58–60,62] have demonstrated that as people age they take longer and expend more effort to prepare a food bolus before swallowing.

Other Changes

Salivary Glands

In early reports, decreased salivary flow was generally considered to be concomitant with increased age.[26,63,64] Recent evidence indicates that the diminished salivary flow often noted in studies of elderly subjects is due to pathologic conditions or pharmacologic effects of medications, rather than aging.[2,5–8,65] Since diminished salivary flow does not occur in healthy, nonmedicated individuals,[66] these findings emphasize that the elderly person may be susceptible to situations and therapies that result in a reduction of saliva availability.

Sense of Taste

The sense of taste is a function of the taste buds in the mouth. Its importance in nutrition lies in the fact that it allows a person to select food in accord with personal desires and needs of the tissues for specific nutritive substances.

Taste Buds. The taste buds are found predominantly on three of the four different types of the tongue papillae (circumvallate, fungiform, and foliate), although they are also located in the epithelium of the palate, tonsillar pillars, and other points around the nasopharynx.[67,68] In early anatomic studies, marked decreases in the numbers and atrophy of the taste buds with aging were reported.[69–71] However, recent investigations indicate there is not a significant loss of taste buds in old age.[72–74]

Taste Sensitivity. Elderly people often complain of altered taste sensations (dysgeusia), decreased ability to perceive taste (hypogeusia), or complete loss of taste (ageusia). Few studies, however, have been able to determine the reasons for these decrements in taste sensitivity.[52,68,75] One explanation is decreased salivary flow, since taste buds react only to dissolved compounds.

Although there is some agreement that taste sensitivity begins to decline after age 55 years, differences in research methods have produced different results.[76] Some studies have indicated that older adults need higher concentrations of the four primary sensations of taste (salty, sour, sweet, bitter) for identification than do children and younger adults.[69,77,78] Others have found that the taste buds detecting saltiness and sweetness are the first to deteriorate and that sensitivity to sour and bitter tastes declines later.[67,70,79–82] The use of psychophysical procedures found only minimal changes in taste sensitivity,[50–52,55] even though a steady decline in taste sensitivity with increasing age is still being found.[49,53,54]

Sense of Smell

Smell is the least researched and understood sense. This is due in part to the location of the olfactory sensory receptors in specialized epithelial tissue of the nasal cavity and in part to the fact that the sense of smell is a subjective phenomenon that is not easily measured. In fact, much of what we call taste is actually smell, which largely determines the flavor and palatability of foods and beverages.[83]

Evidence of a decline in olfactory sensitivity with age is still very limited, and the cause of any decrement remains speculative.[84,85] Some investigators have found reduced smell sensitivity, with the greatest problems in recognition and identification of odors among persons over age 80 years.[86] Others have reported age-related losses with significant individual differences.[87–89] It has also been suggested that poor health and smoking may cause an even greater decline in smell sensitivity than age alone.[89,90]

CHANGES IN ORAL AND CIRCUMORAL STRUCTURES WITH DISEASE

Overview

There are three major characteristics of dental diseases (Table 6-3). Although they are rarely debilitating or life threatening, there are indications that dental diseases make a significant impact on social, economic, and psychologic areas of life, including the quality of life.[91,92] Older adults, however, tend to place minimal importance on their oral health and accept functionally inadequate dentition as an unavoidable consequence of the aging process.

Many of the oral diseases that afflict the elderly are diseases of all age groups. Therefore, preventive dentistry remains an important aspect of their oral health care and should involve all three levels of prevention: (1) preventing initiation of disease, (2) preventing the progression and recurrence of disease, and (3) preventing the loss of function and loss of life.[93]

The prevention of dental disease requires that all individuals see a dentist at least yearly, whether they have natural teeth, no teeth, complete dentures, or teeth and dentures. First, this allows primary prevention procedures to be evaluated and reinforced regularly. Detrimental habits, environmental factors, and nutritional status all affect the likelihood that oral pathology will occur. As an example, poor oral hygiene significantly contributes to the diseases caused or aggravated by bacterial plaque infection,[94] and it is well known that the level of oral hygiene deteriorates with age.[95] Also, regular dental care can lead to early diagnosis and treatment of the pathologic conditions described below.

Table 6-3 The Major Characteristics of Dental Diseases[57]

- *Universality*—Diseases of the oral cavity are the most prevalent of all diseases; dental caries and periodontal disease usually affect most people throughout life.
- *Irreversibility*—The damage derived from the common oral diseases, such as dental decay or bone loss, is irreversible, although treatment can usually intercept its spread.
- *Cumulativeness*—The structural losses induced in the teeth and their supporting alveolar bone by oral diseases are cumulative.

Hard Tissues

Bone

Resorption. Bone resorption is associated with the loss of mineral content, increase in porosity, and generalized atrophy. Clinical observation of alveolar bone resorption has so far failed to provide a clear-cut understanding of the mechanisms responsible. There is a portion of the population that shows bone loss without the other findings usually associated with active periodontal disease. This loss is also seen in the absence of dentition.[96]

Resorption of alveolar bone occurs in two dimensions: The mandible resorbs primarily in a vertical direction, resulting in loss of bone height. The maxilla resorbs primarily in a horizontal direction away from the covering lips and cheeks. This means that the chin will appear to protrude because the maxilla has receded horizontally. This leads to the characteristic "toothless look": a shortening of the distance between the chin and nose and a pulling inward of the lips.

Resorption is greater in the mandible than in the maxilla, and, when severe, constitutes a major problem in the wearing of dentures. The residual bony ridge may become thin and knifelike and unable to withstand the downward compressive forces of a conventional denture.

Osteopenia and Osteoporosis. Osteopenia refers to metabolic bone diseases that are characterized by x-ray findings of a subnormal amount of mineralized bone mass (Chapter 11). The most common osteopenia is osteoporosis, generally defined as a decrease in the quantity of bone, with an increased incidence of fractures from minimal trauma.[97] Osteoporosis is observable within the oral cavity as dental osteopenia.

One of the first signs of osteoporosis is alveolar bone loss, followed by loss in the vertebrae and long bones.[98,99] Indeed, there is a significant correlation between skeletal osteopenia and density of alveolar bone and residual ridges.[100] Radiographically, it appears as diminished bone mass in the mandibular angular cortex, decreased trabeculae, and a diminished alveolar crest.[101,102] Subsequently, it leads to an inadequate amount of bone mass in the mandible, loss or mobility of teeth, edentulousness, and inability to wear dentures.[35] The loss of teeth and the use of ill-fitting dentures also cause extensive alveolar bone or residual ridge atrophy.[103–105]

Although calcium deficiencies and calcium-phosphorus imbalances are contributing factors in the pathogenesis of osteoporosis,[106] prevention and management include not only increased calcium intake, but estrogen therapy, dietary vitamin D, and exercise.[99,107–110] Although fluoride therapy is used extensively in preventive dentistry, its use in the prevention of osteoporosis is still being investigated.[111]

Teeth

Dental Caries (Tooth Decay)—Coronal and Root Surfaces. Dental caries has been considered a disease of young people that stabilizes in the mid-20s and remains dormant until periodontal disease or gingival recession exposes the roots of the teeth and caries of the root surfaces occurs.[93,112,113] However, more recent research indicates that a significant increase in caries, including recurrent decay around restorations, cervical caries at the gingival margin, and root caries, is associated with aging.[16,114–116] Most of the recurrent caries is in the proximal regions of the teeth.[117] Root caries occurs following exposure of the tooth root.[116,118–122]

The diagnosis of dental caries is based on x-ray examination and clinical observation since there is no absolute correlation between the presence or extent of dental decay and symptoms. It is generally recognized that four things are necessary to produce a carious lesion: cariogenic bacteria, a substrate of dietary carbohydrates, a susceptible host (tooth), and time. However, factors that contribute to high caries risk include poor oral hygiene, gingival recession, reduced salivary flow (which increases plaque accumulation), bacterial virulence, and diet.[117,123,124]

Conditions that predispose to xerostomia (dry mouth), such as medications, Sjögren's syndrome, and head and neck irradiation, can promote rampant dental caries in all age groups.[125] In fact, the incidence of root surface caries in elderly people is significantly correlated with a low rate of salivary secretion.[126,127]

Historically, the most effective strategy for preventing dental caries has been increasing tooth resistance to pathogenic plaque through the use of fluorides, by systemic introduction (water, diet) and topical application (professional or self-applied).[128,129] Even fluoridation of other vehicles, such as salt, milk, and sugar have been considered in areas where no reticulated water supplies existed.[111] In xerostomic patients, the development of caries has been avoided largely by daily topical application of either 0.5% sodium fluoride or 0.5% stannous fluoride solutions.[130,131]

Unfortunately, there are few clinical data supporting the use of topical fluoride for prevention of dental caries in geriatric patients with adequate salivary flow.[132–135] Newbrun,[136] however, believes that the elderly population would benefit from the use of fluoride dentifrices, mouth rinses, and gels applied by brush, finger applicator, or plastic tray. The method to be used is dictated by the anticipated susceptibility to decay and the ability of the patient to manage the regimen.

Since both coronal and root caries are plaque-related diseases, measures that limit or inhibit plaque formation should be effective in prevention. Mechanical oral hygiene techniques and chemical antimicrobial agents such as chlorhexidine[137–139] reduce bacterial flora and substrate. Even dietary modification decreases the amount of substrate, acid production, and decalcification of teeth if individuals eliminate or reduce the intake of foods that are soft, sticky, retentive, or high in sugar; and chew firm foods.[14]

Abrasion and Erosion. An aging population with longer retention of teeth is at increased risk for both abrasion (wear of tooth structure by nonmasticatory mechanical forces) and erosion (wear of tooth structure by chemical dissolution). The incidence of both of these conditions increases with age, simply because any damage to the teeth is cumulative. In patients with xerostomia, the diminution in the mucin level of the oral cavity provides less lubrication and protection, posing an even greater risk for abrasion and erosion.

A major etiologic factor of abrasion is overzealous and improper toothbrushing with a hard-bristle brush or an abrasive dentifrice.[140,141] The damage appears as transverse scoring of the tooth surface and tends to be asymmetric in its severity, depending on whether the patient is right-handed or left-handed.[30] Prevention is largely a matter of proper toothbrushing and the use of a soft-bristle brush and toothpaste with minimal abrasivity. Other forms of abrasion result from holding objects with the teeth, chewing tobacco, and using dental floss and toothpicks improperly.

Erosion is a chemical process that occurs when the concentration of acid in the mouth is too high for the saliva to neutralize. The most common causes are chronic ingestion of fruits, fruit juices, and carbonated beverages[142–146]; sucking candies containing phosphorus or citric acid; and gastroesophageal reflux.[147] Erosion can also result from working in an industry that uses or produces acidic materials.[148,149] To prevent dietary erosion, the use of straws with fruit juices and carbonated beverages and substitution of sugar-free candies or gums are indicated.

The lesions of abrasion and erosion look different: the former are characteristically narrow in relation to depth, and areas of erosion are usually saucer-shaped.[30,150] Generally these lesions do not require restorative treatment unless they are extensive or symptomatic.[150]

Hypersensitive Dentin and Cementum. Exposure of dentin or cementum from abrasion, erosion, acute or chronic trauma, or various restorative treatment procedures can lead to hypersensitive dentin and cementum. The teeth are exquisitely sensitive with exposure to any chemical, thermal, tactile, or osmotic stimulus. Although there is great individual variation in pain sensation, hypersensitivity to sour, sweet, cold, hot, and mechanical irritations are most common.[151]

Since hypersensitivity may deter a person from establishing or maintaining adequate oral hygiene procedures, decreasing sensitivity is the first step in treatment. One method is "sealing" the exposed tooth surfaces by applying agents or dentifrices such as fluoride gels and rinses.[152–157] In some cases, dental restoration and even endodontic therapy may be necessary to arrest the progress of the lesion, restore the function and shape of the tooth, and relieve pain.[158]

Tooth Loss and Edentulousness. Tooth loss is an irreversible, cumulative process that is no longer considered a natural consequence of aging. Instead, it is known to be the ultimate sequela of the two most common dental diseases, dental caries and periodontal disease. Nevertheless, tooth loss increases in frequency with age. By age 65 years, approximately 40% of Americans have lost all their teeth; another 20% have lost more than half their teeth.

In all age groups, the total loss of teeth is historically related to increased sugar consumption, combined with ignorance of prevention and insufficient dental manpower resources at the time.[38] Tooth loss in adults over age 35 years has been attributed to periodontal diseases.[159-161] However, recent studies of tooth loss in adult populations indicate that caries is often the cause for tooth extractions.[162-165]

The rate of edentulousness, or total lack of teeth, is declining in the elderly population of the United States. In 1957, 67.3% of persons older than age 65 years were edentulous, whereas only 45.5% were so in 1971.[166] This was largely due to the introduction of preventive and restorative dental procedures. Today, less than 40% of elderly people are edentulous, and this number is rapidly decreasing.

In the recent national survey of employed and older adults, in the group aged 55 to 64 years, less than 15% were edentulous.[16] However, the prevalence of lost teeth was still extensive enough to compromise the employed adults' dentitions and impair function in most of the older adults.[16,167] This means that the fewer missing teeth predicted to occur in the future will lead not only to an increase in tooth-related diseases, but also the continuing need for regular dental care.[168]

Temporomandibular Joint

Dysfunctions of the TMJ have their primary base in the joint mechanism, even though the actual dysfunction may involve the ligaments, muscles, or the bone itself. One-half of the edentulous and one-third of the dentulous older population have signs and symptoms of TMJ disorders,[169] including soreness of the jaw; dull, aching facial pain; severe pain in the joint area; tenderness or pain of the masticatory and facial muscles; dizziness; headaches; impaired hearing or earache; eye pain; chronic fatigue; and popping, clicking, or cracking noise near the ear while opening and closing the mouth.[170-173] These manifestations are dynamic, characterized by periods of quiescence and exacerbation, and have a wide range of expression among patients.[174] However, elderly individuals appear to have more symptoms than younger persons.[175]

The causes of TMJ dysfunction may be external or internal or both. External causes include degenerative joint disease; alveolar bone resorption; and injuries to the head, neck, or mandible. Internally, attrition, malocclusion, and bruxism, in either natural or artificial teeth, can cause the facial muscles and TMJ to quit working together correctly.[176,177]

Diagnostic and treatment decisions are based on symptom reports and clinical examination findings. Management therapies advocated for TMJ dysfunction include applying moist heat to the face; using prescribed muscle relaxants or other medications; massaging the muscles; eating soft and nonchewy foods; counseling; training in biofeedback or relaxation procedures; correcting the "bite" of the teeth; and, in severe cases, surgery.

Soft Tissues

Mucous Membranes/Epithelium

The oral mucosa is composed of both keratinized and nonkeratinized epithelium. In addition, the mouth has a dark, moist environment that is replete with microorganisms. The oral mucosa also may be subjected to several environmental influences, such as smoking; chewing of the lips and cheeks; eating a variety of foods; and sources of trauma, allergy, and carcinogenesis.[178]

Aphthous Ulcer (Canker Sore, Aphthous Stomatitis, Ulcerative Stomatitis). Aphthous ulcers appear as shallow white macules or papules with flat, fairly even borders surrounded by an intense erythematous halo. Each ulcer often is covered with a pseudomembrane. One or more ulcers may be present. They tend to recur and are usually very painful during their acute phase. The pain may interfere with eating, swallowing, and moving the tongue. Aphthous ulcers occur more frequently in women than in men.

Aphthae are found on oral mucosal surfaces that are not bound to underlying bone, especially the buccal and labial mucosa, dorsum of the tongue, floor of the mouth, soft palate, gingivae, lips, and oropharynx. The diagnosis depends mainly on exclusion of similar but more readily identifiable diseases, a history of recurrence, and inspection of the ulcer.

The etiology is still unclear, as it has never been adequately demonstrated that this lesion is due to a virus or any other specific chemical, physical, psychologic, or hormonal cause.[179] Nuts, coffee, chocolate, and citrus fruits often cause flare-ups, but abstinence will not prevent recurrence. Trauma, nutritional deficiencies, stresses of various types, food components, and allergies have been shown to be contributory to the disease.[179–182]

Healing, which usually occurs in 1 to 3 weeks without scarring, may be accelerated slightly by treatment. A new film-forming medication, hydroxypropyl cellulose (Zilactin), brings impressive pain relief and is able to protect the areas of ulceration from irritants, thus allowing patients to eat and drink more normally.[183] Bland antibiotic or anesthetic mouth rinses, topical steroid-antibiotic therapy, and surface protectants can also reduce pain. Sedatives, analgesics, and vitamins may help indirectly. Good oral hygiene and the minimization of mucosal trauma are helpful. Systemic antibiotics are contraindicated.

Ulcerative stomatitis is a general term for multiple ulcerations on an inflamed oral mucosa. It may be secondary to blood dyscrasias, erythema multiforme, bullous lichen planus, acute herpes simplex infection, pemphigoid, pemphigus, and drug reactions. If the lesions cannot be classified, they are referred to as aphthae.

Candidiasis (Moniliasis, Thrush). Candidiasis is the most common opportunistic infection of the mouth, caused by overgrowth of a species of the fungus *Candida.* The species most frequently implicated in oral infections is *C. albicans.* The yeast phase of the fungus is a component of the normal oral flora of most people.[184] It exists in a symbiotic relationship with many of the other oral microorganisms. Because is has such low virulence in the yeast phase, some change must take place in the local environment to produce conditions favorable for its overgrowth and tissue invasion. The change commonly occurs when there is a reduction in host resistance caused by bacterial and viral infection, systemic disease, or medications.

Oral candidiasis generally presents in one of three distinct clinical forms: acute pseudomembranous candidiasis (thrush), acute atrophic candidiasis (antibiotic sore mouth), or chronic atrophic candidiasis (denture sore mouth). Rare forms include chronic hyperplastic candidiasis and chronic mucocutaneous candidiasis.

The lesions of acute pseudomembranous candidiasis consist of either multifocal or diffuse, white, superficial curdlike plaques occurring anywhere in the oral cavity. The infection is called pseudomembranous because the plaques can be scraped off easily, leaving an erythematous or bleeding base. Most other white mucosal lesions cannot be rubbed off.

Acute atrophic candidiasis often follows prolonged antibiotic or steroid therapy and results, clinically, in a painful erythematous mucosa, particularly involving the tongue. The problem usually resolves with cessation of the medications, but antifungal therapy will hasten recovery.

Chronic atrophic candidiasis presents as a slightly granular or irregularly eroded erythematous mucosa under dentures.

Any of these types of candidiasis can be accompanied by angular cheilitis. The diagnosis is based on the varied clinical picture of the surface white patches or erythematous changes and may be confirmed by laboratory culture. Treatment includes elimination of the causative or predisposing factor, if practical, and administration of antifungal agents.[185–190]

Leukoplakia (Benign Keratosis, White Patch). The term leukoplakia is used to describe a thickened, white plaque that will not rub or strip off and is not identifiable clinically or pathologically as any other disease. The lesions may be found on all oral mucous membrane surfaces, varying from a small circumscribed area to an extensive lesion involving a large area of mucosa. They are usually asymptomatic and are discovered on routine dental examination or by patients who feel the thickened plaques in their mouths. Leukoplakia occurs more often in men, and the highest incidence is in the fifth to seventh age decade.[191]

The most common cause of leukoplakia is epithelial hyperplasia, hyperkeratosis, hyperorthokeratosis, dyskeratosis, or acanthosis. These terms refer specifically to reactive conditions of the oral mucosal epithelium, usually in response to an irritant or chronic irritation. The specific etiology is often unknown, but there are risk factors: tobacco, alcohol, deficiency of vitamin A or B complexes, and chronic irritating conditions or habits.[192,193]

Treatment consists of removing all irritants. Failure of a keratotic lesion to regress within 2 weeks after eliminating the apparent cause should arouse suspicion, and the lesion should be biopsied or surgically excised. About 5% of patients with leukoplakia eventually develop squamous cell carcinoma in the area of the white lesion.

Mucositis (Stomatitis). Mucositis and stomatitis are clinical terms describing inflammation, breakdown, and ulceration of the oral mucosal tissues. The disease can vary in its clinical presentation from focal or patchy erythema or ulceration to complete sloughing of the oral mucosa. Secondary hemorrhage is relatively common.

There is a wide variety of causative factors, including chronic mouth breathing, medications, systemic diseases, radiotherapy of the head and neck, and nutritional deficiencies. Patients complain of intense pain, burning, and dysphagia, which lead to an inability to eat or even drink.

Treatment relies heavily on palliation of symptoms, which can be provided by local anesthetic and antacid preparations used singly or in combination. Relief is short-lived, however, since the effect of these agents lasts less than 20 minutes. Benzydamine hydrochloride, a local anesthetic and anti-inflammatory drug, is effective for 1 to 2 hours. The use of any toothpastes or mouthwashes accentuates the problem because of their irritating and desiccating properties.

Radiation-induced mucositis initially appears as reddened and swollen mucosa, but the tissue becomes denuded and ulcerated as therapy continues. The patient experiences pain, burning, and discomfort that is greatly intensified by contact with coarse or highly seasoned foods. Involvement of the pharyngeal mucosa produces difficulties in swallowing and speaking. When therapy ends, spontaneous remission occurs in most patients within several weeks. In the meantime, the use of liquid topical anesthetics in the mouth before mealtimes frequently facilitates eating without discomfort.

Oral Cancer. Oral cancer is clearly a disease of older people; over 98% of cases occur in persons over age 40 years[194,195]; the average age at the time of diagnosis is about 60 years.[196] The male to female ratio is approximately 2:1. It was estimated that in 1990 more than 31,000 new cases of cancer of the lips, tongue, floor of the mouth, palate, gingiva, buccal mucosa, and oropharynx would be diagnosed in the United States.[197] These oral cancers account for about 3.1% of all malignancies.

The most common type of oral cancer is squamous cell carcinoma, accounting for more than 90% of all oral malignancies.[198,199] The remaining 10% are predominantly malignant tumors of minor salivary gland tissue and (rarely) lymphomas, sarcomas, and melanomas.[195]

Clinically, an early cancer may appear as a small white patch (leukoplakia); a red velvety patch (erythroplakia); an aphthouslike, crusting, or traumatic ulcer; an erythematous plaque; a slightly raised lesion with central ulceration and a raised border; a verruciform growth; or a small swelling.[200–203] The most common signs and symptoms of oral cancer are listed in Table 6-4.

Frequently, it is impossible to differentiate between squamous cell carcinomas and the benign non-neoplastic lesions seen in aphthous ulceration, herpes simplex infection, or traumatic ulceration. However, the non-neoplastic lesions are usually painful, and most early oral cancers are painless, becoming symptomatic only after they are large enough to impinge on the sensory nerves.[204]

The cause of oral cancer is not known. A genetic factor is not apparent, but there is a definite increased risk with the use of tobacco and alcohol.[195,196,201,203,205–210] Independently each agent is believed to be associated with an increased incidence of the disease, and the two together may in fact act synergistically.[211] Oral leukoplakia (benign keratosis) is an important precancerous lesion, turning into oral cancer in about 3% to 5% of cases.[212,213] Malignant transformations arising from the oral mucosa are mostly observed between ages 40 and 69 years. Although the peak prevalence is between ages 50 and 59 years, decline is gradual thereafter.[214] Other risk factors for oral cancer include exposure to sunlight, chronic trauma, poor dentition, and history of syphilis infection.[196,199,215]

Table 6-4 Oral Cancer Warning Signals

• Swelling	• Restricted jaw movement
• Lumps, growths, exophytic masses	• Trismus
• White, scaly patches	• Restricted tongue movement
• Red patches	• Difficulty in swallowing
• Oral ulcers (bleed easily, nonhealing)	• Sore throat that does not heal
• Atypic facial pain	• Hoarseness
• Persistent numbness or pain	• Change in denture fit
• Persistent bleeding	• Loose teeth
• Difficulty in chewing	

Oral cancer is a devastating disease with significant morbidity and mortality. Curative treatment consists of surgery, radiation, and chemotherapy, alone or in combination. Unfortunately, despite advances in these therapeutic approaches, only about 50% of patients with oral cancer survive the disease.[216] Of course, survival rates vary substantially depending on the site, ranging from 32% for cancer of the oropharynx to 91% for lip cancer, and on how early in the disease treatment is instituted. The poor overall prognosis for oral cancer is due to the fact that the disease is often detected at advanced stages, after the visual detection of tissue changes or the development of symptoms.

Until the process of carcinogenesis is completely understood and true prevention is possible, early detection and treatment remain the best weapons against malignant disease. However, because there are no reliable methods for early diagnosis of squamous cell carcinoma, biopsy is the only definitive means of diagnosis. A biopsy should be done on any oral lesion that has not responded to therapy or resolved in a 2-week period.

Many of the predisposing factors for oral cancer are potentially avoidable. Preventive education should include delineation of the hazards of tobacco and alcohol, and the need for regular dental care to reduce irritation and mechanical injury and for early detection.

Traumatic Ulcers. Acute trauma (mechanical, thermal, or chemical) is probably the most common cause of oral ulceration[217] and is a frequent problem in the geriatric patient. Ulcers can occur on any mucous membrane surface and are variable in size and shape. The ulcers are raised and have yellow-gray centers surrounded by an erythematous halo. Secondary infections with bacteria or *C. albicans* can occur.

The diagnosis is made primarily by history, since most patients can identify the cause of the trauma. The patient typically complains of an isolated intraoral "sore" with pain or tenderness in the area of the lesion. Symptoms rarely exceed 3 or 4 days, and the lesion heals within 10 to 14 days.[218]

Chronic irritation from decayed or broken teeth and inadequate dentures may lead to chronic ulcers that persist indefinitely. Cheek and tongue biting produce a thin, rough, keratotic film in the area traumatized. Fragments of epithelium are often seen in these cases, due to the continuous chewing on the same area.

Treatment is instituted by avoiding the cause of the trauma and contact with any irritants. Dental care is usually necessary to relieve sources or irritation. Surgical repair of any extensive laceration may be necessary.

Denture-Related Oral Pathology. Dental prosthetic appliances are intended to restore the health and well-being of patients, but they are responsible for many of the most commonly occurring oral lesions among the elderly. Removable appliances (complete or partial dentures) are implicated with greater frequency than are fixed appliances (bridges) because they may become distorted or broken with use and are frequently abused by the patient.[194] Older patients often do not or cannot comply with instructions for proper removal, placement, maintenance and cleanliness of their appliances.

Because dentures fit next to teeth and soft tissue, they must be kept clean to maintain oral health. Plaque, food debris, and calculi collect on dentures just as they do on natural teeth. If left uncleaned, the dentures can be a source of irritation, inflammation, infection, or halitosis.

Partial dentures contribute to increased plaque formation around abutment teeth, which increases gingival inflammation over time.[219–221] Since these appliances can also increase tooth mobility and accelerate bone loss,[222] the reduction of plaque becomes even more important.

Frequently, patients perform their own repairs, relines, or adjustments, which can harm the dentures or oral mucosa. Additionally, all denture wearers should be advised that some servicing or readjustment of dentures is necessary occasionally because of normal changes in the supporting tissues and bone.

Common pathologic changes associated with denture wearing include the problems described below.

Candidiasis. Denture-related candidiasis is by far the most common type of oral candidal infection.[223] The characteristic appearance is that of a slightly granular or irregularly eroded erythematous mucosa that corresponds exactly to the area covered by the upper denture. In some cases, the denture fits poorly and serves as a nutrient reservoir to foster fungal growth.[224] In patients with well-fitting dentures, the stability and peripheral seal of the upper denture allows the fungus to flourish in the absence of normal salivary flow. The condition seldom causes any discomfort.

These fungi are capable of growing on denture surfaces, from which they can infect and reinfect the soft tissues. Management therefore requires that both the denture and the mucosal surfaces be treated. Dentures should be kept scrupulously clean and soaked frequently in antifungal agents, germicides, or chlorhexidine.[224,225] The infected tissue is treated with topical antifungal agents.[185–187,190]

Denture Stomatitis (Denture Sore Mouth, Stomatitis Prosthetica). The true etiology of denture stomatitis, a generalized inflammation associated with denture wearing, is unknown. It has been ascribed to contact hypersensitivity to dental materials, bacterial and candidal infections, tissue reaction to ill-fitting or unclean dentures, residual denture cleanser, medication use, and systemic diseases.[194,223,226,227] It is known to worsen in patients who do not remove their dentures at night or are negligent in denture hygiene.[228,229]

The disease is characterized by a very discrete erythematous reaction that closely follows the outline of the denture. Resolution of the inflammation may be obtained by thoroughly cleaning the denture if it fits well, or by constructing a new one if it is ill-fitting. If candidal organisms are a contributing factor to the stomatitis, the denture may be covered with an antifungal ointment prior to insertion or soaked in an antifungal solution at night.

Traumatic Ulcers (Denture Sore Spots). An unstable or unretentive denture will cause tissue irritation or ulceration because of excess movement. Overextended denture flanges, bone spicules under the dentures, and foods—especially seeds—trapped between the denture and mucosa can also cause ulcerative lesions. The ulcers are small, painful, irregularly shaped lesions usually covered by a necrotic membrane and surrounded by an inflammatory halo. Treatment consists of correcting the underlying cause. Most lesions usually heal promptly.

Periodontium

Periodontal Disease. The most common disease of the periodontium is periodontal disease, a term generally used to describe specific chronic disorders that affect the gingiva, supporting connective tissue, and alveolar bone.[230] It is a chronic, progressive, and destructive condition, and its incidence and severity typically increase with age.[231–234] There is considerable question, however, about whether the increase in severity with age represents age-dependent pathology or the cumulative effects of a lifetime of intermittent destruction.[1]

Periodontal disease commonly develops in two stages, gingivitis and periodontitis. As with dental caries, the major etiologic factor is plaque, which accumulates more rapidly and heavily in elderly people.[235] If the plaque is not removed daily, it will calcify into calculus (tartar). Accumulation of plaque, food, bacteria, and calculi on the tooth surfaces between the tooth and gingiva produces a low-grade inflammation of the gingiva (gingivitis). This is clinically characterized by gingival redness, enlargement, tenderness, and bleeding. Although gingivitis develops more rapidly and with greater severity in older adults,[235] it is reversible with adequate plaque control.

If the inflammatory process is allowed to progress, there is formation of pus (pyorrhea) with or without discomfort or other symptoms. Without drainage, the accumulation of pus leads to acute swelling (periodontal abscess) and pain. When the inflammation extends to the underlying alveolar bone and connective tissue (periodontitis), it loosens the teeth and causes them to be extruded. However, once the teeth are lost, the inflammatory symptoms subside.

The diagnosis depends on a combination of findings, including localized pain, loose teeth, the presence of periodontal pockets, erythema, and swelling or suppuration. A severe case results in a foul odor, inflamed and ulcerated gums, fibrotic tissue, and bleeding. Roentgenograms may reveal the destruction of alveolar bone. Margins of overextended fillings often play a role as local irritating factors. Occlusal trauma, particularly from grinding and teeth-clenching habits, and systemic factors may contribute to periodontal disease, but they do not initiate the disease.[236,237]

The prevention of periodontal disease depends largely on plaque control through meticulous oral hygiene.[238,239] Although there are indications that periodontal breakdown progresses slowly in elderly persons,[234] progression of the disease can be retarded by oral hygiene[234,240,241] and use of antimicrobial agents.[137–139,168] Local drainage and oxygenating mouth rinses (3% hydrogen peroxide in an equal volume of water) will usually reverse any acute symptoms and allow for routine follow-up procedures. In some cases, surgery to reduce excess gum tissue helps prevent the formation of periodontal pockets that predispose to periodontal infections. In advanced disease, extraction of teeth may be necessary.

Necrotizing Ulcerative Gingivitis (Vincent Infection, Trench Mouth). Necrotizing ulcerative gingivitis is an acute, recurring, noncommunicable inflammatory disease of the gingiva resulting from local irritation and organisms in the normal oral flora that invade the gingival tissue when its resistance is lowered. The disease is characterized by redness, swelling, ulceration, bleeding, and pain. The yellowish-gray pseudomembrane that usually covers the ulcerated surface can be removed easily, leaving a raw, bleeding base. In severe cases, there is a fetid odor and foul taste in the mouth. Recurrent attacks can lead to bone loss. Treatment includes eliminating local irritants by careful and thorough oral hygiene procedures. Local anesthetics, as well as antibiotic therapy, may serve as adjuncts to treatment. Caustics are contraindicated.

Tongue

Fissured Tongue. The prevalence of fissured tongue, characterized by cracks on the dorsolateral surfaces of the tongue, increases progressively in each decade of adult life. Fissured tongue is found in varying degrees in approximately 5% of the population. It occurs in 60% of persons after age 40 years.

The fissures are deep, tend to collect food debris and microorganisms, and cause the tongue to be inflamed often. However, the tongue is usually pain free or only mildly tender, even if the fissures become secondarily infected from retained debris and microbes.

Fissuring of the tongue sometimes is associated with deficiency of vitamin B_{12} complex, or it may be genetic. Another cause is correlation with longstanding glossitis.

Treatment consists of brushing the tongue or rubbing it vigorously with a moistened washcloth to provide relief. The scarring is irreversible.

Glossitis. Inflammation of the tongue, usually manifested by considerable atrophy of the filiform papillae, creates a red, smooth appearance. It may be secondary to a variety of diseases such as anemia, nutritional deficiency, drug reactions, systemic infection, and physical or chemical irritations. The diagnosis is usually based on the history and laboratory studies, including cultures as indicated.

Treatment is based on identifying and correcting the primary cause, if possible, and palliating the tongue symptoms as required. When the cause cannot be determined and there are no symptoms, therapy is not indicated.

Glossodynia, Glossopyrosis (Burning Tongue, Chronic Lingual Papillitis). Glossodynia, or painful, burning, itching, stinging tongue, is a distressing symptom that predominantly affects older women.[242] It can accompany atrophy of the tongue papillae and is a prominent feature of the "burning mouth" syndrome. Involvement of the entire tongue or isolated areas, occurring with or without glossitis, may be the presenting symptoms of hypochromic or pernicious anemia, nutritional disturbances, emotional upset, hormonal imbalance, allergies, psychosomatic syndromes (grief, loneliness, despair), or other systemic disorders.[243] Smoking, xerostomia, medication use, and candidiasis may also be causative.

In most cases a primary cause cannot be identified. Cultures are of no value, since the offending organisms usually are also present in the normal oral flora. Dental prostheses, caries, and periodontal disease are usually of no causative significance. Although certain foods may cause flare-ups, they are not the primary causes. Dentifrice ingredients are rare causes of burning and pain of the tongue.

Treatment is mainly empiric, since causative factors usually are not identified. Important approaches include ruling out systemic conditions associated with these symptoms, changing the individual's drug regimen, and reassuring patients that there is no evidence of infection or neoplasia. Ointments and mouth rinses are of no value.

Hairy Tongue. Hairy tongue is characterized by elongated, thick, densely matted, and stained filaments on the dorsum of the tongue that resemble hair. The filaments are hypertrophied or hyperplastic filiform papillae that can be stained yellow, brown, or black.

Normally, the developing papillary tissue cells slide off the tongue during mechanical stimulation. When desquamation is diminished, the papillae become elongated and provide a nidus for materia alba to accumulate, for stains to collect, and for bacteria and fungi to lodge and produce minor infections.[193] Common causes of staining are coffee, tobacco, medications, foods, and chromogenic microorganisms.

Hairy tongue is not a serious condition and is easily eliminated by improving tongue hygiene and promoting desquamation. If candidal organisms are present, the use of antifungal agents is indicated.

Macroglossia. Macroglossia (large tongue) may be congenital or acquired. It is significant in the elderly population because individuals who have been edentulous for many years may develop this condition. The marked use of the tongue to aid in mastication of food results in muscular hypertrophy, a common type of acquired macroglossia. If the patient is able to wear dentures, the tongue muscle may regress, with reduction in the size of the tongue.

Circumoral Tissues

Lips

Angular Cheilitis (Cheilosis, Pseudocheilosis, or Perlèche). Angular cheilitis is a nonspecific inflammation at the oral commissure area bilaterally. It proceeds to a cracking of the angles of the mouth, with well-defined fissures present. The drooling of saliva often aggravates the condition.

The etiology of angular cheilosis is often complex. The combination of bone resorption, muscle atrophy, and tooth loss decreases the distance between the nose and chin, which causes the skin to wrinkle and fold around the mouth. The wrinkling can also accompany a change of bite with old, ill-fitting, or even new dentures. The wrinkled folds collect saliva, *C. albicans,* bacteria, and other contaminants that can cause the infection. Contributing factors include vitamin B complex deficiency, iron deficiency, or both.[63]

Treatment is directed toward unfolding the skin by the fitting of proper dentures; culturing and treating all infections; initiating measures of local hygiene; and, if necessary, giving iron and vitamin supplements.

Squamous Cell Carcinomas. A high risk of lip cancer is associated with the use of tobacco, particularly pipe tobacco, and exposure to ultraviolet radiation. Almost 95% of these cancers develop in the lower lip, where trauma and heat from the pipestem and exposure to the sun are greatest.[244] Atrophy of the lip, thinning of the lip border, and loss of elasticity are early clinical features. Carcinoma of the lip may appear as a crack in the lip surface, a crusting ulcer, or a tumorous growth. The prognosis is very good, unless the lesion is extensive, since metastases develop later and less frequently than from intraoral sites.[195]

Oral Musculature

Dysphagia. Dysphagia (difficulty in swallowing) may render a patient vulnerable to aspiration of saliva or oral intake. Indicators that a swallowing problem is likely to be present include dysarthria, poor control of oral secretions, inability to swallow spontaneously, drooling or gurgling aspirations or regurgitation through the nose, and frequent reflexive coughing.[245,246]

The causes of dysphagia may be neurologic, neuromuscular, or structural. In one study,[59] a significant increase in swallowing dysfunction was seen among older persons taking prescription medications. Conditions that alter the ability to form and prepare a bolus in the oral stage of swallowing can also cause dysphagia.[11]

Dyskinesia. Oral dyskinesia is a movement disorder characterized by severe, dystonic, involuntary movement of the facial, oral, and cervical musculature.[247,248] The involuntary abnormal contractions, mainly of the tongue, lips, and mandible, occur frequently with age in patients who exhibit disturbances of the cerebral stroma or stromal changes of the extrapyramidal motor system.[249–251] Because the movements disappear when the mouth is opened wide, during sleep, or when the patient's attention is distracted, oral dyskinesia tends to be regarded as a disease of the central nervous system.[247,252]

Some studies have reported a close correlation between oral dyskinesia and poor oral conditions.[247,252] One study describing the clinical appearance of this disease in the aged[247] found that its occurrence was associated with missing teeth and use of uncomfortable dentures. It has also been demonstrated that the symptoms of oral dyskinesia respond favorably to dental treatment, such as extractions, new dentures, and adjustment of old dentures.[248,252]

Drug-induced oral dyskinesia, or tardive dyskinesia, is a permanent side effect of long-term neuroleptic (antipsychotic) drug therapy that does not resolve on withdrawl of the drug. The most common movements are tongue protrusion, licking and smacking of the lips, puffing of the cheeks, sucking and chewing, and facial grimacing.[253–256]

Trismus. Trismus is a condition in which tonic spasms of the masticatory muscles limit opening of the mouth. It may develop during or after radiation therapy if these muscles are included in the treatment field. Management is directed toward exercises and various prosthetic appliances to increase the opening capacity of the muscles.

Other

Salivary Glands

Sialolithiasis. Sialoliths, or salivary stones, may form in any of the major or minor salivary glands or their excretory ducts. The most common manifestation of ductal stones, which do not generally cause complete obstruction, is enlargement of the gland and subsequent pain during eating. Both the glandular swelling and pain subside between meals as the entrapped saliva is gradually excreted.

Tumors. Benign and malignant tumors of the salivary glands are more common in older patients, and both the major and minor salivary glands are involved.[257] Overall, neoplasms arising from the minor salivary glands are relatively uncommon compared with those arising from the major salivary glands.[196,258,259] However, most tumors of the minor salivary glands are malignant.[259,260]

Both elderly men and elderly women appear to have an increased risk of salivary gland malignancies; however, little information about the causative factors exists. Radiotherapy is an infrequent etiologic factor.[261] Trauma, infection, stone formation, and the use of alcohol or tobacco are not associated with these tumors.[262]

The survival rates for patients with malignant salivary gland tumors are generally higher than they are for persons with most other oral cancers. Usually, diagnosis and treatment are rendered early and metastasis occurs late in the course of the disease. Long-term follow-up is essential, however, because there is a high rate of recurrence.

Xerostomia (Dry Mouth, Decreased Salivary Flow). Xerostomia, although not a disease concomitant with aging, is a symptom that is often evident in older patients. The main cause is use of medications; other causes include vitamin deficiencies, mouth breathing, stress, and a variety of systemic diseases and their therapies.

Without the antibacterial, cleansing, lubricating, remineralizing, and buffering actions of saliva, the xerostomic individual is at increased risk of developing coronal and root surface caries; abrasion and erosion of tooth surfaces; periodontal disease; atrophic glossitis; traumatic injuries to the mucous membranes; mucosal lesions; infections of the pharynx and salivary glands; and dysfunctions of speech, chewing, swallowing, and taste.[32,263-267] In addition to the damage to teeth and supporting structures, problems with prostheses are also magnified when the mouth is dry. Saliva provides a thin, fluid film between the denture base and underlying soft tissues necessary for the retention and stability of dentures during function.[64,268] Additionally, saliva prevents the hard acrylic or metal surfaces from abrading the oral mucosa. Consequently, frequent denture problems and sores arise, and the patient complains of generalized intraoral soreness during mastication.

Patients may express one or all of the signs and symptoms associated with xerostomia in varying degrees of severity. Some of these include mouth dryness; a fissured tongue; glossodynia or glossopyrosis; candidiasis; rampant caries; oral soreness; sticking of food or lips to the teeth; cracking of lips; difficulty in speaking, chewing, and swallowing; a generalized burning sensation; and ageusia, dysgeusia, or hypogeusia.[64,268] The mucosa becomes dry, rough, and sticky; bleeds easily; and is subject to ulceration or infection.

Prevention and management of xerostomia depends on its etiology (Table 6-5). With drug-induced xerostomia, the responsible drug may be able to be eliminated, reduced in dosage or frequency of administration, or substituted. Management of xerostomia that is irreversible, such as radiation-induced xerostomia, is essentially palliative and accommodative. Small, frequent mouthfuls of water are palatable, inexpensive, and moisten the mouth fairly well. To facilitate chewing and swallowing, most patients with xerostomia moisten and thin foods with sauces, gravies, milk, and other fluids.

Table 6-5 Prevention and Management of Xerostomia

Determine etiology

Alter medication regimen
    Eliminate medication
    Reduce dosage or frequency of administration
    Substitute medication for another with less severe oral side effects

Alleviate complaints
    Increase fluid intake (water or low-sugar beverages); avoid caffeinated drinks
    Avoid dry, bulky, spicy, salty, or highly acidic foods
    Avoid tobacco and alcohol intake
    Humidify air
    Use saliva stimulants (local and systemic agents)
      Local agents
        Sugarless hard candy or lozenges
        Sugarless gum
      Systemic agents
        Pilocarpine drops
        Oral pilocarpine (2.5 to 5.0 mg three times daily before meals)
    Use artificial saliva preparations (containing fluoride)
      Glycerine
      Methylcellulose
    Coat lips and dentures with petroleum jelly

Increase resistance to dental disease
    Have frequent dental examinations
    Use fluorides frequently
    Modify diet
    Control plaque

Artificial saliva preparations provide relief by coating and lubricating the mucosa. Saliva substitutes containing fluoride and fluoride gels are helpful for xerostomic patients at high risk for dental caries. For the lips and dentures, a constant coating of petroleum jelly and frequent oral application of artificial salivas should alleviate some of the problems. However, lemon glycerine swabs should be avoided because of their cariogenic and drying effects. Also, commercial mouth washes should be avoided because they have a high alcohol content and dry the oral mucosa. Similarly, ingestion of alcoholic beverages should be minimized.[269]

Taste Dysfunction

Taste acuity may be affected by oral pathologic conditions, dental diseases, olfactory deficits, medications, malnutrition, smoking, radiation therapy, neurologic deficits, and other systemic disorders.[6] Cues that may indicate alterations in taste sensitivity include decreased or increased appetite, excessive use of seasoning, and excessive use of sugar.[71]

SYSTEMIC DISEASES AND MEDICATIONS AFFECTING ORAL HEALTH

The elderly population suffers from many concurrent acute and chronic diseases, some of which may have oral manifestations or adversely affect oral health. Since 86% of all elderly persons suffer from at least one chronic disease, oral health problems secondary to these diseases may be important.[270] Systemic diseases that affect the oral and circumoral structures are listed in Table 6-6.

Many of the most commonly experienced chronic disease conditions found in the elderly are symptomatically controlled with the proper use of medications. The increased use of medications with advancing age, therefore, is not surprising. Geriatric patients take more drugs because they have more chronic illnesses than do younger patients. The problem of multiple drug use among elderly people not only has serious implications due to pharmacokinetic and pharmacodynamic considerations with aging, but also there are iatrogenic oral manifestations of many drugs (Table 6-7).

In addition to the oral signs and symptoms of properly prescribed and over-the-counter medications that elderly people take, recreational drug abusers experience oral manifestations as well, including advanced generalized periodontal disease, bruxism, numerous abscessed or missing teeth, poor oral hygiene, rampant caries, tooth attrition (secondary to bruxism), and xerostomia.[271-276]

Table 6-6 Oral Manifestations of Systemic Diseases

Disease/Condition	Oral Manifestations
Achlorhydria	Tongue—glossitis
Adrenal insufficiency	Oral infections—increased risk Oral mucosa—pigmentation Taste—loss or distortion Wound-healing response—poor
Agranulocytosis	Gingiva—spontaneous bleeding Hemorrhagic tendency—petechiae Periodontal disease—high incidence Ulcerations—painful, persistent, necrotic
Alcoholism	Breath odor of alcohol Dental caries—high incidence Facial neuralgia, edema Hemorrhagic tendency—ecchymoses, petechiae Lips—angular cheilosis Oral cancer—increased risk Oral hygiene—poor Oral infections—increased risk Oral mucosa—jaundiced, ulcerated Parotid salivary glands—chronic swelling Periodontal disease—chronic (with frequent acute exacerbations) Taste—decreased sensitivity Teeth—attrition, erosion, loss Tongue—glossitis, ulcerated Wound-healing response—delayed Xerostomia
Alzheimer's disease	Dysphagia Oral hygiene—poor, neglected Taste sensitivity—decreased Xerostomia
Amyotrophic lateral sclerosis	Dysarthria Tongue fasciculations—atrophic
Anemia	Burning/sore mouth—mucositis/stomatitis Filiform papillae—atrophic Oral mucosa—pale, atrophic, thin, tender Tongue—glossitis, glossodynia Xerostomia

Table 6-6 continued

Disease/Condition	Oral Manifestations
Anxiety disorders	Burning/sore mouth Dysphagia Xerostomia
Arthritis	TMJ involvement—limited jaw movement
Biliary tract obstruction	Bleeding—excessive, spontaneous Hemorrhagic tendency—petechiae, hematomas
Bipolar disorders	Depressive phase—oral hygiene neglected Manic phase—self-inflicted mucosal abrasion Facial pain syndromes due to mood swings
Bleeding disorders	Intraoral bleeding—ecchymoses, hematomas, petechiae Oral mucosa—jaundiced
Cerebrovascular accident	Chewing difficulty/inability Dysarthria Dysphagia Facial drooping—affects denture fit Gag reflex—decreased Oral motor apraxia Oral sensation—decreased unilaterally
Chorea	Dysarthria Oral dyskinesia
Congenital heart disease	Cyanosis Intraoral hemorrhages, infections Leukopenia, polycythemia, thrombocytopenia
Congestive heart failure	Intraoral bleeding—ecchymoses, petechiae Lips—cyanosis, thinning of vermilion border Oral infections
Coronary arteriosclerotic heart disease	Oral or facial pain—referred
Crohn disease	Aphthous ulcers—high frequency Burning/sore mouth Dental caries—high frequency Oral hygiene—poor

continues

Table 6-6 continued

Disease/Condition	Oral Manifestations
Cyclic neutropenia	Mucositis/stomatitis Oral infections—increased risk Periodontal disease—high incidence Ulcerations—aphthous type
Dementia	Burning/sore mouth Bruxism Dysphagia Facial pain—atypic Poor oral hygiene—chronic Oral injuries—increased susceptibility Periodontal disease—accelerated
Depression	Burning/sore mouth Facial pain syndromes—numerous Oral hygiene—poor Periodontal disease—accelerated Tongue—glossodynia Xerostomia
Diabetes mellitus	Breath odor of ketone Burning/sore mouth—mucositis/stomatitis Candidiasis Dental caries—rampant Gingiva—inflammation Lips—angular cheilitis Mucormycosis Oral infections—increased susceptibility Oral paresthesias Periodontal disease—accentuated, abscesses Taste sensitivity—decreased Teeth—sensitivity Tongue—glossodynia Ulcerations Wound-healing response—delayed Xerostomia
Epilepsy	Gingiva—drug-induced hyperplasia Ulcerations—traumatic
Gonorrhea	Gingivitis Oral abscesses/mucosal lesions/ulcerations Oral mucosa—erythematous Parotitis Pharyngitis/tonsillitis Stomatitis—generalized

Table 6-6 continued

Disease/Condition	Oral Manifestations
Hepatitis	Intraoral bleeding Oral mucosa—pigmentation Taste—loss or distortion
Herpes zoster	Bone—osteoradionecrosis Neuralgia—trigeminal Oral mucosa—lesions, ulcerations, pain Teeth—devitalization, exfoliation
Hypoparathyroidism	Candidiasis
Hypertension	Neuritis
Hyperthyroidism	Dental caries—extensive Periodontal disease—progressive Tongue—tumors (midline of posterior dorsum)
Hypothyroidism	Candidiasis Taste—loss or distortion Teeth—malocclusion Tongue—macroglossia Xerostomia
Immunosuppression	Increased susceptibility to candidiasis; dental caries; infections, local and systemic; intraoral bleeding; periodontal disease; recurrent aphthous ulcers; tumor development
Leukemia	Bone—lesions Burning/sore mouth—mucositis/stomatitis Candidiasis Gingiva—hyperplasia, spontaneous bleeding Hemorrhagic tendency—ecchymoses, hematomas, petechiae Herpetic stomatitis Infections—increased risk Lymphadenopathy Oral mucosa—pallor, lesions Oral paresthesias Ulcerations—painful, persistent, necrotic
Leukopenia	Oral infections—increased risk

continues

Table 6-6 continued

Disease/Condition	Oral Manifestations
Liver disease	Bleeding—excessive, spontaneous Hemorrhagic tendency— ecchymoses,hematomas, petechiae

Lupus erythematosus	Burning/sore mouth
	Candidiasis
	Mandible—immobility
	Oral lesions—bullae, erosions
	Oral mucosa—sloughing
	TMJ—deviation, pain with movement or
	  palpation, joint sounds, locking or
	  dislocation
	Tongue—fissuring, atrophic papillae
	Ulcerations
	Xerostomia

Lymphomas	Burning/sore mouth Candidiasis Cervical lymphadenopathy Extranodal oral tumors Hemorrhagic tendency—ecchymoses, petechiae Infections—increased risk
Malabsorption syndrome	Bleeding—excessive, spontaneous Candidiasis Hemorrhagic tendency—ecchymoses, hematomas, petechiae
Malignant hypertension	Facial paralysis
Multiple myeloma	Amyloid deposits in soft tissue Bone—lesions, pain Soft tissues—tumors Teeth—unexplained mobility
Multiple sclerosis	Dysarthria Xerostomia, drug-induced
Muscular dystrophy	Muscles—weakness, decreased biting force Mouth breathing Tongue—hypertrophy
Myasthenia gravis	Chewing difficulty Dysphagia Gingiva—poor health Mouth breathing

Table 6-6 continued

Disease/Condition	Oral Manifestations
	Muscles—weakness, inability to close mouth Tongue—flaccid
Nephritis	Burning/sore mouth Xerostomia
Neurofibromatosis	Oral neurofibromatous lesions Oral paresthesias Soft tissues—pigmentation Tongue—macroglossia, enlarged lingual papillae
Organ transplants	Oral infections—increased susceptibility Intraoral bleeding—increased susceptibility Tumor development—increased susceptibility
Osteoarthritis	Bone—resorption TMJ—unilateral involvement, dysfunction
Paget's disease	Bone—progressive enlargement
Parkinson's disease	Chewing difficulty Lips—angular cheilitis, tremors Drooling of saliva due to swallowing difficulty (not excessive production) Dysarthria Dysphagia Facial paresthesias, tremors Oral hygiene—poor Tardive dyskinesia, drug-induced Teeth—involuntary bruxism Tongue—tremors Xerostomia, drug-induced
Pemphigus vulgaris	Burning/sore mouth Candidiasis Halitosis Hypersalivation Oral lesions, erosions—bleed easily, painful Ulcerations—raw, red, eroded
Pneumonia	Aspiration—increased susceptibility with dysphagia, poor dentition, poor oral hygiene

continues

Table 6-6 continued

Disease/Condition	Oral Manifestations
Polycythemia	Oral mucosa—cyanosis
Post-traumatic stress disorder	Bruxism Dental caries—increased incidence Oral hygiene—poor Periodontal disease—increased incidence Tongue—glossodynia
Progressive bulbar palsy	Chewing difficulty Dysarthria Jaw muscles—spasticity
Radiation therapy to head/neck	Candidiasis Mucositis Muscles—dysfunction, trismus Oral infections—increased susceptibility Osteoradionecrosis Pulp—pain, necrosis Taste—lost or distorted Teeth—hypersensitivity, radiation caries Xerostomia
Renal disease/dialysis/transplants	Breath odor of urea Calculus—increased formation Candidiasis Dental caries—low incidence Gingiva—pale, undefined, bleeds spontaneously Oral infections—frequent retrograde infectious parotitis Oral mucosa—pallor, uremic stomatitis Renal osteomalacia/osteodystrophy Salivary flow—decreased Taste—metallic Teeth—mobility Tongue—macroglossia, glossodynia Ulcerations—ulcerative stomatitis Wound-healing response—poor
Rheumatoid arthritis	Bone—resorption Muscles—atrophic TMJ—dysfunction Xerostomia

Table 6-6 continued

Disease/Condition	Oral Manifestations

Sjögren's syndrome	Burning/sore mouth—mucositis/stomatitis
	Dental caries—increased susceptibility
	Lips—angular cheilosis, lesions
	Oral mucosa—lesions
	Parotid gland—enlargement
	Periodontal disease—accelerated
	Tongue—glossitis, glossodynia
	Saliva—composition changes: increased
	  sodium, potassium, manganese;
	  decreased calcium
	Taste—loss, distortion
	Xerostomia

Smokeless tobacco use	Gingiva—recession Halitosis Oral mucosa—leukoplakia Oral cancer—increased risk Periodontal disease—accentuated Smell sensitivity—decreased Taste sensitivity—decreased Teeth—abrasion, attrition, erosion, loss
Syphilis	Tongue—interstitial glossitis Oral lesions—chancre, mucous patch, gumma
Temporal arteritis	Orofacial pain
Thrombocytopenia	Hemorrhagic tendency—ecchymoses, hematomas, petechiae
Tobacco smoking	Calculus—increased Gingivitis—increased Hairy tongue Halitosis Smell sensitivity—decreased Taste—loss or distortion Teeth—abrasion Wound-healing response—delayed
Tuberculosis	Lymph node involvement (scrofula) Ulcerations, especially on tongue
Uticaria (angioneurotic anemia)	Swelling—soft tissues
Von Willebrand's disease	Hemorrhagic tendency—ecchymoses, hematomas, petechiae Intraoral bleeding—spontaneous

Table 6-7 Drug-Induced Oral Manifestations

Candidiasis
  Antibiotics
  Antineoplastics
  Corticosteroids
  Diuretics
  Immunosuppressives
  Steroid inhalers

Contact hypersensitivity
  Iodine
  Menthol
  Thymol
  Topical analgesics
  Topical antibiotics

Erythema multiforme
  Anticonvulsants
  Antimalarials
  Barbiturates
  Busulfan
  Chlorpropamide
  Clindamycin
  Codeine
  Isoniazid
  Meprobamate
  Minoxidil
  Penicillins
  Phenolphthalein
  Phenylbutazone
  Propylthiouracil
  Salicylates
  Sulfonamides
  Tetracyclines

Fixed drug eruptions
  Barbiturates
  Chlordiazepoxide
  Sulfonamides
  Tetracyclines

Gingival hyperplasia
  Cyclosporine
  Nifedipine
  Phenytoin sodium

Glossodynia
  Diuretics

Hairy tongue
  Antibiotics
  Corticosteroids
  Sodium perborate
  Sodium peroxide

Hypersalivation/sialorrhea
  Anticholinesterases
  Apomorphine
  Iodides
  Lithium
  Mercurial salts
  Nitrazepam

Infections
  Antineoplastics
  Immunosuppressives
  Corticosteroids (high dose)

Intraoral bleeding/petechiae/purpura
  Antiarrhythmics
  Antibiotics (broad spectrum)
  Anticoagulants
  Aspirin
  Warfarin sodium

Lichenoid mucosal reactions
  Allopurinol
  Antihypertensives
  β-Blockers
  Chloroquine
  Chlorothiazide
  Chlorpropamide
  Dapsone
  Diuretics
  Gold salts
  Mercury compounds
  Nonsteroidal anti-inflammatory agents
  Penicillamine
  Phenothiazines
  Quinidine
  Streptomycin
  Sulfamethoxazole
  Tetracyclines
  Tolbutamide

Table 6-7 continued

Lupus erythematosus
(oral mucosa) reactions
  Gold salts
  Griseofulvin
  Hydralazine hydrochloride
  Isoniazid
  Methyldopa
  Penicillin
  Phenytoin
  Primidone
  Procainamide
  Streptomycin
  Sulfonamides
  Tetracyclines
  Thiouracil

Mucositis/stomatitis
  Antineoplastics
  Gold salts
  Lithium
  Mercurial diuretics

Oral dyskinesias
  Buspirone

Orofacial neuropathies (numbness,
tingling, burning of the face or mouth)
  Acetazolamide
  Antineoplastics
  β-Blockers
  Chlorpropamide
  Ergotamine
  Hydralazine hydrochloride
  Hypoglycemics (oral)
  Isoniazid
  Methysergide
  Nalidixic acid
  Nitrofurantoin
  Phenytoin
  Streptomycin
  Tolbutamide
  Tricyclic antidepressants

Pigmentation (soft tissue)
  Antimalarials
  Busulphan
  Chlorhexidine

  Doxorubicin hydrochloride
  Gold salts
  Mercurial diuretics
  Minocycline
  Phenolphthalein
  Phenothiazines
  Phenytoin
  Silver compounds

Salivary gland enlargement
  Antipsychotics
  Insulin
  Iodides
  Isoproterenol
  Methyldopa
  Phenylbutazone
  Potassium chloride
  Sulfonamides
  Thiocyanate
  Thiouracil
  Warfarin sodium

Salivary gland pain and/or swelling
  Antihypertensives
  Antithyroid agents
  Cytotoxic agents
  Ganglion-blocking agents
  Insulin
  Iodine
  Isoproterenol
  Oxyphenbutazone
  Phenothiazines
  Phenylbutazone
  Potassium chlorate
  Sulfonamides
  Warfarin sodium

Spontaneous oral bleeding
  Anticoagulants
  Antineoplastics

Tardive dyskinesias
  Butyrophenone antipsychotics
  Levodopa
  Phenothiazines
  Thioxanthene

continues

Table 6-7 continued

Taste dysfunction
  Amphetamines
  Benzodiazepines
  Carbimazole
  Chlorhexidine
  Chlorpromazine
  Clofibrate
  D-Penacillamine
  Ethionamide
  Gold salts
  Griseofulvin
  Levodopa
  Lincomycin
  Lithium carbonate
  Methocarbamol
  Metronidazole
  Penicillin
  Phenformin hydrochloride
  Phenindione
  Propranolol
  Quinidine
  Tranquilizers
  Vitamins (excessive use)

Tooth decay (rampant)
  Tricyclic antidepressants

Tooth discoloration
  Chlorhexidine
  Gentian violet
  Stannous fluoride
  Tetracyclines

Ulcerations
  Antiarrhythmics
  Antineoplastics
  Aspirin
  D-Penicillamine
  Gold salts
  Indomethacin
  Meprobamate
  Mercurial diuretics
  Methotrexate
  Methyldopa

Naproxen
Phenylbutazone
Potassium chloride
Propranolol
Spironolactone
Thiazide diuretics
Tolbutamide

Xerostomia
  Amphetamines
  Analgesics
  Anorexiants
  Antiallergics
  Antianxiety agents
  Antiarrhythmics
  Anticholinergics
  Anticonvulsants
  Antidepressants
  Antidiarrheals
  Antihistamines
  Antihypertensives
  Anti-inflammatory agents
  Antinauseants
  Antineoplastics
  Antiparkinsonism agents
  Antipsychotics
  Antispasmodics
  Atropine
  Barbiturates
  Benzodiazepines
  Bronchodilators
  Central nervous system stimulants
  Congestive heart failure medications
  Decongestants
  Diuretics
  Ganglion-blocking agents
  Hypnotics
  Lithium
  Monoamine oxidase inhibitors
  Muscle relaxants
  Narcotics
  Nonsteroidal anti-inflammatory agents
  Phenylbutazone
  Scopolamine
  Sympathomimetics
  Tranquilizers

IMPACT OF NUTRITIONAL STATUS ON ORAL HEALTH

Nutritional status has an important role in oral health. There is a sophisticated system of nutrient interaction that is essential to the formation of healthy teeth and the maintenance of oral and circumoral tissues throughout life.[277–279] The systemic effects of nutrients on oral health, growth and development, cell integrity and renewal, proper function of the tissues and saliva, tissue repair, and resistance and susceptibility to oral diseases (Table 6-8) have been studied by very few researchers and need more attention and understanding. The local effects of food on plaque formation and the resultant oral disease processes, including coronal and root caries, gingivitis, and periodontitis, have been relatively well described.

Plaque Formation

Plaque consists mainly of bacteria and a matrix produced by them that is composed primarily of carbohydrate, protein, salts, and water. From a dietary standpoint, carbohydrates have an important role in initiating plaque formation. Once plaque is present, carbohydrates from food and beverages can diffuse into it and be fermented by the plaque bacteria. The acid produced can dissolve tooth structure, thus leading to carious lesions. Although acids present in food and beverages may also diffuse into the plaque, the result is usually erosion of the tooth surface and not dental caries.

If fermentable carbohydrates are not part of the diet, the acid-producing activity of the plaque will be low. Plaque is still demonstrable in subjects eating a diet devoid of fermentable carbohydrates, but the plaque is thin and structureless.[280] In contrast, subjects eating a sucrose-rich diet have voluminous, turgid plaque formation.

The texture of the diet may also influence dental plaque. Diets containing soft foods increase plaque formation more than those composed of firmer foods. In a study of women on a low calorie diet, the rate of plaque formation increased.[281]

Initially, plaque forms along the tooth-gum margin and gradually spreads across the tooth surface as the bacterial matrix grows. Since dietary carbohydrates contribute to this supragingival plaque formation, they have been implicated as an etiologic agent in the resulting gingival inflammation.[109,282,283]

Dental Caries

Although dental caries is generally accepted as primarily a microbial disease, diet plays a crucial secondary role. The dietary component contributing most to the initiation and progression of the caries process is fermentable carbohy-

Table 6-8 Systemic Effects of Nutrients on Oral Health

Nutrient	Systemic Effect
Barium	Tooth decay resistance
Boron	Tooth decay resistance
Calcium	Bone formation/maintenance Muscle tone maintenance Nerve impulse transmission Tooth formation/maintenance
Calcium-phosphorus balance	Bone maintenance Periodontal maintenance
Copper	Bone formation/maintenance Collagen synthesis Periodontal maintenance Wound healing
Fluorine	Tooth decay resistance
Folic acid	Epithelial integrity Wound healing
Gold	Tooth decay resistance (mild)
Iron	Epithelial integrity Periodontal maintenance
Lead	Tooth decay promotion
Lithium	Tooth decay resistance
Magnesium	Bone formation/maintenance Tooth formation Tooth decay promotion Wound healing
Manganese	Cell membrane formation Tooth decay resistance
Molybdenum	Tooth decay resistance (mild)
Nickel	Wound healing
Phosphorus	Bone formation/metabolism Tooth formation/metabolism Tooth decay resistance
Protein	Epithelial integrity Taste bud renewal Tooth formation Wound healing
Selenium	Tooth decay promotion
Silicon	Bone

Table 6-8 continued

Nutrient	Systemic Effect
Strontium	Tooth decay resistance
Sulfur	Bone maintenance
Vanadium	Bone maintenance Tooth decay resistance
Vitamin A	Epithelial integrity Tooth formation Wound healing
Vitamin B₁	Wound healing
Vitamin B₂	Wound healing
Vitamin B₆	Wound healing
Vitamin C	Epithelial integrity Periodontal maintenance Tooth formation Wound healing
Vitamin D	Bone formation/maintenance Tooth formation
Zinc	Epithelial integrity/metabolism Periodontal maintenance Taste bud renewal Wound healing

drates.[123,284] Biochemical, microbiologic, and animal and human clinical and epidemiologic studies support a causal relationship. Even root surface caries in human populations are enhanced by the ingestion of dietary sugars.[123,124,285]

Normally, before eating, the pH of tooth surface plaque exposed to saliva is close to neutrality (pH 6.5 to 7.0).[286] The ingestion of foods containing fermentable carbohydrates leads to acid production by the cariogenic plaque bacteria on tooth surfaces. The acids cause a rapid drop in pH that can result in demineralization of the tooth substance. If the plaque pH falls below the critical point of about 5.5 and remains there for an appreciable time, the food causing the decrease is likely to support caries initiation and progression.[287,288]

The greatest concentration of acid, or lowest pH, occurs in 5 to 15 minutes,[286] but teeth are attacked by acids for 20 minutes or more. Saliva has a buffering effect that helps to control acid production to some degree, and it contains proteins that act as antibacterial agents. However, in elderly persons who may have reductions in salivary flow and therefore reduced buffering and antibacterial capacity, each acid attack is significantly prolonged.

Dietary Control

There is compelling evidence that dietary control of dental caries requires modification in the form, quantity, frequency, and timing of consumption of carbohydrates.[123,289,290] Sucrose traditionally has been regarded as the form of carbohydrate most detrimental to teeth.[291–293] However, recent research indicates that many of the common simple sugars (glucose, dextrose, fructose, maltose, and lactose) can contribute to the rapid formation of acid by dental plaque.[294,295] Some studies even suggest that complex carbohydrates, such as starches, have the potential to promote caries under certain conditions.[296,297]

Reducing the quantity of fermentable carbohydrates ingested deprives the potentially pathogenic plaque of necessary substrates for growth. It also limits the numbers of cariogenic microorganisms found in the dental plaque.[298,299]

Frequency of consumption is important, since each encounter of bacteria with fermentable carbohydrates can result in acid production, tooth surface demineralization, and the formation of carious lesions.[300,301] There is a strong association between root caries lesions in adults and the frequency of fermentable carbohydrate intake.[124,302] Restricting between-meal snacks containing cariogenic carbohydrates is advised, since frequent sugar consumption, especially between meals, is associated with increased dental caries activity.

The best time to ingest fermentable carbohydrates is with meals. Eating these foods at mealtime will produce less caries than the same foods eaten between meals.[123] One reason for this may be that saliva, the production of which is increased during meals, helps neutralize acid production and clears food from the mouth. This is not true for between-meal snacks. Recently, however, it has been established that increasing salivary flow rates after meals, such as with sugarless gum chewing, helps reduce plaque acids that can cause caries.[303]

Cariogenicity

Cariogenicity refers to the potential that a specific food or diet has for dental caries formation. The local acidogenic activity of the food, not its nutrient content, largely determines its cariogenic potential.[304] Clinical trials to evaluate the cariogenicity of foodstuffs are expensive processes.[288] Studies must last 2 or 3 years, since dental caries develop slowly and are not clinically discernible for many months.

A key determinant of cariogenicity is oral clearance time.[305] When sugar is consumed in foods that adhere to or between tooth surfaces, caries activity has been shown to increase.[306] However, if the fermentable carbohydrate source is eaten with a beverage or in liquid form, the time needed for oral clearance is reduced, resulting in a lower net cariogenic potential. Thus, solid or retentive sugar-containing foods are more cariogenic than sugar-containing foods that are liquid or nonretentive.[304] Likewise, fermentable carbohydrates eaten at meals are less cariogenic than the same ones eaten between meals.[290]

Another indication of cariogenicity is the change in plaque pH associated with food consumption.[299] This measure has been used by a number of investigators to monitor the cariogenicity of particular foods and has been found to relate to oral clearance time. In one study, foods that adhered to the teeth depressed the plaque pH for longer periods than did foods that were removed from the teeth more quickly.[307,308]

The cariogenic potential of preparations of liquid medications is of particular concern for the geriatric patient. These medications frequently include high levels of sucrose, glucose, or fructose as sweeteners. Studies of patients taking sweetened liquid medications demonstrate a significant increase in dental caries, especially with long-term therapy.[309] Sweetened liquid iron supplements, cough syrups, antibiotics, and anticonvulsants have been shown to decrease plaque pH after ingestion.[310,311]

Artificial Sweeteners

Research has been focused on identifying and developing substances that serve as taste-competitive, noncariogenic sugar substitutes. Aspartame and saccharin are the two agents currently available. Cyclamate was banned by the Food and Drug Administration in 1970 because of concerns over its safety. That ban currently is being reconsidered.

Aspartame is noncariogenic, but it is not noncaloric.[312] However, its sweetness is of sufficient intensity (180 times sweeter than sucrose) that only small amounts are required, resulting in a very significant reduction in calories.

Saccharin is 300 times sweeter than sucrose, but is not metabolized by the body and is therefore noncaloric and non-nutritive.[313] Although it has been periodically labeled potentially carcinogenic, studies to date support its safety for human consumption.

Sugar Alcohols

Technically, the sugar alcohols are not sugars, but they are closely related both chemically and biochemically. Since their degrees of sweetness, compared with sugars, are similar, they are used as sugar substitutes.

Sorbitol, mannitol, and xylitol have been used in sugarless chewing gums and candies. Sorbitol- and xylitol-sweetened products appear to be noncariogenic in clinical trials.[288,314–316] Apparently, xylitol is not metabolized by plaque microorganisms at all, and sorbitol is not metabolized rapidly enough to support an active carious process.

In one study, chewing sorbitol gum after consuming potentially cariogenic snacks helped in counteracting the adverse plaque pH measurements.[316] The investigator postulated that the gum not only stimulated salivary flow, which is known to have a high buffering capacity, but allowed the saliva to penetrate between the tooth surfaces to neutralize acid production by plaque microorganisms.

Periodontal Disease

Nutrition has never been implicated as a primary etiologic agent in gingivitis or periodontitis. However, it does play a secondary role by influencing or altering the resistance of the periodontium to the noxious agents and irritants that have a primary etiologic role.[317] The importance of both diet and nutrition in maintaining effective host defense mechanisms to withstand periodontal microbial challenge is well established.[318,319]

Nutrient deficiencies can affect the rate and degree of periodontal disease rather than its initiation. Research suggests that the disease progresses faster and is more severe in patients whose diets do not supply the necessary nutrients.[320–322] However, there is insufficient evidence at this time to justify nutritional therapy as part of periodontal treatment.[279]

Other Oral Conditions

The role, if any, of diet and nutrition in edentulous ridge resorption, mucosal lesions, oral cancer, glossodynia, and taste perception is poorly defined,[279] although intakes of vitamins A and C are associated with a reduced risk of oral cancer.[323,324]

A major reason for poor adaptation to dentures by elderly persons is reduced tissue tolerance resulting from an inadequate diet.[325,326] Thin and friable epithelium covering the edentulous area may not tolerate the forces imposed on it by the hard, unyielding base of the denture.

The composition of saliva is critically dependent on flow rate from the glands, and numerous studies have demonstrated that both the physical consistency and the nutritional quality of the diet influence the structure of the glands as well as the flow rate of saliva.[327–329]

Nutrient Intake and Malnutrition

Inadequate amounts of nutrients can result in fragile, friable oral tissues with a loss of adaptability and tolerance to irritants, and a loss of repair potential.[330] For many nutrient deficiencies, the oral cavity serves as an early warning system.

Because of the rapid tissue turnover and easy visibility of the oral mucosa, it is possible to identify signs of inadequate intake or improper absorption before other organ systems are affected.[331] Although not all nutrient deficiencies have oral manifestations, the most common ones are listed in Table 6-9. Oral signs indicative or suggestive of malnutrition are listed in Table 6-10.

IMPACT OF ORAL HEALTH ON NUTRITIONAL STATUS

There is general agreement that poor oral health is a factor contributing to malnutrition, poor general health, and loss of strength. Although the impact of oral health status alone on dietary intake and nutritional status of the elderly is virtually unknown, any alteration in the anatomic structures or physiologic functions of the oral cavity may play an important role in deterring the elderly from attaining or maintaining a proper diet and nutritional state.

Dietary intake, with respect to food selection, chewing, and swallowing, is integral to the health of the geriatric patient. Many factors influence food selection, including social customs, taste preferences, amount of preparation, and cost.[62,332–334] Chewing is influenced by the status of the oral cavity and the efficiency of the masticatory apparatus. Swallowing depends on adequate lubrication and moisture provided by the salivary glands, as well as sufficient functioning of the oral musculature to form and prepare a food bolus. Clearly, any factor that interferes with food selection, chewing, or swallowing can restrict food intake and thus affect nutritional status.

Dentition Status

Dentition status, inasmuch as it contributes to masticatory efficiency, may exert potent effects on dietary intake. Research suggests that the number of occluding teeth, especially in the posterior segments of the mouth, is correlated with masticatory efficiency.[58,62,335–341] Masticatory efficiency is not only dependent on the number and condition of teeth present, but also on the length of time spent in chewing a bolus of food, and the force exerted when biting.[342]

Impaired masticatory efficiency and biting force have been associated with many oral conditions.[11,33,60,343] These include atrophy of orofacial musculature; oral dyskinesia; trismus; bone loss; tooth attrition, brittleness, mobility, pain, or loss; advanced carious lesions; TMJ dysfunction or dislocation; mucosal atrophy; generalized periodontal disease; gingival enlargement; and ill-fitting dentures.

One commonly held belief is that optimal masticatory efficiency allows an individual to select a wider variety of foods, which leads to a more nutritionally balanced diet.[344–346] It is also suggested that the loss of mechanical chewing

Table 6-9 Nutritional Deficiencies and Related Oral Manifestations

Nutrient Deficiency	Oral Manifestations
Vitamin A	Candidiasis Gingiva—hypertrophy, inflammation Oral mucosa—keratosis, leukoplakia Periodontal disease Taste—decreased acuity Xerostomia
Vitamin B complex	Lips—angular cheilosis Oral mucosa—leukoplakia Periodontal disease Tongue—papillary hypertrophy, magenta color, fissuring, glossitis
Vitamin B$_2$ (riboflavin)	Filiform papillae—atrophic Fungiform papillae—enlarged Lips—shiny, red, angular cheilosis Tongue—magenta color, soreness
Vitamin B$_3$ (niacin) (*pellagra*)	Lips—angular cheilosis Mucositis/stomatitis Oral mucosa—intense irritation/inflammation, red, painful, denuded, ulcerated Tongue—glossitis, glossodynia Tongue (tip/borders)—red, swollen, beefy Tongue (dorsum)—smooth, dry Ulcerative gingivitis
Vitamin B$_6$ (pyridoxine hydrocholoride)	Burning/sore mouth Lips—angular cheilosis Tongue—glossitis, glossodynia
Vitamin B$_{12}$ (cyanocobalamin) (*pernicious anemia*)	Bone loss Burning/sore mouth—mucositis/stomatitis Gingiva—hemorrhagic Halitosis Hemorrhagic tendency—petechiae Lips—angular cheilosis Oral mucosa—epithelial dysplasia Oral paresthesias—burning, numbness, tingling Periodontal fibers—detachment Taste—loss or distortion Tongue—beefy red, glossy, smooth; glossitis, glossodynia, loss of papillae Ulcerations—aphthous type Wound-healing response—delayed Xerostomia

Table 6-9 continued

Nutrient Deficiency	Oral Manifestations
Vitamin C (*scurvy*) or megavitamin C withdrawal	Blood vessels—fragility Bone—abnormal osteoid formation, fragility, loss Burning/sore mouth Candidiasis Gingiva—friability, raggedness, swelling, redness, hemorrhagic tendency Hemorrhagic tendency—petechiae, subperiosteal Oral infections—decreased resistance Periodontal disease—increased susceptibility Teeth—marked mobility, spontaneous exfoliation Wound-healing response—delayed
Vitamin D	Periodontal disease
Vitamin K	Candidiasis Gingiva—bleeding
Calcium	Bone—excessive resorption, loss of mineral, fragility, osteoporosis Hemorrhagic tendency Periodontal disease Teeth—mobility, early loss, edentulism
Copper	Bone—decreased trabeculae, decreased vascularity, fragility
Folic acid	Burning/sore mouth—mucositis/stomatitis Candidiasis Filiform/fungiform papillae—atrophic, loss Gingiva—inflammation Lips—angular cheilosis Tongue—glossitis Tongue (tip/borders)—red, swollen Tongue (dorsum)—slick, bald, pale, or fiery Ulcerations—aphthous type
Iron	Bleeding complications—increased risk Burning/sore mouth Candidiasis Dental caries—increased susceptibility Dysphagia Filiform papillae—atrophic

continues

Table 6-9 continued

Nutrient Deficiency	Oral Manifestations
	Lips—angular cheilosis, pallor
	Oral infections—increased risk
	Oral mucosa—pallor
	Oral paresthesias
	Tongue—atrophic, pale; glossitis, glossopyrosis
	Ulcerations—aphthous type
	Xerostomia
Magnesium	Bone—fragility
	Gingiva—hypertrophy
Phosphorus	Dental decay—increased susceptibility
	Periodontal disease
Protein	Bone—decreased repair
	Epithelium—fragility, burning sensation
	Lips—angular cheilosis
	Oral infections—decreased resistance
	Periodontal disease—increased susceptibility
	Wound-healing response—delayed
Protein-calorie	Bone loss
	Candidiasis
	Necrotizing ulcerative gingivitis
	Periodontal disease
Water	Burning/sore mouth
	Epithelium—dehydration, fragility
	Muscle strength—diminished
	Tongue—glossopyrosis
	Xerostomia
Zinc	Candidiasis
	Dental caries—increased susceptibility
	Epithelial thickening
	Oral mucosa—atrophic
	Periodontal disease—increased susceptibility
	Smell acuity—decreased
	Taste acuity—loss or distortion
	Wound-healing response—delayed
	Xerostomia

Table 6-10 Oral Signs Indicative or Suggestive of Malnutrition

Oral Area	Normal Appearance	Signs Associated with Malnutrition
Teeth	Bright; no caries; no pain	Dental caries; may be missing or erupting abnormally
Gums	Healthy; red; not swollen; no bleeding	Receding; spongy; bleed easily
Tongue	Deep red; not swollen or smooth	Scarlet or magenta color; smooth; raw; swelling; sores; atrophic, hyperemic, or hypertrophic papillae
Lips	Smooth; not swollen or chapped	Redness; swelling of mouth and lips
Face	Uniform color; smooth; pink; healthy appearance; not swollen	Lumpiness or flakiness of skin around mouth
Salivary glands	Face not swollen in gland areas	Parotid enlargement (swollen cheeks)

Source: Adapted from *Nutritional Assessment in Health Programs,* 7th printing, (p 19) by G Christakis with permission of the American Public Health Assocation, © 1984.

efficiency leads to a preference for soft, easy-to-chew foods, which may increase the risk of nutritional deficiencies.[62,109,332,333,336,344,347–352] These foods tend to be high in carbohydrates and calories but low in fiber, protein, iron, calcium, and essential vitamins. Such a diet routinely contains salt and saturated fats in unhealthy amounts for persons with heart disease, and usually lacks vitamin K, which leads to calcium loss in bone.[353]

Edentulousness can affect masticatory function and dietary choice, but its influence on nutritional status is controversial. Some researchers have found that tooth loss is a strong predictor of inadequate nutrition, resulting from problems with biting, chewing, or swallowing foods. Other investigators have found little evidence to indicate that adequate dentition is necessary for geriatric patients to maintain a satisfactory nutritional state.[354,355]

Even the incidence of malnutrition and gastrointestinal disburbances in the older adult appears to be unrelated to impaired masticatory function.[342,345,356–358] In these studies, the percentage of individuals with significantly reduced or inefficient masticatory ability was similar to the percentage of persons with and without overt signs of malnutrition or undernutrition. In addition, various changes in blood chemistry usually associated with malnutrition have not been routinely found in individuals with significantly reduced masticatory ability.[359]

It would appear that replacing missing teeth with partial or complete dentures would improve chewing and limit the risk of nutritional problems. Indeed, the change from poor natural dentition or edentulousness to complete dentures is generally accompanied by improved chewing efficiency and nutritional status,[357,360,361] but there are conflicting observations in the literature.[338,355]

Properly fitted dentures may allow one to choose from a wider selection of food textures. However, denture wearing has been reported to interfere with the ability to eat satisfactorily, talk clearly, and laugh freely.[362,363] Elderly denture wearers also require more time to chew before swallowing than do those with natural teeth.[60]

It is well known that the denture wearer does not have the chewing efficiency enjoyed by the individual with natural teeth. Several studies have shown that significant differences in chewing ability occur among persons with intact natural dentition, individuals with partial prosthetic replacements, and individuals with complete dentures.[338-340,349,364-370] Dental studies have established that the chewing efficiency of an average complete denture wearer is only 15% to 25% of that of an individual with natural teeth.[334,348,366,367,371-373]

Even so, a chewing efficiency as low as 23%, a level attainable with just the 12 maxillary and mandibular anterior teeth, was sufficient to digest the 28 experimental foods in one study of masticatory efficiency and food assimilation.[374] Since the masticatory efficiency attained by the average denture wearer is in this range, most people with dentures should be able to chew food adequately for proper digestion.

The condition of dentures has a direct bearing on an individual's ability to chew. Well-fitting dentures in a healthy mouth can result in better chewing, swallowing, and digestion.[354,357,375] Problems with denture fit, bone shrinkage, and the gum tissues supporting the denture compromise masticatory function and may negatively alter dietary intake.[60] In fact, many denture wearers avoid foods that tend to slip under dentures or are too difficult to manipulate and chew.[376]

Other studies[346,371,377-379] have reported significant variation in the masticatory performance of people who wear dentures. Some individuals are barely able to comminute a test food, whereas others with similar prostheses have a relatively high degree of masticatory proficiency. Furthermore, approximately 5 times more effort is required for the average person wearing complete dentures to pulverize a test food to the same degree as a person with natural dentition. This agrees with previous reports that impaired chewing ability is not usually improved by chewing food longer or by increasing the rate of chewing, but rather by ingesting foods that are softer and easier to chew,[349] or by swallowing larger particles.[338,341,344] Therefore, denture wearers may be more prone to accidental choking from improper mastication.[380-382]

Data from dietary surveys before and after the insertion of new dentures are inconclusive about associated changes in essential nutrient intake.[357,361,383-389]

Before the insertion of new dentures, several essential nutrients are consumed in quantities significantly lower than the recommended daily allowance. After new dentures were placed, shifts in nutrient intake occurred, although the changes were not necessarily beneficial. Subjective evaluations, however, indicated improved chewing efficiency, which aided food digestion, particularly of fibrous foods.

Self-Perceived Chewing Ability

Experimental subjects' evaluations of their own chewing ability have been examined as possible predictors of masticatory efficiency, but most reported results are conflicting.[62,339,340,367,369,370,389-392] There appears to be wide individual variation in the subjective assessment of chewing problems that is not always related to dentition status. For those with poor masticatory efficiency, the lack of a perceived problem is probably due in part to the selection of foods that are easy to chew, or preparation of food in such a way as to facilitate chewing. In fact, perceived ease of chewing is related to subjective estimates of food preference.[339,340,368,369,376,393] In general, denture wearers give lower preference ratings to hard-to-chew foods than do persons with intact or even compromised natural dentition.

Dietary Control of Chewing Difficulties

For those with chewing problems due to dentures or tooth loss, the key is to modify food selection habits and methods of preparing foods for easier chewing. Specific ways to overcome chewing difficulties are listed in Table 6-11.

Oral Cancer

Neoplasms in the oral cavity can interfere with chewing and swallowing because of both pain and infiltration of tissues. Antineoplastic drugs and radiation therapy can alter the character and volume of saliva. In addition, the balance of the oral flora is disrupted, allowing overgrowth of opportunistic organisms such as *Candida* species.

Many patients who undergo radiation therapy for oral cancer become nutritional casualties. Profound loss of appetite is an early and sustained reaction to radiation-induced soreness, xerostomia, taste loss, dysphagia, and nausea and vomiting.[394] Eating becomes a pleasureless and painful chore, and food selection is restricted to items that do not aggravate the oral discomfort, often at the expense of adequate nutrition. When prolonged and severe enough, lack of nutrients can precipitate a nutritional deficiency stomatitis.

Table 6-11 Dietary Control of Chewing Difficulties

- Drink fluids with meals to aid in chewing and swallowing.
- Chop, grind, or mechanically blend foods that are hard to chew.
- Add sources of dietary fiber (stems of vegetables, whole grains, skins of fruits and vegetables, and seeds or berries) that can be cooked, shredded, mashed, ground, or softened with liquids without affecting the fiber content.
- Shred or chop raw vegetables and use them in salads.
- Mash or strain cooked vegetables.
- Buy prechopped vegetables and meat.
- Prepare meats and vegetables in soups, stews, and casseroles.
- Trim meats to remove fat and tough fibers.
- Substitute softer, protein-rich foods such as fish, eggs, peanut butter, cheese, baked beans, ground meats, or yogurt for regular meat.
- Use melted cheese as a sauce on vegetables or toast, to increase protein intake.
- Add extra nonfat dry milk powder to cream soups, cooked cereals, puddings, custards, creamed vegetables, casseroles, and milk beverages, to increase protein and calorie content.
- Use cooked whole-grain cereals such as oatmeal or mixed grains.
- Add bran to hot cereals, baked breads, meat loaf, and casseroles.
- Use fruit juices in place of fruits. Most fruits can be puréed in a blender and the pulp added to juices.
- Avoid sticky foods that adhere to teeth and dentures.
- Use menus from cookbooks written for people with chewing problems.
- Most important, eat a variety of foods from the major food groups each day.

Oral Pain

Oral pain can reduce food intake in both texture and amount. In fact, many patients experiencing dental or facial pain avoid certain foods.[395] As an example, mucositic tissues are sensitive to temperature and pressure, so a semisoft diet that is low in sucrose and citric acid is advised.[396]

Masticatory ability, biting force, and tongue movements are impaired in painful oral conditions, thus influencing the ability to chew many foods. Oral pain can also interfere with swallowing. Conditions that can cause oral pain are listed in Table 6-12.

Saliva

Saliva is essential for taste perception, mastication, and swallowing of foods. It provides the environment for optimal functioning of taste buds and contributes to

Table 6-12 Oral Conditions That Can Be Painful

- Angular cheilosis
- Aphthous ulceration
- Benign mucous membrane pemphigoid
- Burning mouth syndrome
- Candidiasis
- Contact stomatitis
- Dental caries
- Denture stomatitis
- Erythema multiforme
- Glossodynia
- Glossopharygeal neuralgia
- Herpes labialis
- Herpetic stomatitis
- Hypersensitive teeth
- Lichen planus
- Mucositis
- Necrotizing ulcerative gingivitis
- Oral cancer (advanced)
- Periodontal disease
- Pulpal infection
- TMJ dysfunction
- Traumatic ulceration
- Trigeminal neuralgia

ingestion and digestion by forming a mucin-coated food bolus and adequate fluid volume to allow for ready passage along the chewing and swallowing surfaces. The bolus is then digested in the gastrointestinal tract.

When salivary flow is deficient, it causes various stresses on the hard and soft tissues of the mouth, leading to increased oral disease and dysfunction of chewing, swallowing, and taste.[60] The greater concentration of electrolytes in a diminished amount of saliva can result in a salty or metallic taste in the mouth. In addition, decreased ptyalin levels in the reduced salivary flow may affect digestion of chewed particles.

Most xerostomic patients have difficulty eating solid and dry foods,[63,64] which can contribute to changes in nutritional intake patterns.[397,398] Oral pain associated with sialadenitis or sialolithiasis can also impair oral intake. In response, elderly individuals reduce the intake of various foods or switch to foods more easily chewed.

To facilitate chewing and swallowing in severe xerostomia, food must be lubricated with artificial saliva or prepared in liquid or semiliquid form. Saliva substitutes have been shown to improve both chewing and swallowing.[399,400] Many patients moisten foods with sauces, gravies, milk, and other fluids.

Taste and Smell Sensitivity

For the most part, taste and smell determine the flavor of foods and beverages.[400] Reduced acuity of either of these senses many significantly lessen the ability to enjoy food and therefore decrease appetite. Declines in gustation and olfaction, whether with age, chronic disease, or drug use, decrease the flavor and palatability of foods and beverages. Because of this, the senses of both taste and smell are important in food selection.[398,399]

Decreased taste sensitivity is compounded by dental disease or poor oral hygiene.[6,401,402] The causes can be physical, such as debris covering the taste buds, or chemical, as in taste fatigue from constant stimulation by decaying matter in the mouth.[68] Also, chronic dental or periodontal infections might result in the continuous discharge of purulent matter into the mouth, creating a constantly unpleasant taste. Routine oral hygiene has been shown to improve sensitivity to salty and sweet tastes and could improve the elderly patient's appetite.[87]

Saliva has modulating effects on taste sensitivity. A salty taste is detected only when the concentration is above salivary levels of sodium chloride. Saliva diminishes the effect of a sour taste as a result of buffering by salivary bicarbonate. Decreased salivation also alters the taste of many foods.[401,402]

Diminshed taste also may result from altered taste perception.[330] It has long been suspected that denture wearers have a lowered ability to taste,[330,368,403] and edentulous individuals experience a reduction in taste sensitivity after the insertion of complete dentures.[404] Perhaps the taste buds in the hard palate are more insensitive to taste, especially sour and bitter, when covered with dentures.[50,330,405]

Giddon and colleagues[406] compared the ability of denture wearers and persons with natural dentition to differentiate the sweetness of a solid food. It was found that the denture wearers took more than twice as long to render a judgment than did subjects with natural dentition. The denture wearers were unable to distinguish among cookies containing various levels of sucrose.

CONCLUSION

The cumulative effects of aging, disease, and trauma contribute to the wide variety of oral health problems prevalent in the older adult. Although many of these problems can be neither prevented nor cured by diet alone, to ignore nutritional considerations in the oral disease process would be a serious error. Many of the oral problems mentioned previously are associated with dietary deficiencies, excesses, or practices that are detrimental to the oral and circumoral structures. It is imperative that dietary intake provide adequate nutrients to support oral health and function.

There is also a strong association between oral health status and food selection, chewing efficiency, and ability to swallow. Clearly, oral health problems that interfere with any aspects of these factors can restrict food intake and ultimately affect nutritional status.

REFERENCES

1. Somerman MJ, Hoffeld JT, Baum BJ. Basic biology and physiology of oral tissues: overview and age-associated changes. In: Tryon AF, ed. *Oral Health and Aging*. Littleton, Mass: PSG Publishing Co Inc; 1986.

2. Baum BJ. Salivary gland function during aging. *Gerodontics*. 1986;2(2):61–64.

3. Mandel ID. The role of saliva in maintaining oral homeostasis. *J Am Dent Assoc*. 1989;119(2):298–304.

4. Mandel ID, Wotman S. The salivary secretion in health and disease. *Oral Sci Rev*. 1976;8:25–47.

5. Baum BJ. Current research on aging and oral health. *Spec Care Dent*. 1981;1(3):105–109.

6. Baum BJ. Normal and abnormal oral status in aging. *Ann Rev Gerontol Geriatr*. 1984;4:87–105.

7. Baum BJ, Bodner L, Fox PC, et al. Therapy-induced dysfunctions of salivary glands. *Spec Care Dent*. 1985;5(6):274–277.

8. Fox PC, Heft MW, Herrera M, et al. Secretion of antimicrobial proteins from the parotid glands of different aged healthy persons. *J Gerontol*. 1987;42(5):466–469.

9. Spielman AI. Interaction of saliva and taste. *J Dent Res*. 1990;69(3):838–843.

10. Guyton AC. Secretory functions of the alimentary tract. In: Guyton AC, ed. *Textbook of Medical Physiology*. 5th ed. Philadelphia, Pa: WB Saunders Co; 1976.

11. Sonies BC, Stone M, Shawker T. Speech and swallowing in the elderly. *Gerodontology*. 1984;3(2):115–123.

12. Kiyak HA. Psychosocial factors in dental needs of the elderly. *Spec Care Dent*. 1981; 1(1):22–30.

13. Johnson ES, Kelly JE, Van Kirk LE. *Selected Dental Findings in Adults, by Age, Race and Sex: United States: 1960–1962*. Washington, DC: US Public Health Service; 1965. US Dept of Health, Education, and Welfare PHS publication No. 1000 Series 11.

14. National Center for Health Statistics. *Basic Data on Dental Examination Findings for Persons 1–74 years, US 1971–1974*. Washington, DC: Vital and Health Statistics series 11, Data from National Health Survey (HANES), No. 214; 1979.

15. Baum BJ. Characteristics of participants in the oral physiology component of the Baltimore Longitudinal Study of Aging. *Community Dent Oral Epidemiol*. 1981;9(3):128–134.

16. *Oral Health of United States Adults: National Findings*. Bethesda, Md: National Institute of Dental Research; 1987. National Institutes of Health Publication 87-2868.

17. Hand JS, Hunt RJ. The need for restorations and extractions in a non-institutionalized elderly population. *Gerodontics*. 1986;2(2):72–76.

18. Hunt RJ, Srisilapanan P, Beck JD. Denture-related problems and prosthodontic treatment needs in the elderly. *Gerodontics*. 1985;1(5):226–230.

19. Hunt RJ. Periodontal treatment needs in an elderly population in Iowa. *Gerodontics*. 1986;2(1):24–27.

20. Bagramian R, Heller P. Dental health assessment of a population of nursing home residents. *J Gerontol*. 1977;32(2):168–174.

21. Council on Dental Health and Health Planning, Bureau of Economic and Behavioral Research. Oral health status of Vermont nursing home residents. *J Am Dent Assoc*. 1982;104(1):68–69.

22. Beck JD, Ettinger RL. Rational dental care in the long term care facility. *Am Health Care Assoc J*. 1981;7(3):22–24.

23. Empey G, Kiyak HA, Milgrom P. Oral health in nursing homes. *Spec Care Dent*. 1983;3(2):65–67.

24. Yamagata PA, Brattebo SC, Steifel DJ. Use of a dental service in a nursing home. *Spec Care Dent*. 1985;5(2):64–67.

25. Gordon SR. Survey of dental need among veterans with severe cognitive impairment. *Gerodontics*. 1988;4(4):158–159.

26. Baum BJ. Research on aging and oral health: an assessment of current status and future needs. *Spec Care Dent*. 1981;1(4):156–165.

27. Williams TF. Patterns of health and disease in the elderly. *Gerodontics*. 1985;1(6):284–287.

28. Ramazzotto LJ, Curro FA, Gates PE, et al. Calcium nutrition and the aging process: a review. *Gerodontology*. 1986;5(3):159–168.

29. Somerman MJ. Mineralized tissues in aging. *Gerodontology*. 1984;3(2):93–99.

30. Cohen B. Ageing in teeth and associated tissues. In: Cohen B, Thomson H, eds. *Dental Care for the Elderly*. London, England: Year Book Medical Publishers Inc, 1986.

31. Heeneman H, Brown DH. Senescent changes in and about the oral cavity and pharynx. *J Otolaryngol*. 1986;15(4):214–216.

32. Langer A. Oral changes in the geriatric patient. *Compend Contin Educ Dent*. 1981;2(4):258–264.

33. Weiner AA. The psychophysiologic etiology of anxiety in the geriatric dental patient. *Spec Care Dent*. 1985;5(4):174–177.

34. Ettinger RL. *Oral Changes Associated with Aging, Module 2*. Iowa City, Iowa: University of Iowa College of Dentistry, Geriatric Curriculum Series, 1982.

35. Shapiro S, Bomberg TJ, Benson BW, et al. Post-menopausal osteoporosis: dental patients at risk. *Gerodontics*. 1985;1(5):220–225.

36. Murphy TR. The progressive reduction of tooth cusps as it occurs in natural attrition. *Dent Pract*. 1968;19(1):8–14.

37. Fishman LS. Dental and skeletal relationships to attritional occlusion. *Angle Orthod*. 1976;46(1):51–63.

38. Ainamo A, Ainamo J. The dentition is intended to last a lifetime. *Int Dent J*. 1984;34(2):87–92.

39. Begg PR. Stone age man's dentition. *Am J Orthod*. 1984;4(4):298–312.

40. Hand JS, Beck JD, Turner KA. The prevalence of occlusal attrition and considerations for treatment in a noninstitutionalized elderly population. *Spec Care Dent*. 1987;7(5):202–206.

41. Heft MW. Prevalence of TMJ signs and symptoms in the elderly. *Gerodontology*. 1984;3(2):125–130.

42. Miles AEW. Sans teeth: changes in oral tissues with advancing age. *Proc R Soc Med*. 1972;65(9):801–806.

43. Klein DR. Oral soft tissues changes in geriatric patients. *Bull N Y Acad Med*. 1980; 56(8):721–727.

44. Kahane JC. Anatomic and physiologic changes in the aging peripheral speech mechanism. In: Beasley DS, Davis GA, eds. *Aging: Communication Processes and Disorders*. New York, NY: Grune & Stratton; 1981.

45. Koopman CF, Coulthard SW. The oral cavity and aging: symposium on geriatric otolaryngology. *Otolaryngol Clin North Am*. 1982;15(2):293–312.

46. Hill MW. The influence of aging on skin and oral mucosa. *Gerodontology*. 1984;3(1):35–45.

47. Breustedt A. Age-induced changes in the oral mucosa and their therapeutic consequences. *Int Dent J*. 1983;33(3):272–280.

48. Mackenzie IC, Holm-Pedersen P, Karring T. Age changes in the oral mucous membranes and periodontium. In: Holm-Pedersen H, Loe H, eds. *Geriatric Dentistry: A Textbook of Oral Gerontology*. St. Louis, Mo: CV Mosby Co; 1986.

49. Hughes G. Changes in taste sensitivity with advancing age. *Gerontol Clin*. 1969;11:224–230.

50. Hermel J, Schonwetter S, Samueloff S. Taste sensation identification and age in man. *J Oral Med*. 1970;25(2):39–42.

51. Hyde RJ, Feller RP, Sharon IM. Tongue brushing, dentifrice, and age effects on taste and smell. *J Dent Res*. 1981;60(10):1730–1734.

52. Bartoshuk LM, Rifkin B, Marks LE, et al. Taste and aging. *J Gerontol*. 1986;41(1):51–57.

53. Weiffenbach JM, Cowart BJ, Baum BJ. Taste intensity perception in aging. *J Gerontol*. 1986;41(4):460–468.

54. Satoh Y, Seluk LW. Taste threshold, anatomical form of fungiform papillae and aging in humans. *J Nihon Univ Sch Dent*. 1988;30(1):22–29.

55. Bartoshuk LM. Clinical psychophysics of taste. *Gerodontics*. 1988;4(5):249–255.

56. Newton JP, Abel RL, Robertson EM, et al. Changes in human masseter and medial pterygoid muscles with age: a study by computed tomography. *Gerodontics*. 1987;3(4):151–154.

57. Vergo TJ Jr, Papas A. Physiological aspects of geriatric dentistry. *J Dent*. 1984;4(1):10–14.

58. Feldman FS, Kapur K, Alman JE, et al. Aging and mastication: changes in performance and in the swallowing threshold with natural dentition. *J Am Geriatr Soc*. 1980;28(3):97–103.

59. Baum BJ, Bodner L. Aging and oral motor function: evidence for altered performance among older persons. *J Dent Res*. 1983;62(1):2–6.

60. Idowu AT, Graser GN, Handelman SL. The effect of age and dentition status on masticatory function in older adults. *Spec Care Dent*. 1986;6(2):80–83.

61. Elliott JL. Swallowing disorders in the elderly: a guide to diagnosis and treatment. *Geriatrics*. 1988;43(1):95–113.

62. Chauncey HH, Kapur KK, Feller RP, et al. Altered masticatory function and perceptual estimates of chewing experience. *Spec Care Dent*. 1981;1(6):250–255.

63. Langer A. Oral signs of aging and their clinical significance. *Geriatrics*. 1976;31(12):63–69.

64. Massler M. Xerostomia in the elderly. *N Y J Dent*. 1986;56(7):260–261.

65. Tylenda JA, Ship JA, Fox PC, et al. Evaluation of submandibular salivary flow rate in different age groups. *J Dent Res*. 1988;67(9):1225–1228.

66. Baum BJ. Evaluation of stimulated parotid saliva flow rate in different age groups. *J Dent Res*. 1981;60(7):1292–1296.

67. Zegeer LJ. The effects of sensory changes in older persons. *J Neurosci Nurs*. 1986; 18(6):325–332.

68. Whitehead MC. Neuroanatomy of the gustatory system. *Gerodontics*. 1988;4(5):239–243.

69. Cooper RM, Bilash MA, Zubek JP. The effect of age on taste sensitivity. *J Gerontol*. 1959;14(1):56–58.

70. Erickson RI. The elderly patient: a new challenge for dentists. *J Calif Dent Assoc*. 1982;10(5):49–50.

71. Kopac CA. Sensory loss in the aged: the role of the nurse and the family. *Nurs Clin North Am*. 1983;18(2):373–384.

72. Arvidson K. Location and variation in number of taste buds in human fungiform papillae. *Scand J Dent Res*. 1979;87:435–442.

73. Bradley RM. Effects of aging on the anatomy and neurophysiology of taste. *Gerodontics*. 1988;4(5):244–248.

74. Kullaa-Mikkonen A, Kaponen A, Seilonen A. Quantitative study of human fungiform papillae and taste buds: variation with aging and in different morphological forms of the tongue. *Gerodontics*. 1987;3(3):131–135.

75. Weisfuse D, Catalanotto FA, Kamen S. Gender differences in suprathreshold scaling ability in an older population. *Spec Care Dent*. 1986;6(1):25–28.

76. Kiyak HA. Psychological changes associated with aging: implications for the dental practitioner. In: Tryon AF, ed. *Oral Health and Aging*. Littleton, Mass: PSG Publishing Co Inc; 1986.

77. Richter CP, Campbell KH. Sucrose taste thresholds of rats and humans. *Am J Physiol*. 1940;128(1):291–297.

78. Byrd E, Gertman S. Taste sensitivity in aging persons. *Geriatrics*. 1959;14(6):381–384.

79. Hinchcliffe R. Clinical quantitative gustometry. *Acta Otolaryngol (Stockh)*. 1958; 49(6):453–466.

80. Grzegorczyk PB, Jones SW, Mistretta CM. Age-related differences in salt taste acuity. *J Gerontol*. 1979;34(6):834–840.

81. Massler M. Geriatric nutrition: the role of taste and smell in appetite. *J Prosthet Dent*. 1980;43(3):247–250.

82. Baker KA, Didcock EA, Kemm FR, et al. Effect of age, sex and illness on salt taste detection thresholds. *Age Ageing*. 1983;12(2):159–165.

83. Doty RL. A review of olfactory dysfunctions in man. *Am J Otolaryngol*. 1979;1(1):57–79.

84. Mistretta CM. Aging effects on anatomy and neurophysiology of taste and smell. *Gerodontology*. 1984;3(2):131–136.

85. Weiffenbach JM. Taste and smell perception in aging. *Gerodontology*. 1984;3(2):137–146.

86. Venstrom D, Amoore JE. Olfactory threshold in relation to age, sex or smoking. *J Food Sci*. 1968;33(3):264–265.

87. Kimbrell GM, Furchgott E. Effect of aging on olfactory threshold. *J Gerontol*. 1963; 18(10):364–365.

88. Schiffman S, Pasternak M. Decreased discrimination of food odors in the elderly. *J Gerontol*. 1979;34(1):73–79.

89. Doty RL, Shaman P, Applebaum SL, et al. Smell identification ability: changes with age. *Science*. 1984;226(4681):1441–1443.

90. Chalke HD, Dewhurst JR, Ward CW. Loss of sense of smell in old people. *Public Health*. 1958;72(6):223–230.

91. Ettinger RL. Oral disease and its effect on the quality of life. *Gerodontics*. 1987;3(1):103–106.

92. Nikias M. Oral disease and quality of life. *Am J Public Health*. 1985;75(1):11–12.

93. Mandel ID. Preventive dentistry for the elderly. *Spec Care Dent*. 1983;3(4):157–163.

94. Nystrom GP, Adams RA. Oral hygiene and the elderly. In: Tryon AF, ed. *Oral Health and Aging*. Littleton, Mass: PSG Publishing Co Inc; 1986.

95. Kandelman D, Bordeur JM, Simard P, et al. Dental needs of the elderly: a comparison between some European and North American surveys. *Community Dent Health*. 1986;3(1):19–39.

96. Goldberg AF, Gergans GA, Mattson DE, et al. Radiographic alveolar process/mandibular height ratio as a predictor of osteoporosis. *Gerondontics*. 1988;4(5):229–231.

97. Richards M. Osteoporosis. *Geriatr Nurs (New York)*. 1982;3(2):98–102.

98. Krook L, Whalen JP, Lesser GV, et al. Human periodontal disease and osteoporosis. *Cornell Vet*. 1972;62(3):371–391.

99. Lutwak L. Continuing need for dietary calcium throughout life. *Geriatrics*. 1974; 29(5):171–178.

100. Kribbs PJ, Smith DE, Chestnutt CH III. Oral findings in osteoporosis, part II: relationship between residual ridge and alveolar bone resorption and generalized skeletal osteopenia. *J Prosthet Dent*. 1983;50(5):719–724.

101. Bras J, van Ouij CP, Abraham-Inpijn L, et al. Radiographic interpretation of the mandibular angular cortex: a diagnostic tool in metabolic bone loss. *Oral Surg Oral Med Oral Pathol*. 1982;53(5):541–545.

102. Scileppi KP. Bone and joint disease in the elderly. *Med Clin North Am*. 1983;67(2):517–530.

103. Atwood DA. Reduction of residual ridges: a major oral disease entity. *J Prosthet Dent*. 1971;26(3):266–279.

104. Tallgren A. The continuing reduction of the residual alveolar ridges in complete denture wearers: a mixed-longitudinal study covering 25 years. *J Prosthet Dent*. 1972;27(2):120–132.

105. Kribbs PJ, Chesnutt CH. Osteoporosis and dental osteopenia in the elderly. *Gerodontology*. 1984;3(2):101–106.

106. Wical EE, Swoope CC. Studies of residual ridge resorption, part II: the relationship of dietary calcium and phosphorus to residual ridge resorption. *J Prosthet Dent*. 1974;32(1):13–22.

107. Recker RR, Saville PD, Heaney RP. Effect of estrogens and calcium carbonate on bone loss in postmenopausal women. *Ann Intern Med*. 1977;87(6):649–655.

108. Heaney RP, Gallagher JC, Johnston CC, et al. Calcium nutrition and bone health in the elderly. *Am J Clin Nutr*. 1982;36(suppl 5):986–1013.

109. Jakush J. Diet, nutrition, and oral health: a rational approach for the dental practice. *J Am Dent Assoc*. 1984;109(1):20–32.

110. Goodman CE. Osteoporosis: protective measures of nutrition and exercise. *Geriatrics*. 1985;40(4):59–70.

111. Schamschula RG, Barmes DE. Fluoride and health: dental caries, osteoporosis, and cardiovascular disease. *Annu Rev Nutr*. 1981;1:427–435.

112. Banting DW. Epidemiology of root caries. *Gerodontology*. 1986;5(1):5–11.

113. Katz RV. Assessing root caries in populations: the evolution of the root caries index. *J Public Health Dent*. 1980;40(1):7–16.

114. Banting DW, Ellen RP. Carious lesions on the roots of the teeth: a review for the general practitioner. *J Can Dent Assoc*. 1976;42:496–504.

115. Axelsson P, Lindhe J. Effect of controlled oral hygiene procedures on caries and periodontal disease in adults: results after six years. *J Clin Periodontol*. 1981;8(1):239–248.

116. Beck JD, Hunt RJ, Hand JS, et al. Prevalence of root and coronal caries in a noninstitutionalized older population. *J Am Dent Assoc*. 1985;111(6):964–967.

117. Goldberg J, Tanzer J, Munster E, et al. Cross-sectional clinical evaluation of recurrent enamel caries, restoration of marginal integrity, and oral hygiene status. *J Am Dent Assoc*. 1981; 102(5):635–641.

118. Banting DW, Ellen RP, Fillery ED. Prevalence of root surface caries among institutionalized older persons. *Community Dent Oral Epidemiol*. 1980;8:84–88.

119. Billings RJ, Brown LR, Kaster AG. Contemporary treatment strategies for root surface dental caries. *Gerodontics*. 1985;1(1):20–27.

120. Seichter U. Root surface caries: a critical literature review. *J Am Dent Assoc.* 1987; 115(2):305–310.

121. Yanover L. Root surface caries: epidemiology, etiology, and control. *J Can Dent Assoc.* 1987;53:842–859.

122. Wallace MC, Retief DH, Bradley EL. Prevalence of root caries in a population of older adults. *Gerodontics.* 1988;4(2):84–89.

123. Gustafsson BE, Quensel CE, Lanke LS, et al. The Vipeholm dental caries study: the effect of different levels of carbohydrate intake on caries activity in 436 individuals observed for five years. *Acta Odontol Scand.* 1954;11:232–364.

124. Hix JO, O'Leary TJ. The relationship between cemental caries, oral hygiene status, and fermentable carbohydrate intake. *J Periodontol.* 1976;47(7):398–404.

125. Slome BA. Rampant caries: a side effect of tricyclic antidepressant therapy. *Gen Dent.* 1984;32(6):494–496.

126. Ravald N, Hamp SE. Prediction of root surface caries in patients treated for advanced periodontal disease. *J Clin Periodontol.* 1981;8(5):400–414.

127. Kitamura M, Kiyak HA, Mulligan K. Predictors of root caries in the elderly. *Community Dent Oral Epidemiol.* 1986;14(1):34–38.

128. Arnold FA Jr. Fluorine in drinking water: its effect on dental caries. *J Am Dent Assoc.* 1948;136(1):28–36.

129. Ripa LW. Professionally (operator) applied topical fluoride therapy: a critique. *Clin Prevent Dent.* 1982;4(3):3–10.

130. Dreizen S, Brown LR, Handler S, et al. Radiation-induced xerostomia in cancer patients. *Cancer.* 1976;38(1):273–278.

131. Rothwell BR, Richard EL. Diabetes mellitus: medical and dental considerations. *Spec Care Dent.* 1984;4(2):58–65.

132. Swango PA. The use of topical fluorides to prevent dental caries in adults: a review of the literature. *J Am Dent Assoc.* 1983;107(3):447–450.

133. Burt BA, Ismail AI, Eklund SA. Root caries in an optimally fluoridated and a high fluoride community. *J Dent Res.* 1986;65(9):1154–1158.

134. Ripa LW, Leske GS, Forte F, et al. Effect of a 0.05% neutral NaF mouthrinse on coronal and root caries of adults. *Gerodontology.* 1987;6(4):131–136.

135. Sinkford JC. Oral health problems in the elderly: research recommendations. *Gerodontics.* 1988;4(5):209–211.

136. Newbrun E. Prevention of root caries. *Gerodontology.* 1986;5(1):33–41.

137. Gjermo P. Chlorhexidine in dental practice. *J Clin Periodontol.* 1974;1(3):143–152.

138. Bain MJ. Chlorhexidine in dentistry: a review. *N Z Dent J.* 1980;76:49–54.

139. Tonelli PM, Hume WR, Kenney EB. Chlorhexidine: a review of the literature. *Periodont Abstr.* 1983;31:5–10.

140. Saxton CA, Cowell CR. Clinical investigation of the effects of dentifrices on dentin wear at the cementoenamel junction. *J Am Dent Assoc.* 1981;102(1):38–43.

141. Hand JS, Hunt RJ, Reinhardt JW. The prevalence and treatment implications of cervical abrasion in the elderly. *Gerodontics.* 1986;2(5):167–170.

142. Levine RS. Fruit juice erosion: an increasing danger? *J Dent.* 1974;2(2):85–88.

143. Eccles JD, Jenkins WG. Dental erosion and diet. *J Dent.* 1974;2(4):153–159.

144. Reussner GH, Coccodrilli G Jr, Thiessen R Jr. Effects of phosphates in acid-containing beverages on tooth erosion. *J Dent Res.* 1975;54(2):365–370.

145. Mueninghoff LA, Johnson MH. Erosion: a case caused by unusual diet. *J Am Dent Assoc.* 1982;104(1):51–52.

146. Linkosalo E, Markkanen H. Dental erosions in relation to lactovegetarian diet. *Scand J Dent Res.* 1985;93(5):436–441.

147. White DK, Hayes RC, Benjamin RN. Loss of tooth structure associated with chronic regurgitation and vomiting. *J Am Dent Assoc.* 1978;97(5):833–835.

148. Malcolm D, Paul E. Erosion of the teeth due to sulphuric acid in the battery industry. *Br J Industr Med.* 1961;26:249–266.

149. ten Bruggen Cate HJ. Dental erosion in industry. *Br J Indust Med.* 1968;25:249–266.

150. Levy SM. The epidemiology and prevention of dental caries in adults. *Compend Contin Ed Dent.* 1988;(suppl 11):S390–S398.

151. Hong F, Nu Zhong-ying XX. Clinical classification and therapeutic design of dental cervical abrasion. *Gerodontics.* 1988;4(2):101–103.

152. Hodosh M. A superior desensitizer: potassium nitrate. *J Am Dent Assoc.* 1974;88(4):831–832.

153. Tarbet WJ, Silverman G, Fratarcangelo PA, et al. Home treatment for dentinal hypersensitivity: a comparative study. *J Am Dent Assoc.* 1982;105(2):227–230.

154. Collins JF, Gingold J, Stanley H, et al. Reducing dentinal hypersensitivity with strontium chloride and potassium nitrate. *Gen Dent.* 1984;32(1):40–43.

155. Council on Dental Therapeutics. Acceptance of Promise with fluoride and Sensodyne-F toothpastes for sensitive teeth. *J Am Dent Assoc.* 1986;113(4):673–675.

156. Hoyt WH, Bibby BG. Use of sodium fluoride for desensitizing dentin. *J Am Dent Assoc.* 1943;30(3):1372–1376.

157. Berman LH. Dentinal sensation and hypersensitivity: a review of mechanisms and treatment alternatives. *J Periodontol.* 1985;56(4):216–222.

158. Dayton RE, deMarco TJ, Swedlow D. Treatment of hypersensitive root surfaces with dental adhesive materials. *J Periodontol.* 1974;45(12):873–878.

159. Brekhus PJ. Dental disease and its relation to the loss of human teeth. *J Am Dent Assoc.* 1929;16(12):2237–2247.

160. Allen EF. Statistical study of the primary cause of extractions. *J Dent Res.* 1944;23(6):453–458.

161. Pelton WJ, Pennell EH, Druzina A. Tooth morbidity experience in adults. *J Am Dent Assoc.* 1954;49(4):439–445.

162. Cahen PM, Frank RM, Turlot JC. A survey of the reasons for extractions in France. *J Dent Res.* 1985;64(8):1087–1093.

163. Kay EJ, Blinkerhorn AS. The reasons underlying the extraction of teeth in Scotland. *Br Dent J.* 1986;160(8):287–290.

164. Bailit HL, Braun R, Maryniuk GA, et al. Is periodontal disease the primary cause of tooth extraction? *J Am Dent Assoc.* 1987;114(1):40–45.

165. Niessen LC, Weyant RJ. Causes of tooth loss in a veteran population. *J Public Health Dent.* 1989;49(1):19–23.

166. National Center for Health Statistics. Edentulous persons, US 1971. Baltimore, Md: Health Resources Administration; 1974. US Dept of Health, Education, and Welfare publication series 10, No. 29.

167. Brown LJ, Meskin LH. Sociodemographic differences in tooth loss patterns in United States employed adults and seniors, 1985-1986. *Gerodontics.* 1988;4(6):345–362.

168. Yanover L, Banting D, Grainger R, et al. Effect of a daily 0.2% chlorhexidine rinse on the oral health of an institutionalized elderly population. *J Can Dent Assoc.* 1988;54(8):595–598.

169. Budtz-Jorgenson E, Luan WM, Holm-Pedersen P, et al. Mandibular dysfunction related to dental, occlusal and prosthetic conditions in a selected elderly population. *Gerodontics.* 1985;1(1):28–33.

170. Franks AST. Masticatory muscle hyperactivity and temporomandibular joint dysfunction. *J Prosthet Dent.* 1965;15(6):1122–1131.

171. Hansson T, Nilner M. A study of the occurrence of symptoms of diseases of the TMJ, masticatory masculature and related structures. *J Oral Rehabil.* 1975;2(4):313–324.

172. Greene CS, Marbach JJ. Epidemiologic studies of mandibular dysfunction: a critical review. *J Prosthet Dent.* 1982;48(2):184–190.

173. Rugh JD, Solberg WK. Oral health status in the United States: temporomandibular joint disorders. *J Dent Educ.* 1985;49(6):398–406.

174. Jeanmonod A. The diagnosis and treatment of temporomandibular dysfunctions in older, partially or totally edentulous patients. *Int Dent J.* 1982;32(4):339–344.

175. Helkimo M. Epidemiologic surveys of dysfunction of the masticatory system. *Oral Sci Rev.* 1976;7:54–69.

176. Granados JI. The influence of the loss of teeth and attrition on the articular eminence. *J Prosthet Dent.* 1979;42(1):78–85.

177. Richards LC, Brown T. Dental attrition and degenerative arthritis of the temporomandibular joint. *J Oral Rehabil.* 1981;8:293–307.

178. Nesbit SP, Gobetti JP. Multiple recurrence of oral erythema multiforme after secondary herpes simplex: report of case and review of literature. *J Am Dent Assoc.* 1986;112(3):348–352.

179. Antoon JW, Miller RL. Aphthous ulcers: a review of the literature on etiology, pathogenesis, diagnosis, and treatment. *J Am Dent Assoc.* 1980;101(5):803–808.

180. Wray D, Ferguson MM, Mason DK, et al. Recurrent aphthae: treatment with vitamin B12, folic acid, and iron. *Br Med J.* 1975;2(5969):490–493.

181. Nally FF, Blake GC. Recurrent aphthae: treatment with vitamin B12, folic acid, and iron. *Br Med J.* 1975;3(5798):308.

182. Hay KD, Reade PC. The use of an elimination diet in the treatment of recurrent aphthous ulceration of the oral cavity. *Oral Surg Oral Med Oral Pathol.* 1984;57(5):504–507.

183. Rodu B, Russell CM, Ray KL. Treatment of oral ulcers with hydroxypropyl cellulose film (Zilactin®). *Compend Contin Educ Dent.* 1988;9:420–422.

184. Mackowiak PA. The normal microbial flora. *N Engl J Med.* 1982;307(2):83–93.

185. Borelli D, Fuentes J, Leiderman E, et al. Ketoconazole, an oral antifungal: laboratory and clinical assessment of imidazole drugs. *Postgrad Med J.* 1979;55(647):657–661.

186. Yap BS, Bodey GP. Oropharyngeal candidiasis treated with troche form of clotrimazole. *Arch Intern Med.* 1979;139(6):656–657.

187. Bhaskar SN. *Synopsis of Oral Pathology.* 6th ed. St. Louis, Mo: CV Mosby Co; 1981.

188. Dreizen S. Oral candidiasis. *Am J Med.* 1984;77(4D):28–33.

189. Gallagher FJ, Taybos GM, Terezhalmy GT. Clinical diagnosis and treatment of oral candidiasis. *J Indiana Dent Assoc.* 1985;64(2):26–28.

190. Johnson JD, George DI Jr. Treatment of chronic atrophic oral candidiasis with ketonazole (Nizoral): a case report. *J Oral Med.* 1986;41(3):138–144.

191. Waldron CA, Shafer WG. Leukoplakia revisited: a clinicopathologic study of 3256 oral leukoplakias. *Cancer.* 1975;36(4):1386–1392.

192. Gupta PC. Epidemiologic study of the association between alcohol habits and oral leuko-plakia. *Community Dent Oral Epidemiol*. 1984;12(1):47–50.

193. Christen AG, McDonald JL Jr, Klein JA. A primer of relevant facts for smokers. *Dent Teamwork*. 1989;2(1):25–26.

194. Alexander WN. Oral lesions in the elderly. In: Tryon AF, ed. *Oral Health and Aging*. Littleton, Mass: PSG Publishing Co Inc; 1986.

195. Binnie WH, Wright JM. Oral mucosal disease in the elderly. In: Cohen B, Thomson H, eds. *Dental Care for the Elderly*. London, England: Year Book Medical Publishers Inc; 1986.

196. Silverman S Jr, ed. *Oral Cancer*. 2nd ed. New York, NY: American Cancer Society; 1985.

197. Silverberg E, Boring CC, Squires TS. Cancer statistics, 1990. *CA*. 1990;40(1):9–26.

198. Hill MW, Rowe DJ. Influence of aging on oral cancer. *Dent Hyg*. 1982;56(8):26–30.

199. Little JW, Falace DA. Oral cancer. In: Little JW, Falace DA, eds. *Dental Management of the Medically Compromised Patient*. 3rd ed. St Louis, Mo: CV Mosby Co; 1988.

200. Shedd DP. Clinical characteristics of early oral cancer. *J Am Med Assoc*. 1971; 215(6):955–956.

201. Rothman K, Keller A. The effect of joint exposure of alcohol and tobacco on risk of cancer of the mouth and pharynx. *J Chronic Dis*. 1972;25(12):711–716.

202. Shafer WG, Waldron CA. Erythroplakia of the oral cavity. *Cancer*. 1975;36(3):1021–1028.

203. Mashberg A. Erythroplasia: the earliest sign of asymptomatic oral cancer. *J Am Dent Assoc*. 1978;96(4):615–620.

204. Wynder L, et al. Tobacco and alcohol consumption in relation to the development of multiple primary cancers. *Cancer*. 1977;40(4):1872–1878.

205. Moore C. Smoking and mouth-throat cancer. Am J Surg. 1964;108(4):565–569.

206. Silverman S Jr, Griffith M. Smoking characteristics of patients with oral carcinoma and the risk for second oral primary carcinoma. *J Am Dent Assoc*. 1972;85(3):637–640.

207. Williams RR, Horm JW. Association of cancer sites with tobacco and alcohol consumption and socioeconomic status of patients: interview study from the Third National Cancer Survey. *J Natl Cancer Inst*. 1977;58(3):525–547.

208. Mashberg A, Garfinkel L, Harris S. Alcohol as a primary risk factor in oral squamous carcinoma. *CA*. 1981;31(3):146–155.

209. Elwood JM, Pearson JC, Skippen DH, et al. Alcohol, smoking, social and occupational factors in the aetiology of cancer of the oral cavity, pharynx and larynx. *Int J Cancer*. 1984; 34(5):603–612.

210. Brugere J, Guenel P, Leclerc A, et al. Differential effects of tobacco and alcohol in cancer of the larynx, pharynx, and mouth. *Cancer*. 1986;57(2):391–395.

211. Rothman KJ. The proportion of cancer attributable to alcohol consumption. *Prev Med*. 1980;9(2):174–179.

212. Einhorn J, Wersall J. Incidence of oral carcinoma in patients with leukoplakia of the oral mucosa. *Cancer*. 1967;20(12):2189–2193.

213. Squier CA. Smokeless tobacco and oral cancer: a cause for concern? *CA*. 1984;34(5):242–247.

214. Shi HB, Xu GQ, Shen ZY. A retrospective study of oral mucosal diseases in three age groups. *Gerondontics*. 1988;4(5):235–237.

215. Lindqvist C, Teppo L. Epidemiological evaluation of sunlight as a risk factor of lip cancer. *Br J Cancer*. 1978;37(6):983–989.

216. Silverman S Jr, Gorsky M. Epidemiologic and demographic update in oral cancer: California and national data—1973 to 1985. *J Am Dent Assoc*. 1990;120(5):495–499.

217. Peterson DE. Oral mucosal ulcerative lesions. *Pharmacol Dent*. 1986;2(4):1–4.

218. Greer RO. A problem-oriented approach to evaluating common mucosal lesions in the geriatric patient: a survey of 593 lesions in patients over 60 years of age. *Gerodontics*. 1985;1(2):68–74.

219. Ghamrawy EE. Quantitative changes in dental plaque formation related to removable partial dentures. *J Oral Rehabil*. 1976;3:115–120.

220. Brill N, Tryde G, Stoltze K, et al. Ecologic changes in the oral cavity caused by removable partial dentures. *J Prosthet Dent*. 1977;38(2):138–148.

221. Chandler JA, Brudvik JS. Clinical evaluation of patients eight to nine years after placement of removable partial dentures. *J Prosthet Dent*. 1984;51(6):736–743.

222. Rissin L, House JE, Conway C, et al. Effect of age and removable partial dentures on gingivitis and periodontal disease. *J Prosthet Dent*. 1979;42(2):217–223.

223. Budtz-Jorgenson E. Clinical aspects of Candida infection in denture wearers. *J Am Dent Assoc*. 1978;96(3):474–479.

224. Lambert JP, Kolstad R. Effect of a benzoic acid-detergent germicide on denture-borne Candida albicans. *J Prosthet Dent*. 1986;55(6):699–700.

225. Budtz-Jorgensen E, Loe H. Chlorhexidine as a denture disinfectant in the treatment of denture stomatitis. *Scand J Dent Res*. 1972;80:457–464.

226. Nater JP, Groenman NH, Wakkers-Garritsen BG, et al. Etiologic factors in denture sore mouth syndrome. *J Prosthet Dent*. 1978;40(4):367–373.

227. Koopmans ASF, Kippuw N, de Graaff J. Bacterial involvement in denture-induced stomatitis. *J Dent Res*. 1988;67(9):1246–1250.

228. Bastian RJ. Denture sore mouth, aetiological aspects and treatment. *Aust Dent J*. 1976;21:375–382.

229. Arendorf TM, Walker DM. Oral candidal populations in health and disease. *Br Dent J*. 1979;147:267–272.

230. Williams RC. Periodontal disease. *N Engl J Med*. 1990;322(6):373–382.

231. Schei O, Waerhaug J, Lovdal A, et al. Alveolar bone loss as related to hygiene and age. *J Periodontol*. 1959;30(1):7–16.

232. Anderson DL. Periodontal disease and aging. *Gerodontology*. 1982;1(1):19–23.

233. Douglass CW, Gillings D, Sollecito W, et al. National trends in the prevalence and severity of the periodontal diseases. *J Am Dent Assoc*. 1983;107(3):403–412.

234. Page RC. Periodontal diseases in the elderly: a critical evaluation of current information. *Gerodontology*. 1984;3(1):63–70.

235. Holm-Pedersen P, Agerbaek N, Theilade E. Experimental gingivitis in young and elderly individuals. *J Clin Periodontol*. 1975;2(1):14–24.

236. Glickman I, Smulow JB. The combined effects of inflammation and trauma from occlusion in periodontitis. *Int Dent J*. 1969;19:393–407.

237. Ramfjord SP, Ash MM. Significance of occlusion in the etiology and treatment of early, moderate, and advanced periodontitis. *J Periodontol*. 1981;52(9):511–516.

238. Axelsson P, Lindhe J. Effect of controlled oral hygiene procedures on caries and periodontal disease in adults. *J Clin Periodontol*. 1978;5:133–151.

239. Axelsson P, Lindhe J. The significance of maintenance care in the treatment of periodontal disease. *J Clin Periodontol*. 1981;8:281–294.

240. Lindhe J, Haffajee AD, Socransky SS. Progression of periodontal disease in adult subjects in the absence of periodontal therapy. *J Clin Periodontol.* 1983;10:433–442.

241. Lindhe J, Nyman S. The effect of plaque control and surgical pocket elimination on the establishment and maintenance of periodontal health: a longitudinal study of periodontal therapy in cases of advanced periodontitis. *J Clin Periodontol.* 1975;2:67–79.

242. Schmitt RJ, Sheridan PJ, Rogers RS III. Pernicious anemia with associated glossodynia. *J Am Dent Assoc.* 1988;117(6):838–840.

243. Powell FC. Glossodynia and other disorders of the tongue. *Dermatol Clin.* 1987; 5(10):687–693.

244. Hill JH, Deitch RL. Early detection of cancers of the head and neck. *VA Pract.* 1986; 2(9):57–72.

245. Venus CA. Interacting with patients who have communication disorders. *Tex Dent J.* 1990;107(2):11–16.

246. Zimmerman JE, Oder LA. Swallowing dysfunction in acutely ill patients. *Phys Ther.* 1981;61(12):1755–17.

247. Watanabe I, Sato M, Yamane H, et al. Oral dyskinesia of the aged, I: clinical aspects. *Gerodontics.* 1985;1(1):39–43.

248. Watanabe I, Yamane G, Yamane H, et al. Oral dyskinesia of the aged, II: electromyographic appearances and dental treatment. *Gerodontics.* 1988;4(6):310–314.

249. Altrocchi PH. Spontaneous oral-facial dyskinesia. *Arch Neurol.* 1972;26(6):506–512.

250. Pakkenberg H, Fog R. Spontaneous oral dyskinesia. *Arch Neurol.* 1974;31(5):352–353.

251. Altrocchi PH, Forno LS. Spontaneous oralfacial dyskinesia: neuropathology of a case. *Neurology.* 1983;33(6):802–805.

252. Sutcher HD, Underwood RB, Beatty RA, et al. Orofacial dyskinesia: a dental dimension. *J Am Med Assoc.* 1971;216(9):1459–1463.

253. Crane GE. Tardive dyskinesia in patients treated with major neuroleptics: a review of the literature. *Am J Psychiatry.* 1968;124(suppl 8):40–48.

254. Kamen S. Tardive dyskinesia: a significant syndrome for geriatric dentistry. *Oral Surg Oral Med Oral Pathol.* 1975;39(1):52–57.

255. Portnoi VA, Johnson JE. Tardive dyskinesia. *Geriatr Nurs (New York).* 1982;3(1):39–41.

256. Nishioka GJ, Montgomery MT. Masticatory muscle hyperactivity in temporomandibular disorders: is it an extrapyramidally expressed disorder? *J Am Dent Assoc.* 1988;116(4):514–520.

257. Eneroth CM. Salivary gland tumors in the parotid gland, submandibular gland, and the palate region. *Cancer.* 1971;27(6):1415–1418.

258. Richardson GS, Dickason WL, Gaisford JC, et al. Tumors of salivary glands: an analysis of 752 cases. *Plast Reconstr Surg.* 1975;55(2):131–138.

259. Eveson JW, Cawson RA. Salivary gland tumours: a review of 2410 cases with particular reference to histological types, site, age and sex distribution. *J Pathol.* 1985;146(1):51–58.

260. Eveson JW, Cawson RA. Tumours of the minor (oropharyngeal) salivary glands: a demographic study of 336 cases. *J Oral Pathol.* 1985;14(6):500–509.

261. Sener SF, Scanlon EF. Irradiation induced salivary gland neoplasia. *Ann Surg.* 1980;191(3):304–306.

262. McKenna RJ. Tumors of the major and minor salivary glands. *CA.* 1984;34(1):24–39.

263. Mandel I. Relation of saliva and plaque to caries. *J Dent Res.* 1974;53(suppl 2):246–266.

264. Ettinger RL. Xerostomia: a complication of aging. *Aust Dent J.* 1981;26:365–371.

265. Dove J, Sheridan P. Advances in dental research: pilocarpine used to stimulate normal saliva production. *J Am Dent Assoc*. 1985;111(2):310.

266. Atkinson JC, Fox PC. Clinical pathology conference: xerostomia. *Gerodontics*. 1986; 2(6):193–197.

267. Niessen LC, Jones JA. Professional dental care for patients with dementia. *Gerodontology*. 1987;6(2):67–71.

268. Lloyd PM. Xerostomia: not a phenomenon of aging. *Wis Med J*. 1983;82(9):21–22.

269. Jolly DE, Paulson RB, Paulson GW, et al. Parkinson's disease: a review and recommendations for dental management. *Spec Care Dent*. 1989;9(3):74–78.

270. Kelly JF, Winograd CH. A functional approach to stroke management in elderly patients. *J Am Geriatr Soc*. 1985;33(1):48–60.

271. Rosenbaum CH. Did you treat a drug addict today? *Int Dent J*. 1981;31(4):307–312.

272. Chiodo GT, Rosenstein DI. Cocaine use and dental treatment. *Gen Dent*. 1986; 34(3):218–219.

273. Verlander JM, Johns ME. The clinical use of cocaine. *Otolaryngol Clin North Am*. 1981;14(3):521–531.

274. Rappaport A. Dental management of the drug abuser. *N Y State Dent J*. 1972; 38(8):485–491.

275. Carter EF. Dental implications of narcotic addiction. *Aust Dent J*. 1978;23:308–310.

276. Friedlander AH, Mills MJ. The dental management of the drug-dependent patient. *Oral Surg Oral Med Oral Pathol*. 1985;60(5):489–492.

277. McBean LD, Speckmann EW. A review: the importance of nutrition in oral health. *J Am Dent Assoc*. 1974;89(1):109–114.

278. DePaola DP, Kuftinec MN. Nutrition in growth and development of oral tissues. *Dent Clin North Am*. 1976;20(3):441–459.

279. Alfano MC. Diet and nutrition in the etiology and prevention of oral disease. *J Dent Res*. 1980;59(DII):2194–2202.

280. Carlsson J, Egelberg J. Effect of diet on early plaque formation in man. *Odontol Revy*. 1965;16:112–125.

281. Johansson I, Ericson T, Steen L. Studies of the effect of diet on saliva secretion and caries development: the effect of fasting on saliva composition of female subjects. *J Nutr*. 1984; 114(11):2010–2020.

282. Brown AT. The role of dietary carbohydrates in plaque formation and oral disease. *Nutr Rev*. 1975;33(12):353–361.

283. Theilade E, Theilade T. Role of plaque in the etiology of periodontal disease and caries. *Oral Sci Rev*. 1976;9:23–63.

284. Gibbons RJ, van Houte J. Dental caries. *Annu Rev Med*. 1975;26:121–136.

285. Marthaler TM, Froesch ER. Hereditary fructose intolerance: dental status of eight patients. *Br Dent J*. 1967;123:597–000.

286. Englander HR. Anticaries and antiplaque agents. In: Neidel EA, Kroeger DC, Yagiela JA, eds. *Pharmacology and Therapeutics for Dentistry*. St Louis, Mo: CV Mosby Co; 1980.

287. Binns NM. Caries and carbohydrates: a problem for dentists and nutritionists. *Dent Health*. 1981;20(4):5–10.

288. Anonymous. Snacks and caries. *Nutr Rev*. 1987;45(6):169–172.

289. Scheinen A, Makinen KK. The Turku sugar studies I-XXI. *Acta Odontol Scand*. 1974; 32:383–412.

290. Katz S. A diet counseling program. *J Am Dent Assoc.* 1981;102(6):840–845.

291. Falender LG, Leban SG, Williams FA. Postoperative nutritional support in oral and maxillofacial surgery. *J Oral Maxillofac Surg.* 1987;45(4):324–330.

292. Newbrun E. Sucrose, the arch criminal of dental caries. *Odontol Revy.* 1967;18:373–386.

293. Sheiham A. Sucrose and dental caries. *Nutr Health.* 1987;5(1–2):25–29.

294. Makinen KK. The role of sucrose and other sugars in the development of dental caries: a review. *Int Dent J.* 1972;22:363–386.

295. Schachtele CF, Jensen ME. Comparison of methods for monitoring changes in the pH of human dental plaque. *J Dent Res.* 1982;61(10):1117–1125.

296. Mormann JE, Muhlemann HR. Oral starch degradation and its influence on acid production in human dental plaque. *Caries Res.* 1981;15:166–175.

297. Jensen ME, Schachtele CF. The acidogenic potential of reference foods and snacks at interproximal sites in the human dentition. *J Dent. Res.* 1983;62(8):889–892.

298. de Stoppelaar JD, van Houte J, Backer-Dirks O. The effect of carbohydrate restriction on the presence of Streptococcus mutans, Streptococcus sanguis and iodophilic polysaccharide-producing bacteria in human dental plaque. *Caries Res.* 1970;4:114–123.

299. Firestone A, Imfeld T, Schmid R, et al. Cariogenicity of foods. *J Am Dent Assoc.* 1980;101(3):443–444.

300. Mandel ID. Effectiveness of biomedical and biosocial research on improving oral health. *J Public Health Dent.* 1978;38:312–000.

301. Shaw JH. Dietary considerations in oral health. *Fam Community Health.* 1980;3(3):51–60.

302. Papas A, Palmer C, McGandy R, et al. Dietary and nutritional factors in relation to dental caries in elderly subjects. *Gerodontics.* 1987;3(1):30–37.

303. Council on Dental Therapeutics. Consensus: oral health effects of products that increase salivary flow rate. *J Am Dent Assoc.* 1988;116(5):757–759.

304. Hefferren JJ, Harper DS, Osborn JC. Foods, consumption factors and dental caries. *Gerodontics.* 1987;3(1):26–29.

305. Bibby BG, Mundorff SA, Zero DT, et al. Oral food clearance and the pH of plaque and saliva. *J Am Dent Assoc.* 1986;112(3):333–337.

306. Lundquist C. Oral sugar clearance: its influence on dental caries activity. *Odontol Revy.* 1952;3(suppl 1):121–123.

307. Jenkins GN, Kleinberg I. Studies on the pH of plaque in interproximal areas after eating sweets and starch foods. *J Dent Res.* 1956;35:964. Abstract 24.

308. Ludwig TG, Bibby BG. Acid production from different carbohydrate foods in plaque and saliva. *J Dent Res.* 1957;36(1):56–60.

309. Roberts IF, Roberts GJ. Relation of medicines sweetened with sucrose and dental disease. *Br Med J.* 1979;2(6181):14–16.

310. Lokken P, Birkeland JM, Sannes E. pH changes in dental plaque caused by sweetened, iron-containing liquid medicine. *Scand J Dent Res.* 1975;83:279–283.

311. Feigal RJ, Jensen ME. The cariogenic potential of liquid medications: a concern for the handicapped patient. *Spec Care Dent.* 1982;2(1):20–24.

312. Matsukobo T, Myake S, Takaesu Y. Evaluation of aspartame as a non-cariogenic sweetener. *Clin Nutr.* 1984;65:193–196.

313. Alfin-Slater RB, Pi-Sunyer FX. Sugar and sugar susbstitutes: comparisons and indications. *Postgrad Med.* 1987;82(2):46–56.

314. Glass RL. A two-year clinical trial of sorbitol chewing gum. *Caries Res.* 1983;17:365–368.

315. Birkhed D, Edwardsson S, Kalfas S, et al. Cariogenicity of sorbitol. *Swed Dent J.* 1984;8:147–154.

316. Jensen ME. Responses of interproximal plaque pH to snack foods and effect of chewing sorbitol-containing gum. *J Am Dent Assoc.* 1986;113(2):262–266.

317. Spolsky VW, Wolinsky L. The relationship between nutrition and diet and dental caries/periodontal disease. *J Calif Dent Assoc.* 1984;12(9):12–18.

318. Alfano MC. Controversies, perspectives and clinical implications of nutrition in periodontal disease. *Dent Clin North Am.* 1976;20(3):519–548.

319. Slavkin HC. The aging process and nutrition: conception to senescence. *Spec Care Dent.* 1981;1(1):31–36.

320. Stahl SS. Nutritional influences on periodontal disease. *World Rev Nutr Diet.* 1971; 13:277–299.

321. Suomi JD. Prevention and control of periodontal disease. *J Am Dent Assoc.* 1971; 83(6):1271–1287.

322. Charbeneau TD, Hurt WC. Gingival findings in spontaneous scurvy: a case report. *J Periodontol.* 1983;54(11):694–697.

323. Marshall J, Graham S, Mettlin C, et al. Diet in the epidemiology of oral cancer. *Nutr Cancer.* 1982;3(3):145–149.

324. Winn DM, Ziegler RG, Pickle LW, et al. Diet in the etiology of oral and pharyngeal cancer among women from the southern United States. *Cancer Res.* 1984;44(3):1216–1222.

325. Dreizen S. Nutrition and aging. *Spec Care Dent.* 1982;2(6):263–267.

326. Massler M. Influence of diet on denture-bearing tissues. *Dent Clin North Am.* 1984; 28(2):211–221.

327. Dawes C. Effects of diet on salivary secretion and composition. *J Dent Res.* 1970; 49(suppl 6):1263–1272.

328. Buchner A, Screebny LM. Enlargement of salivary glands: review of the literature. *Oral Surg Oral Med Oral Pathol.* 1972;34(2):209–222.

329. Enwonwu CO. Biochemical and morphologic changes in rat mandibular gland in experimental protein-calorie malnutrition. *Exp Mol Pathol.* 1972;16(3):244–269.

330. Cutter CR. Nutrition in the advanced years. *J Tex Dent Hyg Assoc.* 1979;17(2):5–7.

331. Nakamoto T, Mallek HM. Significance of protein-energy malnutrition in dentistry: some suggestions for the profession. *J Am Dent Assoc.* 1980;100(3):339–342.

332. Nizel AE. Role of nutrition in the oral health of the aging patient. *Dent Clin North Am.* 1976;20(3):569–584.

333. Heath MR. Dietary selection by elderly persons, related to dental state. *Br Dent J.* 1972;132(4):145–148.

334. Epstein S. Importance of psychosocial and behavioral factors in food ingestion in the elderly and their ramifications on oral health. *Gerodontics.* 1987;3(1):23–25.

335. Manly RS, Braley LC. Masticatory performance and efficiency. *J Dent Res.* 1950; 29(4):448–462.

336. Manly RS, Shiere FR. The effect of dental deficiency on mastication and food preference. *Oral Surg Oral Med Oral Pathol.* 1950;3:674–685.

337. Yurkstas AA. The effect of missing teeth on masticatory performance and efficiency. *J Prosthet Dent.* 1954;4(1):120–123.

338. Helkimo E, Carlsson GE, Helkimo M. Chewing efficiency and state of dentition: a methodological study. *Acta Odontol Scand.* 1978;36(1):33–41.

339. Wayler AH, Kapur KK, Feldman RS, et al. Effects of age and dentition status on measures of food acceptability. *J Gerontol.* 1982;37(3):294–299.

340. Wayler AH, Chauncey HH. Impact of complete dentures and impaired natural dentition on masticatory performance and food choice in healthy aging men. *J Prosthet Dent.* 1983;49(3):427–433.

341. Oosterhaven SP, Westert GP, Schaub RMH, et al. Social and psychologic implications of missing teeth for chewing ability. *Community Dent Oral Epidemiol.* 1988;16(2):79–82.

342. Mumma RD Jr, Quinton K. Effect of masticatory efficiency on the occurrence of gastric distress. *J Dent Res.* 1970;49(1):69–74.

343. Jenike MA. Tardive dyskinesia: special risk in the elderly. *J Am Geriatr Soc.* 1983;31(2):71–73.

344. Yurkstas AA. The masticatory act: a review. *J Prosthet Dent.* 1965;15(2):248–260.

345. Berry WTC. Mastication, food, and nutrition. *Dent Pract Dent Rec.* 1972;22(7):249–253.

346. Hartsook EI. Food selection, dietary adequacy, and related dental problems of patients with dental prostheses. *J Prosthet Dent.* 1974;32(1):32–40.

347. Yurkstas AA, Manly RS. Value of different test foods in estimating masticatory ability. *J Appl Physiol.* 1950;3(1):45–53.

348. Yurkstas AA, Emerson WH. Dietary selections of persons with natural and artificial teeth. *J Prosthet Dent.* 1964;14(4):695–697.

349. Chauncey HH, House JE. Dental problems in the elderly. *Hosp Pract.* 1977;12(12):81–86.

350. Osterberg T, Steen B. Relationship between dental state and dietary intake in 70-year-old males and females in Goteborg, Sweden: a population study. *J Oral Rehabil.* 1982;9(6):509–521.

351. Chen MK, Lowenstein F. Masticatory handicap, socioeconomic status, and chronic conditions among adults. *J Am Dent Assoc.* 1984;109(6):916–918.

352. Sastry RS. Nutrition study, III: nutritional status of edentulous patients subsequent to complete denture treatment. *J Indian Dent Assoc.* 1984;56(4):145–147.

353. Ramsey WO. Nutritional problems of the aged. *J Prosthet Dent.* 1983;49(1):16–19.

354. Neill DJ, Phillips HI. The masticatory performance and dietary intake of elderly edentulous patients. *Dent Pract.* 1972;22:384–389.

355. Baxter JC. The nutritional intake of geriatric patients with varied dentitions. *J Prosthet Dent.* 1984;51(2):164–168.

356. Rodriquez-Olleros A. Gastritis in the toothless. *Rev Gastroenterol.* 1947;14(3):180–186.

357. Neill DJ, Philips HIB. The masticatory performance, dental state and dietary intakes of a group of elderly army pensioners. *Br Dent J.* 1970;128:581–585.

358. Hunt RJ, Beck JD, Lemke JH, et al. Edentulism and oral health problems among elderly rural Iowans: the Iowa 65 + rural health study. *Am J Public Health.* 1985;75(10):1177–1181.

359. Kapur KK. Optimum dentition in the elderly. In: Chauncey HH, Epstein S, Rose CL, et al, eds. *Clinical Geriatric Dentistry: Biomedical and Psychosocial Aspects.* Chicago, Ill: American Dental Association; 1985.

360. Anderson EL. Eating patterns before and after dentures. *J Am Diet Assoc.* 1971;58(5):421–426.

361. Baxter CJ. Nutrition and the geriatric edentulous patient. *Spec Care Dent.* 1981;1(6):259–261.

362. Straus R, Sandifur JC, Hall DS, et al. Behavioral factors and denture status. *J Prosthet Dent.* 1977;37(3):264–273.

363. Smith JM. Oral and dental discomfort: a necessary feature of old age? *Age Ageing.* 1979;8(1):25–31.

364. Manly RS, Vinton P. A survey of the chewing ability of denture wearers. *J Dent Res.* 1951;30(1):314–321.

365. Abel LF, Manly RS. Masticatory function of partial denture patients among Navy personnel. *J Prosthet Dent.* 1953;3(3):382–392.

366. Yurkstas AA, Emerson WH. Decreased masticatory function in denture patients. *J Prosthet Dent.* 1964;14(5):931–934.

367. Heath MR. The effect of maximum biting force and bone loss upon masticatory function and dietary selection of the elderly. *Int Dent J.* 1982;32(4):345–356.

368. Chauncey HH, Muench ME, Kapur KK, et al. The effect of the loss of teeth on diet and nutrition. *Int Dent J.* 1984;34(2):98–104.

369. Wayler AH, Muench ME, Kapur KK, et al. Masticatory performance and food acceptability in persons with removable partial dentures, full dentures and intact natural dentition. *J Gerontol.* 1984;39(3):284–289.

370. Carlsson GE. Masticatory efficiency: the effect of age, the loss of teeth and prosthetic rehabilitation. *Int Dent J.* 1984;34(2):93–97.

371. Kapur KK, Soman SD. Masticatory performance and efficiency in denture wearers. *J Prosthet Dent.* 1964;14(4):687–694.

372. Kapur KK, Soman SD, Yurkstas A. Test foods for measuring masticatory performance of denture wearers. *J Prosthet Dent.* 1964;14(3):483–491.

373. Haraldson T, Karlsson U, Carlsson GE. Bite force and oral function in complete denture wearers. *J Oral Rehabil.* 1979;6(1):41–48.

374. Farrell JH. The effect of mastication on the digestion of food. *Br Dent J.* 1956; 100(6):149–155.

375. Idowu AT, Handelman SL, Graser GN. Effect of denture stability, retention, and tooth form on masticatory function in the elderly. *Gerodontics.* 1987;3(4):161–164.

376. Ettinger RL. Diet, nutrition, and masticatory ability in a group of elderly edentulous patients. *Aust Dent J.* 1973;18:12–19.

377. Manley RS, Vinton P. A survey of the chewing ability of denture wearers. *J Dent Res.* 1951;30(6):316–321.

378. Farrell JH. Biological aspects of prosthetic dentistry: masticatory effects in patients with and without dentures. *Int Den J.* 1964;14:226–237.

379. Ann L. Biting forces in edentulous patients. *Malays Dent J.* 1966;6:18–31.

380. Bunker PG. The role of dentistry in problems of foreign bodies in the air and food passages. *J Am Dent Assoc.* 1962;64(6):782–787.

381. Wengraf C. Pharyngo-esophageal foreign bodies in denture wearers. *Dent Pract.* 1969; 19:281–282.

382. Anderson DL. Death from improper mastication. *Int Dent J.* 1977;27(4):349–354.

383. Baxter CJ. The nutritional intake of complete denture patients: a computerized study. *J Indiana Dent Soc.* 1980;59(1):14–17.

384. Renaud M, Mercier P, Vinet A. Does the rehabilitation of the masticatory function influence the nutritive value of the diet? *St Marys Hosp Med Bull.* 1982;24:186.

385. Gunne HS, Wall AK. The effect of new complete dentures on mastication and dietary intake. *Acta Odontol Scand.* 1985;43(5):257–268.

386. Gunne HS. The effect of removable partial dentures on mastication and dietary intake. *Acta Odontol Scand.* 1985;43(5):269–278.

387. Rosenstein DI, Chiodo G, Ho JW, et al. Effect of proper dentures on nutritional status. *Gen Dent.* 1988;36(2):127–129.

388. Elmstahl S, Birkhed D, Christiansson U, et al. Intake of energy and nutrients before and after dental treatment in geriatric long-stay patients. *Gerodontics.* 1988;4(1):6–12.

389. Vinton P, Manly RS. Masticatory efficiency during the period of adjustment to dentures. *J Prosthet Dent.* 1955;5(4):477–480.

390. Agerberg G, Carlsson GE. Chewing ability in relation to dental and general health: analyses of data obtained from a questionnaire. *Acta Odontol Scand.* 1981;39:147–153.

391. Lappalainen R, Nyyssonen V. Self-assessed chewing ability of Finnish adults with removable dentures. *Gerodontics.* 1987;3(6):238–241.

392. Ekelund R. Dental state and subjective chewing ability of institutionalized elderly people. *Community Dent Oral Epidemiol.* 1989;17(1):24–27.

393. Gordon SR, Kelley SL, Sybyl JR, et al. Relationship in very elderly veterans of nutritional status, self-perceived chewing ability, dental status, and social isolation. *J Am Geriatr Soc.* 1985;33(5):334–339.

394. Chencharick JD, Mossman KL. Nutritional consequences of the radiotherapy of head and neck cancer. *Cancer.* 1983;51(5):811–815.

395. Locker D, Grushka M. The impact of dental and facial pain. *J Dent Res.* 1987; 66(9):1414–1417.

396. Fattore LD, Baer R, Olsen R. The role of the general dentist in the treatment and management of oral complications of chemotherapy. *Gen Dent.* 1987;35(5):374–377.

397. Cohen T, Gitman L. Oral complaints and taste perception in the aged. *J Gerontol.* 1959;14(3):294–298.

398. Schiffman SS, Moss J, Erickson RP. Thresholds of food odors in the elderly. *Exp Aging Res.* 1976;2(5):389–398.

399. Vissink A, Schaub RMH, van Rijn LJ, et al. The efficacy of mucin-containing artificial saliva in alleviating symptoms of xerostomia. *Gerodontology.* 1987;6(3):95–101.

400. Moeller TP. Sensory changes in the elderly. *Dent Clin North Am.* 1989;33(1):23–31.

401. Corso JF. The sensory effects of aging on man. *Scientia.* 1968;103:362–393.

402. Corso JF. Sensory processes and age effects in normal adults. *J Gerontol.* 1971;26(1):90–105.

403. Henkin RI, Christiansen RL. Taste thresholds in patients with dentures. *J Am Dent Assoc.* 1967;75(1):118–120.

404. Chauncey HH, Wayler AH. The modifying influence of age on taste perception. *Spec Care Dent.* 1981;1(2):68–74.

405. Henkin RI, Christiansen RL. Taste localization on the tongue, palate, and pharynx of normal man. *J Appl Physiol.* 1967;22(2):316–320.

406. Giddon DB, Dreisbach ME, Pfaffman C, et al. Relative abilities of natural and artificial dentition patients for judging the sweetness of solid foods. *J Prosthet Dent.* 1954;4(2):263–268.

Chapter 7

The Aging Gut

Michael D. Cashman

Form and function change in the aged, but because of the functional reserve of most organ systems, changes may not be evident except during stress associated with disease. Function declines with age in various organ systems, but at different rates, and the potential for organ system interaction is high. Sometimes abnormalities are obvious, but nutritional and gut changes are often occult. Organ failure often leads to impaired nutrition because of poor intake, altered metabolic rate, and altered nutritional requirements. Malnutrition contributes to progression of organ failure, making nutrition an important element in the design of treatment.

AGING AND THE GASTROINTESTINAL SYSTEM

Little is known about the morphologic and functional changes of the gastrointestinal system with aging. Available information is mostly derived from studies involving institutionalized subjects. Because of technical limitations associated with the clinical evaluation of gastrointestinal function to differentiate wellness and disease, it is difficult to measure smaller changes of function in a general population. Tests designed to diagnose disease may not be sensitive enough for the study of normal aging, whereas others may be too sensitive and have no clinical or nutritional significance. Contrary to several other organ systems, many more variables affect optimal function of the gastrointestinal tract. Furthermore, the heterogeneity of the elderly population in response to aging, disease, and medications makes the evaluations difficult.

The functional reserve of the gastrointestinal system is greatest in the midgut, pancreas, and liver. This severely limits the clinical significance of observations that suggest less than substantial loss of function. Intestinal segments may adapt, and functional reserves tend to buffer change so that only long-term observations can uncover abnormalities. This is less true for the proximal and distal portions of the gut. Esophageal and gastric disorders usually lead to symptoms associated with eating, whereas colon problems cause difficulties with evacuation. Common gastrointestinal symptoms are often nonspecific and do not indicate the exact nature or severity of disease. Clinical skills are necessary to diagnose these disorders, prognosticate, and prescribe treatment.

This chapter provides a practical view of the impact of aging on normal gastrointestinal function and suggests the implications of common chronic conditions—and altered nutritional requirements—brought about by these changes. In a system that is longitudinally organized, the large number of functions occurring on an autonomic basis makes simplified, standard approaches to feeding for the treatment of disturbed function poorly founded at best and dangerous at worst. This chapter describes some of the complex interrelationships confronting the nutritionist involved in the care and feeding of elderly people.

ESOPHAGUS

Swallowing functions of the oropharynx and esophagus involve the transport of food from mouth to stomach, while preventing nasal reflux, tracheal aspiration, and gastroesophageal reflux. Impaired swallowing is common in elderly individuals, but available evidence indicates that this is due more to the effects of associated diseases than to the intrinsic effects of aging per se. Dysphagia and eating dependence can have a profound impact on nutrition. Common disorders result in malnutrition because of oropharyngeal and esophageal dysphagia. Gastroesophageal reflux frequently is symptomatic and also can lead to dysphagic problems. Symptoms of esophageal dysfunction in elderly people may be difficult to recognize, as they are often atypical and vague, and may not suggest an esophageal problem.[1]

Incidence and Character of Feeding/Swallowing Disorders

The incidence of eating disability in elderly nursing home residents may reach 50%.[2] In such patients, findings of dysphagia are often accompanied by a higher incidence of pneumonia caused by gram-negative microorganisms.[3,4] In an elegant study of nursing home patients, Siebns and colleagues[2] evaluated eating dependence, defined as an impairment of the five components of eating, including behavioral and cognitive ability to recognize food and eat it, normal upper extremity function, oral phase of swallowing, pharyngeal phase of swallowing, and esophageal phase of swallowing. Dependent patients who required physical assistance with eating comprised 32% of the nursing home population. Only 25% ate regular diets, and they demonstrated a higher prevalence of abnormal oral-stage swallowing behavior, including spitting, choking, inability to chew, drooling, nasal regurgitation, squirreling food (retaining food in the buccal pouch), delayed swallowing, and overstuffing of the mouth. Signs of abnormal pharyngeal swallowing included coughing during meals or while drinking, choking during meals, and speaking in a wet-sounding voice. A large portion of the dependent eaters could not be tested for gag reflex or voice quality because they would not or could not follow instructions. Mortality rates were higher in the dependent eaters. These findings, and the results of nursing care in these patients, which were not correlated with weight loss during a 3-month period, suggest that simple bedside observations are effective in identifying this basic clinical problem.

Symptoms of dysphagia may occur in diverse elderly populations in the presence of a cerebrovascular accident (CVA), head and neck surgery, and progressive neurologic disease. Warning signs include a confused mental state that may interfere with the complex sensory and motor functions of eating; dysarthric speech due to weakness or poor control of muscles common to both speech and swallowing; excessive drooling, which can follow neuromuscular impairment of these same mechanisms; coughing and choking on food or sputum; excessive time to consume a meal; unexplained weight loss; difficulty in chewing; pain with swallowing; or lodgment of food. In spite of these correlates it is important to recognize the extensive differential diagnosis for pharyngeal and esophageal dysphagia, some of which represent reversible, treatable lesions.[5] (Figure 7-1).

OROPHARYNGEAL
Cerebrovascular Accident
Neoplasia
Zenkers Diverticulum
Cricopharyngeal Spasm

ESOPHAGEAL
Stricture
Spasm
Neoplasia
Hiatal Hernia
Esophagitis

Figure 7-1 Causes of dysphagia.

Oropharyngeal Physiology

There are three phases to swallowing: oral, pharyngeal, and esophageal. Together the first two take less than 2 seconds; the third takes 3 to 7 seconds. The first two phases involve oropharyngeal transfer. The oral phase begins with the lips closed and the tip of the tongue contacting the upper mouth structure. The tongue is then elevated while a slight elevation of the larynx occurs, resulting in a progressive stripping of the bolus against the hard palate and the tongue into the pharynx. This first phase of swallowing is under voluntary control.

The pharyngeal phase is the most complex neuromuscular aspect of swallowing. The bolus is projected into the esophagus while the airway is protected. When pharyngeal sensation is intact, the medullary swallowing center controls cranial nerve motor impulses, which close the velopharyngeal valve, elevate the larynx, and relax the upper esophageal sphincter. As the bolus passes the upper esophageal sphincter, the vocal cords close and the base of the tongue is forced against the posterior pharyngeal wall. At the conclusion of the pharyngeal phase of swallowing there is forceful contraction of the pharyngeal constrictors followed by descent of the larynx and contraction of the upper esophageal sphincter.[6]

Assessment of Oropharyngeal Function

Oropharyngeal function is assessed by history and observation. Careful observation of the patient's eating will make the magnitude of the problems clear. Subsequent clinical studies may include direct inspection of the pharyngeal and esophageal anatomy, and x-ray observation of its function by barium or cookie swallow. Occasionally, motility studies are necessary for an accurate clinical diagnosis, which permits a proper prescription for diet and eating behavior.

Oropharyngeal Dysphagia

The symptoms of oropharyngeal dysphagia include reflux of fluid out through the nose, persistent cough, a wet hoarseness, overt choking, and a persistent sense of the need to clear the throat. Clinical signs include progressive wasting, dehydration, and recurrent bronchitis. Oropharyngeal dysphagia occurs in elderly subjects because of underlying neurologic disease, muscle weakness, or atrophy. Even elderly asymptomatic patients have demonstrated abnormal swallowing due to poor tone of the pharynx, inadequate opening of the cricopharyngeal sphincter, pooling of barium in the adjacent laryngeal folds, and aspiration into the trachea.[1] Typically, liquids are handled less well than soft foods.[7]

The commonly held belief that patients can localize accurately the causes of dysphagia is not supported by the medical literature. Patients often point to the neck when dysphagia is caused by distal esophageal disease, so this symptom cannot be used to identify pharyngeal dysphagia. Although coughing and choking do indicate either oral or pharyngeal abnormality, the majority of such patients do not cough. Likewise, although coughing during swallowing usually indicates laryngeal penetration, some patients do not cough even though this occurs.

Dysphagia for solid foods is strongly suggestive of anatomic narrowing. Barium swallow studies may be inadequate because of inadequate distention of all segments. A lower esophageal ring is the most commonly missed cause of dysphagia for solid foods.

Mixed dysphagia for liquids and solids can occur in patients with pharyngeal dysphagia due to neurologic injury as well as esophageal motility disorders. Since oropharyngeal dysphagic patients have more difficulty with thin liquids and also have greater airway penetration, dysphagia for water can be a differential feature.

Regurgitation of undigested food may be either of pharyngeal or esophageal origin. Late regurgitation can be caused by Zenker diverticulum or achalasia of the esophagus. Chest pain and heartburn are not reliable in differentiating pharyngeal and esophageal dysphagia.

Drooling and other evidence of oropharyngeal dysfunction are not necessarily accompanied by clinical evidence of more extensive neuromuscular disease. As many as 50% of neurogenic dysphagic patients have no associated abnormalities on screen physical examination, and in many patients no definite neurologic diagnosis can be established at the initial examination.

Combined functional and anatomic abnormalities are common. As many as one third of patients may have multifactorial dysphagia with coincidental abnormalities in both the pharynx and esophagus.[8] These observations support an integrated and thorough assessment of dysphagic symptoms to include the pharyngeal and esophageal mechanisms.

Treatment

Although there is considerable evidence to permit prognostication of behavioral patterns for the extremities and for bulbar and higher cortical functions, after CVA similar correlates for swallowing are limited. In a prospective study, Robbins[9] evaluated patients with isolated left and right CVAs and brain stem CVAs by neurologic examination, computed tomography, video fluoroscopy, selected manometry, and magnetic resonance imaging. All patients demonstrated delayed response of the pharyngeal phase and increased penetration of food. Patients with cortical stroke had increased oral-stage durations for liquid and semisolid foods. Patients with unilateral left and right cortical stroke and those with brain stem CVA also differed from each other. The left cortical CVA group had the most difficulty with the oral stage of swallowing, with incoordination of the lips, mandible, and tongue. The right unilateral CVA patients had increased penetration of the vocal folds by food and an increased risk of aspiration according to video fluoroscopy and history. This aspiration occurred during the delay of the pharyngeal stage of swallowing. Patients with brain stem CVA had relatively normal oral phases, but the most frequent occurrence of aspiration was due to poor airway protection during swallowing and large pharyngeal residuals after swallowing. Manometric studies demonstrated incomplete relaxation of the upper esophageal sphincter as well as delay with respect to pharyngeal contraction.[9]

The different oropharyngeal patterns provide important information for treatment planning, but the general observations, as noted by Siebns and associates,[2] are also important for the selection of appropriate treatment measures. Because patients with left unilateral cortical CVA often demonstrate findings of verbal and oral apraxia, they are not able to swallow on command, which interferes with interpretation of the swallowing study. When these patients are placed in a more natural eating situation, their oral-stage durations were more equivalent to normal and they used postural changes spontaneously to facilitate swallowing. Only 1 of 20 patients required nonoral feeding techniques because of dysphagia.

Patients with right unilateral CVA did not attempt compensation spontaneously for their difficulty in swallowing even though aspiration was commonly observed. Defense of the airway was not very forceful, and over one third of these subjects required nonvolitional feeding.

The group with brain stem CVA demonstrated forceful reflux attempts at coughing, but most required nonvolitional feeding techniques. These observations effectively prognosticate the outcome of therapeutic maneuvers and the need for nonvolitional nutritional support. (Figure 7-2).

Robbins[9] describes three therapeutic categories: compensatory, rehabilitive, or medical. These treatment categories are based on the thorough clinical evaluation described above.

Compensatory therapy involves the introduction of external factors or new combinations of behavior to substitute for defects. These include postural adjustment, supraglottic swallow, food placement, and diet modification. Choices are available in a complex range and are best implemented with speech therapy consultation. They are most effective in the left unilateral CVA group.

Dietary modifications used in combination with posturing are frequently used in the treatment of the stroke patients. Liquids initially are eliminated from the diet because of the likelihood of aspiration during the delayed pharyngeal stage. Occasionally food requiring chewing may need to be eliminated. Tilting the head forward at a 45° angle can facilitate vallecular maintenance of material until the pharyngeal contraction stage is initiated. The size of the bolus must be limited to 2 mL. Patients who cannot carry out instructions often require nonvolitional feeding techniques.

CVA	SIGNS AND SYMPTOMS	ASPIRATION	NEED FOR ENTERAL NUTRITION
Left CVA	Verbal and Oral Apraxia, Spontaneous Compensation with Swallowing	Present	1/20 of Patients
Right CVA	No Spontaneous Compensation with Swallowing	Common	1/3 of Patients
Brain Stem	Normal Oral Phase	Most Frequent	Almost All Patients

Figure 7-2 Swallowing disorders after CVA.

A unique postural compensation was beneficial to the brain stem group. Most of the pooling of the food appeared at the level of the piriform sinuses unilaterally, so that turning the head toward the impaired side facilitated the flow of material through the upper esophageal sphincter, reduced residual material, and reduced or eliminated aspiration.

Rehabilitation therapy involves the retraining of a disordered movement or behavior by repetitive practice. Patients selected for rehabilitative therapy often receive nonvolitional nutritional support because food is not introduced in the treatment regimen until significant progress has been demonstrated. These treatment programs involve oromotor exercises, vocal fold deduction exercises, and thermal sensitization. Several medical/surgical and prosthetic treatments available for the treatment of dysphagia, including intracordal injection, cricopharyngeal myotomy, and palatal reshaping prosthesis, did not prove successful in the study by Robbins.[9] The work done at the Johns Hopkins Swallowing Center demonstrates the necessity of careful clinical and specialized assessment of neurologic deficits and speech pathology combined with nutritional assessment and therapeutic maneuvers.

Esophageal Dysphagia

Esophageal dysphagia is due to a disturbed swallowing mechanism in the body of the esophagus, usually causing a lodgment of food or an awareness of the passage of food through the chest, occasionally with pain. Some patients first present with complete blockage of the esophagus following the ingestion of a piece of meat. Most often dysphagia is caused by anatomic rather than functional changes.

Esophageal motility is probably normal in aged people. Many patients with motility abnormalities attributed to presbyesophagus demonstrate features most consistent with diffuse esophageal spasm with disorganized esophageal contraction waves rather than the progressive peristaltic patterns normally observed with swallowing. Many patients have other conditions, such as diabetes mellitus, senile dementia, and peripheral neuropathy, that most likely account for these abnormalities on the basis of abnormal neuromuscular function.[10] In very old patients, there is a marked decline in the magnitude of esophageal contractions, suggesting smooth muscle weakness, but the clinical importance of this observation is unclear.

Gastroesophageal reflux is a common problem and may be more common in elderly people because of underlying disease and their frequent use of medications that may contribute to it. Gastroesophageal reflux is more common in the upright position and after meals, but it is probably more serious when it occurs in the recumbent position and during sleep. Factors that contribute to its cause include delayed gastric emptying, incompetence of the lower esophageal sphincter, failure of the esophagus to generate waves of peristalsis to clear refluxed material, and the injurious nature of the gastric contents. It is unclear whether age-associated changes may contribute to the frequency of this disorder, but common diseases of the elderly and commonly used medications are known to effect this esophageal dysfunction.[11]

Gastroesophageal reflux may produce no symptoms, even while causing severe injury to the esophagus; but, commonly, patients experience pyrosis or heartburn. Regurgitation may occur with heartburn or independently, with changes in posture, after meals, or at other times. When injury to the esophagus is severe, patients may experience esophageal dysphagia due to esophagitis, or stricture formation. Painful swallowing may accompany dysphagia in some patients. It is increasingly recognized that gastroesophageal reflux may result in pharyngeal reflux or tracheal aspiration, and cause the laryngeal and pulmonary symptoms of change in voice, chronic cough, and recurrent pulmonary infections. Inflammation of the esophagus may also cause iron deficiency anemia resulting from occult blood loss from the inflamed mucosa.

Nutrient requirements probably do not change with gastroesophageal reflux, except in the case of iron deficiency anemia and the metabolic stress brought on by recurrent pulmonary infections. However, dietary modifications are considered an important element of the treatment protocol, which includes postural measures, drug restriction, antacids, motility agents, and histamine 2 (H_2) blockers. Fat, chocolate, peppermint, and alcohol decrease lower esophageal sphincter pressure; coffee, both caffeinated and decaffeinated, stimulates gastric acid secretion; alcohol and fruit drinks irritate the mucosa, probably because of their osmotic effect; and large meals, probably by their volume, delay gastric emptying. Avoiding meals prior to retiring, and elevating the head of the bed with blocks, may be the two most important measures to take to prevent complications of gastroesophageal reflux disease. Drugs that contribute to delayed gastric emptying or increase gastroesophageal reflux are nicotine, anticholinergics, calcium-channel blockers, theophylline, diazepam, and β-adrenergic blocker agonists. Antacids used in the treatment of this condition will increase the dietary load of divalent cations and help to alleviate symptomatic constipation.

The above comments about oropharyngeal dysphagia, esophageal dysphagia, and gastroesophageal reflux disease are especially relevant to the nutritionist participating in the care of elderly patients in acute care hospitals and long-term care facilities, as well as those treated with tube feeding. In elderly patients with esophageal dysphagia, a clinical diagnosis must be sought, rather than attributing symptoms to old age.[7] For most of these patients, specific treatment for the underlying condition is central to the goal of adequate nutrition through dietary management or nutritional support techniques.

STOMACH/DUODENUM

Changes in gastric morphology and function occur with age, but there is meager evidence that these changes are separate and distinct from those of acquired disease. Gastric secretion does not decrease with advanced age unless disease is present.[12] The 20% of elderly patients who have low acid and pepsin secretion have associated atrophic gastritis.[13]

Gastric emptying of solids by the antrum and of liquids by the fundus is elegantly controlled by gastroduodenal regulatory mechanisms responsive to the composition of ingested foods, duodenal contents, and multiple external influences.[14] In healthy elderly people, there is little difference in solid food emptying. Delayed liquid emptying may be attributable to underlying atrophic gastritis.[15,16] Accelerated early gastric emptying of liquids with normal late phases of gastric emptying has been noted.[17] Gastric emptying of a fatty meal may be delayed.[15] However, it is unlikely that these alterations are clinically significant.

Gastritis, a common disorder in elderly individuals, is poorly understood. Type A gastritis involves the fundus of the stomach and is associated with autoimmune findings, including parietal cell antibodies and autoimmune conditions of other organs. Type B gastritis affects the antrum of the stomach without autoimmune associations and is the most common type seen in elderly patients.[18,19] In advanced age, both types of gastritis tend to merge.[20] The cause of type B gastritis is unknown, but recent findings of an association with *Helicobacter pylori,* an organism associated with acute and chronic antral gastritis as well as peptic ulcer disease, have raised speculation about its potential role as a cause of this disease.[21] Vitamin B_{12} deficiency is commonly associated with atrophic gastritis type A[22] (Figure 7-3). Folic acid is also malabsorbed in this condition, but folic acid deficiency probably does not occur because of bacterial synthesis in the small intestine.[23] There is controversy regarding the criteria for the diagnosis of vitamin B_{12} deficiency because of poor predictability of vitamin B_{12} blood levels, the presence of hematologic and neurologic manifestations, and the presence or absence of vitamin B_{12} malabsorption.[24-26]

Although the incidence of peptic ulcer disease is declining for the population at large,[27] evidence suggests that the incidence of gastric ulcer has increased among elderly people.[28] The incidence of ulcer perforation is also increasing.[29] Ulcer disease is more often complicated in older patients, possibly because of malnutrition and concurrent illness.[30] Cimetidine, which may be used in the long-term treatment of peptic disease, can significantly elevate high-density lipoprotein cholesterol in humans, which could represent a favorable risk factor for coronary artery disease.[31] On the other hand, antacids are frequently used by elderly individuals for dyspeptic symptoms.[32] Chronic or high-dose antacid therapy is associated with multiple side effects, including constipation, obstruction, and osteomalacia with use of aluminum antacids; diarrhea, dehydration, and elec-

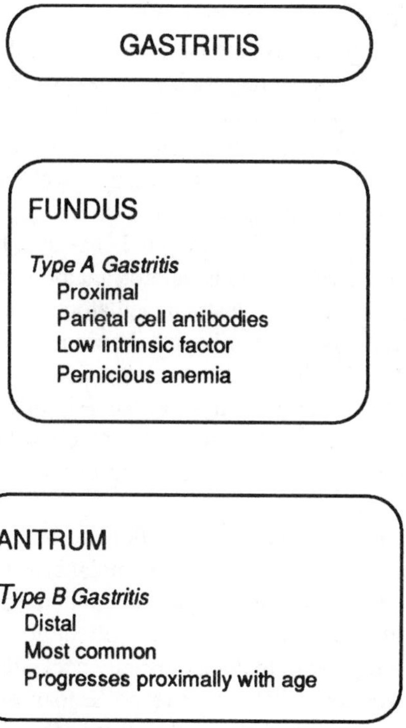

Figure 7-3 Differential features of gastritis.

---

trolyte disturbances with use of magnesium antacids; and hypercalcemia, kidney stones, and acid rebound with use of calcium antacids.[33–35]

Nonsteroidal anti-inflammatory drugs (NSAIDs) play a major role in the pathophysiology and complications of gastroduodenal disease in elderly patients. They are the most commonly prescribed medications for patients over age 65 years.[36,37] A substantial number of patients experience pain, burning, indigestion, nausea, and vomiting while taking these drugs.[38] A variety of mucosal injuries occur with ingestion of NSAIDs, including mucosal hemorrhages, erosions, and acute or chronic ulcers.[39] NSAIDs have also been associated with increased risk of gastrointestinal bleeding.[40]

PANCREAS

Pancreatic Changes with Age

Intraluminal digestion is dependent on pancreatic secretion of enzymes, proenzymes, and bicarbonate. Biliary secretion of bile salts is essential for micelle formation, and biliary bicarbonate contributes to acid neutralization. The meal-stimulated secretion of protein by the pancreas is exceeded only by the lactating mammary gland. The functional reserve is so great that 90% of secretory capacity must be lost before significant maldigestion occurs. The complex control of pancreatic secretion involves the central nervous system and gastric and intestinal mediators. Intestinal trophic substances, recurrent cycles of pancreatic secretion, and nutritional state are determinants of the ability of the pancreas to secrete (Figure 7-4). Extrapancreatic factors, such as acid hypersecretory states, decreased or diverted biliary secretions, altered anatomy of the proximal gastrointestinal tract, impaired release of intestinal mediators, and bacterial overgrowth in the small intestine, can adversely influence intraluminal digestion.

It might be expected that there are age-related changes in both the morphology and function of the aged pancreas, but the clinical significance of these changes is unclear. In elderly patients, malnutrition, hepatobiliary or gastrointestinal surgery, and other factors affecting digestion and absorption could exacerbate the effects of these changes.

Beyond age 70 years, the pancreas is smaller and weighs less. Pancreatic ducts are dilated and there is increased parenchymal fibrosis.[41] Clinical pancreatic insufficiency, resulting in loss of fat, protein, minerals, and fluid in the feces, occurs when pancreatic secretion is less than 10% of normal. Lesser decreases in pancreatic function are difficult to detect, usually necessitating the placement of a nasoduodenal tube to collect secretions in response to meals or injected hormones. Although there is controversy about the presence and extent of pancreatic secretory decline with age, most investigators question its clinical significance. In both human and animal studies there appears to be a linear decline of enzyme output, while volume and bicarbonate concentration increase to a maximum at about the fourth decade of life and then progressively decline.[41-43] Perhaps more insightful is the work by Greenberg and Holt,[44] who demonstrated that the pancreatic enzyme concentrations in aging rats did not adapt to dietary changes as well as they did in younger rats. The enzymes lipase and amylase were studied. The findings suggest that age modifies the effect of gastrointestinal hormones on maintenance of pancreatic mass and enzyme content. Although the clinical significance of these observations is unclear, their potential importance cannot be underemphasized because of the magnification of rather small changes in hormone reactivity or responsiveness, potentially reflecting large changes in secretory rate.[44,45]

Diseases of the Pancreas in the Aged Population

Nutritionists are properly concerned with the potential for dietary or nutritional prevention or moderation of disease processes. The general condition of the

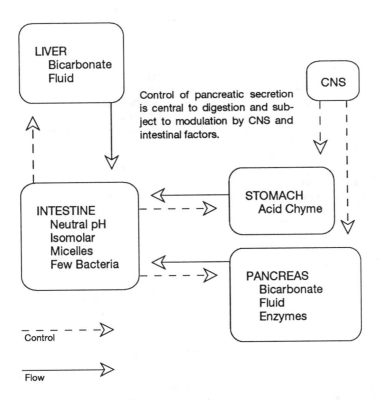

Figure 7-4 Gut interactions. Control of pancreatic secretion is central to digestion and subject to modulation by the central nervous system (CNS) and intestinal factors.

patient and the acuity, severity, and duration of the illness modify this potential (Figure 7-5).

Acute Pancreatitis

Acute pancreatitis is not uncommon in elderly people. It follows the frequency of biliary tract disease and occurs most often in women; but drug-induced acute pancreatitis, most often attributed to diuretics, is also frequent.[46] Age is a negative prognostic factor, as elderly subjects are more likely to die of shock and sepsis.[47,48] The uncomplicated course of this disease usually involves a period of acute illness characterized by pain, nausea, and vomiting. When the disease is more severe, sepsis, pancreatic abscess, and shock complicate the picture. Less ill patients usually recover in a matter of days, with resumption of oral intake; but they may undergo multiple diagnostic and perhaps surgical procedures if retained gallstones are suspected. The management of stress metabolism is the major

ACUTE PANCREATITIS

Occult
    No Oral Intake
    Usual Short Time

    Complicated Course
    Sepsis
    No Oral Intake
    Drainage Has High Protein
        Content
    Usually No Residual
        Pancreatic Insufficiency

CHRONIC PANCREATITIS

Clinical
    Multiple Episodes
    Intake Reduced by Pain
    Chronic Course
    Ethanol As Carbohydrate

    Malnutrition As Late
        Presentation
    Maldigestion
    Steatorrhea

Figure 7-5 Nutrition problems with pancreatitis.

challenge to the nutritionist. Severely ill patients often face protracted periods of bowel rest and drainage of suppurative secretions from the pancreatic bed.

Chronic Pancreatitis

Chronic pancreatitis is of interest to the nutritionist because episodes of symptoms reduce oral intake, while late stages of the disease result in maldigestion due to pancreatic insufficiency. The most common cause of chronic pancreatitis is alcoholism; however, onset after age 60 years is uncommon. Pancreatic insufficiency in asymptomatic elderly people may be accounted for by the presence of either painless disease or chronic primary inflammatory pancreatitis. Painless chronic pancreatitis appears to be more frequent in the sixth and seventh decades. These patients frequently have steatorrhea, diabetes, pancreatic calcification, and weight loss.

Chronic primary inflammatory pancreatitis is exclusively a disease of elderly people. It is seen more frequently in women. Symptoms include mild pain, weight loss, steatorrhea, and low-grade fever. Pancreatic calcifications are absent, but gamma globulin levels are elevated. There is extensive scarring and atrophy of the gland, and response to therapy is unpredictable.[41]

Nutritional Management

The management of pancreatic insufficiency due to chronic pancreatitis is based on the replacement of pancreatic enzymes, dietary modification to minimize the consequences of pancreatic insufficiency, and supplementation of vitamins that may be malabsorbed as a result of this condition. Pancreatic insufficiency most commonly occurs after a long duration of chronic pancreatitis; but it can occur acutely with obstruction of the pancreatic duct by carcinoma, and transiently with acute or relapsing acute pancreatitis. It is likely that visceral protein depletion results in pancreatic insufficiency. Steatorrhea is often a more serious problem than creatorrhea because lipase secretion may decrease more rapidly.[49] Carbohydrate malabsorption also occurs, but its quantitative importance has not been established.[50]

Mild steatorrhea may not be associated with any symptoms. Weight loss may be minimal if food intake is adequate. Enzyme replacement is indicated for weight loss, diarrhea, dyspepsia, and fecal fat excretion exceeding 15 g/d. Some patients also experience reduced pain on pancreatic supplementation.[51] Enzyme preparations are usually given with meals, but even in high doses they do not completely resolve the steatorrhea. Pancreatic extracts may form insoluble complexes with folic acid and interfere with its absorption.[52]

In patients with painful disease, recurrent hospitalizations with reduced or absent oral intake and intake reduced secondary to pain and analgesic use can contribute to the overall picture of malnutrition. Patients who fail to respond may have complicating factors such as primary intestinal disease, bacterial overgrowth, or inactivation of enzyme by gastric acid. Disproportionate acidification of the duodenum because of impaired bicarbonate secretion from the pancreas also occurs. Aluminum hydroxide is effective in reducing steatorrhea during pancreatic enzyme replacement therapy, and H_2 blockers have produced variable results.

Fat-soluble vitamin deficiency occurs despite adequate control of steatorrhea.[53] Nondiabetic retinopathy is improved by vitamin A therapy in patients with pancreatic insufficiency, but zinc malabsorption may also play a role.[54] Vitamin B_{12} malabsorption occurs in chronic pancreatic insufficiency and may be due to a deficiency of a pancreatic factor or impaired proteolysis of vitamin B_{12} binders.[55] Clinical evidence of vitamin B_{12} malabsorption is rare. Dietary treatment of chronic pancreatitis is based on the rationale that a high-fat diet exacerbates steatorrhea and abdominal pain and, therefore, that dietary fat should be restricted to 25% of total calories. Malabsorption of protein prompts the advice of a diet rich in protein. In severe symptomatic chronic pancreatitis, medium-chain triglycerides, which do not require lipolysis but enter the intestinal mucosa directly, can be used as replacement calories. A high-fiber diet is relatively contraindicated in pancreatic insufficiency because fiber may bind as much as 80% to 95% of pancreatic enzymes.[56]

SMALL INTESTINE

Morphology

Because passive absorption is dependent on the surface area of the small intestine, studies have been made of the morphologic changes in the intestinal villous and microvillous membranes that might occur with aging. Animal studies have demonstrated a decrease in the number of villi, villus atrophy, and abnormal villus shape with advancing age, but human biopsy material has not consistently shown such changes. The validity of these early studies is questionable because of a lack of information on the nutritional state of the animals. Although it is not possible to equate normal appearance with normal function, later studies effectively excluded disease- and nutrition-related variables and did not demonstrate an abnormal appearance of the absorptive surface, suggesting that well-being and nutritional state are predominant factors in determining morphology and function.[57]

The epithelial surface of the intestinal villous membrane is normally regenerated at a rapid rate. Replication occurs in the intestinal crypt; then as cells migrate toward the apex of the villus, differentiation and maturation occur. No difference in migration rate has been demonstrated, but the activities of several important enzymes are delayed in aged rats. Although results from older studies conflict with those of more recent studies, based on current information it can be concluded that otherwise healthy, well-nourished, older individuals have no substantial differences in intestinal morphology; however, they may have functional abnormalities because of altered enzyme activity of epithelial cells due to delayed maturation.[57]

Function

Carbohydrate Absorption

The potential for malabsorption is suggested by the alteration of enzyme activity of epithelial cells. Dietary carbohydrates, which approximate 40% of ingested calories, require digestion from the constituent polysaccharide to monosaccharides prior to intestinal absorption. The initial phase of digestion occurs in the intestinal lumen by pancreatic amylase, the secretion of which is well preserved in elderly people. Further hydrolysis of disaccharides and short-chain polysaccharides is accomplished by mucosal cell enzymes. Intestinal biopsies indicate that lactase is not reduced and lactose malabsorption is not responsible for symptoms in healthy elderly patients.[58,59]

The absorption of glucose is difficult to study in elderly subjects because glucose metabolism, body size, and body composition are altered. In vitro studies do not suggest an abnormality of glucose absorption in aged mice.[60,61] One method used to evaluate glucose absorption is to measure hydrogen excretion in the breath. Hydrogen, a product of bacterial fermentation of carbohydrate, is absorbed in the colon and excreted in the breath. Postprandial breath hydrogen excretion studies of elderly patients consuming meals with different amounts of carbohydrate demonstrate excessive excretion of breath hydrogen in one third of people over age 65 years given a 100-g carbohydrate meal. Excessive excretion of hydrogen is also seen in some elderly subjects given as little as 25 to 50 g of carbohydrate.[62]

Carbohydrate absorption is often evaluated by the D-xylose test. D-Xylose, a pentose, is mainly absorbed by diffusion that parallels intestinal absorptive capacity, and it is excreted in urine. Low values may result from incomplete urine collections, impaired renal function, or malabsorption, among others. Earlier studies suggesting impaired xylose excretion in elderly subjects have been dismissed because of the known reduction in urine clearance rate with advanced age. Although D-xylose absorption may decrease in advanced age, this is probably not clinically significant.[63] In the absence of disease it appears that the aged small intestine has normal carbohydrate absorption within the range of clinically important parameters such as symptoms and evidence of malabsorption.

Fat Absorption

The absorption of dietary fats is more complex than that of other nutrients, from a biochemical point of view. Malnutrition associated with steatorrhea and appropriate laboratory studies confirm the diagnosis of malabsorption. Unfortunately, a 72-hour fecal fat collection while the patient is on a fixed dietary fat intake is the standard measure of fat absorption. The absorption of long-chain triglycerides, fatty acids, monoglycerides, and vitamin D occurs as passive diffusion after intraluminal digestion. The limiting factors are dependent on the concentration of bile salts and the unstirred water layer.[64]

The absorbed triglycerides and vitamin D are transferred from the intestinal cell to the lymphatics as chylomicrons and very-low-density lipoproteins (VLDLs). In aged animals, the absorption of radioactively labeled glycerol and vitamin D_3 is decreased, suggesting a defect in the synthesis of chylomicrons and lipoproteins by the enterocyte.[65] This problem may be related to impaired synthesis of essential apoproteins and phospholipids.[66]

Protein Absorption

Protein turnover in the intestine is very high, with respect to the total protein content of the intestine, because of the high synthetic activity related to cell renewal and enzyme production. Although there is controversy as to the amount of protein required to maintain positive nitrogen balance in elderly individuals, there are no studies that suggest any defects in the digestion and absorption of protein in otherwise healthy individuals.

Micronutrient Absorption

It is unclear whether deficiency or disease occurs because of vitamin malabsorption in otherwise healthy elderly people. Research in this area is hampered by the interpretation of blood levels and how they may relate to biochemical effects or tissue stores. Without disease, it is unlikely that malabsorption of vitamins results in significant vitamin depletion.[67] The fat-soluble vitamins A and K may be absorbed more readily by elderly individuals.[68] This is also true of other lipids,[69–71] but the absorption of vitamin D appears to be impaired. Blood levels of 25-hydroxycholecalciferol are lower in elderly subjects, and malabsorption of labeled cholecalciferol has been reported.[72,73] The importance of this observation is emphasized by evidence that calcium absorption appears to be lower in elderly people than it is in younger people, and that osteoporosis and osteomalacia frequently occur in elderly individuals. The mechanism of this malabsorption and the relationship of circulating vitamin D metabolites are unclear, but it appears that there is a reduced adaptation to low dietary intake of calcium. Until the mechanism of vitamin D absorption is more clearly understood, therapeutic options are speculative.[63]

Water-soluble vitamin absorption is probably normal in older adults. Low plasma levels of vitamin C have been correlated with reduced oral intake. No differences of thiamine excretion have been seen in young or elderly subjects. The evidence for folate absorption is inconsistent. Age does not seem to be an independent variable for the ileal absorption of vitamin B_{12}[74] (Chapter 3).

Low serum concentrations of iron and transferrin in aged individuals do not seem to be related to malabsorption of iron, as no such age-related changes have been demonstrated.[75] Iron deficiency in elderly subjects is most often accounted for by intestinal blood loss due to malignant or benign disease, although gastric achlorhydria may account for the reduction of the absorption of nonheme iron[76] (Chapter 10).

Motility

There is little evidence to suggest a clinically important change in small bowel motility in healthy elderly people. This is not true, however, for the changes seen with medical illness or drug effects. In an intestinal motility study of fasting and fed elderly subjects, all three phases of the migrating motor complex were present, and there were no differences in the motility index or duration or velocity of phase III contractions. There was a slight decrease in the motility index and the frequency of contractions after feeding, but there were no differences in the mean amplitude of contractions. It is not known whether these later changes have clinical significance or alter intestinal transit time.[77]

Several clinical studies suggest that subclinical pancreatic insufficiency and bacterial overgrowth in the small intestine are a common cause of malabsorption. However, the results are clouded by problems of concomitant patient selection and systemic or gastrointestinal disease. Therefore, when malabsorption is suspected, a specific diagnosis should be pursued, since it is unlikely that major clinical problems of malabsorption are unique to elderly people.[78–81]

INTESTINAL DISORDERS

Disaccharidase Deficiency

Deficiency of the disaccharidase lactase is the most common disorder of carbohydrate digestion. Its appearance with aging and maturation can be considered normal in most people, with the exception of some northern Europeans, as there is a steady decline in brush border enzymes after weaning. Adults retain about 10% to 30% of intestinal lactase activity and develop symptoms only when they ingest sufficient lactose to exceed lactase production. Lactase deficiency also occurs in the presence of primary intestinal diseases such as viral gastroenteritis, tropical and nontropical sprue, Crohn's disease, bacterial and parasitic infections of the intestine, cystic fibrosis, and ulcerative colitis.

The symptoms of lactase deficiency are nonspecific. Even so, most adults who have this condition are aware of their intolerance to milk because of abdominal cramping, bloating, distention, and possible diarrhea. Symptoms are due to the osmotic effect of unhydrolyzed and unabsorbed lactose shifting fluid into the intestinal tract, resulting in a rapid passage of contents through the intestine into the colon. Colonic bacteria hydrolyze the lactose to lactic acid and short-chain fatty acids, lowering the pH of the stool. Hydrogen produced by this fermentation is absorbed and excreted in the breath, which is a useful test for detecting lactose intolerance. The diagnosis can be confirmed by administering an oral dose of lactose, observing symptoms, and measuring blood glucose levels. When 0.75 to 1.5 g of lactose per kilogram of body weight is administered, the presence of symptoms and a blood glucose concentration of less than 20 mg/dL above the fasting level are considered positive for the disorder. Measurement of breath hydrogen after the ingestion of 50 g of lactose is a more sensitive and specific test. Lactase deficiency in elderly adults is important because of the potential for chronic deficiency of calcium and protein intake. The appearance of lactose intolerance as a new symptom should prompt careful evaluation for the detection of other underlying gastrointestinal disease.[82,83]

Celiac Disease (Gluten-Sensitive Enteropathy)

Celiac disease, also known as gluten-sensitive enteropathy, results from small intestinal mucosal injury caused by dietary exposure to wheat gluten. The classic symptoms of this disease include diarrhea, bloating, and weight loss, which are a result of the profound malabsorption and steatorrhea seen in these patients. The occurrence of this disease in elderly adults is not widely recognized, and its manifestations may be atypical. In contrast to earlier descriptions, recent reports suggest that as many as 25% of patients with celiac disease may be first diagnosed in later years.[84,85] Most patients with this disease do not present with the classic symptoms of diarrhea with steatorrhea, osteomalacia, or anemia; but they may have more subtle findings, including nonspecific gastrointestinal complaints that may be transient or acute. In over half the reported cases, abnormalities of the blood count, including macrocytosis and mild anemia, prompted further investigation.[84] In elderly patients, an abnormally low serum folate level may also indicate the presence of celiac disease.[86]

Cachexia, depression, fatigue, and anemia in older individuals usually lead to consideration of occult malignancy rather than primary gastrointestinal disease. Although the appearance mimicking malignancy appears to be a more common feature of celiac disease in elderly patients, other manifestations are typical but often misdiagnosed (for example, edema attributed to heart disease, osteomalacia attributed to osteoporosis, and wasting due to occult malignancy elsewhere). Elderly patients may present with small intestinal ulcerations, a syndrome of splenic atrophy, villus atrophy and cavitation of mesenteric lymph nodes, or subacute intestinal pseudo-obstruction.[87–89] The diagnosis of celiac disease is dependent on a small bowel biopsy that demonstrates the typical features of a flat mucosa due to villus atrophy. The presence of antigluten immunoglobulin A or immunoglobulin G antibodies in the plasma has a high predictive value as a screening test in adults.[90] The breath hydrogen test differentiates patients with celiac disease from normal subjects but does not identify those who have bacterial overgrowth.[91]

The laboratory features of celiac disease reflect the profound disturbance of absorption in the proximal intestine resulting in steatorrhea and malabsorption of iron and folic acid, but preservation of vitamin B_{12} and bile salt absorption. This dysfunction of intestinal digestion and absorption due to enzyme depletion is secondary to the early exfoliation of maturing enterocytes. These abnormal findings return to normal after treatment with a gluten-free diet; lactase deficiency may persist or be slow to improve.[92]

The treatment of celiac disease in elderly patients consists of the removal of gluten from the diet. Most patients will respond, but those patients with profound malnutrition and debility are at risk for death due to infection and hemorrhage. In such extreme cases, nutritional support measures may be necessary to facilitate the re-establishment of adequate oral feeding. Older patients may require additional training in order to successfully alter their dietary intake. Management of calcium and vitamin D metabolism needs to be attended to and may require oral supplementation. Failure to respond to a gluten-free diet should prompt consideration of underlying complicating diagnoses.

Bacterial Overgrowth

Occult malabsorption caused by bacterial contamination of the small intestine is more common in elderly individuals than is generally recognized. Of 24 patients with unrecognized malabsorption in the presence of clinical malnutrition, 17 were found to have bacterial contamination associated with duodenal/jejunal diverticula, postgastrectomy syndrome, or otherwise normal gastrointestinal anatomy.[93] This condition of overgrowth of abnormal microflora in the small intestine is variously called the blind loop syndrome, stagnate loop syndrome, or small intestinal stasis syndrome. The condition can occur in patients who have abnormal bacterial flora without stasis. The overgrowth of microflora disturbs intraluminal digestion and mucosal function and results in malabsorption of fat, protein, carbohydrate, electrolytes, and vitamin B_{12}. Malnutrition due to steatorrhea and macrocytic anemia due to vitamin B_{12} deficiency frequently develop.

The normal human jejunum is populated by a variable number of transient organisms derived from oral pharyngeal sources. Ileal bacterial populations are somewhat higher and reflect a colonic origin. Protective mechanisms in the proximal gut include acidity of the stomach and the normal cleansing activity of proximal small intestinal motility. Diseases or operations that reduce gastric acidity are correlated with high levels of bacterial contamination, as are conditions that reduce small intestinal motility, such as scleroderma and pseudo-obstruction. Immunologic defenses, the mucous barrier, and bile acids probably play a lesser role in protecting against or reducing bacterial overgrowth. When bacterial contamination of the proximal intestine occurs, anaerobic organisms form a large proportion of the total and result in multiple disturbances of intraluminal digestion and mucosal absorption. The contaminating bacteria deconjugate bile acids, reducing their concentration and thus interfering with fat digestion. Bacterial overgrowth also contributes to denaturation of ingested protein, disturbed function of brush border enzymes, and probable protein loss from injured mucosa. In adults, the D-xylose tolerance test is abnormal because of bacterial fermentation and impaired mucosal absorption. As a result of malabsorption, the end products of bacterial metabolism contribute to diarrhea and water and electrolyte losses.

Malabsorption of vitamin B_{12} is a frequent finding in patients who have bacterial contamination of the small intestine and is due to excessive binding of the vitamin by bacteria, which compete with the normal mechanisms of absorption.

Apparently the mucosal absorptive function for vitamin B_{12} is intact. Bound vitamin B_{12} is excreted in the stool with bacteria. Products of vitamin B_{12} metabolism are physiologically inactive and interfere with intrinsic factor and ileal binding sites as well. Folic acid levels are usually high because of bacterial production of the vitamin in the upper intestine. Nutritional defects of nicotinamide and vitamin D metabolism have been reported.

Clinical investigation of these patients is directed toward defining anatomic defects or disturbed motility that would contribute to stasis, and identifying conditions that reduce bacterial defenses. In addition to the usual diagnostic studies for malabsorption (such as the Schilling test for absorption of vitamin B_{12}, stool examination for fecal fat, and D-xylose absorption studies), measurement of urinary indicans, bile acid breath tests, small bowel biopsy, and collection of intestinal contents for microbiologic analysis are appropriate.[94]

Inflammatory Bowel Disease

Ulcerative colitis and Crohn's disease represent two diagnostic categories of inflammatory diseases of the bowel of unknown etiology. Ulcerative colitis is a mucosal disease limited to the colon and involves the rectum and contiguous parts of the colon proximally to varying degrees. Crohn's disease more typically affects the ileum and proximal portions of the colon and tends to be more segmental, with skipped areas of normal appearing bowel. Because of the involvement of the small intestine and the propensity for chronic perforation of the bowel with fistula and abscess formation, Crohn's disease has, for most patients, a greater negative impact on nutritional state than does chronic ulcerative colitis. Both diseases occur more frequently in young patients, with onset during the teenage years and the 20s. Onset after age 60 years probably accounts for less than 10% of patients. Many patients with the apparent onset of inflammatory bowel disease after age 60 years are probably suffering from ischemic colitis or infectious colitis instead.[95,96]

Of patients over age 60 years who have inflammatory bowel disease, there are those who have had early onset and survived to advanced age with potential complications of intestinal and extraintestinal involvement, sequelae of surgical treatment, and side effects of earlier or continuing medical treatment. There are also those who have had recent onset of this disease, often in the presence of other acute and chronic diseases common in elderly people. Analysis of the nutritional needs of these patients relies on an understanding of the clinical spectrum of the disease, the extent and severity of intestinal involvement, the duration of illness, and the side effects of medical and surgical treatment.

There is a suggestion that some features of late-onset ulcerative colitis distinguish it from early-onset disease. Late-onset disease is less extensive, being more frequently limited to the rectum and the left colon rather than involving the entire colon. Diarrhea is more severe and is accompanied by less bleeding. At the onset of the disease the illness is more protracted, perhaps less responsive to treatment, and has shorter remissions. Of great importance in elderly patients is that significant weight loss, anemia, and frequent hospitalizations are more common.[97]

In elderly adults, many of the symptoms of Crohn's disease, including diarrhea, cramping abdominal pain, fatigue, weight loss, and low-grade fever, might easily be attributed to underlying malignancy. Features that usually alert the clinician to the presence of Crohn's disease include the anorectal manifestations of fistulas and abscesses. Anemia, hypoproteinemia, and malnutrition are caused by the chronic inflammatory process, poor oral intake, increased gastrointestinal losses, and malabsorption. Elderly patients with Crohn's disease are more likely to have left-sided colonic involvement than are younger cohorts, who more commonly have isolated ileal disease.[98]

The treatment of inflammatory bowel disease in older patients does not differ substantially from that in younger patients. Sulfasalazine, corticosteroids, and metronidazole are commonly used drugs. Other immunosuppressants are used for patients with intractable disease. Sulfasalazine has an antifolate effect and may contribute to gastrointestinal side effects that include epigastric discomfort and chronic headache. Corticosteroids can exacerbate diabetes mellitus, cause hypertension, accelerate osteoporosis, and complicate conditions marked by salt and water retention, such as congestive heart failure and renal failure. As in younger patients, older patients with late-onset disease often require surgery.[99]

Published studies of the epidemiology of inflammatory bowel disease may underestimate the true prevalence by 27% to 38%; examination of asymptomatic patients between ages 50 and 75 years during a screening study for colorectal cancer uncovered 8 people with previously undiagnosed inflammatory bowel disease among approximately 18,000 participants.[100]

Radiation Enteritis

Radiation enteritis results from a dose-related injury to the intestine, most commonly associated with radiation treatment of cancer of the cervix, uterus, prostate, rectum, sigmoid, and bladder. As the population ages and more patients become candidates for radiation therapy, this side effect will become more prevalent. In the acute form, radiation enteritis typically causes diarrhea but is usually self-limited; when severe it may be sufficient to interrupt treatment.[101] When the disease has continued beyond 3 months it is considered chronic, and its importance probably is underestimated. Most patients do not seek medical help until serious complications occur.[102]

Radiation therapy typically injures cells that divide rapidly, so that crypt cells in the small intestine are particularly vulnerable. The chronic form of the disease is thought to be due to a progressive, irreversible ischemia that results in a fibrinous peritonitis in which loops of intestine are bound together. Fibrosis, submucosal edema of the bowel wall, and perforation occur. Ulceration of the mucosa is common; deeper ulcerations are associated with perforation. Mucosal areas of atrophy are also present, and scarring results in luminal narrowing.

The severity of radiation injury based on findings and symptoms is categorized as mild, consisting of diarrhea controlled by diet and reassurance; marked, noted by diarrhea and rectal pain and relieved by medications; or severe, characterized by fistulization, perforation, and stricture. Patients with diabetic vascular disease and atherosclerosis are at greatest risk of developing severe radiation enteritis.

The latent period between radiation therapy and the onset of symptoms can be years. Initial symptoms include postprandial fullness, nausea, and cramping, which progress to distention and vomiting. In a retrospective review of 3900 patients at risk for chronic radiation enteritis, O'Brien and colleagues[103] documented the typical course of these patients. Patients with early symptoms were hospitalized and treated with nasogastric suction and intravenous fluids; there were clinical findings of incomplete bowel obstruction. Diets were advanced as tolerated, and patients were discharged on a soft diet. Repeated episodes of partial small bowel obstruction followed, and patients continued to deteriorate over time. Once this cycle of recurrent small bowel obstruction occurred, all patients ultimately required surgical treatment. Bowel obstruction was due to narrowed, thickened bowel wall rather than to associated adhesions. Resection and anastomosis of bowel often were not possible, and bypass of affected segments was required.[103]

Multiple factors contribute to the risk of chronic radiation injury to the bowel, including adhesions due to prior surgery, pelvic inflammatory bowel disease, extremely low body weight, diabetes mellitus, cardiovascular disease, pre-existing vascular compromise of the bowel, and combined chemotherapy and radiation therapy.[104] Some surgeons advise wide excision of affected bowel rather than bypass.[105,106]

Acute Radiation Enteritis

The treatment of acute radiation enteritis consists of the symptomatic use of antidiarrheal agents, including opiates and anticholinergic drugs. Cholestyramine, a bile salt-binding agent, is used based on the hypothesis that injured distal small bowel fails to resorb bile salts. Bile salts entering the colon have a profound secretory effect; binding the salts reduces these effects.[107]

The use of elemental diet therapy to prevent radiation injury has led to conflicting results. McArdle and associates[108] studied the effect of elemental diets prior to and during radiation therapy for invasive bladder cancer, using retrospective controls. A peptide-based formula was given orally, by nasoenteric tube, or by needle jejunostomy; symptoms improved, and small bowel function returned promptly with early passage of flatus and feces. Patients treated with nutritional support had no microscopic damage to the ileum. On electron microscopic examination, there was preservation of the normal glycocalyx, preservation of cell microstructure and tight cell junctions, and greater preservation of brush border enzymes. It is not certain what role, if any, other factors, such as pancreatic biliary secretions or mechanical effects of regular diet, have in the pathophysiology of intestinal injury.[108]

Chronic Radiation Enteritis

Unfortunately, the lesions of chronic radiation enteritis, including mucosal injury, evidence of stricture with bowel stasis, and perforation with fistula formation, are probably not reversible. A variety of treatment programs have been tried with a mixture of results. These include treatments for bile salt diarrhea and bacterial stasis syndrome, and use of a variety of anti-inflammatory agents. Unfortunately, many pathophysiologic factors are probably operating, so the efficacy of low-fat diets, low-residue diets, gluten-free or lactose-deficient diets, and elemental diets remains to be established. Parenteral nutrition has been used to induce weight gain, to correct hypoproteinemia, and to close fistulas.[109]

As noted above, many of these patients eventually have surgical treatment. The results of resection and bypass often result in short bowel syndrome. During the management of the patient with radiation enteritis, it is important to recognize that premorbid malnutrition often is present. Radiated tissues heal poorly, and dehiscence of wounds and infection are common complications. Nutritional rehabilitation must await metabolic recovery from surgery and the initiation of the convalescent phase.

LIVER

Significant morphologic and functional changes in the liver due to aging are of interest to the clinician because alterations in synthetic, excretory, or metabolic processes can affect the response to disease and the disposition of drugs. However, most hepatic changes are due to systemic disease and the liver diseases commonly seen in elderly individuals.

Liver weight decreases after age 50 years, parallel to the anthropometric changes of decreased body weight and muscle mass. In advanced age, the liver becomes disproportionately small.[110] Based on microscopic observations these changes appear to be due to diminished numbers of hepatocytes.[111] Other changes in liver morphology are nonspecific and may be due to extrahepatic processes. There is an increase in portal and periportal fibrosis, and liver cells tend to be larger, with larger or multiple nuclei and nucleoli. Enlargement of the liver cells may be due to compensatory hypertrophy. An increased amount of lipofuscin pigment is present in the Kupffer cells[112,113] and changes in the Golgi apparatus and rough and smooth endoplasmic reticulum may parallel hepatic functional changes seen in older subjects.[114]

Liver Function and Aging

Decreases in liver blood flow from 0.3% to 1.5% per year occur with age.[115,116] Alterations in serum bilirubin, transaminases, alkaline phosphatase, dye tests of hepatic excretion (sulfobromophthalein sodium), and radioactive labeled excretion tests (Rose Bengal) do not occur in elderly people with histologically normal livers.[117] Levels of albumin, a product of hepatic synthesis, are frequently reduced in the elderly. Although albumin metabolism is influenced by many factors, it appears that the rate of albumin synthesis in elderly people is not sensitive to changes in protein intake, suggesting an altered set-point in synthetic rate.[118]

The potential for changes in drug metabolism in the aging liver is of greater concern to clinicians than the apparent minor and probably insignificant changes in morphology and function.[119] The reduction of lean body mass and total body water alters the distribution of water-soluble and fat-soluble drugs (Chapter 13). The disposition and side effects of drugs in elderly patients are of concern.[120] Contrary to conventionally held views, impaired clearance of drugs may not be due to reduced hepatic microsomal enzyme activity. Further study is required to understand this important subject.[121] No generalizations can be made about drug disposition with respect to altered blood flow, drug distribution, and principal metabolic pathways. Nutritional factors can be important, however, as levels of vitamin C and folic acid have been associated with decreased antipyrine clearance in elderly people.[122]

The rate of total body protein synthesis is decreased in older individuals; much of this decrease is presumed to be in the liver.[123] In animal studies, synthesis of nucleic acids and proteins in old liver cells is diminished.[124] There is an increase in the synthesis of faulty proteins; such ''junk'' proteins may account for disturbed drug disposition and function.[125]

Liver Disease in the Elderly Population

Little has been written about the influence of multisystem disease on the liver, which may be of great importance in the elderly. For cardiac, renal, diabetic, stroke, and arthritic patients, among others, the poorly understood intertwining effects of disease, treatment, and complications on nutrition and hepatic function must be considered rationally.

Chronic or acute alcohol use, starvation, protein energy malnutrition, obesity, diabetes mellitus, and hypothyroidism can alter hepatic lipoprotein metabolism and cause fatty liver. Fatty liver can be associated with some element of liver cell necrosis when alcohol or drugs are involved. Fat in liver cells results from an imbalance of oxidation, esterification, or excretion of fatty acids that accumulate from a flux of fatty acids from adipose tissue to the liver. Generally, fatty liver does not interfere with hepatic function but results only in enlargement of the liver. Advanced cases may be associated with cholestasis, portal hypertension, and ascites. Liver cell necrosis accompanying fatty liver is a precursor of a progressive fibrotic process that may lead to cirrhosis.

Nonhepatitis causes of jaundice predominate in elderly patients.[126] Drugs account for 20% of causes of jaundice in this group.[127] Although adverse drug reactions are more common in older subjects, and systemic and hepatic alterations exist that can affect drug disposition, there is little evidence that the elderly liver is more susceptible to drug injury. There is some evidence to suggest that when injury occurs it may be more severe, as in the case of fatal anesthesia-induced liver disease. Commonly used drugs that may have an adverse effect on the liver include NSAIDs, anesthetic agents, antibiotics, antimetabolic agents, antihypertensives, cardiac drugs, and psychotropic drugs.[128,129]

Acute viral hepatitis is most often of the non-A, non-B type associated with blood transfusions. The clinical course of patients over age 60 years is not different from that of younger patients.[130] However, acute type B hepatitis, especially when associated with other illness, has a higher risk of severe disease and hepatic failure.[131,132] In elderly patients with severe liver disease, age adversely affects prognosis.[133]

Primary biliary cirrhosis represents a model of cholestatic liver disease. There is chronic destruction of the bile ducts that results in cirrhosis and eventual liver failure. Although it is usually considered a disease of middle age, the age range of presentation is actually 20 to 80 years.[134] Fatigue and pruritus are the usual presenting symptoms. Since there is no specific treatment for this disease, symptomatic relief and prevention of the nutritional complications are the current treatment aims. Late in the disease, when hepatic cirrhosis and its complications develop, liver transplantation is indicated.

Elderly cirrhotics often are asymptomatic. The cirrhosis is caused by multiple factors and is not an inherent characteristic of aging. The peak incidence of cirrhosis due to alcoholism occurs beyond age 60 years. There may be few clinical indicators of this disease.[135] Patients with primary biliary cirrhosis who are survivors of early-onset disease have associated longstanding metabolic complications at old age.[136,137]

Nutrition in Liver Disease

It is unlikely that there are unique nutritional factors in the cause or treatment of liver disease in elderly patients, but changes that occur in digestion, absorption, and intermediary metabolism as a result of acute or chronic liver cell injury or cholestasis do affect nutrition.

Fatty Liver

Hepatic lipid metabolism can be disturbed at many points and result in fat accumulation. Alcohol increases lipolysis, causing a flow of fatty acids to the liver; increases intrahepatic lipid synthesis; decreases fatty acid oxidation in the liver; increases triglyceride formation; and decreases the release of lipoprotein in the form of VLDLs. It is uncertain where alcohol exerts its greatest effect, but a direct hepatotoxic effect of alcohol is favored.[138] Nutritional deficiency is not essential for the formation of acute fatty liver, but it does seem to have some modifying effect, perhaps increasing the severity of the condition when serious levels of nutritional deficiency exist.[139] The source of fatty acids that accumulate as triglyceride in the liver cell differs depending on the fed state of the individual. Under fasting conditions the source is adipose tissue. During the fed state, triglycerides are of intestinal origin. Stress hormones in acute alcohol intoxication may play a role.[140,141] It is unclear whether alcohol-induced hepatic fatty acid synthesis, decreased oxidation, or decreased secretion of triglycerides is most important.[138] It is generally accepted that alcohol-induced fatty liver is reversible. As many as one third of asymptomatic alcoholics may have fatty liver.[138]

Fatty liver can also have features of cholestasis, with jaundice and abnormal liver-associated enzymes. Some patients with fatty liver due to alcohol ingestion actually develop hepatitis with evidence of liver cell necrosis. These patients often have anorexia, nausea, vomiting, fever, and jaundice.

The treatment of acute alcoholic fatty liver is abstinence from alcohol. Principles of general nutrition dictate a well-balanced diet, adequate protein and calorie intake without overfeeding, and supplementation with vitamins. Prolonged fasting and starvation can produce fatty liver; this is especially true when the classic adaptation to starvation, which involves the change from peripheral oxidation of glucose to oxidation of fatty acid products, is blocked by carbohydrate feeding. In the classic form of starvation disease, kwashiorkor, fatty liver is a feature; it is treated with a high-protein diet.[142] It is probable that the fat in the livers of these patients arises not from mobilization of peripheral fat stores, but rather from glucose administration resulting in intrahepatic lipid synthesis.[143] Low serum levels of albumin and of VLDLs suggest an impairment of hepatic lipoprotein and protein synthesis that is reversible with protein feeding.[144] In fatty liver associated with obesity, insulin resistance and increased levels of free fatty acids are probably secondary to increased adipose tissue mass.[145] Fatty infiltration is reversible by weight reduction. Fatty liver and diabetes are often associated.[142] Obesity, occurring in about 45% of diabetics over age 60 years, may be a more important factor in type II diabetics. Recommendations for treatment include weight reduction and a low-carbohydrate, high-protein diet. Fatty liver seen with total parenteral nutrition is probably due to excessive calorie infusion.

Acute Hepatitis

Whatever the primary cause of acute hepatitis, extensive liver cell necrosis leads to fulminant hepatic failure and impairment of nearly all hepatic functions, including carbohydrate, protein, and lipid metabolism; the catabolic rate is also increased. Hypoglycemia is a common feature of fulminant hepatic failure due to impaired hepatic gluconeogenesis and reduced liver glycogen content. These effects are exacerbated by hyperinsulinemia caused by increased insulin production and increased peripheral insulin resistance.[146]

Characteristic derangements in amino acid metabolism occur in severe liver disease with altered plasma amino acid patterns. More than 85% of the liver must be nonfunctional before these patterns develop. Increased levels of tyrosine, phenylalanine, glutamine, and methionine, and decreased levels of valine, leucine, and isoleucine are seen in chronic hepatic encephalopathy; but in fulminant hepatic failure, branched-chain amino acids are either normal or slightly depressed, while there is a marked elevation of all others, probably representing amino acid release from dying liver cells.[147] The urea cycle, which is responsible for the clearance of metabolic nitrogen, is depressed in fulminant hepatic failure and leads to low urea levels and hyperammonemia.

For patients who have severe hepatic failure, hypoalbuminemia and edema are due to a substantial loss of hepatic protein synthetic activity (to less than 10% of normal). Reduced synthesis of vitamin K-dependent clotting factors can contribute to increased prothrombin time. If patients are unresponsive to vitamin K supplementation, bleeding complications are exacerbated. Low levels of total cholesterol, triglycerides, and esterified cholesterol are seen in fulminant hepatic failure.

For most patients who have acute hepatitis of various etiologies, no specific nutritional treatment measures are necessary unless anorexia, nausea, or vomiting becomes protracted. The anorexia seen in acute liver disease is best managed by a high-carbohydrate diet, with the greatest number of calories provided in the morning meal. If oral intake is poor or not possible, intravenous fluids containing glucose should be provided. In patients who have fulminant hepatic failure, continuous infusions of concentrated glucose sufficient to maintain normal serum glucose levels may be necessary. The negative nitrogen balance seen in fulminant hepatic failure makes the use of protein infusions at the rate of 0.8 to 1 g/kg of body weight rational. However, this often works out to be a practice of compromises because of limited protein tolerance and fluid overload. Lipid emulsions are not recommended in fulminant hepatic failure when hepatic encephalopathy is present. Supplemental vitamins, especially folic acid and vitamins B_6 and B_{12}, should be provided.[148]

Cholestasis

Because of the chronic course of primary biliary cirrhosis, this cholestatic disease has the most profound nutritional consequences. The decreased secretion of conjugated bile salts into the intestine leads to steatorrhea and bone disease.[149–151] Diarrhea, weight loss, and muscle wasting occur in patients when steatorrhea is significant. Reduced intake of neutral triglycerides and substitution of medium-chain triglycerides for calories can be effective in the treatment of this condition, since bile salts are not necessary for medium-chain triglyceride absorption.[150]

Although osteomalacia has been assumed to be the principal bone disease of primary biliary cirrhosis, osteoporosis appears to be more important.[152] Nevertheless, treatment is directed toward correcting calcium and vitamin D metabolism, although the results are mixed. Despite normal 25-hydroxyvitamin D_3 levels achieved by monthly intramuscular injections of vitamin D_3, bone disease continues.[153] Vitamin K deficiency has been demonstrated, and vitamin E deficiency is common in primary biliary cirrhosis.[154] Vitamin A levels are low in primary biliary cirrhosis, but symptoms are not commonly noted. Zinc deficiency has also been reported in association with symptomatic vitamin A deficiency.[155] Cholestryramine, which is used to bind and increase the elimination of bile salts in cholestatic liver disease, contributes to steatorrhea and the malabsorption of fat-soluble vitamins, as well as vitamin C.[156]

Cirrhosis

Inadequate dietary intake is the most likely principal cause of malnutrition in patients with liver disease.[156] Decreased sensitivity to taste and smell may contribute to decreased or altered oral intake in the cirrhotic patient.[157] Factors that contribute to malnutrition include anorexia, nausea, poor palatability of special diets, and the indirect effects of chronic alcohol use and its social consequences.[156] The alcoholic cirrhotic may have both pancreatic insufficiency and injury to the small intestinal mucosa.[158,159] These changes are probably mediated to some extent by nutritional deficiency.[160–162] Steatorrhea, usually of mild extent, is also seen in cirrhotics; whether it is due to the effects of portal hypertension on gut congestion and lymphatic drainage or to diminished bile salt secretion is unclear.[163,164]

Changes in glucose, amino acid, and fat metabolism that occur in cirrhosis resemble those of normal adaptation to prolonged starvation. Calorie requirements of stable alcoholic cirrhotics are no different from those of normal subjects. Ketogenesis and gluconeogenesis are increased, probably reflecting the mobilization of peripheral fats and amino acids and resulting in the typical wasted appearance of patients with advanced cirrhosis.[165] Abnormally high insulin levels due to hypersecretion and reduced hepatic clearance are not associated with the usual inverse relationship and peripheral branched-chain amino acid levels in cirrhotics. Peripheral insulin resistance may account for this abnormality.[166] A protein intake of 0.8 to 1 g/kg of body weight with branched-chain or branched-chain-enriched formulas by oral or parenteral means is appropriate. Lipoprotein metabolism is disturbed in severe hepatic insufficiency. The major defects appear to be due to impaired triglyceride release by the liver rather than to disturbances of peripheral fat oxidation; lipid emulsions therefore are probably contraindicated in patients who have advanced, severe, acute liver disease. Supplementation with folic acid, vitamins B_6 and B_{12}, and multivitamins is rational. A trial of parenteral vitamin K administration when low prothrombin levels exist is common.

Clinically significant vitamin B deficiency has been demonstrated in alcoholic patients with macrocytosis, megaloblastic changes, or microcytic anemia associated with low serum folate levels, and peripheral neuropathy is often associated with low thiamine levels; nicotinic acid and riboflavin deficiencies are often seen.[167] Septicemia frequently may accompany end-stage cirrhosis, resulting in metabolic stress.[168]

Hepatic Encephalopathy

Hepatic encephalopathy occurs as a syndrome of impaired mental function in the setting of severe, acute, or chronic liver disease. Factors that contribute to it are multiple, and they differ depending on the clinical circumstances. The diagnosis is based on clinical features, including disturbed consciousness, which ranges from sleepiness to coma and occasionally delirium. Personality changes are most remarkable in patients who have chronic liver disease. It may be difficult to differentiate the effects of alcohol from those of hepatic encephalopathy. Specialized testing may be needed in mild cases. With advanced disease, there is gross confusion, disturbed speech, and a flapping tremor. Hepatic coma is graded on a scale of 1 through 5: grade 1, confused state with altered mood and behavior with psychometric defects; grade 2, drowsiness and inappropriate behavior; grade 3, stupor, ability to obey simple commands, inarticulate speech, marked confusion; grade 4, coma; grade 5, deep coma, no response to painful stimuli.

In fulminant hepatic failure, the syndrome is due to liver cell necrosis. In cirrhosis, it is due to portal-systemic shunting with other precipitating factors. In fulminant hepatic failure, the finding of hepatic encephalopathy indicates a very poor prognosis, although the symptoms are reversible if the liver recovers. In cirrhosis, the reversibility depends on the inciting factors. These findings suggest that a metabolic agent or agents interfere with normal cerebral activity. The specific nature and mechanism of action is unknown.

Current theories of hepatic encephalopathy are based on the hypotheses that the agent is nitrogenous; arises from the colon as a result of intestinal bacterial action; is present in the portal venous system; normally would be metabolized by the liver; and, under the clinical circumstances of hepatic encephalopathy, is able to enter the brain and impair function. In fulminant hepatic failure, the liver cells are unable to metabolize the agent. In cirrhotic liver, blood bypasses the liver by portal-systemic shunting. Candidate toxins include amino acids (eg, methionine), aromatic amino acids, and γ-aminobutyric acid. The production of these agents and their transport to and into the brain, as well as brain function, can be modified by serum amino acid imbalance, alkalosis, and hypoxemia.[169]

Treatment of hepatic encephalopathy is pragmatic. Medical measures are directed at precipitating factors and at identifying and treating sources of infection, gastrointestinal bleeding, and electrolyte disturbances. Toxic medications and alcohol are withdrawn. Sources of nitrogen load are eliminated or reduced. If excess nitrogen is suspected in the intestines, they are purged; diuretics are discontinued, and antibiotics may be administered to decrease bacterial ammonia production. The synthetic disaccharide lactulose is not digested by the human intestinal mucosa but is broken down by colonic bacteria to produce fatty acids yielding a low fecal pH; it alters colonic bacterial populations to reduce ammonia production. Although the mechanism of action is uncertain, total fecal output is increased, as well as fecal nitrogen. Lactitol is an alcohol analogue of lactose and has similar effects. This new product may be better tolerated than lactulose because it can be taken in tablet form.[170]

While these measures are undertaken, dietary protein is discontinued and calories are provided in carbohydrate form intravenously or by enteral feeding tube. As the patient improves, protein is added in 20-g increments on alternate days in divided doses of 4 meals. In chronic encephalopathic patients, it may be necessary to restrict protein intake.[171] The appropriateness of vegetable versus meat protein diets is controversial but some authors have demonstrated advantages.[171–173] The ratio of aromatic to branched-chain amino acids is reduced in hepatic encephalopathy, and infusions of aromatic amino acids have been used in its treatment; but it is difficult to justify their use, considering their high cost.[174]

Ascites

The formation of cirrhotic ascites is another serious manifestation of liver failure. The accumulation of a protein-rich fluid in the peritoneal cavity occurs as a result of venous outflow obstruction in the liver. This results in an elevated hydrostatic pressure of the liver sinusoid, transudation of plasma into the space of disse, and increased liver lymph flow. When the capacity of the lymphatic system is exceeded, fluid begins to accumulate in the peritoneal cavity. Factors contributing to the shift of fluid include low levels of plasma albumin, resulting in a low plasma oncotic pressure. In response to baroreceptors in the liver, the kidney is less able to excrete a salt load, which results in a net retention of sodium. A second alteration in renal function is impaired excretion of water loads. This multiple organ system dysfunction in patients with advanced cirrhotic ascites makes patient management and dietary treatment complex.

Although the presence of ascites dictates the need to determine its exact cause and to exclude other treatable disorders, the presence of ascites per se does not demand treatment. When ascites is massive or tense it can interfere with respiration; can cause discomfort; and (when extreme) can contribute to herniation and necrosis of the umbilicus, resulting in spontaneous rupture and death. A traditional approach to the treatment of ascites involves a therapeutic trial of bed rest and sodium restriction. When a careful history reveals a recent substantial increase in salt intake or exacerbation of a reversible liver disease, the prognosis for response is quite good. However, patients with cirrhotic ascites require a more substantial restriction of sodium intake than do typical patients with heart disease. Restrictions as low as 250 to 500 mg of sodium per day are often required. This represents a significant challenge to meeting other dietary goals.

If diuresis is not evident within several days, the diuretic spironolactone may be effective in nonazotemic patients. In addition to azotemia, hyperkalemia may limit the usefulness of spironolactone. Patients taking spironolactone should not use potassium-containing salt substitutes because of this potential complication. Weight loss should be limited to 1 kg/d. Patients with peripheral edema can tolerate a large volume. In addition to the dietary restriction of salt, at least 50 g of high biologic protein and a 2000-kcal/d diet are usually recommended. Fluid restriction is not required unless serum sodium levels are below 130 mmol/L.[175]

One treatment that is gaining popularity is large-volume paracentesis. A volume of 4 to 6 L of fluid can be withdrawn safely with fewer complications than occur with standard diuretic programs. In patients without peripheral edema, albumin infusions are necessary to prevent volume contraction and azotemia. Fluid is withdrawn over 20 to 30 minutes and is followed by an infusion of 40 g of salt-poor albumin.[176] The advantages of this approach are that it can be accomplished in an outpatient setting with less utilization of hospital resources. The goals of nutritional management are to assure adequate dietary intake with salt restriction to avoid recurrence, although some patients are able to eliminate salt and water loads more effectively as treatment progresses.

COLON

Like the gallbladder and the appendix, the colon is not essential for health and well-being. However, for many elderly people the colon is a major source of symptoms and disease. The most important function of the colon is its role as a reservoir and final processor of fecal residue. Water, electrolytes, bile salts, and short-chain fatty acids are absorbed. Of the physiologic processes of motility, secretion, and absorption, movement disorders predominate.

Little is known about age-related alterations in structure and function of the colon. Biopsy specimens from healthy elderly subjects have demonstrated mucosal atrophy, alteration of mucosal glands, muscularis mucosa hypertrophy, increased connective tissue, and changes of atherosclerosis.[177] Electron microscopic cytologic changes in nuclei, cytoplasm, and cell organelles have also been noted but are of questionable significance. The most significant functional change that occurs with aging is constipation; the most important morphologic change is diverticular disease.

Constipation

Two mechanisms of chronic constipation are known: colon dysmotility and disordered defecation. Contributing causes include drug effects, neurologic disease, structural abnormalities, and systemic disease. Although constipation often is attributed to diet, behavior, and inactivity, it is a condition of multiple causes. It is a symptomatic disease with decreased frequency of bowel movements, difficult passage, passage of hard stools, or a sensation of incomplete evacuation. In nonconstipated adults, intestinal transit time does not appear to be increased.[178] Normal bowel habits range from three per week to two per day.[179] About 30% of aged women use laxatives regularly. Frequent laxative use has been attributed to social attitudes brought about by popular misconceptions in the early part of the 20th century.[180] Elderly people who chronically consume laxatives have demonstrated prolonged transit time as well as electromyographic and physiologic changes in colorectal and anal function.[176,181,182]

Postprandial sigmoid, rectosigmoid, and rectal motility in healthy elderly people is not altered.[183] Abnormalities of anorectal function in elderly people include decreased maximal basal and squeeze pressures of the anal canal; higher rectal pressures with distention; reduced tolerance for rectal distention; and progressive neuropathic damage to the nerves of the anal sphincters, which occurs most frequently in women and is probably related to childbirth. Many of these factors also contribute to the risk of incontinence in elderly people.[184]

A strategy for the effective treatment of chronic constipation involves a careful diagnostic classification and search for underlying and complicating factors. Patients with slow-transit constipation, established by a prolonged colonic transit study, and normal colonic anatomy have either colonic atonia with retention of markers in the right colon or outlet dysfunction with delay of rectosigmoid emptying.[185] Some of these patients may actually suffer from a neuropathic disorder similar to the functional abnormalities found in the esophagus, proximal gastrointestinal tract, and bladder.[186] Patients with outlet dysfunction due to impaired sensory perception or disturbances of anatomy that cause impaired expulsion do not respond to laxatives. These patients may respond to biofeedback or surgical procedures. If transit studies suggest outlet obstruction, further diagnostic evaluation of anorectal physiology is necessary. Patients with normal-transit constipation have either a defecatory disorder or a misperception of what normal bowel function should be.[187,188]

Dietary treatment of constipation invariably involves the addition of dietary or supplemental fiber.[189] An increase of 25% to 40% in fiber intake is accompanied by prevention or elimination of constipation in up to 60% of patients; transit time is also reduced.[190] An intake of 10 to 20 g of bran daily usually is required; initially this almost invariably causes altered bowel habits, distention, and occasional discomfort. Stool bulking is contraindicated in patients who are severely debilitated or who have obstruction as an element of their disease. Course bran has a greater laxative effect than fine bran. The concept that the water-holding capacity of bran is the mechanism by which it works may not be true, as similar modifications of stool consistency, weight, and ease of passage were experienced by subjects taking indigestible plastic particles.[191] For elderly patients who have used laxatives for years, it is not reasonable to adhere slavishly to a concept of fiber supplementation without laxatives when results of therapeutic efforts dictate otherwise.

When bran supplementation is impractical, preparations containing psyllium seed at a dosage of 1 teaspoon twice daily as a hydrophilic agent is effective when accompanied by generous amounts of fluid. Since these agents can obstruct the esophagus, they should be avoided in patients with dysphagia or known esophageal strictures. Sugar-containing supplements may alter diabetic control. Many other laxatives commonly used may lead to a cathartic colon or toxic systemic effects. Lactose may be used, but mineral oil is not recommended because of its interference with fat-soluble vitamin absorption and its potential for pulmonary aspiration. Anthracine purgatives are known to cause degeneration of the myoneural chains of the colon.[180]

Diverticulosis

Diverticulosis is a common disorder of elderly individuals, occurring in 30% of those over age 60 years and 60% of those over age 80 years.[192] The disease is usually asymptomatic. Symptomatic uncomplicated diverticulosis is thought to be essentially the same as irritable bowel syndrome. Diverticulitis is an inflammatory disease that causes obstruction and bleeding. Most pathophysiologic concepts have included the idea of a specific motility disorder resulting in increased intraluminal pressure. Although diverticulosis increases in frequency with age, among active elderly people there is no difference in fecal output.[193] There has been no demonstrated increased sigmoid colon pressure with age.[194] Although muscular layers are greatly thickened in diverticular disease, the morphology of muscle cells is normal. There is no evidence that intrinsic changes in muscle cells account for the thickening associated with diverticulosis. There is a progressive elastosis of the taeniae coli compared with normal structures, which supports the concept of a shortening or contracture of the colon as an initiating factor in the development of diverticulosis. This results in a greater cross-section mass of both longitudinal and circular muscle fibers of the muscularis propria. The luminal dimensions are decreased, and therefore higher pressures can be developed with contraction of these circular muscle folds. The length of the taeniae do respond to fecal bulk. Rural Africans consuming a high-fiber diet have a redundant sigmoid colon with a generous lumen.[195]

The usual dietary measures prescribed in diverticulosis are identical with those used in the treatment of irritable bowel syndrome or chronic constipation. Patients with high levels of sigmoid colon obstruction or stenoses, like their constipated cohorts, may be intolerant of usual amounts of dietary or supplementary fibers, so that symptoms of constipation may need to be treated somewhat independently.

CONCLUSION

Although changes in structure and function of the gastrointestinal tract do occur with aging, they do not seem to be clinically significant in the healthy elderly population. Enzyme and bicarbonate secretions by the pancreas are diminished; whether this is a result of lessened or faulty enteral stimulation or intrinsic age-related pancreatic insufficiency is not clinically relevant because of the huge pancreatic secretory reserve. Mucosal regeneration of the small bowel is accompanied by functional enzyme-related differentiation, which has been noted to be reduced in laboratory animals; but it does not approach clinical significance nor has it been demonstrated to be important in human studies. Alteration in motility could have far-reaching effects, but to date clinical problems appear to be caused by disease rather than aging. Alterations resulting from disease have to be the focus for the diagnosis and treatment of malnutrition in the setting of gastrointestinal dysfunction in the elderly.

Chewing and swallowing problems are the most easily recognized causes of nutritional failure because of poor intake, notwithstanding the frequent drug-induced alterations of taste, nausea, or disturbed mood or attention, which also reduce intake. Simple clinical observations can identify these disorders and lead to appropriate diagnostic studies to enable treatment plans. Disturbances of digestion and absorption in the midgut are more occult and difficult to differentiate. A knowledgeable diagnostic approach based on pathophysiologic principles often requires treatment by trial and error when multiple problems exist. Here the collaboration of the dietitian and physician is most important.

The effects of functional gastrointestinal disorders, such as constipation, on dietary intake are difficult to quantify. A lifetime of learned behavior can exasperate attempts at a very scientific approach and necessitate a practical and compromising plan for successful management to include good nutrition goals. In the care of the very old, ethical and spiritual issues may come to dominate the theme of respectful care.

REFERENCES

1. Pelemans W, Vantrappen G. Oesophageal diseases in the elderly. *Clin Gastroenterol.* 1985;14(4):635–656.

2. Siebens H, Trupe MA, Hilary A, et al. Correlates and consequences of eating dependency in institutionalized elderly. *J Am Geriatr Soc.* 1986;34:192–198.

3. Dorff GL, Rytel MW, Farmer SG, et al. Etiologies and characteristic features of pneumonias in a municipal hospital. *Am J Med Sci.* 1973;266:349–358.

4. Ebright JR, Rytel MW. Bacterial pneumonia in the elderly. *J Am Geriatr Soc.* 1980;28:220.

5. Miller RM. Evaluation of swallowing disorders. In: Groher ME, ed. *Dysphagia: Diagnosis and Management.* Stoneham, Mass: Butterworth Publishers; 1984.

6. Dobie RA. Rehabilitation of swallowing disorders. *American Family Physician.* 1978; 17(5):84–95.

7. Castell DO. Dysphagia in the elderly: likely causes of oropharyngeal dysphagia in elderly patients. *J Geriatr Soc.* 1986;34(3):248.

8. Ravich WJ. Classification of dysphagia on the basis of the clinical examination. In: *Second Symposium on Dysphagia.* Baltimore, Md: The Johns Hopkins Swallowing Center; March 1988.

9. Robbins J. Approaches to rehabilitation of neurogenic dysphagia. In: *Second Symposium on Dysphagia.* Baltimore, Md: The Johns Hopkins Swallowing Center; March 1988.

10. Hollis JB, Castell DO. Esophageal function in elderly men. *Ann Intern Med.* 1974;80: 371–374.

11. Mold JW, Rankin RA. Symptomatic gastroesophageal reflux in the elderly. *J Am Geriatr Soc.* 1987;35(7)649–659.

12. Kekki M, Sipponen P, Siuraha M. Age behavior of gastric acid secretion in males and females with a normal antral body and body mucosa. *Scand J Gastroenterol.* 1983;18(8):1009–1016.

13. Bock OA, Arapakis G, Witts LJ, et al. The serum pepsinogen level with special reference to the histology of the gastric mucosa. *Gut.* 1963;4:106–111.

14. Minami H, McCallum RW. The physiology and pathophysiology of gastric emptying in humans. *Gastroenterology.* 1984;86(6):1592–1610.

15. Moore JG, Tweedy C, Christian PE, et al. Effect of age on gastric emptying of liquid solid meals in man. *Dig Dis Sci.* 1983;28(4):340–344.

16. Frank EB, Lange R, McCallum RW. Abnormal gastric emptying in patients with atrophic gastritis with or without pernicious anemia. *Gastroenterology.* 1981;80(5):1151.

17. Kupfer RM, Heppell M, Haggith JW, et al. Gastric emptying and small bowel transit rate in the elderly. *J Am Geriatr Soc.* 1985;33(5):340–343.

18. Stricklin RG, Mackay IR. A reappraisal of the nature and significance of chronic atrophic gastritis. *Am J Dig Dis.* 1973;18:426–440.

19. Siurala M, Isokoski M, Varis K, et al. Prevalence of gastritis in a rural population: bioptic study of subjects selected at random. *Scand J Gastroenterol.* 1968;3:211–223.

20. Kekki M, Villako K, Tamm A, et al. Dynamics of antral and fundal gastritis in an Estonian rural population sample. *Scand J Gastroenterol.* 1977;12(3):321–324.

21. Barthel JS, Westblom TU, Havey AD, et al. Gastritis and *Campylobacter pylori* in healthy asymptomatic volunteers. *Arch Intern Med.* 1988;148(5):1149–1151.

22. Krasinski SD, Russell RM, Samloff IM, et al. Fundic atrophic gastritis in an elderly population: effect on hemoglobin and several serum nutritional indicators. *J Am Geriatr Soc.* 1986;34(11):800–806.

23. Russell RM, Krasinski SD, Samloff IM, et al. Folic acid malabsorption in atrophic gastritis: possible compensation by bacterial folate synthesis. *Gastroenterology.* 1986;91(6):1476–1482.

24. Supiano MA. Atrophic gastritis and B_{12} deficiency. *J Am Geriatr Soc.* 1987;35(5):478. Letters to the Editor.

25. Herbert V. Don't ignore low serum cobalamin (vitamin B_{12}) levels. *Arch Intern Med.* 1988;148:1705–1707.

26. Carmel R, Sinow RM, Siegel ME, et al. Food cobalamin malabsorption occurs frequently in patients with unexplained low serum cobalamin levels. *Arch Intern Med.* 1988;148:1715–1719.

27. Elashoff JD, Grossman MI. Trends in hospital admissions and death rates for peptic ulcer in the United States from 1970 to 1978. *Gastroenterology.* 1980;78(2):280–285.

28. Sonneberg A. Changes in physician visits for gastric and duodenal ulcer in the United States during 1958–1984 as shown by National Disease and Therapeutic Index. *Dig Dis Sci.* 1987;32(1):1–7.

29. Walt R, Katschinski B, Logan R, et al. Rising frequency of ulcer perforation in elderly people in the United Kingdom. *Lancet.* 1986;1:489–492.

30. Myren J. The natural history of peptic ulcer views in the 1980s. *Scan J Gastroenterol.* 1983;18(8):993–997.

31. Franceschini G, Montanari G, Cittella C, et al. Cimetidine increases HDL cholesterol, particularly in the HDL3 subfraction. *Metabolism.* 1985;34(7):597–599.

32. Stewart RB, Hale WE, Marks RG. Antacid use in an ambulatory elderly population: a report from Dunedin program. *Dig Dis Sci.* 1983;28(12):1062–1069.

33. Gerbino PP, Gans JA. Antacids and laxatives for symptomatic relief in the elderly. *J Am Geriatr Soc.* 1982;30:S81–S85.

34. Girotti MJ, Ruddan J, Cohanim M. Amphojeloma: antacid impaction in a critically ill patient. *Can J Surg.* 1984;27(4):379–380.

35. Godsall JW, Baron R, Insogna KL, et al. Vitamin D metabolism in bone histomorphometry in a patient with antacid induced osteomalacia. *Am J Med.* 1984;77(4):747–750.

36. Baum C, Kennedy DL, Forbes MB, et al. Drug utilization in the geriatric age group. In: Moore SR, Teal TW, eds. *Geriatric Drug Use: Clinical and Social Prospective.* New York, NY: Pergamon Press; 1985:63–69.

37. Baum C, Kennedy DL, Forbes MB. Utilization of nonsteroidal antiinflammatory drugs. *Arthritis Rheum.* 1985;28(6):686–692.

38. Coles LS, Fries JF, Kraines RG, et al. From experiment to experience: side effects of nonsteroidal anti-inflammatory drugs. *Am J Med.* 1983;74:820–828.

39. Silvoso GR, Ivey KJ, Butt JH, et al. Incidence of gastric lesions in patients with rheumatic disease on chronic aspirin therapy. *Ann Intern Med.* 1979;91:517–520.

40. Bartle WR, Gupta AK, Lazor J. Nonsteroidal anti-inflammatory drugs and gastrointestinal bleeding: a case-control study. *Arch Intern Med*. 1986;146:2365–2367.

41. Laugier R, Sarles H. The pancreas. *Clin Gastroenterol*. 1985;14(4):749–756.

42. Snook JT. Effect of age and long-term diet on exocrine pancreas of the rat. *Am J Physiol*. 1975;228(1):262–268.

43. Kim SK, Weinhold PA, Calkins DW, et al. Comparative studies of the age-related changes in protein synthesis in the rat pancreas and parotid gland. *Exp Gerontol*. 1981;16(1):91–99.

44. Greenberg RE, Holt PR. Influence of aging upon pancreatic digestive enzymes. *Dig Dis Sci*. 1986;31(9):970–977.

45. Greenberg RE, McCann PP, Holt PR. Trophic responses of the pancreas differ in aging rats. *Pancreas*. 1988;3(3):311–316.

46. Bourke JB, Mead GM, McIllmurray MB, et al. Drug associated primary acute pancreatitis. *Lancet*. 1978;1:706–708.

47. Ranson JH, Pasternack BS. Statistical methods for quantifying for severity of clinical acute pancreatitis. *J Surg Res*. 1977;22(2):79–91.

48. Corfield AP, Cooper MJ, Williamson RCN. Acute pancreatitis: a lethal disease of increasing incidence. *Gut*. 1985;26:724–729.

49. DiMagno EP, Malagelada JR, Go VL. Relationship between alcoholism and pancreatic insufficiency. *Ann N Y Acad Sci*. 1975;252:200–207.

50. Mackie RD, Levine AS, Levitt MD. Malabsorption of starch in pancreatic insufficiency. *Gastroenterology*. 1981;80:1220. Abstract.

51. Isaksson G, Ihse I. Pain reduction by an oral pancreatic enzyme preparation in chronic pancreatitis. *Dig Dis Sci*. 1983;28(2):97–102.

52. Russell RM, Dutta SK, Oaks EV, et al. Impairment of folic acid absorption by oral pancreatic extracts. *Dig Dis Sci*. 1980;25(5):369–373.

53. Dutta SK, Bustin MP, Russell RM, et al. Deficiency of fat-soluble vitamins in treated patients wth pancreatic insufficiency. *Ann Intern Med*. 1982;97:549–552.

54. Toskes PP, Greenberger NJ. Acute and chronic pancreatitis. *Dis Mon*. 1983;29:1–81.

55. Toskes PP, Hansell J, Cerda J, et al. Vitamin B_{12} malabsorption in chronic pancreatic insufficiency. *N Engl J Med*. 1971;284:627–632.

56. Lankisch PG, Creutzfeldt W. Therapy of exocrine and endocrine pancreatic insufficiency. *Clin Gastroenterol*. 1984;13(3):985–999.

57. Holt PR, Kotler DP, Pascal RR. Delayed enterocyte differentiation: a defect in aging rat jejunum. *Clin Res*. 1982;30:496A.

58. Welsh JD, Poley JR, Bhatia M, et al. Intestinal disaccharidase activities in relation to age, race and mucosal damage. *Gastroenterology*. 1978;75:847–855.

59. Rorick MH, Scrimshaw NS. Comparative tolerance of elderly from different ethnic backgrounds to lactose-containing and lactose-free dairy drugs. *J Gerontol*. 1979;34:191–196.

60. Klimas JE. Intestinal glucose absorption during the life-span of a colony of rats. *J Gerontol*. 1968;23:529–532.

61. Calingaert A, Zorzoli A. The influence of age on 6-deoxy-D-glucose accumulation by mouse intestine. *J Gerontol*. 1965;20:211–214.

62. Feibusch J, Holt PR. Impaired absorptive capacity for carbohydrates in the elderly. *Am J Clin Nutr*. 1979;32:942.

63. Holt PR. The small intestine. *Clin Gastroenterol*. 1985;14(4):689–723.

64. Hollander D, Ruble PE Jr. Beta-carotene intestinal absorption: bile, fatty acid, pH, and flow rate effects on transport. *Am J Physiol.* 1978;235(6):E686–E691.

65. Holt PR, Dominguez AA. Intestinal absorption of triglyceride and vitamin D_3 in aged and young rats. *Dig Dis Sci.* 1981;26:1104–1115.

66. Geokas MC, Conteas CN, Majumdar AP. The aging gastrointestinal tract, liver, and pancreas. *Clin Geriatr Med.* 1985;1(1):177–205.

67. Holt PR. Intestinal absorption and malabsorption. In: Texter EC, ed. *The Aging Gut.* New York, NY: Masson Publishing USA; 1983.

68. Krazinski SD, Dallal GE, Russell RM. Aging changes vitamin A absorption characteristics. *Gastroenterology.* 1985;88:1715.

69. Hollander D, Morgan D. Increase in cholesterol intestinal absorption with aging in the rat. *Exp Gerontol.* 1979;14:201–205.

70. Hollander D, Morgan D. Aging: its influence on vitamin A intestinal absorption in vivo by the rat. *Exp Gerontol.* 1979;14:301–305.

71. Hollander D, Dadufalza VD, Sletten EG. Does essential fatty acid absorption change in aging? *J Lipid Res.* 1984;25:129–134.

72. Barragry JM, France MW, Crless D, et al. Intestinal cholecalciferol absorption in the elderly and in younger adults. *Clin Sci Mol Med.* 1978;55(2):213–220.

73. Gallagher JC, Lawrence BR, Eisman J, et al. Intestinal calcium absorption and serum vitamin D metabolites in normal subjects and osteoporotic patients. *J Clin Invest.* 1979;64:729–736.

74. Nelson JB, Casteli DO. Effects of aging on gastrointestinal physiology. *Prac Gastroenterol.* 1988;12:28–35.

75. Marx JJM. Normal iron absorption and decreased red cell iron uptake in the aged. *Blood.* 1979;53:204–211.

76. Jacobs P, Bothwell T, Charlton RW. Role of hydrochloric acid in iron absorption. *J Appl Physiol.* 1964;19:187–188.

77. Anuras S, Sutherland J. Jejunal manometry in healthy elderly subjects. *Gastroenterology.* 1986;86:1016.

78. Pelz KS, Gottfried SP, Soos E. Intestinal absorption studies in the aged. *Geriatrics.* 1968;23:149–153.

79. Montgomery RD, Hainey MR, Ross IN, et al. The aging gut: a study of intestinal absorption in relation to nutrition in the elderly. *Q J Med.* 1978;47:197–211.

80. Price HL, Gazzard BG, Dawson AM. Steatorrhoea in the elderly. *Br Med J.* 1977;1:1582–1584.

81. Sklar M, Kirsner JB, Palmer WL. Gastrointestinal disease in the aged. *Med Clin North Am.* 1956;40:223–337.

82. Bayless TM, Rothfeld B, Massa C, et al. Lactose and milk intolerance: clinical implications. *N Engl J Med.* 1975;292(22):1156–1159.

83. Bond JH, Levitt MD. Use of breath hydrogen (H_2) in the study of carbohydrate absorption. *Am J Dig Dis.* 1977;22(4):379–382.

84. Swinson CM, Levi AJ. Is coeliac disease underdiagnosed? *Br Med J.* 1980;281:1258–1260.

85. Kirby J, Fielding JF. Very adult coeliac disease: the need for jejunal biopsy in the middle aged and elderly. *Ir Med J.* 1984;77:35–36.

86. Hallert C, Gothard R, Norrby K, et al. On the prevalence of adult coeliac disease in Sweden. *Scand J Gastroenterol.* 1981;16:257–261.

87. Robertson DAF, Dixon MF, Scott BB, et al. Small intestinal ulceration: diagnostic difficulties in relation to coeliac disease. *Gut.* 1983;24:565–574.

88. Matuchansky C, Collin R, Helmet J, et al. Cavitation of mesenteric lymph nodes, splenic atrophy and a flat small intestinal mucosa: report of six cases. *Gastroenterology.* 1984;87:606–614.

89. Dawson DJ, Sciberras CM, Whitwell H. Coeliac disease presenting with intestinal pseudo-obstruction. *Gut.* 1984;25:1003–1008.

90. Friis SU, Gudmand-Hoyer E. Screening for coeliac disease in adults by simultaneous determination of IgA and IgG gluten antibodies. *Scand J Gastroenterol.* 1986;21(9):1058–1062.

91. Corazza GR, Strocchi A, Gasbarrini G. Breath hydrogen and celiac disease. *Gastroenterology.* 1987;93(1):53–58.

92. Pena AS, Truelove SC, Whitehead R. Disaccharidase activity and jejunal morphology in coeliac disease. *Q J Med.* 1972;41:457–476.

93. McEvoy A, Dutton J, James OFW. Bacterial contamination of the small intestine is an important part of the occult malabsorption in the elderly. *Br Med J.* 1983;287:289–293.

94. Isaccs PET, Kim YS. The contaminated small bowel syndrome. *Am J Med.* 1979;67:1049–1057.

95. Brandt LJ, Boley S, Goldberg L, et al. Colitis in the elderly: a reappraisal. *Am J Gastroentol.* 1981;76:239–245.

96. Tedesco FJ, Hardin RD, Harper RN, et al. Infectious colitis endoscopically simulating inflammatory bowel disease: a prospective evaluation. *Gastrointest Endosc.* 1983;29:195–197.

97. Zimmerman J, Gavish D, Rachmilewitz D. Early and late onset ulcerative colitis: distinct clinical features. *J Clin Gastenterol.* 1985;7(6):492–498.

98. Brocklehurst JC. Colonic disease in the elderly: aging and bowel habit. *Clin Gastroenterol.* 1985;14(4):725–747.

99. Brandt LJ, Boley SJ, Mitsudo S. Clinical characteristics and natural history of colitis in the elderly. *Am J Gastroenterol.* 1982;77(6):382–386.

100. Mayberry JF, Ballantyne KC, Hardcastle JD, et al. Epidemiologic study of asymptomatic inflammatory bowel disease: the identification of cases during a screening programme for colorectal cancer. *Gut.* 1989;30(4):481–483.

101. Joslin CA, Smith CW, Malik A. The treatment of cervix cancer using high activity cobalt-60 sources. *Br J Radiol.* 1972;45:257–270.

102. Yeoh EK, Horowitz M. Radiation enteritis. *Surg Gynecol Obstet.* 1987;165:373–379.

103. O'Brien PH, Jenrette JM III, Garvin AJ. Radiation enteritis. *Am Surg.* 1987;53:501–504.

104. Cox JD, Byhardt RW, Wilson F, et al. Complications of radiation therapy and factors in their prevention. *World J Surg.* 1986;10:171–188.

105. Galland RB, Spencer J. Surgical management of radiation enteritis. *Surgery.* 1986;99(2):133–138.

106. Harling H, Balslev IB. Radical surgical approach to radiation injury of the small bowel. *Dis Colon Rectum.* 1986;29(6):371–372.

107. Arlow FL, Dekovich AA, Priest RJ, et al. Bile acids in radiation-induced diarrhea. *South Med J.* 1987;80(10):1259–1261.

108. McArdle AH, Reid EC, Laplante MP, et al. Prophylaxis against radiation injury. *Arch Surg.* 1986;121:879–885.

109. Miller DH, Ivey M, Young J. Home parenteral nutrition in treatment of severe radiation enteritis. *Ann Intern Med.* 1979;91:858–860.

110. Calloway NO, Foley CF, Lagerbloom P. Uncertainties in geriatric data, II: organ size. *J Am Geriatr Soc.* 1965;13:20–28.

111. Thomas FB, Clausen KP, Greenberger NJ. Liver disease in multiple myeloma. *Arch Intern Med.* 1973;132:195–202.

112. Tauchi H, Sato T. Effective environmental conditions upon age changes in the human liver. *Mech Ageing Dev.* 1975;4(1):71–80.

113. Schaffner F, Popper H. Nonspecific reactive hepatitis in aged and infirm people. *Am J Dig Dis.* 1959;4(5):389–399.

114. Schmucker DL. Age related changes in hepatic fine structure: a quantitative analysis. *J Gerontol.* 1976;31(2):135–143.

115. Landowne M, Stanley J. Aging of the cardiovascular system. In: Shock NW, ed. *Ageing: Some Social And Biological Aspects.* Washington, DC: American Association for the Advancement of Science; 1960.

116. Bender AD. The effect of increasing age on distribution of peripheral blood flow in man. *J Am Geriatr Soc.* 1965;13:192–198.

117. Kampmann JP, Sinding J, Moller-Jorgensen I. Effect of age on liver function. *Geriatrics.* 1975;30(8):91–95.

118. Gersovitz M, Munro HN, Udall J, et al. Albumin synthesis in young and elderly subjects using a new stable isotope methodology: response to level of protein intake. *Metabolism.* 1980; 29(11):1076–86.

119. Kitani K. Hepatic drug metabolism in the elderly. *Hepatology.* 1986;6(2):316–319. Editorial.

120. Crooks J, O'Mallery K, Stevenson IH. Pharmacokinetics in the elderly. *Clin Pharmacokinet.* 1976;1(4):280–296.

121. Woodhouse KW, Mutch E, Williams FM, et al. The effect of age on pathways of drug metabolism in human liver. *Age Ageing.* 1984;13(6):328–334.

122. Smithard DJ, Langman MJ. The effect of vitamin supplementation upon antipyrine metabolism in the elderly. *Br J Clin Pharmacol.* 1978;5(2):181–185.

123. Young VR, Steffee WP, Pencharz PB, et al. Total human body protein synthesis in relation to protein requirements at various ages. *Nature.* 1975;253:192–194.

124. Geokas MC, Conteas CN, Majumdar AP. The aging gastrointestinal tract, liver, and pancreas. *Clin Geriatr Med.* 1985;1(1):177–205.

125. James OFW. Gastrointestinal and liver function in old age. *Clin Gastroenterol.* 1983; 12(3):671–691.

126. Mooney H, Roberts R, Cooksley WGE, et al. Alterations in the liver with ageing. *Clin Gastroenterol.* 1985;14(4):757–771.

127. Gibinski K, Fajt E, Suchan L. Hepatitis in the aged. *Digestion.* 1973;8(3):254–260.

128. Ludwig J, Baggenstoss AH. Cirrhosis of the aged and senile cirrhosis: are there two conditions? *J Gerontol.* 1970;25:244–248.

129. Ludwig J, Axelsen R. Drug effects on the liver: an updated tabular compilation of drugs and drug-related hepatic diseases. *Dig Dis Sci.* 1983;28(7):651–666.

130. Goodson JD, Taylor PA, Campion EW, et al. The clinical course of acute hepatitis in the elderly patients. *Arch Intern Med.* 1982;142:1485–1488.

131. Fenster LF. Viral hepatitis in the elderly: an analysis of 23 patients over 65 years of age. *Gastroenterology.* 1965;49:262–271.

132. Saint EG. Infectious hepatitis in older age groups. *Med J Aust.* 1952;2:613–619.

133. Sherlock S. Acute hepatic failure. In: *Diseases of the Liver Biliary System*. 8th ed. Boston, Mass: Blackwell Scientific Publications Inc; 1989:117.

134. Kaplan M. Primary biliary cirrhosis. *N Engl J Med*. 1987;316(9):521–528.

135. James OFW. Gastrointestinal and liver function in old age. *Clin Gastroenterol*. 1983;12(3):671–691.

136. Hislop WS, Hopwood D, Bouchier IA. Primary biliary cirrhosis in elderly females. *Age Ageng*. 1982;11:153–159.

137. Lehman AB, Bussendine MF, James OF. Primary biliary cirrhosis: a different disease in the elderly? *Gerontology*. 1985;31(3):186–194.

138. Alpers DH, Sabesin SM. Fatty liver: biochemical and clinical aspects. In: Schiff L, Schiff ER, eds. *Diseases of the Liver*. 6th ed. Philadelphia, Pa: JB Lippincott Co; 1987.

139. Lieber CS. Alcohol-nutrition interaction: 1984 update. *Alcohol*. 1984;1(2):151–157.

140. Lieber CS, Spritz N. Effects of prolonged ethanol intake in man: role of dietary, adipose, and endogenously synthesized fatty acids in the pathogenesis of the alcoholic fatty liver. *J Clin Invest*. 1966;45:1400–1411.

141. Reboucas G, Isselbacher JJ. Studies on pathogenesis of ethanol induced fatty liver, 1: synthesis and oxidation of fatty acids by the liver. *J Clin Invest*. 1961;40:1355.

142. Alpers DH, Sabesin SM. Fatty liver: biochemical and clinical aspects: In: Schiff L, Schiff ER, eds. *Diseases of the Liver*. 6th ed. Philadelphia, Pa: JB Lippincott Co; 1987.

143. Katz J, McGarry JD. The glucose paradox: is glucose a substrate for liver metabolism? *J Clin Invest*. 1984;74:1901–1909.

144. Flores H, Pak N, Maccioni A, et al. Lipid transport in kwashiorkor. *Br J Nutr*. 1970;24:1005–1011.

145. Flatt JP. Role of increased adipose tissue mass in the apparent insulin insensitivity of obesity. *Am J Clin Nutr*. 1972;25:1189.

146. Chase R, Sullivan SR, Bloom DB. Insulin, glucagon, and amino acid imbalance in fulminant hepatic failure. *Gut*. 1977;18:A953.

147. Rosen HM, Yoshimura N, Hodgman JM, et al. Plasma amino acid patterns in hepatic encephalopathy of differing etiology. *Gastroenterology*. 1977;72(3):483–487.

148. Fiaccadori F, Magnani G, Pedretti G. Nutritional status in acute liver damage. In: Barbara L, Ed. *Nutrition & Gastrointestinal Disease*. New York, NY: Raven Press; 1987:241–251.

149. Atkinson M, Nordin BE, Sherlock S. Malabsorption and bone disease in prolonged obstructive jaundice. *Q J Med*. 1956;25:299–312.

150. Ros E, Garcia-Puges A, Reixach M, et al. Fat digestion and exocrine pancreatic function in primary biliary cirrhosis. *Gastroenterology*. 1984;87:180–187.

151. Lanspa SJ, Chan AT, Bell JS III, et al. Pathogenesis of steatorrhea in primary biliary cirrhosis. *Hepatology*. 1985;5(5):837–842.

152. Hodgson SF, Dickson ER, Wahner HW, et al. Bone loss and reduced osteoblast function in primary biliary cirrhosis. *Ann Intern Med*. 1985;103(6, pt 1):855–860.

153. Skinner RK, Long RG, Sherlock S, et al. 25-Hydroxylation of vitamin D in primary biliary cirrhosis. *Lancet*. 1977;1:720–721.

154. Epstein O. Nutritional therapy in women with primary biliary cirrhosis. *Geriatr Med Today*. 1983;2(10):48–60.

155. Herlong HF, Russell RM, Maddrey WC. Vitamin A and zinc therapy in primary biliary cirrhosis. *Hepatology*. 1981;1(4):348–351.

156. Mezey E. Progress in hepatology: liver disease and nutrition. *Gastroenterology.* 1978;74:770–783.

157. Burch RE, Sackin DA, Ursick JA, et al. Decreased taste and smell acuity in cirrhosis. *Arch Intern Med.* 1978;138:743–746.

158. Baraona E, Pirola RC, Lieber CS. Small intestinal damage and changes cell population produced by ethanol ingestion in the rat. *Gastroenterology.* 1974;66:226–234.

159. Rubin E, Rybak BJ, Lindenbaum J, et al. Ultrastructural changes in the small intestine induced by ethanol. *Gastroenterology.* 1972;63:801–814.

160. Mezey E, Jow E, Slavin RE, et al. Pancreatic function and intestinal absorption in chronic alcoholism. *Gastroenterology.* 1970;59:657–664.

161. Mezey E, Potter JJ. Changes in endocrine pancreatic function produced by altered dietary protein intake in drinking alcoholics. *Johns Hopkins Med J.* 1976;138(1):7–12.

162. Mezey E. Intestinal function in chronic alcoholism. *Ann NY Acad Sci.* 1975;252:215–227.

163. Malagelada JR, Pihl O, Linscheer WG. Impaired absorption of micellar long-chain fatty acid in patients with alcoholic cirrhosis. *Am J Dig Dis.* 1974;19(11):1016–1020.

164. Vlahcevic ZR, Buhac I, Farrar JT, et al. Bile acid metabolism in patients with cirrhosis: kinetic aspects of cholic acid metabolism. *Gastroenterology.* 1971;60:491–498.

165. Owen OE, Trapp VE, Reichard GA Jr, et al. Nature and quantity of fuels consumed in patients with alcoholic cirrhosis. *J Clin Invest.* 1983;72(5):1821–1832.

166. Marchesini G, Bianchi G, Zoli M, et al. Plasma amino acid response to protein ingestion in patients with liver cirrhosis. *Gastroenterology.* 1983;85(2):283–290.

167. Leevy CM, Baker H, TenHove W, et al. B complex vitamins in liver disease of the alcoholic. *Am J Clin Nutr.* 1965;16:339–346.

168. Gradual N, Milman N, Kirkegaard E, et al. Bacteremia in cirrhosis of the liver. *Liver.* 1986;6(5):297–301.

169. Sherlock S. *Diseases of the Liver and Biliary System.* 8th ed. Boston, Mass: Blackwell Scientific Publications; 1989.

170. Morgan MY, Holly KE, Stambuk D. Lactitol versus lactulose in the treatment of chronic hepatic encephalopathy: a double blind randomized crossover study. *J Hepatol.* 1987;4:236–244.

171. Greenberger NJ, Carley J, Schenker S, et al. Effect of vegetable and animal protein diets in chronic hepatic encephalopathy. *Dig Dis.* 1977;22:845–855.

172. Uribe M, Marquez MA, Ramos GG, et al. Treatment of chronic portal systemic encephalopathy with vegetable and animal protein diets: a controlled crossover study. *Dig Dis Sci.* 1982;27:1109–1116.

173. Jonung T, Jeppsson B, Aslund U, et al. A comparison between meat and vegan protein diet in patients with mild chronic hepatic encephalopathy. *Clin Nutr.* 1987;6:169–174.

174. Rossi-Fanelli F, Cascino A, Cagiano C. Branched chain amino acids in the management of hepatic encepholopathy. *J Clin Nutr Gastroenterol.* 1987;2:44.

175. Rocco VK, Ware AJ. Cirrhotic ascites: pathophysiology, diagnosis and management. *Ann Intern Med.* 1986;105:573–585.

176. Quintero E, Geines P, Arroyo V, et al. Paracentesis versus diuretics in the treatment of cirrhosis with tense ascites. *Lancet.* 1985;1:611–612.

177. Yamajata A. Histopathological studies of the colon due to age. *Jpn J Gastroenterol.* 1965;62:224–235.

178. Melkerson M, Anderson H, Bosaeus I, et al. Intestinal transit time in constipation and nonconstipated geriatric patients. *Scand J Gastroenterol.* 1983;18:593–597.

179. Connell AM, Hilton C, Irvin G. Variations in bowel habit in two population samples. *Br Med J.* 1965;2:1095–1099.

180. Brocklehurst JC. Colonic disease in the elderly. *Clin Gastroenterol.* 1985;14(4):725–747.

181. Frieri G, Parisi F, Corazziari E, et al. Colonic electromyography in chronic constipation. *Gastroenterology.* 1983;84:737–740.

182. Shoulder P, Keighley MRB. Changes in colorectal function in severe idiopathic chronic constipation. *Gastroenterology.* 1986;90:414–420.

183. Loening-Baucke V, Apuras S. Sigmoidal and rectal motility in healthy elderly. *J Am Gerontol Soc.* 1984;32(12):887–891.

184. Bannister JJ, Abouzekry L, Read NW. Effect of aging on anorectal function. *Gut.* 1987;28:353–357.

185. Martelli H, Devroede G, Arhan P, et al. Mechanisms of idiopathic constipation: outlet obstruction. *Gastroenterology.* 1978;75(4):623–631.

186. Watier A, Devroede G, Duranceau A, et al. Constipation with colonic inertia: a manifestation of systemic disease? *Dig Dis Sci.* 1983;28(11):1025–1033.

187. Read MW, Timms JM. Defecation in the pathophysiology of constipation. *Clin Gastroenterol.* 1986;15(4)937–965.

188. Wald A, Stoney B, Hinds JP, Psychological profiles in patients with constipation associated with normal and slow colonic transit. *Gastroenterology.* 1988;95(3):892.

189. Hull C, Greco RS, Brooks DL, et al. Alleviation of constipation in the elderly by dietary fibre supplementation. *J Am Geriatr Soc.* 1988;28(9):41–44.

190. Anderson H, Bosaens I, Falkheden T, et al. Transit time in constipated geriatric patients during treatment with a bulk laxative and bran: a comparison. *Scand J Gastroenterol.* 1979;14(7):821–826.

191. Tomlin J, Read NW. Laxative properties of indigestible plastic particles. *Br Med J.* 1988;297(5):1175–1176.

192. Parks TG. Natural history of diverticular disease of the colon. *Clin Gastroenterol.* 1975;4(1):53–69.

193. Eastwood MA, Watters DAK, Smith AN. Diverticular disease: is it a motility disorder? *Clin Gastroenterol.* 1982;11(3):545–561.

194. Weinreich J, Anderson D. Intraluminal pressure in the sigmoid colon, II: patients with sigmoid diverticula and related conditions. *Scand J Gastroenterol.* 1976;11(6):581–586.

195. Burkitt DP. Epidemiology of cancer of the colon and rectum. *Cancer.* 1971;28:3–13.

Chapter 8

Aging and the Cardiovascular System

Jeanne P. Goldberg

The maximal life span of humans, about 114 years, has remained unchanged over time, while life expectancy in the United States has increased dramatically over the past several decades, reaching a high of 74.8 years in 1986.[1] By 2030, it is expected that the percentage of those living to age 65 years and beyond will double, accounting for 25% of the total population (Chapter 1). Given the fixed upper limit of the human life span, the objective of chronic disease prevention in the growing population of elderly people should be to delay the onset of diseases, and the resulting disabilities, to that limit.[2]

Diseases of the heart and blood vessels are by far the most important cause of morbidity and mortality among elderly individuals, rising logarithmically with age. Elderly people, who contribute 68% of all deaths in the United States annually, account for 78% of all deaths attributed to coronary heart disease (CHD). Among those individuals who reach age 65 years, more than half will suffer a cardiovascular catastrophe. Morbidity is similarly prevalent in this age group. In 1981, of the population aged 65 years or older, 28% reported significant health impairments related to heart conditions, including angina pectoris, congestive heart failure, and rhythm disturbances.[3]

It is widely agreed that primary efforts to prevent cardiovascular disease should begin with altering life style habits during middle age; many experts believe that these efforts should begin considerably earlier (Chapter 17). Prevention activities include maintaining ideal body weight, detecting and treating hypertension, maintaining a blood lipid profile consistent with minimizing risk, smoking cessation, and increased physical activity. Most of these risk factors are closely linked to dietary factors (Table 8-1).[4] However, the relevance of risk factor modification among older populations remains a matter of conjecture, based to a great extent on extrapolation of findings from studies conducted on younger populations.

Although no controlled intervention trials have focused specifically on the elderly segment of the population, the fact that the dramatic decline in the

Table 8-1 Risk Factors for Atherosclerosis

Not reversible
  Aging
  Male sex
  Genetic traits—positive family history of premature atherosclerosis
Reversible
  Cigarette smoking
  Hypertension
  Obesity
Potentially or partially reversible
  Hyperlipidemia/hypercholesterolemia or hypertriglyceridemia or a combination
  Hyperglycemia; diabetes mellitus
  Low levels of high-density lipoproteins
Other possible factors
  Physical inactivity
  Emotional stress or personality type

Source: Reprinted from *Principles of Geriatric Medicine* by R Andres, EL Bierman, and WR Hazzard (Eds) with permission of McGraw-Hill, © 1985.

---

cardiovascular mortality rate has included them argues in favor of risk reduction efforts in this group.[3] Dietary recommendations for elderly people must be based on our currently limited knowledge of the benefits of risk factor modification in older populations and on appropriate modifications for individuals with frank disease. Recommendations must be made within a framework that acknowledges the universal importance of a nutritionally adequate diet and the unique constellation of constraints that might make it difficult to achieve that goal. Moreover, interventions that will reduce risk should take into account the potential for diminishing morbidity and disability that result from cardiovascular disease.[5]

THE DISEASE PROCESSES

Decline in cardiovascular function is a major physical impairment associated with aging from middle age onward. Loss of cardiovascular reserve capacity can be attributed to three factors: age-associated changes, physical deconditioning associated with an increasingly sedentary life style, and changes associated with atherosclerotic cardiovascular disease. The relative contribution of each of these factors is unclear.[6] It is clear, however, that environmentally induced atherosclerotic changes play a major role in this process.

Atherosclerosis, thickening and hardening of the intima (the lining of the coronary arteries), underlies most cardiovascular disease in elderly individuals;

hypertension and diabetes act as important contributing factors. The development of atherosclerosis is believed to result from years of interaction between intrinsic aging processes and environmental factors—including diet—superimposed on unknown, predisposing genetic factors[7] (Figure 8-1). At least two lines of evidence suggest that atherosclerosis is not simply the result of unmodified biologic aging processes. The first line of evidence is that mammalian species age without developing atherosclerosis; second, there are populations that realize the human life span without clinical evidence of the disease.[8]

Changes do occur in the arteries during normal aging. A slow, apparently continuous, symmetric increase in the thickness of the interior walls of the arteries

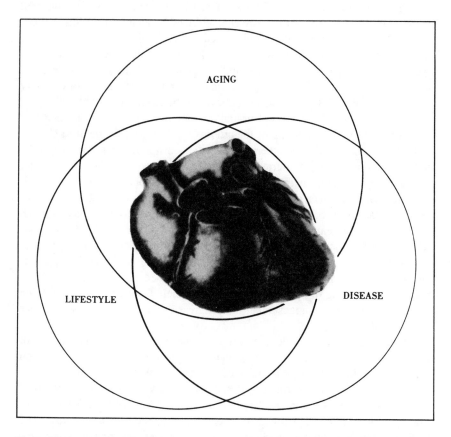

Figure 8-1 Age-related changes in cardiac structure and function interact to alter the presentation of cardiovascular disease in the elderly. *Source*: Reprinted with permission from *Cardiovascular Medicine* (1985; March: 38), Copyright © 1985, Physicians' World.

results from the gradual accumulation of smooth muscle cells from the middle layer of the vessels, surrounded by additional connective tissue. In addition, there is a progressive accumulation of both sphingomyelin and cholesterol ester. These age-associated changes result in a gradual increase in the rigidity of the vessels. Larger arteries may become dilated, elongated, and tortuous. Aneurysms (balloonings of the arterial wall) may form in areas of expanding arteriosclerotic plaques. These wear-and-tear changes often depend on the diameter of the vessel and tend to occur where vessels branch and curve, and at anatomic attachment points.[8]

Although these structural changes are considered to be a normal part of the aging process, atherosclerotic changes are believed to be strongly influenced by environmental factors, especially diet. The lesions of atherosclerosis are generally classified into three categories: fatty streaks, fibrous plaques, and complicated lesions (Figure 8-2). Fatty streaks are characterized by an accumulation of lipid-filled smooth muscle cells and are surrounded by lipid in the lining of the vessels. Whether they are the earliest lesions is a matter of debate. They are universal, appearing in the aorta by age 10 years, and occupying as much as 50% of the aortic surface by age 25 years. The age-related increase in the surface area of coronary arteries involved with fatty streaks is believed to be readily reversible.[9]

Fibrous plaques, which are not ubiquitous among populations, are elevated areas of thickening in the lining of the arteries. They represent the most characteristic lesions of progressive atherosclerosis, appearing first in the intima of the abdominal aorta, coronary arteries, and carotid arteries during the third decade, and gradually increasing with advancing age. A fibrous plaque is firm, elevated, and dome shaped, with an opaque, glistening surface that bulges into the lumen of the affected artery. It consists of an accumulation in the arterial intima of smooth muscle cells rather heavily laden with cholesterol and surrounded by other lipids, collagen, elastic fibers, and other substances. The protrusion of fibrous plaques into the lumina of arteries reduces their diameter. The cholesterol in plaques closely resembles that in plasma lipoproteins. Raised lesions are thought to develop in the setting of a disruption of the endothelial cell continuity overlying fatty streaks. Evidence suggests that the progression of raised lesions continues into very old age.[10]

Complicated lesions are calcified fibrous plaques exhibiting various degrees of necrosis, thrombosis, and ulceration. Increasing necrosis, accumulation of cell debris, and weakening of the arterial wall increase the likelihood of rupture of the interior wall, causing hemorrhage. Arterial emboli may occur when fragments of plaque dislodge into the lumen. The thickening of plaque and the formation of thrombi (clots) lead to narrowing of blood vessels, reduced blood flow, and impaired organ function.[8] Arteries narrowed by raised lesions are more vulnerable to occlusion or blockage than are normal arteries.

The extent of the surface area of coronary arteries involved with fatty streaks increases in men during the second and third decades of life and remains constant

A
B

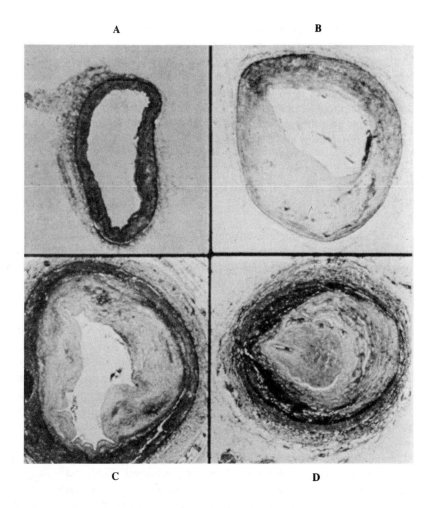

C
D

Figure 8-2 **A,** Normal artery; **B,** moderate atherosclerosis; **C,** severe atherosclerosis vessel wall; and **D,** severe atherosclerosis with occlusive thrombus. *Source:* Courtesy of the National Heart, Lung, and Blood Institute, National Institutes of Health, Bethesda, Maryland.

through the remainder of their lives. However, the development of raised lesions, which gradually impair blood flow, continues. In women, the extent of fatty streaks increases to about age 50 years, but the development of raised lesions lags nearly 20 years behind that for men.

Interventions designed to prevent clinical complications of raised, atherosclerotic lesions have focused on men aged 40 to 50 years for several reasons.

First, raised lesions generally appear earlier in men than in women. Second, associated with the first observation, risk of death from CHD increases in men at an earlier age than in women. Finally, the greatest likelihood of reversing the atherosclerotic process focuses on the smaller, less mature plaques.[11] However, several recent studies have demonstrated significant regression of larger fatty lesions.[12-14] Fibrous, calcified lesions may be prevented from further progression, but they probably do not regress. To date, there have been no clinical interventions trials with elderly subjects.

RISK FACTORS AND THEIR MODIFICATION IN ELDERLY SUBJECTS

Coincidentally with the increased publicity focused on CHD as a cause of death, death rates from CHD began to decline. This decline, which began in 1950, has continued. Between 1968 and 1976, CHD death rates in the adult population declined 20%. Among individuals over age 65 years, there was a decline of between 13% and 27%. Even among men and women aged 85 years and older, the death rate dropped 17% and 21%, respectively.[15] The most recent figures show an overall decline in deaths from CHD between 1985 and 1986.[1] A key question is whether this decline is associated only with better survival rates attributable to improved medical management or whether a decline in incidence also is a contributing factor. For example, a large decline in age-specific incidence rates between the early 1960s and mid-1970s has been demonstrated in a prospective study of both blue-collar and white-collar workers. However, the rate of decline was steeper among the white-collar workers.[16] Among the subjects in the oldest age group, the decline was 22%.

A number of risk factors predict the likelihood of developing a clinical atherosclerotic event, but only some of them can be altered (Table 8-1). Research conducted for over four decades has identified a series of diet-related factors associated with the incidence of cardiovascular disease and the development and progression of the underlying atherosclerosis. The role of dietary fats in regulating circulating lipoprotein levels and the role of body weight in affecting both blood lipoprotein levels and blood pressure are of particular importance. Dietary sodium also has a role in hypertension.[17]

Blood Lipids

Patterns of atherogenic blood lipid levels and their relationship to risk of CHD differ among older men and women. Total serum cholesterol and low-density lipoprotein (LDL) cholesterol fractions tend to plateau in men after age 60 years; in women, serum cholesterol levels rise until age 70 years, and levels actually exceed those seen in men[18] (Figure 8-3). However, the proportion of total serum cholesterol as high-density lipoprotein (HDL) cholesterol remains stable from age 40 years to age 80 years in men. HDL cholesterol levels, which are substantially higher in women, decline slightly, but they remain higher than HDL cholesterol levels in men. HDL cholesterol is inversely correlated with weight and is likely to be lower in individuals with impaired glucose tolerance.[19] It is also lower among individuals who have suffered a coronary event.[19]

In the Framingham study, the relative predictive power of the major cardiovascular risk factors weakens with age for both men and women.[20] Among 35-year-old men with total cholesterol levels of 310 mg/dL, the risk of suffering a coronary event was 5.2 times greater than among those with total cholesterol

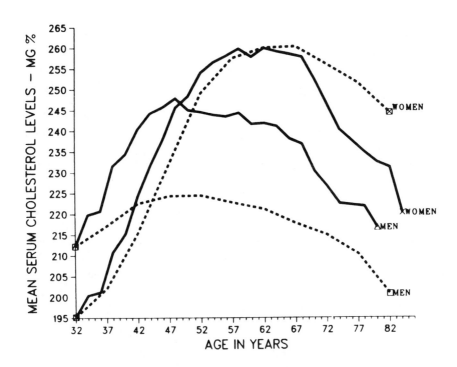

Figure 8-3 Average age trends in serum cholesterol levels for cross-sectional and cohort data. Framingham study, examinations 1 to 16. □, Cross-sectional sample of men; ⊠ cross-sectional sample of women; ∆, cohort of men; ×, cohort of women. *Source*: Reprinted with permission from *Nutrition Reviews* (1988;46:68-78), Copyright © 1988, Springer-Verlag.

levels of 185 mg/dL. However, by age 65 years the relative risk at the higher cholesterol level is only 1.1. Among 45-year-old women with total cholesterol levels of 310 mg/dL, the risk of a coronary event is 2.5 times that of women with total cholesterol levels of 185 mg/dL. However, by age 65 years that risk diminishes to 1.1. Barrett-Connor and colleagues[21] found a significant predictive effect of total cholesterol in groups of men and women aged 65 to 79 years who were followed for 9 years. Recent data from the Framingham study confirm the long-term predictive power of serum cholesterol levels in individuals aged 65 years and older. For each 1% increase in total cholesterol, there is a 2% increase in the incidence of CHD among those 60 to 70 years old.[22]

In the Framingham study, fractioning serum cholesterol into atherogenic LDL and protective HDL cholesterol restores the predictive power of total cholesterol demonstrated at younger ages.[19] A ratio of either LDL cholesterol to HDL cholesterol or total cholesterol to HDL cholesterol is highly predictive of CHD in elderly people. In men, this atherogenic lipid ratio plateaus at age 54 years; in women, it continues to rise until age 80 years but still remains lower than that for men. These observations still do not provide clear evidence that modifying lipoprotein levels at older ages will prevent further progression of atherosclerotic disease among elderly people.

A number of factors affect blood lipid levels. Total serum cholesterol and LDL cholesterol are elevated by excess calories, saturated fat, and dietary cholesterol. They can be lowered by weight reduction, increased dietary unsaturated fats, and water-soluble dietary fiber.[23] Although evidence for the effectiveness of these dietary modifications among elderly people is lacking, that should not preclude individual trials with standard approaches, particularly in the presence of other risk factors and for individuals who are concerned about their serum cholesterol levels.

The National Cholesterol Education Program (NCEP) was developed by the National Heart, Lung, and Blood Institute in 1985[24] as a means to reduce coronary morbidity and mortality related to elevated blood cholesterol levels. The NCEP Expert Panel on Detection, Evaluation, and Treatment of high blood cholesterol was charged with responsibility for developing population-based strategies to shift the distribution of cholesterol levels of the entire population to a lower range.[25] It was also asked to develop guidelines for patient-centered approaches that identify individuals at high risk who would benefit from intervention efforts. The Panel recommends that total cholesterol cutoff points for relative risk for CHD be uniform for men and women of all ages. The Panel acknowledges that there is little direct clinical trial evidence for the benefits of intervention among those aged 60 years and older, and that the LDL cholesterol and CHD association diminishes with age. However, the fact that some association remains, and that evidence from clinical trials with younger individuals suggests that lowering the LDL cholesterol level is of benefit after a myocardial infarction in individuals with advanced disease, argue for attempting to lower LDL cholesterol levels when indicated. Beyond that, the Panel's report points out that, since older age increases the risk of CHD, lowering total cholesterol levels in elderly individuals could result in substantial reductions in morbidity and mortality rates. Modifications of this general approach may be warranted, especially at extreme age.[23]

The Panel has also developed a set of recommendations based on total cholesterol levels[25] (Table 8-2). A second set of criteria for classification and treatment has been developed for those individuals in whom elevated total serum cholesterol levels have indicated a need for lipoprotein analysis[25] (Table 8-3). The outline for dietary modifications is presented in Table 8-4.[25] Modifications in the Step-One diet are similar to the dietary modifications recommended by the American Heart Association as part of a population-based strategy for lowering serum cholesterol:

1. A total of no more than 30% of calories is provided by fat, less than 10% of calories from saturated fat. Polyunsaturated fats provide up to 10% of the calories; monounsaturates provide the remainder.
2. Between 50% and 60% of calories should come from carbohydrates.
3. Between 10% and 20% of calories should come from protein.
4. Cholesterol should be limited to less than 300 mg/d.
5. Calories should be adjusted to achieve and maintain ideal weight.

Table 8-2 Initial Classification and Recommended Follow-up Based on Total Cholesterol*

Classification, mg/dL

<200	Desirable blood cholesterol
200–239	Borderline-high blood cholesterol
≥ 240	High blood cholesterol

Recommendation for follow-up

Total cholesterol <200 mg/dL	Repeat within 5 years
Total cholesterol 200-239 mg/dL	
Without definite CHD or 2 other CHD risk factors (one of which can be male sex)	Provide dietary information and recheck annually
With definite CHD or 2 other CHD risk factors (one of which can be male sex)	Lipoprotein analysis; further action based on LDL cholesterol level
Total cholesterol ≥ 240 mg/dL	Lipoprotein analysis; further action based on LDL cholesterol level

*CHD, Coronary heart disease; LDL, low-density lipoprotein.

Source: Reprinted with permission from *Archives of Internal Medicine* (1989;148:36-69), American Medical Association.

Table 8-3 Classification and Treatment Decisions Based on LDL-Cholesterol*

Classification, mg/dL

<130	Desirable LDL cholesterol
130–159	Borderline high-risk LDL cholesterol
≥160	High-risk LDL cholesterol

	Initiation Level, mg/dL	Minimal Goal, mg/dL
Dietary treatment		
Without CHD or 2 other risk factors†	≥160	<160‡
With CHD or 2 other risk factors†	≥130	<130
Drug treatment		
Without CHD or 2 other risk factors†	≥190	<160
With CHD or 2 other risk factors†	≥160	<130

*LDL, Low-density lipoprotein; CHD, coronary heart disease.

†Patients have a lower initiation level and goal if they are at high risk because they already have definite CHD, or because they have any two of the following risk factors: male sex, family history of premature CHD, cigarette smoking, hypertension, low high-density lipoprotein cholesterol, diabetes mellitus, definite cerebrovascular or peripheral vascular disease, or severe obesity.

‡Roughly equivalent to total cholesterol level of <240 mg/dL or <200 mg/dL as goals for monitoring dietary treatment.

Source: Reprinted with permission from *Archives of Internal Medicine* (1989;148:36-69), American Medical Association.

Two other dietary modifications, targeted toward risk reduction of cardiovascular disease, have gained widespread attention in the popular press. They include the use of fish oils and water-soluble fibers, particularly oat bran.

The Panel believes that specific recommendations for increasing consumption of highly polyunsaturated omega-3 fatty acids, found mainly in fish oils, is unwarranted for several reasons. They have been shown to lower both triglyceride and LDL cholesterol levels when given in high doses and substituted for saturated fats. Moreover, there is no evidence that they reduce the risk for CHD, and whether long-term use will lead to undesirable side effects is unknown.[26] Finally, evidence from epidemiologic studies suggests an association of reduced risk from consumption of fish of any type, independent of omega-3 fatty acid levels.[27] The Panel specifically does not recommend the use of fish oil capsules.[26]

Water-soluble fibers found in oat products and beans, if consumed in large amounts (as much as 15 to 25 g/d), have also been reported to lower plasma cholesterol by 5% to 15%.[28,29] However, the Panel does not make specific recommendations for increasing fiber consumption as a component of the Step-One diet. Similarly, no specific recommendations are made for alcohol, which has

Table 8-4 Dietary Therapy of High Blood Cholesterol Level

Nutrient	Recommended Intake	
	Step-One Diet	Step-Two Diet
Total fat	Less than 30% of total kcal	Less than 30% of total kcal
Saturated fatty acids	Less than 10% of total kcal	Less than 7% of total kcal
Polyunsaturated fatty acids	Up to 10% of total kcal	Up to 10% of total kcal
Monounsaturated fatty acids	10%–15% of total kcal	10%–15% of total kcal
Carbohydrates	50%–60% of total kcal	50%–60% of total kcal
Protein	10%–20% of total kcal	10%–20% of total kcal
Cholesterol	< 300 mg	< 200 mg
Total Calories	To achieve and maintain desirable weight	To achieve and maintain desirable weight

Source: Reprinted with permission from *Archives of Internal Medicine* (1989;148:36-69), American Medical Association.

been shown to raise HDL cholesterol levels. Specific dietary modifications are presented in Table 8-5. The goal of dietary therapy is to reduce elevated cholesterol levels while maintaining a nutritionally adequate diet. Serum cholesterol measurement, and an assessment of adherence to the diet, should be conducted at 4 weeks, 6 weeks, and 3 months. If the total serum cholesterol goal is achieved, the LDL cholesterol level should be measured as confirmation that it has dropped to the desired level. If this occurs, long-term monitoring should include quarterly evaluation for 1 year, and twice-yearly visits after that. At each visit, total serum cholesterol should be measured and diet and behavior modifications reviewed.

If the goal on the Step-One diet is not met, a second trial on the same diet or progression to the Step-Two diet is indicated, with measurement at similar intervals for monitoring and maintenance as for Step-One. On the Step-Two diet, total fat remains at 30% of total calories, but saturated fat is reduced further, to 7%, and cholesterol to 200 mg. Recent evidence indicates that a marked reduction in total fat is not necessary to lower LDL levels satisfactorily if saturated fat is reduced. Although diets with fat levels as low as 20% of total calories may facilitate weight reduction, they have low satiety value and are not well accepted. A minimum of 6 months of intensive dietary therapy and counseling usually should precede the use of drugs, except where levels of LDL cholesterol exceed 225 mg/dL, or where CHD exists. Drug therapy should be added to dietary therapy, not substituted for it.

Table 8-5 Recommended Dietary Modifications to Lower Blood Cholesterol

Foods	Step-One Diet Choose	Decrease
Fish, chicken, turkey, lean meats*	Fish, poultry without skin, lean cuts of beef, lamb, pork, veal, shellfish	Fatty cuts of beef, lamb, pork; spareribs, organ meats, regular cold cuts, sausage, hot dogs, bacon, sardines, roe
Skim milk and low-fat milk, cheese, yogurt,* dairy substitutes	Skim or 1% fat milk (liquid, powdered, evaporated), buttermilk	Whole milk (4% fat) (regular, evaporated, condensed), cream, half-and-half, 2% fat milk, imitation milk products, most nondairy creamers, whipped toppings
	Nonfat (0% fat) or low-fat yogurt	Whole-milk yogurt
	Low-fat cottage cheese (1% or 2% fat)	Whole-milk cottage cheese (4%)
	Low-fat cheeses, farmer or pot cheeses (all of these should be labeled no more than 2–6 g fat per ounce)	All natural cheese (eg, blue, Roquefort, Camembert, Cheddar, Swiss), low-fat or "light" cream cheese, low-fat or "light" sour cream, cream cheeses, sour cream
	Sherbet, sorbet	Ice cream
Eggs*	Egg whites (2 whites equal 1 whole egg in recipes), cholesterol-free egg substitutes	Egg yolks
Fruits and vegetables*	Fresh, frozen, canned, or dried fruits and vegetables	Vegetables prepared in butter, cream, or other sauces
Breads and cereals	Home-baked goods using unsaturated oils sparingly, angel food cake, low-fat crackers, low-fat cookies	Commercial baked goods: pies, cakes, doughnuts, croissants, pastries, muffins, biscuits, high-fat crackers, high-fat cookies
	Rice, pasta	Egg noodles

continues

Table 8-5 continued

| Foods | Step-One Diet | |
	Choose	Decrease
	Whole-grain breads and cereals (oatmeal, whole-wheat, rye, bran, multigrain)	Breads in which eggs are a major ingredient
Fats and oils*	Baking cocoa	Chocolate
	Unsaturated vegetable oils: corn, olive, rapeseed (canola oil), safflower, sesame, soybean, sunflower	Butter, coconut oil, palm oil, palm kernel oil, lard, bacon fat
	Margarine or shortenings made from one of the unsaturated oils listed above, diet margarine	
	Mayonnaise, salad dressings made with unsaturated oils listed above, low-fat dressings	Dressings made with egg yolk
	Seeds and nuts	Coconut

*Limit lean meat, chicken, turkey, and fish to 6 oz/d. Have at least 2 servings of very-low-fat dairy products per day. Include fruits and/or vegetables at every meal. Up to 6 to 8 teaspoons of unsaturated vegetable oil is acceptable. Limit nuts and peanut butter, which are high in fat and calories.

Blood Pressure

Hypertension in elderly individuals is generally classified in three ways.[30] Isolated hypertension is defined as systolic blood pressure greater than 160 mm Hg with an accompanying diastolic pressure less than 95 mm Hg. Predominant systolic hypertension is characterized by a disproportionate elevation in systolic pressure compared with a slightly elevated diastolic pressure. Two formulas are used to express the expected relationship:

$$\text{Expected systolic pressure} = 3/2 \times \text{diastolic pressure}$$

or

$$\text{Expected systolic pressure} = (\text{diastolic pressure} - 15) \times 2$$

Combined systolic and diastolic hypertension, characteristic of essential hypertension, consists of a proportional increase in both systolic and diastolic pressures continuing into old age. For diagnostic purposes, hypertension has been variously defined as systolic pressure exceeding 130 mm Hg to 200 mm Hg, or diastolic pressure between 90 and 120 mm Hg. In the Framingham study, hypertension was defined as greater than 160 mm Hg for systolic pressure and greater than 95 mm Hg for diastolic pressure. According to this definition, 22% of men and 34% of women aged 65 to 74 years were hypertensive.[31]

Hypertension is the most powerful predictor of stroke and the risk factor most readily amenable to treatment. It is also extremely common among elderly people, doubling the overall mortality and tripling cardiovascular mortality.[32] An age-adjusted increased risk of death from all causes and from cardiovascular causes during 24 years of follow-up in the Framingham study was at least twice that of subjects with blood pressure at or below 140/95 mm Hg.

Longitudinal observations from the Framingham study show different patterns for systolic and diastolic pressures in men and women. Among women there is an almost linear rise in systolic pressure, with obesity acting as a significant contributing factor. Diastolic pressure rises until the early 60s and then declines. In men, systolic pressure peaks in middle age and then levels off, whereas diastolic pressure rises until the mid-50s and then declines.[18]

The rise in blood pressure with age that is observed in most countries does not occur among some primitive populations, which may indicate that hypertension is not an inevitable consequence of aging.[30] Until recently, however, isolated systolic hypertension was widely viewed as a benign disease of older persons and was thought to be a physiologic adaptation necessary for the perfusion of aging organ systems. Antihypertensive therapy was commonly believed by practicing physicians to be of little value and too dangerous in individuals over age 65 years.

Isolated systolic hypertension (ISH), usually a reflection of diminished distensibility of the aorta, has recently been estimated to exist in 14.4% of the men and 22.8% of the women in the Framingham heart study, occurring as the end-point of several contributing factors.[32] These include the effects of systolic hypertension on arterial wall compliance, inducing a gradual reduction in diastolic pressure and increased pulse pressure. The disproportionate rise in systolic pressure is consistent with a progressive loss of elasticity, and the fact that it is predominantly systolic pressure that rises does not make it less dangerous. In fact, evidence from the Framingham study indicates that no measure is superior to systolic pressure in predicting cardiovascular events in general, and stroke in particular—the hypertensive event most closely related to blood pressure elevation.[30]

The recent statement of the Working Group on Hypertension in the Elderly[33] outlines a diagnostic and treatment program for the management of elevated blood pressure in elderly individuals. The rationale for the program is based on findings from both observational and interventional studies. Both the Hypertension Detection and Follow-up Program and the Australian National Blood Pressure Study have demonstrated a reduction in cardiovascular morbidity and mortality in patients aged 60 to 90 years with diastolic hypertension. The incidences of fatal and nonfatal stroke were reduced by 45.5% and 26%, respectively. The European Working Party on High Blood Pressure demonstrated a reduction in cardiovascular mortality of 38%.[33]

Since clinical trials conducted to assess the benefits of antihypertensive therapy have routinely used diastolic pressure as the measurement of interest, most evidence regarding the relationship between ISH and increased risk of cardiovascular disease comes from epidemiologic studies.[34-36] One study found a two- to fivefold excess risk of cardiovascular death over 2 years[34]; a second study found an excess mortality of 51% among insured individuals with hypertension[35]; and a third study found a stroke incidence 2.5 times higher than among individuals with normal blood pressure.[36] The Systolic Hypertension in the Elderly Program (SHEP), a prospective intervention study of antihypertensive therapy currently underway, will provide a more detailed protocol for the treatment of ISH in elderly patients.[33]

Based on available evidence, the Working Group on Hypertension in the Elderly has made several recommendations for the detection and treatment of hypertension of elderly people.[33] The first step in the management protocol consists of two dietary measures, calorie control and sodium restriction. Both of these interventions have serious practical limitations, the former with respect to compliance and the latter with respect to variability in physiologic response. Weight loss has been shown to have an independent antihypertensive effect on blood pressure.[37,38] Unfortunately, the success rate for long-term weight maintenance is limited. Not all hypertensives experience a drop in blood pressure on reduced sodium intake. It has been suggested that there is, in all likelihood, a continuum of response, and that older individuals are more likely to benefit from sodium restriction.[18]

If diet is not effective, drug therapy should be initiated. The choice of medication is based on the coexistence of both risk factors and disease.[39] Diuretics are often the drugs of choice for elderly patients. They were evaluated during the feasibility trial for the SHEP and were found to be both effective and acceptable. The possibility of particular sensitivity to the hypokalemic effects of diuretics among elderly people suggests that serum potassium should be monitored closely and that extra emphasis should be placed on including generous amounts of potassium-rich foods in the diet. Although potassium supplements reportedly can help offset the effects of a high sodium intake, cost and the potential hazards associated with their use make them impractical.[17] Sodium restriction, used in conjunction with diuretics, has been shown to reduce dependence on antihypertensive medications.[18]

Alcohol is associated with increased blood pressure; caffeine, however, is not.[17] Evidence for relationships between blood pressure and other nutrients is more sparse, and their relationship to hypertension in elderly people is unclear.

The long-term effects of increased calcium and magnesium, modification of food intake, and vegetarian diets on hypertension in older subjects remain to be explored.[17]

A reasonable protocol for appropriate measures for the dietary management of hypertension, which is feasible for elderly people, has been suggested.[40] It includes the following:

- Reduce weight when indicated
- Restrict sodium intake to 2 g/d (88 mmol/d)
- Supplement potassium only in the presence of hypokalemia, since intake will increase on a lower sodium intake
- Supplement magnesium and calcium only when a deficiency exists, making sure not to reduce dietary calcium when the diet is modified to reduce sodium levels
- Increase fiber and lower saturated fat intake, which may be of benefit for other reasons and may help lower blood pressure
- Restrict alcohol to 2 oz/d

Obesity

The relationship of obesity to increased risk for cardiovascular disease in elderly individuals remains controversial, with some studies indicating increased risk at both extremes of the weight distribution curve.[41] Much of the controversy is explained by the confounding effects of smoking, coexisting disease, and inadequate follow-up.[18] However, the preponderance of evidence suggests that obesity heightens other atherogenic risk factors and thereby contributes to increased risk. The relationships between weight and cardiovascular risk are presented in Figure 8-4.[42]

Data from the Framingham study at 30-year follow-up demonstrate a continuous relationship between obesity and coronary morbidity and mortality (stronger in men than in women). Obesity is associated with both blood pressure and serum lipoprotein levels. In the Framingham study,[43] correlation between relative weight and either systolic or diastolic pressure declined steadily over adult life. Havlik and colleagues,[44] using the body mass index (wt/ht^2) (BMI) and blood pressure, reported similar declines in men over the age range 30 to 70 years. Harlan and associates[45] showed a reduction in association between BMI and systolic blood pressure in older women. The weaker association at older ages remains significant for men, but not for women.

In the Framingham study, the correlation between relative body weight and total plasma cholesterol is not significant over age 50 years for men; for women, it is

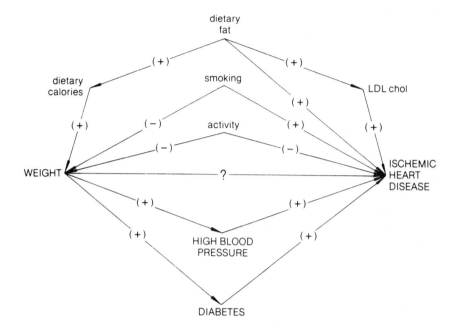

Figure 8-4 Interactions and confounding effects in the relationships between body weight and ischemic heart disease. LDL chol, low-density lipoprotein cholesterol. *Source*: Reprinted with permission from *Annals of Internal Medicine* (1985;103:1003-1005), Copyright © 1985, American College of Physicians.

significant only among 35- to 39-year-olds.[46] Further analyses showed that, over age 50 years, BMI is no longer significantly associated with LDL cholesterol in either sex. However, the strong inverse relationship between HDL cholesterol and BMI remains statistically significant, even among subjects aged 70 to 79 years.[46,47] Therefore, the benefits of maintaining optimal weight for height are associated with a positive effect on HDL cholesterol levels.[6]

The effects of weight change on blood lipid profiles, however, are considerable. In the Framingham study, the investigators found that a 10-unit change in weight relative to height was associated with a change in serum total cholesterol of 11 mg/dL in men and 6.3 mg/dL in women. There was no diminution in these relationships among older age groups.[48] Both Wolf and Grundy[49] and Zimmerman and colleagues[50] found modest increases in HDL cholesterol with weight reduction. A 10-unit change in relative weight also resulted in a change of 6.6 and 4.5 mm/Hg in men and women, respectively.[48]

Both blood lipids and blood pressure are sensitive to degree of obesity. National surveys have found that the relative weights of men increased between the 1950s and the mid-1970s, and that increased fatness has occurred among 65- to 74-year-old men. This suggests that weight reduction has not contributed to declining serum cholesterol levels in men, and that increased fatness may even have blunted the trend. Among women, relative weights decreased at young and middle ages, but no trend has emerged among the older cohort.[6]

A small but significant drop in age-specific blood pressure over the past 22 years has been observed,[51] despite increased relative weight. More effective control of obesity, and especially the prevention of weight gain in middle adult life, is of potentially great value in further reducing CHD mortality. Direct evidence for long-term benefits of weight reduction is lacking, and likely to remain so. The inability to achieve and maintain sustained weight loss is widely documented.[52] Moreover, it is impractical to conduct a controlled trial with random assignment of subjects to a weight reduction program. Few data compare the relative risks associated with weight fluctuation and sustained obesity. In the Framingham study, weight at younger ages has been found to be an important predictor of cardiovascular disease.[53,54] Relative weights at the time of initial examination predicted a 26-year incidence of CHD and cardiac failure in men, independent of risk factors associated with increased fatness. In women, there was an independent association between relative weight and CHD, stroke, cardiac failure, and cardiovascular mortality. The relative risk of CHD 25 years later in a group of men ranging in age from 45 to 57 years at time of entry into the study who reported weight fluctuation during young adulthood was double that for men whose weight remained stable or increased.[55]

Weight reduction has been shown to confer substantial improvement in the cardiovascular risk profile. Therefore, it is recommended for elderly individuals who are 20% or more above desirable weight as defined by BMIs of 27.2 for men and 26.9 for women. In individuals with diabetes, hypertension, dyslipidemia, and gout, lesser degrees of overweight should be reversed.[18]

Dietary Modification for Cardiovascular Risk Reduction

The decline in CHD mortality that began in the 1960s coincided with considerable changes in the American diet. Between 1960 and 1974, egg consumption declined 14%, milk and cream by 25%, butter by 50%, and animal fat by 39%. Per capita use of margarine increased 33%, poultry by 50%, and fish by 30%.[56–58] A comparative analysis of dietary data obtained over more than 20 years from epidemiologic studies of middle-aged Americans shows the impact of these altered food habits on fat intake. Energy derived from total and saturated fat declined by 2% to 3%, and dietary cholesterol consumption declined between 100 and 200 mg/d. The decline in saturated (S) fat intake and the increase in polyunsaturated (P) fats raised the dietary P:S ratio from 0.25 to 0.5 by the mid-1970s.[59]

Information about elderly people is limited. However, among elderly individuals in Boston,[60] it was found that men in their 80s and 90s consumed diets in which 35% of calories came from fat, the P:S ratio was 0.4, and their cholesterol intake averaged 300 to 400 mg/d. These data are similar to those from the Lipid Research Clinics Prevalence Study.[61]

Studies of secular trends in blood lipid levels have shown that serum total cholesterol began to decline in the late 1950s across the broad age span from 20 to 74 years. Data from the large national health surveys and from the Framingham study have shown substantial decreases among individuals of both sexes.[6] Data from the Baltimore Longitudinal Study extend this observation to men in their 70s and 80s. Therefore, the decline in blood total cholesterol over the past 25 years is consistent with dietary changes, even among older age groups.[6]

Consideration of further dietary modifications for elderly persons must address two questions. First, are the dietary modifications of value for older people? Second, are the proposed changes feasible? A consistent observation in elderly people has been their extremely low energy intakes. Since intake of essential nutrients is closely related to calorie intake, the risk of nutrient deficiencies rises in older groups. Further calorie restriction carries with it the potential danger of increasing the risk of nutrient deficiencies. For weight reduction, it is perhaps more reasonable to suggest increased physical activity rather than further decreases in calorie intake.

Any dietary modification in older individuals should begin with a careful assessment to determine both the nutritional adequacy of the diet and the level of intake of nutrients to be modified. In particular, current and usual levels of sodium intake should be assessed before dietary modifications are made. In order to succeed, the diet plan should be developed in cooperation with the patient, allowing for differences in cultural patterns and taste preferences. The concept that only 30% of calories should come from fat, and just 10% from saturated fat, is difficult for many individuals to apply to their diets. To be effective, the nutrition counselor must develop unique methods of communicating simple concepts to older individuals who are expected to modify their diets. A nutrition counselor who prescribes diets modified in calories, fat, and sodium to older subjects and neglects to teach them how to select and prepare the diets is likely to see failure and noncompliance by these individuals.

CONCLUSION

Recommendations for cardiovascular disease prevention for older people are extensions of recommendations for younger age groups; they focus primarily on

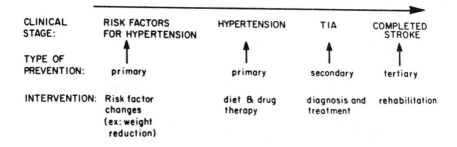

CLINICAL STAGE:	RISK FACTORS FOR HYPERTENSION	HYPERTENSION	TIA	COMPLETED STROKE

Figure 8-5 Progression in the focus of stroke prevention, based on degree of disease present. TIA, Transient ischemic attack. *Source*: Reprinted with permission from *Epidemiologic Reviews* (1988;10:48-64), Copyright © 1988, Johns Hopkins University, School of Hygiene and Public Health.

functional ability or the full spectrum of conditions associated with advancing age, largely because the efficacy of prevention in elderly people is undetermined.[5] Prevention efforts for elderly individuals might more appropriately be viewed in a three-stage model, as shown in Figure 8-5. The model for consideration of intervention strategies for the management of hypertension can be applied to other cardiovascular risk factors as well. The development of more effective nutritional interventions for elderly people requires a series of steps. First, it is essential to define appropriate risk factors and effective modifiers for the natural history of disease; second, to define outcomes meaningful to elderly individuals in terms of the burden of illness; and, third, to identify critical points of intervention to prevent disability.

REFERENCES

1. National Center for Health Statistics. Advance report of final mortality statistics, 1986. *Monthly Vital Statistics Report*. 1988;37:6(suppl). Hyattsville, Md: US Public Health Service. US Dept of Health and Human Services publication PHS 88-1120.

2. Bierman EL, Hazzard WR. Middle age: strategies for the prevention or attenuation of the chronic diseases of aging. In: Andres R, Bierman EL, Hazzard WR, eds. *Principles of Geriatric Medicine*. New York, NY: McGraw-Hill Book Co; 1985.

3. *Technology and Aging in America*. US Congress, Office of Technology Assessment, OTA-NS-264. Washington, DC: US Office of Technological Assessment; 1985.

4. Bierman EL. Aging and atherosclerosis. In: Andres R, Bierman EL, Hazzard WR, eds. *Principles of Geriatric Medicine*. New York, NY: McGraw-Hill Book Co; 1985.

5. Fried LP, Bush TL. Morbidity as a focus of preventive health care in the elderly. *Epidemiol Rev*. 1988;10:48–64.

6. McGandy RB. Nutrition and the aging cardiovascular system. In: Hutchinson ML, Munro HN, eds. *Nutrition and Aging*. Orlando, Fla: Academic Press Inc; 1986.

7. Lakatta EG. Health, disease and cardiovascular aging. *Cardiovasc Med.* 1985 (March):38.

8. Bierman EL. Arteriosclerosis and aging. In: Finch CE, Schneider EL, eds. *Handbook of the Biology of Aging.* New York, NY: Van Nostrand Reinhold Co; 1985.

9. McGandy RB. Atherogenesis and aging. In: Chernoff R, Lipschitz DA, eds. *Health Promotion and Disease Prevention in the Elderly.* New York, NY: Raven Press; 1988.

10. Waller BF, Roberts WC. Cardiovascular disease in the very elderly. *Am J Cardiol.* 1983; 51:403–421.

11. Hennerici M, Rautenberg W, Trockel U, et al. Spontaneous progression and regression of small carotid atheromata. *Lancet.* 1985;1:1415–1419.

12. Blankenhorn DH. Prevention or reversal of atherosclerosis: review of current evidence. *Am J Cardiol.* 1989;63:38H–41H.

13. Cashin-Hemphill L, Sanmarco ME, Blankenhorn DH. Augmented beneficial effects of co-lestipol-niacin therapy at four years in the CLAS trial. Presented at the American Heart Association Annual Meeting; November, 1989.

14. Ornish DM, Scherwitz W, Brown SE, et al. Adherence to lifestyle changes and reversal of coronary atherosclerosis. Presented at the American Heart Association Annual Meeting; November, 1989.

15. Rosenberg HM, Klebba AJ. Trends in cardiovascular mortality with a focus on ischemic heart disease: United States 1950–1976. In: Havlik RJ, Feinleib M, eds. *Proceedings of the Conference on the Decline in Coronary Heart Disease Mortality.* Washington, DC: Conference on Decline in Coronary Heart Disease Mortality; 1979. US Dept of Health, Education, and Welfare publication NIH 79-1610.

16. Pell S, Fayerweather WE. Trends in the incidence of myocardial infarction and in associated mortality and morbidity in a large employed population. *N Engl J Med.* 1985;312:1005–1011.

17. Kaplan NM. Non-drug treatment of hypertension. *Ann Intern Med.* 1985;102:359–373.

18. Kannel WB. Nutrition and the occurrence and prevention of cardiovascular disease in the elderly. *Nutr Rev.* 1988;46:68–78.

19. Castelli WP, Doyle JT, Gordon T, et al. HDL cholesterol and other lipids in coronary heart disease. *Circulation* 1977;55:767–772.

20. Kannel WB, Gordon T, eds. *The Framingham Study: An Epidemiological Investigation of Cardiovascular Disease.* Section 27. Washington, DC: US Public Health Service; 1971. US Dept of Health, Education, and Welfare publication NIH 1740-0320.

21. Barrett-Connor E, Suarez L, Kjaw K, et al. Ischemic heart disease risk factors after 50. *J Chronic Dis.* 1984;27:103–114.

22. Castelli WP, Wilson PWF, Levy D, et al. Cardiovascular risk factors in the elderly. *Am J Cardiol.* 1989;63:12H–19H.

23. Blum CB, Levy R. Current therapy for hypercholesterolemia. *JAMA* 1989;261:3582–3587.

24. Lenfant C. New national cholesterol education program. *Cardiovasc Med.* 1985;10:39–40.

25. Expert Panel: Report of the national cholesterol education program expert panel on detection, evaluation, and treatment of high blood cholesterol in adults. *Arch Intern Med.* 1989;148:36–69.

26. Committee on Diet and Health, National Research Council. *Diet and Health: Implications for Reducing Chronic Disease Risk.* Washington, DC: National Academy Press; 1989.

27. Kromhout D, Bosschieter EB, Coulander CDL. The inverse relationship between fish consumption and 20-year mortality from coronary heart disease. *N Engl J Med.* 1985;312:1205–1209.

28. Anderson JW, Story L, Sieling B, et al. Hypocholesterolemic effects of oat-bran or bean intake for hypercholesterolemic men. *Am J Clin Nutr.* 1984;40:1146–1155.

29. VanHorn L, Liu K, Parker D, et al. Serum lipid response to oat product intake with a fat-modified diet. *J Am Diet Assoc*. 1986;86:759–764.

30. Kannel WB. Hypertension and aging. In: Finch CE, Schneider EL, eds. *Handbook of the Biology of Aging*. New York, NY: Van Nostrand Reinhold Co; 1985.

31. Kannel WB, Brand FN. Cardiovascular risk factors in the elderly. In Andres R, Bierman EL, Hazzard WR, eds. *Principles of Geriatric Medicine*. New York, NY: McGraw-Hill Book Co; 1985.

32. Wilking SVB, Belanger A, Kannel WB, et al. Determinants of isolated systolic hypertension. *JAMA*. 1988;260:3451–3455.

33. The Working Group on Hypertension in the Elderly. Statement on hypertension in the elderly. *JAMA*. 1986;256:70–74.

34. Kannel WB. Implications of Framingham study data for treatment of hypertension: impact of other risk factors. In: Laragh JH, Buhler FR, Seldin DW, eds. *Frontiers in Hypertension Research*. New York, NY: Springer-Verlag Inc; 1981.

35. Blood Pressure Study 1979. Chicago, Ill: Society of Actuaries and Association of Life Insurance Medical Directors of America; 1980.

36. Shekelle RB, Ostfeld AM, Klawans HL Jr. Hypertension and risk of stroke in an elderly population. *Stroke*. 1974;5(1):71–75.

37. Reisen E, Frohlich EG, Messerli FH, et al. Cardiovascular changes after weight reduction in obesity hypertension. *Ann Intern Med*. 1983;98:315–319.

38. Maxwell MH, Kushiro T, Dornfeld LP, et al. Blood pressure changes in obese hypertensive subjects during rapid weight loss: comparison of restricted versus unchanged salt intake. *Arch Intern Med*. 1984;144:1581–1584.

39. Weber MA, Neutel JM, Chung DG. Hypertension in the aged: a pathologic basis for treatment. *Am J Cardiol*. 1989;63:25H–32H.

40. Kaplan NM. Non-pharmacologic therapy of hypertension. *Med Clin North Am*. 1987; 71:921–933.

41. Jarret RJ. Is there an ideal body weight? *Br Med J*. 1986;293:493–495.

42. Stallones R. Epidemiologic studies of obesity. In: Foster WR, Burton BT, eds. Health implications of obesity. *Ann Intern Med*. 1985;103(6 pt 2):1003–1005.

43. Kannel WB, Gordon T. *An Epidemiologic Investigation of Cardiovascular Disease*. Section 5. Washington, DC: US Public Health Service; 1968. US Dept of Health, Education, and Welfare publication.

44. Havlik RJ, Hubert HB, Fabsitz RR, et al. In: Weight and hypertension. *Ann Intern Med*. 1983;98(2 pt 5):855–859.

45. Harlan WR, Hull AL, Schmouder RL, et al. High blood pressure in older Americans: the first national health and nutrition examination survey. *Hypertension*. 1984;6(pt 1):802–809.

46. Jannel WB, Gordon T, Castelli WP. Obesity, lipids, and glucose intolerance: the Framingham study. *Am J Clin Nutr*. 1979;32:1238–1245.

47. Wilson PWF, Garrison RJ, Abbott RD, et al. Factors associated with lipoprotein cholesterol levels: the Framingham study. *Arteriosclerosis*. 1983;3:273–281.

48. Ashley FW Jr, Kannel WB. Relation of weight change to changes in atherogenic traits: the Framingham study. *J Chronic Dis*. 1974;27:103–114.

49. Wolf RN, Grundy SM. Influence of weight reduction on plasma lipoproteins in obese patients. *Arteriosclerosis*. 1983;3:160–169.

50. Zimmerman J, Kaufman NA, Fainaru M, et al. Effective weight loss in moderate obesity on plasma lipoprotein and apolipoprotein levels and on high density lipoprotein composition. *Arteriosclerosis*. 1984;4:115–123.

51. Drizd T, Dannenberg AL, Engel A. Blood pressure levels in persons 18–74 years of age in 1976–80, and trends in blood pressure from 1960 to 1980 in the United States. *Vital Health Stat.* 1986;234(11):1–68.

52. Brownell KD. Public health approaches to obesity and its management. In: Breslow L, Fielding JE, Lave LB eds. *Annual Review of Public Health.* Palo Alto, Calif: Annual Reviews Inc; 1986.

53. Dannenberg A, Drizd T, Horan M, et al. CVD. *Epidemiology Newsletter.* January 1985, 68. Abstract.

54. Higgins M, Kannel WB, Garrison R, et al. Hazards of obesity: the Framingham experience. *Acta Med Scand.* 1987;723(suppl):23–26.

55. Hubert HB, Feinleib M, McNamara PM, et al. Obesity as an independent risk factor for cardiovascular disease: a 26-year follow-up of participants in the Framingham heart study. *Circulation.* 1983;67:968–977.

56. Hamm P, Shekelle RB, Steinler J. Large fluctuations in body weight during young adulthood and twenty-five year risk of coronary death in men. *Am J Epidemiol.* 1989;29:312–318.

57. Stamler J. Hypertension, blood lipids and cigarette smoking as co-risk factors for coronary heart disease: discussion. *Ann N Y Acad Sci.* 1978;304:140–146.

58. Slattery ML, Randall DE. Trends in coronary heart disease mortality and food consumption in the United States between 1909 and 1980. *Am J Clin Nutr.* 1988;47:1060–1067.

59. Walker WJ. Changing U.S. lifestyle and declining vascular mortality: a retrospective. *N Engl J Med.* 1983;308:649–651.

60. McGandy RB, Russell RM, Hartz SC, et al. Nutritional status survey of healthy noninstitutionalized elderly: energy and nutrient intakes from three-day records and nutrient supplements. *Nutr Res.* 1986;6:785–798.

61. Goor R, Hosking JD, Dennis BH, et al. Nutrient intakes among selected North American populations in the Lipid Research Clinics Prevalence Study: composition of fat intake. *Am J Clin Nutr.* 1985;41:299–311.

Chapter 9

The Aging Renal System

Robert D. Lindeman

The accuracy and simplicity with which renal clearance studies can be performed, requiring only timed urine samples and blood samples drawn at the midpoints of these collection periods, make the kidney an ideal organ for studying the physiologic changes that occur with aging. Many descriptive studies performed in the 1950s and 1960s on cross-sectional populations show mean changes in renal function in each age group. In 1958, the Baltimore Longitudinal Study of Aging was initiated at what is now the Gerontology Research Center of the National Institute of Aging, and up to 30 years of information is available to add substantially to our knowledge of the normal aging process.

Controversy still remains as to the pathophysiology of the decline in renal function observed with age. Cross-sectional and longitudinal studies show a mean loss approximating 1 mL/min per year in glomerular filtration rates (GFR), and other physiologic renal functions parallel this change. Is this all due to superimposed, often undetectable, pathologic processes, or is there a progressive involutional loss of function that is inevitable? Do hyperperfusion and hyperfiltration develop in residual nephrons of aging persons, leading to development of glomerulosclerosis as seen in rats and in humans with diabetes mellitus? Does vasoconstriction or a decrease in protein intake in elderly persons account for a portion of the loss in kidney fι ιction?

CHANGES IN RENAL MORPHOLOGY WITH AGE

The weight of both kidneys, about 50 g at birth, increases to 270 g in the third and fourth decades and thereafter decreases to 185 g in the ninth decade.[1] The loss of renal mass is principally from the cortex and is primarily vascular in origin, with the most significant changes occurring at the capillary level. The number of glomerular tufts per unit area and the number of glomerular and tubular cells decrease, while the size of individual cells increases with age.[2]

A detailed description of the course of ischemic obsolescence of glomeruli has been provided by several investigators.[3,4] Initially, there is progressive collapse of the glomerular tuft with wrinkling of the basement membranes, followed by a simplification and reduction in the vascular channels. Hyaline is deposited within both the residual glomerular tuft and the space of Bowman's capsule. Identifiable structures rapidly disappear. The obsolete glomerulus may be resorbed and disappear entirely; resorption is suggested because of the scantiness of the cellular response and residual scar. This process can leave a single vessel in place of the glomerular capillary, thus producing a shunt between the afferent and efferent arterioles. Ljungvist[5] and Takazakura and colleagues[6] confirmed the presence of these shunts in the juxtamedullary glomeruli. In the cortical area, atrophy resulted in an abrupt termination of the arteriole (Figure 9-1).

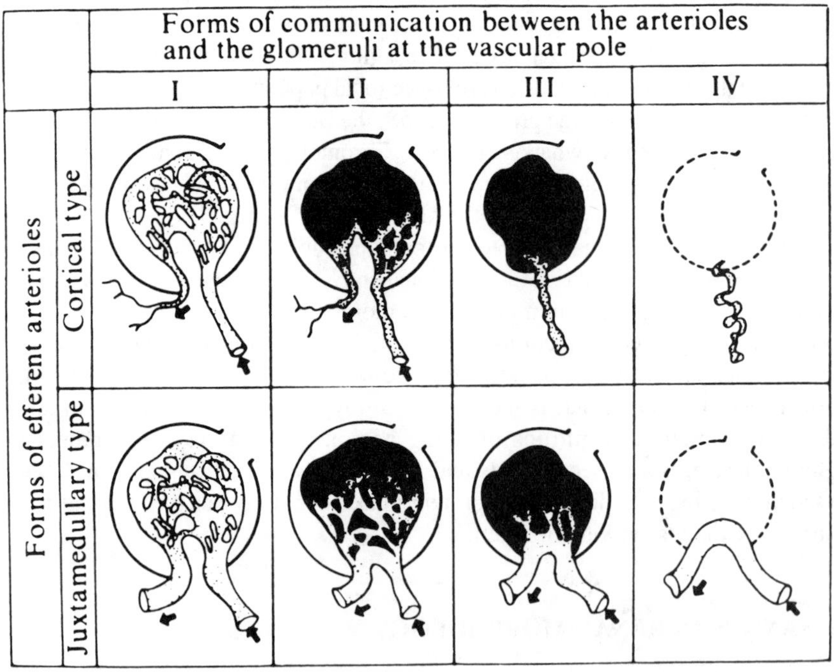

Figure 9-1 The arteriole-glomerular units are classified into two basic types, cortical and juxtamedullary. Cortical glomeruli are shown in various stages of degeneration, terminating in complete atrophy of the arteriolar-glomerular units. The vasculature in the juxtamedullary glomeruli shows a shunt forming between the afferent and efferent arterioles. *Source:* Reprinted with permission from *Kidney International* (1972;2:224–230), Copyright © 1972, International Society for Nephrology.

CHANGES IN RENAL FUNCTION WITH AGE

Glomerular Filtration Rate

A number of studies have been reported that show an age-related decline in renal function after age 30 years[7] (Figure 9-2). All of these cross-sectional studies indicate that the rate of decline in the GFR approximates 1 mL/min per year. Rowe

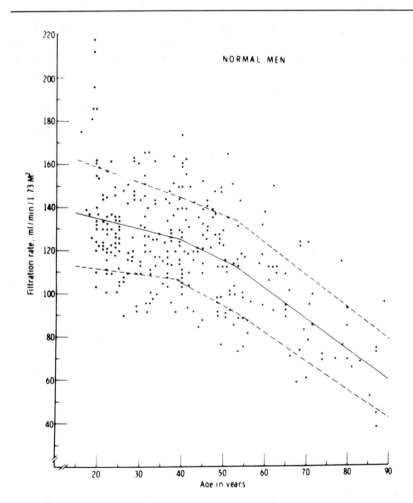

Figure 9-2 Glomerular filtration rates (inulin clearances) per 1.73 m_2 in normal men versus age in 38 studies. The solid and broken lines represent 1 standard deviation. *Source:* Reprinted by permission from Wesson, *Physiology of the Human Kidney,* New York, Grune & Stratton, 1969.

and colleagues[8] reported a 10-year analysis of the first large-scale longitudinal study of renal function. Serial true creatinine clearances were obtained on 884 community-dwelling volunteers at 12- and 18-month intervals (Baltimore Longitudinal Study of Aging). The cross-sectional analysis (Figure 9-3) provided data similar to those observed in other studies. An analysis of the serial creatinine clearances (longitudinal analysis) showed that there was an accelerating decline in creatinine clearances similar to that observed in cross-sectional studies, indicating that selective mortality and cohort differences had no significant impact on the cross-sectional results.

Although mean creatinine clearance rates fell from 140 mL/min per 1.73 m² at age 25 to 34 years to 97 mL/min per 1.73 m² at age 75 to 84 years, mean serum creatinine concentrations rose insignificantly from 72 to 74 μmol/L (0.81 to 0.84 mg/100 mL). The reduction in creatinine clearance with age is accompanied by a reduction in daily urinary creatinine excretion, reflecting the decreased creatinine production from decreased muscle mass. The net effect is a near-

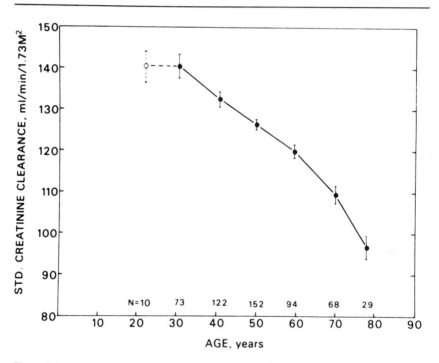

Figure 9-3 Cross-sectional differences in standard creatinine clearance with age. The number of subjects in each age group is indicated above the abcissa. Values plotted indicate means ± standard error of the mean. *Source:* Reprinted with permission from *Journal of Gerontology* (1976;31:155–163), Copyright © 1976, Gerontological Society of America.

constancy of mean serum creatinine concentrations with GFR reductions. The practical implication of these observations is that serum creatinine concentrations in older persons must be interpreted with this effect in mind when these data are used to determine or modify dosages of drugs cleared completely or partially by the kidneys, eg, digoxin and aminoglycoside antibiotics. The Cockcroft-Gault formula is used to estimate creatinine clearance from serum creatinine concentration:

Men $\quad C_{cr} = (140 - \text{age}) (\text{wt in kg})/72 \times \text{serum creatinine (mg/100mL)}$
Women $C_{cr} = C_{cr} \times 0.85$

More recent observations reported from this longitudinal study[9,10] indicate that there are a number of subjects, even some in the older age categories, who show no decrease in their creatinine clearance when studied serially at 12- to 18-month intervals. The mean decrease in creatinine clearance for 254 normal subjects (free of renal and urinary tract disease and untreated with diuretics or antihypertensives) was 0.75 mL/min per year. Figure 9-4 shows the individual regression slopes plotting creatinine clearance versus age. The slopes of the creatinine clearances versus time fell into a normal (gaussian) distribution around this mean. One third of the subjects followed had no decrease in renal function (positive slope of creatinine clearance versus time). Some of these subjects actually showed a statistically significant increase ($P < .05$) in creatinine clearance with age. These observations may have important implications in understanding the pathophysiology of the decrease in renal function with age, as discussed later in this chapter.

Renal Blood (Plasma) Flow

The quantity of blood perfusing the kidney, generally estimated by measuring *p*-aminohippuric (PAH) acid clearances, decreases with age at a rate greater than that of the inulin clearances.[7] The PAH clearance at low serum PAH concentrations measures effective renal plasma flow (ERPF). All PAH that reaches renal tubular cells is secreted into the tubular fluid (urine) in a single pass through the kidney. The percentage of PAH cleared, compared with renal plasma flow as measured by direct-flow techniques (extraction ratio), is 92%; this percentage is similar in young and old subjects. The PAH clearances fall from a mean of 649 mL/min during the fourth decade to a mean of 289 mL/min during the ninth decade.[11]

The decrease in renal blood flow with age without a proportionate decrease in blood pressure is indicative of either vascular impedance due to intraluminal pathology (atheromata, sclerosis) or an increase in renal vascular resistance due to vasoconstriction. Since renal blood flow can be increased transiently by admin-

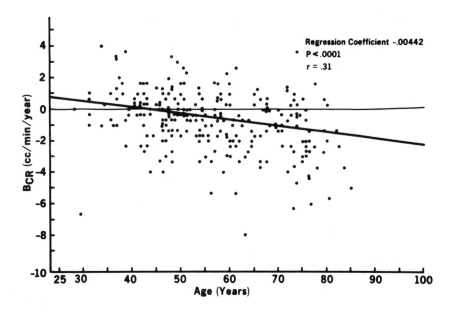

Figure 9-4 Regression coefficients plotting change in creatinine clearance versus time in years (B_{cr}) for 254 normal subjects (free of renal and urinary tract disease and untreated with diuretics and antihypertensive agents) versus age in years. Subjects who had positive B_{cr} values had slopes indicating an increase in creatinine clearances with age. *Source:* Reprinted with permission from *Journal of American Geriatrics Society* (1985;33:278–285), Copyright © 1985, American Geriatrics Society.

istration of vasodilators or pyrogens in both young and old subjects, a vasoconstrictive or reversible component must be implicated in the regulation of renal circulation in both age groups. Administration of a pyrogen produced a greater vasodilation of the arteriolar system in the kidneys of older subjects than in the kidneys of young subjects, suggesting that a greater vasoconstriction exists in the resting state.[12]

Hollenberg and colleagues[13] provided conflicting information in their xenon washout studies; they found that the perfusion of the outer cortical nephrons decreased more with age than did perfusion of the corticomedullary nephrons. Whether this selective decrease in cortical nephron perfusion was due to sclerotic changes in the small arcuate arterioles or represented a selective vasoconstriction of the peripheral vasculature was investigated. Acetylcholine increased renal blood flow in both young and old subjects, but the effect was much more striking in the young subjects. In contrast, the vasoconstrictor responses to angiotensin were similar in the young and old subjects. These studies suggest that the renal vasculature in the aged subject is in a relatively greater state of baseline vasodilation compared with the renal vasculature of the young subject, in contrast to the studies conducted by McDonald and associates.[12]

Because the cortical component of blood flow decreased more rapidly than did mean flow rate, it was thought that cortical nephrons are more severely affected by age than are juxtamedullary nephrons. Since the juxtamedullary nephrons have a higher filtration fraction than do cortical nephrons, a selective loss of the latter would explain the increase in the mean filtration fraction (GFR/ERPF) observed with age. An alternative, but less likely, explanation for the increase in filtration fraction observed with age is that the efferent arteriole is disproportionately vasoconstricted compared with the afferent arteriole, thereby increasing the filtration pressure in the glomerular capillary bed.

Maximal Tubular Transport Capacity

The tubular maximum for iodopyracet (Diodrast) or PAH secretory transport decreases with age at a rate nearly parallel to the decrease in inulin clearance.[7] The tubular maximum for secretion of PAH is measured by determining PAH clearances and subtracting inulin clearances at increasingly higher serum PAH concentrations until a maximal clearance of PAH is obtained. This gives a measure of the maximal amount of PAH that the tubules can secrete. The tubular maximal rate for glucose resorption also decreases at a rate closely paralleling the decrease in inulin clearance.

Although the reduction in the secretory and resorptive tubular maximums with age could be explained by a progressive loss of whole functioning nephrons, animal experiments also have shown fewer energy-producing mitochondria,[14] lower enzyme concentrations,[14,15] lower concentrations of total or sodium–potassium–activated adenosine triphosphatase (ATPase),[16] decreased sodium extrusion and oxygen consumption,[17] and decreased tubular transport capacity in the tubular cells[14] in old compared with young kidneys. Therefore, aging not only reduces the population of functioning nephons but also produces changes in the basic biochemistry of the tubular cell even though no changes in tubular function per se can be detected by using available clearance techniques in human studies.

Concentrating and Diluting Ability

A decrease in the kidneys' concentrating ability with age has been well documented.[7] In the Baltimore Longitudinal Study of Aging analysis,[18] 12 hours of water deprivation increased urine osmolality to a mean of 1109 mOsm/L in young subjects, 1051 mOsm/L in middle-aged subjects, and 882 mOsm/L in old subjects.

Attempts to relate the decrease in concentrating ability to a more rapid decrease in GFR than in solute load, resulting in an osmotic or solute diuresis per residual nephron (which would impair concentrating ability) were not successful. Rowe and associates[18] suggested that the development of a continuity between juxtamedullary afferent and efferent arterioles[5,6] would increase medullary blood flow, and this is supported by the observations of Hollenberg and colleagues.[13] This relative increase with age in medullary blood flow per nephron would result in an enhanced removal of solute (washout) from the medullary interstitium, thereby decreasing concentrating ability.

Maximal urine osmolality after infusion of large amounts of vasopressin was significantly decreased in older subjects undergoing water diuresis.[19] This decrease appears most likely to be the result of diminished medullary tonicity rather than a defect in the ability of the kidney tubule to respond to vasopressin; elderly persons responded normally to graded doses of vasopressin insufficient for the kidney to concentrate urine to its maximal concentration.[20] Elderly persons were better able to achieve urine isotonicity with a lower dose of vasopressin than were younger subjects.

Maximal diluting ability, as measured by minimal urine osmolality achieved with water loading, also decreases with age.[20] A comparison of free water clearance per unit of nephron mass (GFR) reveals little difference between young and old, suggesting that there is no basic defect in the ability to produce a dilute urine.

Urine Acidification

Despite the decrease in renal function with age, blood pH, pCO_2, and bicarbonate values of aged persons without renal disease do not differ from the values observed in young subjects under basal conditions.[21] The decreases in blood pH and bicarbonate concentrations after ingestion of an acid load are prolonged in elderly persons. The minimal urine pH values achieved after an acid load are similar in young and old subjects. A much larger percentage of the ingested acid load as measured by total acid excretion (ammonium plus titratable acid [TA] minus bicarbonate) was excreted over an 8-hour period by the young subjects, compared with the older subjects. However, if total acid excretion in 8 hours is factored by GFR, similar rates of excretion are obtained. The young subjects excreted a greater percentage of their total acid as ammonium, compared with older subjects, presumably because there was an increase in urinary buffers responsible for titratable acid (eg, phosphate, creatinine) per unit of GFR in older subjects. This varies with dietary protein and, although dietary protein generally decreases in older subjects, it does not decrease as rapidly as GFR; therefore, TA/GFR increases. Agarwal and Cabebe[22] subsequently reported that elderly subjects showed a small pH gradient defect and ammonium excretion was reduced significantly in elderly subjects even after correction for GFR. These investigators attempted to select older patients who had GFRs more similar to those observed in the young.

Glomerular Permeability

Little information exists to indicate that glomerular permeability changes with age in humans. VanZonneveld[23] found an increasing incidence of proteinuria in a population survey of persons over age 65 years. Nevertheless, by age 85 years, only a minority of patients had evidence of clinical proteinuria. Glomerular permeability to free hemoglobin, determined by factoring free hemoglobin clearances by inulin clearances in healthy young and old subjects, did not change with age.[24] Furthermore, there was no difference between young and old subjects in glomerular permeability to a spectrum of dextrans of different molecular weights.[25]

AGE-RELATED CHANGES IN RENAL RESPONSE TO ENVIRONMENTAL ALTERATIONS

Epstein and Hollenberg[26] found that older subjects failed to conserve sodium as rapidly or efficiently as did younger subjects. The half-lives of urinary sodium excretions when old patients were placed on a restricted dietary salt intake were much longer compared with young subjects in the same circumstance. Elderly persons have lower plasma renin activities and urinary aldosterone excretions both on an unrestricted salt diet and after 3 to 6 days of salt restriction.[27,28] However, the mechanism explaining this decreased plasma renin activity and aldosterone excretion in elderly individuals remains unknown; ie, is it a renal or an extrarenal defect? This unexplained phenomenon probably accounts for the decreased ability of elderly subjects to conserve sodium when challenged with a low-salt diet. It may also account for the propensity of elderly subjects to develop hyperkalemia when given potassium supplements, as discussed in Chapter 4.

Similarly, there is a marked decrease in the ability of elderly people to convert 25-hydroxyvitamin D_3 to 1,25-dihydroxyvitamin D_3.[29] This appears to be related to a deficiency of 1α-hydroxylase enzyme activity in old kidneys as compared with young kidneys. Again, whether this is related to renal or extrarenal influences remains unclear. This is just one of the factors that may contribute to deficient vitamin D activity in older persons, which, in turn, may contribute to the development of senile osteoporosis.

PATHOPHYSIOLOGY OF AGE-RELATED DECLINE
IN RENAL FUNCTION

As discussed earlier, cross-sectional studies of normal subjects over a wide age range indicate that there is a mean decrease in renal function with age that accelerates in the oldest age groups. It remains unclear whether this decrease is due to a progressive involutional change with loss of nephron units and a decline in cellular function throughout the life of the individual or whether renal function remains stable until intermittent pathologic processes produce acute or chronic injuries and impairments. For example, undetected glomerulonephritis caused by immunologic injury after an infection, pyelonephritis due to bacterial or viral infection, acute tubular injury or interstitial nephritis due to a drug reaction, and vascular occlusion with resultant ischemic injury are pathologic processes that lead to impairment of renal function.

Normal cells (eg, fibroblasts), when placed in culture medium, have a finite life span in that the population-doubling potential of these cells is inversely related to the age of the donor.[30] Normal cells cannot be maintained in a state of active proliferation or even in a functional state in culture medium for a period of time in excess of the specific age of the species from which the cells were obtained. As cultured normal cells approach the end of their life spans, a number of biochemical decrements occur that indicate the approaching loss of divisional capacity much like that observed in tubular cells showing fewer energy-producing mitochondria, lower enzyme concentrations, lower concentrations of sodium-potassium–activated ATPase activity, decreased sodium transport and oxygen consumption, and diminished tubular transport in old kidneys compared with young kidneys. These sequences of glomerular loss in the absence of overt lesions in the large or small vessels, as described by Ljungvist[5] and Takazakura and colleagues,[6] suggest that nephron loss occurs normally without an overt vascular lesion.

On the other hand, the studies reported earlier[9,10] from the Baltimore Longitudinal Study of Aging, on a cohort of male volunteers followed between 1958 and 1981, provide evidence that the decrease in renal function observed with age may be the result of intervening pathologic processes rather than a relentless involutional process. One third of the normal subjects showed no decrease in renal function (positive slope of creatinine clearance plotted against time) (Figure 9-4).

Friedman and associates,[31] for example, used scintillation scanning techniques to localize defects in kidney function in elderly persons with no past history of renal disease. They found abnormal scans in 25 of 35 elderly patients with a mean age of 75 years and mean creatinine clearance of 53 mL/min; 16 patients showed focal areas of diminished uptake that were thought to represent ischemic lesions.

Asymptomatic bacteriuria may be another contributor to decreased renal function in the aged. Dontas and colleagues[32] found that 27% of clinically healthy residents of the Athens House for the Aged had persistent bacteriuria, and the mean inulin clearances (70 versus 81 mL/min) were lower in this group. These are just two representative studies that indicate that pathologic changes must contribute, at least in part, to the observed decline in renal function with age. In a longitudinal study in which subjects were followed for periods up to 24 years, the failure of all subjects to show some decline in renal function indicates that a decline in renal function with age is not inevitable, ie, the result of an involutional aging process.

COMPENSATORY RENAL HYPERTROPHY

Unilateral nephrectomy causes compensatory hypertrophy in the normal remaining kidney[33,34]; however, the rates of enlargement and increased function are much lower in the old than they are in the young. The number of glomeruli does not increase after birth, so that compensatory enlargement cannot be attributed to an increase in the number of nephrons. In studies of young animals, cellular hyperplasia predominates, whereas in older animals cellular hypertrophy is the chief response.[33] This is supported by studies of cell counts, counts of mitosis, RNA:DNA ratios, and measures of double-stranded DNA replications. Even though the kidneys of older animals enlarge primarily by hypertrophy, the rate of hypertrophy is less than that observed in younger animals. The role of growth factors in producing these differences in young and old animals is discussed later. The relative failure to regenerate new cells in the older person becomes important when the responses to the numerous insults and injuries received by the kidney over the life span of the individual are assessed.

ROLE OF HYPERPERFUSION, HYPERFILTRATION, AND RENAL RESERVE

When the population of normal glomeruli is reduced by surgical ablation or renal disease in the rat model, the remaining glomeruli react with an "adaptive" hyperperfusion and hyperfiltration.[35] This glomerular hyperfiltration disrupts the integrity of the capillary membrane, resulting in proteinuria, accumulation of mesangial deposits, and initiation or acceleration of the loss of renal function through a process of developing glomerular sclerosis. This phenomenon of hyperfiltration also is seen in humans in the remaining kidney after uninephrectomy, in uncontrolled diabetes mellitus, and acutely after the ingestion of protein or infusion of amino acids. Restriction of protein, calories, or phosphate delays the renal progression. The earlier the underfeeding starts, the more the renal problems are delayed. Brenner and colleagues[36] proposed that the progressive decline in renal function in persons with primary renal disease, with hypertension, with diabetes mellitus, and with age could be related to this hyperperfusion and hyperfiltration, resulting in glomerular sclerosis. The mechanisms are illustrated in Figure 9-5.

Both glomerular filtration rate and kidney size are increased in early diabetes mellitus, producing changes in humans similar to those observed in animal models with remnant kidney or renal disease.[37] The state of glomerular hyperperfusion and hyperfiltration created by abnormal carbohydrate metabolism is corrected when the carbohydrate metabolism is normalized. Glomerulosclerosis with impaired glomerular filtration develops in diabetes with hyperperfusion and hyperfiltration of long duration.

Hypertension in diabetic animal models hastens the development of glomerulosclerosis. When hypertension is experimentally induced using the kidney Goldblatt model (clipped and unclipped renal arteries), asymmetry of the renal lesions is seen.[38] In the unclipped kidneys exposed to elevated systemic pressures, more severe glomerulosclerosis is seen than in the clipped kidney, where reduced systemic pressure occurs. Similarly, normotensive diabetic rats have less severe lesions compared with hypertensive diabetic animals.[39]

Not all evidence favors the theory that hyperfiltration leads to glomerulosclerosis in humans. Uninephrectomy does not lead to impairment in renal function in transplant donors followed for a mean duration of 6 years.[40] Hyperperfusion and hyperfiltration in humans does not necessarily lead to glomerulosclerosis and progression of renal insufficiency. Fine[41] has proposed the concept that "glomerular tolerance" to injury as well as perfusion pressure determines whether or not glomerulosclerosis will develop.

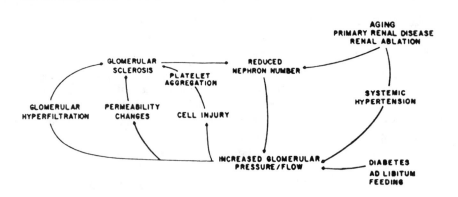

Figure 9-5 Role of increased glomerular pressures and flows leading to the development of glomerular sclerosis. *Source:* Reprinted with permission from *American Journal of Medicine* (1986;80:435), Copyright © 1986, Cahners Publishing Company.

Bosch and associates[42] quantified the increase in GFR and ERPF after an oral protein load and termed this increase "renal functional reserve capacity." In four normal subjects, they showed a mean increase in GFR (creatinine clearance) from 105 to 171 mL/min after an 80-g protein meal. They theorized that this represented the ability of the kidney under periods of stress to increase flow and filtration. If the kidney reaches the point where it is hyperperfusing and hyperfiltering at all times, it seems likely that it is susceptible to damage resulting from glomerular sclerosis. Using low (40 g/d), normal (70 g/d), and high (90g/d) protein diets, they also showed that GFR varied directly with protein intake from a mean of 101 mL/min on the low-protein diet to a mean of 127 mL/min on the high-protein diet.

Since the GFR increases more than the ERPF, the mechanisms for the GFR increase would appear to be due to a vasodilatation of the afferent arteriole. One might suspect that this would increase the filtration pressure in the glomerulus more than would other vasodilator agents, especially the converting enzyme inhibitors, which act by vasodilating the efferent arteriole, thereby subjecting the kidney to greater damage (glomerulosclerosis).

The same investigators[43] further showed that patients with underlying renal disease lost some to all of this ability to increase their GFR after an oral protein load and suggested that loss of this ability meant that they were already hyperfiltering. Since others[44] have demonstrated that limitations of protein intake in patients with chronic renal disease reduces the rate of progression of renal insufficiency, it has been speculated that a low-protein diet might restore renal functional reserve and thereby provide protection to the kidneys. Rodriguez-Iturbe and colleagues[45] compared creatinine clearances before and after a high-protein meal in 25 kidney donors and 35 patients with poststreptococcal glomerulonephritis with those of 44 normal control subjects. The mean increase in GFR in the postacute nephritis and nephrectomy patients was 18% compared with 58% in the control subjects, suggesting that the first two groups had a diminished renal reserve capacity. Infusions of amino acids and dopamine to increase GFR also have been used to quantify renal reserve[46] but offer no advantages other than a more rapid onset of action.

Older persons, or a sample of older persons, may have lost their "renal reserve," indicating that they already are hyperperfusing and hyperfiltering. The studies of Hollenberg and associates[13] suggest that older patients are in a relative state of renal vascular vasodilatation. Such individuals might be at risk for the development of glomerulosclerosis and might benefit from protein restriction, particularly if this allows a renal reserve to be re-established.

Recent investigations identifying epidermal growth factor (EGF), and suggesting perhaps other humoral mediators exist to modulate this effect, should provide answers in the near future on the mechanisms involved, offering other alternatives for protection and management. EGF is a 6000-d peptide (53 amino acids), which is a potent multiplication (mitogenic) and maturation factor for cells and a modifier of many kinds of secretory cells. It was first isolated from mouse submandibular (salivary) glands, but mouse and human EGF are very similar in structure and function. EGF receptors have been identified by immunostaining techniques in the thick ascending limb of Henle's loop and early distal convoluted tubule. Unilateral nephrectomy greatly increases EGF concentrations in these sites and in the urine.[47] Furthermore, pre-EGF messenger RNA also increases in these sites after unilateral nephrectomy, suggesting that EGF is synthesized there. It does not appear, however, that this source of EGF contributes to circulating EGF.

Although EGF has been reported to be synthesized in sites other than salivary glands (eg, duodenum, kidney tubule), removal of the salivary glands from mice (sialoadenectomy) produced EGF deficiency.[48] Kidneys of EGF-deficient mice failed to undergo compensatory hypertrophy after unilateral nephrectomy, causing renal insufficiency. The kidneys of animals receiving EGF replacement, as in animals without sialoadenectomy, developed compensatory hypertrophy without renal insufficiency.

An increase in dietary proteins (from 6% to 24%) was associated with a doubling of urinary EGF.[49] Furthermore, protein feeding results in hypertrophy of the thick ascending limb of Henle's loop.[50] Finally, there is an age-related decrease in urinary EGF.[51]

When these pieces of information are put together, it appears that the process of compensatory hypertrophy, and regeneration or repair of injured kidney tissue, may be mediated through stimulation of growth factors, such as EGF; or the response (receptor activity) may be modified with age, making repair slower and perhaps less optimal. This presents a challenging new area of investigation for those involved in both renal and aging research.

CONCLUSION

Most renal functions decline with age at a rate similar to that observed for the GFR and ERPF. Cross-sectional and longtitudinal population studies have suggested that this progressive decline in renal function results from an inevitable (involutional) loss of cellular function ending ultimately in cell death, and this suggestion is supported by studies of cell culture and tubular function in aging rats. More recent longitudinal studies of individual patients indicate that there are many patients, some of whom are old, who go for decades with no evidence of a decline in renal function. This suggests that the decline in renal function observed with age is related to the superimposition of pathologic processes, often asymptomatic or at least undetected. The concept of ''ideal'' or ''successful'' aging as opposed to ''usual'' aging has emerged as a result of similar findings in other organ systems.[52]

REFERENCES

1. Roessle R, Roulet F. *Mass und Zahl in der Pathologie*. Berlin, Germany: F Springer; 1932.

2. Goyal VK. Changes with age in the human kidney. *Exp Gerontol*. 1982;17:321–331.

3. MacGallum DB. The bearing of degenerating glomeruli on the problem of the vascular supply of the mammalian kidney. *Am J Anat*. 1939;65:69–103.

4. McManus JFA, Lupton CH Jr. Ischemic obsolescence of renal glomeruli. *Lab Invest*. 1960; 9:413–434.

5. Ljungvist A. Structure of the arteriole-glomerular units in different zones of the kidney. *Nephron*. 1964;1:329–337.

6. Takazakura E, Wasabu N, Handa A, et al. Intrarenal vascular changes with age and disease. *Kidney Int*. 1972;2:224–230.

7. Lindeman RD, Goldman R. Anatomic and physiologic age changes in the kidney. *Exp Gerontol*. 1986;21:379–406.

8. Rowe JW, Andres R, Tobin J, et al. The effect of age on creatinine clearance in men: a cross-sectional and longtitudinal study. *J Gerontol*. 1976;31:155–163.

9. Lindeman RD, Tobin JD, Shock NW. Association between blood pressure and the rate of decline in renal function with age. *Kidney Int*. 1984;26:861–868.

10. Lindeman RD, Tobin JD, Shock NW. Longitudinal studies on the rate of decline in renal function with age. *J Am Geriatr Soc*. 1985;33:278–285.

11. Davies DF, Shock NW. Age changes in glomerular filtration rate, effective renal plasma flow, and tubular excretory capacity in adult males. *J Clin Invest*. 1950;29:496–507.

12. McDonald RF, Solomon DH, Shock NW. Aging as a factor in the renal hemodynamic changes induced by a standardized pyrogen. *J Clin Invest*. 1951;5:457–462.

13. Hollenberg NK, Adams DF, Solomon HS, et al. Senescence and the renal vasculature in normal man. *Circ Res*. 1974;34:309–316.

14. Barrows CH, Jr, Falzone JA Jr, Shock NW. Age differences in the succinoxidase activity of homogenates and mitochondria from the livers and kidneys of rats. *J Gerontol*. 1960;15:130–133.

15. Burich RJ. Effects of age on renal function and enzyme activity in male C57 BL/6 mice. *J Gerontol*. 1975;30:539–545.

16. Beauchene RE, Fanestil DD, Barrows CH Jr. The effect of age on active transport and sodium-potassium activated ATPase activity in renal tissue of rats. *J Gerontol*. 1965;20:306–310.

17. Proverbio F, Proverbio T, Marin R. Ion transport and oxygen consumption in kidney cortex slices from young and old rats. *Gerontology*. 1985;31:166–173.

18. Rowe JW, Shock NW, De Fronzo RA. The influence of age on the renal response to water deprivation in man. *Nephron*. 1976;17:270–278.

19. Miller JH, Shock NW. Age differences in the renal tubular response to antidiuretic hormone. *J Gerontol*. 1953;8:446–450.

20. Lindeman RD, Lee TD, Jr, Yiengst MJ, et al. Influence of age, renal disease, hypertension, diuretics, and calcium on the antidiuretic response to suboptimal infusions of vasopressin. *J Lab Clin Med*. 1966;68:206–223.

21. Adler S, Lindeman RD, Yiengst MJ, et al. Effect of acute acid loading on urinary acid excretion by the aging human kidney. *J Lab Clin Med*. 1968;72:278–289.

22. Agarwal BN, Cabebe FG. Renal acidification in elderly subjects. *Nephron*. 1980;26:291–293.

23. VanZonneveld RJ. Some data on the genito-urinary system as found in old-age surveys in the Netherlands. *Gerontol Clin.* 1959;1:167–173.

24. Lowenstein J, Faulstick DA, Yiengst MJ, et al. The glomerular clearance and renal transport of hemoglobin in adult males. *J Clin Invest.* 1961;40:1172–1177.

25. Faulstick D, Yiengst MJ, Ourster DA, et al. Glomerular permeability in young and old subjects. *J Gerontol.* 1962;17:40–44.

26. Epstein M, Hollenberg NK. Age as a determinant of renal sodium conservation in normal man. *J Lab Clin Med.* 1976;87:411–417.

27. Crane MG, Harris JJ. Effect of aging on renin activity and aldosterone excretion. *J Lab Clin Med.* 1976;87:947–959.

28. Weidman P, DeMyttenaere-Burzstein S, Maxwell MH, et al. Effect of aging on plasma renin and aldosterone in normal man. *Kidney Int.* 1975;8:325–333.

29. Armbrecht HJ, Zenser RV, Davis BB. Effect of age on the conversion of 25-hydroxyvitamin D_3 to 1,25-dihydroxyvitamin D_3 by kidney of rats. *J Clin Invest.* 1980;66:1118–1123.

30. Hayflick L. The cell biology of human aging. *N Engl J Med.* 1976;295:1302–1308.

31. Friedman SA, Raizner AE, Rosen H, et al. Functional defects in the aging kidney. *Ann Intern Med.* 1972;76:41–45.

32. Dontas AS, Papanayiotou P, Marketos SG, et al. The effects of bacteriuria on renal functional patterns in old age. *Clin Sci.* 1968;34:73–81.

33. Phillips TL, Leong G. Kidney cell proliferation after unilateral nephrectomy as related to age. *Cancer Res.* 1967;2:286–292.

34. Boner G, Shelp WD, Neton M, et al. Factors influencing the increase in glomerular filtration rate in the remaining kidney of transplant donors. *Am J Med.* 1973;55:169–174.

35. Hostetter TH, Olson JL, Rennke HG, et al. Hyperfiltration in remnant nephrons: a potentially adverse response to renal ablation. *Am J Physiol.* 1981;9:F85–F93.

36. Brenner MB, Meyer TW, Hostetter TH. Dietary protein intake and the progressive nature of kidney disease: the role of hemodynamically mediated glomerular injury in the pathogenesis of progressive glomerular sclerosis in aging, renal ablation and intrinsic renal disease. *N Engl J Med.* 1973;307:652–712.

37. Mogensen CE, Andersen MJF. Increased kidney size and glomerular filtration rate in early juvenile diabetes. *Diabetes.* 1973;22:706–712.

38. Mauer SM, Steffes MW, Azar S, et al. The effects of Goldblatt hypertension on development of the glomerular lesions of diabetes mellitus in the rat. *Diabetes.* 1978;27:738–744.

39. Bank N, Klose R, Aynedjian HS, et al. Evidence against increased glomerular pressure initiating diabetic nephropathy. *Kidney Int.* 1987;31:898–905.

40. Miller IJ, Suthanthiran M, Riggio RR, et al. Impact of renal donation: long term clinical and biochemical follow-up of living donors in a single center. *Am J Med.* 1985;79:201–208.

41. Fine LG. Preventing the progression of human renal disease: have rational therapeutic principles emerged? *Kidney Int.* 1988;33:116–128.

42. Bosch JP, Saccaggi A, Lauer A, et al. Renal functional reserve in humans: effect of protein intake on glomerular filtration rate. *Am J Med.* 1983;75:943–950.

43. Bosch JP, Lauer A, Glabman S. Short-term protein loading in assessment of patients with renal disease. Am J Med. 1984;77:873–879.

44. Barsotti G, Morelli E, Giannoni A, et al. Restricted phosphorus and nitrogen intake to slow the progression of chronic renal failure: a controlled trial. *Kidney Int.* 1983;24(suppl 16):278–284.

45. Rodriguez-Iturbe B, Herrera J, Garcia R. Response to acute protein load in kidney donors and in apparently normal postacute glomerulonephritis patients: evidence for glomerular hyperfiltration. *Lancet*. 1985;2:461–464.

46. Ter Wee PM, Rosman JB, VanDerGiest S, et al. Renal hemodialysis during separate and combined infusion of amnio acids and dopamine. *Kidney Int*. 1986;29:870–874.

47. Rall LB, Scott J, Bell GI, et al. Mouse prepro-epidermal growth factor synthesis by the kidney and other tissues. *Nature*. 1985:313:228–231.

48. Uchida S, Tsutsumi O, Hise MK, et al. Role of epidermal factor in compensatory renal hypertrophy in mice. *Kidney Int*. 1988;33:387. Abstract.

49. Gung A, Badr KF, Orth DN, et al. Effect of dietary protein and uninephrectomy on urinary epidermal growth factor excretion. *Kidney Int*. 1988;33:376. Abstract.

50. Bouby N. Influence of dietary protein on adenylate cyclase activity of the medullary thick ascending limb. *Kidney Int*. 1987;31:430. Abstract.

51. Uchihashi M, Hirata Y, Fujita T, et al. Age-related decrease in urinary excretion of human epidermal growth factor. *Life Sci*. 1982;31:679–683.

52. Rowe JW, Kahn RL. Human aging: usual and successful. *Science*. 1987;237:143–149.

Chapter 10

Impact of Nutrition on the Age-Related Declines in Hematopoiesis

David A. Lipschitz

The production of hematopoietic cells involves a complex interaction between proliferating marrow stem cells, a unique stroma, and a series of diffusible molecules that regulate the production of erythroid, myeloid, and megakaryocytic elements. The high cellular turnover makes the bone marrow particularly susceptible to nutritional deprivation leading to significantly compromised function. The aging hematopoietic system is characterized by a decline in reserve capacity that makes it particularly susceptible to environmental insults that are known to affect the bone marrow adversely. This review discusses the effects of age on the hematopoietic system and the role of nutrition in the common hematologic problems seen in elderly people.

EFFECT OF AGE ON THE HEMATOPOIETIC SYSTEM

Pluripotent Stem Cells

All immunohematopoietic elements are derived from a small pool of pluripotent stem cells that are characterized by a unique self-renewal capacity.[1] They have the ability to divide and yield a progenitor cell committed to differentiating into a specific cell lineage, and an identical daughter cell, thus maintaining the pluripotent stem cell pool size. These morphologically unidentifiable cells are referred to as colony-forming unit—spleen (CFU-S) because they form colonies when marrow is injected into lethally irradiated mice recipients. One of the major questions about the aging of the hematopoietic system is whether or not CFU-S have a finite replicative capacity. Studies using serial transplantation to assess finite replicative capacity have yielded conflicting results. When cells are subjected to in vivo serial transfer by repeated injection into lethally irradiated recipients, they gradually lose their ability to replicate.[2,3] Recent evidence has suggested that results of serial transplantation may well be the result of methodologic artifact.[4,5] Even if their life span is finite, it is clear that CFU-S have a vastly redundant reserve capacity, enabling production of hematopoietic cells in numbers that far exceed the maximal life expectancy of the animal.[6] This point is further highlighted by the observation that as few as 20 CFU-S are able to reconstitute the bone marrow of lethally irradiated mice.[7] There is in vivo evidence that CFU-S have a heterogeneous self-renewal capacity. Young CFU-S with a high self-renewal capacity produce older CFU-S with decreasing self-renewal capacity and greater differentiation potential.[2]

The effect of age on CFU-S senescence has been studied in long-term bone marrow culture. Several studies have shown an inverse relationship between donor age and maintenance of hematopoiesis in this long-term bone marrow culture system.[8,9] Additional studies using this in vitro culture system have shown that CFU-S with high replicative history are more likely to be recruited into the committed cell compartments than are CFU-S that have divided fewer times.[10] Additional evidence for a finite life span comes from a series of elegant studies that examined stem cell kinetics in long-term marrow culture subjected to various doses of irradiation.[11,12]

Effect of Age on Normal Marrow Function

The CFU-S divide into an identical daughter cell and progenitor cells committed to differentiation, and, in the case of hematopoiesis, into myeloid, erythroid, megakaryocytic, and macrocytic precursors (Figure 10-1). There are two forms of erythroid progenitor cells. The first is a more primitive precursor, which forms large colonies in cultures containing high concentrations of erythropoietin, and is referred to as a burst-forming unit—erythroid (BFU-E). This precursor is thought to give rise to a more mature progenitor cell that develops colonies in culture at shorter intervals and at lower erythropoietin concentrations. It is referred to as a colony-forming unit—erythroid (CFU-E) and is the immediate precursor of the proerythroblast, which is the first morphologically identifiable erythroid element. Committed myeloid progenitors include the colony-forming unit—culture (CFU-C), which is the immediate precursor of the myeloblast. A primitive progenitor cell that gives rise to megakaryocytes (CFU-MEGG) and to macrophages (CFU-M) can also be identified under appropriated culture conditions. Morphologically recognizable hematopoietic cells proliferate and mature in a transit or amplification compartment, eventually giving rise to terminally differentiated cells that continually enter the peripheral blood (Figure 10-1).

Recent studies have examined the effect of age on committed hematopoietic progenitor cell number and on the number of differentiated cells in the various marrow compartments. In both animals and humans, no age-related declines in

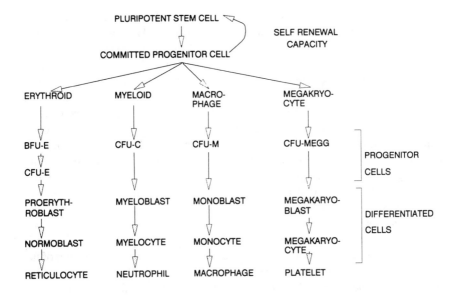

Figure 10-1 The production of terminally differentiated cells of various lineages is derived from a small pool of pluripotent stem cells (CFU-S) with a unique self-renewal capacity. They give rise to progenitor cells of specific lineages that divide and differentiate, resulting in the daily production of the required amounts of hematopoietic elements.

any bone marrow element can be demonstrated when carefully selected subjects are examined in the basal state.[13,14] These observations strongly suggest that marrow function can be adequately maintained, and that no measurable declines occur as a consequence of age per se. The aging process is characterized, however, by a significant reduction in reserve capacity, so that abnormalities not present in the basal state become apparent when the response to maximal stimulation is examined. Udupa and Lipschitz[15,16] have undertaken a number of studies in which they examined hematopoietic function in animals exposed to increased stimulation. Both in vivo and in vitro studies have shown that the hematopoietic response to increased stimulation in old mice is blunted and more variable. Furthermore, greater pathologic abnormalities are noted in response to infection or protein deficiency.

DOES ANEMIA OCCUR AS A CONSEQUENCE OF NORMAL AGING?

Anemia is the most common hematologic problem associated with aging. The high prevalence of anemia is best illustrated from a series of epidemiologic studies conducted in the United States, Canada, and Europe.[17-23] In women older than age 59 years, anemia occurs as frequently as that observed in women of childbearing age. In men, a definite increase in the prevalence of anemia is found in older age groups. Studies from Great Britain are particularly important because they have determined the incidence of anemia in a large number of subjects older than age 60 years. In both men and women, the prevalence of anemia increased significantly with each successive decade.[19-22] An analysis of the second national Health and Nutrition Survey (HANES II) demonstrated a significant reduction in hemoglobin levels with advancing age in apparently healthy men and a minimal, although significant, decrease in elderly women.[23] Based on a lower normal limit of 140 g/L, a very large percentage of elderly men were anemic. This study proposed that the reduction in hemoglobin in elderly men is a consequence of aging and suggested that age-specific reference standards be adopted for hemoglobin concentration for the elderly population.

In hospitalized and institutionalized elderly people, the incidence of anemia is even higher. A survey of patients admitted to the Geriatric Evaluation Unit of the John L. McClellan Memorial Veterans' Hospital in Little Rock, Ark., revealed that 58% had hemoglobin values lower than 140 g/L. In the institutionalized elderly, the incidence of anemia in men ranges from 30% to 50% and for women the incidence ranges from 25% to 40%. Studies conducted in many nursing home settings have also demonstrated anemia to be a very common medical problem.

A major unanswered question is whether this anemia reflects the normal aging process or is the result of an identifiable pathologic process. Close evaluation has revealed that the cause of anemia is usually not obvious in ambulatory, apparently healthy, elderly people.[24] These subjects had evidence of mild marrow failure characterized by significant reductions in the number of bone marrow CFU-C and CFU-E and decreases in marrow-differentiated erythroid and myeloid cells.[25] The elderly men and women who had unexplained anemia also had lower peripheral leukocyte and platelet counts (Figure 10-2). Another unanswered question is whether this unexplained anemia results from the aging process or some other related abnormality. Animal models indicate that basal hematopoiesis is unaltered with aging and that a true anemia does not occur; therefore, other etiologies must be considered for the anemia occurring in elderly humans.[13,14] This possibility is strengthened by the recent finding that anemia is extremely rare in very affluent, healthy, elderly communities. In one study conducted in New Mexico, none of the elderly subjects studied were anemic, and none developed anemia during a 5-year follow-up.[26]

Epidemiologic studies provide additional clues to the etiology of the anemia in the elderly. Cross-sectional studies invariably demonstrate a higher prevalence of anemia in low socioeconomic populations.[17,23] These groups also have a high prevalence of other nutritional deficiencies. Comprehensive nutritional and hematologic evaluations were conducted on a group of 73 healthy veterans living in a

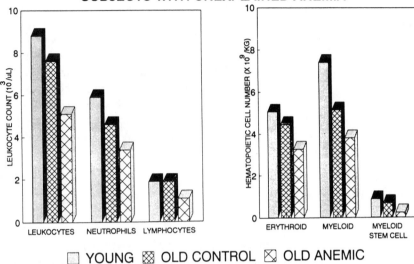

Figure 10-2 Peripheral blood counts (left panel) and hematopoietic precursor number (right panel) in groups of healthy young subjects and groups of carefully selected elderly subjects with or without an unexplained anemia. *Source:* Reprinted with permission from *Blood* (1984;63:502), Copyright © 1984, Grune & Stratton, Inc.

domiciliary facility; a high prevalence of anemia was found in this population. Multivariate analysis showed that age was the major variable affecting declines in immunologic measurements but was not an important factor in the prevalence of anemia. In contrast, serum albumin, transferrin, and prealbumin, which often are used to assess nutritional status, appeared to be good predictors of anemia. This information provides indirect information that a nutritional variable may contribute to the unexplained anemia in these elderly populations.

If nutrition does account for the unexplained anemia seen in healthy elderly populations, mechanisms other than simple deficiencies must be considered. Based on the animal data described above, it is likely that significantly less stress is required to result in alterations in erythropoiesis in elderly people. Therefore, a nutritional deficiency not usually severe enough to affect the hematopoietic system in younger subjects may account for the anemia observed in the elderly population. Other possibilities that may modulate or cause anemia in the elderly include marginal deficiencies of one or more nutrients acting alone or in combination over prolonged periods of time. It is also possible that the delivery of nutrients to the target organ may be affected by aging, or that nutrient and cell interactions may be compromised in elderly people.

The above discussion suggests that nutrition accounts for the unexplained anemia seen in elderly individuals. At the current time this is no more than a hypothesis that requires a great deal of further study. There are other possibilities worthy of consideration. For example, there is some evidence that elderly subjects with anemia have higher sedimentation rates than do nonanemic elderly.[27] This has led to the suggestion that the anemia reflects an acute or chronic disease process. However, iron-deficient erythropoiesis, which characterizes the anemia of inflammation or chronic disease, was not present. It remains likely, however, that a relatively minor inflammatory or chronic stress may result in anemia only in an elderly population.

HEMATOLOGIC MANIFESTATIONS OF PROTEIN ENERGY MALNUTRITION IN THE ELDERLY

A high incidence of protein-energy malnutrition (PEM) has been reported in hospitalized elderly patients. The incidence is also very high in nursing homes and in other long-term care settings.[28] The disorder is characterized by hypoalbuminemia, increased protein and energy requirements, and declines in immune and hematologic function. Anemia is invariably present in patients with PEM, the features being identical with those that occur as the "anemia of chronic disease," and with inflammatory processes.[29] In both men and women the hemoglobin concentration ranges from 100 to 120 g/L. The disorder is associated with an impaired ability of the reticuloendothelial system to recycle iron from senescent red cells. As a result, serum iron concentrations are low and the transferrin saturation is less than 20%. These findings indicate the presence of iron-deficient erythropoiesis, which also occurs in iron deficiency anemia that most commonly results from blood loss. In this disorder, iron stores are absent and, as a result, the serum ferritin level, which is a relatively accurate measure of iron stores, is reduced (usually less than 50 μg/L) and total iron-binding capacity (TIBC) is increased. In contrast, iron stores are normal or increased in the anemia associated with chronic disease and in the anemia associated with PEM. This is reflected in a normal to elevated serum ferritin level (<60 μg/L) and a low TIBC (<45 μmol/L). In elderly people the immunohematopoietic sequelae of PEM tend to be more severe than they are in younger individuals. This may well relate to the diminished reserve capacity that is believed to exist in elderly individuals. Furthermore, the effects of age on the immune and hematologic systems are remarkably similar to the declines in function noted in PEM. The effects of age and PEM on declines in function may well be additive, resulting in more severe abnormalities in older individuals. An example of this additive effect is provided by the observations made of the effect of age and protein deficiency on neutrophil function in mice.[30] Lipschitz and Udupa[30] have shown that, although neutrophil function is compromised in aged mice and in young mice fed a low-protein diet, the reduction is not sufficient in either case to compromise the neutrophil's ability to phagocytose or kill bacteria. In contrast, the reserve capacity of the neutrophil is markedly compromised when aged mice are fed a low-protein diet. Neutrophils obtained from these animals are clearly pathologic and have a marked impairment of their ability to phagocytose and kill bacteria (Figure 10-3). These results may explain the high prevalence of severe bacterial infections in hospitalized, malnourished elderly people. They also emphasize that the reduced reserve in cellular function as a consequence of aging results in increased susceptibility to external stress.

The most appropriate definition of PEM is that it is a metabolic response to stress associated with increased requirements for calories and protein.[31] It may be that elderly people are more susceptible to PEM and develop pathologic conditions more rapidly and with less stress than do younger subjects. The stresses that result in this disorder include trauma, infection, and other acute or chronic inflammatory conditions. Considering these pathophysiologic facts, it is likely that the hema-

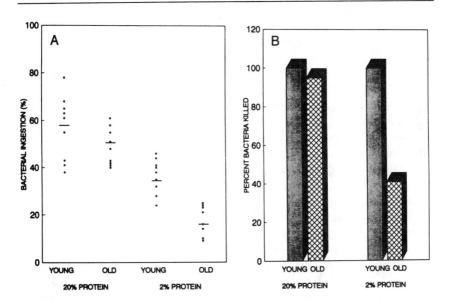

Figure 10-3 Bacterial ingestion (panel A) and percentage bacteria killed (panel B) in neutrophils obtained from the peritoneal cavity of young (aged 6 months) or old mice (aged 24 months) fed a 20% (normal) or 2% protein diet for 3 weeks. The results demonstrate that phagocytosis and bacterial killing are significantly compromised only in the old animals fed the low-protein diet. *Source:* Reprinted with permission from *Journal of Gerontology* (1986;41:690), Copyright © 1986, The Gerontology Society of North America.

tologic changes noted in these patients reflect the underlying disease and only indirectly relate to a nutritional problem.

Clinical studies have shown that the initial responses to stress that characterize PEM are beneficial and assist the patient in developing an optimal response to the underlying primary pathology. Since acute stress is associated with severe anorexia, patients rarely if ever consume sufficient calories or protein to meet their daily needs. In young subjects, inadequate nutrient intake for a period of up to 10 days usually does not affect outcome adversely. Thereafter, inadequate protein and calorie intake results in further lowering of serum albumin and worsening of hematologic, immunologic, and hepatic function, which can affect outcome adversely. In elderly subjects, the time period before PEM exerts a negative effect is likely to be much shorter than that observed in younger subjects. In elderly individuals, failure to meet nutrient needs after a period as brief as 2 to 3 days can lead to further lowering of the serum albumin, worsening immunohematologic function, and increased morbidity. It is essential, therefore, that the presence of PEM be appropriately diagnosed and managed in elderly people.

Lipschitz and Mitchell[29] have studied the effects of nutritional rehabilitation on the hematologic system in elderly subjects with PEM who did not have terminal disease. They confirmed previous reports that adequate nutritional support improves delayed cutaneous hypersensitivity and increases lymphocyte count. In addition, marked improvements in the hematologic system were demonstrated. Correction of the nutritional deficits resulted in a highly significant increase in the hemoglobin concentration, which was accompanied by a return of both serum iron levels and TIBC to normal ranges. Simultaneously, serum ferritin levels fell, presumably as a result of redistribution of iron from stores to the circulating erythrocyte mass (Figure 10-4). In selected individuals, they also demonstrated that improved nutritional status was accompanied by significant increases in the number of bone marrow-differentiated cells and immature stem cells. The observation that delivery of adequate nutrition resulted in a prompt rise in both serum iron level and TIBC is of great interest, particularly since these changes occurred long before any other improvement in the clinical status was noted. This observation provides the strongest evidence for a nutritional role in the hematopoietic alterations occurring in PEM.

The overall interpretation of the improved immunohematopoietic function in malnourished elderly subjects is extremely difficult. Any hospitalized elderly patient who has PEM also has coexisting medical conditions (including infection, dehydration, and psychoneurologic changes) that will affect immune and hematologic function. Therefore, the overall improvement seen with nutritional rehabilitation may reflect an overall improvement of the medical status of the patient.

To examine this possibility more closely, Lipschitz and colleagues[32] studied the effects of increased feeding on the immune and hematologic status of mildly

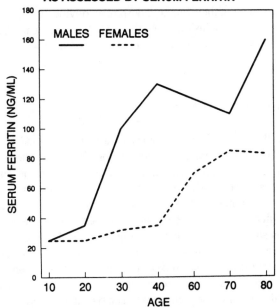

**EFFECT OF AGE ON TISSUE IRON STORES
AS ASSESSED BY SERUM FERRITIN**

Figure 10-4 Estimation of tissue iron stores by serum ferritin determinations in a healthy population ranging in age from 10 years to 80 years. The results demonstrate a significant age-related increase in serum ferritin in both men and women, reflecting a gradual increase in tissue iron stores. *Source:* Reprinted with permission from *Blood* (1976;48:449), Copyright © 1976, Grune & Stratton, Inc.

malnourished, elderly, homebound subjects. These individuals were underweight, had evidence of inadequate food intake, were invariably anemic, and had diminished immune function. By providing polymeric dietary supplements between meals, it was possible to increase total calorie and protein intake by 50% for a total of 16 weeks. A significant improvement in nutritional status occurred; weight gain, increased serum albumin and transferrin, and significant increases in selected vitamins and minerals were seen. Despite this improved nutritional profile, immune function or hematologic status remained unchanged. No anergic subject demonstrated improved delayed cutaneous hypersensitivity, T and B cell function remained abnormal, and the hemoglobin concentration did not increase.

This study, and one on more severely malnourished elderly, suggests that nutritional deficiencies aggravate immune and hematopoietic function in elderly subjects. Correction of coexisting disease and nutritional rehabilitation in the severely malnourished is associated with measurable improvements in host defense parameters. Mildly malnourished elderly individuals who have changes in immune and hematopoietic function similar to those seen in healthy elderly do not show an improvement in their function despite an obviously improved nutritional status. A reasonable conclusion from these studies is that neither protein nor calorie deprivation accounts for the immune and hematologic changes seen in elderly people.

IRON DEFICIENCY ANEMIA

Throughout the world, iron deficiency as a result of blood loss is the most common nutritional problem and accounts for significant morbidity in Third World countries. In the United States, iron deficiency anemia is very common in premenopausal women, during pregnancy, and in infants and children. The disorder is not as common in older men and women and, when present, invariably indicates significant pathology.[33,34] In both men and women, a progressive increase in iron stores occurs with advancing age. This has been demonstrated in numerous studies that have shown an age-associated increase in serum ferritin in both men and women (Figure 10-5). In older men, tissue iron stores average 1200 mg. In older women, iron stores increase from an average of 300 mg to 800 mg in the decade after the menopause. The rise in iron stores clearly relates to

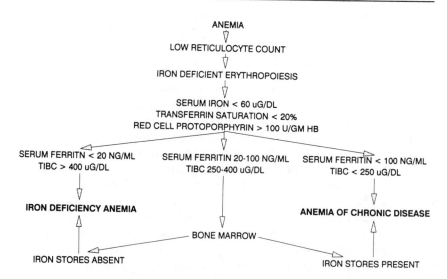

Figure 10-5 A rational approach to the workup of a patient with iron-deficient erythropoiesis caused by either iron deficiency or the anemia of chronic disease.

improved iron balance as a consequence of cessation of menstruation.[35] As a result, in contrast to younger women, iron deficiency is not the most common cause of anemia in ambulatory, healthy, elderly people.[24,25] In the hospital setting, however, iron deficiency anemia is more common in elderly patients. In a number of studies of elderly, hospitalized subjects, the prevalence of anemia ranged from 6.4% to 41%.[36–39] In 21% to 90% of the patients, the etiology of the anemia was thought to be caused by iron deficiency. This information must be interpreted with some caution, as the criteria for the diagnosis of anemia varied and in many cases only serum iron concentration and TIBC were used to make the diagnosis. However, it is apparent that iron deficiency is a common problem in hospitalized people.

When iron deficiency does occur in elderly individuals, it is almost invariably caused by gastrointestinal blood loss. The common causes of blood loss anemia in elderly patients are listed in Table 10-1. The etiology of this blood loss in both elderly men and elderly women must be assumed to be gastrointestinal malignancy until proved otherwise. Depending on the patient's medical condition, an aggressive attempt to define the cause of the anemia should be undertaken, whether or not occult blood is detected in the stool. Comprehensive evaluation of the gastrointestinal tract, including radiography and endoscopy, frequently will identify a malignancy or the presence of polyps that accounts for the blood loss. Other common causes of blood loss from the gastrointestinal tract include atrophic gastritis and angiodysplasia of the large bowel.

Iron deficiency anemia primarily must be distinguished from other disorders that are characterized by the presence of iron-deficient erythropoiesis. These include the anemia of chronic disease and the anemia associated with inflammation and, as described above, protein-energy malnutrition.[40] The major defect in these disorders appears to be an impaired ability of the reticuloendothelial cells to recircuit the iron derived from previously phagocytosed erythrocytes. As a result, serum iron levels are low, iron supply to the marrow is inadequate, and iron-deficient erythropoiesis develops. In contrast to iron deficiency, tissue iron stores are normal or increased rather than absent. The mechanism accounting for the reticuloendothelial abnormality is not well understood. Other factors contributing to this anemia include a modest reduction in erythrocyte survival. The erythropoietin response to the level of the anemia is frequently reduced, but in some circumstances has been shown to be normal or increased.

Figure 10-5 lists an approach to distinguishing whether iron deficiency is caused by iron deficiency anemia or by chronic disease or inflammation. In both, there is evidence of iron-deficient erythropoiesis characterized by a low serum iron level and low transferrin saturation. Transferrin saturation is the percentage of circulating transferrin that is saturated with iron; it is calculated by dividing the serum iron value by the TIBC and expressing the result as a percentage. The free erythrocyte protoporphyrin is also elevated in iron-deficient erythropoiesis. How-

Table 10-1 Major Causes of Iron Deficiency in the Elderly

Gastrointestinal blood loss
  Tumors
    Polyps
    Carcinoma of the colon
    Carcinoma of the stomach

  Peptic ulcer disease
    Gastric
    Duodenal

  Drugs
    Nonsteroidal anti-inflammatory drugs
      Aspirin
      Indomethacin
    Anticoagulants

  Miscellaneous Causes
    Angiodysplasia of the large bowel
    Hiatal hernia
    Hemorrhoids
    Diverticulosis

Other sources of blood loss
  Genitourinary blood loss
    Carcinoma of the uterus and cervix
    Hematuria (rare)

  Miscellaneous
    Frequent blood drawings in hospitalized patients
    Thrombocytopenia
    Coagulopathies

---

ever, a saturation below 16% favors iron deficiency. Although microcytosis does occur in the anemia of chronic disease, a mean corpuscular volume below 75 fL is very unusual. The major distinguishing feature between the two disorders is the absence of iron stores in iron deficiency and its presence in chronic disease or inflammation. In classic iron deficiency anemia, the serum ferritin level is less than 20 µg/L and the TIBC is greater than 72 µmol/L. In the anemia of inflammation, serum ferritin is usually greater than 100 µg/L provided that iron stores are adequate. In this circumstance, TIBC is usually less than 45 µmol/L. Frequently the serum ferritin and the TIBC yield equivocal results. This is particularly likely in patients with inflammatory disorders complicated by iron deficiency. For example, a patient with active rheumatoid disease and iron deficiency caused by drug-induced gastrointestinal blood loss may demonstrate confusing blood chemistries. In a patient like this, the serum ferritin level is usually above 12 µg/L but less than 100 µg/L. Despite the presence of inflammation, this type of patient will respond to oral iron therapy with a significant increase in hemoglobin. A reasonable recommendation for subjects with anemia and inflammatory disorders is to consider a trial of oral iron when the ferritin level is less than 100 μg/L. Alternatively, the diagnosis of iron deficiency can be made definitively by demonstrating absent hemosiderin iron in a bone marrow aspirate. In the anemia of chronic disease, sideroblasts are absent but hemosiderin iron is readily seen in marrow macrophages.

Once the diagnosis has been made, initial therapy should be directed at correcting the underlying pathologic process that resulted in the iron deficiency. In most cases, the iron deficiency can be corrected by oral administration of an iron salt. Ferrous sulfate in either tablet form or as an elixir should be given three times per day with meals[41]; the usual dose contains 60 mg of elemental iron. An adequate response to iron therapy is an increase in the hemoglobin concentration of approximately 0.5 g weekly. Elderly patients appear to respond as rapidly to oral iron as do younger individuals.[42] Side effects, which include nausea, vomiting, epigastric discomfort, constipation, and diarrhea, are common causes for cessation of medication. The best approach to minimize these complications is to reduce the dose and assure that iron therapy is administered with meals. In some elderly subjects there may be value in prescribing one tablet daily to diminish polypharmacy and aid with compliance. A slow-release iron preparation may be more appropriate when prescribing iron on a daily basis. Failure to respond is not uncommon and usually results from noncompliance or continued bleeding. Once these possibilities have been excluded, an incorrect diagnosis or a contributing condition such as renal impairment, infection, or neoplasia should be considered. In the rare patient who does not respond to oral iron, parenteral iron therapy may be considered. This should be reserved for those individuals proven to have iron malabsorption or when noncompliance is a serious problem.

The importance of treating with oral iron only when indicated cannot be overemphasized. There is evidence that as many as 83% of elderly subjects have received oral iron therapy unnecessarily.[43] This contributes to the common problem of polypharmacy in the elderly, may result in major gastrointestinal side effects and excessive accumulation of body iron stores, and may delay or prevent the detection of occult gastrointestinal blood loss.

FOLIC ACID

Folic acid deficiency in elderly people can result from inadequate intake. As a general rule, however, pathologic deficiencies occur only when decreased intake is accompanied by increased requirements, as occurs in alcoholics or in patients with gastrointestinal malabsorption. Epidemiologic studies conducted in Great Britain indicate that significant folate deficiency is relatively common, with significantly low erythrocyte folate levels occurring in 8% to 14% of subjects examined.[44] Generally, folate nutriture in ambulatory, healthy Americans is adequate, although levels below the lower limit of normal are common in low socioeconomic groups.[45] Dietary recall information suggests that a large fraction of older individuals consume well below the recommended dietary allowance of 400 μg/d. In three separate studies, intakes ranging from 129 to 300 μg/d have been reported.[46–48] In a Canadian study of elderly men, intake averaged 150 μg daily. The inadequate intake, coupled with the relatively uncommon incidence of biochemical deficiency, probably relates to the unrealistically high recommended daily intake. It must be emphasized, however, that folate balance in older individuals is marginal and that significant deficiencies are likely to develop rapidly if intake is further compromised by illness or if demand for the vitamin is increased.

Megaloblastic anemia due to folate deficiency in elderly people usually occurs in association with other medical problems. Of these, chronic alcoholism is the most important. In alcoholics, significant folate deficiency results from a combination of inadequate dietary intake combined with decreased absorption and altered folate metabolism.[49,50] Intestinal malabsorption is rare in the elderly but can present or manifest with isolated megaloblastic anemia caused by folate deficiency.

Drugs are another common cause of folate deficiency. Phenytoin (Dilantin) causes folate deficiency by a direct effect on the ability of cells to incorporate thymidine into DNA.[49] In addition, the drug suppresses the gut enzyme folic acid conjugase, which is responsible for the conversion of polyglutamates to monoglutamates. Inhibition of the enzyme results in impaired folate absorption. The common use of combinations of sulfamethoxazole with trimethoprim in elderly individuals with chronic urinary tract infections can also result in folate deficiency. Trimethoprim inhibits dihydrofolate reductase and hence prevents the formation of the active tetrahydrofolate. Although macrocytosis is common in patients consuming drugs that interfere with folate metabolism, frank anemia is rare. Finally, folate deficiency has been reported in elderly individuals who have hemolytic anemia. The presence of increased erythrocyte production results in increased folate requirements that frequently cannot be met from diet alone.

Significant folate deficiency results in ineffective erythropoiesis and a classic megaloblastic anemia. The disorder should be diagnosed by the detection of features of ineffective erythropoiesis, which include a low absolute reticulocyte count and evidence of intramedullary hemolysis, suggested by an indirect bilirubin level of greater than 0.6 mg/dL and an elevated lactic acid dehydrogenase level. The presence of macrocytosis (mean corpuscular volume >100 fL) suggests either vitamin B_{12} or folate deficiency. The diagnosis is confirmed by the presence of pathologically low serum (<2 nmol/L) and erythrocyte (<227 nmol/L) folate concentrations. Oral folate is the treatment of choice.

CONCLUSION

There is compelling evidence that nutritional factors contribute to, or account for, age-related changes in the hematopoietic system. A clear relationship exists between the prevalence of anemia and socioeconomic status, the disorder being common in groups in whom poverty is prevalent and rare in affluent elderly people. In low socioeconomic populations a relationship exists between the prevalence of anemia and other nutritional deficiencies. Furthermore, nutritional deprivation reversibly aggravates hematologic changes in the elderly. If nutritional factors do contribute to the anemia seen in relatively healthy elderly individuals, mechanisms other than simple single-nutrient deficiencies must be considered. In older people, erythropoietic reserve is diminished, resulting in abnormalities under less stressful conditions than is likely to occur in younger subjects. A minor nutritional deficit that would cause no abnormality in young people may result in anemia in elderly individuals. Clearly, further research is required to unravel the complex nature of the interrelationships among age, nutrition, disease in general, and hematopoiesis in particular. Iron and folate are common nutritional causes of hematologic abnormalities in elderly subjects. In the case of both nutrients, deficiency that is severe enough to result in anemia occurs only in the presence of an associated pathologic process. Gastrointestinal blood loss is the major cause of iron deficiency. Increased folate requirements, altered metabolism, or decreased absorption invariably accompany the presence of significant folate deficiency.

REFERENCES

1. Schofield R. The pluripotent stem cell. *Clin Haematol*. 1979;8:221.

2. Schofield R, Lord BI, Kyffin S, et al. Self maintenance capacity of CFU-s. *J Cell Physiol*. 1980;103:355.

3. Albright JA, Makinodan T. Decline in the growth potential of spleen-colonizing bone marrow stem cells of long lived aging mice. *J Exp Med*. 1976;144:1204.

4. Harrison DE, Astle CM, Delaittre JA. Loss of proliferative capacity in immunohemopoietic stem cells caused by serial transplantation rather than aging. *J Exp Med*. 1978;147:1526.

5. Ross EAM, Anderson H, Micklem HS. Serial depletion and regeneration for the murine hematopoietic system: implication for hematopoietic organization and the study of cellular aging. *J Exp Med*. 1982;155:432.

6. Harrison DE. Normal production of erythrocytes by mouse marrow continues for 73 months. *Proc Natl Acad Sci U S A*. 1972;70:3184.

7. Spangrude GJ, Heimfeld S, Weissman IL. Purification and characterization of mouse hematopoietic stem cells. *Science*. 1988;261:58.

8. Mauch P, Greenberger JS, Botnick L, et al. Evidence of structured variation in self-renewal capacity within long-termed bone marrow cultures. *Proc Natl Acad Sci U S A*. 1980;77:2927.

9. Lipschitz DA, McGinnis SK, Udupa KB. The use of long term marrow culture as a model for the aging process. *Age*. 1983;6:122.

10. Mauch P, Botnick LE, Hannon EC, et al. Decline in bone marrow proliferative capacity as a function of age. *Blood.* 1982;60:245.

11. Hellman S, Botnick L, Hannon EC, et al. Proliferative capacity of murine hematopoietic stem cells. *Proc Natl Acad Sci U S A.* 1978;75:490.

12. Reincke U, Hannon EC, Rosenbalt M, et al. Proliferative capacity of murine hematopoietic stem cells in vitro. *Science.* 1982;215:1619.

13. Williams LH, Udupa KB, Lipschitz DA. An evaluation of the effect of age on hematopoiesis in the mouse. *Exp Hematol.* 1985;14:827.

14. Boggs DR, Patrene KD. Hematopoiesis and aging, III: anemia and a blunted erythropoietic response to hemorrhage in aged mice. *Am J Hematol.* 1985;19:327.

15. Udupa KB, Lipschitz DA. Erythropoiesis in the aged mouse, I: response to stimulation in vivo. *J Lab Clin Med.* 1984;103:574.

16. Udupa KB, Lipschitz DA. Erythropoiesis in the aged mouse, II: response to stimulation in vitro. *J Lab Clin Med.* 1984;103:581.

17. *Ten-State Nutrition Survey.* Washington, DC: US Dept of Health, Education, and Welfare publication HSM 72-8132; 1968–1970.

18. *Nutrition Canada.* National Survey, Ottawa, Ont, Canada: Information Canada; 1973.

19. Parson PL, Whithey JL, Kilpatrick GS. The prevalence of anemia in the elderly. *Practitioner.* 1965;195:656.

20. Hill RD. The prevalence of anemia in the over-65s in a rural practice. *Practitioner.* 1967;217:963.

21. Myers MA, Saunders CRG, Chalmers DG. The hemoglobin level of fit elderly people. *Lancet.* 1968;2:261.

22. McLennan WJ, Andress GR, Macleod C, et al. Anaemia in the elderly. *Q J Med.* 1973;52:1.

23. Yip R, Johnson C, Dallman PR. Age-related changes in laboratory values used in the diagnosis of anemia and iron deficiency. *Am J Clin Nutr.* 1984;39:427.

24. Lipschitz DA, Mitchell CO, Thompson C. The anemia of senescence. *Am J Hematol.* 1981;11:47.

25. Lipschitz DA, Udupa KB, Milton KY, et al. Effect of age on hematopoiesis in man. *Blood.* 1984;63:502.

26. Garry PJ, Goodwin JS, Hunt WC. Iron status and anemia in the elderly. *J Am Geriatr Soc.* 1983;31:389.

27. Dallman PR, Yip R, Johnson C. Prevalence and causes of anemia in the United States, 1976–1980. *Am J Clin Nutr.* 1984;39:437.

28. Rudman D, Mattson DE, Nagraj HS, et al. Antecedents of death in the men of a Veterans Administration nursing home. *J Am Geriatr Soc.* 1987;35:496.

29. Lipschitz DA, Mitchell CO. The correctability of the nutritional, immune and hematopoietic manifestations of protein calorie malnutrition in the elderly. *J Am Coll Nutr.* 1982;1:17.

30. Lipschitz DA, Udupa KB. Influence of aging and protein deficiency on neutrophil function. *J Gerontol.* 1986;41:690.

31. McMahon MM, Bistrian BR. The physiology of nutritional assessment and therapy in protein calorie malnutrition. *Dis Mon.* In press.

32. Lipschitz DA, Mitchell CO, Milton KY. Nutritional evaluation and supplementation of elderly participants in a "Meals on Wheels" program. *J Parenter Enter Nutr.* 1985;9:343.

33. Hershko C, Levy S, Matzner Y, et al. Prevalence and causes of anemia in the elderly in Kiryat Shmoneh, Israel. *Gerontology.* 1979;25:42.

34. MacPhail AP, Bothwell TH, Torrance JD, et al. Iron nutrition in Indian women at different ages. *S Afr Med J*. 1981;59:939.

35. Cook JD, Finch CA, Smith NJ. Evaluation of iron status of a population. *Blood*. 1976;48:449.

36. Bedford PD, Wollner L. Occult intestinal bleeding as a cause of anaemia in elderly people. *Lancet*. 1958;1:1144.

37. Evans DMD, Pathy MS, Sanerkin NG, et al. Anaemia in geriatric patients. *Gerontol Clin*. 1968;10:228.

38. Matzner Y, Levy S, Grossowicz N, et al. Prevalence and causes of anemia in elderly hospitalized patients. *Gerontology*. 1979;25:113.

39. Kalchthaler T, Tan ME. Anemia in institutionalized elderly patients. *J Am Geriatr Soc*. 1980; 28:108.

40. Hillman RS, Finch CA. *Red Cell Manual*. Philadelphia, PA: FA Davis Co; 1985.

41. Brise H. Influence of meals on iron absorption in oral therapy. *Acta Med Scand*. 1962; 171(suppl 376):39.

42. Fulcher RA, Hyland CM. Effectiveness of once daily oral iron in the elderly. *Age Ageing*. 1981; 10:44.

43. Reizenstein P, Ljunggren G, Smedby B, et al. Overprescribing iron tablets to elderly people in Sweden. *Br Med J*. 1979;2:962.

44. Elwood PC, Shinton NK, Wilson CID, et al. Haemoglobin, vitamin B_{12} and folate levels in the elderly. *Br J Haematol*. 1971;21:557.

45. Rosenberg IH, Bowman BB, Cooper BA, et al. Folate nutrition in the elderly. *Am J Clin Nutr*. 1982;36:1060.

46. Chanarin I. The folate content of foodstuffs and the availability of different folate analogues for absorption. In: *Getting the Most Out of Food*. London, England: Van den Bergh & Jurgens; 1975.

47. Jagerstad M, Westesson AK. Folate Bergstrom B, Nordin A, Akesson B, et al. eds. In: *Nutrition and Old Age*. Oslo: Universities Forlaget; 1979.

48. *Nutrition Canada*. Food Consumption Patterns Report. Ottawa, Ont, Canada: Department of National Health and Welfare; 1979.

49. Lindenbaum J, Roman MJ. Nutritional anemia in alcoholism. *Am J Clin Nutr*. 1980;33:2727.

50. Chanarin I. *The Megaloblastic Anaemias*. 2nd ed. Oxford, England: Blackwell Scientific Publications Ltd; 1979.

Chapter 11

Skeletal Aging

Christine Snow-Harter and Robert Marcus

The integrity of the human skeleton begins to decline with the onset of bone loss in early adult life. This bone loss is a result of aging and of alterations in physical activity and reproductive endocrine status. The specific mechanisms that lead to severe bone losses in some people, but not in others, is not completely understood. However, considerable interest has been directed toward clarifying the elements that determine peak bone mass at maturity and its subsequent decline. In many cases, bone loss does not result in disability. However, in some individuals, this bone loss can be devastating.

Osteoporosis, the end result of extensive bone loss, is a disease characterized by bone porosity; it appears clinically as fractures of the spine, wrist, and hip. Vertebral fractures are more common in women, while hip fractures are more evenly distributed between sexes and tend to occur at a later age. Osteoporosis is traditionally divided into primary and secondary forms; the primary disorder occurs as a consequence of reproductive failure and aging and the secondary disorder reflects specific disease processes, such as thyrotoxicosis (Chapter 12). Riggs and associates[1,2] have proposed that primary osteoporosis be further divided into two distinct clinical entities, which they have called type I (postmenopausal) and type II (senile) osteoporosis. The factors contributing to the development of each type are delineated in Table 11-1.

This chapter considers current views regarding changes in bone mass with age, as well as hypothesized mechanisms of bone accretion and loss. Before these specific issues are discussed, however, a brief review of some fundamental aspects of skeletal organization, function, and assessment would be valuable.

ORGANIZATION OF THE SKELETON

The skeleton can be considered to be organized into two compartments, peripheral and axial. The peripheral (cortical) skeleton constitutes 80% of skeletal

289

Table 11-1 Type I (Postmenopausal) and Type II (Senile) Osteoporosis

Contributing Factor	Type I	Type II
Age (y)	51–75	>70
Sex ratio (F:M)	6:1	2:1
Type of bone loss	Mainly trabecular	Trabecular and cortical
Fracture sites	Vertebrae and distal radius	Vertebrae and hip
Parathyroid function	Decreased	Increased
Calcium absorption	Decreased	Decreased
Main causes	Factors related to menopause	Factors related to aging

Source: Adapted with permission from JL Riggs and JL Melton, "Involutional Osteoporosis" in *New England Journal of Medicine* (1986;314:1676), Copyright © 1986, Massachusetts Medical Society.

---

mass and is composed primarily of compact plates (lamellae) organized around central nutrient canals. The shafts of long bones consist almost entirely of cortical bone that envelopes the central marrow cavity.

Trabecular (cancellous) bone comprises about 70% (by volume) of the central (axial) skeleton and is characterized by a high degree of porosity. It consists of a honeycomb of vertical and horizontal bars called trabeculae that are filled with varying fractions of red and yellow marrow. The metaphyseal ends of long bones also contain trabecular bone, but they contain no red marrow in the adult. Since marrow elements are the source of osteoclast precursors, the nature of remodeling activity in the metaphyses is not comparable to that of the axial skeleton, and these regions cannot be considered a valid surrogate for predicting axial changes. It recently has been shown that vertebral bodies contain about 35% trabecular bone by weight, which, although much less than previous estimates, still greatly exceeds the trabecular component of peripheral bones.[3]

On close examination, the differences between cortical and trabecular bone are striking. As seen in Figure 11-1A,[4] cortical bone is a tight composite of plates exhibiting virtually no intralamellar space. By contrast, the lattice of trabecular bone is easily observed in Figure 11-1B.[5] Bone loss seems to occur earliest in trabecular bone, possibly because there is a much higher surface prevalence of remodeling units.[6]

MEASUREMENT OF BONE MINERAL DENSITY

Initial assessments of bone mass and its changes with age were conducted with postmortem anatomic specimens and morphometric analyses of radiographs. During the past two decades, several newer methods have been applied to this

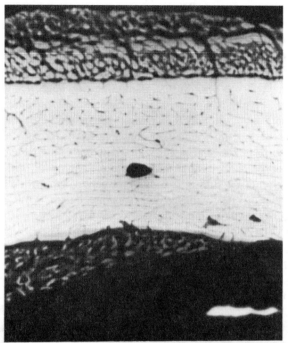

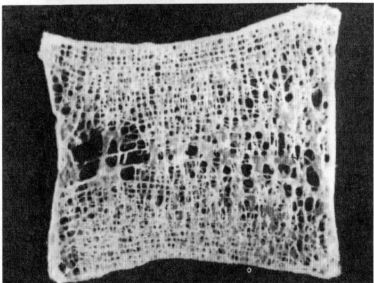

B

Figure 11-1 A, Sagittal section of ulnar compact bone from a turkey; **B,** Sagittal section of vertebral trabecular bone from a 55-year-old woman. *Source*: Reprinted from *Bone Histomorphometry: Third International Workshop*, by WSS Jee and AM Parfitt (Eds) with permission of Societé Nouvelle de Publications, © 1981.

problem. Noninvasive methods now include single- and dual-photon absorptiometry (SPA and DPA) and quantitative computed tomography (QCT).[7] Iliac crest biopsy has been the primary invasive measurement.

Accurate, noninvasive measurement of bone mass emerged with the development of photon absorptiometry and CT. SPA is based on the attenuation of a narrowly focused photon beam (usually iodine [125]) by bone. The measurements are accurate and precise and suited to regions of the body in which variations in soft tissue composition (fat versus lean mass) are minimal, such as the forearm, leg, or heel (ie, the cortical skeleton). Although estimates of cortical bone density in any region correlate reasonably well with whole-body bone mineral, they have a very poor reflection of the central trabecular skeleton.

Isotopes that emit photons at two energies permit application of the photon absorptiometry principle to the central skeleton; current DPA machines use gadolinium #153, with energies of 44 and 100 keV, while dual-energy x-ray absorptiometry (DEXA) uses a dual-energy x-ray beam. The subject is recumbent while a photomultiplier tube records transmission from an isotope or x-ray source located under the scanning table. The lumbar spine can be scanned in about 20 minutes with DPA and 5 minutes with DEXA. Radiation exposures from DPA and DEXA are approximately 10 mrem and 5 mrem, respectively. Since the detector recognizes all transmitted photons, estimates of bone density by this technique will include not only vertebral trabecular bone, but also such cortical elements as spinous and transverse processes. DPA is accurate and precise, with a coefficient of variation for replicate measurements of about 2.5%. DEXA, the most advanced of the dual-energy techniques, has lower precision error than DPA (<0.5%) with shorter examination time and less radiation exposure. Recent software modifications permit some equipment to measure whole-body and regional skeletal mineral. The DEXA has software available that accurately and precisely measures mineral density of the proximal femur. With photon absorptiometry, mineral densities are reported as grams of mineral per square centimeter of bone area.

QCT has been used frequently to determine trabecular bone density of the lumbar spine.[8] The subject lies on the scanning table above a set of materials of known and varying densities. The operator selects a region of pure trabecular bone for analysis, and the mineral density, given as milligrams per cubic centimeter of bone volume, is computed. Although this technique can be modified for any region of the skeleton, most work has involved the lumbar spine, for which commercial software is available. For healthy, nonosteoporotic subjects, the coefficient of variation of repeated measurements by experienced operators may be as low as 1.6%. Radiation exposure, usually 500 to 1000 mrems, is modest but considerably greater than that with photon absorptiometry.

Neutron activation analysis measures total body calcium and correlates extremely well with DPA ($r > .99$).[9] However, prohibitive expense limits its application.

Transiliac bone biopsy is an invasive technique that provides a core sample of largely trabecular bone bordered by internal and external cortices. In most cases, transverse cylindric cores are obtained approximately 2 cm posterior to the anterior superior iliac spine, just inferior to the iliac crest. Biochemical and histologic analyses performed on these biopsies yield information regarding bone mass, adequacy of bone mineralization, and, when the bone has been previously labeled with tetracycline, dynamic aspects of bone turnover.[10] Recent applications of this technique also permit assessment of the degree to which trabecular elements are connected to each other and the magnitude of spaces between adjacent trabeculae, ie, the connectivity of trabecular bone.[11]

ROLE OF BONE REMODELING

Bone exhibits three fundamental activities: modeling, repair, and remodeling. Modeling refers to the process by which the characteristic shape of a bone is achieved and maintained. Repair is the regenerative response to fracture. Remodeling is a continuous cycle of destruction and renewal of bone that occurs throughout life in humans, primates, and some other mammals.

Bone adapts to imposed stress or lack of stress by forming or losing tissue. This process is mediated through remodeling. Remodeling is performed by individual, independent bone remodeling units comprising osteoclasts (bone-resorbing cells) and osteoblasts (bone-forming cells). In a maintenance situation, remodeling may be somewhat inefficient, as small deficits appear to persist on completion of each cycle. Over the years, the accumulating deficits account for the bone loss associated with age.[6] The basis for this conclusion is the reported age-related decline in mean wall thickness of trabecular bone from iliac crest bone biopsies.[12,13]

Bone hypertrophy occurs when stress is applied in excess of normal levels. Osteoblastic activity exceeds osteoclastic resorption, leading to a net gain in bone. Net loss occurs when resorption is greater than formation. Burr and associates[14] suggest that accumulated fatigue-related microdamage at the level of the osteon (bone cell) stimulates the remodeling process. Osteoclastic activity removes the damaged material so that osteoblasts can deposit matrix and mineral along the paths of imposed stress. When microdamage accumulation is slow, remodeling is able to keep pace, and skeletal integrity is maintained. However, when damage accumulation is more rapid, such as from a sudden and sustained major increase in exercise level, the remodeling scavenger function may not provide adequate protection against fatigue damage; fracture then may result.

CHANGES IN BONE MASS WITH AGE

The traditional view of age-related bone loss was clearly enunciated by the landmark studies of Garn et al.[15] By using careful measurements of metacarpal cortical thickness from hand radiographs, they described a characteristic trajectory of bone mass that was similar in men and women and was observed in virtually all ethnic groups. By this model, bone is gained during adolescence, reaches a plateau level sometime during the third decade, and remains stable until approximately age 50 years, after which progressive gradual loss is observed. This model was confirmed by a number of independent laboratories and was supplemented with the observation that the initial loss of bone at age 50 years is temporarily more rapid in women, presumably because of the effects of menopause.[16] Experience with newer noninvasive methods, such as SPA, remain consistent with this model.[17–19] Hui and colleagues[19] used SPA to measure forearm density in 268 Caucasian women aged 50 to 95 years. They observed the expected decline in forearm density beginning at age 50 years, but reported an increase in forearm bone mineral density at age 86 years (Figure 11-2). The investigators attributed this late increase to a gain in density of the periosteal envelope in compensation for endosteal (medullary cavity of the bone) loss. Additional research using a large population of elderly individuals is necessary to substantiate this conclusion.

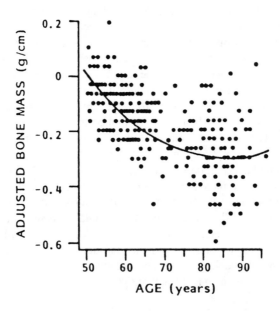

Figure 11-2 Average bone mass for each woman adjusted for body size against her mean age during time of measurement. *Source*: Reprinted with permission from *Journal of Chronic Diseases* (1982;35:715–725), Copyright © 1982.

Although the age-related decline in bone mineral density of the radius provides an accurate description of the trajectory of appendicular (limb) cortical bone mass, it was difficult for many years to validate its applicability to other areas of the cortical skeleton, such as the proximal femur, or to the axial or trabecular skeleton. In fact, pioneering studies with postmortem material[20-22] clearly indicated that loss of axial bone mass occurred earlier than one would predict from the forearm data. Subsequent analyses of iliac crest biopsy material confirm this view.[23-25]

There is unanimous agreement, using multiple techniques, that trabecular bone is lost with age and that axial density is substantially lower in older subjects than in young people. Controversy today concern the timing of the onset of axial bone loss and whether or not there is accelerated loss at menopause.

ONSET OF BONE LOSS

A decline in bone density has been reported to begin after the second,[2] third,[26] fourth,[27] or fifth[28] decade. Both measurements of anatomic specimens and results from biopsy studies indicate that axial bone loss occurs as early as the third decade.[24,29,30] In particular, iliac crest biopsy data have suggested that trabecular bone mass declines significantly in women before menopause. Meunier and colleagues[23] showed an age-related loss of trabecular bone volume from iliac crest specimens that appeared to begin as early as the third decade. However, this study could be criticized because the material was obtained from victims of accidents and sudden death and therefore might not be representative of a normal population. Marcus and colleagues[24] examined trabecular bone volume in 62 iliac crest biopsy specimens taken from active women with normal menstrual function. They found that trabecular bone volume was negatively correlated with age, and there was an annual predicted loss of 0.7% of the original bone volume in women aged 18 to 45 years (Figure 11-3). The cumulative effect over a span of 30 years might amount to a loss of 25% of original trabecular bone volume before the age of menopause is reached. Once again, questions might be raised about the normalcy of this study group, since all subjects had undergone biopsy for preliminary staging of Hodgkin's disease. However, the great majority of women proved to have only limited disease, and all were active, normally menstruating women at the time of biopsy. More recently, Birkenhager-Frenkel and associates[25] conducted iliac crest biopsies on 94 healthy men and women aged 20 to 80 years and reported a correlation of trabecular bone volume with age for premenopausal women that was the same as that observed by Marcus and colleagues.[24] Since their population included elderly individuals, they also reported that the women had accelerated trabecular bone loss beginning at age 50 years.

Trabecular vertebral specimens have been shown to follow the same pattern as iliac crest bone samples. Mosekilde and Mosekilde[31] examined postmortem

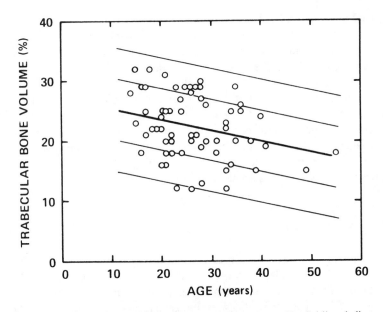

Figure 11-3 Trabecular bone volume (iliac crest biopsies) versus age. Parallel lines indicate mean ± 1 and 2 standard deviations. *Source*: Reprinted with permission from *Calcified Tissue International*, (1983;35:406–409), Copyright © 1983, Springer-Verlag.

trabecular samples of the first lumbar vertebra from 42 normal individuals, aged 15 to 87 years, and found a significant age-related decrease in vertebral bone volume, beginning early in the third decade (Figure 11-4). An accelerated loss at age 50 years was not observed in the women, but that may have been due to the small sample size. Therefore, although concerns remain about the limited nature of the data base, both postmortem and in vivo anatomic evidence support the concept that early loss of trabecular bone occurs in women.

The development of DPA and QCT as noninvasive measurements of axial and trabecular bone mass has permitted evaluation of this issue on a much larger scale. Measurements of spine density in both normal and osteoporotic groups of patients have revealed both a linear and a nonlinear loss of bone with age. One of the major problems with these studies is the difficulty in predicting longitudinal changes from cross-sectional analyses. Depending on the number of subjects and the measurement technique, some investigators have reported regressions of bone mineral with age that fit a linear model, in which the loss of lumbar bone mineral remains constant from young adulthood; others have described an exponential model, in which loss is minimal or nonsignificant before age 50 years (or to menopause in women), followed by a significant linear decline thereafter.[32]

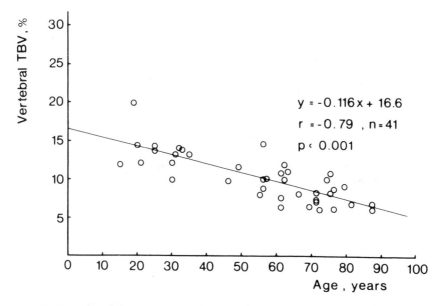

Figure 11-4 Relationship between age and percentage of trabecular bone volume in postmortem vertebral specimens. *Source*: Reprinted with permission from *Bone* (1988;9:195–199), Copyright © 1988, Societe Nouvelle des Publications Medicales et Dentaires.

Results with use of DPA and QCT to determine changes in bone density have been variable. Some groups have observed significant axial bone loss before age 50 years[33–36] and others have failed to show such a change.[26–28,37–40] Madsen[33] suggested a linear loss with age. This investigator examined lumbar spine densities of 41 women and 5 men aged 20 to 93 years (mean = 61 years) and found a decrease of 0.5% per year. A similar pattern was later observed by Riggs and associates,[34] who reported DPA spine densities for a large group of healthy women across the age range of 20 to 80 years. The best description of these data in women was a single negative correlation, the slope of which indicated a loss of axial bone mass over the entire adult age span of about 1% per year (Figure 11-5). Similar measurements in normal men also gave a negative regression with age, although the slope was somewhat less than half that observed with women. Riggs et al[34] concluded that there was no evidence of an increased rate of loss in axial bone mass in women after age 50 years. Buchanan and associates[35] measured vertebral bone density (QCT) in 74 healthy premenopausal women aged 18 to 48 years. They found a linear regression with age ($r = -.39$, $P = .0006$) and concluded that vertebral trabecular bone loss begins during or prior to the third decade. In a cross-sectional study of 214 normal women aged 35 to 80 years,

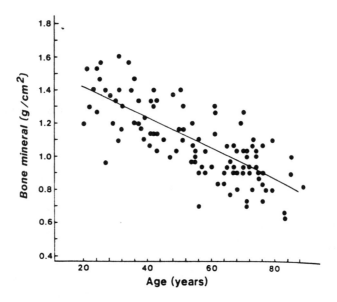

Figure 11-5 Regression of bone mineral density of lumbar spine on age in 105 normal women. *Source*: Reprinted with permission from *Journal of Clinical Investigation* (1981;67:328–335), Copyright © 1981, American Society for Clinical Investigation.

Hansson and Roos[36] observed no differences in the rate of bone loss of the third lumbar vertebra when groups of different ages were compared, a pattern previously reported by Riggs and associates.[34] They concluded that menopause does not have a direct effect on bone loss and that events occurring in the premenopausal years need to be considered in the prevention of osteoporosis.

Other investigators have failed to find a significant loss prior to age 50 years,[26–28,37–40] and they report that the major loss begins at the time of menopause. The reasons for discrepancies among investigators are not clear. The principal difficulty may arise from the fact that the vast majority of these studies are cross-sectional analyses. Although such studies may provide valid insights into population changes across time, they cannot distinguish secular trends and are subject to multiple confounding factors. For example, the observation of a bone density of age 40 years that is lower than that at age 20 years could reflect loss of bone over this 20-year period, but it is also consistent with an interpretation that peak bone mass is significantly higher in today's 20-year-old women than was true 20 years ago. Therefore, a number of important geographic, ethnic, dietary, and physical activity differences within and between study populations could account for the differences observed in the literature. In addition, Sambrook and colleagues[32] have recently shown that the population size necessary to detect subtle changes in regression slope with certainty is far greater than that of any reported study. This is particularly relevant to detecting a menopausal acceleration of bone loss.

CHANGES AT MENOPAUSE

Two issues arise when considering the changes in trabecular bone loss that occur at menopause. The first issue is whether there is support for the onset of significant bone loss around the time of menopause. The second issue is whether the first few years past menopause exhibit an acceleration in rate of loss that later subsides. The majority of studies confirm that if bone loss has not started earlier, it certainly is present during the menopausal years. The question remains, however, whether a transient increase in rate of loss, specifically due to the loss of endogenous estrogen, can be demonstrated.

The majority of studies confirm that trabecular bone loss accelerates at menopause.[26–28,37–40] Using DPA, Gallagher and colleagues[37] measured spine density on 392 normal women aged 20 to 80 years and reported that the largest decrease in density occurred in the first 5 years following menopause. They found a 3.4% per year decline in the second year, a 1.7% per year decline in the fourth year, and 0.8% per year in the ninth year, a time during which bone loss slowed. Cann and associates[39] used QCT to measure spine density and found that values for trabecular bone mineral remain stable until menopause, then decline rapidly for 5 to 8 years, followed by a continued, but slower, decrease. Similarly, QCT measurements of spine density by Firooznia and colleagues[40] showed the same trend. Their results from studying 132 normal women demonstrated increased vertebral trabecular bone loss (2% per year to 8% per year) from ages 50 to 60 years. An accelerated loss of trabecular vertebral bone also has been demonstrated following surgical menopause.[41]

A few cross-sectional studies have reported a linear decline in bone loss beginning at age 50 years. Aloia and colleagues[28] measured lumbar spine density with DPA in 159 healthy women (aged 20 to 70 years) and reported significant losses at menopause, occurring in a linear relationship with age. From a sample of 70 healthy women (aged 20 to 88 years), Krølner and Pors Nielsen[27] observed a constant loss (1.4% per year) in the rate of spine density from ages 50 through 88 years (Figure 11-6). Although they observed a loss beginning at age 34 years, the investigators reported that the linear slope in premenopausal women (triangles in Figure 11-6) did not differ significantly from zero. In the same report, Krølner and Pors Nielsen[27] examined spine density of 59 normal women in a longitudinal study. These women had their spine density measured by DPA 2 times within 3 to 19 months (mean = 10.5 months). The premenopausal group (n = 27) had no significant loss, whereas the postmenopausal women (n = 32) exhibited a decline

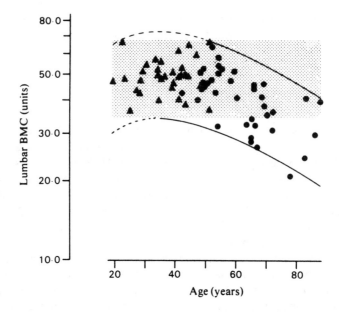

Figure 11-6 Lumbar spine bone mineral content in 70 normal women in relation to age. Triangles represent premenopausal women; circles represent postmenopausal women. *Source*: Reprinted with permission from *Clinical Science* (1982;62:329–336), Copyright © 1982, Biochemical Society.

of 1.6% to 7.1% per year. The 12 women within 5 years of menopause demonstrated a mean decrease of 6.5% per year, supporting an accelerated loss in the first 5 years past menopause.

To summarize, bone loss in women is a result of both aging and menopause. From the published studies it seems that trabecular bone loss begins prior to age 50 years and that it increases at menopause. Certainly more longitudinal studies are indicated in light of the data presented by Krølner and Pors Nielsen.[27] The linear loss reported by Riggs and colleagues[34] is often cited as the progression of bone loss in women. However, as suggested by the work of Sambrook and colleagues,[32] the data may not be representative of the population of women at-large.

PEAK BONE DENSITY

Although considerable attention has been given to the onset of bone loss, a paucity of data exists concerning the issue of when peak bone density is achieved. It has been assumed that maximal bone mass is reached at some time during the third decade. However, recent data indicate that it is likely that this assumption will need to be revised. Densitometric evidence as well as previous anatomic and bone biopsy studies[20] permit the conclusion that peak bone density may occur in late adolescence. Gilsanz and associates[42] used CT to measure trabecular vertebral density in female adolescents (aged 14 to 19 years; $n = 24$) and young adults (aged 25 to 35 years; $n = 24$). They found that the adolescent group had significantly higher vertebral density than the young adult group and concluded that peak bone density occurs around the time of cessation of longitudinal growth. This group also reported[43] significantly higher vertebral bone density following puberty in both girls and boys. The values measured at puberty remained stable through late adolescence, indicating that the subjects had reached their peak bone mass directly after puberty. Unpublished observations from our laboratory support the notion that peak bone density is reached in adolescence. We used DPA to measure spine density on 84 healthy girls and women from ages 12 to 30 years. A significant increase in lumbar spine BMD ($p<0.01$) was observed from 12 to 17 years ($n=31$), whereas no significant change was demonstrated between the ages of 18 and 30 years ($n=53$). Although preliminary, these results indicate that peak bone density is reached much earlier than previously reported.

LOSS IN BONE MASS AND BONE STRENGTH

Most patients with compression fractures of the vertebra, wrist, and hip have low bone density. Consequently, the compressive strength of trabecular bone relative to bone mass has been studied by many investigators.[31,44–49] Results indicate that bone strength depends not only on bone mass, but also on bone quality and architecture. Research by Mosekilde and Mosekilde[31] elucidates this formulation. They have shown that significant decreases in ash density (bone mass) corresponded to biomechanical properties of vertebral trabecular bone in normal men and women aged 15 to 87 years in whom biomechanical competence declined as much as 90% on some parameters while ash density declined only 48% to 50%. The investigators concluded that the loss of bone strength with age is much more pronounced than is the concurrent loss of bone mass (ash density), and they attributed the discrepancy in percentage decline to the loss in continuity of the trabecular lattice with increasing age.

In a young person, the architecture of load-bearing vertebral trabecular bone is characterized by thick vertical planes and columns that are crossed by thinner horizontal trabeculae. Maximal support (strength) is gained by the connection of all trabecular elements.[50] With age, the trabecular framework changes. The structural changes that occur in the three-dimensional trabecular network, in concert with a decline in bone mass, lead to extreme losses in bone strength.

The nature of these modifications in trabeculae is a topic of great research interest. There is debate as to whether the loss in strength is due to a disappearance of horizontal trabeculae, leading to increased trabecular spacing, or merely thinning of both vertical and horizontal structural supports. However, Parfitt and colleagues[11] reported that trabeculae from iliac crest biopsies were disconnected and often disappeared, leaving hollow areas in the matrix. Recently, Weinstein and Hutson[51] measured trabecular microarchitecture directly on iliac crest biopsies and reported both decreased trabecular width and increased trabecular separation with age. They concluded that loss of trabeculae may occur after the elements become thin enough for complete penetration by osteoclasts.

In addition to iliac crest samples, vertebral trabecular specimens also have exhibited alterations in microarchitecture. Mosekilde[49] analyzed cylindric trabecular specimens from the central third vertebral body of normal men and women and found a significant age-related decrease ($r = -.71$) in mean horizontal trabecular thickness as well as significant increases in spacing between the horizontal and vertical trabeculae ($r = .79$ and $r = .75$, respectively). These changes are illustrated in Figure 11-7.

In conclusion, the loss in bone strength with age seems to be a result of both trabecular thinning and disappearance of trabeculae. Although it is suggested that trabecular elements can be thickened but not replaced,[51] further research is indicated to determine how various intervention techniques can modify the microarchitecture of trabecular bone.

MECHANISMS OF BONE MASS REGULATION

As previously stated, alteration in remodeling activity is the final common pathway to modifications in bone mineral density. Primary controllers of this process include physical activity, calcium nutriture, and reproductive endocrine status.

Physical Activity

The estimated loss of bone from its peak in young adulthood to age 80 years is comparable to the reported 35% to 45% decline in muscle strength during the same life span.[52] Since a clear relationship between muscle strength and bone mass has been established,[22,53–55] physical activity has gained attention as a method for improving bone mass. The mechanisms by which the skeleton responds to activity are yet to be defined, but the evidence suggests that bone mass increases in response to application of mechanical stress.[56–58] Data from numerous studies strongly support the notion that the bone mass of athletes exceeds that of sedentary individuals.[59–63] Not only does bone density appear to be higher in physically active people, but the literature suggests that exercise reduces the rate of age-

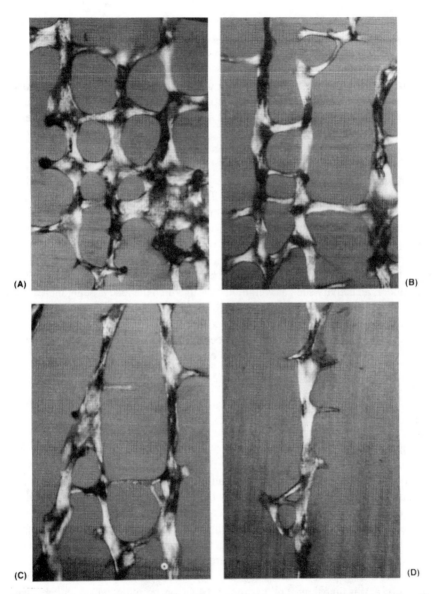

Figure 11-7 A, a 50-year-old man with an almost perfect, continuous trabecular network; **B,** a 58-year-old man with discernible thinning of the horizontal trabeculae and some loss of continuity; **C,** a 76-year-old man with continued thinning of the horizontal trabeculae and wider separation of the vertical structures; **D,** an 87-year-old woman with advanced breakdown of the whole network, showing unsupported vertical trabeculae. (Original magnification × 8). *Source*: Reprinted with permission from *Bone* (1988;9:247–250), Copyright © 1988, Societe Nouvelle des Publications Medicales et Dentaire.

related bone loss.[64–66] There is a small amount of literature on exercise intervention suggesting that mechanical stress from activity increases bone density.[67–71] However, problems with these studies include nonrandomization, lack of adequate controls, and inappropriate exercise protocols.

Currently it is not known which type of exercise is best for improving bone mass. For example, weight-bearing activity, such as walking, jogging, and running, has been suggested as the most appropriate form of activity for elderly women. However, Cavanaugh and Cann[72] failed to find an increase in spinal bone mineral density in postmenopausal women who engaged in 1 year of brisk walking three times per week. Either the type of exercise program (walking) was not appropriate for bone, or the walking program should have been performed at greater frequency, duration, or intensity. This idea introduces another issue in the area of research on exercise and bone mass; that is, which components of an exercise program—duration, frequency, or intensity—are most important in producing increases in bone mass? Based on the conclusions of Carter and colleagues,[58] increasing the load of an activity should be a superior osteogenic stimulus to an increase in the number of cycles (repetitions) of an activity. With this model, an activity such as weight lifting, in which the load is being increased, would produce greater changes in bone mineral density than an activity such as running, in which the load does not change as much as the cycles change. It is apparent that extensive investigation is needed to clarify these research questions. A comprehensive treatment of this topic can be found elsewhere.[73]

Calcium Nutriture

The skeleton is the repository for 99.5% of the total body calcium and constitutes a source of mineral that can support plasma calcium levels at times of need. The published literature concerning relationships between dietary calcium and skeletal integrity is complex and frequently ambiguous[74–76] and is not detailed here, although a few summary statements are in order.

The recommended dietary calcium intake for adolescent boys and girls is 1200 mg, a figure derived primarily from balance studies. Since the 2 or 3 years that constitute the pubertal growth spurt are accompanied by deposition of 60% of final bone mass, dietary inadequacy may impose far greater constraints on bone formation at this time than at other times of life. Consumption figures indicate that the calcium intake of American men corresponds reasonably well to recommended levels at most ages, but that median intakes for American girls are substantially below target levels by age 11 years, and they never recover. It is likely that calcium undernutrition has an important influence on peak bone mass in women (Chapter 4).

During the third through fifth decades, growth has stopped, and robust compensatory mechanisms permit rapid adaptation to even severe dietary restriction. Therefore, it should not be surprising that calcium nutritional state appears not to be a major influence on the rate of bone loss during this period;[77] as a corollary, it is unlikely that calcium supplementation will exert important beneficial effects on bone mass during this period. It is ironic that this population is the target for the greatest portion of calcium supplement advertising.

At menopause, the initial acceleration in bone loss in women reflects loss of endogenous estrogen, and it has little relationship to dietary calcium. Riis and colleagues[78] showed only modest effects on bone loss when early-menopausal women were given supplemental calcium. However, the habitual dietary calcium of Danish women approximates 1100 mg, considerably higher than that in the United States, so what may have been a marginal effect for Danish women might be more substantial for their American counterparts.

After age 60 years, the early effects of estrogen deficiency have subsided, whereas the compensatory mechanisms for accommodating dietary deficiencies have become less efficient in both men and women. It is considered likely that disruption of these mechanisms leads to secondary hypersecretion of parathyroid hormone, leading to support of plasma calcium at the expense of aggravated bone loss[79,80] (Chapter 12). At this time attention to proper calcium nutriture, whether from dietary calcium or from supplementation with calcium or vitamin D, is rational; adequate intake has been shown to have beneficial effects on bone mass.[75,76]

Reproductive Endocrine Status

Formidable evidence supports an important role for gonadal function in the acquisition and maintenance of bone mass. Hypogonadal boys and girls have substantial deficits in both cortical and trabecular bone mineral. The loss of endogenous androgen or estrogen during adult life regularly leads to accelerated loss of bone mineral, an effect that is particularly striking when it occurs at an early age, such as after oophorectomy in a young woman.

In women, the loss of estrogen has dual effects. Decreased efficiency of intestinal and renal calcium homeostasis increases the level of calcium intake necessary to maintain calcium balance. In addition, evidence shows that estrogen directly affects bone cell function,[81–83] and this interaction is thought to underlie the accelerated bone loss of early estrogen deficiency. In terms of bone remodeling, estrogen deficiency permits osteoclasts to resorb bone with greater efficiency. This may lead to perforation of trabeculae, with no scaffold left for initiation of bone formation. Therefore, entire trabecular elements may be eliminated. Replacement of estrogen at menopause protects bone mass and affords significant protection against risk for osteoporotic fractures.[84] Estrogen deficiency may have an overwhelming influence on bone mass even when adequate attention is given to other important influences on bone health. For example, women athletes who experience interruption of menstrual function lose bone, despite regular exercise at high density.[62]

The skeletal role of androgens is less well understood. Testosterone deficiency is an important contributor to osteoporosis in men, and replacement therapy restores bone mass. However, the mechanisms by which androgens interact with the skeleton are not known. Specific receptors for testosterone have not yet been demonstrated in bone cells. One known action for androgens is to increase muscle mass, so it is possible that the androgenic effects on bone secondarily reflect the increased mechanical loading that would occur if muscle mass were to increase. Finally, evidence suggests that circulating androgens make a significant contribution to peak bone mass in women.[85]

CONCLUSION

Extensive published literature documents important contributions of physical activity, calcium nutriture, and reproductive endocrine status to the acquisition and maintenance of bone mass. For too long, many investigators in osteology have maintained parochial interests in one or another of these areas, championing its particular importance while occasionally denigrating the relevance of others. It is now clear that, to understand the regulation of bone mass and to design rational strategies to improve it, consideration of these several influences as an integrated whole will be required.

REFERENCES

1. Riggs JL, Melton JL III. Involutional osteoporosis. *N Engl J Med*. 1986;314:1676–1684.

2. Riggs BL, Wahner HW, Melton JL III, et al. Rates of bone loss in the appendicular and axial skeletons of women: evidence of substantial vertebral bone loss before menopause. *J Clin Invest*. 1986;77:1487–1491.

3. Nottestad SY, Baumel JJ, Kimmel D, et al. The proportion of trabecular bone in human vertebrae. *J Bone Miner Res*. 1987;2:221–229.

4. Rubin CT, Lanyon LE. Regulation of bone mass by mechanical loading: the effect of peak strain magnitude. *Calcif Tissue Int*. 1985;37:411–417.

5. Arnold JS. Trabecular patterns and shapes in aging and osteoporosis. In: Jee WSS, Parfitt AM, eds. *Bone Histomorphometry: Third International Workshop*. Paris, France: Societé Nouvelle de Publications; 1981.

6. Marcus R. Normal and abnormal bone remodeling in man. *Adv Intern Med*. 1987;38:129–141.

7. Mazess RB. The noninvasive measurement of skeletal mass. In: Peck WA, ed. *Bone and Mineral Research Annual*. New York, NY: Elsevier Science Publishing Co Inc; 1981;1.

8. Cann CE, Genant HK. Precise measurement of vertebral mineral content using computed tomography. *J Comput Assist Tomogr*. 1980;4:493–500.

9. Mazess RB, Peppler WW, Chesnut CH III, et al. Total body bone mineral and lean body mass by dual-photon absorptiometry, II: comparison with total body calcium by neutron activation analysis. *Calcif Tissue Int*. 1981;33:361–363.

10. Burnell JM, Baylink DJ, Chesnut CH III, et al. Bone matrix and mineral abnormalities in postmenopausal osteoporosis. *Metabolism*. 1982;31(11):1113–1120.

11. Parfitt AM, Mathews HE, Villanueva AR, et al. Relationships between surface, volume and thickness of iliac trabecular bone in aging and in osteoporosis. *J Clin Invest*. 1983;72:1396–1409.

12. Kragstrup J, Melsen F, Mosekilde L. Thickness of bone formed at remodeling sites in normal iliac trabecular bone: variations with age and sex. *Metab Bone Dis & Relat Res*. 1983;5:17–21.

13. Lips P, Courpron P, Meunier PJ. Mean wall thickness of trabecular bone packets in the human iliac crest: changes with age. *Calcif Tissue Res*. 1978;26:13–17.

14. Burr DB, Martin RB, Schaffler MB, et al. Bone remodeling in response to in vivo fatigue damage. *J Biomech*. 1985;12:189–200.

15. Garn SM, Rohman CG, Nolan P Jr. The developmental nature of bone changes during aging. In: Birren JE, ed. *Relations of Development and Aging*. Springfield, Ill: Charles C Thomas Publisher; 1966.

16. Meema HE, Meema S. Cortical bone mineral density versus cortical thickness in the diagnosis of osteoporosis: a roentgenological-densitometric study. *J Am Geriatr Soc*. 1969;17:120–141.

17. Mazess RB. On aging bone loss. *Clin Orthop*. 1982;165:239–252.

18. Smith DM, Khairi MRA, Norton J, et al. Age and activity effects on rate of bone mineral loss. *J Clin Invest*. 1976;58:716–721.

19. Hui SL, Wiske PS, Norton JA, et al. A prospective study of change in bone mass with age in postmenopausal women. *J Chronic Dis*. 1982;35:715–725.

20. Arnold JS, Bartley MH, Bartley DDS, et al. Skeletal changes in aging and disease. *Clin Orthop*. 1966;49:37.

21. Trotter M, Broman GE, Peterson RP. Densities of bones of white and Negro skeletons. *J Bone Joint Surg*. 1960;42-A:58.

22. Doyle F, Brown J, LaChance C. Relation between bone mass and muscle weight. *Lancet*. 1970;1:391–393.

23. Meunier P, Courpron P, Edouard C, et al. Physiological senile involution and pathological rarefaction of bone. *Clin Endocrinol Metab*. 1973;2(2):239–256.

24. Marcus R, Kosek J, Pfefferbaum A, et al. Age-related loss of trabecular bone in premenopausal women: a biopsy study. *Calcif Tissue Int*. 1983;35:406–409.

25. Birkenhager-Frenkel DH, Courpron P, Hupscher EA, et al. Age-related changes in cancellous bone structure. *Bone Miner*. 1988;4:197–216.

26. Geusens P, Dequeker A, Verstraeten A, et al. Age-, sex-, and menopause-related changes of vertebral and peripheral bone population study using dual and single photon absorptiometry and radiogrammetry. *J Nucl Med*. 1986;27:1540–1549.

27. Krølner B, Pors Nielsen S. Bone mineral content of the lumbar spine in normal and osteoporotic women: cross-sectional and longitudinal studies. *Clin Sci*. 1982;62:329–336.

28. Aloia JF, Vaswani A, Ellis K, et al. A model for involutional bone loss. *J Lab Clin Med*. 1985;106:630–637.

29. Weaver JK, Chalmers J. Cancellous bone: its strength and changes with aging and in evaluation of some methods for measuring its mineral content. *J Bone Joint Surg*. 1966;48A:289–299.

30. Arnold JS. Amount and quality of trabecular bone in osteoporotic vertebral fractures. *Clin Endocrinol Metab*. 1973;2:221–238.

31. Mosekilde L, Mosekilde L. Iliac crest bone volume as a predictor for vertebral compressive strength, ash density and trabecular bone volume in normal individuals. *Bone* 1988;9:195–199.

32. Sambrook PN, Eisman JA, Furler SM, et al. Computer modeling and analysis of cross-sectional bone density studies with respect to age and the menopause. *J Bone Miner Res*. 1987;2(2):109–114.

33. Madsen M. Vertebral and peripheral bone mineral content by photon absorptiometry. *Invest Radiol*. 1977;12:185–188.

34. Riggs BL, Wahner HW, Dann WL, et al. Differential changes in bone mineral density of the appendicular and axial skeleton with aging. *J Clin Invest*. 1981;67:328–335.

35. Buchanan JR, Myers C, Lloyd T, et al. Early vertebral trabecular bone loss in normal premenopausal women. *J Bone Miner Res*. 1988;3:583–587.

36. Hansson T, Roos B. Age changes in bone mineral of the lumbar spine in normal women. *Calcif Tissue Int*. 1986;38:249–251.

37. Gallagher JC, Goldgar D, Moy A. Total bone calcium in normal women: effect of age and menopause status. *J Bone Miner Res*. 1987;2(6):491–496.

38. Nilas L, Gotfredsen A, Hadberg A, et al. Age-related bone loss in women evaluated by the single and dual photon technique. *Bone Miner*. 1988;4:95–103.

39. Cann CE, Genant HK, Kolb FO, et al. Quantitative computed tomography for prediction of vertebal fracture risk. *Bone* 1985;6:1–7.

40. Firooznia H, Golimbu C, Rafii M, et al. Quantitative computed tomography assessment of spinal trabecular bone, I: age-related regression in normal men and women. *J Comput Tomogr*. 1984;8:91–97.

41. Genant HK, Cann CE, Ettinger B, et al. Spinal mineral loss in oophorectomized women. *JAMA*. 1980;244:2056–2059.

42. Gilsanz V, Gibbons DT, Carlson M, et al. Peak vertebral density: a comparison of adolescent and adult females. *Calcif Tissue Int*. 1988;43:260–262.

43. Gilsanz DT, Roe TF, Carlson M, et al. Vertebral bone density in children: effect of puberty. *Radiology*. 1988;166:847–850.

44. Galante J, Rostoker W, Ray RD. Physical properties of trabecular bone. *Calcif Tissue Res*. 1970;5:236–246.

45. Townsend PR, Raux P, Rose RM, et al. The distribution and anisotropy of the stiffness of cancellous bone in the human patella. *J Biomech*. 1975;8:199–201.

46. Lindahl O. Mechanical properties of dried defatted spongy bone. *Acta Orthop Scand*. 1976;47:11–19.

47. Martens M, VanAudekerche R, Delport P, et al. The mechanical characteristics of cancellous bone of upper femoral region. *J Biomech*. 1983;16:971–983.

48. Mosekilde L, Mosekilde L, Danielson CC. Biomechanical competence of vertebral trabecular bone in relation to ash density and age in normal individuals. *Bone*. 1987;8:79–85.

49. Mosekilde L. Age-related changes in vertebral trabecular bone architecture: assessed by a new method. *Bone*. 1988;9:247–250.

50. Parfitt AM. Age-related structural changes in trabecular and cortical bone: cellular mechanisms and biomechanical consequences. *Calcif Tissue Int*. 1984;36:123–128.

51. Weinstein RS, Hutson MS. Decreased trabecular width and increased trabecular spacing contribute to bone loss with aging. *Bone*. 1987;8:137–142.

52. Johnson T. Age-related differences in isometric and dynamic strength and endurance. *Phys Ther.* 1982;62:985–989.

53. Aloia JF, Cohn SH, Babu T, et al. Skeletal mass and body composition in marathon runners. *Metabolism.* 1978;27:1793–1796.

54. Sinaki M, Offord K. Physical activity in postmenopausal women: effect on back muscle strength and bone mineral density of the spine. *Arch Phys Med Rehabil.* 1988;69:277–280.

55. Sinaki M, McPhee MC, Hodgson SF. Relationship between bone mineral density of spine and strength of back extensors in healthy postmenopausal women. *Mayo Clin Proc.* 1986;61:116–122.

56. Rubin CT, Lanyon LE. Regulation of bone mass by mechanical strain magnitude. *Calcif Tissue Int.* 1985;37:411–417.

57. Rubin CT, Lanyon LE. Regulation of bone formation by applied dynamic loads. *J Bone Joint Surg.* 1984;66:397–402.

58. Carter DR, Fyrie DP, Whalen RT. Trabecular bone density and loading history: regulation of connective tissue biology by mechanical energy. *J Biomech.* 1987;20:785–794.

59. Nilsson BE, Westlin NE. Bone density in athletes. *Clin Orthop.* 1971;77:179–182.

60. Huddleston AL, Rockwell D, Kulund DN, et al. Bone mass in lifetime tennis players. *JAMA.* 1980;244:1107–1109.

61. Dalen N, Olsson KE. Bone mineral content and physical activity. *Acta Orthop Scand.* 1974;45:170–174.

62. Marcus R, Cann C, Madvig P, et al. Menstrual function and bone mass in elite women distance runners: endocrine metabolic features. *Ann Intern Med.* 1985;102:158–163.

63. Jacobson PC, Beaver W, Grubb SA, et al. Bone density in women: college athletes and older athletic women. *J Orthop Res.* 1984;2:328–332.

64. Talmadge RV, Stinnett SS, Landwehr JT, et al. Age-related loss of bone mineral density in non-athletic and athletic women. *Bone Miner.* 1986;1:115–125.

65. Brewer V, Meyer BM, Keele MS, et al. Role of exercise in prevention of involutional bone loss. *Med Sci Sports Exerc.* 1983;15:445–449.

66. Smith EL, Reddan W, Smith PE. Physical activity and calcium modalities for bone mineral increase in aged women. *Med Sci Sports Exerc.* 1981;13:60–64.

67. Smith EL, Smith PE, Ensign CJ, et al. Bone involution decrease in exercising middle-aged women. *Calcif Tissue Int.* 1984;36:S129–S138.

68. Krølner B, Toft B, Pors Nielsen S, et al. Physical exercise as prophylaxis against involutional bone loss: a controlled trial. *Clin Sci.* 1983;64:541–546.

69. White MK, Martin RB, Yeater RA, et al. The effects of exercise on the bones of post-menopausal women. *Int Orthop.* 1984;7:209–214.

70. Williams JA, Wagner J, Wasnich R, et al. The effect of long-distance running on appendicular bone mineral content. *Med Sci Sports Exerc.* 1984;16:223–227.

71. Dalsky G, Stocke KS, Ehsani AA. Weight-bearing exercise training and lumbar bone mineral content in postmenopausal women. *Ann Intern Med.* 1988;108:824–828.

72. Cavanaugh DJ, Cann CE. Brisk walking does not stop bone loss in postmenopausal women. *Bone.* 1988;9:201–204.

73. Marcus R, Carter DR. The role of physical activity in bone mass reguation. *Adv Sports Med Fitness.* 1988;1:63–82.

74. Marcus R. The relationship of dietary calcium to the maintenance of skeletal integrity in man: an interface of endocrinology and nutrition. *Metabolism.* 1982;31:93–101.

75. Marcus R. Calcium intake and skeletal integrity: is there a critical relationship? *J Nutr.* 1986;117:631–635.

76. Heaney RP. Nutritional factors in bone health. In: Riggs BL, Melton JL, eds. *Osteoporosis: Etiology, Diagnosis, and Management.* New York, NY, Raven Press; 1988.

77. Riggs BL, Wahner HW, Melton LJ III, et al. Dietary calcium intake and rates of bone loss in women. *J Clin Invest.* 1987;80:979–982.

78. Riis B, Thomsen K, Christiansen C. Does calcium supplementation prevent postmenopausal bone loss: a double-blind controlled clinical study. *N Engl J Med.* 1987;316:173–177.

79. Young G, Marcus R, Minkoff JR, et al. Age-related rise in parathyroid hormone in man: the use of intact and midmolecule antisera to distinguish hormone secretion from retention. *J Bone Miner Res.* 1987;2:367–374.

80. Eastell R, Health H III, Kumar R, et al. Hormonal factors: Pth, vitamin D and calcitonin. In: Riggs BL, Melton JL, eds. *Osteoporosis: Etiology, Diagnosis, and Management.* New York, NY: Raven Press; 1988.

81. Eriksen EF, Colvard DS, Berg NJ, et al. Evidence of estrogen receptors in normal human osteoblast-like cells. *Science.* 1988;241:84.

82. Komm BS, Terpenning CM, Benz DJ, et al. Estrogen binding, receptor mRNA, and biologic response in osteoblast-like osteosarcoma cells. *Science.* 1988;241:81–83.

83. Gray TK, Flynn TC, Gray KM, et al. 17b-estradiol acts directly on the clonal osteoblast cell line UMR 106. *Proc Natl Acad Sci U S A.* 1985;84:6267.

84. Lindsay R. Sex steroids in the pathogenesis and prevention of osteoporosis. In: Riggs BL, Melton LJ, eds. *Osteoporosis: Etiology, Diagnosis, and Management.* New York, NY: Raven Press; 1988.

85. Buchanan JR, Myers C, Lloyd R, et al. Determinants of trabecular bone density in women: the role of androgens, estrogen and exercise. *J Bone Miner Res.* 1988;3:673–680.

Chapter 12

Endocrine Aspects of Nutrition and Aging

John E. Morley and Zvi Glick

Hormones play a major role in the regulation of nutrient intake and utilization within an individual. Conversely, nutritional status can markedly affect circulating hormone levels. Treatment of a number of endocrine disorders (eg, diabetes mellitus and osteoporosis) involves dietary modification.

With advancing age, there are several alterations in circulating hormone levels and hormonal action. Some of these changes are related to the multiple diseases often present in older individuals, while other changes are due to aging per se. The loss of functional reserve in many endocrine organs increases the propensity for the elderly to develop deficiency diseases, eg, diabetes mellitus, hypothyroidism, and hypogonadism. With advancing age, there is a tendency for endocrine disease to present with atypic or nonspecific symptoms, making diagnosis increasingly difficult. Weight loss is the classic nonspecific presentation of endocrine disease in elderly people.

In this chapter, the interactions of the endocrine system and nutrition are examined, and the impact of aging and its modulation of these interactions is described. More detailed information on the effect of aging on hormones are reported elsewhere.[1,2]

NUTRITIONAL ASPECTS OF DIABETES MELLITUS

Diabetes mellitus occurs in approximately 18% of the population between ages 65 and 75 years.[3] The diagnosis is missed in almost half of older patients with frank diabetes. In many older patients with diagnosed diabetes mellitus, the diabetes is inadequately treated.[4]

In general, older subjects tend to have an impaired glucose tolerance compared with younger subjects; however, recent data suggest that only 10% of the variance in total serum glucose response to an oral glucose load can be attributed to age.[5]

The level of body weight and physical activity appears to have a more important role in the pathogenesis of the hyperglycemia of aging. Table 12-1 lists the major factors thought to play a role in the pathogenesis of the hyperglycemia of aging and the development of type II diabetes mellitus.

While fasting and postprandial glucose levels increase slightly with age, the basic definition for treatable diabetes mellitus should not change. Treatment should be instituted when any individual has two fasting plasma glucose levels greater than 7.8 mmol/L. Alternatively, 2-hour postprandial values greater than 10.0 mmol/L on two or more occasions would also suggest the need for treatment.

Regardless of the causes of diabetes mellitus in the elderly, there is increasing evidence that reasonable control of glucose will improve the patient's quality of life, as well as possibly decrease morbidity and mortality rates. The major reasons for control of diabetes in elderly people are listed in Table 12-2. The special features of diabetes mellitus in elderly individuals have been the subject of a number of recent reviews.[6–8] At present, it is recommended that the blood glucose be maintained between 5.6 and 11.1 mmol/L for all diabetics over age 70 years.

Treatment of Diabetes Mellitus

The modalities for treatment of diabetes mellitus in elderly subjects are the same as those used in younger subjects: diet, exercise, oral medications, and insulin. In 1674, Sir Thomas Willis advised patients with diabetes mellitus to have gummy and starchy foods. Since then, diabetologists have made a variety of recommendations about what should constitute the appropriate diet for diabetic patients. In 1986, the National Institutes of Health (NIH) consensus panel made the following recommendations on diet for patients with non–insulin-dependent diabetes mellitus[9]: If the patient is overweight, caloric restriction to 500 to 1000 kcal below daily requirements is recommended to promote gradual weight loss. The diet should have less than 30% of the calories as fat and 50% to 60% of calories as carbohydrate. Saturated fats should be less than 10% of total calories, and cholesterol intake should be less than 300 mg/d. Sucrose may be added up to 5%

Table 12-1 Major Factors Involved in the Pathogenesis of the Hyperglycemia of Aging and Type II Diabetes Mellitus

1. Poor second-phase insulin secretion
2. Failure to inhibit hepatic glucose production
3. Insulin receptor and postreceptor defect
4. Obesity
5. Lack of physical activity

Table 12-2 Reasons To Control Diabetes Mellitus in Elderly People

Prevention of acute complications
  Diabetic coma
  Complications related to hyperosmolality
    Diuresis leading to incontinence and nocturia
    Visual disturbances
    Falls related to above two factors
    Poor outcome following stroke
    Increased pain perception
    Cognitive dysfunction
  Complications related to altered function of circulating blood cells
    Worsening peripheral vascular disease due to decreased erythrocyte deformability
    Increased prevalence of myocardial infarction and stroke due to increased platelet stickiness
Prevention of chronic complications*
  Neuropathic complications
  Diabetic retinopathy
  Diabetic nephropathy

*There is some evidence that these complications occur more rapidly in late-onset diabetes.

---

of the carbohydrate calorie intake in mixed meals. Although foods high in soluble fiber may be used to replace other carbohydrates, purified fiber supplements are not recommended. Carbohydrate calories promote hyperinsulinemia and elevate circulating triglycerides. Furthermore, high dietary protein content may be harmful to kidney and retinal microvasculature. Certain complex carbohydrates, such as beans or pasta, produce less hyperglycemia than do other carbohydrates, such as potatoes and bread; they have a lower "glycemic index." While this phenomenon is well established for a single meal, its effect over prolonged periods is less well established. Finally, there are no studies on dietary intervention in ambulatory individuals over age 70 years. A study of elderly nursing home patients suggested that the "diabetic" diet resulted in no better glycemic control than did a regular diet.[10] For these reasons, it is difficult to make a firm recommendation on the ideal diet for the older diabetic.

Cross-sectional studies have shown that the impaired glucose tolerance of aging is significantly related to the level of physical fitness or activity.[7] Only one prospective trial of the effects of exercise on glucose tolerance has been carried out in men over age 60 years. While glucose levels did not change, both insulin and C peptide levels were lower.[11] In addition, high-density lipoprotein cholesterol levels increased and triglyceride levels decreased. Exercise trials in patients with type II diabetes mellitus have failed to show a major advantage of short-term exercise programs over diet alone.[12] However, two trials that lasted 5 and

11 months did find improvements in glucose tolerance without change in body weight.[13,14] Besides the possible beneficial effects of exercise on glucose tolerance, exercise training may also improve cardiovascular fitness, lipid profiles, hypertension, osteopenia, and psychologic function in diabetic patients. Risks of exercise in diabetics include hypoglycemia, ketosis, dehydration, myocardial ischemia, arrhythmias, acceleration of proliferative retinopathy, increased proteinuria, and trauma (particularly in patients with neuropathy). The NIH consensus panel concluded that the effect of exercise on metabolic control in non–insulin-dependent diabetes mellitus is often variable and of small magnitude.[15] Pacini and colleagues[16] have demonstrated that normal weight, physically active older subjects have normal insulin-binding capacity, insulin sensitivity, and insulin secretory capacity in response to a glucose stimulus. Studies of long-term exercise programs need to be undertaken before a formal recommendation for an exercise prescription can be given.

The sulfonylurea oral hypoglycemic agents produce their major effect by stimulating insulin release from pancreatic B cells through a different signal recognition system than that by which glucose stimulates insulin release. Chlorpropamide should never be used in subjects over age 60 years because it produces prolonged hypoglycemia and hyponatremia. The prevalence of hypoglycemia with other sulfonylureas is less than that with chlorpropamide; nevertheless, elderly people are always at increased risk for developing hypoglycemia. The combination of insulin and sulfonylureas has not been proven to be effective.

Biguanides are no longer available in the United States. Drugs such as metformin have the advantage of producing anorexia as well as enhancing insulin action. However, in elderly diabetics, the danger that these drugs might produce lactic acidosis makes their use problematic. Acarbose, an amylase inhibitor, has been used to smooth the glycemic response to meals. It does, however, appear to produce an unacceptable amount of gastrointestinal side effects in some patients. Tetrahydrolipostatin, a drug that reduces fat absorption, may prove useful in the treatment of diabetes mellitus in the future. In massively obese subjects, long-term use of anorectic agents, such as fluoxetine, may be useful.

Chronic insulin deficiency is similar to starvation in that both conditions are catabolic states that lead to cachexia. The catabolic state of uncontrolled diabetes mellitus is readily reversed by insulin therapy. For this reason, and those listed in Table 12-2, insulin should not be withheld from elderly patients whose glucose levels cannot be reduced below 11.1 mmol/L. At present, human insulin is recommended as the insulin of choice to decrease the formation of anti-insulin antibodies; however, polymerization of human insulin at therapeutic dosage levels does lead to some antibody formation.

Older diabetics may have up to a 20% error when drawing up their insulin into a syringe.[17] For this reason, older diabetics with visual deficiencies should use syringe magnifiers or dose gauges. Some patients also benefit from using needle guides and vial holders.

Micronutrient Status and Diabetes Mellitus

Diabetes mellitus produces a number of effects on vitamin and mineral status of patients.[18] Many of these changes are similar to those seen with aging (Table 12-3). Elderly people often have a decreased zinc intake and are at risk for developing zinc deficiency when illness occurs (Chapter 5). Diabetes mellitus is associated with decreased zinc absorption and hyperzincuria.[19] Zinc deficiency is associated with poor wound healing, poor immune function, immune dysfunction, and anorexia.[20] In addition, zinc is cosecreted from pancreatic islets and enhances insulin binding, suggesting a possible role of zinc in the pathogenesis of some forms of diabetes. Pharmacologic zinc administration has been demonstrated to improve immune function[21] and foot ulcer healing[22] in patients with deficient zinc status.

Chromium has been suggested to have a role in normal glucose homeostasis. Deficiency of chromium (Chapter 5) or its biologically active form, glucose tolerance factor, has been implicated in the glucose intolerance of aging.[23] The main sources of glucose tolerance factor include brewer's yeast, liver, and kidney.

Table 12-3 Comparison of the Effects of Type II Diabetes Mellitus and Aging on Micronutrients

Micronutrient	Changes in Type II Diabetes Mellitus*	Changes with Aging *
Vitamins		
A	N	N
B$_1$	N	N
B$_6$	N or ↓	↓
B$_{12}$	N or ↓	↓
C	↓	N or ↓
25-hydroxyvitamin D$_3$	N	↓
E in serum	N	N
E in platelets	↓	↑
Trace elements		
Zinc	N or ↓	↓
Chromium	N	↓
Copper	N or ↑	↑
Manganese	↑	?
Selenium	?	N or ↓

*N, Normal; ↑, increased; ↓, decreased.

Source: Adapted with permission from *Journal of American Geriatrics Society* (1987;35:435–447), Copyright © 1987, American Geriatrics Society.

In most double-blind studies, chromium supplementation has failed to reverse the hyperglycemia of aging. In one recent small study, the combination of chromium and nicotinamide resulted in a minor diminution of the glucose response to oral glucose, but it did not alter fasting glucose levels.[24]

Copper and ceruloplasmin levels are elevated in type II diabetes mellitus. Copper deficiency induced experimentally results in elevated total cholesterol levels.[25]

Thiamine is essential for the transport of metabolized glucose from the Embden-Meyerhof pathway into the Krebs cycle. The elevated levels of erythrocyte transketolase activity (an indirect measure of thiamine status) in type II diabetes mellitus may be related to the poor availability of intracellular glucose. When malnourished patients receive glucose, they may utilize all of the available thiamine, resulting in Wernicke's syndrome. Conversely, in malnourished patients, thiamine administration may result in hypoglycemia.

Diabetes mellitus may be associated with pernicious anemia. Vitamin B_{12} deficiency should be suspected in any diabetic patient with macrocytic anemia, posterior column neuropathy, or dementia. Recent studies have suggested that low vitamin B_{12} levels, in the absence of macrocytic anemia, may explain the cognitive dysfunction seen in elderly individuals.

Vitamin C in large doses acts as a reducing agent and can interfere with glucose measurements in both urine and serum.

Diabetes Mellitus in Long-Term Care

The management of diabetes mellitus in the long-term care setting is steeped in mythology. It should be realized that hypoglycemic reactions occur infrequently in institutionalized patients, permitting reasonable control of diabetes mellitus in this population.[26] In a study of diabetic patients in a nursing home, it was found that one in five were 20% below average body weight.[26] Weight loss often leads to improved glycemic control in nursing home patients. Awareness of weight loss in this population is important since it may necessitate a reduction in insulin or oral hypoglycemic dosage. As previously mentioned, there is little evidence that an American Dietetic Association/American Diabetic Association diabetic diet is appropriate for diabetic patients in long-term care.

Generally, the management of diabetes mellitus in older patients is the same as that in younger patients. In elderly patients, diabetes mellitus can interact with the normal aging process to produce major changes in micronutrient requirements. In particular, older diabetics are at risk for developing minor degrees of zinc deficiency. When instituting dietary changes in older diabetics, care needs to be taken not to produce protein-calorie malnutrition. This is particularly true of patients residing in nursing homes.

THYROID FUNCTION

With advancing age, there is no change in the circulating levels of total thyroxine or triiodothyronine or the free hormone values.[1] However, this apparent stability of the circulating thyroid hormones belies the underlying physiologic turmoil that results in the hypothalamic-pituitary-adrenal axis with advancing age. There is a decreased production of thyroid hormones with aging that is counterbalanced by a decreased thyroid hormone degradation. In addition, there is a tendency for diminished feedback of thyroid hormones, leading to a mild increase in thyrotropin (TSH) levels, particularly in women. In older men, there is an increased prevalence of failure for TSH to respond to thyrotropin-releasing hormone (TRH).

In subjects under age 60 years, the prevalence of hypothyroidism tends to be 1% or less, whereas in those over age 60 years, the prevalance rises to 4% to 7%.[27] Between 7% and 12% of patients with hyperthyroidism are over age 60 years.[1] While there are limited changes in circulating thyroid hormones with aging, when illness supervenes, there can be major changes in thyroid hormones that can mimic the changes seen with hypothyroidism.[28] These changes are delineated in Table 12-4. Malnutrition is a particularly common cause of the euthyroid sick syndrome in elderly people.

Atypic presentations of thyroid disease become increasingly common with advancing age. One study estimated that only 10% of older patients with biochemical hypothyroidism were suspected of having thyroid disease on clinical examination.[29] The classic hyperkinetic state, thyromegaly, and eye signs of hyperthyroidism may be replaced by heart failure, apathy, and unexplained weight loss in elderly persons—the so-called apathetic hypothyroidism.[30] For these reasons, it is recommended that all patients over age 60 years who are admitted to

---

Table 12-4 Typical Changes in Thyroid Hormone Levels with Various Diseases*

Hormone	Aging	Hyperthyroid	Hypothyroid	Euthyroid Sick
Thyroxine	N	↑	↓	N or ↓
Triiodothyronine	N	↑	N or ↓	↓
Uptake	N	↑	↓	↑
Free thyroxine index	N	↑	↓	N or ↓
TSH				
Normal	N	N	↑	N or ↑
Supersensitive	N	↓	↑	↓, N, ↑
Response to TRH	↓	↓	↑	↓

*N, Normal; ↑, increased; ↓, decreased.

the hospital or who have unexplained weight loss, fatigue, depression, dementia, or atrial fibrillation be screened biochemically for thyroid disease.[28]

Nutritional Aspects of Thyroid Disease

The classic nutritional change associated with hyperthyroidism is weight loss. Thyroid hormones produce a marked increase in the basal metabolic rate. The exact mechanism by which thyroid hormones increase the metabolic rate remains controversial.[31] There is an increase in mitochondrial size, number, and surface area, and thyroid hormone stimulates mitochondrial turnover. Thyroid hormone also increases Na^+, K^+-adenosine triphosphatase activity. Pharmacologic concentrations of thyroid hormone produce uncoupling of oxidative metabolism in vitro.

Thyroid hormone results in stimulation of both protein synthesis and degradation. In hyperthyroidism, the predominance of protein degradation leads to loss of muscle mass, muscle weakness, and a negative nitrogen balance. In younger subjects, hyperthyroidism is often associated with hyperphagia, which tends to offset the weight loss to some degree. However, anorexia occurs in up to 30% of older hyperthyroid subjects.

Hyperthyroidism is associated with an increase in glucose utilization and a depletion of liver glycogen. While fasting glucose levels are generally normal in hyperthyroidism, glucose intolerance is present in approximately half of these patients.[32] In hypothyroidism, there is decreased glucose absorption from the gastrointestinal tract and a reduction in peripheral glucose utilization. A flat glucose tolerance curve is not unusual in hypothyroidism.

In hyperthyroid subjects, there is an increase in free fatty acid and triglyceride levels and a decrease in cholesterol levels.[31] In hypothyroidism, fat cell lipolysis in response to catecholamines is reduced.[31] Free fatty acid levels are normal or slightly decreased in hypothyroidism.[31] Plasma triglyceride levels are markedly increased secondary to a marked decrease in the triglyceride removal rate.[33] Cholesterol levels are also increased in hypothyroidism; more than four fifths of hypothyroid patients have cholesterol levels greater than 250 mg/dL.[34] The increase is mostly in low-density lipoprotein cholesterol. Cholesterol secretion in the bile is markedly decreased in hypothyroidism.

Osteopenia commonly is present in hyperthyroidism, and the development of hyperthyroidism aggravates the normal age-related bone loss. Mild hypercalcemia commonly is seen in hyperthyroidism. Calcium absorption is decreased and calcium excretion is increased in hyperthyroidism. In hypothyroidism, there is a mild decrease in the rate of calcium deposition in bone.

The alterations in vitamin status that occur in thyroid disease are outlined in Table 12-5.[35,36] Decreased dark adaptation occurs occasionally in hyper-

Table 12-5 Effects of Thyroid Diseases on Vitamin Status*

Vitamin	Hypothyroid	Hyperthyroid
Vitamin A	↑	↓
Retinol-binding protein	↑	↓
Thiamine		
Erythrocyte transketolase	?	↓
In vitro thiamin pyridinylase (thiammase)	?	None†
Riboflavin	?	↑
Pyridoxine		
Xanthurenic acid excretion after tryptophan administration	?	↑ ‡
Vitamin B_{12}	↓ or N§	↓
Folate	N	?
Vitamin C	N	N
25-Hydroxyvitamin D_3	N	N
1,25-Hydroxyvitamin D_3	↑	↓
α-Tocopherol (vitamin E)	↑	↓

*N, Normal; ↑, increased; ↓, decreased.
†The decrease in erythrocyte transketolase suggests thiamine deficiency, but the failure of in vitro thiamine augmentation suggests other causes.
‡Suggests pyridoxine deficiency.
§About 5% to 10% have pernicious anemia.

---

thyroidism and may be related to diminished vitamin A levels in this disorder. The characteristic yellow color of the skin of hypothyroid patients is due to increased carotene values secondary to decreased conversion of carotene to vitamin A.

Effects of Nutritional Status on Thyroid Hormones

There is increasing evidence that vitamin status may alter thyroid function. Vitamin A deficiency in animals leads to mild increases in circulating thyroid hormones in the presence of normal TSH secretion, suggesting a resetting of the hypothalamic-pituitary axis in response to thyroid hormones.[37] Vitamin A excess lowers circulating total thyroid hormone levels, but not free hormone levels, as the dialyzable function of thyroid hormones increases.[38] In animals, thiamine administration decreases the weight loss seen when pharmacologic amounts of thyroid hormone are administered.[39] Riboflavin deficiency diminishes the hepatic deiodination of thyroxine.[40] Vitamin E may attenuate the effects of thyroid hormone on some of its target organs.[41] These findings and others suggest that a careful study of vitamin status in elderly patients with hyperthyroidism is warranted.

ADRENAL CORTEX

Aging produces only minor changes in the hypothalamic-pituitary-adrenal axis. There are mild decreases in both cortisol production and clearance rates; as a result, plasma cortisol levels remain unchanged with aging.[1] In addition, with advancing age there is a decreased sensitivity of the anterior pituitary to negative feedback by circulating cortisol.[42] Therefore, with advancing age there is an increased prevalence of failure of dexamethasone to suppress cortisol adequately.

Less than 10% of patients with Addison's disease (hypoadrenalism) are over age 60 years.[43] Nutritional and clinical manifestations are commonly seen in patients with Addison's disease. These include weakness, easy fatigability, vomiting, constipation or diarrhea, abdominal pain, salt craving, weight loss, hypoglycemia, hyponatremia, and hyperkalemia. Additional manifestations include hyperpigmentation and postural hypotension.

The clustering of hypertension, hypokalemia, diabetes mellitus, and osteopenia is suggestive of Cushing's syndrome. However, in elderly people all of these conditions occur commonly, and the presence of multiple disease states represents a more likely finding. The classic appearance of patients with Cushing's syndrome is central obesity with thin arms and legs, although weight loss may occur in elderly individuals. The screening test for Cushing's syndrome is the failure of 1 mg of dexamethasone to suppress cortisol levels below 138 mmol/L. In elderly patients, failure of dexamethasone suppression may be secondary to depression, Alzheimer's disease, obesity, or alcoholism.

While Cushing's syndrome is rare in elderly individuals, ectopic corticotropin syndrome secondary to tumors, eg, oat cell carcinoma of the lung, is relatively common. These patients are usually cachectic rather than obese, have severe proximal muscle weakness, hypokalemic alkalosis, mental changes, and hyperpigmentation. Patients with ectopic corticotropin fail the dexamethasone suppression test and have relatively high circulating corticotropin levels.

In elderly people, by far the most common cause of elevated cortisol levels is exogenous cortisol administration. The use of steroids in elderly patients should be limited to situations in which they are absolutely essential, and the steroids should be tapered off as rapidly as possible. Exogenous steroid use is a major cause of osteopenia; patients receiving steroids should receive calcium prophylactically and possibly vitamin D supplementation, as steroids inhibit the conversion of 25-hydroxyvitamin D_3 (25(OH)D_3) to 1,25dihydroxyvitamin D_3 (1,25(OH)$_2D_3$).

Nutritionally, glucosteroids promote the conversion of protein to carbohydrate (gluconeogenesis). This leads to a negative nitrogen balance, an increase in circulating glucose, and increased liver glycogen. Corticosteroids also reduce hexose transport into the cells, which further increases circulating glucose levels and produces a secondary hyperinsulinemia. Patients receiving corticosteroids who develop frank diabetes mellitus usually require insulin therapy rather than oral hypoglycemic agents.

Cortisol increases DNA synthesis in human adipose cells in vitro. Cortisol promotes hyperphagia and mobilization of free fatty acids. Pharmacologic doses of cortisol elevate triglyceride levels.

Other Adrenal Hormones

Plasma levels and urinary excretion of aldosterone tend to fall with advancing age.[44] Active renin levels also fall with advancing age.[45] These changes increase the propensity of older subjects to develop hyperkalemia secondary to hyporeninemic hypoaldosteronism. This is particularly common in patients with diabetes mellitus and mild renal failure.

In contrast to the relative preservation of cortisol secretory dynamics, dehydroepiandrosterone (DHEA) secretion declines dramatically with advancing age.[46] In animals, DHEA administration prolongs life span, which may be related to its ability to reduce weight.[47] In men, DHEA-sulfate (DHEA-S) has been suggested to be inversely related to death from cardiovascular disease.[48] Diminished levels of DHEA and DHEA-S are associated with hypercholesterolemia[49] and hypertension.[50] The mechanism by which DHEA deficiency promotes atherosclerosis is uncertain but may be related to excessive stimulation of lipogenesis by reduced nicotinamide-adenine dinucleotide phosphate (NADPH).

WATER METABOLISM

Elderly people are at increased risk for developing disturbances of water metabolism. Both dehydration and hyponatremia occur with increasing frequency in elderly subjects. Phillips and colleagues[51] have demonstrated that even healthy elderly subjects fail to respond adequately to mild dehydration. In part, this failure to develop an appropriate thirst response may be secondary to an impaired secretion of angiotensin.[52] This has led to the concept that elderly people live in a "water desert" and that hospitalized elderly patients need a prescription of at least 1 L of fluid intake per day.

There is greater argipressin release for a given osmotic stimulus in elderly subjects compared with younger subjects.[53] Older subjects also have a decrease in free water clearance in response to argipressin, predominantly related to the age-related fall in glomerular filtration rate.[54] Atrial natriuretic factor (ANF) is released by volume overload and acts on the kidney to increase glomerular filtration rate and induce natriuresis. Recently, ANF levels have been demonstrated to be elevated in elderly individuals.[55]

These hormonal changes explain why hyponatremia occurs commonly in elderly people. Many institutionalized elderly persons have the syndrome of inappropriate secretion of antidiuretic hormone, which may lead to hyponatremia; tube feeding represents another major cause of hyponatremia in institutionalized elderly people.

GROWTH HORMONE AND INSULIN GROWTH FACTORS

There is evidence that growth hormone secretion is mildly impaired with advancing age.[1] A single study in medically impaired elderly subjects found adequate nitrogen retention and free fatty acid increase after growth hormone administration, but impaired urinary hydroxyproline secretion.[56] This highly limited study is the basis for the claim that metabolic responses to growth hormone are impaired in elderly persons.

In contrast to the minor decreases in growth hormone with aging, plasma levels of insulin-like growth factor I (somatomedin C) are markedly decreased with advancing age.[57] Insulin-like growth factor I (IGF I) levels are also decreased by malnutrition. In malnourished, institutionalized elderly patients, the levels of IGF I are even lower than those seen in healthy elderly people, suggesting an interaction between nutrition and aging in these individuals.[58]

Rudman[59] has suggested that the growth hormone "menopause" that occurs with advancing age may explain a number of the normal changes seen with aging. These include the diminished nitrogen retention, the decrease in lean body mass, the increase in adipose tissue, and some of the osteopenia characteristically associated with aging. Studies are presently under way to determine whether growth hormone administration can have a salutary effect on the catabolic effects seen in some malnourished elderly people.

MALE HYPOGONADISM

With advancing age, sexual dysfunction occurs with increasing frequency. Kinsey and colleagues[60] reported that impotence occurred in 18.6% of 60-year-old men and 75% of 80-year-old men. Over age 50 years, one in three men who are examined by a physician are impotent.[61] The causes of impotence in older men are multifactorial.[62] The major cause for the increasing prevalence of impotence with advancing age is arteriosclerosis. Medications also have an important role in the pathogenesis of impotence. Nutritionally, it has been found that a small subset of older impotent men has low serum zinc levels and hyperzincuria.[63] Approximately half of these subjects improve after the administration of pharmacologic amounts of zinc.

Hypogonadism occurs with increasing frequency with advancing age. While testosterone levels may remain normal in some healthy elderly men, in the majority of older men there is a marked decrease in testosterone and bioavailable testosterone.[64] Both luteinizing hormone and follicle-stimulating hormone levels tend to increase with advancing age in an attempt to compensate for the decreased levels of testosterone.[65] However, in a number of older individuals, the hypothalamus fails to detect the decrease in testosterone adequately, resulting in the development of hypothalamic hypogonadism.[62]

Testosterone not only plays a role in maintaining normal sexual function (libido and potency), but also has a number of effects that enhance the general well-being of the individual.[66] Testosterone promotes nitrogen retention, maintains muscle mass, protects bone from excessive calcium loss, helps to maintain erythrocyte mass, and produces a general feeling of well-being. For these reasons, it is recommended that testosterone replacement therapy be instituted in all subjects with proven hypogonadism, regardless of whether or not they desire to have sexual intercourse. In patients receiving testosterone, regular rectal examinations need to be conducted to detect prostatic growth.

CALCIUM METABOLISM

Both calcium intake and calcium absorption diminish with advancing age[1] (Chapter 4). With advancing age, there is a decrease in vitamin D synthesis in the skin[67] and decreased activity of 1α-hydroxylase in the kidney[68] (Chapter 3). Recent studies have clearly demonstrated that at least a proportion of older individuals has a decrease in $25(OH)D_3$ and its active metabolite, $1,25(OH)_2$ D_3.[68] Lower vitamin D levels are particularly prevalent in institutionalized and housebound elderly people who are rarely exposed to sunlight and who have low calcium intakes.

These changes tend to lead to a decrease in ionized calcium which, in turn, results in a compensatory increase in parathyroid hormone (PTH) levels.[69] Calcitonin levels may decline slightly with advancing age.[70] As already mentioned, the age-related declines in IGF I and testosterone also impinge on calcium metabolism. The changes in calcium metabolism that occur with age are summarized in Figure 12-1.

Seventeen percent of patients with hyperparathyroidism are over age 60 years.[71] Clinically, hyperparathyroidism is often characterized by vague complaints, including anorexia, weight loss, weakness, abdominal symptoms, cognitive disturbances, polyuria, and dehydration. Diagnosis is made by demonstrating elevated calcium and PTH levels. Treatment consists of surgical removal of the parathyroid adenoma. In postmenopausal women, estrogen therapy has been shown to lower mild hyperparathyroidism. In the differential diagnosis of

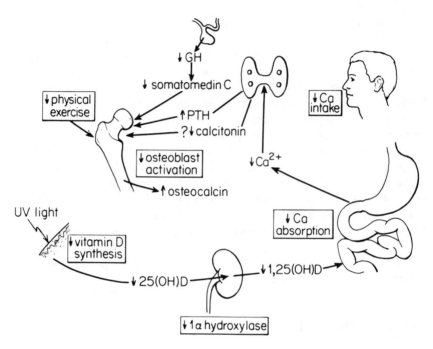

Figure 12-1 Overview of the effects of aging on calcium metabolism. GH, Growth hormone; PTH, parathyroid hormone. *Source:* Reprinted with permission from *Journal of American Geriatrics Society* (1988;36:845–859), Copyright © 1988, American Geriatrics Society.

hypercalcemia, it should be remembered that megadoses of vitamin A activate cathepsin D, resulting in increased PTH secretion and elevated calcium levels.

A detailed discussion of osteopenia in elderly people is presented elsewhere[67] (Chapter 11). In the postmenopausal (type I) osteopenia, clearly estrogen deficiency represents the major problem. The etiologic factors involved in type II osteopenia are multifactorial and include a variety of nutritional factors such as low calcium intake, a high-protein diet that produces hypercalciuria, late-onset lactase deficiency, coffee consumption, alcoholism, lack of physical exercise, and cigarette smoking. Recently, boron supplementation has been demonstrated to reduce the urinary excretion of calcium.[72]

HORMONAL REGULATION OF ENERGY BALANCE

The early phase of aging typically is associated with a positive energy balance and an increase in adiposity, but a decrease in lean body mass.[73] While lean body mass continues to decline in the last phase—often seen beyond age 65 years—negative energy balance often is maintained.[74] Protein-energy malnutrition occurs in this age group at an alarming frequency.[20] In elderly people, both energy intake and output typically are reduced, but reduction in intake exceeds the reduced output, leading to the observed loss in energy stores, including lean body mass.

Control of energy intake and output involves complex autonomic, hormonal, and metabolic mechanisms that are only partially understood. It is therefore difficult to identify, with any level of certainty, the age-related dysfunctions responsible for the status of negative energy balance in elderly individuals.

Hormonal Control of Energy Intake

The control mechanism of food intake has central and peripheral components. The primary central structures are in the hypothalamus, and include the ventromedial hypothalamus (VMH), lateral hypothalamus (LH), and paraventricular nucleus (PVN).[75] The primary peripheral aspects are thought to include the gastrointestinal tract, liver, and adipose tissue, and are thought to involve some key hormones and metabolites.[76,77]

Whatever effect a peripheral hormone or metabolite has on feeding, its effect will be encoded into the neurotransmitter system in the hypothalamus, and a behavioral feeding response will be elicited subsequent to the specific neurotransmitter signal. Accordingly, discussion of hormone influences on feeding must include the neurotransmitter system (neurohormones), exerting a direct effect in the hypothalamus, and hormones secreted in the periphery.

Neurohormones

Monoamines. Norepinephrine, dopamine, and serotonin all have important roles in determining feeding behavior.[75] Direct injection of norepinephrine into the VMH or PVN will stimulate feeding; its administration into the LH will inhibit feeding. This effect of norepinephrine is mediated through α-adrenergic receptors in the VMH and β-adrenergic receptors in the LH.[75] Brain tissue from aged rats has an impaired capacity for synthesis and regulation of α- and β-adrenergic receptors. This impairment has been demonstrated in the cortex and cerebellum,[78] but it has not been studied in the hypothalamus.

The effects of serotonin on feeding also appear to depend on the type of serotonin receptor, with a decrease in feeding induced by 1_B receptor agonist in the PVM and an increase in feeding with a 1_A receptor agonist.[79] Dopamine neurotransmitters have also been thought to have a role in controlling feeding behavior, but the effects of aging on either the serotonin or the dopamine feeding system have not been studied.

Neuropeptides. Several peptide neurotransmitters have been found in recent years in mammalian brain. These include cholecystokinin (CCK), bombesin, substance P, neurotensin, opioids, neuropeptide Y (NPY), and others.[80] A number of these peptides were shown to decrease feeding after central administration. However, a reduced food intake need not imply a physiologic role for these neuropeptides in modulating feeding behavior, as their effect may be secondary to nonspecific behavioral effects. The administration of either opioid peptides[81] or NPY[82] was reported to stimulate feeding, suggesting a physiologic role for these neuropeptides. Moreover, the opioid antagonist, naloxone, suppresses food intake.[81] Recently it was reported that older rats display a much smaller response to opioid agonists and antagonists.[83] Older rats also have a lower concentration of opioid peptides in the hypothalamus.[81] Aging is thus associated with a decreased opiate-based feeding drive, but the relative importance of the latter in anorexia of aging is not clear. The orexigenic effect of NPY does not appear to be age-dependent.[84]

Peripheral Hormones

Growth Hormone. Administration of growth hormone into experimental animals stimulates food intake and growth of lean, but not adipose, tissue[85] (Glick Z, Groesbeck MJ, Parlow AF. January 1980. Unpublished observations). A similar effect was reported in humans. [86] It is not clear to what extent small changes in growth hormone activity (within the normal range) influence food intake or whether the reduction in growth hormone activity, which is often observed in elderly subjects (vide supra), contributes to their anorexia.

Insulin. Daily single injections of insulin stimulate food intake and produce obesity.[76] Moreover, the hyperphagia and obesity that develop after placement of lesions in the ventromedial hypothalamus are contributed to by a vagally mediated insulin hypersecretion induced by the lesions.[76,77] The stimulatory effect of insulin on food intake is thought to result from its lipolytic effect, which decreases availability of endogenous substrate to the tissues and to specific glucose-sensitive hypothalamic sites.[76,77] The role of age-associated hyperglycemia (impaired glucose tolerance) in the anorexia of aging is not known.

Glucocorticoids. The stimulatory effect of norepinephrine administered in the PVN of the hypothalamus on food intake is absent in adrenalectomized rats; it is restored with corticosterone.[87] Also, peak hormone concentration in blood is observed before onset of feeding.[88] However, corticosterone administered into nonadrenalectomized rats has little or no effect on food intake.[89] Combined, these data suggest that glucocorticoids have an important "permissive" role in the central control mechanism of feeding. In both animals and humans, glucocorticoid hyperactivity is associated with a redistribution of body energy stores toward increased adiposity and decreased lean body mass.[90] In humans, this is known as Cushing's syndrome, which is rare in elderly persons.

Thyroid Hormone. Thyroid hormone stimulates food intake,[91] but this effect appears to be secondary to a stimulated metabolic rate and a compensatory replenishment of the greater energy losses.

Gonadal Steroids. The gonadal steroid estrogen suppresses food intake in female subjects; its site of action is thought to be in the VMH.[92] Food intake is decreased during days of estrus (high estrogen) and increased during diestrus (low estrogen).[93] Castration of female rats leads to overeating and obesity.[77] Testosterone, on the other hand, increases food intake and lean tissue growth, while decreasing body fat.[94]

Although there is little change in estrogen levels, bioavailable testosterone levels are reduced in the majority of elderly people. These sex hormone changes would be compatible with reduced ingestion with advancing age.

Gastrointestinal Hormones. Peripheral injections of a variety of gastrointestinal hormones and other peptides into rats reduce food intake. These peptides include CCK, bombesin, gastrin-releasing peptide, glucagon, somatostatin, substance P, and neurotensin.[81] However, the physiologic significance of these hormones in producing normal satiety is not clear.[95,96] It has been proposed that CCK exerts a weak effect on food intake, amounting to some 10% to 20% of the total intake at a single meal.[80] Higher than normal serum levels of CCK were observed in elderly men, perhaps contributing to their anorexia.[97] Silver and colleagues[98] have reported an increased ability of pharmacologically administered CCK-8 to decrease feeding in older mice compared with younger mice.

Hormonal Control of Energy Output

Energy output may be divided into the following components: basal metabolic rate, physical activity, and thermic effect of feeding. A brief discussion of each of these components, their hormonal mediators, and how they interact is necessary to present a complete discussion of the control of hormones on energy balance.

Basal Metabolic Rate

Basal metabolic rate (BMR) accounts for about 1400 to 1600 kcal, constituting about 60% to 75% of total energy expenditure. It has several major metabolic origins. It is thought to reflect the energy cost of protein and, to a much smaller extent, carbohydrate and fat turnover. It reflects the activity of the sodium pump, the cost of maintaining muscle tone, and the work done by involuntary muscles (heart, respiratory, and gastrointestinal).[99–102] It originates primarily in, and therefore is highly correlated with, lean body mass; men, having a greater lean body mass, have a higher BMR than do women.

BMR is governed by thyroid hormones through a mechanism that is not fully understood. The hormone stimulates activity of the sodium pump[103] as well as protein turnover[104]; protein turnover is stimulated through enhancement of protein breakdown via lysosomal proteinases[104] and through stimulation of protein synthesis in conjunction with other anabolic hormones, ie, insulin and growth hormone. Triiodothyronine stimulates release of both insulin[105] and growth hormone.[106] Triiodothyronine is also required for sympathetic activation,[107] which can, in turn, stimulate metabolic rate.

BMR is reduced in elderly people some 10% to 20%[108,109]; it is thought that this decline in metabolic rate reflects, by and large, the reduced lean body mass.[108] The reduction in BMR is accompanied by a decrease in the rate of protein turnover,[110] but with no clear change in activity of the sodium pump in the small number of tissues examined.[111]

The metabolic origins for the age-dependent compositional changes have not been clearly identified. Activities of growth hormone and testosterone, which promote lean tissue growth, are reduced with aging; this may contribute to the shift in balance from lean to adipose tissue. A decreased trophic effect of the autonomic nervous system on muscle and a decreased capacity for muscle fiber regeneration have also been suggested.[112]

Physical Activity

Physical activity is an important determinant of energy balance status. Muscle mass is increased and adiposity is decreased with physical training.[73] In elderly people, there is usually a decline in physical activity[73] imposed by age-related conditions such as cardiovascular disease, musculoskeletal disease, osteopenia, obesity, and others. In addition, there is a decline in physical working capacity ($\dot{V}o_2max$), amounting to about 10% per decade between ages 25 and 65 years. The latter means that the same physical tasks require a greater physical effort in elderly people. Elderly individuals retain the ability to enjoy the benefit of training,[113] and physical training can correct these age-related changes in physical working capacity by as much as 50%. The level of physical activity is not under hormonal control but is determined by motivational factors.

Thermic Effect of Feeding

The thermic effect of feeding[114,115] represents two components: an obligatory component and an adaptive component. In the obligatory component, heat is a by-product of the metabolic cost of converting the ingested macronutrient into body glycogen, protein, and fat.[116] It amounts to an average of 5% to 10% of the energy value of the food. It is minimal after fat intake and maximal after protein intake.[116]

In the adaptive component, heat is the primary end-product. In rodents, this heat is produced exclusively in the brown adipose tissue, where substrate oxidation is uncoupled from phosphorylation.[117]

In rodents, the brown fat has the potential of dissipating a large portion of the caloric intake; but in humans, the capacity for adaptive thermogenesis is relatively small, apparently because of the small quantity of brown fat in humans.[118,119] Thermogenic activity of brown adipose tissue is controlled primarily by norepinephrine released from a dense sympathetic innervation of this tissue.[118] Insulin[119] and glucagon,[120] which are released in response to feeding, stimulate thermogenesis of brown adipose tissue in rodents, whereas glucocorticoids[77] inhibit it.

In rodents, the capacity for feeding-induced thermogenesis declines rapidly after sexual maturity is reached.[121] In old rats, there is a 30% decrease in brown adipose tissue mass, a twofold decrease in β-adrenergic receptors (primarily due to receptors of the β_1 subtype), and a decrease in the activation of adenylate cyclase.[122] These biochemical abnormalities may contribute to the decreased capacity for feeding-induced thermogenesis in older animals. An analogous reduction in adaptive thermogenesis in humans would contribute to the observed age-related decrease in energy expenditure.

CONCLUSION

Nutrition and the endocrine system are closely integrated. Nutritional status influences glandular activities, while endocrine function can have marked influences on nutrient requirements and status. With advancing age, changes occur in both endocrine and nutritional status.

Several factors enhance development of diabetes mellitus in elderly people, including weight gain, decreased physical activity, and defective mechanisms for insulin secretion and action. Although the efficacy of the American Dietetic Association/American Diabetic Association diet for glucose control in elderly diabetics is not clear, there is no better dietary recommendation for them at the present time. Long-term exercise programs are beneficial to elderly diabetics and should be encouraged.

A hypothyroid state is much more prevalent in elderly people than in young people. In elderly individuals, hypothyroidism is often contributed to by the presence of malnutrition. In the hyperthyroid elderly person, the rise in metabolic rate is not fully compensated for by a corresponding rise in voluntary food intake. Thyroid status can have profound effects on vitamin and calcium requirements, and their proper intake should be monitored in hyperthyroid elderly people.

Aging produces only minor changes in the hypothalamic-pituitary-adrenal axis. Diseases of the adrenal cortex, ie, Addison's disease and Cushing's syndrome, are not common in elderly people. However, ectopic corticotropin production, secondary to tumors, is relatively common. Steroid treatment should be used in elderly patients with extreme caution, as it can cause negative nitrogen and calcium balances as well as hyperglycemia and resistance to insulin.

Growth hormone secretion is mildly reduced in the elderly, but IGF I is markedly reduced. These may contribute to the diminished nitrogen retention and increased adiposity observed with aging. Another possible contributor to the decline in nitrogen retention in elderly persons is reduced serum testosterone levels. However, the main cause for impotence in elderly men is thought to be arteriosclerosis and not reduced testosterone levels.

In elderly individuals, both energy intake and output are reduced, but reduction in intake often exceeds output. In experimental animals aging is associated with reduced opioid-based feeding drive and with a greater suppression of feeding by CCK, but the possible role of these events in the development of the anorexia of aging humans is not known. The smaller energy expenditure observed in elderly people is brought about by a reduced basal metabolic rate, by reduced physical activity, and possibly by a reduced thermic response to feeding.

REFERENCES

1. Mooradian AD, Morley JE, Korenman SG. Endocrinology in aging. *Dis Mon*. 1988; 34:395–461.

2. Morley JE. Geriatric endocrinology. In: Mendelsohn G, ed. *Diagnosis and Pathology of Endocrine Disease*. Philadelphia, Pa: JB Lippincott Co.; 1988.

3. Harris MI, Hadden WC, Knowler WC, et al. Prevalence of diabetes and impaired glucose tolerance and plasma glucose levels in U.S. population aged 20–74 years. *Diabetes*. 1987;4:523–534.

4. Morley JE, Korenman SG. Aging. In: Bagdale JD, ed. *The Year Book of Endocrinology*. Chicago, Ill: Year Book Medical Publishers; 1988.

5. Zavaroni I, Dall'Aglio E, Bruschi F. Effect of age and environmental factors on glucose tolerance and insulin secretion in a worker population. *J Am Geriatr Soc*. 1986;34:271–278.

6. Morley JE, Mooradian AD, Rosenthal MJ, et al. Diabetes mellitus in elderly patients: is it different? *Am J Med*. 1987;83:533–544.

7. Rosenthal MJ, Hartnell JM, Morley JE, et al. UCLA geriatric grand rounds: diabetes in the elderly. *J Am Geriatr Soc*. 1987;35:435–447.

8. Lipson LG. Diabetes in the elderly: diagnosis, pathogenesis and therapy. *Am J Med*. 1986;80(suppl 5A):10–21.

9. National Institutes of Health Panel. Consensus development conference on diet and exercise in noninsulin-dependent diabetes mellitus. *Diabetes Care*. 1987;10:639–644.

10. Coulston A, Mandelbaum D, Reaven G. Dietary management of nursing home residents with diabetes: diabetic versus regular diet. *Clin Res*. 1988;36:95A.

11. Seals DR, Hagberg JM, Hurley BF, et al. Effects of endurance training on glucose tolerance and plasma lipid levels in older men and women. *JAMA* 1984;252:645–649.

12. Krotkiewski M, Lonnroth P, Mandroukas K, et al. The effects of physical training on glucose metabolism in obesity and type 2 (noninsulin-dependent) diabetes mellitus. *Diabetologia*. 1985; 28:881–890.

13. Saltin B, Lindgarde F, Houston M, et al. Physical training and glucose tolerance in middle-aged men with chemical diabetes. *Diabetes*. 1979;28(suppl 1):30–32.

14. Bogardus C, Ravussin E, Robbins DC, et al. Effects of physical training and diet therapy on carbohydrate metabolism in patients with glucose intolerance and noninsulin-dependent diabetes mellitus. *Diabetes*. 1984;33:311–318.

15. Karam JH. Therapeutic dilemmas in type II diabetes mellitus: improving and maintaining B-cell and insulin sensitivity. *West J Med*. 1988;148:685–690.

16. Pacini G, Valerio A, Beccaro F, et al. Insulin sensitivity and beta-cell responsivity are not decreased in elderly subjects with normal OGTT. *J Am Geriatr Soc*. 1988;36:317–323.

17. Puxty JAM, Hunter DM, Burr WA. Accuracy of insulin injection in elderly patients. *Br Med J*. 1983;287:1762–1763.

18. Mooradian AD, Morley JE. Micronutrient status in diabetes mellitus. *Am J Clin Nutr*. 1987;45:877–895.

19. Kinlaw WB, Levine AS, Morley JE, et al. Abnormal zinc metabolism in type II diabetes mellitus. *Am J Med*. 1983;75:273–277.

20. Morley JE. Nutritional status of the elderly. *Am J Med*. 1986;81:679–695.

21. Niewoehner CB, Allen JI, Boosalis M, et al. The role of zinc supplementation in type II diabetes mellitus. *Am J Med*. 1986;81:63–68.

22. Hallbook T, Lanner E. Serum-zinc and wound healing of venous leg ulcers. *Lancet*. 1972; 2:780–782.

23. Wallach S. Clinical and biochemical aspects of chromium deficiency. *J Am Coll Nutr*. 1985;4:107–120.

24. Urberg M, Zemel MD. Evidence for synergism between chromium and nicotinic acid in the control of glucose tolerance in elderly humans. *Metabolism*. 1987;36:896–899.

25. Klevay LM. Hypercholesterolemia in rats produced by an increase in the ratio of zinc to copper ingested. *Am J Clin Nutr*. 1978;26:1060–1065.

26. Mooradian AD, Osterweil D, Petrasek D, et al. Diabetes mellitus in elderly nursing home patients: a survey of clinical characteristics and management. *J Am Geriatr Soc*. 1988;36:391–396.

27. Robuschi G, Safran M, Braverman LE. Hypothyroidism in the elderly. *Endocr Rev*. 1987;8:142–153.

28. Morley JE, Slag MF, Elson MK, et al. The interpretation of thyroid function tests in hospitalized patients. *JAMA*. 1983;249:2377–2379.

29. Lloyd WA, Goldberg IJL. Incidence of hypothyroidism in the elderly. *Br Med J*. 1961; 2:1256–1258.

30. Morley JE. The aging endocrine system. *Postgrad Med*. 1983;73:107–120.

31. Loeb JN. Metabolic changes in hyperthyroidism. In: Ingbar SM, Braverman LE, eds. *Werner's The Thyroid*. Philadelphia, Pa: JB Lippincott Co; 1986.

32. Kreines K, Jett M, Knowles HC. Observations in hyperthyroidism of abnormal glucose tolerance and other traits related to diabetes mellitus. *Diabetes*. 1965;14:740–744.

33. Nikkala EA, Kekki M. Plasma triglyceride metabolism in thyroid disease. *J Clin Invest*. 1972;51:2103–2111.

34. Watanakunakom C, Hodges RE, Evans TC. Myxedema. *Arch Intern Med*. 1965;116: 183–187.

35. Rivlin RS. Vitamin metabolism in hyperthyroidism. In: Ingbar SM, Braverman LE, eds. *Werner's The Thyroid*. Philadelphia, Pa: JB Lippincott Co; 1986.

36. Rivlin RS. Vitamin metabolism in hypothyroidism. In: Ingbar SM, Braverman LE, eds. *Werner's The Thyroid*. Philadelphia, Pa: JB Lippincott Co; 1986.

37. Morley JE, Damassa DA, Gordon J, et al. Thyroid function and vitamin A deficiency. *Life Sci*. 1978;22:1901–1906.

38. Morley JE, Melmed S, Reed A, et al. The effect of vitamin A on the hypothalamic-pituitary-thyroid axis. *Am J Physiol*. 1980;238:E174–E179.

39. Drill VA. Interrelationships between thyroid function and vitamin metabolism. *Physiol Rev*. 1942;23:355–372.

40. Galton VA, Ingbar SM. Effects of vitamin deficiency on the *in vitro* and *in vivo* deiodination of thyroxine in the rat. *Endocrinology*. 1965;77:169–174.

41. Postelnicu D. Action of an antioxidant substance (alpha tocopherol) on the myocardium of rats treated with thyroxine. *Stud Cercet Endocrinol*. 1972;23:175–182.

42. Oxenburg GF, Pomara N, McIntyre IM. Aging and cortisol resistance to suppression by dexamethasone: a positive correlation. *Psychiatry Res*. 1983;10:125–130.

43. Irvine WJ, Barnes EW. Addison's disease, ovarian failure and hypoparathyroidism. *Clin Endocrinol Metab*. 1975;4:379–434.

44. Gregerman RI, Bierman EL. Aging and hormones. In: Williams RM, ed. *Textbook of Endocrinology*. *6th ed*. Philadelphia, Pa: WB Saunders Co; 1981.

45. Tsundo K, Abe K, Goto T. Effect of age on the renin-angiotensin-aldosterone system in normal subjects: simultaneous measurement of active and inactive renin, renin substrate, and aldosterone in plasma. *J Clin Endocrinol Metab*. 1986;62:384–389.

46. Parker LN, Odell WD. Decline of adrenal androgen production as measured by radioimmunoassay of urinary conjugated dehydroepiandrosterone. *J Clin Encocrinol Metab*. 1978;47:600–602.

47. Pashko LL, Schwartz AG. Effect of food restriction, dehydroepiandrosterone or obesity on the binding of 3H-7,12 dimethylbenz (a) anthracene to mouse skin DNA. *J Gerontol*. 1983;38:8–12.

48. Barrett-Connor E, Shaw KT, Yen SSC. A prospective study of dehydroepiandrosterone sulfate, mortality and cardiovascular disease. *N Engl J Med*. 1986;315:1519–1524.

49. Sonka J, Fassati M, Fassati P. Serum lipids and dehydroepiandrosterone excretion in normal subjects. *J Lipid Res*. 1968;9:769–772.

50. Nowaczynski W, Fragachon F, Silah J. Further evidence of altered adrenocortical function in hypertension: dehydroepianodrosterone excretion rate. *J Physiol (Lond)*. 1964;56:650–651.

51. Phillips PA, Rolls BJ, Ledingham JGG. Reduced thirst after water deprivation in healthy elderly men. *N Engl J Med*. 1984;311:753–759.

52. Yamamoto T, Harada H, Fukeiyama J, et al. Impaired arginine-vasopressin secretion associated with hypoangiotensinemia in hypernatremic dehydrated elderly patients. *JAMA*. 1988;259:1039–1042.

53. Helderman JH. The impact of normal aging on the hypothalamic-neurohypophyseal-renal axis. In: Korenman SG, ed. *Endocrine Aspects of Aging*. New York, NY: Elsevier-North Holland; 1982.

54. Lindeman RD, Lee TD Jr, Yiengst MJ. Influences of age, renal diseases, hypertension, diuretics, and calcium on the antidiuretic responses to suboptimal infusions of vasopressin. *J Lab Clin Med*. 1966;68:206–223.

55. Ohashi M, Fujia N, Nawata H. High plasma concentrations of human atrial natriuretic polypeptide in aged men. *J Clin Endocrinol Metab*. 1987;64:81–85.

56. Manson J McK, Wilmore DW. Positive nitrogen balance with human growth hormone and hypocaloric intravenous feeding. *Surgery*. 1986;100:188–197.

57. Florini J, Prinz PN, Vitiello MV. Somatomedin-C levels in healthy young and old men: relationship to peak and 24 hours integrated levels of growth hormone. *J Gerontol*. 1985;40:2–7.

58. Rudman D, Nagraji HS, Mattson DE. Hyposommatomedinemia in the nursing home patient. *J Am Geriat Soc*. 1986;34:427–430.

59. Rudman D. Growth hormone, body composition and aging. *J Am Geriatr Soc*. 1985;33: 800–807.

60. Kinsey AC, Pomeroy WB, Martin CE. *Sexual Behavior in the Human Male*. Philadelphia, Pa: WB Saunders Co; 1948.

61. Slag MF Morley JE, Elson MK, et al. Impotence in medical clinic outpatients. *JAMA*. 1983;249:1736–1740.

62. Morley JE. Impotence. *Am J Med*. 1986;80:897–905.

63. Billington CJ, Levine AS, Morley JE. Zinc status in impotent patients. *Clin Res*. 1983; 31:714A. Abstract.

64. Kaiser FE, Viosca SP, Morley JE, et al. Impotence and aging: clinical and hormonal factors. *J Am Geriatr Soc*. 1988;36:511–519.

65. Baker HWG, Berger HG, deKretser DM, et al. Changes in the pituitary testicular system with age. *Clin Endocrinol (oxf)*. 1976;5:349–372.

66. Mooradian AD, Morley JE, Korenman SG. Biological actions of androgens. *Endoc Rev*. 1987;8:1–28.

67. MacLaughlin J, Holick MF. Aging decreases the capacity of human skin to produce vitamin D_3. *J Clin Invest*. 1985;76:1536–1538.

68. Armbrecht HJ, Zenser TV, Davis BB. Effect of age on the conversion of 25-hydroxyvitamin D_3 to 1,25-dihydroxyvitamin D_3 by kidney of rat. *J Clin Invest*. 1980;66:1118–1123.

69. Morley JE, Gorbien MJ, Mooradian AD, et al. UCLA geriatric grand rounds: osteoporosis. *J Am Geriatr Soc*. 1988;36:845–859.

70. Somaan NA, Anderson GD, Adam-Mayne ME. Immunoreactive calcitonin in mother, neonate, child and adult. *Am J Obstet Gynecol*. 1975;121:622–625.

71. Sier HC, Hartnell J, Morley JE, et al. UCLA geriatric grand rounds: primary hyperparathyroidism and delirium in the elderly. *J Am Geriatr Soc*. 1988;36:157–170.

72. Nielson FH, Hunt CD, Mullen LM, et al. Effect of dietary boron on mineral, estrogen, and testosterone metabolism in postmenopausal women. *FASEB J*. 1987;1:394–397.

73. Shepard JW. Interrelationships of exercise and nutrition in the elderly. In: Armbrecht HJ, Prendergast J, Coe R, eds. *Nutritional Intervention in the Aging Process*. New York, NY: Springer-Verlag; 1984.

74. Frisancho AR. New standards of weight and body composition by frame size and height for assessment of nutritional status of adults and the elderly. *Am J Clin Nutr*. 1984;40:808–819.

75. Leibowitz SF. Brain monoamines and peptides; role in the control of eating behavior. *Fed Proc*. 1986;45:1396–1403.

76. LeMagnen J. Body energy balance and food intake: a neuroendocrine regulatory mechanism. *Physiol Rev*. 1983;63:314–386.

77. Bray GA. Autonomic and endocrine factors in the regulation of food intake. *Brain Res Bull*. 1985;14:505–510.

78. Greenberg LH. Regulation of brain adrenergic receptors during aging. *Fed Proc*. 1986; 45:55–59.

79. Morley JE, Blundell JE. The neurobiological basis of eating disorders: some formulations. *Biol Psychiatry.* 1988;23:53–78.

80. Morley JE. Neuropeptide regulation of appetite and weight. *Endocr Rev.* 1987;8:256–287.

81. Morley JE, Levine AS, Yim GK, et al. Opioid modulation of appetite. *Neurosci Biobehav Rev.* 1983;7:281–305.

82. Morley JE, Levine AS, Gosnell BA, et al. Effect of neuropeptide Y on ingestive behaviors in the rat. *Am J Physiol.* 1987;252:R599–R609.

83. Gosnell BA, Levine AS, Morley JE. The effects of aging on opioid modulation of feeding in rats. *Life Sci.* 1983;32:2793–2799.

84. Morley JE, Hernandez EN, Flood JF. Neuropeptide Y increases food intake in mice. *Am J Physiol.* 1987;253:R516–R522.

85. York DA, Bray GA. Dependence of hypothalamic obesity on insulin, the pituitary, and the adrenal gland. *Endocrinology.* 1972;90:885–894.

86. Bray GA. *The Obese Patient.* Philadelphia, Pa: WB Saunders Co; 1976:9. Saunders Monographs on Major Problems in Internal Medicine.

87. Leibowitz SF, Roland CR, Hor L, et al. Noradrenergic feeding elicited via the paraventricular nucleus is dependent upon circulating corticosterone. *Physiol Behav.* 1984;32:857–864.

88. Dalman MF. Viewing the ventromedial hypothalamus from the adrenal gland. *Am J Physiol.* 1984;246:R1–R12.

89. Freedman MR, Castunguay TW, Stern JS. Effect of adrenalectomy and corticosterone replacement on meal patterns of Zucker rats. *Am J Physiol.* 1985;249:R584–R594.

90. Hollifield G. Glucocorticoid-induced obesity: a model and a challenge. *Am J Clin Nutr.* 1968;21:1471–1474.

91. Donhoffer SZ, Vonotzky J. The effect of thyroxine on food intake and selection. *Am J Physiol.* 1947;150:334–339.

92. Wade GH, Zucker I. Modulation of food intake and locomotor activity in female rats by diencephalic hormone implants. *J Comp Physiol Psychol.* 1978;72:328–336.

93. Wade GH, Zucker I. Development of hormonal control over food intake and body weight in female rats. *J Comp Physiol Psychol.* 1970;70:213–220.

94. Numez AA, Grundman M. Testosterone affects food intake and body weight of weanling male rats. *Pharmacol Biochem Behav.* 1982;16:933–936.

95. Glick Z. Intestinal satiety with and without upper intestinal factors. *Am J Physiol.* 1979; 236:R142–R146.

96. Billington CJ, Levine AS, Morley JE. Are peptides truly satiety agents? a method for testing neurohormonal satiety effects. *Am J Physiol.* 1983;245:R920–R929.

97. Khalil T, Walker JP, Wiener J, et al. Effect of aging on gallbladder contraction and release of cholecystokinin-33 in humans. *Surgery.* 1985;98:423–429.

98. Silver AJ, Flood JF, Morley JE. Effect of gastrointestinal peptides on ingestion in young and old mice. *Peptides.* 1988;9:221–226.

99. Garrow J. *Energy Balance and Obesity in Man.* New York, NY: American Elsevier; 1974.

100. Keynes RD. The energy cost of active transport. In: Bolis L, Manddrell HP, Schmidt-Nielsen K, eds. *Comparative Physiology: Functional Aspects of Structural Materials.* Amsterdam, Netherlands: North Holland Publishing Co; 1975.

101. Waterlow JC, Garlick PJ, Millward DJ. *Protein Turnover in Mammalian Tissues and in Whole Body.* New York, NY: Elsevier-North Holland; 1978.

102. Newsholme EA. A possible metabolic basis for the control of body weight. *N Engl J Med.* 1980;302:400–405.

103. Guernsey DL, Edelman IS. Regulation of thermogenesis by thyroid hormones. In: Oppenheimer JH, Samuels HH, eds. *Molecular Basis of Thyroid Hormone Action.* New York, NY: Academic Press; 1983.

104. Millward DJ. Human protein requirements: the physiological significance of changes in the rate of whole body protein turnover. In: Garrow JW, Holliday D, eds. *Substrate and Energy Metabolism in Man.* London, England: John Libbey; 1985.

105. Mariash CN, Oppenheimer JH. Thyroid hormone: carbohydrate interaction. In: Oppenheimer JH, Samuels HH, eds. *Molecular Basis of Thyroid Hormone Action.* New York, NY: Academic Press; 1983.

106. Towle HC. Effects of thyroid hormones on cellular RNA metabolism. In: Oppenheimer JH, Samuels HH, eds. *Molecular Basis of Thyroid Hormone Action.* New York, NY: Academic Press; 1983.

107. Rothwell NJ, Saville ME, Stock MJ. Sympathetic and thyroid influences on metabolic rate in fed, fasted, and refed rats. *Am J Physiol.* 1982;243:R339–R346.

108. Lipson LG, Bray GA. Energy. In: Chen LH, ed. *Nutritional Aspects of Aging.* Cleveland, Ohio: CRC Press; 1986.

109. Chernoff R, Lipschitz DA. Nutrition and aging. In: Shils ME, Young VR, eds. *Modern Nutrition in Health and Disease.* 7th ed. Philadelphia, Pa: Lea & Febiger; 1988.

110. Young VR. Impact of aging on protein metabolism. In: Armbrecht HJ, Prendergast JM, Coe RM, eds. *Nutritional Intervention in the Aging Process.* New York, NY: Springer-Verlag; 1984.

111. Guernsey DL, Koebbe M, Thomas JE, et al. An altered response in the induction of cell membrane (Na⁺K⁺) ATPase by thyroid hormone is characteristic of senescence in cultured human fibroblasts. *Mech Ageing Dev.* 1986;33:283–293.

112. Evans MJ. Exercise and muscle metabolism in the elderly. In: Hutchinson ML, Munro HN, eds. *Nutrition and Aging.* New York, NY: Academic Press; 1986.

113. Hagberg JM. Effect of training on the decline of VO_{2max} with aging. *Fed Proc.* 1987; 46:1830–1833.

114. Glick Z. The thermic effect of a meal. *J Obes Weight Regul.* 1987;6:170–178.

115. Rothwell NJ, Stock MJ. Diet-induced thermogenesis: concepts and mechanisms. *J Obes Weight Regul.* 1987;6:162–169.

116. Flatt JP. The biochemistry of energy expenditure. In: Bray GA, ed. *Recent Advances in Obesity Research: Proceedings of the 2nd International Congress on Obesity.* London, England: Newman Publishing; 1978.

117. Himms-Hagen J. Brown adipose tissue metabolism and thermogenesis. *Ann Rev Nutr.* 1985;5:69–94.

118. Astrup A, Bulow J, Madsen J, et al. Contribution of BAT and skeletal muscle to thermogenesis induced by ephedrine in man. *Am J Physiol.* 1985;248:E507–E515.

119. Glick Z, Teague RJ, Bray GA. Effect of prandial glucose on brown fat thermogenesis: possible implications in dietary obesity. *J Nutr.* 1984;114:286–291.

120. Billington CJ, Bartness TJ, Briggs J, et al. Glucagon stimulation of brown adipose tissue growth and thermogenesis. *Am J Physiol.* 1987;252:R160–R165.

121. Rothwell NJ, Stock MJ. Effects of age on diet-induced thermogenesis and brown adipose tissue metabolism in the rat. *Int J Obes.* 1983;7:583–589.

122. Scarpace PJ, Mooradian AD, Morley JE. Age-associated decrease in beta-adrenergic receptors and adenylate cyclase activity in rat brown adipose tissue. *J Gerontol.* 1988;43:B65–B70.

Chapter 13

Pharmacology, Nutrition, and the Elderly: Interactions and Implications

Jeffrey B. Blumberg and Paolo Suter

There is a growing recognition of the clinically significant relationship between pharmacology and nutrition, especially in the elderly population. Although much of the early information on this topic had been based on anecdotal reports, current understanding of the interactions among pharmacotherapeutics, nutrition, and aging has been reviewed and compiled such that many adverse outcomes can now be predicted and avoided.[1–10] The adverse consequences of drug-nutrient interactions in the elderly can include nutritional deficiency, drug toxicity, loss of drug efficacy and disease control, and unwanted changes in body weight.

Adverse drug reactions are responsible for significant morbidity and mortality among the elderly. Even though the elderly comprise 12% of the population of the United States, they consume more than 25% of all prescription drugs and experience 30% of the adverse drug reactions reported to the Food and Drug Administration.[11] While the relative contribution of drug-drug interactions and drug-nutrient interactions to this problem among elderly people has not been established, both situations share common ground: the presence of multiple disease states, the practice of polypharmacy, the poor nutritional status of elderly individuals, and the age-related changes in pharmacokinetics and pharmacodynamics.

EXTENT AND PATTERNS OF DRUG USE BY THE ELDERLY

The growing numbers of elderly people and the multiple pathologic processes that affect them appear, inevitably, to lead to increased use of drugs in old age. Clinicians manage most illnesses in elderly patients with prescription drugs. Moreover, conditions such as memory loss, confusion, and changed sleep patterns are also treated with drug therapy by some physicians. Four of every five individuals over age 65 years are afflicted with chronic conditions such as heart disease, hypertension, arthritis, and diabetes; 35% have three or more of these problems.[12] Many older patients living at home take 3 or more different drugs daily; in institutions the quantity frequently increases to 10 or more different drugs per day.[13] This situation carries with it an increased likelihood of overprescribing practices, including inappropriate or excessive drug use, excessive dosage, and overlong drug use.

Cardiovascular drugs (eg, digitalis glycosides, diuretics, antiarrhythmics, anti-hypertensives, and anticoagulants) are the medication class most often prescribed for older patients, followed by psychoactive drugs (eg, neuroleptics and sedative-hypnotics) and gastrointestinal drugs (eg, histamine$_2$ [H$_2$] blockers and lax-atives)[13–15] (Table 13-1). More than 60% of the elderly population regularly use nonprescription drugs, especially non-narcotic analgesics such as acetaminophen, antacids, antihistamines, and nutrient supplements.[16,17] Interestingly, the 10 most common medical conditions reported by elderly people during health interviews include (by rank) arthritis, hearing problems, heart diseases, hyperten-sion, visual handicaps, digestive diseases, chronic sinusitis, mental and nervous disorders, genitourinary tract problems, and circulatory problems.[18] Therefore, despite the patterns of illness among older adults, actual prescribing practices and use of over-the-counter drugs may be different from the incidence of diseases (Table 13-1).

The problems associated with trying to provide rational drug treatment for older people can be categorized as extrinsic issues (ie, drug prescription and drug compliance) and intrinsic issues (ie, age-related pharmacokinetic and pharmaco-dynamic changes).[19] Polypharmacy prescribing patterns provide elderly patients with more drugs than they can reasonably be expected to cope with in a practical way; this situation leads to difficulty with compliance and greatly increases the risk of drug-drug and drug-nutrient interactions. In the context of multiple diseases, treatment without drugs is often insufficiently explored, although the risk-benefit ratio is higher in older adults than in young people.

Table 13-1 Patterns of Drug Use by the Elderly

| Therapeutic Class of Drug | Percentage of Prescriptions for Patients Aged Over 65 Years | | | |
	United Kingdom	Germany	Netherlands	Belgium
Peripheral vasodilators	68	67	68	65
Cardiac drugs	68	59	60	57
Diuretics	60	57	51	54
Antihypertensives	53	64	51	31
Psycholeptics	38	41	26	33
Antirheumatics	43	37	25	31

Source: Adapted from IMS International Audit of Prescribing in General European Practice, 1981.

It has been noted that the withdrawal of drug treatment once the initial indication has resolved often requires greater initiative and discipline than the original act of prescribing. "Inherited therapy," when drugs started in middle age are automatically continued, is common among elderly people. The need for periodic reevaluation of all drugs prescribed on a chronic basis is an essential component of rational drug therapy.[20] There is now evidence that long-term drug treatment with some compounds (eg, hypnotics, diuretics, cardiotonic glycosides, and nonsteroidal anti-inflammatory agents) is not necessary for many patients.

Issues concerning compliance are not unique to elderly people, although they are more vulnerable to problems associated with packaging and labeling, difficult-to-follow regimens, and poor physician-patient communication about drug use. Attention must also be directed to the self-prescribing practices of the older individual; ubiquitous over-the-counter drugs and worthless antiaging remedies may interfere with other drugs and nutrients. Intrinsic factors of prescribing for the geriatric patient are discussed below.

AGE-RELATED PHARMACOKINETIC CHANGES

Aging produces changes in pharmacokinetics (absorption, disposition, excretion) such that any given maintenance dose can lead to a higher steady-state concentration during repeated drug administration[21-23] (Table 13-2). However, most studies of drug kinetics and efficacy have been conducted in young and middle-aged patients, and relatively few controlled scientific data are available from geriatric patients. Therefore, increased drug monitoring is essential in elderly individuals, since the clinical base for quantitatively predicting changes in pharmacokinetics is not available for all compounds. Lower initial doses are usually used in treating elderly patients.

Absorption

The age-related physiologic changes in the gastrointestinal tract that could affect drug absorption, such as decreases in gastric emptying, splanchnic blood flow, and intestinal motility, are overcome to a considerable degree by the very large capacity of the system for passive absorption of small-molecular-weight compounds. Drugs absorbed via active transport may be affected by the age-related decline in the efficiency of these mechanisms.[24] The presence of chronic diseases and the interference of foods can further alter drug pharmacokinetics.

Table 13-2 Physiologic Changes Relevant to Pharmacokinetics in the Elderly

Pharmacologic Characteristics	Age-Related Changes*
Absorption	↓ Absorptive surface
	↓ Splanchnic blood flow
	↑ Gastric pH
	↓ Gastrointestinal motility
	↓ Gastric secretion
	↓ Pancreatic trypsin
	↓ Gastric emptying
Distribution	↓ Lean body mass
	↓ Total body water
	↓ Serum albumin
	↑ Body fat
	↑ Serum α-glycoprotein
	↓ Cardiac output
	↓ Cerebral blood flow
	↑ / ↓ Membrane permeability
Metabolism	↓ Liver mass
	↓ Hepatic blood flow
	↑ / ↓ Enzyme activity/inducibility
Excretion	↓ Renal blood flow
	↓ Glomerular filtration
	↓ Tubular secretion

* ↑ , Increased; ↓ , decreased; ↑ / ↓ , change dependent on specific drug.

Distribution

Age-related changes in body composition, such as the increase in adipose tissue and loss of skeletal muscle, can affect drug distribution. These changes are more marked in women than in men. The linear increase with age in the elimination half-life of diazepam, a fat-soluble drug, has been attributed to a larger volume of distribution.[25,26] Plasma protein binding of drugs also alters drug distribution and is affected by age-related declines in serum albumin levels. Decreased protein binding in the presence of lowered albumin levels has been demonstrated for antipyrine, meperidine, phenytoin, propranolol, salicylates, and warfarin.[27,28] Although many drugs exhibit decreased binding (increased free fraction) in elderly subjects, a few show increased binding because of a greater affinity for α_1-acid glycoprotein, which increases with age, than for albumin.[29] Although protein-binding changes are important factors in determining dosage, concomitant alteration in the volume of distribution and in the metabolic clearance of the total drug make a direct relationship difficult to establish.

Metabolism

Pharmacokinetic studies suggest that diminished hepatic oxidative (phase I) metabolism reduces the clearance of many drugs in elderly patients; however, this decline is not universal, due in part to the differential effects of aging on individual cytochrome P-450 isozymes.[21,30] A decrease in the metabolic clearance of drugs such as antipyrine, barbiturates, diazepam, and phenylbutazone is indicative of reduced oxidative drug-metabolizing enzyme activity in elderly people.[28,31,32] Such reduced biotransformation capacity accordingly reduces total drug clearance and causes higher steady-state plasma concentrations during repeated dosage (Table 13-3). Drugs principally biotransformed via phase II conjugation reactions seem to be less influenced by age.[21,33] However, recent studies with nonhuman primates indicate that conclusions drawn from the extensive data on hepatic metabolism in rodent experiments may not be completely relevant to humans.[34–36] It has been suggested that the decline in liver size with age in humans, which does not occur in rats, may also account for the lower drug-metabolizing capacity in older adults.[34,37]

Excretion

Most drugs and their metabolites are eliminated via urinary excretion. The reduction of renal function (ie, glomerular filtration, tubular secretion, and total renal plasma flow) and the decrease in nephrons and renal mass underlie the slower rate of drug elimination in elderly individuals[28,38] (Chapter 9). Diminished renal function may be the most important single factor responsible for altered drug levels in older people (Table 13-4). Dosages should be adjusted in older patients by taking into account their reduced creatinine clearances, not their serum creatinine levels. If such measurements cannot be obtained, nomograms exist that

---

Table 13-3 Drugs Showing Reduction in Hepatic Biotransformation in the Elderly

Alprazolam	Meperidine hydrochloride
Antipyrine	Norepinephrine
Carbenoxolone sodium	Nortriptyline hydrochloride
Chlordiazepoxide	Phenytoin
Chlormethiazole	Piroxicam
Clobazam	Propanolol
Desalkylfurazepam	Quinidine
Desmethyldiazepam	Quinine
Indocyanine green	Theophylline
	Verapamil

Table 13-4 Drugs Showing a Reduction in Renal Excretion in the Elderly

Acetylprocainamide	Kanamycin
Amikacin	Lithium carbonate
Ampicillin	Methotrexate
Atenolol	Pancuronium bromide
Azapropazone	Penicillin
Cefuroxime	Phenobarbital
Cephalothin	Procainamide hydrochloride
Cephradine	Propicillin
Cimetidine	Quinidine
Digoxin	Sotalol hydrochloride
Dihydrostreptomycin	Streptomycin
Doxycycline	Sulfamethizole
Ethambutol	Tetracycline
Gentamicin	Tobramycin

adjust for the expected change related to both age and sex.[39] In addition to the normal decline in renal function with aging, a variety of conditions (eg, congestive heart failure, dehydration, hypotension, and diabetes) can further reduce renal elimination of drugs.[40]

AGE-RELATED PHARMACODYNAMIC CHANGES

Despite the various alterations in pharmacokinetics that occur with different drugs in elderly patients and the associated changes in drug efficacy and toxicity, there remains a significant residue of altered responsiveness; this can be explained by differences in sensitivity to the drugs.[23] Pharmacodynamic theories suggest that such altered pharmacologic effects result from age-related changes in drug receptors, homeostasis, or tissue sensitivity. Pharmacodynamic explanations are difficult to test in vivo, and most studies depend on comparisons of correlations of drug effects versus simultaneously measured plasma drug concentrations, ie, demonstrating different responses between young and old subjects with similar tissue exposures to the drug.

Receptors

Mechanisms for age-related alterations in target tissue sensitivity could include changes in receptor number or affinity, receptor regulation, or translation of binding into a response. Elderly patients are less responsive to β-adrenergic agonists and more responsive to β-adrenergic antagonists as a result of alterations in the cyclic adenosine monophosphate second-messenger system;[41,42] on the other hand, α-adrenergic receptors do not appear to change with age.[43] Age-related changes have also been documented for brain benzodiazepine receptors and several hormone receptors.[44] The pharmacologic effects of cholinergic agonists increase with age, while those of parasympathetic antagonists produce less response in the heart rates of elderly patients. The beneficial effects of anticholinergics have been reported to decrease while their adverse side effects become more hazardous to elderly subjects. The progressive depletion of brain dopamine with age enhances the risk of drug-induced extrapyramidal side effects. Baroreceptor sensitivity is responsible for the high incidence of drug-induced orthostatic hypotension.[45] Age-related alterations in receptor-drug interactions are difficult to evaluate because of the influence of confounding factors such as disease, previous drug exposure, and nonreceptor drug-binding sites.

Homeostasis

A reduced homeostatic vitality may be the basis of some examples of increased drug sensitivity among elderly people. The ventilatory response to hypoxic challenge is affected by age, with direct consequences for hypoxic disease states and drug therapy. Elderly individuals also show a decreased response to dietary challenges to acid-base balance; eg, ammonium chloride will lower blood pH and prolong recovery time more markedly in old subjects than in young subjects, despite identical resting steady-state conditions. Older people are also less able to regulate blood glucose levels, pulse rate, blood pressure, and oxygen consumption, but to varying degrees. These variations are great enough to preclude clinically useful generalizations.[46,47]

Tissue Sensitivity

As discussed above, mechanisms for age-related alterations in target tissue sensitivity often appear to be based on changes in receptor number, affinity, or signal translation. However, many altered drug actions can be ascribed partially to age-related changes in the cardiovascular, endocrine, and central nervous systems. With age, decreases in cellular brain mass, sensory conduction time, and cerebral blood flow may contribute to a greater vulnerability to adverse drug effects such as confusion, falls, and urinary incontinence.[44] Changes with age in the cardiovascular system result in a decreased response of the heart to stress and catecholamines and altered sensitivity to the toxic effects of some drugs. Alterations in pancreatic and adrenal hormone levels result in decreased glucose tolerance with age and an increased susceptibility of older patients to drug-induced hypoglycemia.[48] With age there is a progressive decline in pulmonary function and a greater rigidity of the lung, which may cause an exaggerated respiratory depression after administration of narcotic analgesics. Decreases in thyroid hormone levels can make elderly individuals less sensitive to β-adrenergic sympathomimetics and more sensitive to digitalis and drug-induced hypothermia.[49] An age-related reduction in the synthesis of hepatic blood-clotting factors may underlie an increased sensitivity to oral anticoagulant drugs. Declines in immune responsiveness may alter the expected efficacy of antibiotic and antiviral medications. Physiologic losses of vestibular and cochlear hair cells and ganglia make geriatric patients more susceptible to irreversible drug-induced hearing loss.

FOOD CHOICE AND NUTRITIONAL STATUS OF THE ELDERLY

Economic, physical, psychosocial, and pathologic factors may significantly affect elderly people's accessibility to food (Table 13-5). These elements may result from lack of money to purchase food; physical disability; loss of a spouse, affecting motivation to cook and eat; isolation from family and community; limited knowledge concerning balanced diets; and existing disease processes. Chronic conditions such as arthritis, impaired hearing and vision, and coronary heart disease, as well as other physical disabilities, may affect health such that the ability to carry out food-related activities (eg, shopping and cooking) is significantly affected. Reduced appetite and food intake due to decreases in taste sensitivity, inability to chew, or problems in swallowing make eating more difficult and less pleasurable. Age-related changes in body composition and physiologic function also alter the dietary requirement for some nutrients.

Table 13-5 Factors Affecting Food Choices of the Elderly

Primary Factors
  Poverty
  Social isolation/depression
  Loss of spouse
  Physical disability
  Poor dentition
  Inadequate knowledge of nutrition

Secondary Factors
  Chronic drug therapy
  Gastrointestinal disorders/malabsorption
  Disease/pathologic processes
  Alcoholism

National surveys reveal that substantial numbers of elderly people are seriously lacking in adequate intake of some nutrients. The most common dietary deficiency in older adults is in intake of calories and calcium. In some studies, over half of the respondents fail to meet the recommended level of calorie intake and two thirds have less than adequate calcium intake. Decreasing energy intake with advancing age has important implications for the diet in terms of protein, vitamins, and minerals. Allowances for these nutrients assume that elderly people actually consume levels of energy that considerably exceed the amounts of food actually consumed. Dietary quality becomes difficult to assure when overall energy intake is low; prudent diets in elderly individuals require a careful selection of nutrient-dense foods. Energy intake decreases more rapidly in the very old because of disabilities that limit physical activity. Many elderly eat few fruits and vegetables, particularly vitamin A- and vitamin C-rich varieties. Despite the widespread use of enriched breads and cereals, low intake of the B-complex vitamins is common in the aged. Many studies demonstrate, however, that elderly people who take advantage of community services providing nutritional support, particularly those in congregate settings, show improved overall dietary intake and nutritional status.

Although the prevalence of nutrient supplementation among elderly people is high, exceeding 50% in some areas, the use of such supplements often appears irrational and inappropriate to their needs.[50] As with drug regimens, there can be serious problems in compliance with nutritional therapies for chronic disease.[51] The generally poor nutritional status of hospitalized and institutionalized elderly patients has been well documented.[52]

DRUG EFFECTS ON NUTRITIONAL STATUS

Several classification schemes have been proposed to categorize the ways in which drugs affect nutritional status.[53] While many of these schemes provide a sense of coherence and organization to the topic, there are difficulties or limitations with each scheme. The reason for this situation is the lack of any comprehensive theory underlying the numerous biochemical and clinical observations that have been reported. For the purpose of this discussion it is useful to employ the same scheme used to illustrate the interaction between aging and pharmacokinetics.

Absorption

The best described and most frequent type of drug-nutrient interaction results from drug-induced alteration of nutrient absorption.[54] Drugs cause malabsorption by exerting an effect in the intestinal lumen or by impairing the absorptive ability of the gastrointestinal mucosa. These effects can be limited and specific for a particular nutrient, or they can be general and can affect an entire class of nutrients, such as fat-soluble vitamins or trace minerals. Drugs may decrease nutrient bioavailability by a variety of mechanisms, including adsorption of the nutrient itself or of bile acids, therefore inhibiting the intraluminal phase of fat digestion and absorption. Drugs may form insoluble precipitates or chelate with a nutrient. Drugs may affect the environment of the gastrointestinal lumen through changes in pH, motility, or composition of bacterial flora (Table 13-6).

Some drugs may damage the intestinal mucosa and destroy the structure of the villi and microvilli, resulting in an inhibition of brush-border enzymes and intestinal transport systems needed for nutrient absorption. The malabsorptive effect of colchicine, neomycin, and p-aminosalicylic acid appears to be the result of such mucosal injury.[55]

Drugs may also interfere with nutrient absorption through secondary mechanisms. Drugs can impair digestion of food directly via initial adverse effects on gastric or intestinal secretion, pancreatic exocrine function, or hepatic bile secretion. Cimetidine and other H_2 blockers, because of their inhibitory effects on gastric acid production, reduce the liberation of vitamin B_{12} from its protein-bound state, making it less available for association with intrinsic factor.[56] Furthermore, in elderly individuals who have atrophic gastritis, changes in bacterial flora result in colonies with an increased avidity for vitamin B_{12}, making the nutrient less bioavailable.[57] Chronic effects of hepatotoxic drugs, notably alcohol, include maldigestion with reduced absorption of fats and fat-soluble vitamins.[58] Direct systemic effects of a drug on one nutrient may have secondary consequences for another nutrient. For example, drugs such as isoniazid[59] and cimetidine,[60] which inhibit the hepatic or renal hydroxylation of vitamin D, and those such as phenytoin[61] and phenobarbital,[62] which promote the catabolism of

---

Table 13-6 Examples of Drug-Induced Alteration of Nutrient Absorption

Drug	Mechanism	Impaired Absorption
Cholestyramine resin	Adsorption	Vitamin K
Aluminum hydroxide	Precipitation	Phosphate
Tetracycline	Chelation	Calcium
Mineral oil	Solubilization	Beta carotene
Sodium bicarbonate	Change in pH	Folate
Sulfasalazine	Enzyme inhibition	Folate
Sulfonamide	Change in bacterial flora	Vitamin B_1
Acarbose	Change in motility	Sugars
Colchicine	Mucosal injury	Vitamin B_{12}

vitamin D metabolites, produce a functional deficiency of vitamin D with a secondary impairment in calcium absorption.

Hypolipidemic drugs of the absorbable and nonabsorbable types may improve lipid status and decrease the risk of coronary artery disease, but they pose nutritional hazards.[63] Cholestyramine is a basic anion-exchange resin that binds salts and impairs the absorption of a number of nutrients, including carotene, vitamins A, B_{12}, D, K, and folic acid; and the minerals calcium, iron, and zinc.[64] Clofibrate and colestipol have similar, although less pronounced, effects.

Several classes of over-the-counter drugs may induce adverse nutritional effects. It has been suggested that drug-induced malnutrition in elderly people is commonly due to their excessive use of over-the-counter drugs such as antacids, laxatives, and non-narcotic analgesics.[65] Antacids formulated with aluminum and magnesium hydroxides form nonabsorbable phosphates in the gut lumen and may induce hypophosphatemia[66] with the development of proximal limb muscle weakness, malaise, paresthesias, anorexia, and secondary syndromes of hypomagnesemia/tetany,[67] and osteomalacia.[68] These antacids have also been associated with impaired absorption of riboflavin, copper, and iron. Excessive use of sodium bicarbonate can result in sodium overload and may render the pH of the jejunum sufficiently alkaline to decrease the absorption of folic acid.[69]

Laxative abuse is common among elderly individuals. Stool softeners such as mineral oil, if taken at mealtime or in the postprandial absorptive period, prevent the absorption of carotenes and fat-soluble vitamins via solubilization. Overuse of diphenylmethane derivatives, including phenolphthalein and bisacodyl, may result in severe malabsorption with steatorrhea; decreased glucose, calcium, potassium, and vitamin D absorption; and protein-losing enteropathy.[70] Osteomalacia resulting from excessive laxative use has been reported.[71] Laxatives such as dioctyl sulfosuccinates, which alter electrolyte transport, have also been associated with potassium deficiency due to gastrointestinal losses and failure of colonic reabsorption.[72] Laxative-induced malabsorption may be related to the loss of structural integrity of intestinal epithelial cells and protein-losing enteropathy secondary to potassium depletion.[73] In elderly patients, the risks of hypokalemia and potassium deficiency with the attendant hazards of cardiac arrhythmias, digitalis toxicity, and hyperglycemia are associated with concurrent use of laxatives and thiazide diuretics.[74]

Anti-inflammatory drugs such as aspirin and indomethacin produce multiple small hemorrhages of the gastrointestinal mucosa, leading to iron deficiency anemia and decreased absorption of vitamin C.[75] Chronic aspirin therapy is also associated with folic acid deficiency and macrocytic anemia; the greatest risk occurs in patients with a low intake of folic acid.[76] Colchicine has been noted to decrease the absorption of protein, fat, lactose, carotene, vitamin B_{12}, sodium, potassium, and bile acids as a result of villous damage.[77]

Metabolism

Drugs may act to inhibit the essential intermediary metabolism of a nutrient, or promote its catabolism (Table 13-7). While these actions are sometimes put to therapeutic advantage (eg, with oral anticoagulants [vitamin K antagonists such as coumarin] and antineoplastics [folic acid antagonists such as methotrexate]), examples of unwanted interference must also be recognized. Drug interference of vitamin D metabolism with secondary impairment of calcium absorption can result in osteomalacia. Anticonvulsants may interfere with osteocalcin-related bone mineralization processes via interruption of vitamin K metabolism.[78] Anticonvulsants and sedatives/hypnotics that induce hepatic microsomal drug-metabolizing enzymes may increase the demand for folic acid sufficiently to precipitate signs of deficiency.[79] Isoniazid[80] and hydralazine[81] may inhibit pyridoxal kinase sufficiently to produce clinical symptoms of vitamin B_6 deficiency. Triamterene, for example, is a potent inhibitor of dihydrofolate reductase and may induce megaloblastosis in some patients.[82]

Excretion

Drugs may act to increase the excretion of a nutrient by displacement from plasma protein-binding sites, chelation, or reduction of renal reabsorption. Aspirin competes for folic acid-binding sites on serum proteins and enhances the vitamin's excretion.[83] Long-term administration of penicillamine for rheumatoid arthritis results in chelation of essential minerals such as copper and zinc.[84] Although diuretic therapy effectively decreases the resorption of sodium, it also enhances the renal excretion of calcium, chromium, magnesium, potassium, and zinc.[85]

Food Intake

In addition to their direct effects on absorption, metabolism, and excretion of nutrients, drugs also may affect nutritional status by altering food intake

---

Table 13-7 Drug-Induced Alteration of Nutrient Metabolism

Drug	Mechanism	Impaired Metabolism
Isoniazid	Inhibits pyridoxal kinase	Vitamin B_6
Cephalosporin	Inhibits reductase/carboxylation	Vitamin K
Phenytoin	Induces hepatic microsomal enzymes	Folic acid
Triamterene	Inhibits dihydrofolate reductase	Folic acid

(Table 13-8). Several drugs have been noted to alter food intake, primarily through changes in appetite or the senses of taste and smell, or through their adverse gastrointestinal side effects.[86] Drugs may be hyperphagic or hypophagic, but the effects of drugs on appetite are strongly influenced by situational factors.[87] Psychotropic agents, such as the phenothiazines and benzodiazepines, improve mood and psychologic function with a consequent increase in food intake in some individuals; however, in elderly patients, whose rate of drug metabolism is slow, these drugs may induce somnolence and disinterest in food. Amitriptyline hydrochloride and related tricyclic antidepressants appear to stimulate appetite, but in elderly subjects they can cause behavioral agitation that interferes with eating.[88] The oral hypoglycemic agents may stimulate appetite by pancreatic release of insulin.

Brief or prolonged periods of anorexia associated with drug therapy are often due to effects on the gastrointestinal tract. Antineoplastic drugs induce nausea, vomiting, and aversion to food.[89] Cardiac glycosides produce anorexia accompanied by nausea; high-dose treatment may result in digitalis cachexia.[90] Several antihypertensive drugs (eg, hydralazine, minoxidil, and diazoxide) are also associated with side effects of anorexia, nausea, vomiting, and diarrhea. Alcohol abuse can cause anorexia, but even elderly social drinkers tend to have lower food intakes than do age-matched nondrinkers. Some drugs (eg, lithium carbonate) produce an abnormal, unpleasant taste sensation (dysgeusia). A few drugs may also induce an unusual desire for certain foods, such as has been reported by patients taking diuretics who crave salt. Some drugs may induce untoward problems in the mouth that affect food intake, eg, dry mouth (xerostomia) resulting from the anticholinergic action of tricyclic antidepressants and tran-

---

Table 13-8 Drug-Induced Alteration of Food Intake

Hypophagic Drugs	Hyperphagic Drugs	Drugs Producing Hypogeusia/Dysgeusia
Actinomycin D	Amitriptyline hydrochloride	Amydricaine
Alcohol	Anabolic steroids	Amylocaine hydrochloride
Amphetamine	Benzodiazepines	Captopril
Cisplatin	Buclizine hydrochloride	Clofibrate
Cocaine	Chlorpropamide	d-Penicillamine
Diethylpropion hydrochloride	Chlortetracycline	Encainide
Fenfluramine hydrochloride	Cyproheptadine	5-Fluorouracil
Hydroxyurea	hydrochloride	Griseofulvin
Mazindol	Glucocorticoids	Lincomycin
Methotrexate	Phenothiazines	Lithium carbonate
Phenethylbiguanide	Reserpine	Methimazole
Phenmetrazine	Tolbutamide	Methylthiouracil
hydrochloride		Oxyfedrine

quilizers, gingival hyperplasia from phenytoin, oral ulcerations from captopril, and parotid inflammation from guanethidine.

FOOD EFFECTS ON DRUG THERAPY

The clinical effects of foods on drug absorption and disposition, particularly in elderly patients and during chronic care, has not been well studied. Nonetheless, food and food components have been shown to interact with drugs in various ways.[91] Food may influence both the absorption and presystemic metabolism of drugs, and these effects may be caused by food intake or by different nutrients or additives, food/fluid volume, or polycyclic hydrocarbons present in grilled foods. Whether the changes induced by food are clinically significant depends both on the type of drug and the extent of the change. Food-induced changes in drug therapy can be examined in much the same fashion as drug-induced changes in nutritional status.

Absorption

Food and its constituents can influence drug absorption as a result of physical or chemical interactions between the food product and the drug, or because of physiologic changes in the gastrointestinal tract induced by eating or drinking. The net effect of this interaction may be that drug absorption is reduced, slowed, or increased by food intake.[92]

Food can act to alter the rate of gastric emptying and drug dissolution in the stomach. It can also increase the viscosity of the gastric medium, decreasing the rate of drug diffusion to mucosal absorption sites. Food can act as a mechanical barrier, preventing drug access to the mucosal surface. Food components can also act to complex or chelate drugs. The effect of food on drug absorption may also be dependent on the drug formulation. Generally, enteric-coated tablets appear to be most affected by foods, and drugs in solution may be least affected.[93]

Several food-related effects on gastrointestinal function that also affect drug absorption and may augment age-related changes include alteration in gastric emptying time; intestinal motility; splanchnic blood flow; and alteration in the secretion of bile, gastric acid, and digestive enzymes.[94] The β-blocker drugs, propranolol and metoprolol, are better absorbed after meals because of food-related increases in splanchnic blood flow and reduced first-pass metabolism in the intestinal mucosa or liver.[95]

When the effect of food on drug absorption is related to interactions between the food and the drug in the gastrointestinal tract, then the timing of drug intake in relation to mealtime is of practical importance. Acetaminophen absorption, for example, is five times more rapid after fasting than after consumption of a high-carbohydrate meal containing large amounts of pectin.[96] Foods can also interfere with the mucosal transfer of drugs absorbed by active transport. Drugs such as levodopa and methyldopa, with structures similar to amino acids, are absorbed by the transport mechanism for amino acids.[97] Competition for transport between the drug and amino acids from protein in the diet diminish drug uptake and appears responsible for the "on-off" phenomenon of levodopa in patients with Parkinson's disease.[98] In elderly patients, particularly those who have difficulty with mastication or who have had gastric surgery, long-term cimetidine administration, coupled with high fiber intake, may lead to the formation of phytobezoars.[99]

The effects of changes in gastric emptying time on drug absorption are dependent on the water solubility of the drug; drugs with very low solubility are better absorbed when they remain longer in the stomach, as they will do after large, hot, or high-fat meals.[100] For drugs that are weak bases (such as amitriptyline hydrochloride, diazepam, and pentazocine), gastric emptying rate is critical, as absorption occurs in the less acidic intestine. The gastric emptying time is approximately 50 minutes in young, healthy volunteers but greater than 120 minutes in subjects over age 77 years.[101] Food-induced decreases in gastric clearance can cause more of drugs such as digoxin, levodopa, and penicillin to be metabolized in the stomach and less of the unchanged drug to be available for absorption, resulting in an erratic therapeutic response.[27] Changes in gastric emptying affect mainly drugs that are rapidly absorbed or that have a short biologic half-life.

Distribution

Nutritional influences on drug distribution appear to be limited to the large reduction of plasma albumin seen in poorly nourished geriatric patients. However, even in well-nourished, healthy elderly individuals, albumin concentrations have been found to be lower than those in young adults.[102] Therefore, for extensively protein-bound drugs, such as diazepam and warfarin, a reduced binding capacity in old age results in an increase in the drugs' free fractions so lower ranges of therapeutic and toxic plasma concentrations can be anticipated.[103] Dietary fats may modify drug distribution; free fatty acids compete for anionic binding sites on plasma albumin, increasing the pharmacologic activity of displaced drugs.

Metabolism

Diet and nutritional status may have a marked effect on the way drugs are metabolized, although studies in this area have rarely been conducted on elderly subjects.[104] As previously noted, rates of drug metabolism decrease with age, so this type of interaction is likely to be more marked in older adults.[105] In studies conducted on healthy young men given antipyrine or theophylline during sequential feeding of high-carbohydrate, high-fat, or high-protein diets, the rate of drug elimination was slowest when the high-carbohydrate diet was fed and fastest during the high-protein period.[106,107] The high-fat diet produced a small decrease in the rate of antipyrine loss but did not alter theophylline pharmacokinetics. Reduced drug clearance has been demonstrated in lactovegetarians, whose diets are characterized by a low-protein intake.[108] Balanced-protein diets produce an acid urine, whereas low-protein diets usually result in an alkaline urine. Many elderly patients switch to low-protein diets with advancing age, and drug elimination patterns consequently may change.

Subjects who switch between saturated and polyunsaturated dietary fats show a concurrent alteration in plasma lipids but no change in cytochrome P-450–mediated drug metabolism.[109] In cases of mild or moderate undernutrition, particularly in adults, the rate of drug metabolism has been found to be either normal or slightly increased.[110] Only in severely malnourished adults with nutritional edema is drug metabolism impaired, with significant increases in plasma half-life of the drug.[111]

Natural non-nutrient components of the diet may exert a profound influence on the rate of drug metabolism, and these effects may occur rapidly after food ingestion. Indolic compounds in vegetables of the Brassica family, eg, cabbage and Brussels sprouts, stimulate the rate of drug metabolism in humans.[112] Flavones (bioflavonoids) occurring in citrus and other fruits, and polycyclic aromatic hydrocarbons generated during charcoal broiling, stimulate liver microsomal drug metabolism.[113] However, it has not been established whether elderly people are as susceptible as younger people to this type of hepatic enzyme induction. Alterations of intestinal microflora produced by changes in the dietary level or source of protein or fiber may also influence intestinal drug metabolism.

EFFECT OF NUTRIENT SUPPLEMENTS ON DRUG THERAPY

Nutrient supplements are required by those on chronic drug regimens when a risk of progressive nutrient depletion exists as well as when a nutrient deficiency induced by the drug is present[17] (Table 13-9). Appropriate levels of vitamin supplementation have been proposed for specific drug therapies.[6] It is not unusual that drug-related depletion of nutrients in geriatric patients is complicated by dietary inadequacy or disease states that induce nutrient deficiencies. Despite such well-justified therapeutic needs for nutrient supplementation, it is important to recognize the extensive nature of self-prescribed supplement use among older adults. The estimated prevalence of nutrient supplementation in the elderly ranges from 30% to 70%.[50] In one survey of middle-class elderly individuals who had no

Table 13-9 Chronic Drug Therapy and Nutrient Supplementation

Drug	Supplement
Antacids	Folic acid
Aspirin	Folic acid, iron, vitamin C
Chlortetracycline	Calcium, vitamin C, vitamin B_2
Cholestyramine resin	Vitamins A, D, K, folic acid
Colestipol	Vitamins A, D, K, folic acid
Estrogens/progestin	Vitamin B_6, folic acid
Hydralazine hydrochloride	Vitamin B_6
Indomethacin	Iron
Isoniazid	Vitamin B_6, niacin, vitamin D
Pencillamine	Vitamin B_6
Phenothiazines	Vitamin B_2
Phenytoin	Folic acid, vitamin D, vitamin K
Primidone	Vitamin K
Rifampin	Vitamin B_6, niacin, vitamin D
Sulfasalazine	Folic acid
Tetracycline	Calcium, vitamin B_2, vitamin C
Triamterene	Folic acid

known medical illnesses and who were not taking prescription medications, the prevalence of nutrient supplement use was 60%.[114] While several of the factors discussed above suggest that there may be valid reasons to recommend nutrient supplementation for older adults, current trends indicate that their supplementation regimens are not always appropriate; ie, self-selected supplements are not based on the individual's actual needs.

High-dose vitamin supplementation has been noted to produce an alteration of some drug effects. Megadoses of vitamin E potentiate the action of the anticoagulant warfarin and produce hemorrhage by further depressing the levels of vitamin K-dependent coagulation factors.[115] Vitamin D supplements can induce hypercalcemia and precipitate cardiac arrhythmias in patients receiving digitalis.[116] The administration of supplemental calcium can cause a recurrence of atrial fibrillation in patients maintained on verapamil.[116] Excessive doses of vitamin C acidify the urine and may alter drug pharmacokinetics; acidic drugs are more readily absorbed and basic drugs are more rapidly excreted from acidic urine.[117] Large doses of vitamin C may also inhibit the anticoagulant response of warfarin.[118] Niacin supplements may have an additive vasodilating effect, producing postural hypotension in patients receiving hypertensive drugs of the sympathetic blocking type, such as clonidine hydrochloride.[116] An increase in seizure frequency and a corresponding decrease in serum phenytoin levels have been reported in epileptic patients receiving high-dose folic acid supplements.[119]

IMPLICATIONS FOR AGING

The long list of identified drug-nutrient interactions does not implicate the production of a clinically significant adverse effect whenever the specific ingredients, ie, the drug prescription and low intake of a nutrient, are present. However, both the nutrition- and drug-related risk factors for adverse interactions are greatest in elderly subjects because of the concomitant presence of age-associated conditions[120] (Table 13-10). The nutrient intakes of most older people are less than desirable, so they present with suboptimal nutritional status at the outset of drug therapy. Elderly individuals are often prescribed multiple drugs requiring frequent administration over long periods of time. Age-associated diseases, changes in body composition, and changes in physiologic function contribute to substantial alterations in drug pharmacokinetics and pharmacodynamics. Therefore, it is important to recognize the multifactorial diet-drug-age-disease interrelationships in determining the benefits and risks of any specific therapeutic intervention.

Table 13-10 Risk Factors for Drug-Induced Nutrient Deficiency in the Elderly

Drug-Associated Factors
  Dose
  Duration
  Frequency
  Polypharmacy

Nutrition-Associated Factors
  Nutritional quality of diet
  Initial nutritional status
  Use of nutrient supplements
  Temporal relation between meals and drug administration

Age-Associated Factors
  Gastrointestinal changes
  Hepatic changes
  Renal changes
  Body composition changes
  Homeostatic changes
  Receptor-mediated changes
  Tissue sensitivity changes

Pathologic Factors
  Cardiovascular disease
  Gastrointestinal malabsorption
  Liver disease
  Renal disease

The medical treatment of geriatric patients often tends to include practices that do not fully consider the risk factors that contribute to drug-nutrient interactions. Physician advice to older patients to take medication with foods to decrease gastrointestinal side effects and enhance compliance may increase the chance of adverse interactions. Drug-nutrient interactions may also occur as a result of the common practice of passing drugs down nasogastric tubes used for enteral feeding. This practice can induce blockage of the tube or reduce bioavailability because of physical incompatibility between the enteral formula and the drug. As discussed above, drug metabolism and efficacy may also be affected simply by changing the diet (eg, the protein content) or the timing between meals and drug administration. These situations point out the importance of close and frequent communication among physicians, dietitians, and pharmacists on the health care team. The widespread use of nutrient supplements among elderly people may adversely or beneficially influence the therapeutic outcome of drug treatment. Relatively frequent and careful evaluation through drug monitoring and nutritional assessment becomes critical in the geriatric patient.[121]

CONCLUSION

Nutritional deficiencies have been linked to increased susceptibility to disease and behavioral changes. Drug-induced vitamin and mineral deficiencies can lead to a host of symptoms, including anorexia, bone pain, confusion, and malaise, that mimic what are frequently considered as signs of old age.[121] Prolonged nutrient deficiencies can also result in conditions such as anemia, laryngitis and bronchitis,[122] carpal tunnel syndrome,[123] and postoperative confusion.[124] As described, the interactions between drugs and diet have implications for therapeutic outcome; and, unless the health care team is aware of such relationships, the problem may be wrongfully attributed to other factors such as age. Application of existing knowledge about the relationships among pharmacology, nutrition, and aging can directly contribute to minimizing the iatrogenic impact of drug-nutrient interactions.

Carefully controlled clinical trials as well as hospital- and community-based epidemiologic studies are needed to identify further the risk factors associated with drug-nutrient interactions in geriatric patients. In some cases, the effects of age on drug disposition and action are of less importance than the effects of inappropriately concurrent drug and meal intakes, unscheduled changes in dietary regimens, or ill-considered polypharmacy regimens. There is therefore a need to develop methods of communication to transfer this information to geriatric patients and to their care givers, including physicians, nurses, pharmacists, dietitians, and home care personnel. Means of communication between care givers and educational programs within geriatric institutions must be developed further so that the potential consequences of changes in diet or drug therapies are recognized by the appropriate individuals. While more research is necessary to identify and characterize the mechanisms and symptoms of drug-nutrient interactions in the geriatric patient, much can be done now through education and communication to recognize the risks and avoid their adverse consequences.

REFERENCES

1. Powers DE, Moore AG. *Food-Medication Interactions*. Tempe, Ariz: F-M I Publishing; 1983.

2. Roe DA, ed. *Drugs and Nutrition in the Geriatric Patient*. New York, NY: Churchill-Livingstone Inc; 1984.

3. Roe DA, Campbell TC, eds. *Drugs and Nutrients: The Interactive Effects*. New York, NY: Marcel Dekker Inc; 1984.

4. Basu TK. *Drug-Nutrient Interactions*. Deckenham, England: Croom Helm; 1988.

5. Roe DA. *Drug-Induced Nutritional Deficiencies*. Westport, Conn: Avi Publishing; 1985.

6. Roe DA. *Handbook: Interactions of Selected Drugs and Nutrients in Patients*. Chicago, Ill: The American Dietetic Association; 1982.

7. Roe DA. *Diet and Drug Interactions*. New York, NY: Van Nostrand Reinhold; 1989.

8. Blumberg JB. Drug-nutrient interrelationships. In: Calkins E, Davis P, Ford A, eds. *The Practice of Geriatrics*. Philadelphia, Pa: WB Saunders Co; 1986.

9. Blumberg J. Clinical significance of drug-nutrient interactions. *Trans Pharmacol Sci*. 1986; 7:33–35.

10. Hershey LA. Avoiding adverse drug reactions in the elderly. *Mt Sinai J Med*. 1988;55: 244–250.

11. Young FE. Clinical evaluation of medicine used by the elderly. *Clin Pharmacol Ther*. 1987; 42:666–669.

12. Kovar MG. Health of the elderly and use of health services. *Public Health Rep*. 1977;92: 9–19.

13. Chen LH, Liu S, Cook-Newell ME, et al. Survey of drug use by the elderly and possible impact of drugs on nutritional status. *Drug-Nutr Interact*. 1985;3:73–86.

14. Cusak B, Denham MJ, Kelly JG, et al., eds. *Clinical Pharmacology and Drug Treatment in the Elderly*. Edinburgh, Scotland: Churchill Livingstone; 1984.

15. Shapiro S, Avery KT, Carpenter RD. Drug utilization by a non-institutionalized ambulatory elderly population. *Gerodontics*. 1986;2:99–102.

16. Rikans LE. Drugs and nutrition in old age. *Life Sci*. 1986;39:1027–1036.

17. Lamy PP. Nonprescription drugs and the elderly. *Am Fam Physician*. 1989;39:175–179.

18. Lofholm P. Self-medication by the elderly. In: Kayne KC, ed. *Drugs and the Elderly*. Los Angeles, Calif: University of Southern California Press; 1979.

19. Swift CG. Prescribing in old age. *Br Med J*. 1988;296:913–915.

20. Lamy P. The elderly and drug interactions. *J Am Geriatr Soc*. 1986;34:586–592.

21. Greenblatt DJ, Sellers EM, Shader RI. Drug disposition in old age. *N Engl J Med*. 1982;306: 1081–1088.

22. Schmucker DL. Drug disposition in the elderly: a review of the critical factors. *J Am Geriatr Soc*. 1984;32:144–149.

23. Blumberg JB. A discussion of drug metabolism and actions in the aged. *Drug-Nutr Interact*. 1985;4:99–106.

24. Robertson D. Drug handling in old age. In: Brocklehurst JC, ed. *Geriatric Pharmacology and Therapeutics*. Oxford, England: Blackwell Scientific Publications Ltd; 1984.

25. Klotz U, Avant GR, Hoyumpa A, et al. The effects of age and liver disease on the disposition and elimination of diazepam in adult man. *J Clin Invest*. 1975;55:347–359.

26. Greenblatt DJ, Allen MD, Harmatz JS. Diazepam disposition determinants. *Clin Pharmacol Ther*. 1980;27:301–312.

27. Lamy PP. Nutrition, drugs, and the elderly. *Clin Nutr (Phila)*. 1983;2:9–14.

28. Cohen JL. Pharmacokinetic changes in aging. *Am J Med*. 1986;80:31–38.

29. Wallace SM, Verbeeck RK. Plasma protein binding of drugs in the elderly. *Clin Pharmacokinet*. 1987;12:41–72.

30. Kamataki T, Maeda K, Shimada M, et al. Age-related alteration in the activities of drug-metabolizing enzymes and contents of sex-specific forms of cytochrome P-450 in liver microsomes from male and female rats. *J Pharmacol Exp Ther*. 1985;233:222–228.

31. Greenblatt DJ, Allen MD, Harmatz JS, et al. The effects of age and liver disease on the disposition and elimination of diazepam in adult man. *J Clin Invest*. 1975;55:347–359.

32. Crooks J, O'Malley K, Stevenson IH. Pharmacokinetics in the elderly. *Clin Pharmacokinet*. 1976;1:280–285.

33. Vestal RE, Woods JA, Branch RA, et al. Studies of drug disposition in the elderly using model compounds. In: Kitani K, ed. *Liver and Aging*. Amsterdam, Netherlands: Elsevier-North Holland; 1978.

34. Kitani K. Hepatic drug metabolism in the elderly. *Hepatology*. 1986;6:316–319.

35. Sutter MA, Gibson G, Williamson LS, et al. Comparison of the hepatic mixed function oxidase systems of young, adult and old non-human primates (*Macaca nemiestrina*). *Biochem Pharamcol*. 1985;34:2983–2987.

36. Maloney AG, Schmucker DL, Vessey DS, et al. The effects of aging on the hepatic microsomal mixed-function oxidase system of male and female monkeys. *Hepatology*. 1986;6: 282–287.

37. Kitani K. The role of the liver in the pharmacokinetic and pharmacodynamic alterations in the elderly. In: Waddington JL, O'Malley K, eds. *Therapeutics in the Elderly*. Amsterdam, Netherlands: Elsevier Scientific Publishers BV; 1985.

38. Davies DF, Shock NW. Age changes in glomerular filtration rate, effective renal plasma flow, and tubular excretory capacity in adult males. *J Clin Invest*. 1950;29:496–507.

39. Rowe JW, Andres R, Tobin JD, et al. Age-adjusted standards for creatinine clearance. *Ann Intern Med*. 1976;84:567–569.

40. Chan GL, Matzke GR. Effects of renal insufficiency on the pharmacokinetics and pharmacodynamics of opioid analgesics. *Drug Intell Clin Pharm*. 1987;21:773–783.

41. Roth GS. Hormone receptor changes during adulthood and senescence: significance for aging research. *Fed Proc*. 1979;38:1910–1914.

42. Feldman RD, Limbird RE, Nadeau J, et al. Alterations in leukocyte beta-receptor affinity with aging: a potential explanation for altered beta-adrenergic sensitivity in the elderly. *N Engl J Med*. 1984;310:815–819.

43. Scott PJ, Reid JL. The effect of age on the response of human isolated arteries to nor-adrenaline. *Br J Clin Pharmacol*. 1982;13:237–239.

44. Lamy, PP. Age-associated pharmacodynamic changes. *Methods Find Exp Clin Pharmacol*. 1987;9:153–159.

45. Gribbin B, Pickering TG, Sleight P, et al. Effect of age and high blood pressure on baroreflex sensitivity in man. *Circ Res*. 1971;29:424–431.

46. Kohn RR. Human aging and disease. *J Chronic Dis.* 1983;16:5–21.

47. Vestal RE. Drug use in the elderly: a review of problems and special considerations. *Drugs.* 1978;16:358–382.

48. Lamy PP. *Prescribing for the Elderly.* Littleton, Mass: PSG Publishing Co Inc; 1980.

49. Orlander P, Johnson DG. Endocrinologic problems in the aged. *Otolaryngol Clin North Am.* 1982;15:439–449.

50. Hartz SC, Blumberg JB. Use of vitamin and mineral supplements by the elderly. *Clin Nutr (Phila).* 1986;5:130–136.

51. Glanz K. Compliance with dietary regimens. *Prev Med.* 1980;9:787–791.

52. Colucci RA, Bell SJ, Blackburn GL. Nutritional problems of institutionalized and free-living elderly. *Compr Ther.* 1987;13:20–28.

53. Roe DA. Concurrent interactions of drugs with nutrients. In: Linder MC, ed. *Nutritional Biochemistry and Metabolism with Clinical Applications.* New York, NY: Elsevier Science Publishing Co Inc; 1985.

54. Roe DA. Nutrient and drug interactions. *Nutr Rev.* 1984;42:141–154.

55. Roe DA. Pathological changes associated with drug-induced malnutrition. In: Sidransky H, ed. *Nutritional Pathology.* New York, NY: Marcel Dekker Inc; 1985.

56. Streeter AM, Goldston KJ, Bathur FA, et al. Cimetidine and malabsorption of cobalamine. *Dig Dis Sci.* 1982;27:13–16.

57. Kassarjian Z, Russell RM. Hypochlorhydria: a factor in nutrition. *Annu Rev Nutr.* 1989;9: 271–285.

58. Liber CS. Alcohol, protein nutrition, and liver injury. In: Winick M, ed. *Nutrition and Drugs.* New York, NY: John Wiley & Sons; 1983.

59. Brodie MJ, Boobis AR, Hillyard CJ, et al. Effect of isoniazid on vitamin D metabolism and hepatic monooxygenase activity. *Clin Pharmacol Ther.* 1981;30:363–367.

60. Bengoa JM, Bolt MJG, Rosenberg IH. Hepatic vitamin D-25-hydroxylase inhibition by cimetidine and isoniazid. *J Clin Med.* 1984;104:546–552.

61. Robbro OT, Christiansen C, Lund M. Development of anticonvulsant osteomalacia in epileptic patients on phenytoin treatment. *Acta Neurol Scand.* 1974;50:527–532.

62. Hahn TJ, Birge SJ, Sharp CR, et al. Phenobarbital-induced alterations in vitamin D metabolism. *J Clin Invest.* 1972;51:741–748.

63. Miettinen TA. Effects of hypolipidemic drugs on bile acid in man. *Adv Lipid Res.* 1981;18: 65–97.

64. West RJ, Lloyd JK. The effect of cholestyramine on intestinal absorption. *Gut.* 1975;16: 93–98.

65. Roe DA. Adverse nutritional effects of OTC drug use in the elderly. In: Roe DA, ed. *Drugs and Nutrition in the Geriatric Patient.* New York, NY: Churchill-Livingstone Inc; 1984.

66. Lotz M, Zisman E, Bartter C. Evidence for phosphorus depletion syndrome in man. *N Engl J Med.* 1968;278:409–415.

67. Rud RK, Singer FR. Magnesium deficiency and excess. *Annu Rev Med.* 1981;32:245–259.

68. Insogna KL, Bordley DR, Caro JF, et al. Osteomalacia and weakness from excessive antacids. *JAMA.* 1980;244:2544–2546.

69. Benn A, Swan CJH, Cooke WT, et al. Effect of intraluminal pH on the absorption of pteroylmonoglutamic acid. *Br Med J.* 1971;16:148–150.

70. Fleming BJ, Genuth SM, Gould AB, et al. Laxative-induced hypokalemia, sodium depletion and hyperreninemia: effects of potassium and sodium replacement on the renin-angiotensin-aldosterone system. *Ann Intern Med.* 1975;83:60–62.

71. Frame B, Guiang HL, Frost HN, et al. Osteomalacia induced by laxative (phenolphthalein) ingestion. *Arch Intern Med.* 1971;128:794–796.

72. Donowitz M, Binder HJ. Effect of dioctylsulfosuccinate on colonic fluid and electrolyte movement. *Gastroenterology.* 1975;69:941–950.

73. Heiser WD, Warshaw AL, Waldeman TA, et al. Protein losing gastroenteropathy and malabsorption associated with factitious diarrhea. *Arch Intern Med.* 1968;68:839–851.

74. Roe DA. Drug interference with the assessment of nutritional status. *J Clin Lab Med.* 1981;1: 647–664.

75. Leonards JH, Levy G. Gastrointestinal blood loss during prolonged aspirin administration. *N Engl J Med.* 1973;289:1020.

76. Gouf KR, McCarthy C, Read AE, et al. Folic acid deficiency in rheumatoid arthritis. *Br Med J.* 1964;1:212–216.

77. Race TF, Paes IC, Faloon WW. Intestinal malabsorption induced by oral colchicine: comparison with neomycin and cathartic agents. *Am J Med Sci.* 1970;259:32–41.

78. Keith DA, Gundberg CM, Japour A, et al. Vitamin K-dependent proteins and anticonvulsant medication. *Clin Pharmacol Ther.* 1983;34:529–532.

79. Maxwell JD, Hunter J, Stewart DA, et al. Folate deficiency after anticonvulsant drugs: an effect of hepatic enzyme induction? *Br Med J.* 1972;1:297–299.

80. Vilter RW. The vitamin B_6-hydrazide relationship. In: Harris RS, Loraine JA, Wool IG, eds. *Vitamins and Hormones.* New York, NY: Academic Press; 1964.

81. Kirkendall WM, Page EB. Polyneuritis occurring during hydralazine therapy: report of two cases and discussion of adverse reactions to hydralazine. *JAMA.* 1958;167:427–432.

82. Corcino J, Waxman S, Herbert V. Mechanism of triamterene-induced megaloblastosis. *Ann Intern Med.* 1970;73:419–424.

83. Lawrence VA, Lowenstein JE, Eichner ER. Aspirin and folate binding: in vivo and in vitro studies of serum binding and urinary excretion of endogenous folate. *J Lab Clin Med.* 1984;103: 944–948.

84. Day AT, Golding JR, Lee PN, et al. Penicillamine in rheumatoid disease: a long term study. *Br Med J.* 1974;1:180–183.

85. Wester PO. Zinc during diuretic treatment. *Lancet.* 1975;1:578.

86. Pawan GLS. Drugs and appetite. *Proc Nutr Soc.* 1974;33:239–244.

87. Syiel JN, Liddle GW, Lacey WW. Studies of the mechanism of cyproheptadine-induced weight gain in human subjects. *Metabolism.* 1970;19:192–200.

88. Paybel PS, Mueller PS, DeLa Vergne PM. Amitriptyline weight gain and carbohydrate craving: a side effect. *Br J Psychiatry.* 1973;123:501–507.

89. Morrison SD. Origins of anorexia in neoplastic disease. *Am J Clin Nutr.* 1978;31:1104–1107.

90. Banks T, Ali N. Digitalis cachexia. *N Engl J Med.* 1974;290:746.

91. Roe DA. Food, formula and drug effects on the disposition of nutrients. *World Rev Nutr Diet.* 1984;43:80–94.

92. Toothaker RD, Welling PG. The effect of food on drug bioavailability. *Annu Rev Pharmacol Toxicol.* 1980;20:173–199.

93. Rosenberg HA, Bates TR. The influence of food on nitrofurantoin bioavailability. *Clin Pharmacol Ther.* 1976;20:227–232.

94. Gibaldi M. *Biopharmaceutics and Clinical Pharmacokinetics*. Philadelphia, Pa: Lea & Febiger; 1977.

95. McLean AJ, Isbister C, Bobik A, et al. Reduction of first-pass hepatic clearance of propranolol by food. *Clin Pharmacol Ther*. 1981;30:31–34.

96. Lamy PP. *Prescribing for the Elderly*. Littleton, Mass: PSG Publishing Co Inc; 1980.

97. Gillespie NG, Mena I, Cotzias GS, et al. Diets effecting treatment of parkinsonism with levodopa. *J Am Diet Assoc*. 1973;62:525–532.

98. Nutt JG, Woodward WR, Hammerstad JP, et al. The "on-off" phenomenon in Parkinson's disease: relation to levodopa absorption and transport. *N Engl J Med*. 1984;310:483–488.

99. Nichols TW. Phytobezoar formation: a new complication of cimetidine therapy. *Ann Intern Med*. 1981;95:70–73.

100. Welling PG. Influence of food and diet on gastrointestinal drug absorption: a review. *J Pharmacokinet Biopharm*. 1977;5:291–315.

101. Evans MA, Triggs EJ, Cheung M. Gastric emptying in the elderly: implications for drug therapy. *J Am Geriatr Soc*. 1981;29:201–207.

102. McLennan WJ, Martin P, Mason BJ. Protein intake and serum albumin levels in the elderly. *Gerontology*. 1977;27:360–367.

103. Richey DP, Bender AD. Pharmacokinetic consequences of aging. *Annu Rev Pharmacol Toxicol*. 1977;17:49–65.

104. McDannell RE, McLean AEM. Role of nutritional status in drug metabolism and toxicity. In: Sidransky H, ed. *Nutritional Pathology*. New York, NY: Marcel Dekker Inc; 1985.

105. O'Malley K, Crooks J, Duke E, et al. Effect of age and sex on human drug metabolism. *Br Med J*. 1971;3:607–609.

106. Conney AH, Pantuck EJ, Kuntzman R, et al. Nutrition and the chemical biotransformation in man. *Clin Pharmacol Ther*. 1977;22:707–716.

107. Alvares AP, Anderson KE, Conney AH, et al. Interactions between nutritional factors and drug biotransformations in man. *Proc Natl Acad Sci USA*. 1976;73:2501–2504.

108. Mucklow JC, Caraher MT, Henderson DB, et al. Relationship between individual dietary constituents and antipyrine metabolism in Indo-Pakistani immigrants to Britain. *Br J Clin Pharmacol*. 1982;13:481–486.

109. Anderson KE, Conney AH, Kappas A. Nutrition and oxidative drug metabolism in man: relative influence of dietary lipids, carbohydrate and protein. *Clin Pharmacol Ther*. 1979;26:493–501.

110. Krishnaswamy K. Drug metabolism and pharmacokinetics in malnutrition. *Trans Pharmacol Sci*. 1983;4:295–297.

111. Krishnaswamy K, Naidu AN. Microsomal enzymes and malnutrition as determined by plasma half-life of antipyrine. *Br Med J*. 1977;1:538–542.

112. Pantuck EJ, Pantuck CB, Garland WA, et al. Stimulatory effect of Brussels sprouts and cabbage on human drug metabolism. *Clin Pharmacol Ther*. 1979;25:88–95.

113. Lasker JM, Wuang MT, Conney AH. In vivo activation of zoxazolamine metabolism by flavone. *Science*. 1982;216:1419–1421.

114. Garry PJ, Goodwin JS, Hunt MA, et al. Nutritional status in a healthy elderly population: dietary and supplemental intakes. *Am J Clin Nutr*. 1982;36:319–331.

115. Anonymous. Megavitamin E supplementation and vitamin K-dependent carboxylation. *Nutr Rev*. 1983;41:268–270.

116. Garbadian-Ruffalo SM. Alterations in drug effects secondary to vitamin supplementation. *Intern Med*. 1984;5:129–137.

117. Levy G, Leonards JR. Urine pH and salicylate therapy. *JAMA*. 1971;217:81.

118. Rosenthal G. Interaction of ascorbic acid with warfarin. *JAMA*. 1971;215:1671–1672.

119. Rall TN, Schleifer LS. Drugs effective in the therapy of the epilepsies. In: Gilman AG, Goodman LS, Gilman A, eds. *The Pharmacological Basis of Therapeutics*. New York, NY: Macmillan Publishing Co; 1980.

120. Roe DA. Drug-nutrient interactions in the elderly. *Geriatrics*. 1986;41:57–74.

121. Lamy PP. Effects of diet and nutrition on drug therapy. *J Am Geriatr Soc*. 1982;30:S99.

122. Nauss KM. Vitamin A and human response. *Nutr & MD*. 1982;8:1–5.

123. Ellis J, Folgers K, Levy M, et al. Therapy with vitamin B_6 with and without surgery for treatment of patient's idiopathic carpal tunnel syndrome. *Res Commun Chem Pathol Pharmacol*. 1981;33:331–335.

124. Older MWJ, Dickerson JWT. Thiamin and the elderly orthopaedic patient. *Age Ageing*. 1982; 11:101–106.

Chapter 14

Nutritional Assessment of the Elderly

Carol O. Mitchell and Ronni Chernoff

One of the more challenging aspects of providing nutrition to elderly individuals is the determination of their nutritional status. Aging has an effect on many of the commonly used anthropometric, biochemical, and hematologic analyses used to assess nutritional status in younger adults. Adding to the difficulty of evaluating results of these measures is the fact that people age at individual rates, therefore contributing to the heterogeneity of the older group. In order to make a considered judgment about the need for nutritional interventions or the possibility of nutritional depletion that may have an impact on health, it is necessary to conduct a thorough, multifaceted nutritional assessment that examines many aspects of the individual to present the most complete picture possible. To evaluate the individual adequately, a thorough nutritional assessment should be made, including appraisal of physical appearance, oral health, social and environmental situation, potential physical and psychologic disabilities, and medical and drug history; performance of anthropometric measurements; evaluation of biochemical, hematologic, and immune function; and obtainment of a comprehensive dietary history.

Conducting a comprehensive nutritional assessment is an important component of providing quality health care to elderly people; malnutrition may contribute to the depletion of reserve capacity, or the ability to respond rapidly and appropriately to a physiologic insult. Malnutrition may be unrecognized in elderly subjects because many of the changes that are seen with inadequate nutrition are often associated with changes that occur with aging. Severely malnourished individuals are easier to identify than those who are mildly or moderately malnourished, since they will not manifest the overt signs of malnutrition. Many health care professionals are not attuned to the important role that nutrition has in the maintenance of health throughout life; therefore, subclinical or marginal nutritional deficits may go unnoticed and undocumented.[1]

CLINICAL ASSESSMENT

Physical Assessment

Malnutrition is the consequence of chronically inadequate intake of essential nutrients.[2] Replenishment of normal tissue requires protein, energy, vitamins, and minerals in amounts adequate to replace old cells with new ones, to repair damaged cells and tissues, and to make substrate for protein compounds such as antigens, hormones, and enzymes. For many anabolic processes, vitamins and minerals serve as cofactors in metabolic cycles that drive these physiologic mechanisms. When chronic malnutrition of one or more essential nutrients exists, there may be physical manifestations that result and are associated with the primary functions of the deficient nutrients.[2] It is very important to look at the individual being assessed; a great deal can be ascertained about nutritional status by carefully assessing the state of hair, skin, nails, musculature, eyes, mucosa, and other physical attributes. Many of the consequences of specific nutrient deficiencies are listed in Table 14-1.

Another clinical manifestation associated with nutritional deficiencies in elderly people is fluid imbalance. Overhydration that contributes to edema is probably less of a nutritional problem than is dehydration. Presentation of dehydration in elderly individuals is described in Table 14-2. Dehydration is often caused by inadequate ingestion of free fluids and is a potentially precarious state for older people.[3,4] Total body water is decreased with changes in body composition that occur with aging—alterations in thirst and osmoreceptor sensitivities and impairment of renal capacity to conserve water or to concentrate urine efficiently.[5] Factors that may contribute to risk of dehydration in elderly subjects are listed in Table 14-3.

Many nutritional deficiencies are manifested in the oral cavity; therefore, an oral examination should be included in an assessment of nutritional status[6] (Chapter 6). The condition of an individual's mouth (number and looseness of teeth; presence of caries or plaque; presence of—or need for—dentures and how well they fit; condition of periodontal tissues and tongue; presence of lesions; and condition of the lips and skin around the mouth) can be evaluated easily without invasive procedures. Individuals who have difficulty in chewing because of loose teeth, poorly fitting dentures, or oral lesions have a tendency to eat soft foods, which are usually high in fat and refined carbohydrate and low in most essential nutrients. It is valuable to assess the individual's ability to chew, swallow, and self-feed while evaluating the condition of the teeth, tongue, gums, and oral mucosa. Poor oral status may be both the etiology and manifestation of poor nutrition.

Table 14-1 Clinical Signs of Nutritional Deficiencies*

Nutrient	Clinical Deficiency Symptoms
Vitamin A	Eyes—Bitot's spots; conjunctival and corneal xerosis (dryness); keratomalacia Skin—follicular hyperkeratosis; xerosis Hair—coiled, keratinized
Vitamin D	Bone—bowlegs; beading of ribs; pain; epiphyseal deformities
Vitamin E	Possible anemia
Vitamin K	Skin—subcutaneous hemorrhage; ecchymoses (bruises easily)
Thiamine (vitamin B₁)	Neurologic—mental confusion; irritability; sensory losses; weakness, parethesias; anorexia Eyes—ophthalmoplegia Cardiac—tachycardia; cardiomegaly; congestive heart failure Other—constipation; sudden death
Niacin (vitamin B₂)	Skin—nasolabial seborrhea; fissuring eyelid corners; angular fissures around mouth; papillary atrophy; pellagrous dermatitis Neurologic—mental confusion Other—diarrhea
Riboflavin	Skin—nasolabial seborrhea; fissuring and redness around eyes and mouth; magenta tongue; genital dermatosis Eyes—corneal vascularization
Pyridoxine (vitamin B₆)	Skin—nasolabial seborrhea; glossitis Neurologic—parethesias; peripheral neuropathy Other—anemia
Folic acid	Skin—glossitis; hyperpigmentation of tongue; pallor Neurologic—depression Other—diarrhea; anemia
Pantothenic acid	Other—headache; fatigue, apathy; nausea; sleep disturbances
Ascorbic acid (vitamin C)	Skin—petechiae, purpura; swollen, bleeding gums Other—bone pain; dental caries; depression; anorexia; delayed wound healing
Vitamin B₁₂	Skin—glossitis; skin hyperpigmentation; pallor Neurologic—ataxia; optic neuritis; parethesias; mental disorders Other—anemia; anorexia; diarrhea
Biotin	Skin—pluckable, sparse hair; pallor; seborrheic dermatitis Neurologic—depression Other—anemia; fatigue
Iron	Skin—pallor; angular fissures; glossitis; spoon nails; pale conjunctiva Other—enlarged spleen

Table 14-1 continued

Nutrient	Clinical Deficiency Symptoms
Zinc	Skin—seborrheic dermatitis; poor wound healing Eyes—photophobia Other—dysgeusia
Iodine	Other—large, swollen tongue; goiter
Protein	Skin—dull, dry, easily pluckable hair; "flaky paint" dermatitis; edema
Protein energy	Skin—loss of subcutaneous fat; dull, dry, easily pluckable hair; decubitus ulcers; muscle wasting

*Data compiled from several sources.

Physical Disabilities

Nutritional status may be affected by changes in physical ability to perform normal functions of life. Eating behavior is influenced by many factors, including taste and smell changes and the ability to feed oneself. These alterations may not be correctable, but they might be improved if they are first recognized as contributing to nutritional intake problems. Some of these changes occur slowly, and the individual adapts to them with little effort; others occur as the result of acute illness, and they require an intervention to accommodate them.

One change that occurs with aging, although at different rates among elderly people, is an alteration in taste and smell sensitivity. Diminishment in taste and

Table 14-2 Presentation of Dehydration in the Elderly

- Mucosal xerosis
- Swollen tongue
- Sunken eyeballs
- Elevated body temperature
- Decreased urine output
- Constipation
- Nausea and vomiting
- Decreased blood pressure
- Mental confusion
- Acute renal failure
- Altered drug effects
- Electrolyte disturbances

Table 14-3 Risk Factors for Dehydration in the Elderly

- Anorexia
- Laxative abuse
- Diuretic abuse
- Disability
- Confinement to chair or bed
- Depression
- Cognitive dysfunction
- Confusion
- Central nervous system impairment
- Diarrhea, vomiting, hemorrhage
- Incontinence
- Unconsciousness
- Dependence on tube or parenteral feeding
- Inability to feed self
- Presence of four or more chronic conditions
- Use of four or more medications
- Presence of chronic infections

smell acuity contribute to decreased enjoyment of food.[7] Bland, tasteless, odorless food will not be very appetizing and will not be eaten. Loss of certain taste sensations, particularly sweet and salt, may contribute to stronger sour or bitter taste sensations.[8] The magnitude and etiology of taste sensation remains somewhat controversial,[9–11] due in part to the accuracy and validity of the methodologies used in studying the senses of taste and smell; however, improved oral hygiene may help enhance taste sensations.[12] Unless an individual is deficient in zinc, vitamin A, or the B vitamins, supplementing the diet with these nutrients will not correct loss of taste.

Other sensory losses may affect nutrition, although in less direct ways. Loss of vision and hearing will contribute to social isolation and changes in eating behaviors. A decrease in visual acuity will limit shopping and cooking activities. Loss of hearing will also tend to restrict social activities.[13]

Physical disabilities that affect nutritional status in elderly people are related to chronic illnesses or problems with motor or cognitive function.[14,15] Chronic illness can affect appetite and alter nutrient needs, and eventually may lead to tube or parenteral feeding dependency (Chapter 15). Multiple chronic illnesses can lead to polypharmacy, which may have an impact on absorption, metabolism, and requirements for specific nutrients (Chapter 13). Assessing the types and doses of various prescription and over-the-counter medications is an essential component of a thorough nutritional assessment.

Motor skills that enable elderly individuals to remain independent are important factors in their health and nutrition maintenance. The ability to move around unencumbered by walkers or wheelchairs is important for getting out of the house or being restricted to living quarters. Fine motor skills are necessary for the preparation and consumption of food. Assessing an individual's ability to self-feed should be an essential component of a nutritional evaluation of individuals who have been institutionalized or have had a debilitating illness such as a stroke.

Cognitive and Psychologic Function

It is very difficult to prove a relationship between cognitive function and nutritional status, but tests with standardized instruments designed to measure abstract thinking and problem-solving ability suggest a correlation.[16] A case might be made for the effect of depressed nutritional status on these cognitive measures, but the causal relationship between these variables has not been determined. It is well recognized, however, that weight loss occurs in patients with senile dementia, such as Alzheimer's disease, but it is difficult to define the etiology of the weight loss.[17–19] Poor memory, loss of feeding skills, hyperactive behavior, anorexia associated with polypharmacy, and depression may contribute to poor dietary intake. Depression occurs commonly in institutionalized people and is recognized as a treatable cause of weight loss.[20] Changes in cognitive or psychologic function must be elicited from family members or care givers, and should be considered as possible etiologies in a chronically malnourished elderly patient.

Socioeconomic Factors

Exploring the environment in which elderly people live is important to an understanding of their nutrition and health status. Financial resources, living situation, degree of independence, level of education, and social support systems are all factors that may influence nutritional intake. Many elderly people live on a fixed income, which limits their purchasing power when the cost of living increases. Of course, there is a large population of older people who have financial resources to meet their needs, but many do not. The ability to purchase fresh fruits, vegetables, and meats may be limited, and this limitation may contribute to reliance on high-calorie, low-nutrient-density foods such as those high in carbohydrates and fats. Dietary supplements (eg, vitamin and mineral preparations), however, are used by some older individuals who probably do not require nutritional supplementation.[21]

Financial resource is a factor that determines living arrangements. Individuals who have adequate incomes may still live in their own homes. There are many alternatives to housing that are available for those who cannot afford to live alone or who need support in their activities of daily living, including group or foster homes, congregate living situations, retirement homes, and minimum to skilled care facilities. For elderly individuals who choose to live at home or alone, there are congregate meal programs, home meal programs, and home health aides. Several studies indicate that elderly people who live alone or in institutions have dietary intakes below recommended levels.[22,23]

Educational level is linked to both income and nutritional status. Several studies have indicated that level (years) of education is associated with the dietary intake of several nutrients, such as protein, iron, calcium, and several B vitamins.[22,24,25]

Health and nutritional status have also been linked with accessibility of social support systems. There appears to be a relationship between health status and social and community support systems, such as senior citizens' centers, churches, and other community groups.[26] This type of extended support system contributes to a sense of extended family and belonging to a caring group.

Examination of as many of these factors as possible in a nutritional assessment will contribute to a clearer picture of an individual's functional ability, life style, and health problems that may interfere with nutritional intake. A clinical assessment will add another dimension to the commonly used tools of nutritional assessment: anthropometric measurements; biochemical, hematologic, and immune evaluations; and dietary histories.

ANTHROPOMETRIC ASSESSMENT

The major physiologic effect of malnutrition, either undernutrition or overnutrition, is a detrimental alteration of body composition. Protein-energy malnutrition (PEM) is first evidenced by loss of lean body mass and fat tissue. If the loss of available energy reserve (undernutrition) is severe enough, it can result in a significantly increased incidence of morbidity or mortality. Obesity (overnutrition) is characterized by an abnormal increase in body fat tissue, contributing to an increased risk for many chronic diseases.

Anthropometry is the technique by which the severity and composition of these morphologic changes can be evaluated easily. It also provides a method of monitoring the appropriateness of nutritional therapy. The anthropometric measurements most commonly used for assessing nutritional status are height, body weight, circumferences, and skinfold thicknesses.[27] For various reasons, the usefulness of these measures as predictors of nutritional status in the elderly is questionable. Major benefits of anthropometry over other nutritional assessment procedures are the ease with which the measurements can be accomplished, their relatively low cost, and their noninvasive nature, all of which make anthropometry particularly desirable for use in an aged population. However, the ability to obtain adequate and reproducible data is dependent on being able to obtain accurate measurements, and many elderly individuals have physical impairments that make this difficult and often impossible. Another drawback of anthropometry is the lack of appropriate standards with which to compare results.

There are well-known physiologic changes in stature and body composition that occur with normal aging that must be considered when using anthropometric measurements to assess nutritional status.[28] A progressive decrease in height with age is well documented and has been attributed to changes in the integrity of the vertebral column, with postural changes due to generalized osteoporosis.[29-31] An average decrease in height of 1.2 cm per 20 years postmaturity for whites and blacks of both sexes has been reported;[32,33] other cross-sectional studies have estimated the rate of loss in stature to be between 0.5 and 1.5 cm per decade.[30,34-36] A more recent longitudinal study observed a decrease in stature of 0.5 cm per year in white, healthy, middle-class, elderly men and women.[37]

Weight and body composition have also been shown to change with age[38-43] (Figure 14-1). Weight tends to increase until the early 40s in men and the early 50s in women, to hold relatively steady for the next 15 to 20 years, and to decrease thereafter.[39,41-43] A decrease in lean body mass is characteristic of aging, regardless of energy intake.[40] Along with the loss of protein mass, there is an increase in the proportion of body weight as adipose tissue. There is approximately a 10% increase in total body fat in an elderly subject above that carried as a young adult. This increase in fat is not always visually evident because of the higher proportion of fat deposited around internal organs, particularly in women.[40] Subcutaneous fat on the extremities decreases with age, while fat tends to increase on the trunk.[44-46] This shift in body composition can complicate the interpretation of skinfold and circumference measurement data as predictors of total body fat.[47]

A major objective of anthropometry in nutritional assessment is to establish an individual's protein-energy reserve compared with normal ranges.[48] This presents a perplexing problem when using anthropometric measures to assess nutritional status in elderly subjects because of the lack of appropriate standards with which to compare the obtained data.[47] Therefore, extreme care must be used when interpreting results of anthropometric measures; anthropometry must be used in conjunction with clinical, laboratory, dietary, and psychosocial data.

Weight for Height

Almost all of the currently used indicators of appropriate body weight, as well as other measures of lean body mass, require knowledge of the individual's height. Accurate measurements of stature are particularly difficult to obtain from most aged subjects because the physical changes that occur with aging make it difficult or even impossible for many elderly people to stand erect. Chronic diseases, such

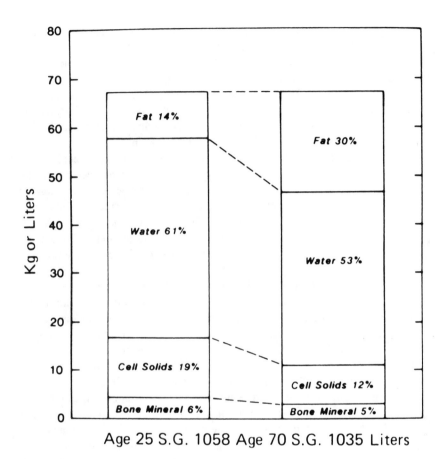

Age 25 S.G. 1058 Age 70 S.G. 1035 Liters

Figure 14-1 A comparison of body composition compartments in a 25-year-old man and a 75-year-old man. *Source:* Reprinted from *Biological Aspects of Aging*, (pp 59–78) by N.W. Shock (Ed) with permission of Columbia University Press, © 1962.

as arthritis, osteoporosis, and Parkinson-like disorders, which affect the neuromuscular systems, contribute to this problem. Individuals who have severe kyphosis (curvature of the spine) and bowing of the legs present major problems in obtaining accurate measures of height.[27]

Additional problems are related to the fact that these same diseases may result in an actual decrease in height due to a compression of the vertebral disc space.[31] Since height is used as a constant reference point in many weight/height-related measurements, it is difficult to know whether to use actual height as best measured or maximal height of the individual as a young adult.[49]

To measure stature in elderly subjects who are able to stand unaided in an erect position, the following standardized procedure, as described in the *Anthropometric Standardization Reference Manual*[50] and adapted for elderly subjects,[51] is recommended: The subjects should be measured without shoes and in little or light clothing to allow viewing of the position of the body. They should stand on a flat surface that is at a right angle to the vertical board of a stadiometer. They should stand up straight, with heels close together, legs as straight as possible, arms at the sides, and shoulders relaxed. The head should be in the Frankfort horizontal plane; ie, the line of vision should be perpendicular to the body; the headboard is then lowered onto the crown of the head. The subject should then take a deep breath; the stature measurement is recorded to the nearest 0.1 cm or ⅛ in at maximal inspiration. A repeated measurement should be taken to assure reliability and should agree within 1 cm or ½ in of the first measurement. The degree of kyphosis or bowing of the legs should be noted. A sliding bar attached to a beam balance may also be used to measure height; however, this device is generally less accurate.[47]

Because of the problems described, alternative methods for estimating stature in the elderly have been investigated.[52,53] Arm span is highly correlated with stature when an individual reaches his or her maximal height, before age-associated changes occur in the vertebral column.[28,54] Studies indicate that racial differences between American blacks and whites occur in the relationship between arm span and stature.[32] Arm span includes both arms and the breadth of the shoulders, and is measured with the subject's arms outstretched maximally. Problems similar to those encountered in measuring stature due to kyphosis, osteoporosis, and arthritis can prevent the use of arm span measurement in this group. As a result, total arm length (TAL) has been evaluated as an alternative measure.[52] TAL is measured from the tip of the acromial process of the scapula to the end of the styloid process of the ulna. This study indicates that, although height decreases with age, arm measurements do not change to the same degree. Therefore, it seems likely that TAL could be a useful value for the development of anthropometric standards for the elderly; however, further studies are required to determine the reliability and interpretation of this measurement before its routine clinical use can be advocated.[52]

For those elderly individuals who cannot stand erect, recumbent anthropometric techniques have been developed that can be used to estimate stature from knee height measurements[53]; weight can be estimated by using recumbent measurements of arm and calf circumferences, subscapular skinfold thickness, and knee height.[55] The clinical application of these and other recumbent measures, along with detailed descriptions of the measuring techniques, have been reported elsewhere.[51] For elderly individuals who have severe neuromuscular deformities, the best measurement of height may be obtained by measurement of individual body segments. Segment lengths should be measured between specific bony landmarks and as vertical distances between a flat surface and a bony landmark, but they should not be measured from joint creases[56] (Figure 14-2).

Weight

Body weight is one of the simplest and most routinely collected anthropometric indices used to monitor individuals,[57] and is used as a rough estimate of body energy stores. Body weight is a composite measure of total body size, reflecting everything inside the personal envelope,[58] but it provides no information relating to body composition. Absolute weight may stay constant over time, but the proportions of lean muscle mass and fat may change, as seen in many elderly individuals.[33]

To increase the reliability and reproducibility of repeated measures, standardized procedures should be followed.[59] The subject should always be weighed in the same type clothing, preferably in a lightweight gown or underclothing. Because of diurnal variations in weight, it is best to weigh at the same time of day, before eating and after voiding. These conditions should be recorded each time to help to understand extreme variations in the measurement.

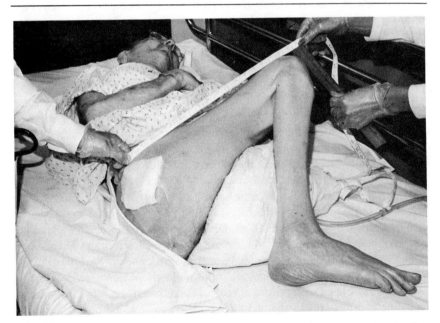

Figure 14-2 An example of segmental measurements in an elderly, cachectic, contracted patient. Measurement points are from one bony prominence to another bony landmark. (Courtesy of the John L. McClellan Memorial Veterans' Hospital.)

For ambulatory persons who can stand unaided, an upright beam scale with movable weights is the most accurate and reliable. One with a wide base and a hand support is best because most elderly individuals are unsteady and need this support to position themselves before accurate measurements can be taken. Subjects should stand with their feet over the center of the platform. Measurements should be recorded to the nearest 0.1 kg or ¼ lb. A chair scale may be needed for persons who are unable to stand unaided. For the nonambulatory, bedfast patient, it is necessary to use a bed scale; recumbent measures developed to estimate weight can be used.[55] Every scale should be calibrated periodically against a set of standard weights.

As with most nutritional assessment parameters, it is useful to be able to compare a given weight of an individual with that of an ideal weight for a healthy subject of the same sex, age, and stature. This presents a problem, however, since there are no universally accepted standards available for evaluation of weight in very old persons.[27] The Metropolitan Life Insurance Company height and weight tables for 1959[60] and 1983[61] are commonly used standards (Table 14-4). These tables represent weights associated with the lowest mortality rate for persons of various height and body frames. These data were compiled to represent persons up to age 59 years; however, the 1983 tables have been shown to be appropriate for older individuals.[62] Body frame is determined by measuring elbow breadth as described by Frisancho and Flegel.[63] A recent study comparing several reported methods of determining frame size showed that elbow breadth was not the most acceptable measure based on the assumptions inherent in use of frame size determinations.[64] No data exist on the reliability of determining frame size in very old people.

The National Center for Health Statistics has published reference data that include weights for older subjects up to age 74 years[65] (Table 14-5). These data make it possible to locate the 5th through 95th percentile values for weight of an elderly person of any given height. The 50th percentile value is probably a reasonable standard for most active elderly patients. It has been recommended that the 5th percentile value is the acceptable standard for completely inactive patients.[66]

Limited data on average or reference weight are available on persons over age 74 years. Master and Lasser[67] published average height-weight tables for persons aged 64 years and older (Table 14-6). Drawbacks associated with these data are that there were only a limited number of subjects included in the groups aged 85 years and older and that the subjects were predominantly white men and women and may not be representative of most elderly populations.[27] There are limitations associated with the use of each of the different standards. All of these should be considered, and the one most representative of the population being evaluated should be selected. It is important that the standards selected be recorded and used consistently by all members of the health care team.

Table 14-4 Metropolitan Life Insurance Company Height and Weight Tables, 1983

Height		Men		
Feet	Inches	Small Frame	Medium Frame	Large Frame
5	2	128–134	131–141	138–150
5	3	130–136	133–143	140–153
5	4	132–138	135–145	142–156
5	5	134–140	137–148	144–160
5	6	136–142	139–151	146–164
5	7	138–145	142–154	149–168
5	8	140–148	145–157	152–172
5	9	142–151	148–160	155–176
5	10	144–154	151–163	158–180
5	11	146–157	154–166	161–184
6	0	149–160	157–170	164–188
6	1	152–164	160–174	168–192
6	2	155–168	164–178	172–197
6	3	158–172	167–182	176–202
6	4	162–176	171–187	181–207

Weights at ages 25 to 59 years based on lowest mortality. Weight in pounds according to frame (in indoor clothing weighing 5 lb, shoes with 1-in heels).

Height		Women		
Feet	Inches	Small Frame	Medium Frame	Large Frame
4	10	102–111	109–121	118–131
4	11	103–113	111–123	120–134
5	0	104–115	113–126	122–137
5	1	106–118	115–129	124–140
5	2	108–121	118–132	128–143
5	3	111–124	121–135	131–147
5	4	114–127	124–138	134–151
5	5	117–130	127–141	137–155
5	6	120–133	130–144	140–159
5	7	123–136	133–147	143–163
5	8	126–139	136–150	146–167
5	9	129–142	139–153	149–170
5	10	132–145	142–156	152–173
5	11	135–148	145–159	155–176
6	0	138–151	148–162	158–179

Weights at ages 25 to 59 years based on lowest mortality. Weight in pounds according to frame (in indoor clothing weighing 3 lb, shoes with 1–in heels).

Table 14-5 Average Weights for U.S. Men and Women, 1971–1974

Sex and Height	Age Group (yr)			
	35–44	45–54	55–64	65–74
Men	Weight (lb)			
62 in	143	147	143	143
63 in	148	152	147	147
64 in	153	156	153	151
65 in	158	160	158	156
66 in	163	164	163	160
67 in	169	169	168	164
68 in	174	173	173	169
69 in	179	177	178	173
70 in	184	182	183	177
71 in	190	187	189	182
72 in	194	191	193	186
73 in	200	196	197	190
74 in	205	200	203	194
Women				
57 in	125	129	132	130
58 in	129	133	136	134
59 in	133	136	140	137
60 in	137	140	143	140
61 in	141	143	147	144
62 in	144	147	150	147
63 in	148	150	153	151
64 in	152	154	157	154
65 in	156	158	160	158
66 in	159	161	164	161
67 in	163	165	167	165
68 in	167	168	171	169

Estimated values from regression equations of weight on height for specified age groups.
NOTE: Examined persons were measured without shoes; clothing weight ranged from 0.20 to 0.62 lb, which was not deducted from weights shown.
Adapted from Weight by Height and Age for Adults 18–74 years: United States, 1971–74, Office of Health Research, Statistics and Technology, National Center for Health Statistics, U.S. Dept. of Health and Human Services.

A more clinically useful and predictive factor than relative body weight is the evaluation of changes in weight over a given period of time[57]; therefore, a careful history of previous weight gain or loss should be obtained. For a very old individual or an acutely ill, elderly patient, one must usually seek the help of a close family member or care provider to ascertain this information. Extreme differences in either weight gain or loss over very short durations are most probably related to shifts in fluid balance rather than to alterations in nutritional status.[68] Recommen-

Table 14-6 Average Height-Weight Table for Persons Aged 65 Years and Older

Height (in)	Men Ages 65–69	Ages 70–74	Ages 75–79	Ages 80–84	Ages 85–89	Ages 90–94
61	128–156	125–153	123–151			
62	130–158	127–155	125–153	122–148		
63	131–161	129–157	127–155	122–150	120–146	
64	134–164	131–161	129–157	124–152	122–148	
65	136–166	134–164	130–160	127–155	125–153	117–143
66	139–169	137–167	133–163	130–158	128–156	120–146
67	140–172	140–170	136–166	132–162	130–160	122–150
68	143–175	142–174	139–169	135–165	133–163	126–154
69	147–179	146–178	142–174	139–169	137–167	130–158
70	150–184	148–182	146–178	143–175	140–172	134–164
71	155–189	152–186	149–183	148–180	144–176	139–169
72	159–195	156–190	154–188	153–187	148–182	
73	164–200	160–196	158–192			

Height (in)	Women Ages 65–69	Ages 70–74	Ages 75–79	Ages 80–84	Ages 85–89	Ages 90–94
58	120–146	112–138	111–135			
59	121–147	114–140	112–136	100–122	99–121	
60	122–148	116–142	113–139	106–130	102–124	
61	123–151	118–144	115–144	109–133	104–128	
62	125–153	121–147	118–144	112–136	108–132	107–131
63	127–155	123–151	121–147	115–141	112–136	107–131
64	130–158	126–154	123–151	119–145	115–141	108–132
65	132–162	130–158	126–154	122–150	120–146	112–136
66	136–166	132–162	128–157	126–154	124–152	116–142
67	140–170	136–166	131–161	130–158	128–156	
68	143–175	140–170				
69	148–180	144–176				

dations for evaluating the significance of weight change over time have been published.[48] Similar recommendations specifically for evaluating the anorexia of aging were made at a recent conference on nutrition in the elderly.[69]

Skinfold and Circumference Measures

Body weight is one indication of available energy stores; however, it is desirable to evaluate the composition of these stores and the severity of loss of lean muscle tissue versus adipose tissue. Depletion of lean muscle mass is more critical because of the role protein plays in body function. At present, the most clinically applicable procedure for evaluating the degree of muscle loss and adipose mass depletion is anthropometry, particularly skinfold and circumference measurements. These techniques have particular limitations in elderly subjects, due in part to the previously mentioned physical alterations in body composition associated with aging. In addition to the changes in lean muscle tissue and adipose tissue, other factors exist that make these measures more difficult to interpret in elderly subjects. With aging there are changes in elasticity, hydration, and compressibility of the skin and changes in subcutaneous adipose and connective tissues that can alter the relationship of skinfold thickness measurements to body composition[70] as well as affect both the accuracy and precision of the skinfold measurements. Additional problems relating to technique become apparent when working with elderly subjects who have loose skin on the arms and upper body. Therefore, it is imperative that standardized techniques be used[59] and any major abnormalities in skin and fat distribution be noted.

Skinfold Measures

Skinfold measurements are relatively simple to obtain, are less affected by hydration status than is weight, and are independent of height. Skinfold measurements have been shown to correlate with body fat measured by more sophisticated techniques.[71-75] Formulas have been developed for predicting total body fat from one skinfold[76] and from multiple skinfold measurements.[71] Data from a large study of elderly subjects indicated that skinfold measurements on the trunk may be more reliable predictors of body fat in men, whereas skinfold measurements on the extremities seem to be more accurate in women.[72] In elderly people, the use of multiple skinfold measurements should add to the reliability of the predicted value of body fat. Numerous equations have been developed to determine body composition from skinfold measurements, all of which use various combinations of measurements from different sites.[77]

While there is no universal agreement about whether to use right-side or left-side body measures, it is very important that the same side of the body always be used for both skinfold and circumference measurements of a given subject. The most commonly used anatomic sites for skinfold measurements are triceps, biceps, subscapular, and suprailiac. The following methods for identifying these sites and performing the measurements are taken from the *Anthropometric Standardization Reference Manual*.[78]

Triceps skinfold is measured at a point midway between the lateral projection of the acromial process of the scapula and the inferior margin of the olecranon. This point is determined by using a tape measure with the subject's elbow flexed to 90°. The midpoint is marked on the lateral side of the arm. Subjects are measured while standing, if possible; if not, they should be propped upright in a chair or bed. The skinfold is measured with the arm hanging loosely and comfortably at the subject's side. The triceps skinfold is picked up with the left thumb and index finger, approximately 1 cm proximal to the marked level, and the calipers are applied to the skinfold at the marked level. The skinfold should be held for the duration of the measurement. The measurement site must be in the midline posteriorly when the palm is directed anteriorly.

Biceps skinfold is measured by lifting the skin on the anterior aspect of the upper arm, directly above the center of the cubital fossa at the same level as the triceps skinfold. The crest of the fold should run parallel to the long axis of the arm. The subject stands, facing the measurer, with the arm relaxed at the side and the palm directed anteriorly.

Subscapular skinfold is measured by lifting the skin 1 cm under the inferior angle of the scapula with the shoulder and arm relaxed at the side of the body. To locate the site, the measurer palpates the scapula, running the fingers inferiorly and laterally along its vertebral border until the inferior angle is identified. For obese or elderly subjects, gentle placement of the subject's arm behind the back aids in identifying the site. The skinfold thickness is recorded to the nearest 0.1 cm.

Suprailiac skinfold is measured in the midaxillary line immediately superior to the iliac crest. The skinfold is grasped just posterior (about 2 cm) to the midaxillary line, following the natural cleavage lines of the skin. The crest of the fold should be horizontal. The caliper jaws are applied about 1 cm from the fingers holding the skinfold, and the thickness is recorded to the nearest 0.1 cm.

Equations for calculating total body fat and fat-free mass from the sum of the four skinfold measurements are given in Table 14-7. The most widely used data for evaluating skinfold and circumference measurements in elderly subjects are those from a cross-sectional sampling of American subjects aged 25 to 74 years from the national Health and Nutrition Examination Surveys I and II.[65] These data are presented in Tables 14-8 and 14-9. Recently available percentile norms for upper-arm anthropometry in white men and women aged 60 to 89 years are presented in Table 14-10.[79]

Circumference Measurements

Circumferences are measurements that record the size of cross-sectional and circumferential dimensions of the body. They can be used alone, in combination with skinfold measurements, or in combination with other circumferences to help evaluate nutritional status. Specific techniques for measuring circumferences have been described.[80] These measurements require the use of a tape measure, which should be flexible but nonstretchable and should have markings on only one side, in either metric or English units. Circumferences should be recorded with the zero end of the tape held in the left hand above the remaining part of the tape, which is

Table 14-7 Calculation of Fat and Fat-Free Mass

1. Determine the patient's age and weight in kilograms
2. Measure the following skinfolds in millimeters: biceps, triceps, subscapular, suprailiac
3. Compute Σ by adding four skinfold values
4. Compute the logarithm of Σ
5. Apply one of the following age- and sex-adjusted equations to calculate body density (D)(g/mL):

Equations for men:

Age Range (y)	
17–19	$D = 1.1620 - 0.0630 \times (\log \Sigma)$
20–29	$D = 1.1631 - 0.0632 \times (\log \Sigma)$
30–39	$D = 1.1422 - 0.0544 \times (\log \Sigma)$
40–49	$D = 1.1620 - 0.0700 \times (\log \Sigma)$
50+	$D = 1.1715 - 0.0779 \times (\log \Sigma)$

Equations for women:

Age Range (y)	
17–19	$D = 1.1549 - 0.0678 \times (\log \Sigma)$
20–29	$D = 1.1599 - 0.0717 \times (\log \Sigma)$
30–39	$D = 1.1423 - 0.0632 \times (\log \Sigma)$
40–49	$D = 1.1333 - 0.0612 \times (\log \Sigma)$
50+	$D = 1.1339 - 0.0645 \times (\log \Sigma)$

6. Fat mass is then calculated as:

$$\text{Fat mass (kg)} = \text{body weight (kg)} \times [(4.95/D) - 4.5]$$

7. Fat-free mass is then calculated as:

$$\textit{Fat-free mass (kg)} = \text{body weight (kg)} - \text{fat mass (kg)}$$

Source: Reprinted with permission from JV Durnin and J Womersley, "Body fat assessed from total body density and its estimation from skinfold thickness" in *British Journal of Nutrition* (1974;32:77), Copyright © 1974, Cambridge University Press.

---

held by the right hand. The tape should be maintained in a horizontal position, touching the skin and following the contours of the limb, but not compressing underlying tissue. The tension applied to the tape by the evaluator affects the validity and reliability of the measurement. The mid-upper arm circumference is measured at the midpoint between the acromial process of the scapula and olecranon. This location is the same as that marked for the triceps and biceps skinfolds. The measurement is made with the elbow extended and the arm relaxed and hanging just away from the side of the trunk, with the palm facing the thigh.

Table 14-8 Average Mid-Upper-Arm Muscle Circumference in Adults

Age (y)	Average Circumference (cm)	
	Men	Women
45–54	28.2	22.7
55–64	27.8	22.8
65–74	26.8	22.8

Source: Reprinted with permission from *American Journal of Clinical Nutrition* (1981;34:2530), Copyright © 1981, American Society for Clinical Nutrition.

The mid-upper-arm circumference (MAC), in conjunction with the triceps skin-fold (TSF) measurement, can be used to calculate the arm-muscle circumference (AMC) and the arm-muscle area (AMA), both of which are estimates of the amount of muscle or lean tissue in the body. Formulas that can be used for these calculations are as follows:

1. AMC (cm) = MAC (cm) − (3.14 × TSF (mm))
2. AMA (cm²) = AMC²/12.56

Reference standards are given in Tables 14-8 and 14-9.

Another measure of lean body mass (LBM) is the creatinine height index (CHI), which has been used to assess nutritional status in the elderly.[81] Creatinine is formed irreversibly from the metabolism of creatine and creatine phosphate found primarily in muscle tissue. The daily production of creatinine is related to the total LBM content of the body, and has been shown to be remarkably consistent from day to day.[82] The CHI has been adopted for evaluation of LBM in young, healthy adults and in hospitalized patients who may be protein-energy malnourished.

Table 14-9 Average Triceps Skinfold Thickness in Adults

Age (y)	Average Thickness (mm)	
	Men	Women
35–44	12	23
45–54	11	25
55–64	11	25
65–74	11	23

Source: Reprinted from 1971–1975 National Health Survey, Vital and Health Statistics Series No. 219, U.S. Department of Health and Human Services, Public Health Service, 1981.

Table 14-10 Percentile Norms for Measurements of Upper-Arm Anthropometry

Sex and Age (y) Group	No. in Sample	Mean	5th	10th	25th	50th	75th	90th	95th
Triceps skinfold thickness									
— mm —									
Women									
60–89	496	25.2	12.5	14.4	18.5	24.0	30.8	38.1	43.6
60–69	146	27.2 ± 10.2*	13.0	14.7	20.7	26.2	33.0	40.3	47.2
70–79	239	25.1 ± 9.3	13.0	15.0	18.0	23.7	31.0	38.3	41.5
80–89	111	23.3 ± 9.7	10.9	12.9	16.7	21.8	27.5	34.6	43.4
Men									
60–89	250	22.5	5.7	7.6	11.5	20.4	31.8	42.1	45.8
60–69	86	21.9 ± 13.6	4.9	6.9	10.8	18.0	31.9	45.1	49.3
70–79	115	23.5 ± 13.3	6.3	7.9	12.0	22.0	32.7	41.8	45.4
80–89	49	21.6 ± 11.0	5.8	8.0	11.5	21.0	29.6	37.5	40.5
Mid-upper-arm circumference									
— cm —									
Women									
60–89	496	30.0	23.3	25.1	27.0	29.7	32.7	35.9	38.1
60–69	146	31.1 ± 4.8	23.5	25.6	27.7	30.6	33.7	37.5	39.9
70–79	239	30.0 ± 4.1	23.5	25.5	27.1	29.5	32.5	35.5	37.8
80–89	111	28.8 ± 4.6	22.5	23.5	26.0	28.8	31.6	34.5	36.4
Men									
60–89	250	30.4	24.9	26.6	28.7	30.4	32.2	34.6	36.3
60–69	86	30.5 ± 3.0	25.1	27.3	29.0	30.5	32.4	34.2	35.7
70–79	115	30.7 ± 3.1	25.3	26.8	29.0	30.7	32.4	34.6	36.6
80–89	49	29.6 ± 3.5	23.4	24.9	27.6	29.6	31.5	35.3	36.5
Mid-upper-arm muscle circumference									
— cm —									
Women									
60–89	496	22.0	16.7	17.7	19.8	21.9	24.3	26.9	28.3
60–69	146	22.6 ± 3.6	17.8	18.4	20.2	22.3	24.6	27.5	29.2
70–79	239	22.1 ± 3.5	16.7	17.8	19.8	21.9	24.2	26.7	28.2
80–89	111	21.4 ± 4.1	15.2	16.7	19.1	21.3	24.2	26.7	27.5
Men									
60–89	250	23.3	16.6	18.1	20.5	23.4	26.2	28.4	29.7
60–69	86	23.7 ± 4.4	16.1	18.0	20.5	23.7	26.7	28.9	31.7
70–79	115	23.3 ± 4.1	17.0	18.2	20.4	23.4	26.3	28.4	28.7
80–89	49	22.8 ± 3.3	16.6	18.2	20.7	22.8	24.9	27.3	28.6

continues

Table 14-10 continued

Sex and Age (y) Group	No. in Sample	Mean	Percentile						
			5th	10th	25th	50th	75th	90th	95th
Mid-upper-arm muscle area									
					cm²				
Women									
60–89	496	39.9	22.2	25.0	31.1	38.0	47.1	57.7	63.8
60–69	146	41.6 ± 13.5	25.1	27.0	32.6	39.6	48.3	60.3	67.6
70–79	239	39.8 ± 12.7	22.1	25.1	31.2	38.0	46.7	56.6	63.2
80–89	111	37.9 ± 13.3	18.4	22.3	29.0	36.1	46.5	56.8	60.2
Men									
60–89	250	44.6	22.0	26.2	33.5	43.6	54.4	64.1	70.4
60–69	86	46.0 ± 16.5	20.7	25.8	33.4	44.8	56.8	66.7	79.7
70–79	115	44.6 ± 14.6	23.0	26.4	33.3	43.7	54.8	64.3	65.7
80–89	49	42.3 ± 11.8	21.9	26.5	34.2	41.5	49.4	59.1	64.9

*Mean ± standard deviation.

Source: Adapted from G Falciglia, "Upper arm anthropometric norms in elderly white subjects." Copyright The American Dietetic Association. Adapted by permission from *Journal of the American Dietetic Association*, Vol. 85: 1296, 1985.

Several problems are associated with this measurement as a clinical tool in elderly individuals. The measurement requires an accurately timed, 24-hour urine collection, which is very difficult (and often impossible) to obtain from elderly patients. In addition, creatinine excretion must be related to an individual's measured height, which sometimes is difficult to obtain in elderly subjects, as discussed previously. Another problem relates to the fact that LBM decreases with age, and with this decrease there will be a decrease in creatinine excretion unrelated to nutritional status. Many elderly individuals have compromised renal function; if this is the case, urinary creatinine excretion may not be a reliable measure.[83] The usefulness of the CHI as a tool with which to predict PEM in an elderly population has been evaluated.[47] This research indicated that CHI was a more accurate predictor of PEM in elderly men than in elderly women.

BIOCHEMICAL MEASURES

A number of biochemical measures are available for use in the assessment of nutritional status. They can be categorized into two groups based on the diagnostic ability of the results.[83] The first group relies on nonspecific indices of nutritional status, and the second group uses nutrient-specific indices of nutritional status. The first group includes determinations of the plasma proteins, which are usually easier to obtain than the nutrient-specific analyses that can detect subclinical micronutrient deficiencies.

As with anthropometric measures, problems exist with the use of biochemical indices in the assessment of elderly people. Factors other than nutrient intake are known to influence biochemical marker levels in the body. General state of health; past and present history of diseases; and use and abuse of alcohol, tobacco, medications, and over-the-counter drugs can produce alterations in biochemical data. These factors are of particular concern in elderly individuals. There is also a lack of age-adjusted reference data for appropriate interpretation of available results.

Protein

Several biochemical measurements are available that reflect dietary protein intake as well as body protein stores. Among these, analyses of serum albumin, transferrin, and total iron-binding capacity (TIBC) are the most readily available and least expensive. Transport proteins with more rapid turnover (eg, prealbumin and retinol-binding protein) may be more sensitive to changes in protein nutriture, but tests for these are less readily available. The level of circulating serum albumin is the most consistently used measure of visceral protein status because of its high reliability as a prognostic marker of PEM. Albumin is the major visceral protein produced by the liver, and its synthesis is dependent on an adequate supply of protein and, to a lesser degree, total energy intake.[84] It has been used extensively as a marker of the degree of PEM, has been shown to correlate positively with postsurgical outcome,[85] and has been reported to be a good prognostic indicator of hospital survival in elderly patients.[86]

Serum albumin levels appear to be only minimally affected by aging, although some studies indicate a slight reduction in the rate of albumin synthesis in aged subjects.[87] Hypoalbuminemia has been shown to be a reliable predictor of protein malnutrition in elderly people.[47,88] In a recent study evaluating several nutritional indices for their predictive ability of mortality of elderly hospitalized patients, a serum albumin level of <3 gm/dl was found to be the best single predictor of mortality; it has been suggested that this value could provide early identification of elderly people who are at increased risk of death.[86]

Even though decreased albumin levels are almost always present in malnourished individuals, caution, along with astute clinical judgment, must be exercised in their interpretation. Many of the concurrent diseases that are common in elderly people are known to alter plasma protein concentrations. Therefore, depressed serum albumin levels due to diminished production in liver diseases, and excess losses as a consequence of renal or gastrointestinal disease or protein-losing enteropathy, must be ruled out before this measure can be used as a reliable indicator of nutritional status. In addition, plasma albumin concentrations are directly influenced by hydration status. Any situation that results in a decrease in plasma volume will cause an artificially high serum albumin level unrelated to protein intake or albumin synthesis. Depressed levels of serum albumin are seen when plasma volume is expanded, as would occur in a patient with congestive heart failure or renal disease. Albumin values in these individuals might appear to be deceptively low and unrelated to nutritional status. Very old and acutely ill elderly patients are often confined to bed for extended periods of time, which can contribute to depressed albumin levels.[89]

After taking into account the clinical findings described above, a serum albumin level of less than 3.5 gm/dl is suggestive of chronic PEM and warrants further evaluation. Albumin has a relatively long half-life (approximately 14 to 20 days), which explains its slow response to nutritional therapy. A refeeding period of at least 2 weeks usually is required before consistent improvement in serum albumin levels can be noted. Aggressive refeeding in a severely malnourished elderly patient often will result in a further decrease in serum albumin level before an increase is seen. This phenomenon is attributed to the redistribution of extracellular and intracellular fluids.

Another major visceral protein often used for monitoring nutrition status is serum transferrin. It is usually considered a more sensitive marker of protein nutriture than albumin, because its half-life is approximately 9 days. However, its usefulness in an aged population is complicated by the fact that there is a strong negative correlation between circulating transferrin and tissue iron stores.[90,91] With advancing age, tissue iron stores increase and, as a result, serum transferrin levels are reduced.[92,93] Thus, some healthy elderly individuals may have transferrin values in the range commonly associated with nutritional deficiency.[94] This fact should always be considered before assuming that reductions in transferrin levels are due to protein malnutrition. Conversely, in individuals who have decreased iron stores, serum transferrin may be within the normal range, even in the presence of PEM.[94]

Often direct measures of serum transferrin are not available, necessitating the estimation of transferrin from TIBC.[93] This is usually accomplished by using the following formula:

$$[\text{TIBC (mg/dL)} \times 0.8] - 43$$

This may not be the best formula to use in all circumstances, however, and it has been suggested that each laboratory run its own regression analysis to determine a laboratory-specific formula for the estimation of transferrin levels from TIBC.[83]

Thyroxine-binding prealbumin (PA) and retinol-binding protein (RBP) are two serum proteins synthesized in the liver that have very rapid turnover rates and small body pool sizes; they are therefore sensitive to any changes affecting their synthesis and catabolism.[95] Because of these properties, they may be excellent indicators of subclinical malnutrition and may aid in the long-term management and monitoring of high-risk elderly patients.[96]

RBP is a glycoprotein with a half-life of approximately 12 hours; it is involved in the transport of retinol from the liver to peripheral tissues. Its synthesis is responsive to the need for retinol transport; therefore, circulating serum levels may reflect vitamin A status, not just protein nurture. In addition, inflated levels of RBP can be seen in patients with renal failure, and the levels may be depressed in patients with liver disease. RBP circulates while bound to PA as a PA-RBP complex. PA has a half-life of 2 days and is responsible for the transport of thyroxine. Its synthesis is not dependent on vitamin A status.

The concentration of PA-RBP complex is decreased in the presence of protein-energy metabolism, responds positively to nutritional therapy, and has been shown to be useful as a prognostic indicator of nutritional status.[97–100] However, like albumin, both RBP and PA are acute-phase reactants and therefore are directly affected by infections and inflammatory states. PA is considered a negative acute-phase reactant because levels decrease after acute stress. This decrease is due to an interruption of hepatic synthesis rather than to increased catabolism or urinary excretion,[101] and is influenced by hormonal changes rather than lack of available nutritional substrate. Discretion should be used before ascribing any change in these proteins to nutritional circumstances if either of these conditions exists. There are no data to indicate that RBP and PA are altered in elderly people. However, more research is needed to determine the effect of aging on the synthesis and catabolism of these visceral proteins.

IMMUNOLOGIC MEASURES

The association between nutritional status and immunocompetence is complex and multifactorial.[102–105] However, one of the strong associations noted is that PEM is accompanied by a reduction in host defense, demonstrated by anergy measured by delayed cutaneous hypersensitivity and lymphocytopenia. Immunologic dysfunction is associated with infections, cancer, and autoimmune diseases and may be a serious problem in elderly adults.

The immune system does not function as efficiently in older individuals as it does in younger individuals. The cell-mediated immune system is related to the T cell system, which is responsible for the delayed cutaneous hypersensitivity response; responses to certain autoimmune diseases; responses to some bacteria, viruses, and fungi; and responses to cancers. An absolute decrease in the number of T cells with a relative increase in the number of T suppressor cells has been described in elderly subjects.[94,106] One explanation is a progressive decline in thymic function and the production of thymic hormone with advanced age. These factors contribute to the increase in immature lymphocytes and the related decrease in helper/inducer T lymphocytes.[106] These and other changes that occur in immune function are very similar to the changes that are often seen with PEM.[107,108]

The most commonly used assay for immunocompetence is antigen-recall skin testing. The ability to demonstrate a response to recall antigens diminishes with age.[109,110] This same effect has been demonstrated in PEM.[103,109,110] The similarity of the effects of the aging process and those of PEM on immune function makes the usefulness of routine immunologic testing in elderly subjects difficult to interpret. A relationship between anergy and mortality in a nursing home population has been shown,[111] and there appears to be evidence that restoration of some immune function in malnourished, elderly patients can be induced by nutritional repletion.[106] The contribution of measures of immune function to the assessment of nutritional status in elderly people is difficult to isolate and therefore must be evaluated within the context of all the previously identified parameters.

HEMATOLOGIC MEASURES

Epidemiologic evidence indicates that anemia is fairly common among elderly subjects.[112,113] (Chapter 10). Whether the anemia is related to the aging process or to nutritional factors is difficult to determine. There is a strong similarity between the alterations in hematologic function seen with advancing age and those seen with PEM. In a study that examined multiple indicators of nutritional status in malnourished, elderly subjects, refeeding corrected most nutritional indicators (weight, serum albumin level, vitamin and mineral levels) but did not correct immunologic and hematologic indices (eg, hemoglobin level).[94]

Hematologic indices such as hematocrit, hemoglobin level, and total lymphocyte count are often available in the medical record since they are routinely obtained on admission to the hospital; they should be followed and changes noted. In a free-living or long-term care environment where complete blood counts are not obtained on a regular basis, it is probably more valuable to follow other nutritional indicators that will provide more reliable nutritional data, such as weight, serum albumin level, and dietary intake.

DIETARY ASSESSMENT

Dietary assessment of elderly subjects should provide insight into both present and past nutrient consumption habits. Finding the methods that can best accomplish this task is complicated by the physical and psychologic impairments often seen in this group. While quantitative methods often may be impossible, a qualitative assessment can be used to identify those individuals who are at risk for nutrient deficiencies. These methods should be able to uncover those who are having problems consuming an adequate diet, those who limit their intake to one or two foods or categories of food, those who follow unusual dietary patterns, or those who exclude an important food or food group.[114] Methods available for collecting dietary intake data include diet histories with food frequency checks, food records kept over a specific time period, and 24-hour dietary recalls. All of these methods rely on the cooperation of the elderly subject and the knowledge and skills of the interviewer. Many hospitalized and institutionalized elderly patients are not competent enough to provide accurate self-reported dietary intake information. When this is encountered, the use of a surrogate source is advocated; surrogates include the spouse, child, or close relative or friend of the patient. For a very old individual, it may be difficult to find a person who can provide data adequate to reflect an accurate description of eating habits. In a recent review of the use of surrogate measures of dietary intake in elderly subjects, it was concluded that surrogate dietary data may introduce misclassification in analytic investigations but that it may be useful in descriptive studies.[115]

Dietary histories elicit information regarding what subjects generally eat, and are based on food frequency checklists. Checklists should be constructed so that food intake over time can be estimated and should minimize the variation of day-to-day intake. Additional data should be gathered concerning food likes and dislikes; socioeconomic factors such as transportation availability, cooking facilities, and income status; information on health-related special dietary requirements; and use of alcohol and over-the-counter drugs. In a recent review by Hankin,[116] the following recommendations were made regarding the development of a diet history questionnaire for studies of older persons:

1. The questionnaire should include items that are representative of the population's usual diet to permit valid associations with biochemical and clinical findings. Both regional and ethnic foods should be included.
2. The questionnaire should provide both qualitative and quantitative information on the usual intake of foods, nutrients, and other dietary components. This can best be accomplished through the use of visual prompts: food models, common household measuring equipment, or actual photographs of serving sizes of different foods.
3. The questionnaire should be objective. Food items and groups should be clearly defined, the range of serving sizes specified, and the method of recording frequencies clearly presented. This will help to reduce variations among interviewers and will increase clarity and comprehension among the older subjects.

4. The validity of the questionnaire must be determined as accurately as possible.
5. The reproducibility of the questionnaire should be assessed by pretesting it on a random sample of the study population on two different occasions and assessing agreement of the two sets of data. This will also help identify potential problems that may occur in the administration of the instrument.

A simplified diet history questionnaire may be adequate for use in an elderly population, because the diets of these individuals are usually less varied than those of younger subjects. This is a result of the physiologic, sociologic, and economic changes that are often encountered in this group.[116] Dietary history and food frequency questionnaires, if administered properly, are very time consuming and require a well-trained, experienced professional interviewer. The subjectivity involved in describing a usual eating pattern makes this method vulnerable to memory lapses and psychologic tendencies to exaggerate or minimize self-described behavior.[117]

Another method often used to assess the nutrient intake of free-living elderly persons is the self-written dietary food record. A 7-day record is considered to be of an optimal length to obtain a more representative sample of usual intake. The food record technique places most of the responsibility on the subject, and is therefore less time consuming for the interviewer. However, this method can be used reliably only for individuals who are well motivated and who can read and write. Level of education is often a factor in determining who will complete a 7-day record[118]; the length of the food record is often a factor relating to compliance. The accuracy of record keeping has been shown to decline before the end of 7 days[118]; therefore, for an older person a 3-day record may be adequate, but it should include one weekend day. Physical abnormalities, such as arthritis or uncontrollable tremors as a result of neurologic damage, may make it very difficult for some elderly people to write. Alterations in eating patterns are often noted by individuals who record their intakes.

The 24-hour recall is used more often than any other technique for assessing dietary intake and the subsequent nutrient status of free-living as well as institutionalized or hospitalized elderly people. The reliability of this method has been questioned for use in this group.[119] Factors that may interfere with the reliability of the method relate to dependence on memory; short-term memory is one of the first physiologic functions to show changes with advancing age.

CONCLUSION

Assessing nutritional status in elderly individuals is a challenging task for nutrition professionals because of the age- and disease-related alterations of parameters commonly used to evaluate nutritional condition. To assess nutritional status properly, a multifaceted evaluation of the individual is necessary to develop a comprehensive picture of nutritional state. A thorough evaluation should include a physical assessment, including an examination of skin, hair, nails, eyes, oral mucosa, and musculature; fluid balance; physical disability; sensory losses; medical, cognitive, and psychologic problems; and socioeconomic conditions. Measures of body composition, such as anthropometric measures including height, weight, skinfold thicknesses, and muscle circumferences can be used to estimate protein and energy stores. Biochemical, immunologic, and hematologic assessments contribute to a more comprehensive evaluation of nutritional status and provide some valuable biomarkers by which to track changes in nutritional status over time. A dietary history will contribute to a more complete profile of an individual's nutritional state and may serve to identify potential nutritional problems that are not obvious to the observer.

An evaluation of nutritional status will help to detect individuals who are at risk for malnutrition before the overt presentation of such a condition. Malnutrition may interfere with the successful treatment of acute medical conditions, with the ability of an individual to recover from an insult or injury, or with an adequate response by the immune system to fight infection. Nutrition assessment will help to identify patients who may benefit from successful nutritional intervention before heroic measures are needed to restore nutritional integrity.

REFERENCES

1. Buzina R, Bates CJ, van der Beek J, et al. Workshop on functional significance of mild-to-moderate malnutrition. *Am J Clin Nutr.* 1989;50:172–176.

2. McLaren DS. Clinical manifestations of nutritional disorders. In: Shils ME, Young VR, eds. *Modern Nutrition in Health and Disease.* 7th ed. Philadelphia, Pa: Lea & Febiger; 1988.

3. Lavizzo-Mourey R, Johnson J, Stolley P. Risk factors for dehydration among elderly nursing home residents. *J Am Geriatr Soc.* 1988;36:213–218.

4. Chernoff R, Lipschitz DA. Nutrition and aging. In: Shils ME, Young VR, eds. *Modern Nutrition in Health and Disease.* 7th ed. Philadelphia, Pa: Lea & Febiger; 1988.

5. Rowe J. Renal system. In: Rowe JW, Besdine RW, eds. *Health and Disease in Old Age.* Boston, Mass: Little Brown & Co; 1982.

6. Knapp A. Nutrition and oral health in the elderly. *Dent Clin North Am.* 1989;33(1):109–125.

7. Jurdi-Haldeman D, Napier AK. Perceived relationships between taste and smell acuity and food intake in the elderly. *Top Clin Nutr.* 1988;3(4):4–8.

8. Rosenberg IH, Russell RM, Bowman BB. Aging and the digestive system. In: Munro HN, Danford DE, eds. *Nutrition, Aging, and the Elderly.* New York, NY: Plenum Publishing Corp; 1989.

9. Grzegorczyk PB, Jones SW, Mistretta CM. Age related differences in salt taste acuity. *J Gerontol.* 1979;34:834–840.

10. Miller IJ. Human taste bud density across adult age groups. *J Gerontol.* 1988;43(1):B26–30.

11. Chauhan J, Hawrysh ZJ, Gee M. et al. Age-related olfactory and taste changes and interrelationships between change and nutrition. *J Am Diet Assoc.* 1987;87:1543–1550.

12. Langan MJ, Yearick ES. The effects of improved oral hygiene in taste perception and nutrition of the elderly. *J Gerontol.* 1976;31:413–418.

13. Chernoff R. Aging and nutrition. *Nutr Today.* 1987;22(2):4–11.

14. Chernoff R. Nutrition and chronic conditions. *Top Geriatr Rehabil.* 1989;5(1):69–78.

15. Kohrs MB, Czajka-Narins DM, Nordstrom JW. Factors affecting nutritional status of the elderly. In: Munro HN, Danford DE, eds. *Nutrition, Aging, and the Elderly.* New York, NY: Plenum Publishing Corp; 1989.

16. Goodwin JS, Goodwin JM, Garry PJ. Association between nutritional status and cognitive functioning in a healthy elderly population. *JAMA.* 1983;249:2917–2921.

17. Franklin CA, Karkeck J. Weight loss and senile dementia in an institutionalized elderly population. *J Am Diet Assoc.* 1989;89(6):790–792.

18. Sandeman P, Adolfsson R, Nygren C, et al. Nutritional status and dietary intake in institutionalized patients with Alzheimer's disease and multiinfarct dementia. *J Am Geriatr Soc.* 1987;35:31.

19. Chandra V, Bharucha NE, Schoenberg BS. Conditions associated with Alzheimer's disease at death: case-control study. *Neurology.* 1986;36:209.

20. Morley JE. Death by starvation: a modern American problem? *J Am Geriatr Soc.* 1989; 37:184–185. Editorial.

21. Gray GE, Paganini-Hill A, Ross RK. Dietary intake and nutrient supplement use in a Southern California retirement community. *Am J Clin Nutr.* 1983;38:122–128.

22. O'Hanlon P, Kohrs MB, Hilderbrand E, et al. Socioeconomic factors and dietary intake of elderly Missourians. *J Am Diet Assoc.* 1983;82:646–653.

23. Baker H, Frank O, Thind IS, et al. Vitamin profiles in elderly persons living at home or in nursing homes, versus profile in healthy young subjects. *J Am Geriatr Soc.* 1979;27:444–450.

24. Singer JD, Granahan P, Goodrich NN, et al. Diet and iron status, a study of relationships: United States, 1971–1974. *Vital Health Stat* [11]. 1982;229.

25. McGandy RB, Russell RM, Hartz SC, et al. Nutritional status survey of healthy noninstitutionalized elderly: energy and nutrient intakes from three day records and nutrient supplements. *Nutr Res.* 1986;6:785–798.

26. McIntosh WA, Shifflet PA. Influence of social support systems on dietary intake of the elderly. *J Nutr Elderly.* 1984;4(fall):5.

27. Blackburn GL, Bistrian BR, Maini BS. Nutritional and metabolic assessment of the hospitalized patient. *J Parenter Enter Nutr.* 1977;1:11–22.

28. Mitchell CO, Lipschitz DA. Detection of protein-calorie malnutrition in the elderly. *Am J Clin Nutr.* 1982;35:398–406.

29. Rossman J. The anatomy of aging. In: Rossman J, ed. *Clinical Geriatrics.* Philadelphia, Pa: JB Lippincott Co; 1979.

30. Dequeker JV, Baeyens JP, Classens J. The significance of stature as a clinical measurement of aging. *J Am Geriatr Soc.* 1969;17:169–179.

31. Miall WE, Ashcroft MT, Lovell HG, et al. A longitudinal study of the decline of adult height with age in two Welsh communities. *Hum Biol.* 1967;39:445–454.

32. Trotter M, Bleser G. The effect of aging on stature. *Am J Phys Anthropol.* 1951;9:311–324.

33. McPherson JR, Lancaster DR, Carroll JC. Stature changes with aging in black Americans. *J Gerontol.* 1978;33:20–25.

34. Young CM, Blondin J, Tensuan R, et al. Body composition studies of "older" women, thirty to seventy years of age. *Ann N Y Acad Sci.* 1963;110:598–607.

35. Norris AH, Lundy T, Shock NW. Trends in selected indices of body composition in men between the ages 30 and 80 years. *Ann N Y Acad Sci*. 1963;110:623–639.

36. Hertzog KP, Garn SM, Hempy HO. Partitioning the effects of secular trend and aging on adult stature. *Am J Phys Anthropol*. 1969;31:111–116.

37. Chumlea WC, Garry PJ, Hunt WC, et al. Serial changes in stature and weight in a healthy elderly population. *Hum Biol*. 1988;60:918–925.

38. Abraham S, Lowenstein FW, Johnson CL. *Preliminary Findings of the First Health and Nutrition Examination Survey, United States, 1971–72: Dietary Intake and Biochemical Findings*. National Center for Health Statistics; US Dept of Health, Education, and Welfare publication HRA 74-1219-1. Washington, DC: US Government Printing Office; 1974.

39. Elahi VK, Elahi P, Andres R. A longitudinal study of nutritional intake in men. *J Gerontol*. 1983;38:162–180.

40. Forbes GB. The adult decline in lean body mass. *Hum Biol*. 1976;48:161–166.

41. Garth S, Young R. Concurrent fat loss and fat gain. *Am J Phys Anthropol*. 1956;14:497–504.

42. Hejda S. Skinfold in old and long-lived individuals. *Gerontology*. 1963;8:201–297.

43. Stoudt HW, Damon A, McFarland R, et al. Weight, height and selected body dimensions of adults, United States, 1960–1962. *Vital Health Stat* [11]. 1963;35.

44. Enzi G, Gasparo M, Biondetti PR, et al. Subcutaneous and visceral fat distribution according to sex, age, and overweight, evaluated by computed tomography. *Am J Clin Nutr*. 1987;45:7–13.

45. Borkan GA, Hults DE, Gerzof SG, et al. Comparison of body composition in middle-aged and elderly males using computed tomography. *Am J Phys Anthropol*. 1985;66:289–295.

46. Baumgartner RN, Heymsfield SB, Roche AF, et al. Quantification of abdominal composition by computed tomography. *Am J Clin Nutr*. 1989;50:221–226.

47. Mitchell CO, Lipschitz DA. The effect of age and sex on the routinely employed measurements used to assess the nutritional status of hospitalized patients. *Am J Clin Nutr*. 1982;36:340–349.

48. Heymsfield SB, McManus CB, Nixon DW, et al. Anthropometric assessment of adult protein-energy malnutrition. In: Wright RA, Heymsfield S, eds. *Nutritional Assessment*. Boston, Mass: Blackwell Scientific Publications Inc; 1984.

49. Lipschitz DA, Mitchell CO. Nutritional assessment of the elderly: special considerations. In: Wright RA, Heymsfield S, eds. *Nutritional Assessment*. Boston, Mass: Blackwell Scientific Publications Inc; 1984.

50. Gordon CC, Chumlea WC, Roche AF. Stature, recumbent length, and weight. In: Lohman TG, Roche AF, Martorell R, eds. *Anthropometric Standardization Reference Manual*. Champaign, Ill: Human Kinetics Publishers Inc; 1988.

51. Chumlea WC, Roche AF, Mukherjee D. *Nutritional Assessment in the Elderly Through Anthropometry*. 2nd ed. Columbus, Ohio: Ross Laboratories; 1987.

52. Mitchell CO, Lipschitz DA. Arm length measurement as an alternative to height in nutritional assessment of the elderly. *J Parenter Enter Nutr*. 1982;6:226–229.

53. Chumlea WC, Roche AF, Steinbaugh ML. Estimating stature from knee height for persons 60 to 90 years of age. *J Am Geriatr Soc*. 1985;33:116–120.

54. Harris JA, Jackson CM, Patterson DG, et al. *The Measurement of Man*. Minneapolis, Minn: University of Minnesota Press; 1930.

55. Chumlea WC, Guo S, Roche AF, et al. Prediction of body weight for the non-ambulatory elderly from anthropometry. *J Am Diet Assoc*. 1984;88:564–568.

56. Martin AD, Carter JEL, Hendy KC, et al. Segment lengths. In: Lohman TG, Roche AF, Martorell R, eds. *Anthropometric Standardization Reference Manual*. Champaign, Ill: Human Kinetics Publishers Inc; 1988.

57. Dwyer JT, Coleman A, Krall E, et al. Changes in relative weight among institutionalized elderly adults. *J Gerontol*. 1987;42:246–251.

58. Roche AF. Anthropometric variables: effectiveness and limitations. In: *Assessing the Nutritional Status of the Elderly: State of the Art. Report of the Third Ross Roundtable on Medical Issues*. Columbus, Ohio: Ross Laboratories; 1982.

59. Sullivan DH, Patch GA, Baden AL, et al. An approach to assessing the reliability of anthropometrics in elderly patients. *J Am Geriatr Soc*. 1989;37:607–613.

60. Metropolitan Life Insurance Company. New weight standards for men and women. *Stat Bull Metrop Insur Co*. 1959;40:1–4.

61. Metropolitan Life Insurance Company. Metropolitan height and weight tables. *Stat Bull Metrop Insur Co*. 1989;64:2–9.

62. Russell RM. Evaluating the nutritional status of the elderly. *Clin Nutr*. 1983;2:4–8.

63. Frisancho AR, Flegel PN. Elbow breadth as a measure of frame size for U.S. males and females. *Am J Clin Nutr*. 1983;73:311–314.

64. Novascone MA, Smith EP. Frame size estimation: a comparative analysis of methods based on height, wrist circumference, and elbow breadth. *J Am Diet Assoc*. 1989;89:964–966.

65. Frisancho AR. New standards of weight and body composition by frame size and height for assessment of nutritional status of adults and the elderly. *Am J Clin Nutr*. 1984;40:808–819.

66. Clark NG. Nutritional support of elderly patients, II: proposed answers. *Clin Consult*. 1982; 2:5–9.

67. Master AM, Lasser RP. Tables of average weight and height of Americans aged 65 to 94 years: relationship of weight and height to survival. *JAMA*. 1960;172:661.

68. Chernoff R, Mitchell CO, Lipschitz DA. Assessment of the nutritional status of the geriatric patient. *Geriatr Med Today*. 1984;3:129–141.

69. Mooradian AD. Nutrition modulation of life span and gene expression. In: Morley JE, moderator. Nutrition in the elderly. *Ann Intern Med*. 1988;109:890–904. Report of a conference.

70. Chumlea WC, Baumgartner RN. Status of anthropometry and body composition data in elderly subjects. *Am J Clin Nutr*. 1989;50:1158–1166.

71. Durnin JV, Womersley S. Body fat assessed from total body density and its estimation from skinfold thickness: measurements of 481 men and women aged from 16 to 72 years. *Br J Nutr*. 1974; 32:77–79.

72. Steen B, Bfroce A, Isaksson B, et al. Body composition in 70-year-old males and females in Gothenburg, Sweden: a population study. *Acta Med Scand Suppl*. 1977;611:87–112.

73. Wilmore JH, Behnke AR. Predictability of lean body weight through anthropometric assessment in college men. *J Appl Physiol*. 1968;25:349–355.

74. Watson PE, Watson JD, Batt RD. Total body water volumes for adult males and females estimated from simple anthropometric measurements. *Am J Clin Nutr*. 1980;33:27–39.

75. Latin RW, Johnson SC, Ruhling RO. An anthropometric estimation of body composition of older men. *J Gerontol*. 1987;42:24–28.

76. Butterworth CE, Blackburn GL. Hospital malnutrition and how to assess the nutritional status of a patient. *Nutr Today*. 1975;10:8–18.

77. Fox EA, Boylan ML, Johnson L. Clinically applicable methods for body fat determination. *Top Clin Nutr*. 1987;2:1–9.

78. Harrison GG, Buskirk ER, Carter JEL, et al. Skinfold thickness and measurement technique. In: Lohman TG, Roche AF, Martorell R, eds. *Anthropometric Standardization Reference Manual.* Champaign, Ill: Human Kinetics Publishers Inc; 1988.

79. Falciglia G, O'Connor J, Gedling E. Upper arm anthropometric norms in elderly white subjects. *J Am Diet Assoc.* 1988;88:569–574.

80. Callaway CW, Chumlea WC, Bouchard C, et al. Circumferences. In: Lohman TG, Roche AF, Martorell R, eds. *Anthropometric Standardization Reference Manual.* Champaign, Ill: Human Kinetics Publishers Inc; 1988.

81. Mitchell CO, Lipschitz DA. Creatinine height index in the elderly. In: *Assessing the Nutritional Status of the Elderly: State of the Art. Report of the Third Ross Roundtable on Medical Issues.* Columbus, Ohio: Ross Laboratories; 1982.

82. Bloch L, Schoenheimer R, Rittenberg D. Rate of formation and disappearance of body creatinine in normal animals. *J Biol Chem.* 1941;138:155–161.

83. Morrow FD. Assessment of nutritional status in the elderly: application and interpretation of nutritional biochemistries. *Clin Nutr.* 1986;5:112–120.

84. Mobarhan S. The role of albumin in nutritional support. *J Am Coll Nutr.* 1988;7:445–452.

85. Mullen JL, Buzby GP, Waldman MT, et al. Prediction of operative morbidity and mortality by preoperative nutritional assessment. *Surg Forum.* 1979;30:80–82.

86. Agarwal N, Acevedo F, Leighton LS, et al. Predictive ability of various nutritional variables for mortality in elderly people. *Am J Clin Nutr.* 1988;48:1173–1178.

87. Munro HN. Nutrition and ageing. *Br Med J.* 1981;37:83–88.

88. Finucane P, Rudra T, Hsu R, et al. Markers of the nutritional status in acutely ill elderly patients. *Gerontology.* 1988;34:304–304.

89. Eisenberg S. Postural changes in plasma volume in hypoalbuminemia. *Arch Intern Med.* 1963;112:544–549.

90. Lipschitz DA, Cook JD, Finch CA. The clinical evaluation of serum ferritin as an index of iron stores. *N Engl J Med.* 1974;290:1213–1216.

91. Bothwell TH, Charlton R, Cook J, et al. *Iron Metabolism in Man.* Oxford, England: Blackwell Scientific Publishers Ltd; 1979;295–297.

92. Lipschitz DA, Mitchell CO, Thompson C. The anemia of senescence. *Am J Hematol.* 1981; 11:47–54.

93. Awad MO, Barford AV, Grindulis KA, et al. Factors affecting the serum iron-binding capacity in the elderly. *Gerontology.* 1982;28:125–131.

94. Lipschitz DA, Mitchell CO. The correctability of nutritional, immune, and hematopoietic manifestations of protein-caloric malnutrition in the elderly. *J Am Coll Nutr.* 1982;1:16–23.

95. Winkler MF, Gerrior SA, Pomp A, et al. Use of retinol-binding protein and prealbumin as indicators of the response to nutrition therapy. *J Am Diet Assoc.* 1989;89:684–687.

96. Prendergast JM. Nutritional evaluation of the institutionalized elderly. In: Armbrecht HJ, Prendergast JM, Coe RM, eds. *Nutritional Intervention in the Aging Process.* New York, NY: Springer-Verlag; 1984.

97. Kergoat MJ, Leclerc BS, PettitClerc C, et al. Discriminant biochemical markers for evaluating the nutritional status of elderly patients in long-term care. *Am J Clin Nutr.* 1987;46: 849–861.

98. Ingenbleek Y, DeVisscher M, DeNayer P. Measurements of prealbumin as an index of protein-calorie malnutrition. *Lancet.* 1972;2:106–108.

99. Carpentier YA, Barthel J, Bruyns J. Plasma protein concentration in nutritional assessment. *Proc Nutr Soc.* 1982;41:405–417.

100. Bourry J, Milano G, Caldani C, et al. Assessment of nutritional proteins during the parenteral nutrition of cancer patients. *Ann Clin Lab Sci*. 1982;12:158–162.

101. Ramsden D, Prince H, Burr A, et al. The inter-relationship of thyroid hormones, vitamin A and their binding proteins following acute stress. *Clin Endocrinol (Oxf)*. 1978;8:109–122.

102. Cunningham-Rundles S. Effects of nutritional status on immunological function. *Am J Clin Nutr*. 1982;35:1202–1210.

103. Bistrian BR, Blackburn GL, Scrimshaw N, et al. Cellular immunity in semistarved states in hospitalized adults. *Am J Clin Nutr*. 1975;28:1148–1155.

104. Meakins JL, Pietsch JB, Bubenick O, et al. Delayed hypersensitivity: indicator of acquired failure of host defenses in sepsis and trauma. *Surgery*. 1977;82(3):349–355.

105. Chandra RK, Scrimshaw NS. Immunocompetence in nutritional assessment. *Am J Clin Nutr*. 1980;33:2694–2497.

106. Thompson JS, Robbins J, Cooper JK. Nutrition and immune function in the geriatric population. *Clin Geriatr Med*. 1987;3(2):309–317.

107. Katz AE. Immunity and aging. *Otolaryngol Clin North Am*. 1982;15(2):287–291.

108. Delafuente JC, Meuleman JR, Nelson RC. Anergy testing in nursing home residents. *J Am Geriatr Soc*. 1988;36:733–735.

109. Chandra RK. Serum thymic hormone activity in protein energy malnutrition. *Clin Exp Immunol*. 1979;38:228.

110. Stiehm ER. Humoral immunity in malnutrition. *Fed Proc*. 1980;39:3093.

111. Cohn JR, Hohl CA, Buckley CE III. The relationship between cutaneous cellular immune responsiveness and mortality in a nursing home population. *J Am Geriatr Soc*. 1983;3:808–809.

112. Lipschitz DA. Nutrition, aging, and the immunohematopoietic system. *Clin Geriatr Med*. 1987;3(2):319–328.

113. Lipschitz DA. Nutrition and the aging hematopoietic system. In: Hutchinson ML, Munro HN, eds. *Nutrition and Aging*. New York, NY: Academic Press; 1986.

114. Caliendo MA. Validity of the 24-hour recall to determine dietary status of elderly in an extended care facility. *J Nutr Elderly*. 1981;1:57–66.

115. Samet JM. Surrogate measures of dietary intake. *Am J Clin Nutr*. 1989;50:1139–1144.

116. Hankin JH. Development of a diet history questionnaire for studies of older persons. *Am J Clin Nutr*. 1989;50:1121–1127.

117. Mahalko JR, Johnson LK, Ballagher SK, et al. Comparison of dietary histories and seven-day food records in a nutritional assessment of older adults. *Am J Clin Nutr*. 1985;42:542–553.

118. Gersovitz M, Madden JP, Smiciklas-Wright H. Validity of the 24-hr dietary recall and seven-day record for group comparisons. *J Am Diet Assoc*. 1978;73:48–55.

119. Bowman BB, Rosenberg IH. Assessment of the nutritional status of the elderly. *Am J Clin Nutr*. 1982;35:1142–1144.

Chapter 15

Nutritional Support in the Elderly

Ronni Chernoff

It is well known that nutrition plays a key role in the recovery from acute and chronic illnesses; that the elderly segment of the population consumes the greatest percentage of health care resources[1]; and that approximately 50% of hospitalized patients who receive enteral feedings are over age 65 years (Chernoff R, Lipschitz DA. 1985. Unpublished data). Therefore, it becomes essential that the provision of nutritional therapies, particularly as enteral or parenteral infusions, is done with special consideration to the unique needs of elderly individuals. Many of these specific needs have been addressed in the examination of macronutrient and micronutrient needs and in the discussion of nutritional assessment in previous chapters. However, it is important to review these particular requirements with consideration of the benefits and limitations of nutritional support methodologies. Appropriate selection of nutritional interventions may be key to successful nutritional rehabilitation, correction of nutritional deficits, restoration of nutritional reserves, and avoidance of difficult ethical dilemmas.

INDICATIONS FOR NUTRITIONAL SUPPORT

Gradual loss of weight is a common occurrence among elderly individuals, although the etiology of the weight loss is undetermined. Involuntary weight loss may occur with a variety of acute and chronic illnesses, such as cancer, sepsis, diabetes, and renal disease; however, weight loss in elderly subjects may not have an obvious cause.[2–4] Anorexia or diminished nutrient intake usually is associated with the loss of weight. Morley and colleagues[5] describe this syndrome as the "anorexia of aging" and have suggested that the diminished nutrient intake is a consequence of decreased metabolic rate and reduced energy output. Inadequate food intake due to compromised socioeconomic circumstances, depression or dementia, and functional dependency may also contribute to slow, chronic weight loss. Sometimes weight is maintained because of lack of activity and reduced requirements for energy, but chronic malnutrition may occur because of a deficit of essential nutrients other than energy. Depletion of nutrient stores, particularly tissue stores of water-soluble vitamins, may not be apparent until a physiologic insult such as an illness, an accident, or emotional stress occurs. When an individual who is chronically undernourished encounters physical stress, his or her physical condition may deteriorate rapidly and unexpected complications may occur. Repletion of nutrient stores and restoration of nutritional and reserve capacity may require aggressive nutritional intervention—enteral or parenteral support.

Protein-energy malnutrition is often secondary to a primary disease process such as cancer, chronic cardiac conditions, chronic pulmonary diseases, renal or hepatic diseases, and gastrointestinal disorders.[6] One of the profound consequences of protein-energy malnutrition in elderly individuals is impairment of immune function. Immune responses are affected by age (Chapter 14), independently of nutritional condition; but a compromised nutritional status contributes to an additional depression of the immune system.[7,8] This situation may prove life-threatening in seriously ill individuals because of the increased risk of infection and a decreased ability to mobilize host defenses.

If protein-energy malnutrition is suspected in seriously ill patients, it is important to use clinical judgment to set therapeutic priorities and to select and initiate nutritional interventions. Major medical problems take priority over nutritional deficits and must be corrected before nutritional intervention is considered. Priorities include the management of infection; the control of blood pressure; and the restoration of metabolic, fluid, and electrolyte balances. It is important to monitor fluid and electrolyte equilibration during the acute phase of an illness or at the time of admission to an acute care facility to establish the validity of certain nutritional markers. Nutritional indicators may appear to change after fluid and electrolyte therapy is instituted, because of serum dilution or rehydration effects. True serum values are necessary for an accurate assessment of nutritional condition and the need for nutritional support intervention.

Even in the absence of overt protein-energy malnutrition, there may be an indication for nutritional support. Medical condition, diagnosis, prognosis, and treatment plans are all factors in the decision to provide nutritional intervention therapies. A patient who suffers from multiple chronic conditions is less likely to respond swiftly to an acute insult and may need support through the critical phase. Patients who may not be able to eat for extended periods of time because of coma, stroke, head injuries, oral surgery, or gastrointestinal injuries or impairments may be candidates for nutritional support. Patients who are chronically ill and cannot ingest adequate amounts of nutrients because of anorexia, side effects of drugs such as those used in chemotherapy, or severe limitations on nutrient or fluid intake for therapeutic purposes may be candidates for nutritional support. Having gastrointestinal disease (eg, malabsorption, maldigestion, or motility disorders), surgery, or obstruction may contribute to the need for nutritional support. If the gastrointestinal tract cannot be used, parenteral nutrition is a viable option.

Even in stable, long-term-care patients, chronic undernutrition may be a problem, despite the lack of active disease processes. Patients who require long-term care may have inadequate dietary intakes because of dementia or the need for help with feeding.[9,10] The need for help with feeding may be a significant factor for both dependent and apparently independent nursing home patients, not only for adequate energy intake but also for nutrient density.[10] For patients who have permanent disabilities that interfere with adequate nutrient ingestion, absorption, or utilization, nutritional support may become a necessity for continued life.

ORAL SUPPLEMENTS

The optimal method for nutritionally supporting patients who are at risk for malnutrition is to feed them a nutritionally dense, well-balanced diet. Patients should be encouraged to eat as much as possible within the limits of their disabilities, oral health status, and medical conditions. It has been reported that only 10% of elderly people who have protein-energy malnutrition can ingest nutrients adequate to overcome their nutritional deficits.[11] However, since food is such an important part of life, being the focus of social, cultural, religious, and family gatherings, it is important to encourage elderly individuals to maintain their normal diets as long as they are able.[12,13] Unless there is a compelling need or a specific request from the patient, restricting certain nutrients from the diet may contribute to unforeseen problems. Many older people have difficulty in discriminating between moderation in eating habits and the elimination of entire groups of food products. Limiting intake of many foods may lead to previously unseen nutritional deficiencies. Liberalizing diet restrictions may lead to a more palatable diet and more interest in food, and may not have a negative impact on medical interventions for chronic disease; it is possible that the patient may enjoy food more and consume a diet that reduces the risk of nutritional problems. A thorough dietary history is essential before changes in the diets of patients or clients are initiated.

Dietary Supplements

There are many options available to supplement the diets of individuals who are at risk for malnutrition. Carbohydrate and protein powders are available that can be added to the patient's usual diet to increase the nutrient density without changing the flavor, texture, or color. Vitamin supplements are readily available to compensate for vitamins and minerals that may be lacking in an individual's diet. In a recent study conducted on elderly Australians, the use of dietary supplements (eg, bran or wheat germ) or vitamin and mineral supplements had no effect on incidence of illness or use of medical resources; however, individuals who used such supplements did have more favorable dietary habits and were more nutritionally aware than those who did not use supplements.[14] Data are inconclusive as to the contribution of supplements to the nutritional value of the diets of elderly Americans.[15,16]

For people who have unpredictable appetite levels, snacks can be prepared in advance to be available as desired. These might include crackers; cheese; hard-cooked eggs; peanut butter; fresh fruit; small meals, such as half a sandwich and a glass of milk or juice; soup; milkshakes or fruit frappés; or oral nutritional supplements. Commercially available nutritional supplements may be nutritionally complete or may provide only a portion of the recommended dietary allowances (RDAs) for adults. Elderly patients who have chewing, swallowing, or feeding problems or gastrointestinal impairments may require either liquid diets or supplemented diets for extended periods of time because of their inability to ingest adequate nutrients from regular food. Consideration of fluid, mineral, or macronutrient (eg, protein) restrictions is essential to selection of an appropriate supplement in long-term-care patients. Many elderly individuals experience problems with chronic cardiac, renal, pulmonary, and hepatic diseases that contribute to fluid or protein limitations. Careful evaluation of the nutritional profile of supplements is necessary to meet therapeutic guidelines for individual patients.[17]

Many elderly patients, especially African-Americans and Hispanics, are lactose deficient or have conditions that temporarily render them lactose deficient (severe malnutrition, sprue, bacterial overgrowth, chemotoxicity); these individuals may need lactose-free nutritional supplements in place of milkshakes, custards, or cream soups.[17]

Commercial Liquid Supplements

Oral supplementation of patients' diets with commercially available liquid formulas has been shown to be efficacious in elderly cancer patients,[18] long-term-care patients,[19] and homebound elderly people.[20] In a study by Ching and associates,[18] nutritional status was maintained in a group of elderly cancer patients undergoing various cancer treatment modalities through supplementation with commercially available nutritional supplements. Nine long-term-care patients benefited from the addition of a nutritional supplement to their diets, in a study reported by Andersson and colleagues.[19] Although the volume of food consumed did not change appreciably in this group of patients, they achieved positive nitrogen balances as a result of increased protein, calorie, and fat intakes. In a study of homebound elderly who were dependent on home-delivered meals, the impact of oral nutritional supplements was significant based on overall nutritional intake.[20] The composition of oral liquid supplements changes regularly. It is important to obtain current information from industry representatives about available products.

Nutritional intervention can be accomplished successfully by use of oral supplements; however, there are patients who cannot ingest adequate nutrients because of oral problems (eg, malignancies, wired jaws, lesions associated with chemotherapy or radiation therapy, fungus infections, mucositis, obstructions); cognitive problems (eg, dementia, coma); functional impairments (eg, due to stroke or head or spinal cord injury); or increased nutrient needs associated with hypermetabolic states, cancer, thermal injuries, malnutrition, or malabsorption. For these patients and others who cannot obtain sufficient nutrients via the oral route, there are alternative methods for providing nutrition to elderly individuals in need of nutritional support. Enteral feeding by tube is the next option to consider, especially if the patient has a functional gastrointestinal tract.

ENTERAL FEEDING

Aggressive nutritional support via enteral feeding has been shown to be efficacious in restoring nutritional status in individuals who are unable to orally ingest adequate nutrients.[17,21] Enteral feeding by tube provides a reasonably safe, cost-effective method of providing protein, calories, vitamins, minerals, trace elements, and fluid while preserving or restoring a functional bowel surface.[7,21–23] Because most enteral solutions can be prepared in a nonsterile environment, can be administered without special equipment, and are relatively inexpensive, the choice of enteral solutions for nutritional support of elderly patients is a reasonable one.

Selection of Enteral Feeding Route

Enteral feeding solutions can be effectively delivered to the stomach, duodenum, or jejunum, but relative benefits and risks must be carefully evaluated when selecting an enteral feeding route for a specific patient. Feeding into the stomach, via either a nasogastric or a gastrostomy feeding tube, takes advantage of the normal physiologic processes of digestion and absorption.

Gastric Feeding

The stomach acts to digest food through secretion of acid and hormones, contributes to regulation of pH, and controls release of partially digested meals into the small intestine. Release of liquid food into the small intestine is affected by osmoreceptors in the jejunum that delay emptying of hyperosmolar or hypoosmolar solutions; by acid solutions; by solutions with a high level of fatty acids, with a high nutrient density, or with high or low temperature; and by drugs such as narcotic analgesics and anticholinergic agents.[24] Although there are many advantages to feeding into the stomach, there are potential risks, primarily associated with aspiration. In elderly patients the risk of aspiration may be associated with high levels of gastric residuals or an impaired or absent gag reflex.[21]

Nasogastric feeding has been the most commonly used method throughout the history of enteral feeding because of the near-normalcy that it evokes.[25] For centuries, the administration of liquid meals through a tube into the stomach provided nutrition to individuals who could not otherwise obtain adequate nutrients. Until the development of the Dobbhoff feeding tube and others like it (all of which are made from new-technology compounds that allow for soft, nonirritating, flexible tubes), the hazards of nasogastric feeding included the development of otitis media and nasopharyngeal lesions, aspiration, and voluntary tube removal. Even with the new materials and advanced technology, risks are still encountered with nasogastric tube feeding. In a recent case report, difficulty with nasal breathing due to the presence of a nasogastric tube contributed to respiratory failure in an elderly woman who was tube-feeding dependent as a result of a stroke.[26] Evaluation of nasal patency is an important step prior to the insertion of a nasogastric feeding tube.

Placement of a nasogastric tube is the most easily achieved since it can be accomplished at the bedside, needs a minimal amount of equipment, and can be performed by nurses. There are risks associated with the placement of nasogastric tubes that should be prepared for by the individual placing them. Placement of a tube by an inexperienced practitioner can lead to trauma associated with insertion of the tube (eg, esophageal perforation, pneumothorax, pulmonary hemorrhage, pleural effusion, bronchopleural fistula formation, pneumonia) or with aspiration.[26–30] Placement of feeding tubes may lead to other complications that, although uncommon, are potentially dangerous. For example, Lipman and colleagues[29] reported cases of nasopulmonary tube placement that resulted in pneumothorax in one patient and pneumonia and hydrothorax in another.

Despite these potential problems with tube insertion, nasogastric feeding can be used in both acute and chronic care patient settings. Feeding solutions may be administered continuously by using a slow-drip gravity method or an enteral feeding pump that maintains a constant rate of flow. In the acute care setting, nasogastric feeding is a commonly used means of providing short-term enteral nutritional support. However, increasing numbers of long-term-care patients are being fed by the enteral tube route; nasogastric feeding can be provided safely for long periods of time[31–33] (Chernoff R, Lipschitz DA, Milton KY. 1988. Unpublished data).

If the indications are that tube feeding will be required for extended periods of time; or if the patient is confused, demented, or combative, leading to inadvertent dislodgment of the feeding tube and putting the patient at serious risk of aspiration or mechanical complications,[33] the establishment of a permanent gastrostomy should be considered.[31,34–36] Permanent gastrostomies avoid most of the complications associated with nasogastric tube feeding, but there are some problems that occur with indwelling gastric tubes. Because access is accomplished through an incision in the abdominal wall, complications include intra-abdominal leakage of gastric contents, potentially causing peritonitis; leakage around the catheter insertion site, causing skin excoriation; and migration of the catheter into the abdominal cavity or pylorus.[36] Percutaneous endoscopic gastrostomy is an alternate method that may be used with some success in long-term tube-fed patients.[37–39] Clinicians must carefully evaluate elderly patients for the suitability of this method as part of their care; older patients who are malnourished may have mucosal thinning and skin fragility, which should be considered when placing a gastrostomy tube endoscopically. An organized appraisal of the value of this tube-feeding method should be conducted in long-term tube-fed patients to assure its safety. In most cases, gastrostomy feeding is an efficacious method to use in elderly patients.

Jejunal Feeding

Jejunal feedings are usually used when there is an obstruction in the upper gastrointestinal tract or stomach; when there is potential for the exacerbation of gastric disease, such as ulcers; when gastric dysfunction, such as atrophic gastritis or achlorhydria, exists; or when an individual has had surgery that precludes esophageal or gastric feeding.[40] Jejunal access has distinct advantages for patients who cannot be fed via the upper gastrointestinal tract, but it also has some potential risks that must be considered when selecting an enteral feeding route. Jejunostomies reduce the risk of gastroesophageal reflux and aspiration, a major consideration in elderly patients; however, jejunostomy tube placement frequently requires surgical procedures, which have their own risks.[41] Jejunostomy feeding should be considered if enteral support will be required for an extended period of time and the upper gastrointestinal tract will not be viable for feeding. Caution must be exercised to avoid inadvertent or purposeful tube dislodgment. Partial extraction of a jejunostomy tube can cause leakage of formula or intestinal contents into the peritoneum, leading to peritonitis.[42,43] The use of an indwelling jejunostomy tube should be carefully considered for elderly patients who require nutritional support; placement of a jejunal catheter should be seen as a solution for a long-term problem that will necessitate extended enteral nutritional support.

Selection of Enteral Formulas

Many factors must be considered when selecting an enteral feeding formula for an elderly patient.[21,44,45] Some of these factors include an estimation of the duration of tube-feeding dependency, the location of the feeding tube, the energy and protein requirements of the patient, the ability of the patient to digest and absorb nutrients, and the expense and availability of the product to be infused.

In a limited, short-term situation that is characterized by an acute episode, patients probably will be fed nasogastrically, although if the illness required gastrointestinal surgery, an indwelling gastric or jejunal catheter may be in place. In either of these short-term, acute situations, a formula can be selected to meet specific short-term needs. High-protein, high-calorie, predigested, or specially designed nutritional products can be selected to meet unique needs related to the medical condition. Acutely ill individuals may require disease-specific formulas that are part of the treatment plan. Elderly patients who have been undernourished for an extended period of time may have the additional problem of compromised absorptive capacity, for which a dilute solution or a partially predigested formula may be needed. Whenever enteral feeding is considered for an elderly patient, early feeding protocols should be followed with some caution. It is wise to start with a dilute solution that is infused slowly, to assure tolerance before moving to full-strength, full-volume feeding.

The vast majority of elderly patients who are sustained on tube-feeding formulas are chronically ill and will be tube-feeding dependent for extended periods of time. Selecting a formula for use with long-term tube-fed patients requires consideration of energy, protein, vitamin, mineral, and fluid needs. Although energy needs may be lower owing to a decrease in energy output and a slower basal metabolic rate, requirements for other nutrients remain the same, with only small variations. The challenge this represents is that small volumes of formula often do not provide the levels of protein, vitamins, minerals, and trace elements that are needed to maintain nutritional status.

Recent evidence emphasizes the need for careful formula selection for patients who will be dependent on tube feedings for 6 months or longer. Chernoff and colleagues[46] examined serum levels of trace minerals (including zinc and selenium) and trace proteins (carnitine and taurine) in long-term tube-fed elderly patients. They found deficiencies of selenium and low levels of carnitine and taurine in all the subjects who had been maintained on tube feedings for 6 months or longer; these deficiencies were corrected with the substitution of an enteral formula that contained small amounts of these nutrients. These nutrients have important roles in immune function (selenium) and fat metabolism (carnitine and taurine) and are important in long-term nutrition status. These data suggest that use of supplemented formulas should be considered for individuals who will be tube-feeding dependent for extended periods of time.

Even with supplemented formulas, adequate volumes must be infused to achieve an adequate intake of all nutrients. Inadequate volumes of enteral solutions may also be a factor in inadequate hydration of chronically tube-fed individuals.

Nutrient levels for tube-fed patients should meet basic needs for protein (approximately 1 g/kg of body weight); the RDAs for vitamins, minerals, and trace elements for adults over age 50 years; and fluid requirements of approximately 1500 mL/d. Fluid requirements can be met by providing at least 1 mL/kcal ingested, 30 mL/kg of body weight, or 125% of the volume of the formula. Of particular importance is the fact that the vast majority of enteral formulas require more than 1500 mL or 1500 kcal to meet 100% of the RDAs. Underfeeding of essential nutrients can be a chronic problem in enteral feeding-dependent elderly individuals, as described above.

Consideraton must be given to the patient's metabolic status, gastrointestinal function, and diagnosis. Most long-term tube-fed patients can be supported by using a standard, 1 kcal/mL formula that provides the RDA or greater for vitamins and minerals.[47] There is rarely a demand for disease-specific, predigested, or nutrient-dense formulation; however, there may be indications for high-nitrogen products, such as for decubitus ulcer healing.[48] Unfortunately, the development of decubitus ulcers may be related in part to chronic undernutrition.

Delivery of Enteral Feeding

The first consideration in determining what schedule to establish for enteral feeding is the site of tube placement. The location of the tube may determine how the formula should be infused. If the infusion site is the stomach, there may be more options because the stomach acts as a natural reservoir, controlling release of nutrient solution into the duodenum. Because the stomach regulates the flow of formula into the small bowel, enteral feedings can be administered either by intermittent or continuous flow without serious concern about osmolarity, nutrient concentration, or formula visocity. If a patient has a compromised or absent gag reflex, then a feeding site that minimizes the risk of aspiration should be selected. However, if infusion occurs distal to the stomach, either pump-controlled intermittent or continuous feeding is the choice. Since the reservoir function of the stomach is lost, solutions should not be infused more rapidly than the small bowel can safely absorb. Too rapid infusion or too large a volume may cause problems with poor absorption or diarrhea.

There is considerable diversity of opinion among nutrition professionals about how to infuse tube feeding solutions effectively. The route, formula concentration, and flow rate should be dictated by patient tolerance. In older patients, individual tolerance should be the guide for formula feeding progression.[49] The primary goal should be to provide an adequate volume of formula to meet patient needs while maintaining a safe, tolerable method of infusion.

Complications of Enteral Feeding

There are many risks associated with enteral feeding in elderly patients (Table 15-1); some of these have already been described, but some complications must be addressed more specifically.

It is not uncommon to encounter elderly patients who will not tolerate enteral feeding tubes. Even small-bore, flexible tubes may be uncomfortable; patients are resistant to tube placement and become agitated; and elderly, confused patients may partially dislodge tubes, which can contribute to more serious complications.[50] Small-bore tubes are susceptible to clogging, kinking, and migration. One of the most frequent causes of clogging is the use of enteral feeding tubes for administering crushed medications. The only medications that should be put into feeding tubes are those that are dissolved in a liquid or are in fluid form. The internal diameter of the tube should permit the tube-feeding formula of choice to flow easily; more viscous formulas should only be administered through a moderate-sized tube (eg, 12 French).

Table 15-1 Potential Enteral Feeding Problems in Elderly Patients

Risk Factor	Problem
Decreased gastric emptying	Gastric retention → aspiration
Hiatal hernia	Gastric reflux → aspiration
Dislocation of tube	Muscosal ulceration
	Pulmonary infusion
Altered glucose tolerance	Hyperglycemia → dehydration → altered mental status
Inadequate water	Hypernatremia
	Hyperchloremia
	Azotemia
Decreased energy needs	Inadequate intake of nutrients
Decreased bowel motility	Constipation → fecal impaction
Achlorhydria	Increased susceptibility to bacterial contamination
Polypharmacy	Changes in formula osmolarity
	Interference with drug absorption
	Diarrhea
Confusion	Tube dislocation → aspiration

Source: Reprinted from *Clinical Nutrition: Enteral and Tube Feeding* (p. 395) by JL Rombeau and MD Caldwell (Eds) with permission of W.B. Saunders Company, © 1990.

Some enteral formulas leave a precipitate on the interior walls of the tube, which eventually leads to clogging. Flushing the tube regularly with liquid, such as water, under pressure minimizes this problem. Since all tube-fed patients require additional free fluid, flushing the tube with water will help to meet this need.

Tube location should be monitored at periodic intervals, especially after an episode of vomiting or when there is evidence that the patient has pulled on the tube.[21] Migration of the feeding tube can contribute to complications of aspiration, pulmonary infections, and gastrointestinal dysfunction.[50] Pulmonary complications are frequently, but not always, related to aspiration. Risk of aspiration can be minimized by always elevating the patient's head or the head of the bed when tube formula is being infused; by using pump-administered feeding; and by using tubes that are placed in the duodenum or jejunum. Particular attention should be paid to patients who have had strokes or neurologic or esophageal diseases that contribute to an impaired gag reflex or swallowing difficulties.

Gastrointestinal complications that may be encountered include bloating, nausea, vomiting, diarrhea, and constipation. Frequently these problems can be alleviated by slowing the rate of the enteral infusion; altering the feeding regimen to a slow, controlled, continuous drip; or changing the formula. Diarrhea is the most commonly experienced gastrointestinal problem associated with tube feeding.

Diarrhea may be related to a number of conditions that affect elderly, hospitalized, or institutionalized patients. In the past, the use of milk-based formulations caused diarrhea, bloating, and gastrointestinal discomfort in lactase-deficient patients. There is now a greater understanding of the extent of this problem, and since the mid-1970s there has been a vast array of lactose-free products from which to choose. Bacterial contamination of tube-feeding formulas appeared to be a cause of diarrhea; this problem has also been minimized with the availability of commercially prepared products. Homemade formulas were made from blended meats, strained vegetables, cooked cereals, puréed fruit, milk powder, juices, and other ingredients that could be contaminated easily by skin-, air-, and water-borne bacteria.[51]

Diarrhea can be caused by many different kinds of medications; when diarrhea is encountered, it is wise to review the drug profile to identify any drug that might be causing the problem. Diarrhea can also be the result of a too-rapid infusion or a hyperosmolar formulation. Feeding regimens should be slowed to allow the patient time to adapt to the formula. Individuals who have been chronically undernourished may have incompetent bowel surfaces that contribute to malabsorption. Concentrated or hyperosmolar feeding will lead to a watery diarrhea that can be reduced or corrected by diluting the formula and feeding it slowly.

One solution to the problem of diarrhea in tube-fed patients has been the addition of soluble fiber to the enteral feeding products. There is some evidence that fiber may resolve the diarrhea in tube-fed patients.[52–54] There have also been investigations that discuss some of the potential problems associated with fiber-supplemented enteral feedings.[55,56] A conservative approach is most appropriate in elderly patients. If diarrhea is present and the cause is not apparent (eg, medications), adding one or two cans (feedings) of a fiber-containing product to the patient's feeding regimen may resolve the problem.

Many other problems unique to older patients require clinical considerations that may not be included in standard enteral feeding protocols. Some of these are itemized in Table 15-2.

PARENTERAL NUTRITION

Although enteral nutritional support is the preferred method of nutritional intervention for patients who are unable to ingest adequate nutritional substrate orally, the parenteral route may be used. There are very few data, and a great many unanswered questions, about the efficacy and safety of intravenous feeding in elderly patients. A multitude of studies has examined the use of parenteral nutritional support in different populations with assorted diagnoses, but none of them has examined the tolerance for parenteral nutrition in elderly individuals.

The customary source of calories in parenteral solutions is hypertonic glucose solutions. Standard formulas are often greater than 20% glucose. It is known that glucose tolerance deteriorates with advancing age,[57] but the threshold of glucose infusion that can be administered safely to elderly patients has not been thoroughly investigated; the simultaneous infusion of insulin to enhance the absorption of intravenous glucose also warrants more careful study.

The use of intravenous fat emulsions has become a routine part of parenteral nutritional support. Lipid systems may prove to be very effective in elderly patients who are fluid restricted or who have glucose intolerance; however, lipid clearance rates and efficiency are usually not investigated prior to their use. The ability of elderly patients to adequately tolerate lipid emulsions is an area for further investigation. If lipids are well tolerated and rapidly cleared by older patients, their use in lipid-based peripheral parenteral systems might be very valuable. A combination of peripheral intravenous infusion and oral or enteral feedings might serve to provide an excellent source of nutrition, encourage the patient to take food or fluids by mouth or tube, and preserve gut integrity and function.

Protein solutions should be tolerated equally as well by elderly patients as they are by younger individuals. Limitations of protein infusion in older patients parallel those in younger patients and are usually associated with organ system dysfunction. Since parenteral nutrition solutions are aqueous, patients are usually well hydrated unless there is an excess of electrolytes in the formulation. The maintenance of hydration status in parenteral feeding-dependent patients is essential to a successful course of therapy.

Table 15-2 Considerations When Tube Feeding Elderly People

Clinical Condition	Therapeutic Consideration
Functionally dependent with inadequate nutrient intake	Dental status Ability to feed without assistance Therapeutic restrictions Cost *Consider oral supplements, puddings, snacks*
Protein-energy malnutrition treated by enteral nutrition	Calorie density Protein level Volume tolerance Renal function Cost *Consider high-nitrogen, high-calorie formula until nutritional status is restored, then provide adequate calories, nitrogen*
Diarrhea	Rate/volume of feeding Medication profile Fat content of formula Osmolarity of formula *Consider decrease in rate/volume for brief period, use of fiber-containing formula*
Long-term tube feeding dependency	Placement of tube Adequate caloric intake Availability of pump Cost *Consider gastrostomy feeding with a formula providing complete nutrition*
Decubitus ulcers	Calorie level Protein level *Consider high-calorie, high-protein formula*
Constipation	Residue content of diet Fluid intake Medical profile Ambulation *Consider fiber-containing diet with extra free water; increase physical activity if possible*
Intolerance to nasogastric tube	Type of tube Anticipated length of tube dependency Gastrointestinal physiology *Consider soft, pliable, small-bore tube; gastrostomy, jejunostomy*

Source: Reprinted from *Clinical Nutrition: Enteral and Tube Feeding* (p. 394) by JL Rombeau and MD Caldwell (Eds) with permission of W.B. Saunders Company, © 1990.

As with other forms of nutritional therapy, adequate vitamins, minerals, and trace elements must be provided in the basic formulation to meet unique nutrition needs. Older patients must be monitored very carefully to ensure adequate hydration; sufficient calories, protein, and micronutrients; maintenance or correction of metabolic status; and positive therapeutic effects. There is some risk, particularly of air emboli, venous thrombosis, and sepsis, associated with parenteral feeding. Careful, close monitoring of the elderly, parenterally fed patient is the prudent course.[21,58]

HOME NUTRITIONAL SUPPORT

It is conceivable that elderly patients may be sent home with nutritional support when their medical condition stabilizes. Because of the management problems associated with the complex administration of parenteral feedings, the most likely method for home nutritional support is enteral feeding. Age-related changes in elderly patients must be considered when deciding to send them home with nutritional support.[59]

Impairments that may have an impact on the success of home nutritional support include alterations of vision; compromised hearing; loss of fine motor skills, coordination, and strength; and cognitive dysfunction. All of these age-related changes limit the patient's ability to understand and follow directions, recognize and correct potential problems, and communicate with care givers and medical personnel. Successful nutritional support is dependent on the capacity of the patient and care giver to manage care and obtain advice and guidance when problems arise.

Another factor of major importance is a thorough evaluation of the social circumstances in which the patient resides. The patient's financial situation, including access to private health insurance or Medicare or Medicaid, Social Security benefits, and other sources of support, should be assessed. The availability of other social service systems should be explored as well. The home environment should be surveyed to appraise the availability of space needed for storage and formula preparation. The motivation of both patient and care giver to undertake the responsibilities associated with home nutritional support must also be evaluated by a professional.

One viable alternative, assuming that Medicare or other health insurance is available, is use of the services of a home nutritional support company. This type of service may be more efficient because it can provide regular formula delivery, minimize the need for storage space, respond rapidly to problems, offer a reliable product, and provide regular monitoring. With careful advance planning, nutritional support can be safely and effectively provided to elderly patients.

CONCLUSION

Nutritional support, whether in the acute, chronic, or home care setting, can be safely and successfully used in elderly patients. Careful attention must be given to gastrointestinal function, unique nutrient needs, tube site location, feeding regimen, and disease-specific requirements. Parenteral, enteral, and oral nutritional support may be used singly or together, as needed. Some caution must be built into the protocols developed for elderly patients; metabolic changes can occur rapidly and must be addressed quickly to avoid serious problems. Nutritional support can be an important component of life-saving or life-sustaining treatments in elderly individuals.

REFERENCES

1. Besdine RW. The data base of geriatric medicine. In: Rowe JW, Besdine RW, eds. *Health and Disease in Old Age*. Boston, Mass: Little Brown & Co; 1982.

2. Martin KI, Sox HC, Krupp JR. Involuntary weight loss: diagnostic and prognostic significance. *Ann Intern Med*. 1981;95:568.

3. Rabinovitz M, Pitlik SD, Leifer M, et al. Unintentional weight loss: a retrospective analysis of 154 cases. *Arch Intern Med*. 1986;146:186.

4. Olsen-Noll CG, Bosworth MF. Anorexia and weight loss in the elderly. *Postgrad Med*. 1989;85(3):140–144.

5. Morley JE, Silver AJ, Fiatarone M, et al. Geriatric grand rounds: nutrition and the elderly. *J Am Geriatr Soc*. 1986;34:823–832.

6. Lipschitz DA. Protein calorie malnutrition in the hospitalized elderly. *Prim Care*. 1982;9(3):531–543.

7. Chernoff R, Lipschitz DA. Enteral feeding and the geriatric patient. In: Rombeau JL, Caldwell MD, eds. *Clinical Nutrition Enteral and Tube Feeding*. 2nd ed. Philadelphia, Pa: WB Saunders Co; 1990.

8. Goodwin JS, Burns EL. Aging, nutrition, and immune function. *Clin Appl Nutr*. 1991;1(1):85–94.

9. MacLennan WJ, Martin P, Mason BJ. Causes for reduced dietary intake in a long-stay hospital. *Age Ageing*. 1975;4:175–180.

10. Nguyen NH, Flint DM, Prinsley DM, et al. Nutrient intakes of dependent and apparently independent nursing home patients. *Hum Nutr Appl Nutr*. 1985;39A:333–338.

11. Lipschitz DA, Mitchell CO. The correctability of the nutritional, immune, and hematopoietic manifestations of protein calorie malnutrition in the elderly. *J Am Coll Nutr*. 1982;1:17–25.

12. Letsou AP, Price LS. Health, aging, and nutrition. *Clin Geriatr Med*. 1987;3(2):253–260.

13. Pories WJ. Feeding the elderly patient. *N C Med J*. 1988;49(12):632–635.

14. Horwath CC, Worsley A. Dietary supplement use in a randomly selected group of elderly Australians. *J Am Geriatr Soc*. 1989;37:689–696.

15. Garry PJ, Goodwin JS, Hunt WC, et al. Nutritional status in a healthy elderly population: dietary and supplemental intakes. *Am J Clin Nutr*. 1982;36:319–331.

16. O'Hanlon P, Kohrs MB. Dietary studies of older Americans. *Am J Clin Nutr*. 1978;31:1257–1269.

17. Bernard MA, Rombeau JL. Nutritional support for the elderly patient. In: Young EA, ed. *Nutrition, Aging and Health*. New York, NY: Alan R Liss Inc; 1986.

18. Ching N, Grossi C, Zurawinsky H, et al. Nutritional deficiencies and nutritional support therapy in geriatric cancer patients. *J Am Geriatr Soc*. 1979;27:491–494.

19. Andersson H, Falkheden T, Petersson I. A study on liquid diet in geriatric patients. *Aktuel Gerontol*. 1979;9:417–421.

20. Lipschitz DA, Mitchell CO, Steele RW, et al. Nutritional evaluation and supplementation of elderly subjects participating in a "Meals on Wheels" program. *J Parenter Enter Nutr*. 1985;9(3):343–347.

21. Sullivan DH. Nutritional support for elderly patients. In: Morley JE, Glick Z, Rubenstein LZ, eds. *Geriatric Nutrition: A Comprehensive Review*. New York, NY: Raven Press; 1990.

22. Levine GM, Deren JJ, Steiger E, et al. Role of oral intake in maintenance of gut mass and disaccharide activity. *Gastroenterology*. 1974;67:975–982.

23. Tilson MD. Pathophysiology and treatment of short bowel syndrome. *Surg Clin North Am*. 1980;60:1273–1284.

24. Moran JR, Greene HL. Digestion and absorption. In: Rombeau JL, Caldwell MD, eds. *Clinical Nutrition Enteral and Tube Feeding*. 2nd ed. Philadelphia, Pa: WB Saunders Co; 1990.

25. Randall HT. The history of enteral nutrition. In: Rombeau JL, Caldwell MD, eds. *Clinical Nutrition Enteral and Tube Feeding*. 2nd ed. Philadelphia, Pa: WB Saunders Co; 1990.

26. Hernandez OG, Nelson S, Haponik EF, et al. Obligate nasal breathing in an elderly woman: increased risk of nasogastric tube feeding. *J Parenter Enter Nutr*. 1988;12(5):531–532.

27. Miller KS, Tomlinson JR, Sahn SA. Pleural pulmonary complications of enteral tube feedings. *Chest*. 1985;88:230–233.

28. Woodall BH, Winfield DF, Bisset GS. Inadvertent tracheobronchial placement of feeding tubes. *Radiology*. 1987;165:727–729.

29. Lipman TO, Kessler T, Arabian A. Nasopulmonary intubation with feeding tubes: case reports and review of the literature. *J Parenter Enter Nutr*. 1985;9(5):618–620.

30. McWey RE, Curry NS, Schabel SI, et al. Complications of nasoenteric feeding tubes. *Am J Surg*. 1988;155(Feb):253–257.

31. Sundaram R, Megna D, Sibley J. Long-term tube feeding in the aged. *N Y State J Med*. July 1979:1226.

32. Heitkemper MM, Williams S. Prevent problems caused by enteral feeding: know about complications before they arise. *J Gerontol Nurs*. 1985;11(7):25–30.

33. Meer JA. Inadvertent dislodgment of nasoenteral feeding tubes: incidence and prevention. *J Parenter Enter Nutr*. 1987;11(2):187–189.

34. Sriram K, Palac B. Nasogastric feeding in the elderly, *JAMA*. 1984;252(13):1682.

35. Ciocon JO, Silverstone FA, Graver LM, et al. Tube feedings in elderly patients: indications, benefits, and complications. *Arch Intern Med*. 1988;148:429–433.

36. Pomerantz MA, Salomon J, Dunn R. Permanent gastrostomy as a solution to some nutritional problems in the elderly. *J Am Geriatr Soc*. 1980;28(3):104–107.

37. Miller RE, Kummer BA, Tiszenkel HI, et al. Percutaneous endoscopic gastrostomy: procedure of choice. *Ann Surg*. 1986;204:543–545.

38. Larson DE, Fleming CR, Ott BJ, et al. Percutaneous endoscopic gastrostomy: simplified access for enteral nutrition. *Mayo Clin Proc*. 1983;58:103–107.

39. Silberman H. *Parenteral and Enteral Nutrition*. 2nd ed. San Mateo, Calif: Appleton & Lange; 1989.

40. Kirkland ML. Enteral and parenteral access. In: Skipper A, ed. *Dietitian's Handbook of Enteral and Parenteral Nutrition*. Gaithersburg, Md: Aspen Publishers Inc; 1989.

41. Rombeau JL, Palacio JC. Feeding by tube enterostomy. In: Rombeau JL, Caldwell MD, eds. *Clinical Nutrition Enteral and Tube Feeding*. 2nd ed. Philadelphia, Pa: WB Saunders Co; 1990.

42. Lambaise RE, Dorfman GS, Cronan JJ, et al. Percutaneous alternatives in nutritional support: a radiologic perspective. *J Parenter Enter Nutr*. 1988;12(5):513–520.

43. Blebea, J, King TA. Intraperitoneal infusion as a complication of needle catheter feeding jejunostomy. *J Parenter Enter Nutr*. 1985;9(6):758–759.

44. Bell SJ, Pasulka PS, Blackburn GL. Enteral formulas. In: Skipper A, ed. *Dietitian's Handbook of Enteral and Parenteral Nutrition*. Gaithersburg, Md: Aspen Publishers Inc; 1989.

45. MacBurney MM, Russell C, Young LS. Formulas. In: Rombeau JL, Caldwell MD, eds. *Clinical Nutrition Enteral and Tube Feeding*. 2nd ed. Philadelphia, Pa: WB Saunders Co; 1990.

46. Chernoff R, Milton KY, Lipschitz DA. The effect of enteral formula supplementation on carnitine, taurine and selenium status in long-term tube fed patients. *J Parenter Enter Nutr*. 1991;15(1):365.

47. Berner Y, Morse R, Frank O, et al. Vitamin plasma levels in long-term enteral feeding patients. *J Parenter Enter Nutr*. 1989;13(5):525–528.

48. Chernoff R, Milton KY, Lipschitz DA. The effect of a high protein formula (Replete) on decubitus ulcer healing in long term tube fed institutionalized patients. *J Am Diet Assoc*. 1990;90(9):S:A130.

49. Sullivan DH, Chernoff R, Lipschitz DA. Nutritional support in long-term care facilities. *Nutr Clin Pract*. 1987;2(1):6–13.

50. Sullivan DH, Moriarty MS, Chernoff R, et al. Patterns of care: analysis of the quality of nutritional care routinely provided to elderly hospitalized veterans. *J Parenter Enter Nutr*. 1989;13(3):249–254.

51. Chernoff R, Bloch AS. Liquid feedings: considerations and alternatives. *J Am Diet Assoc*. 1977;70(4):389–391.

52. Zimmaro DM, Rolandelli RH, Koruda MJ, et al. Isotonic tube feeding formula induces liquid stool in normal subjects: reversal by pectin. *J Parenter Enter Nutr*. 1989;13(1):117.

53. Slavin JL, Nelson NL, McNamara EA, et al. Bowel function of healthy men consuming liquid diets with and without dietary fiber. *J Parenter Enter Nutr*. 1985;9(3):317–321.

54. Scheppach W, Burghardt W, Bartram P, et al. Addition of dietary fiber to liquid formula diets: the pros and cons. *J Parenter Enter Nutr*. 1990;14(2):204–209.

55. Hart GK, Dobb GJ. Effect of fecal bulking agent on diarrhea during enteral feeding in the critically ill. *J Parenter Enter Nutr*. 1988;12(5):465–468.

56. Heymsfield SB, Roongspisuthipong C, Evert M, et al. Fiber supplementation of enteral formulas: effects on the bioavailability of major nutrients and gastrointestinal tolerance. *J Parenter Enter Nutr*. 1988;12(3):265–273.

57. Andres R. Aging and diabetes. *Med Clin North Am*. 1971;55:835–846.

58. Chernoff R, Lipschitz DA. Total parenteral nutrition: considerations in the elderly. In: Rombeau JL, Caldwell MD, eds. *Clinical Nutrition: Parenteral Nutrition*. Philadelphia, Pa: WB Saunders Co; 1986;2.

59. Chernoff R. Home nutrition support in elderly patients. *Clin Nutr*. Jan/Feb 1987;6(1):36–39.

Chapter 16

Nutrition Services for Older Americans

Barbara Millen Posner and Elyse Levine

The American populace's advancing life expectancy, which has been called the "graying of America," is the result of significant strides in the prevention and treatment of infectious illnesses during early life, improved nutrition, reduced infant mortality, and the better management of chronic diseases that are associated with aging. Watkin[1] notes that the human life span has reached 115 years; today the average life expectancy at birth is 75 years, compared with 47 years in 1900.[2] Men who reach age 65 years live an average of an additional 14.5 years, and women live 19 more years. The median age of the population has risen from 29.4 years in 1960 to 32.1 years in 1987[3]; the proportion of those aged 65 years and older, currently estimated at 12%, is expected to increase to 25% through the year 2030[4] (Chapter 1).

Further advances in life expectancy and the quality of life of older persons will depend on continued improvements in health, the prevention and early treatment of diseases (Chapter 17), and better understanding of the aging process. Nutritional interventions and related services will play a major role in the promotion of successful aging, as suggested by the Surgeon General[5(p.18)]: "Sound public education directed toward this group [the older population]—and professional education directed toward individuals who care for older Americans—should focus on dietary means to reduce risk factors for chronic disease, to promote functional independence, and to prevent the adverse consequences of use of medications."

The purpose of this chapter is to summarize the characteristics that place the older population at particular risk of nutritional problems and to describe the evolution of United States policies, programs, and services that are aimed at improving the nutritional status of older Americans. Many of the available services and programs that are discussed are relatively new and compete for federal and state funding and private reimbursement. Nutrition programs and services are but one part of a dynamic public health system that has changed

415

dramatically in recent years and is currently undergoing major alterations. As cost-containment concerns, prospective payment systems, and alternative health insurance strategies continue to evolve, the health care and related nutrition programs and services will change as well. We therefore attempt to discuss nutritional issues in the context of the evolving health care system. The gaps in nutrition services are identified, and the need for a unified, integrated, and comprehensive group of nutrition-related policies and programs is addressed.

HEALTH AND NUTRITIONAL STATUS

The role of diet in the major health problems that affect American adults is both etiologic and palliative in nature. For example, whereas proper and balanced nutrition may promote health, excess calories in relation to energy needs can lead to weight gain and obesity, which may increase risk for cardiovascular disease, diabetes, and possibly certain forms of cancer. Consequently, dietary intervention has a central role in the prevention and treatment of many chronic diseases (Chapter 17). It is also well known that appetite loss and significant unexplained weight loss are hallmarks of risk in older persons with acute and chronic illnesses; therefore, proper nutrition is a mainstay of institution-based acute or chronic care. In practice, nutrition services in community-based or home-based health care settings have received less attention, despite their importance.

The overall health status of people aged 65 years and older appears to be improving. The extent to which their nutritional status is changing and the nature of the nutritional changes are less certain. About two thirds of the older population consider themselves in good to excellent health and perceive that they have adequate access to health, supportive, social, and rehabilitative services.[6] The proportion of older persons with undiagnosed health problems, such as hypertension, is decreasing; likewise, percentages of those who are well managed medically seems to be increasing.[6] It would appear that many older people receive health and related social services that result in a perceived, relatively high level of well-being. Nonetheless, significant numbers of older persons, indeed one third or more of those aged 65 years and older, consider their health to be poor.[6] About 85% of elderly people have one or more nutrition-related chronic conditions.[7] Substantial numbers of older individuals continue to have undiagnosed medical problems, and many appear to have chronic conditions that are unstable or, at best, poorly managed from a health care standpoint.[4-6] It appears that, although the health of the older population is improving, there are major segments of that population with unmet health needs and concerns.

From the nutritional perspective, it is difficult to ascertain the prevalence and types of problems in the older population. The major reason for this uncertainty is the relative scarcity of information concerning historic and current dietary patterns, nutritional status, and related health problems in the elderly. The older age groups traditionally have been under-represented or unstudied in national nutrition monitoring efforts such as the Household Consumption Surveys by the United States Department of Agriculture (USDA) and the National Health and Nutrition Examination Survey (NHANES) by the United States Department of Health and Human Services.[8,9] These information deficits will be corrected by more complete population sampling strategies and emphasis on older persons, which are being planned for future studies, including the USDA's Household Food Consumption Survey, NHANES III (begun in 1988), and a new segment of the USDA's Continuing Survey of Food Intakes by Individuals.[5] In the interim, a limited number of public policy statements, national studies, and research on selected samples of older people may provide some perspective on the major nutritional problems of this population.

PUBLIC POLICY STATEMENTS

Since 1979, when the Surgeon General published his report on disease prevention and health promotion,[10] dozens of national and international committees have emphasized the need to lower population intakes of dietary fats, particularly saturated fats, and cholesterol; have encouraged weight reduction and maintenance of ideal body weight; have suggested limited alcohol consumption; and have recommended increased dietary levels of complex carbohydrates, fiber, calcium, iron, and fluoride. Reports that have placed an emphasis on the older adult population have further noted the need to deliver preventive dietary guidance throughout adulthood. Recommendations concerning dietary intake and specific nutrition services are summarized in Tables 16-1 and 16-2, respectively. These reports have emphasized the unique nutritional needs and problems of older people. They have pointed to needs for clinical nutritional care and dietary counseling, particularly among the majority of older people who suffer from chronic diseases. Additionally, these reports have noted that the age-associated changes in metabolic requirements, alterations in tissue function, and nutrient utilization with aging have major dietary implications. It is stated that older adults will benefit from diets that are relatively low in calories (yet sufficient to maintain ideal body weight) but dense in essential nutrients. The susceptibility of the older population to health fraud has also resulted in recommendations for cooperation between the public and private sectors in providing mass communication of sound nutrition education to older people.[4,13] In addition, the paucity of information on characteristics of older people and environmental circumstances that increase nutritional risk is emphasized as a major research need.

Table 16-1 Dietary Recommendations for Older People

Originating Agency, Year	Recommended Dietary Allowance (RDA)	Energy Needs/Ideal Body Weight (IBW)	Calcium Needs	Use of Supplements
National Research Council, 1989[11]	Recommendations for total energy, thiamin, riboflavin, and niacin lower than levels recommended for younger adults; all other nutrients consistent with recommendations for younger adults	Recommended average energy allowance is 30 kcal/kg for both men and women aged 51 years and older, based on median heights and weights	Consume low- or nonfat dairy products and dark-green vegetables to maintain calcium intake at RDA levels; use of supplements to increase calcium intake above RDA not recommended	Avoid taking dietary supplements in excess of the RDA in any one day
The Surgeon General's Report, 1988[5]	Use current until age-specific RDAs are developed	Engage in physical activity to maintain IBW and delay onset of chronic disease	Consume foods to meet the RDA; use calcium supplements if medically necessary	Advisable only with counseling from qualified health professional
Surgeon General's Workshop, 1988[4]				Federal agencies should provide health professionals information on efficacy and safety of commonly used supplements

NUTRITIONAL EXCESSES

The elderly suffer from nutritional problems that span the continuum from nutrient excesses to deficiencies. Studies of diet and health in the free-living older population suggest, on average, that the problems of food and nutrient excess appear to affect more people than do nutrient deficiencies. For example, the estimated mean dietary intake of older people appears relatively high in total fat (particularly saturated fat), cholesterol, and sodium.[17] This pattern of intake is thought to contribute to some of the major health concerns of adults, namely cardiovascular disease, certain cancers, diabetes, and obesity. The apparent contributions of higher-fat animal food products and convenience foods in the American diet are also cited as factors in these conditions.[5,17] As much as 40% of the older population may suffer health problems that arise in part from dietary excesses, such as excess body weight, dyslipidemia, glucose intolerance, and hypertension.[18] These conditions may be further aggravated by inactivity, age-related alterations in nutrient utilization, and changes in tissue or organ function.[4,5,18]

Factors Related to Nutritional Excesses

As with other groups, we have a limited understanding of food purchasing and dietary patterns that result in dietary excesses in the older population. Often the consumption patterns reflect habits accumulated over a lifetime. Contributing to these habits are numerous sociologic, psychologic, and demographic factors. Although it is beyond the scope of this chapter to delve into these complex relations, two studies warrant discussion here.

Grotkowski and Sims'[19] study of dietary practices among older adults found that dietary intake was influenced by the person's level of nutrition knowledge and self-confidence in that knowledge, a variety of health and nutrition beliefs, and socioeconomic status. Among the beliefs and attitudes that affect food purchasing are that nutrition is important for overall health status, that food and nutrient supplements could be medicinal, and that vitamins and minerals are necessary for health. Attitudes or misconceptions about weight reduction regimens also appeared to influence food and nutrient intake.

More recently, a cluster analysis of food consumption patterns of older adults[20] yielded 8 clusters which showed socioeconomic and geodemographic differences. For example, living in a Southern state increased the likelihood of being in clusters characterized by ''light-eaters,'' and having higher intakes of sugar (especially among rural dwellers) and legumes (especially among nonwhites). Consumers of large amounts of salty snacks and soup were mainly white, non-Southern, rural residents who ate at home more. Frequent consumption of meals outside the home

Table 16-2 Recommendations for Nutrition Services for Older People

Originating Source, Year	Nutritional Assessment and Guidance/Counseling	Public Nutrition Education	Food Services
The Surgeon General's Report, 1988[5]	To be provided within institutional and community-based services for older adults, including homebound elderly	Called for more research on methods, program strategies that promote adequate food consumption, elimination of health fraud	Should be required to pay special attention to meeting energy/ nutrient needs of older clients, including frail and homebound elderly
Surgeon General's Workshop, 1988[4]	Recommended that assessment be done at admission or enrollment in all institutional or community-based health services for older adults; recommended services of RD or nutrition professional; addressed need for health professionals to coordinate community-based services	Recommended that health-related agencies and associations develop and coordinate messages to meet needs of elderly; utilize advanced communication techniques appropriate to older adults; develop and disseminate successful public/ private sector models for health promotion	
American Dietetic Association, 1987[12]	To be integrated into institutionally based health care facilities; private or group medical, health maintenance, and preferred provider practice settings; and ambulatory, home health, and social service settings	Nutrition education is part of the continuum of health care for older adults, to be incorporated into all ambulatory, home, and institutional health care services	
Select Committee on Aging, 1984[13]		Called for Congress to increase funds for health education and consumer information; DHHS should establish an office to coordinate consumer health	

ADA/ITT Continental Baking, 1982[14]	education and act as a clearinghouse on unproven medical remedies	Specific recommendations for private sector and government to develop nutrition education materials that address the special needs of older Americans, disseminate the information through the media and existing service networks, and combat misinformation; special focus advised on drug-nutrient relationships, biochemical changes that occur with aging, dental health, and nutrition in chronic and acute diseases	Recommended that all food delivery systems and programs should contain some form of nutrition education insofar as possible without hampering the delivery of foods
White House Conference on Food, Nutrition and Health, 1981[15]	Committee resolution recommended reimbursement of nutritional assessment or counseling provided by RDs from Medicaid/Medicare; private insurance coverage was opposed in a minority report	Called for a task force appointed by the president to devise and execute a program for nutrition education through the mass media; recommended that laws be strengthened to require public service time on radio and television; advocated use of mass media for training neighborhood leaders	
National Conference on Nutrition Education, 1980[16]	Advocated Medicaid/Medicare reimbursement for nutrition education services	Recommended the development of national nutrition education policy with specific provision for nutritionally vulnerable persons; increased use of mass media recommended for public nutrition education programs	

was a predictor of higher fat intake among older adults, as was residence in Northern states. Higher alcohol consumption was found in clusters that contained more urban residents; men had higher incomes and lived in non-Southern states, but women with higher alcohol intake were more likely to have lower incomes and live in Southern states. Further research in these areas is important to guide clinical intervention and the development of policies related to older persons.

NUTRIENT DEFICIENCIES

While problems of dietary excesses are prevalent in older Americans, it is equally important to note that there appear to be distinct subgroups of elderly people who are at particular risk of malnutrition. In studies of national scope, low dietary levels of energy, calcium, magnesium, and vitamin B_6 have been reported among certain groups of older persons.[5,9,17,21] Regional studies and investigations on selected samples of older people have further suggested that protein-calorie malnutrition is prevalent, particularly among hospitalized, homebound, and very frail elderly people.[22–25] Additionally, there have been reports that low, but significant, proportions of the institutionalized and noninstitutionalized older population are at risk for deficiencies related to vitamins B_{12} and B_6, thiamine, nicotinic acid, ascorbic acid, iron, and folate[26,27] (Chapter 3). The National Research Council recently lowered the recommended dietary allowances (RDAs) for vitamin B_6, folate, and iron,[11] which may change the status of subjects originally classified as consuming lower than recommended levels of these nutrients. However, regardless of the RDAs, it is estimated that about 1 in 20 noninstitutionalized elderly people may have clinical symptoms or biochemical evidence of vitamin or mineral deficiencies.[28] A somewhat higher prevalence of nutritional deficiencies has been reported among institutionalized people.[5,18]

RISK OF MALNUTRITION IN THE ELDERLY

Major predictors of low levels of food and nutrient intake among elderly people include poverty, homelessness or social isolation, health frailty and the associated reduced functional capacity, low levels of nutrition knowledge, and susceptibility to fraudulent health and nutrition claims.[5,13,21–24,26,27,29] Balsam and Rogers[30] found that older people who comprise ethnic and linguistic minority groups are more likely to need nutritional services.

Low Income

Numerous studies have reported the relationship between income and poor nutritional status in the noninstitutionalized population.[9,17,19,22,23,31,32] The

Surgeon General's report[5] acknowledged that poverty is a major problem among older people and that it is often linked to inadequate levels of nutrient intake. In 1986, the United States Census reported that 12.4% of the noninstitutionalized population over age 65 years, or 3.5 million people, had incomes below the poverty level. Another 2.3 million (8%) were classified as "near-poor" (incomes 125% of the poverty level). Poverty is particularly prevalent among minorities; almost one third of elderly blacks (31%) and one fourth of elderly Hispanics (23%) are estimated to be poor, in contrast to one of every nine (11%) elderly whites. Among older women, 15% are poor compared with 8% of older men. Also, one fourth of older people who live alone or with nonrelatives are poor, whereas only 6% of elderly individuals who live with their families are poor.[33]

In a recent study of noninstitutionalized elders, over half of the 3602 respondents reported that they did not have enough money to purchase the food they needed. This study focused on economically needy elderly people, particularly those who were recipients of community-based social support services.[21] Although the proportion of the elderly population with economic constraints may be overestimated by this sample, the association between lower income and risk of inadequate food intake seems quite apparent.

Social Isolation

Lower nutrient intakes have been found in adults who are more socially isolated[18,21,25,34,35] (ie, those who live alone or who are less likely to be in contact with family members or other people). House et al[36] recently reported that social isolation was a consistent predictor of morbidity and mortality from chronic disease. Both the 1986 Census report[33] and the National Health Interview Survey on Housing Supplement on Aging[37] reported that about 8.3 million people over age 65 years, or one third of the noninstitutionalized older population, were living alone. The numbers of older adults who live alone increased 68% between 1970 and 1986.[33] Those who live alone tend to be older (average age 75.2 years), widowed, female, and have no living children or siblings. Of those over age 65 years, 14% reported that they had no one to care for them for even a few days if the need arose, while the majority would rely on family (69%) or others (17%).[37] One study of predominantly low-income elderly people[21] suggested that 28.3% had no one to provide assistance at home if illness confined them to bed. Low income and social isolation also appear to be inextricably linked.

Frailty and Loss of Functional Capacity

Poor health and limited functional capacity have repeatedly been found to lower the nutritional well-being of older people.[5,18,21] Often nutritional problems are heralded by loss of appetite, prolonged reduction in food intake, and significant weight loss. Loss of appetite may result from chronic illness and confinement to bed, diminished taste and smell sensations, poor oral health, or neuromuscular or skeletal abnormalities that can make chewing or swallowing difficult. Feelings of social isolation and depression can also contribute to appetite loss. In a survey of low-income elderly people,[21] 38.2% reported skipping one or more meals a day and 17% reported periods of appetite loss at least once a week. Unexplained weight loss appeared in about one fifth (20.2%) of respondents.

Functional limitations resulting from acute or chronic illnesses can reduce an elderly person's ability to shop for and prepare foods. Nearly one fifth (18.3%) of lower-income elders have reported their inability to leave home without assistance or to prepare their own food (17.2%). The 1984 Health Interview Survey reported that 10.5% of the noninstitutionalized elderly could not complete their food shopping without assistance and that 6.2% required assistance with meal preparation.[38]

Poor Nutrition Knowledge

The low levels of nutrition knowledge observed among many older people have been identified by many researchers as a key contributor to poor food choices.[14,16,39,40] The need for nutrition education efforts among older people has been the subject of national forums, including the 1969 White House Conference on Nutrition and Health,[41] the joint ITT/American Dietetic Association conference on nutrition education for older Americans,[14] and the Surgeon General's workshop on health promotion and aging.[4]

Among the most dramatic consequences of inadequate nutrition information among older people is their susceptibility to fraud. Over 30% of health fraud victims in the United States are older people, and it is thought that misconceptions about nutriton are a major contributor to the susceptibility to frauds.[13]

Several studies in older populations indicate significant gaps in their nutrition knowledge.[19,39,42–45] A nutrition knowledge quiz administered to over 300 participants in federally funded nutrition programs for older people in New England suggested that, on average, older people could correctly answer only half the test items.[46] This is consistent with earlier research.[39,45] Significantly lower nutrition knowledge scores were found in those who described their health as poor.

Interest in nutrition and health is high among older people, yet they perceive only limited numbers of reliable sources of information to which they can refer.[42] The older population has preferred sources of health and nutrition information that differ from those of other age groups. Their styles of learning differ as well. The mass media are frequently cited as a primary source of health and nutrition information for elderly people. The print medium has the learning advantage of being self-paced, an important factor for this population.[47,48] Other sources are family, friends, and—to a lesser extent—professionals, including physicians, nurses, and dietitians.[39,46,49]

Limitations in knowledge can relate to deficits in nutrition facts that influence food purchasing, menu planning, and the like.[50] Grotkowski and Sims[19] found that older people often do not recognize their needs for nutrition information. Over 65% of a sample they studied reported that their own food intake was "excellent" in meeting recommended levels of nutrients, whereas only 30% actually consumed foods that met 66% to 100% of standards.

Influences on Food Purchases and Intake

Food marketing experts, such as Jacoby and colleagues[51] and Ruddell,[52] have provided evidence that food-purchasing habits and related nutrient intake are extremely complex consumer behaviors. They describe processes whereby consumers utilize information such as diet-related health claims as well as product characteristics (eg, price and brand) in making food-purchasing decisions. Consumers, they suggest, attempt to integrate newly acquired information with their attitudes, preferences, and past experiences in making food choices. Their resulting food purchases lead to a pattern of dietary intake over time that is balanced, excessive, or inadequate in essential nutrients (Figure 16-1).

Knowledge of food consumption behaviors and influencing factors such as the media will contribute to the development of educational, counseling, and treatment efforts to improve the nutritional well-being of older people. This seems particularly important in the prevention and treatment of diet-related chronic diseases that affect nearly all individuals over age 65 years. In addressing the public-policy considerations related to the health and nutritional needs of the older population, the Surgeon General recommended that "Health promotion messages from the public and private sectors should utilize advanced communication techniques, recognizing different life-styles, decrements in vision and hearing, different cultural experiences and different learning styles that are common to older people."[5]

PROVIDING NUTRITION SERVICES TO OLDER PERSONS

A wide range of interventional strategies could be considered for meeting the nutritional needs of older persons, as summarized in Table 16-2. The nature and appropriateness of these services tend to depend on the characteristics of the people served, their nutritional problems, and the settings in which services are provided. For example, the mix of nutrition services provided within a rural

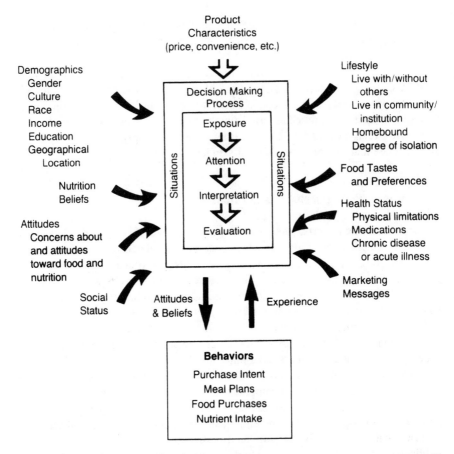

Figure 16-1 Information processing related to food purchases and consumption in older adults.[51–54]

community may be quite different from those provided to urban elderly; likewise, nutrition services provided in hospitals may differ in nature and frequency of provision compared with those provided to ambulatory or homebound elderly.[4]

The earliest community-based nutrition services that were available to older people were initiated by the United States Department of Agriculture in the 1960s.

These "services" were essentially income transfers to economically disadvantaged people to assist with food purchases.

The Food Stamp Act of 1964 and its 1977 revisions entitled eligible households to receive a food stamp benefit in the form of food coupons that could be used to purchase grocery items at retail outlets. The intent of the program was to eliminate financial barriers to adequate food consumption and to improve the food and nutrient intake as well as nutritional status of participating people or households. The food stamp program continues to distribute stamps to eligible households and, in some states, older people may benefit from a direct income transfer as cash instead of food coupons.

The advent of the federal Medicare and Medicaid programs, also begun in the 1960s, provided guidelines and a mechanism for reimbursement of nutritional care services to older people during periods of hospitalization. Currently, Medicare and Medicaid also allow for the reimbursement of "medically necessary" nutrition services that are provided incidentally to the provision of medical care in hospital, long-term care, and alternative care settings (eg, ambulatory care centers, health maintenance organizations [HMOs], group or solo medical practices, and hospices). Since the types of services considered appropriate and their mechanisms for funding vary from setting to setting, they are discussed separately. In general, it is important to define the categories of nutrition services that may be needed by older people.

The nutrition services offered within the context of the food stamp program and through Medicare and Medicaid provide a sharp contrast and help establish the range of nutrition services for older people that has emerged over the past 30 years. Services can involve clinical treatments, such as nutrition screening, assessment, monitoring, and evaluation; education and counseling; or enteral and parenteral nutritional support. Services may also include food services and ancillary activities such as meal preparation in congregate, institutional, or home settings; or transportation and shopping assistance.

Among the clinical nutrition care services, nutrition screening is a focused activity that is designed to identify people who need a particular program or type of nutrition service.[59,60] Screening is usually conducted by community agencies, programs, or clinic personnel to identify those at high risk for nutritional problems or to determine special considerations in managing an individual's situation (eg, edentulousness, confinement to bed, food allergies or preferences, and therapeutic diet needs). Nutritional assessment determines the individual's nutritional status and identifies significant nutritional problems, and investigates the problems'

Table 16-3 Nutrition Programs for Older Adults

Program	Type of Intervention	Funding Source	Eligible/Available Services	Percent of Older Population Served
Nutrition Program for Older Americans	Congregate and home meals, therapeutic diets	DHHS OHDS AoA	Meals; transportation; shopping assistance; limited nutrition education, information and referral	10% to 13% of population aged 60+ years[3,55]
Food Stamps	Income subsidy	USDA Social Security	Coupons for food purchases or cash equivalent	50% to 80% of the eligible low-income elderly[56]
Meals-on-Wheels America	Direct food delivery	Private	Home meals that complement weekday congregate programs; attention to needs of homebound elderly	*< 1%[57]
Healthy Older Americans	Health education	DHHS PHS AoA	Public health and nutrition programs for older Americans	—
Medicare/Medicaid	Third-party payment system	DHHS HCFA SSA	Covers medical and related services provided by participating hospitals, HMOs, private medical practices, ambulatory centers, rehabilitation and skilled nursing facilities, home health agencies, and hospice programs. Eligible nutrition services vary depending on the setting of care and the deemed medical necessity. Home meals, enteral/parenteral nutrition, and weight reduction are particularly limited	Virtually all people over age 65 years eligible (but in 1985, 400,000 eligible people reportedly lacked coverage by either program)[58]

| Blue Cross/Blue Shield | Third-party payment system | Private | Highly variable depending on the provider | — |
| VA Health Care Facilities | Health care delivery | PHS Veterans Administration | Clinical services are integrated into all VA-funded facilities and programs | — |

AoA = U.S. Department of Health and Human Services, Administration on Aging
DHHS = U.S. Department of Health and Human Services
HCFA = U.S. Department of Health and Human Services, Health Care Financing Administration
HMO = Health maintenance organization.
OHDS = U.S. Department of Health and Human Services, Office of Human Development Services
PHS = U.S. Department of Health and Human Services, Public Health Services
SSA = Social Security Administration
USDA = U.S. Department of Agriculture

*New Program
—figures unknown

etiologies and possible solutions.[59,60] Trained professionals with a relatively complex and comprehensive set of clinical and laboratory techniques conduct the assessments. Monitoring nutritional status is a process whereby assessments are conducted at predetermined, regular intervals, allowing an assessment of the change in an individual's or population's nutritional status over time. Evaluation studies provide a mechanism by which to assess the impact of nutrition services in terms of the changing nutritional status and health of those served. These studies may include estimates of the costs of providing care, the potential cost savings that result from nutritional interventions, or the improved overall status of individuals or households that receive nutritional services. Education and counseling may occur on a one-on-one level or in groups with families or consumers. It is ideally carried out by professionals who are trained in the needs and learning strategies of older people. Nutritional support is a specialized form of clinical nutritional care that involves the planning and management of parenteral and enteral feedings. These services are discussed further by the American Dietetic Association in its publication *Nutrition Services Payment Systems*.[60] The benefits and costs of these services were also recently reviewed.[61]

At present, no single organization or provider coordinates nutrition services planning and implementation for older people in either the institutional or non-institutional setting. Relevant activities may be carried out independently by hospital nutrition departments, consultants to skilled nursing facilities, hospital discharge and social service planning units, community-based area agencies on aging, Social Security offices, and congregate and home nutrition programs. The result is a service network that is only loosely integrated and contains gaps in available services for older individuals.

It is generally recognized that there is a need to better integrate and coordinate the health and nutrition services of older individuals. The concept of a "continuum of health care" has been proposed and was first defined in a 1982 California law as "a coordinated continuum of diagnostic, therapeutic, rehabilitative, supportive and maintenance services that addresses the health, social, and personal needs of (older) persons."[62] It was recognized that older people may receive health care services and related benefits in a variety of settings (at home, in the community, or within institutions) and that the providers of necessary services may have diverse backgrounds, resources, and orientations.[62] For example, food stamps may be handled by community agencies and personnel whose expertise lies in income-related services and programs. Adult day care and home care may be handled by local community social service agencies who provide a number of benefits (shopping assistance, social services) and refer clients to other programs and services (eg, homemakers and home health aides).

The diagnosis and treatment of chronic disease and the management of terminal illness may be carried out by a network of community-based health and social service providers (eg, health centers, HMOs, ambulatory care centers, private practitioners' offices, or hospices). Institutions (eg, hospitals, rehabilitation centers, and skilled nursing facilities) provide acute and chronic care. Increasingly, hospitals are providing short-term care; providers in less costly, alternative care settings deliver follow-up care.[12,63,64]

Among the Surgeon General's recent recommendations regarding public nutrition policies for the aging population, it was suggested that nutrition services, with emphasis on nutritional assessment and "guidance," be offered in both institution- and community-based settings of health care. It was also recommended that other providers of social and support services for older people recognize and tailor nutrition services to the particular conditions of their clients.

These recommendations are similar to those proposed by the American Dietetic Association (ADA) in its position paper on nutrition and aging.[12] The ADA recommended that nutrition services be included throughout the continuum of health care services for the elderly. Posner and Krachenfels[59] describe a continuum of nutrition care services and programs for the elderly that would be carried out in institution- and community-based settings as needed. Balsam and Rogers[30] describe a range of community-based nutrition service options based at Title III sites that includes community meal programs, food pantries, shopping assistance, home-delivered meals, and nutrient supplements. A model for the possible integration of nutrition, health, and social services for older people is summarized in Figure 16-2.

Many of the nutrition services described above are currently available to older individuals. However, they often operate within severe funding constraints and, as a consequence, reach relatively few older people. There are also major restrictions placed on the provision of certain types of services, depending upon the setting. The following sections of this chapter provide a description of available community nutrition programs for the elderly, and a summary of strategies that exist for the reimbursement of nutrition care services provided by professional nutrition personnel in institutional and community settings.

COMMUNITY-BASED PROGRAMS FOR OLDER ADULTS

Title IIIc Nutrition Program for Older Americans

In 1972, the Older Americans Act of 1965 (OAA) was amended to establish a national Nutrition Program for Older Americans (NPOA). This program distributes funding under Title IIIc of the OAA to states and United States territories for a national network of programs that provide congregate and home-delivered meals for elderly people. Nutrition programs are required to provide at least one meal a day that meets one-third of the recommended dietary allowances (RDA) and to operate 5 or more days a week.[65]

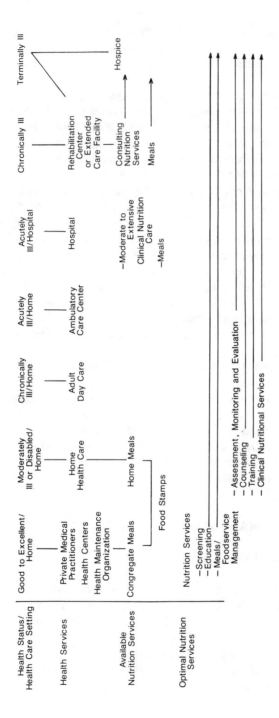

Figure 16-2 Continuum of nutritional services for the elderly. *Source:* Reprinted with permission from *Clinics in Geriatric Medicine* (1987;3[2]:261–274), Copyright © 1987, W.B. Saunders Company.

As of 1988, federal funding for the Title IIIc program was nearly $430 million, and an additional $273 million were available to provide supportive services such as transportation to meal sites, shopping assistance, information and referral, outreach, and—to a limited extent—nutrition counseling and education.[66] Title IIIc nutrition programs request grant funds through their state or Area Agencies on Aging (AAAs). Each state has an Office on Aging, which coordinates community programs for its elderly citizens. In 1987, there were over 15,000 Title IIIc nutrition program sites nationally that served 2.8 million people in congregate settings, and an additional 729,000 frail people who received home meals (Administration on Aging. Unpublished data released January 29, 1988).

In its report, Prevention 86/87, the United States Department of Health and Human Services (DHHS) summarized federal expenditures for health promotion and disease prevention among all age groups and minority groups in the population. The Title IIIc program, included in the Office of Human Development Service budget, accounted for over three fourths of expenditures by DHHS for health promotion and disease prevention.[67]

The nutrition programs gain additional spending power from a cash/commodity entitlement program supported by the USDA. Nutrition programs may elect to receive food commodities, cash at a fixed amount of about $0.57 per meal served to eligible participants per year or a flexible combination of food and cash. This support from the USDA amounted to $136 million in 1988.[68,69] Other sources of funding are realized from donations from older participants toward meal costs, and private or public donations for the ongoing provision of services.

Separate federal funding was established in 1980 under Title VI of the OAA to emphasize the delivery of congregate and home meals to Indians and native Alaskans. In 1987, 131 tribal organizations operated meal programs under a $7.4 million budget.[70]

Many evaluations of the impact of the Title III nutrition programs have been conducted.[71-77] It appears that this program has been able to attract "high-risk" older people, to improve the nutritional content of their diets, and to provide beneficial socialization and recreation. Balsam and Rogers[30] found that many NPOA sites were compelled to become innovative in meeting the nutritional needs of its participants. Beyond the congregate and home meals that are required by law, these researchers found that many nutrition programs across the nation had begun to add provisions for therapeutic diets; food pantries; ethnic meals; luncheon clubs; acceptance of food stamps for meal payments; alternative meal sites (eg, diners); breakfast, weekend, and evening meals; and meals for the homeless older population.

While evaluations of NPOA have demonstrated its impact, it appears that programs often overlook the particularly "needy" segments of the population, including socially isolated; homeless; ethnic and linguistic minorities; and extremely functionally impaired, homebound elderly individuals.[30] It is also increasingly clear that NPOA and other community programs are being pressured to provide services to larger numbers of frail and homebound elderly. The greater number of those with unmet needs has resulted, in part, from the recent trends for early discharge of older patients from hospitals before they completely recover and with their more complicated medical conditions. In many areas of the country, requests for nutrition services, particularly Meals-on-Wheels, have increased two- and threefold. These increased demands are likely to continue as cost containment continues to be a major influence on hospital-based care.

The provision of nutrition education within the NPOA programs and the relative impact of these educational efforts has been more dubious than the success of meal delivery. A national evaluation of NPOA suggested that nutrition education was a poorly defined service, highly variable from site to site, and difficult to evaluate.[71] Selected studies have found little impact of organized nutrition education on the nutrition knowledge of older NPOA participants.[42,71,73] Recognition of this problem led to amendments of the Older Americans Act to support the redesign and development of nutrition education efforts. However, this aspect of the program has not received funding authorization and remains unresolved.

Meals-on-Wheels America

A major gap in the services within certain Title IIIc sites is the limited availability of weekend and holiday meals. Meals-on-Wheels America is a national project that attempts to fill this need by raising private funding to complement existing services. It is an example of private/public sector partnership that has been espoused as the solution to the needs of growing numbers of elderly people. The project began in New York City in 1981, and by 1989 had expanded to 30 communities across the country.[57,78] In these communities, food preparation and delivery are integrated into existing NPOA programs. Funds are raised through foundations, media exposure, direct mail campaigns to businesses, and a variety of other efforts. Plans for expansion include attention to the needs of the home-bound elderly.

Administration on Aging/Public Health Service Joint Initiative on Health Promotion for Older Americans

Some Title IIIc nutrition program sites have benefited from a joint initiative on health promotion by the Administration on Aging (AoA) and the Public Health Service (PHS) that began in 1983. As described by FallCreek and colleagues,[79] the cooperative effort was designed to facilitate the collaboration between state and local health departments, state and federal agencies, and appropriate volunteer agencies in the development and implementation of health promotion programs for elderly citizens. AoA and PHS provide materials for designing and implementing community programs, including directories, media materials, and special instructional materials for older adults. The American Association of Retired Persons (AARP) received funding for a 3-year period beginning in 1988 to assist the coordination of these joint initiatives.

Food Stamps

The USDA food stamp program, which was authorized by the 1964 Food Stamp Act, provides an income supplement to low-income households in the form of coupons used to purchase food. About 2 million American households headed by older people, or between 40% and 80% of those within the population who are eligible, currently participate in the food stamp program. Reasons cited for nonparticipation by eligible older people include the "stigma of welfare" associated with the program's income means test, lack of information on program availability, and the perceived complexity of the application process.[56] To encourage participation by those residents aged 65 years and older, Wisconsin and California converted the food stamp benefit to a cash equivalent and added it to the individual's monthly supplemental security income (SSI) check. SSI provides a guaranteed minimal income to the nation's aged (those aged 65 years and older), blind, and disabled people.

Results concerning the impact of food stamps on the nutritional status of participating households have been inconclusive. Butler et al[80] concluded that elderly food stamp participants consumed levels of nutrients that were similar to those of nonparticipants who had otherwise similar characteristics. They suggested that food stamps act more as an income supplement than as a mechanism whereby nutrient intake per se is increased. In contrast, Akin and colleagues[81] found that food stamp participants consumed higher levels of many nutrients than did members of nonparticipating households with similar incomes. It seems clear, however, that food stamps provide a significant income benefit to its participants and that this may further extend the limited resources of participating households.

Coordinated Volunteer Services

A Gallup poll reported that 45% of the adult population (80 million people) were volunteering a total of 19.5 million hours in 1987.[82] Individual contributions by volunteers to services for older people are difficult to measure, but a large study sponsored by the Robert Wood Johnson Foundation requires discussion. The Foundation provided up to $150,000 in grants for 3 years to 25 "coalitions" of volunteers based in churches and synagogues. Between 1983 and 1986, over

11,000 volunteers took part in these programs and served 26,000 people. Older individuals in need of volunteers' services were referred to the grantee churches and synagogues by community agencies, family, and friends. The activities of the volunteer coalitions were diverse and were designed to complement existing services. Shopping, transportation, and meal preparation were among those services most requested by older people who contacted these coalitions. While the Foundation project was successful in coordinating volunteer efforts, a report on the project[83] emphasized that volunteer programs cannot replace formal programs, nor can they thrive without a paid staff to manage the individual volunteers.

NUTRITION SERVICES PAYMENT SYSTEMS

Nutrition services are made available to older people through the network of federal- and state-funded programs such as food stamps and the Title IIIc program. As described previously, however, these programs generally emphasize the needs of a particular older population segment (eg, the economically disadvantaged, as in the case of food stamps), and have generally been designed to provide a specific type of nutrition service (eg, meals, income subsidies, shopping assistance, and food stamps). Another system designed for supporting the delivery of nutrition services, particularly therapeutic services carried out by professionals, is the third-party payment system. The major third-party payers are Medicare, Medicaid, Blue Cross/Blue Shield, and other commercial insurance carriers. These payers reimburse the costs of providing medical and health-related services, including certain nutrition care functions, to individuals in a range of institutional, community-based, or home settings. A summary of the general guidelines that determine the nature and extent of coverage for nutrition services within each of these reimbursement mechanisms is found in Table 16-2.

Most third-party payers do not provide precise definitions of the types of nutrition services for which they will provide coverage. Rather, they typically maintain a generalized description of the services that may be eligible for reimbursement in an individual's case. They also tend to provide "standard conditions of participation" that must be met by a provider (ie, hospital, agency, or practitioner) in order to receive reimbursement for services provided to third-party beneficiaries.

To understand the third-party payer system more completely with respect to coverage for nutrition services, one has to differentiate the third-party payers (eg, Medicare), the settings in which care is provided (eg, hospital, skilled nursing facility, or HMO), and the type of nutrition service. It would be impossible to provide an in-depth discussion of the nutrition service-related policies for all third-party payers by care setting in this chapter. However, the following is an overview of policies and procedures that affect reimbursement of nutrition services by third-party payers in alternative health care settings. Two available resources should be mentioned: (1) Parver[84] prepared a comprehensive report for the ADA on policies for nutrition care service coverage and reimbursement under Medicare, Medicaid, Blue Cross/Blue Shield, and other commercial carriers; and (2) the ADA published procedures for implementing a nutrition services payment system, including service definitions and documentation, fee setting, billing, and patient monitoring procedures.[60]

The types of nutrition services that may or may not be covered by third-party payers, depending on the health care setting, are food services, including meal preparation and delivery, menu planning, and diet prescription; nutrition care, such as nutritional screening and assessment, nutrition care planning, evaluation of nutrition services, education and counseling, and referral services; and specialized nutritional support via enteral and parenteral feedings. Food services or meal preparation/delivery per se are generally reimbursed by third-party payers only if a person is hospitalized or is a resident of a skilled nursing facility or hospice program. Clinical nutrition care may be reimbursed if it is generally judged to be "medically necessary" on a case-by-case basis; third-party payers typically have more explicit guidelines governing what is a reasonable nutrition service, depending on the health care setting. The level of reimbursement may vary depending on the specific policy and its provisions for deductables and copayments. The reimbursement of parenteral and enteral nutrition support services is quite controversial, particularly in the home setting. Such services currently undergo particularly close scrutiny among all of the third-party payers for the determination of necessity.

MEDICARE

The Medicare program, which receives its statutory authority under Title XVIII of the 1965 Social Security Act, is administered by the Health Care Financing Administration (HCFA) of the DHHS. Medicare is a federal health insurance system whereby hospitals, physicians, and other health care providers receive reimbursement for services they provide to Medicare beneficiaries (ie, eligible people aged 65 years and older and the disabled of all ages). The Medicare program consists of two parts: part A, which covers inpatient hospital care, skilled nursing care, home health care, hospice care, and care provided through an HMO; and part B, which covers "medical and other services" including physicians' services (hospital-based, community-based, or home-based care); other clinical, therapeutic, or rehabilitative professional services deemed to be "incident to the provision of medical care," such as physical and speech therapy and nutrition services as determined to be appropriate; outpatient hospital services; medical equipment; prosthetic devices; diagnostic tests; and other items and services as specified by Medicare.

There are significant differences between Medicare coverage and reimbursement for inpatient hospital care and alternative settings (eg, nursing homes, patients' homes, clinics, and HMOs). The inpatient care coverage is carrried out under what is termed a prospective payment system, which is based on reimbursement rates set for given medical diagnoses, adjusted to some extent depending on the severity of a patient's disease. Outside the hospital, reimbursement for services and equipment is judged according to "reasonable" cost on the basis of charges incurred, rather than a particular cost per diagnosis.

Medicare reimbursement claims are processed by private entities, generally insurance carriers, who have contracted with HCFA to determine the appropriateness of the claim for reimbursement. These entities are called "intermediaries" (in the case of Medicare part A) or "carriers" (in the case of Medicare part B).

Hospital-Based Care

The Medicare program part A component covers hospital-based care, including the following "core" inpatient services: bed and board; nursing and related services; diagnostic or therapeutic services; and drugs, biologicals, equipment, or other services and items ordinarily furnished to inpatients. Medicare part B covers the physician's component of inpatient care and related services as previously described.

The rates of Medicare reimbursement to hospitals for costs incurred in patient care are fixed and based on 470 diagnosis-related groups (DRGs). There is a flat reimbursement rate for each DRG regardless of the services that a patient receives, including nutrition care.

There is only limited flexibility within the Medicare reimbursement guidelines to adjust hospital reimbursement rates for patients who have unusually long hospital stays or multiple, complicated diagnoses. As a consequence, the DRG-based fixed payment system creates an incentive for hospitals that are able to limit patients' lengths of stay and encourages early patient discharge. The hospital must determine the mix of services that it will provide and must determine how it will balance quality of care against cost efficiency. The services a patient receives (ie, medical, nursing, food services, and nutrition care services) essentially compete for Medicare reimbursement within the hospital environment. The extent to which nutrition services are provided will, in part, depend on how they are perceived within the institutional framework. Nutrition services that are perceived as increasing the hospital's cost of providing care may be limited or not provided. Those nutrition services that are perceived as improving patients' rates of recovery or reducing hospital stays for a given diagnosis may be incorporated into the hospital's "core services." This decision is made at the institutional level and is not regulated by the third-party payers. When provided, nutrition services are not reimbursed separately but are covered as part of the hospital's routine costs.

The Medicare program sets specific "conditions of participation" that must be met in order for the hospital to receive Medicare funding. Several of these conditions pertain to nutrition. From a nutritional perspective, a hospital that receives Medicare payments must have an organized dietary department, but the guidelines do not specify that it be headed by a registered dietitian. A consulting dietitian must be available to meet with medical and nursing staff and instruct patients on diet modifications, write diet histories, and participate in ward rounds and conferences. Diets must be recorded on patients' charts, and orders for therapeutic diets must appear there as well. Meals must be consistent with diet orders and must meet the National Research Council's RDAs. While these guidelines provide general criteria for hospital nutrition services, they leave considerable latitude for determining the type and organization of these services and the availability of nutrition professionals for the provision of clinical nutrition care.

An additional factor that may determine the mix of available nutrition services in the hospital setting is a voluntary hospital accreditation process that is carried out by the Joint Commission on Accreditation of Healthcare Organizations (Joint Commission). Hospitals that participate in this process, including about 5200 of the 6700 hospitals that participate in Medicare,[59] are required to maintain a set of basic nutrition care services, including routine dietary screening; nutritional assessment of individual patients; clinical nutrition care (including the availability of both enteral and parenteral nutrition); dietary counseling; and the administration of safe, appropriate, and sanitary food service operations.[59] The Joint Commission guidelines add further emphasis on the availability of qualified nutrition professionals in the provision of both food service and clinical nutrition care activities.

There appears to be specific wording in the Medicare policy that denies coverage for nutritional supplements such as enteral feedings in the hospital setting; supplements are considered to be "self-administered drugs" and ineligible for coverage.[84]

Post-Hospital Care

Medicare part A benefits also include coverage for "extended care" services provided after a hospitalization within settings such as rehabilitation facilities and skilled nursing facilities. There are guidelines that define eligibility based on the length of prior hospitalization and that limit the length of care in these facilities. Criteria for reimbursement of services in these facilities are similar to those for

Medicare part A hospital services and generally allow those services that are available in a hospital setting as described above.

Ambulatory Nutrition Services

Medicare part B may cover nutrition services provided in hospital ambulatory centers or private physicians' offices if they are deemed "incident to medical care." Guidelines concerning nutrition services carried out in the hospital ambulatory center require that the nutrition professional be an employee of the hospital. Nutrition services provided in a private practice must be carried out by a professional who is an employee of the physician, rather than a private contractor; the physician must also be present to supervise the nutrition care. Nutrition services in hospital-based ambulatory centers and private practice settings are billed by the hospital or medical practice as a medical visit and are reimbursed as such.

Health Maintenance Organizations

An HMO participating in the Medicare program must offer its Medicare beneficiaries the full range of services that are available to all HMO clients. The HMO legislation does include nutrition education and counseling as an allowable service but does not specify that these services be carried out by a professional with a specific background. Cost-containment concerns guide the development of the available services of HMOs, similar to the hospital setting. For these reasons, the profiles of nutrition services paid for by HMOs differ considerably across the nation.

Home Health Agencies

Home health agency services may be reimbursed under both Medicare parts A and B. To qualify, a patient or beneficiary must be homebound, under a physician's care, and in need of skilled nursing or speech or physical therapy. There are no limits to the number of home visits a person can receive and, unlike institution-based skilled nursing or rehabilitative care, the beneficiary need not have been hospitalized prior to receiving home care. Home services that are considered appropriate for reimbursement are generally those that would be provided under hospital-based care. Meals-on-Wheels, however, is specifically excluded since it is not a component of hospital care.

Home health agencies are reimbursed on a "reasonable cost" basis for visits; these rates include the administrative component of arranging care. In addition, the home health agency receives a negotiated overhead rate. Conditions for participation require that, as part of administrative overhead, the agency must develop a treatment plan for each client, including his or her diet. Therefore, nutrition services are allowable under the agency's administrative costs. Home visits by nutrition professionals are generally not allowed as separate visits; rather, the nutrition professionals' time should be reflected in administrative costs and their level of effort reflective of the agency's case load. Parenteral and enteral nutrition products can be reimbursed under Medicare part B but must not be billed separately (ie, they are also included as an administrative cost).

Hospice Care

Medicare part A covers hospice care services, but guidelines specify limits on the length of allowable coverage and set ceilings on the total cost of service reimbursement per client. Many hospice programs across the country elect not to participate in the Medicare program because of these ceilings. Unlike other settings of care, dietary counseling is reimbursed directly. However, nutrition professionals are not designated as preferred providers of these services.

MEDICAID

Medicaid is a federal/state program that is funded under Title XIX of the Social Security Act. It is difficult to generalize about Medicaid reimbursement for services, since each state determines the types of services it provides, based on its particular population's needs and its resources. However, Medicaid "conditions of participation" within a given setting of care are generally identical with those under the Medicare program. Generally, nutrition services would be reimbursable along with other types of competing services as part of the provider's allowable administrative overhead (home health agency); the provider's fixed-payment package (HMO); or as a service "incident to" ongoing medical care (hospital ambulatory care or private medical practice). Medicaid also has guidelines for adult day care and personal care services provided to older people that are over and above those provided under Medicare. Despite similarities in coverage, Medicaid is generally considered more restricted than the Medicare program.

BLUE CROSS/BLUE SHIELD AND OTHER COMMERCIAL CARRIERS

The Blue Cross/Blue Shield plans across the nation generally cover hospital-based nutrition services as part of the patient's allowable per diem reimbursement rather than separately, as with the Medicare program. Similarly, coverage for home health agency nutrition services occurs as part of the agency's overhead rate, not as a separate service. Hospital-based ambulatory nutrition services and private practice-based nutrition services are reimbursed as a medical visit if "incident to" medical care coverage. As Blue Cross/Blue Shield plans differ from state to state, their treatments of nutrition service coverage vary as well.

There is considerable variability in reimbursement for nutrition services by other commercial insurance carriers. Regrettably, it is beyond the scope of this chapter to provide an assessment on a carrier-by-carrier basis.

DEPARTMENT OF VETERANS AFFAIRS SYSTEM

The federally funded Department of Veterans Affairs (VA) is not a third-party payment system, but warrants attention. The VA supports a network of hospitals and long-term care, rehabilitative, and other facilities that provide health and related services to United States Armed Forces veterans. The VA clinical nutrition services have received considerable attention, and are perhaps better defined than those systems supported by the third-party payers described above. The VA promotes the diagnosis and treatment of nutrition-related problems by an interdisciplinary professional staff that includes registered dietitians. Nutrition care is not limited to hospital settings but is encouraged in all VA-sponsored treatment centers. For example, obesity is a condition that is included under VA guidelines for nutrition services conducted by VA personnel.

The VA has also instituted a community access program that establishes partnerships between the VA and community services. Services include nutrition activities, such as elder veterans' luncheon clubs, sponsored jointly with the Title IIIc nutrition programs.[85]

CONCLUSION

The health and nutritional status of older people has improved in this century, but significant numbers continue to have unmet needs for food and nutritional services. The most prevalent nutritional problems of people aged 65 years and older are the nutrition-related chronic diseases, including heart disease, diabetes, and cancer, which affect most older people. There are also distinct groups of elderly people—notably the socially isolated, the very frail, and the economically disadvantaged—who suffer from apparent nutrient deficiencies. The factors and personal characteristics that place the older population at risk of nutrition problems are poorly understood. Considerable future research in both basic and applied settings is needed to resolve these information deficits.

The programs and services that are available to meet the nutritional needs of older people are limited and only loosely integrated. No single agency or entity plans, coordinates, or provides nutrition services to older people in home, community, or institutional settings. Generally, the available federally and privately funded nutrition programs and services are designed to provide a particular service (such as Meals-on-Wheels) under specific and restrictive conditions. Within the third-party payment system, the allowable nutrition services vary considerably, depending on the location of care and an individual's medical status. Third-party payers (ie, Medicare, Medicaid, and Blue Cross/Blue Shield) rarely stipulate that nutrition services be provided by professionals with specialized training in nutrition.

The nutritional needs and problems of older people and the potential benefits of expanded research in this area are recognized at federal and state levels. Greater federal attention is needed to develop more explicit guidelines for providing nutrition services to elderly people in the full range of community- and institution-based health care settings. Federal and private health care providers and third-party payers would be advised to explore mechanisms whereby home, community, and institutional services could be coordinated so that the nutritional needs of elderly people are met. There is also further need to support research to document the costs and benefits of nutritional services for elderly people.

REFERENCES

1. Watkin DM. *Handbook of Nutrition, Health and Aging*. Park Ridge, NJ: Noyes Publications; 1983.

2. National Center for Health Statistics. *Health, United States—1987*. US Dept of Health and Human Services publication PHS 88-1232. Washington, DC: US Government Printing Office; 1988.

3. Soldo BJ, Agree EM. *America' a Elderly*. Population Bulletin 43(3). Washington, DC: Population Reference Bureau Inc; September 1988.

4. *Surgeon General's Workshop on Health Promotion and Aging*. Washington DC: US Government Printing Office No. 1988-201-875/83669; 1988.

5. *Surgeon General's Report on Nutrition and Health*. Washington, DC: US Public Health Service; 1988. US Dept of Health and Human Services publication 88-50210.

6. National Center for Health Statistics. *Aging in the Eighties: Preliminary Data from the Supplement on Aging to the National Health Interview Survey*. Hyattsville, Md: National Center for Health Statistics; 1986. Advance Data from Vital and Health Statistics, N 115. US Dept of Health and Human Services publication PHS 86-1250.

7. Health of the Elderly. *Metropolitan Life Foundation Statistical Bulletin*. January-March 1982;63(1):2–5.

8. US Dept of Agriculture. *Nutrient Intakes: Individuals in 48 States, Year 1977–78*. Report No. I-2. Washington, DC: US Government Printing Office; 1978.

9. Carroll MD, Abraham S, Dresser CM, eds. *Dietary Intake Source Data: U.S., 1976-1980, NHANES I,II*. Hyattsville, Md: National Center for Health Statistics; 1983.

10. *Heatlhy People: Surgeon General's Report on Health Promotion and Disease Prevention.* Washington DC: US Government Printing Office; 1979. Dept of Health, Education, and Welfare Publication PHS 79-55071.

11. Food and Nutrition Board, National Research Council. *Recommended Dietary Allowances.* 10th rev ed. Washington, DC: National Academy Press; 1989.

12. Posner BM, Fanelli MT, Krachenfels MM, et al. Position of the American Dietetic Association: nutrition, aging, and the continuum of health care. *J Am Diet Assoc.* 1987;87(3):344–347.

13. House Select Committee on Aging, Subcommittee on Health and Long-Term Care. *Quackery: A $10 Billion Scandal.* Washington, DC: US Government Printing Office publication No. 98-435; 1984.

14. Posner BM. Nutrition education for older Americans: national policy recommendations. *J Am Diet Assoc.* 1982;80(5):455–458.

15. *Process Proceedings.* In: Final Report 1981, White House Conference on Aging, Volume 2. Washington, DC: US Government Printing Office; 1981.

16. National Conference on Nutrition Education. Specific recommendations: low income and elderly populations. *J Nutr Educ.* 1980;12(2suppl):128–130.

17. US Dept of Health and Human Services and US Dept of Agriculture. *Nutrition Monitoring in the U.S.: A Report from the Joint Nutrition Monitoring Evaluation Committee.* Washington, DC: US Government Printing Office; US Public Health Service; 1986. US Dept of Health and Human Services publication PHS 86-1255.

18. Posner BM. *Nutrition and the Elderly.* Lexington, Mass: Heath & Co; 1979.

19. Grotkowski M, Sims L. Nutrition knowledge, attitudes and dietary practices of the elderly. *J Am Diet Assoc.* 1983;47:263–268.

20. Akin JS, Guilkey DK, Popkin BM, et al. Cluster analysis of food consumption patterns of older Americans. *J Am Diet Assoc.* 1986;86:616–624.

21. *A National Survey of Nutritional Risk Among the Elderly.* Washington, DC: Food Research and Action Center; 1987.

22. *Ten-State Nutrition Survey, V: Dietary.* Atlanta, Ga: Centers for Disease Control; 1972. US Dept of Health and Human Services publication HSM 72-8133.

23. Guthrie HA, Black K, Madden JP. Nutritional practices of elderly citizens in rural Pennsylvania. *Gerontologist.* 1972;12:330–335.

24. Posner BP, Smigelski CG. Dietary characteristics and nutrient intake in an urban homebound population. *J Am Diet Assoc.* 1987;87(4):452–456.

25. Roe DA. Nutritional surveillance of the elderly: methods to determine program impact and unmet need. *Nutr Today.* 1989;24(5):24–29.

26. Vaughan LA, Manore MM. Dietary patterns and nutritional status of low income, free-living elderly. *Food Nutr News.* 1988;60(5):27–30.

27. Bailey LB. Vitamin B_{12} status of elderly persons from urban low-income households. *J Am Geriatr Soc.* 1980;28:276–278.

28. Suter PM, Russell RM. Vitamin requirements of the elderly. *Am J Clin Nutr.* 1987;45:501–512.

29. *Final Report of the 1981 White House Conference on Aging: A National Policy on Aging.* Washington, DC: US Government Printing Office; 1981;1.

30. Balsam AL, Rogers BL. *Service Innovations in the Elderly Nutrition Program: Strategies for Meeting Unmet Needs.* Boston, Mass: Tufts University School of Nutrition; 1988.

31. Allen JE, Gadson KE. *Nutrient Consumption Patterns of Low-Income Households.* Technical Bulletin No. 1685. Washington, DC: Economic Research Service, US Dept of Agriculture; June 1983.

32. Blanciforti L, Green R, Lane S. Income and expenditure for relatively more versus relatively less nutritious food over the life cycle. *Am J Agric Econ.* 1981;63(2):225–260.

33. American Association of Retired Persons and Administration on Aging, US Dept of Health and Human Services. *A Profile of Older Americans.* Long Beach, Calif: American Association of Retired Persons; 1987.

34. Rao DB. Problems of nutrition in the aged. *J Am Geriatr Soc.* 1973;21:362.

35. Lockniskar M. Nutrition and health symposium: University of Texas at Austin, 1988 summary report. *Nutr Today.* 1988;23(5):31–37.

36. House JS, Landis KR, Umberson D. Social relationships and health. *Science.* 1988;241:540–544.

37. National Center for Health Statistics, 1986. *Aging in the Eighties, Age 65 Years and Over and Living Alone, Contacts with Family, Friends, and Neighbors.* Preliminary Data from the Supplement on Aging to the National Health Interview Survey: United States, January-June, 1984, No. 116. Hyattsville, Md: US Public Health Service; 1986.

38. National Center for Health Statistics, 1987. *Aging in the Eighties: Functional Limitations of Individuals Age 65 Years and Over.* Preliminary Data from the Supplement on Aging to the National Health Interview Survey: United States No. 133. Hyattsville, Md: US Public Health Service; 1987.

39. Fanelli M: An assessment of the nutrition education needs of congregate meal program participants. *J Nutr Educ.* 1987;19(3):131–137.

40. Light L. Cameras help the elderly to improve food patterns. *J Nutr Educ.* 1976;8(2):80.

41. White House Conference on Food, Nutrition and Health: Panel IV-4. *Popular Education and How to Reach Disadvantaged Groups.* Washington, DC: US Government Printing Office; 1970.

42. Hersey J, Glass L, Crocker P. *Aging and Health Promotion: Market Research for Public Education.* NTIS Accession, No. PB84-211150; 1984.

43. Betts N, Vivian V. Factors related to the dietary adequacy of noninstitutionalized elderly. *J Nutr Elderly.* 1985;4(4):3–13.

44. Caliendo MA, Smith J. Factors influencing the nutrition knowledge and dietary intake of participants in the Title III-C meal program. *J Nutr Elderly.* 1981;1(3/4):65–77.

45. Fanelli M, Abernethy M. A nutritional questionnaire for older adults. *Gerontologist.* 1986;26(2):192–197.

46. Levine E, Posner B. Media use and nutrition knowledge of Title IIIc congregate meal participants in New England. *J Am Diet Assoc.* 1989;89(9 suppl):A-124.

47. Phillips L, Sternthal B. Age differences in information processing: a perspective on the aged consumer. *J Market Res.* 1977;14:444–457.

48. Stephens N. Media use and media attitude changes with age and time. *J Advertis.* 1981;1:38–45.

49. Connel C, Crawford C. How people obtain their health information: a survey in two Pennsylvania counties. *Public Health Rep.* 1988;2:189–195.

50. Gilbert SB. Health promotion for older Americans. *Health Values.* 1986;10(3):38–46.

51. Jacoby J, Chestnut R, Fisher WA. A behavioral process approach to information acquisition in nondurable purchasing. *J Market Res.* 1978;15:532–544.

52. Rudell F. *Consumer Food Selection and Nutrition Information.* Westport, Conn: Praeger Publishers Division; 1979.

53. Sharlin J. *Food Consumption Behavior and Blood Cholesterol Levels in Women and Men.* Boston, Mass: Tufts University School of Nutrition; 1990.

54. Marketing Sciences Institute. *Determinants of Food Consumption in American Households.* Report No. 82-112. Cambridge, Mass: Marketing Sciences Institute; 1982.

55. Administration on Aging. *Fact Sheet.* Washington, DC: Administration on Aging; March 1988.

56. US Senate Special Committee on Aging. *Developments in Aging: 1986. A Report of the Special Committee on Aging.* Washington DC: US Government Printing Office ASI No. 25144.3; 1987.

57. *Meals-On-Wheels America: More Meals for the Homebound Through Public/Private Partnerships: A Technical Assistant Guide.* New York, NY: New York City Department for the Aging; 1989.

58. *Americans at Risk: The Case of the Medically Underinsured.* US Senate Special Committee on Aging; 1985.

59. Posner B, Krachenfels M. Nutrition services in the continuum of health care. *Clin Geriatr Med.* 1987;3(2):261–274.

60. American Dietetic Association. *Nutrition Services Payment Systems: Guidelines for Implementation.* Chicago, Ill: American Dietetic Association; 1985.

61. Disbrow DD. The costs and benefits of nutrition services: a literature review. *J Am Diet Assoc.* 1989;89(4suppl).

62. Monteith M. Role of nutritionists in community-based long term care. Presented at the Annual Meeting of the American Dietetic Association; September 15, 1983; Anaheim, Calif.

63. Rubin DC. Waxing of the gray, waning of the green. In: Committee on an Aging Society, Institute of Medicine and the National Research Council, eds. *America's Aging: Health in an Older Society.* Washington, DC: National Academy Press; 1985.

64. Bezold C, Carlson RJ, Peck JC. *The Future of Work and Health.* Dover, Mass: Auburn House Publication Co; 1986.

65. Dept of Health and Human Services, Office of Human Development Services, Administration on Aging. *Older American's Act of 1965, As Amended.* Washington, DC: US Government Printing Office No. 1985-527-317:30451; 1985.

66. Administration on Aging. 1988 Allotments: Information Memorandum No. AoA-IM-88-7; 1988.

67. *Prevention 86/87, Federal Programs and Progress.* Washington, DC: Public Health Service, OHDS; 1987.

68. National Association of Nutrition and Aging Services Programs: *The Aging Networks Guide to USDA.* Grand Rapids, Mich: National Association of Nutrition and Aging; 1988.

69. Administration on Aging. Information Memo AoA-IM-FY-90-5: Title IIIc nutrition program participation in the USDA Cash/Commodity Entitlement Program, 1990.

70. Office of Economic Opportunity: *Catalog of Federal Domestic Assistance.* June 1988;294–295.

71. Kirschner Associates Inc. and Opinion Research Corporation. *Longitudinal Evaluation of the National Nutrition Program for the Eldery.* Washington, DC: Administration on Aging; 1980. US Dept of Health, Education, and Welfare publication 80-20249.

72. Caliendo MA. Factors influencing the dietary status of participants in the national nutrition program for the elderly, I: population characteristics and nutritional intakes. *J Nutr Elderly.* 1980;1(1):23–39.

73. LeClerc H, Thornbury ME. Dietary intakes of Title III meal program recipients and nonrecipients. *J Am Diet Assoc.* 1983;83(5):573–577.

74. Kohrs MB, O'Hanlon P, Eklund D. Title VII nutrition program for the elderly, I: contribution to one day's dietary intake. *J Am Diet Assoc.* 1978;72(5):487–492.

75. Kohrs MB. Association of participation in a nutritional program for the elderly with nutritional status. *Am J Clin Nutr*. 1980;33:2643–2656.

76. Zandt SV, Fox H. Nutritional impact of congregate meals programs. *J Nutr Elderly*. 1986;5(3):31–43.

77. Nestle M, Lee PR, Fullarton JE. *Nutrition and the Elderly: A Working Paper for the Administration on Aging*. Policy Paper No. 2. San Francisco, Calif: Aging Health Policy Center, University of California; 1983.

78. Sainer JS. The big apple has a big heart. *Aging*. 1983;341(October/November):2–7.

79. FallCreek SJ, Allen BP, Halls DM. *Health Promotion and Aging*. San Francisco, Calif: Aging Health Policy Center, University of California; 1985.

80. Butler JS, Ohls JC, Posner BM. The effect of the food stamp program on the nutrient intake of the eligible elderly. *J Hum Resources*. 1985;20(3):405–419.

81. Akin JS, Guilkey DK, Popkin BM, et al. The impact of federal transfer programs on the nutrient intake of elderly individuals. *J Hum Resources*. 1985;20(3):382–404.

82. Independent Sector. *Giving and Volunteering in the U.S.: Summary of Findings*. Washington, DC: 1988.

83. *Interfaith Volunteer Caregivers: A Special Report No. 1*. Princeton, NJ: The Robert Wood Johnson Foundation; 1989.

84. Parver AK. *Coverage and Reimbursement Policies for Nutrition Care Services*. Chicago, Ill: American Dietetic Association; 1986.

85. *VA Community Access Program*. Boston, Mass: Veterans Administration; 1989.

Chapter 17

Health Promotion and Disease Prevention in the Elderly

Ann Sorenson, Nancy Chapman, and David N. Sundwall

If then commitment is made at every level, we ought to achieve our goals and older Americans, who might otherwise have suffered disease and disability, will instead be healthy people.[1]

Good health is the key factor in maintaining an independent and productive life. Health promotion and disease prevention activities interrupt or slow the progression of aging and disease before pathologic changes become irreversible. The expected outcome of health promotion must reach beyond longevity to the goal of an acceptable quality of life, without debilitating physical or mental disabilities.[2,3]

Preventive measures seek to detect early the precursors and risk factors for diseases and to intervene rapidly.[4] Previous chapters in this volume discuss prevention and treatment strategies of specific age-related syndromes. This chapter offers health promotion as a more global approach to health care that focuses on an individual's life style and general well-being, regardless of any special health problem. For example, smoking cessation improves physical stamina and lessens susceptibility to infections, while it reduces the risk of lung cancer and heart disease.

In the health promotion context, public health education unifies the message and avoids confusing the public with disjointed proscriptions and recommendations for distinct diseases. The generalized direction of health promotion guidance, however, often handicaps fund-raising abilities for biomedical research, health care delivery, and public education. Campaigns to "cure or prevent" life-threatening or immediate diseases often command more public attention and funding.

Nevertheless, one of the most significant advancements of the past decade has been the convergence of opinion on what constitutes a "proper diet" for the general public. It is worth noting that the largest voluntary health organizations, the American Cancer Society, the American Heart Association, and the American Diabetes Association, have all invested a significant proportion of their health promotion activities in dietary recommendations. While it is widely recognized that cancer, heart disease, and diabetes represent the ''big killers'' of our citizens, the association between dietary factors and these diseases is less well known.

In addition to understanding the current scientific consensus on what constitutes good and proper nutrition, health professionals must also be aware of the multitude of fraudulent and false claims made that promote nutritional products. Many Americans suffer from unsubstantiated fears of dietary risks, and it is incumbent on health professionals to be able to ease these fears when appropriate.

To meet the needs of their patients and the public, health practitioners and educators are challenged to employ three health promotion, as well as disease treatment, strategies:

1. Educate individuals on ways to promote good health by adopting better life style habits and a safer local environment.
2. Assist people to identify their own genetic/familial predispositions and risk factors for specific diseases.
3. Promote public awareness of the myths as well as the realities pertaining to good health.[5,6]

TYPES OF PREVENTION

Several levels of prevention exist in current practice. Primary prevention, synonymous with health promotion, seeks to prevent disease in susceptible people by reducing their exposure to risk factors or by altering susceptibility. The basic messages recommend a better diet, more exercise, smoking cessation, better sanitation, and accident prevention. Primary prevention uses education to encourage individuals to modify behaviors. This approach also manipulates the local environment to facilitate healthy behaviors, such as taking measures to shift from the use of saturated fats to unsaturated fats in the diet, or prohibitions against smoking in public places.

Secondary prevention is the early detection and treatment of disease. The objective is to cure—or at least slow—the disease process, and to prevent complications and disability. Screening programs are the hallmark of secondary prevention at the community level. Public health officials and private practitioners share responsibility for conducting these programs.

Tertiary prevention attempts to minimize the ill effects of diseases once they have occurred and to rehabilitate the patient's remaining capacities. Rehabilitation depends on multidisciplinary teamwork of various health professionals, including physical and behavioral therapists, physicians, nurses, and nutritionists.

Prevention of disease or mitigation of disability can improve the quality of life at any age. Anyone can benefit from gains in function, fewer periods of acute illness, and less need for long-term care.[1] Prevention strategies can also conserve health resources. In 1988, those over age 65 years represented 12% of the population but accounted for more than 30% ($175 billion) of public health care costs. Health care expenditures by older people totaled $73 billion—an average of $2,394 per individual (Table 17-1).[7,8] Over the past decade, these expenditures grew from under 13% in 1977 to an average of more than 18% of their 1988 personal income for health care.[9–11]

With the older age group as the fastest-growing segment of the population, these health care cost estimates signal the need to examine strategies that might lower expenditures, such as health promotion and disease prevention for those over age 65 years. In the next 25 years, the number of people over age 60 years will double; and those over 85 years are projected to increase in number the fastest of any age group.[12]

GENERAL CONSIDERATIONS FOR SUCCESSFUL HEALTH PROMOTION AND DISEASE PREVENTION

Successful preventive health care strategies must be practical, feasible, and effective. Several criteria suggest ways to maximize available financial resources and health manpower:

Table 17-1 Per Capita Health Care Cost for People Aged 65 Years and Older

Year and Source	Total Care	Hospital	Physician	Nursing Home	Other Care
1988 total	5,749	2,374	1,244	1,197	934
Private	2,421	406	620	695	700
Consumer	2,394	395	620	685	694
• Direct out of pocket	1,691	98	287	670	635
• Insurance	463	248	149	15	52
• Medicare premium	240	49	184	0	7
Other private	27	11	0	10	5
Government	3,328	1,968	623	503	234
Medicare	2,303	1,602	580	20	101
Medicaid	677	115	18	429	115
Other government	348	251	25	54	18
Cost/income (%)	18.12	2.99	4.69	5.18	5.25
Per capita mean income	30,521				

Source: Congressional Record—Extension of Remarks: Elderly Health Care Costs likely to rise to one-fifth of income, Representative Edward R. Roybal (D, CA) March 23, 1989; PE 979.

- Direct prevention toward diseases or disabilities that have a significant impact on the quality or length of life.
- Ensure that acceptable methods of treatment or intervention are available.
- Institute early detection to improve the prognosis of the disease.
- Make available reliable and cost-effective methods of detection.
- Implement risk modifiers that prevent or substantially reduce disease.
- Verify that the prevalence and impact of the health end-point is great enough to justify the cost of prevention, detection, or treatment.[13,14]

Although they are sometimes difficult to quantify in economic measures, the effects of age-related diseases such as heart disease, cancer, and osteoporosis are so great that even a small reduction of disease prevalence translates into substantial savings in health care expenditures and lost productivity.[15] Because the quality of life often eludes cost-benefit determinations, some critics overlook this outcome of health promotion and contend that costs of many disease prevention/health promotion programs exceed the medical costs to treat disease. Policy makers and economists need to factor in improved quality of life as well as reduced mortality and morbidity rates when allocating financial resources for health care.[16]

When resources are limited, public health programs usually concentrate on the most effective programs to reach the broadest constituency. For example, the prevention and detection of hypertension has emerged as a national priority because of its high prevalence, its role in multiple diseases, and the potential for successful intervention.[17] Since 1972, the National Heart, Lung, and Blood Institute has sponsored the National High Blood Pressure Detection and Education Program. Decreasing excess intakes of sodium and reducing obesity hold the most promise in reducing hypertension and are advocated by most public health programs.[18] Limiting alcohol consumption and increasing intake of potassium, magnesium, fiber, and unsaturated fats may also alter blood pressure status at a reasonably low cost of intervention. However, more clinical research studies are needed before specific recommendations for the public can be made.[17]

HEALTH PROMOTION AND DISEASE PREVENTION FOR OLDER ADULTS

Advancing primary prevention for those over age 65 years requires a change in attitude that accepts the growing proof that individuals of any age may benefit from adopting health-promoting behaviors.[3] Health professionals must dismiss the attitude that diseases of old age are irreversible and inevitable. Life expectancy has been extended, accounting for the growth in population of those over age 85 years. In fact, those who are presently age 65 years can expect to live an additional 17 years (19 years for women and 14.5 years for men).[10]

Although demonstrated advantages of preventive services for older people are limited, emerging research is quite convincing. Research on cancer etiology suggests that a 10- to 20-year latent period exists between events that may induce some cancers and the clinical expression of the disease. Based on an average 15-year latency period, cancer detected after age 70 years could have begun between ages 55 and 60 years. Hence, many of the quarter of a million cancers induced in people after age 60 might have been prevented by primary prevention measures, such as smoking cessation and dietary changes.[11]

Table 17-2 lists the most common causes of death in people over age 65 years. It is obvious that older people are more susceptible not only to chronic diseases, but also to acute diseases, such as food poisoning, infections, pneumonia, and orthostatic hypotension.[10,19–21] Most of these conditions are responsive to aggressive preventive health care. The growth of community "wellness" services or activities for older people signals a growing commitment to postponing disease and disabilities in older persons. By 1985, 37 states had initiated community wellness programs for seniors.[22]

Over the past 20 years, some of the major causes of morbidity and mortality in old age have declined, although the extent to which health promotion efforts are responsible has not been determined. Over these two decades, stroke deaths declined 55%, heart attacks decreased 40%, and substantial progress has been made in hypertension control.[1] Evidence indicates that those who reach old age in good health tend to stay healthy until shortly before death, often well into the seventh or eighth decade of life.[23]

Table 17-2 Most Common Causes of Death in Persons Over Age 65 Years (Rate per 100,000)

	Age (rank)		
Cause	65–74	75–84	>85
All causes	2,848	6,399	15,224
Heart disease	1,103(1)	2,749(1)	7,251(1)
Atherosclerosis		88(8)	488(5)
Malignant neoplasm	835(2)	1,272(2)	1,604(3)
Stroke	177(3)	626(3)	1,884(2)
Chronic pulmonary disease	141(4)	270(4)	331(6)
Diabetes	59(5)	126(6)	217(8)
Pneumonia/influenza	54(6)	216(5)	883(4)
Accidents and complications	50(7)	107(7)	257(7)
Auto accidents	12.6	17.9	14.0
Chronic liver disease	39(8)		
Nephritis/nephrosis	27(9)	76(9)	201(9)
Septicemia	20(10)	51(10)	142(10)
Suicide	34	48	52

Additional Factors Affecting Health Promotion and Disease Prevention in Older People

Planning preventive care packages and counseling approaches for older people requires considerations in addition to those for younger adults. People over age 65 years have special concerns about their own mosaic of disease afflictions.[1,6,10,24–26] Most older people suffer from one or more chronic diseases or syndromes, and total risk increases as a function of the number of individual risk factors.[27]

Some diseases and conditions, such as coronary heart disease, may manifest themselves differently in older ages than at younger ages.[3] For example, elevated serum cholesterol becomes less predictive of heart disease-related morbidity in an older individual (Chapter 8). In fact, a low serum cholesterol level is a predictor of mortality in people of advanced age.[28–31] Lower serum levels are associated with increased risk of cancer and hemorrhagic stroke.

Some chronic conditions common in old age have competing risk factors.[32] For example, obesity is a major risk factor for heart disease, diabetes, and other chronic diseases, but modest obesity is protective for osteoporosis.[5] Conversely, low body weight is a significant risk factor for hip fracture.[33]

In older people, functional disabilities associated with chronic diseases become as important as preventing onset of the disease.[13,14] Of the population aged 65 years who live independently, 24% have some degree of functional impairment; 15% are unable to perform major activities; and 11% are less impaired. Of those who are dependent on others for daily care, 6% are in nursing homes and 14% are homebound.[13,34] Table 17-3 shows the distribution of limitations in various activities in daily living by age and sex.[7]

The common aging process and the attendant dysfunctions occur in all individuals to some extent, although at different rates and to different degrees over the normal life span.[11,35] Age-dependent changes in taste,[36] smell,[37] kidney function,[38] bone loss,[5] and skin[39] occur in almost everyone. Some dysfunctions may produce age-related morbidity such as urinary incontinence, falls and fractures, sensory impairment, malnutrition, depression, and poor dentition.[13]

Although data are sparse, existing studies report important differences among various minority populations, and by gender, in the severity and prevalence of degenerative conditions of later life. Osteoporosis may be less severe in elderly blacks than in nonblacks, whereas diabetes is more common among native Americans compared with the general population. Women have a higher prevalence for most age-related conditions of old age except those with the mortality risk (ie, prevalence and incidence rates are similar). Women therefore live longer, but in poor health and with disabilities.

Table 17-3 Sources of Functional Limitations in Older People by Age and Sex

| | Distribution of Limitations in the Population | | | |
| | Age >65 y | | Age >75 y | |
Limitation: Difficulty in	Men	Women	Men	Women
Shopping	7.3	14.1	12.3	23.1
Heavy housework	13.7	30.8	18.7	40.0
Light housework	4.9	8.7	7.6	14.0
Getting outside	6.3	11.8	9.8	19.4
Walking	15.5	20.9	20.5	29.2
Walking up 10 steps	19.1	28.5	24.6	37.0
Lifting 10 lb	8.2	18.6	11.4	27.2
Lifting 25 lb	22.9	45.8	29.0	57.8
Using toilet	3.1	5.1	4.6	8.4

AGING VERSUS PATHOLOGY

Differentiating age-related from age-dependent disorders challenges clinicians and researchers. Age-related diseases and disorders have specific temporal patterns. They display incidence peaks and then decline in frequency with advancing age. Ulcerative colitis, gout, peptic ulcers, and some cancers are age-related diseases. Therefore, if the initiating factors can be determined and then prevented or treated, the diseases might never appear in older persons.[40]

Age-dependent diseases are directly correlated with age and closely related to the usual aging processes. Coronary heart disease, adult-onset diabetes, and Alzheimer's disease are examples of age-dependent diseases. Most disability of old age is increasingly associated with these age-dependent conditions, which are, ultimately, the primary causes of death and disability[13] in persons over age 65 years.[3]

Major sources of morbidity appear in Table 17-4, and may overlap and differ from primary causes of death presented in Table 17-2. Heart disease, digestive conditions, respiratory problems, and cancer afflict people over age 65 years most often. Renal disease, diabetes, osteoporosis, dementias (including Alzheimer's disease), and cancer are also frequent causes of ill health in the elderly. Table 17-5 shows the distribution of the main health problems that cause disability.

Prevention is especially important when there is no generally acceptable treatment for a disease.[32] Osteoporosis, a case in point, demonstrates the need for prevention strategies throughout life. Adolescent and young women need to increase their intake of dietary calcium to achieve maximal peak bone mass,[32,41] but older women also need adequate calcium intake to slow the rate of bone mineral loss.[32] There has been a general failure to recognize the need for increased

Table 17-4 Most Common Causes of Morbidity in Persons Over Age 65 Years*

Rank	First-Degree Diagnosis	Rate per 1000			All Diagnosis	Rate per 1000		
		Total	Men	Women		Total	Men	Women
1	Circulatory system†	1122	245	217	Circulatory system†	4635	869	838
2	Digestive system	426	146	156	Endocrine, nutrition, metabolism and immune disorders	1286	144	360
3	Respiratory system†	366	126	121	Respiratory system†	1199	331	297
4	Neoplasms	348	83	109	Digestive diseases	1169	317	359
5	Injury and poisoning†	260	142	109	Genitourinary tract	956	220	381
6	Genitourinary tract	246	80	126	Neoplasms	778	177	214
7	Musculoskeletal system	186	76	86	Ill-defined condition	729	215	227
8	Endocrine, nutrition, metabolism, and immune disorders	153	35	54	Musculoskeletal system	699	160	230
9	Nervous system and sense organs	102	37	41	Injury and poisoning†	570	299	229
10	Mental disorders†	88	80	68	Supplementary class	559	149	518
	Total	1382	1160	1589	Total	4280	3617	4902

*Data based on inpatients discharged from a short stay in the hospital.
†Rates are higher in men.

Table 17-5 Distribution of Illnesses That Cause Disability in People Over Age 65 Years

Condition	% Women	% Men
Arthritis/rheumatism	31.6	16.3
Heart conditions	22.0	25.3
Hypertension	11.1	6.1
Urinary incontinence	9.3	6.5
Visual impairment*	8.6	7.6
Diabetes	6.4	6.2
Impairment of lower extremities and hips	5.7	4.0
Mental and nervous conditions†	3.8	2.0
Impairment of back and spine	3.8	2.7
Hearing impairments	2.7	2.0
Asthma	2.0	2.2

*Cataracts.
†Rate for depression 147/1000. Rate for Alzheimer's disease 112/1000 (5% to 10% > age 65 years; 35% > age 85 years).

calcium beyond childbearing years despite altered patterns and excretion that commonly occur with advancing age.

To develop appropriate preventive and health promotion strategies for older people, health professionals must ask the following questions:

1. Do all people develop age-dependent diseases as a consequence of aging processes if they live long enough?
2. Are age-dependent diseases preventable?
3. What are the risk factor profile and disease mosaic of the target audience?
4. Which factors are (1) the most life-threatening or debilitating, (2) likely to progress most rapidly, or (3) most likely to be cured or arrested?

Role of the Health Care Provider

Disease prevention and health promotion in old age are dependent on sensitizing educators and health professionals to the special needs of older people and the risk factors affecting older individuals.

STRATEGIES FOR DISEASE PREVENTION AND HEALTH PROMOTION IN OLD AGE

Additional questions for which answers are also needed include when and which health promotion strategies should be initiated and what criteria should be used to set health priorities for older individuals. But, because older people of the same chronologic age differ appreciably in functional capacity and health status, some programs should be developed for free-living older people while others should be targeted to institutionalized or homebound older persons.

Successful interventions take into account the past and present life styles of older people—their socioeconomic status, medical histories, personal environment, and drug regimens.[42] Of course, the strong role that genetics plays in longevity and disease patterns cannot be overlooked.[43]

How well older individuals respond to preventive therapies will depend on how long they ate too much fat, smoked, were inactive, abused alcohol, or followed other high-risk behaviors. Regular risk assessments of older individuals aid in designing the most appropriate health promotion messages. It is important to assess several factors before making appropriate recommendations for people over age 65 years:

- dietary guidelines and nutrient intake recommendations
- socioeconomic determinants
- trends in food supply
- eating patterns
- nutritional and dietary status
- use of dietary supplements
- physical activity
- smoking habits
- alcohol abuse
- medications
- food safety
- health fraud

Individuals are more likely to comply with dietary recommendations tailored to their personal situations than with general information. An analysis of changes in the socioeconomic conditions, cultural factors, and the food supply provides insight into an older person's eating patterns, developed over a lifetime. Assisting families to understand, tolerate, and support older members' curious eating habits may reduce urgency to institutionalize them and may help an older family member's easy transition into a household, on discharge from an institution.[44] For older people, the frequency of meals and food preferences and taboos can connect them to a familiar past; ignoring these factors can heighten resistance to change.

Dietary Guidelines for the General Public

Two recent documents, the 1988 *Surgeon General's Report on Nutrition and Health*[45] and the 1989 National Research Council's (NRC) *Report on Diet and Health*,[46] summarize the consensus of the scientific community and make dietary and health recommendations for the general public.[15] The advice reinforces the United States Department of Health and Human Services/Department of Agriculture *Dietary Guidelines for Americans*,[47] which are appropriate for any age.

These two reports recommend (1) reducing dietary fats and cholesterol; (2) limiting salt intakes; (3) limiting the use of alcohol; (4) maintaining adequate but not excessive protein intakes; (5) eating more fruits, vegetables, and complex carbohydrates; (6) balancing caloric intake with expenditure to maintain a healthy weight; and (7) avoiding the use of dietary supplements in excess of the NRC's recommended dietary allowances (RDAs).[48] Both documents caution against unsafe dietary practices, health fads, and outright health fraud, much of which is directed at older persons.[49]

Most dietary guidelines are based on the NRC's RDAs for almost all healthy people.[48] The RDAs are based on data collected mainly from men aged 20 to 30 years. Extrapolating a requirement for an individual to a population is difficult because of the variability of physiologic, sociologic, and health status determinants, and the ability of individuals to adapt to a wide range of nutrient intakes. Factors such as phytates, oxalates, or the form of a nutrient can alter the bioavailability, absorption, metabolism, or excretion of nutrients derived from foods.[48–50] Thus, following the RDAs does not ensure nutritional adequacy (or inadequacy with consumption of lesser amounts), but it provides reasonable protection for generally healthy people who eat a variety of foods in their normal diet.

Aging may increase requirements for some nutrients, primarily minerals,[50,51] and may reduce adaptability to changes in nutritional intake;[22,48,51] requirements for some nutrients may increase with age while requirements for others, mainly lipid-soluble vitamins, may decrease.[52–54] It was anticipated that the 10th edition of *Recommended Dietary Allowances* would establish separate recommendations for those aged 51 to 75 years and those older than age 76 years.[50] The RDA committee concluded that data were insufficient to establish separate RDAs for people over age 70 years, because of the disparities between chronologic and physiologic aging and the higher prevalence of chronic diseases with advancing age.

The 10th edition RDA, published in October 1989, adds RDAs for vitamin K and selenium and changes the recommendations for vitamins C, B_6, B_{12}, and folate and for calcium, magnesium, iron, and zinc. A comparison of the 1980 RDAs to the 1989 RDAs for adults is presented in Table 17-6. The 1989 RDAs for women are generally the same as or lower than those for men. For those over age

Table 17-6 Ninth (1980) and Tenth (1989) Editions of the Recommended Dietary Allowances for Adults

| | Men | | | | Women | | | |
| | Age 25–50 y | | Age 51+ y | | Age 25–50 y | | Age 51+ y | |
Nutrients	1980	1989	1980	1989	1980	1989	1980	1989
Weight (lb)	154	174	154	170	120	138	120	143
Height (in)	70	70	70	68	64	64	64	63
kcal/d	2700*	2900	2400†	2300	2000*	2200	1800†	1900
Protein (g)	56	63	56	63	44	50	44	50
Fat-soluble vitamins								
Vitamin A (mg re)‡	1000	1000	1000	1000	800	800	800	800
Vitamin D (mg)	5	5	5	5	5	5	5	5
Vitamin E (mg)	10	10	10	10	8	8	8	8
Vitamin K (mg) (new)	—	80	—	80	—	65	—	65
Water-soluble vitamins								
Vitamin C (mg)	60	60	60	60	60	60	60	60
Thiamine (mg)	1.4	1.5	1.2	1.2	1.0	1.1	1.0	1.0
Riboflavin (mg)	1.6	1.7	1.4	1.4	1.2	1.3	1.2	1.2
Niacin (mg ne)§	18	19	16	15	13	15	13	13
Vitamin B_6 (mg)	2.2	2.0	2.2	2.0	2.0	1.6	2.0	1.6
Folate (mg)	400	200	400	200	400	180	400	180
Vitamin B_{12} (mg)	3.0	2.0	3.0	2.0	3.0	2.0	3.0	2.0
Minerals								
Calcium (mg)	800	800	800	800	800	800	800	800
Phosphorus (mg)	800	800	800	800	800	800	800	800
Magnesium (mg)	350	350	350	350	300	280	300	280
Iron (mg)	10	10	10	10	18	15	10	10
Zinc (mg)	15	15	15	15	15	12	15	12
Iodine (mg)	150	150	150	150	150	150	150	150
Selenium (mg) (new)	—	70	—	70	—	55	—	55

*Ages 23 to 50 years.
†Ages 51 to 75 years.
‡re, Retinol equivalents.
§ne, Nicotinamide equivalents.

51 years, new recommendations increased protein and substantially reduced folate and vitamin B_{12}. For women over age 51 years, zinc decreased slightly. Most other new recommendations for groups aged 51 + years parallel those for younger adults except for lower values for thiamine, niacin, and vitamin B_6 (Chapter 3).

RDAs specific for older people may be necessary as knowledge of the relationship between certain diseases and nutritional status is better articulated. Furthermore, it has been suggested that a separate dietary recommendation for older people should specify what level of nutrient is required to (1) prevent nutrient defiency syndromes (minimum), (2) maintain tissue saturation or optimal function (desirable), (3) reduce risk or treat degenerative diseases (pharmacologic), and (4) prevent toxic effects (toxic).[50,55] For example, an increasing prevalence of atrophic gastritis, with accompanying hypochlorhydria and compromised absorption, may require higher intakes of calcium, zinc, and some B vitamins.[56] For the present, the new RDAs are the best and most authoritative nutrient intake guidelines available.

Socioeconomic Determinants

Previous family structures, gender roles, employment opportunities, education, and economic stability affect food choices of older people. Sensitivity to these determinants enhances the effectiveness of dietary interventions. Individuals born between 1910 and 1930 who experienced food shortages during the Depression, who consumed more carbohydrates and less fat, and who produced fewer children to support them in old age, may be more parsimonious, more dependent on Social Security, and may make more regimented food choices. People born between 1940 and 1950 who ate more processed foods, who consumed more simple sugars and fewer complex carbohydrates, and who had more employment opportunities expect economic security, more leisure time, and more diverse diets.[57]

Current place of residence and economic status can also determine access to food sources and health care services. Successful preventive measures will accommodate the limitations of existing circumstances, such as a lack of transportation, improper cooking utensils and storage facilities, or physical impairments that narrow food choices and restrict certain nutrients.[58]

Older persons residing in central cities, small towns, and rural areas may have limited access to social and health services, nutrition programs, and food stores. Because older residents in urban and rural areas are often less educated and poorer than suburban residents, their risk of nutritional problems increases.[59] Individuals living in rural areas also tend to eat foods higher in salt, sugar, fat, and cholesterol.[60]

Living alone also raises the risk of poor nutritional status, especially for men.[61] In 1985, individuals over age 65 years were generally white, women, and noninstitutionalized; after age 80 years, men and blacks are more likely to survive. Overall, 67% of older people live with a spouse or others, 30% live alone, and 5% (generally over age 85 years) live in nursing homes. Directing single older adults to senior nutrition programs or arranging for home care assistance, including food purchasing and preparation, can improve their nutritional status.

Although growing numbers of people reach old age with adequate resources, older adults are more likely than younger adults to be poor or to live on fixed incomes. For some, Medicare, Medicaid, and frequently indexed Social Security benefits have decreased the inevitable poverty many elders faced in the past; but more than two out of every five older people are poor or economically vulnerable.[62] Poverty rates increase for those aged 85 years and over, nonwhites, women, and people living alone. For those living on fixed or low incomes, food price inflation can shrink the food budget. Health professionals should encourage older people with limited incomes to participate in the food stamp program, the senior nutrition program, and the commodity supplemental food program for seniors.

Food Supply

Food supply data provide a historic perspective on foods available over the lifetime of today's elderly. Since 1909, per capita food supply data, although not individual food intakes (individual food intake information was not collected until the mid-1960s), show significant shifts in macronutrient and micronutrient composition, as well as total energy available.[63]

From 1909 to 1985, dietary fat increased from 31% of total calories to 42%. Fat has partially replaced carbohydrates as an energy source. Vegetable oils, salad dressing, margarines, and shortenings have accounted for the largest increases. Although declining, animal sources remain the largest source of fat in the food supply. Over 80 years, saturated fats as a proportion of total fats have declined and polyunsaturated fats have increased. Monounsaturated fat consumption has not changed.

Most micronutrients—vitamins and minerals—have increased in the food supply because of fortification of processed foods, introduction of nutrient-rich produce strains, and changes in food preferences. Enrichment of grain products has increased levels of thiamine, riboflavin, niacin, and iron in the food supply. Fortification of fruit drinks and increased intakes of citrus fruits have contributed to the rise in available ascorbic acid. New vitamin A-rich vegetables and fortified margarines and dairy products have augmented the vitamin A content in the food supply. Calcium in the food supply has increased with increased use of low-fat milk and cheeses. Declines in grain products have accounted for slight declines in folic acid and magnesium.

Eating Patterns

If clinicians use knowledge of food preferences and eating frequencies of aging people when counseling them, it will contribute to their acceptance of dietary advice. Older adults surveyed in HANES II chose low-fat milk and cheese from the milk group; grapefruits and melon from the fruit group; potatoes and tomatoes from the vegetable group; bread, biscuits, and muffins from the grain group; and ground beef from the meat group.[64] The 1977–1978 National Food Consumption Survey data show that one third of older adults used whole-grain products and that older people were the highest users of eggs, skim milk, vegetables, fruits, and soups, and the lowest users of soft drinks compared with other adults.[65]

Nutritional and Dietary Status

Undetected disease and use of dietary supplements or medications complicate the task of defining nutrient needs of various strata of older persons; however, recommendations have been made and are described briefly here; some of these recommendations are discussed in more detail in other chapters of this book.

Fluid Consumption

Decreased fluid consumption and an age-related loss of body water pose real threats to many older people. Dehydration is often undetected; the decrease in thirst sensation common in old age increases the risk of dehydration and leads to electrolyte imbalances.[66] Hypodipsia also occurs as a result of changes in renal function, mental dysfunction, or use of diuretics. Dietary advice must routinely emphasize fluid replacement at levels appropriate for an individual's electrolyte status, type of feeding (ie, oral, enteral, or parenteral), and presence of incontinence.[67] Adequate water intake (eg, 30 mL/kg of body weight or approximately 1 mL of water for each calorie ingested)[68] is reasonable and important to normal renal and bowel function.[69,70]

Energy and Body Weight

Significant declines in energy intake among aging people could be related to many factors: (1) decreased physical exercise, (2) loss of lean body mass, (3) depression, (4) living alone, (5) loss of sensory acuity, (6) anorexia-inducing medications, (7) poorly-fitting dentures, and (8) decrease in income.

In the Baltimore Longitudinal Study of Aging, the average energy expenditure of male executives declined from 2700 kcal/d at age 30 years to 2100 kcal/d at age 80 years.[71] A more recent 6-year longitudinal study found that daily energy intakes decreased about 12 kcal/d per year for men and 4 kcal/d per year for women. Lower fat intakes accounted for most of the reduction.[72] National data report the lowest mean energy intakes for those over age 75 years, about 1800 kcal for men and 1350 kcal for women.[73]

As energy requirements decline for those over age 65 years, nutrient needs remain stable or perhaps increase. Recommendations for nutrient intakes should be stated in terms of nutrients by weight per 1000 kcal or per unit of lean body mass for those over age 65 years.[74] Lower energy intakes do not impair health as long as the nutrient density of the diet remains adequate to meet nutrient needs.[10] In fact, energy deprivation, at least in animals, appears to have a beneficial effect on immune status, although the mechanism is unknown.[75]

Increasing energy expenditure can help balance energy intakes and achieve appropriate body weight for individuals who are overweight for height. Determinations of obesity in older people should account for the fact that approximately 1.2 cm of height is lost for each 20 years past maturity.[76] Friscancho[77] has suggested new standards for weight and body composition by frame size and height to assess geriatric nutritional status. Master and associates[78] also proposed revising weight and height charts that compensated for loss in height in individuals aged 65 to 94 years. These measures developed specifically for older people will help to assess the true prevalence of over- and underweight among older people and evaluate effects of inappropriate weight on health status. To estimate more accurately the lean body mass in geriatrics, creatine/height indices may need to be revised, based on reduced creatine clearance, reduced creatine production, and reduced height of older people.[79]

A rapid, unexplained weight loss or anorexia in older people often heralds the onset of overt symptoms of a protein-calorie type of malnutrition (PCM). Symptoms may include dehydration, loss of lean body mass, loss of protein status, and confusion.[67,80–82] Whether PCM is a symptom of intercurrent disease or a syndrome of unknown origin, this condition is a strong predictor of morbidity and mortality in older people and has been estimated to be present in 35% to 65% of older people in long-term or acute care facilities.[34,82] Caution is needed in interpreting these results, because no nutritional status standards or measures exist for older people.[83]

Protein

The 1989 RDA for protein has been increased from 56 g/d to 60 g/d for adult men and from 44 g/d to 50 g/d for women[48] (Table 17-6). Declining protein intakes, protein absorption, and protein synthesis do not appear to affect deleteriously older populations with no evidence of wasting diseases.[84]

Some clinicians are concerned that protein intakes in substantial excess of the RDA may contribute to the decline of renal function that commonly begins after the fourth decade of life;[85] however, there is evidence that even older, chronically ill, elderly people can tolerate high protein intakes with no measurable changes in renal function.[86] Nitrogen requirements do increase with the physiologic stress (ie, infections, fractures, surgery, and burns) common in older people[86] or with the use of protein-bound drugs.[87]

The quantity and type of protein best able to meet the needs of older people are unknown. Free-living elderly should be advised to consume moderate amounts of protein and avoid high and low extremes.

Lipids

Over the past 30 years, blood cholesterol levels for adults in the United States have declined, but for postmenopausal women, blood cholesterol levels increase to higher levels than seen in men after age 60 years. Dietary cholesterol and total fat intakes are decreasing in older adults,[88] but mean cholesterol (461 mg for men, 316 mg for women)[10] and total fat (34% of total cholesterol)[71] remain above recommended levels for lowering the risk of coronary heart disease. Furthermore, in one study, higher intakes of animal fats and saturated fatty acids and lower intakes of polyunsaturated fatty acids depressed the circulating essential fatty acids in institutionalized elderly people.[89] Because of the recent evidence linking low serum cholesterol levels to stroke, cancer, and other causes of morbidity,[28–30] and high cholesterol levels to risk of heart disease, people of advanced age should be counseled on how to maintain moderate serum levels of fat and cholesterol (Chapter 8).

Vitamins and Minerals

Intakes of most nutrients except vitamin C and vitamin A decline with decreases in energy intakes. In dietary surveys of older people, dietary calcium, vitamin A, thiamine, riboflavin, and iron either approached or failed to meet the RDAs, as did their energy intakes. Biochemical or clinical signs of deficiency, however, rarely accompanied (<5% on average) observed low intakes.[10,90,91]

Based on the observed nutrient status of older populations, the RDA Committee lowered the requirements for folate, vitamin B_6, and vitamin B_{12} for those over age 51 years, below recommendations for adults aged 25 to 50 years (Table 17-6) (Chapter 3). The 1989 RDA for zinc was decreased from 15 mg/d to 12 mg/d for women.

Maintaining adequate intakes of calcium and fluoride may mitigate several problems of old age, including osteoporosis, hypertension, and possibly colon cancer.[17,48,92,93] Low calcium intakes combined with poor calcium absorption, attenuated by high intakes of fiber;[94] protein;[95] lactase deficiency;[96] calcium-binding drugs;[39] and physiologic changes,[97] are of particular concern for postmenopausal women who have high rates of forearm and spinal fractures.[98,99]

Both men and women are at high risk for hip fractures after the eighth decade of life.[100] Estrogen replacement, exercise, and increased intakes of calcium (1000 to 1500 mg/d)[101,102] have been shown to diminish bone loss[103,104] and reduce osteoporosis-related fractures.[39]

Assessment of calcium intakes and risk factors for calcium deficiency or osteoporosis should be routine. For elders with lactose intolerance, advice on appropriate dietary sources can supplant the need for calcium supplementation. For some, calcium supplements may be necessary to obtain 1200 to 1500 mg of calcium per day. Some forms of calcium may decrease magnesium retention in bone, adversely affect kidney function, or decrease iron absorption; therefore, a physician should select the proper calcium salt and dosage (Chapter 4). Additional supplementation with Vitamin D (100,000 IU twice yearly)[105] and fluoride (50 to 80 mg) is still experimental. Because of possible side effects,[106] vitamin D and fluoride supplementation are recommended only for high-risk patients under the care of a clinical expert.

Older people who absorb higher levels of fat-soluble vitamins, because of a thinner water layer in the gut, are more susceptible to vitamin D toxicity than are younger adults. On the other hand, RDAs for vitamin D might be too low for older people[90] who have reduced vitamin D synthesis in the skin, low vitamin D intakes, less exposure to the sun, or impaired 1α-hydroxylation.[107] For housebound older individuals to maintain adequate serum vitamin D, increased sun exposure (30 min/d)[108] combined with low-dose supplementation (ie, 10 μg/d)[90] or a twice-per-year regimen of 2.5 mg of vitamin D_2[105] is recommended.

Use of Dietary Supplements

Whether to prevent deficiency diseases, treat a specific disorder or symptom (eg, tiredness, leg cramps, or urinary tract infection), or to assure good nutrition, a large number of elderly people use dietary supplements.[46] Use of supplements by older people has increased from an estimated 1% in 1975[109] to estimates of 40% nationwide in 1980.[110] Among those over age 65 years, supplement intakes ranged from 34% of men and 46% of women in a health screening program[111] to 62% of men and 69% of women in a Southern California retirement community.[112]

Because of drug regimens, poor economic status, living alone, physiologic decline, or disease process, many older individuals have inadequate intakes or poor absorption of certain nutrients. Supplements may be needed but, even then, in quantities no more than 50% to 150% of the RDAs.[48] Analyses of national survey results suggest that supplement users may not be the people most in need of them.[113–116]

Supplement use does not necessarily correlate with potential deficiencies,[117] nor does use relate to the users' perceived adequacy of their diets.[118] Approximately half of those who use supplemental vitamins take multivitamins, particularly vitamins C and E.[119,120] There is no evidence that older individuals are deficient in either vitamin E[121] or vitamin C,[122] nor that taking high dosages of self-prescribed vitamin E[123] and vitamin C[124] supplements retard aging or prevent atherosclerosis or cancer.

The benefits of supplements to the health of users is often unclear.[125] Pharmacologic levels of nutrients are administered in many studies. Sometimes benefits ascribed to one supplement, such as fish oil capsules, may be related to secondary contaminating vitamins (eg, vitamins A or E) in the mixture.[126] Dietary supplementation does not routinely improve morbidity or nutritional status for older people,[127] but it may improve some functions. Zinc supplements improved immune functions in several studies,[10] generally where zinc deficiencies existed. Zinc also aided wound healing,[50] especially leg ulcers, in the elderly.[128] Vitamin E may improve immune function and help elderly people resist disease.[129,130]

Excess vitamin and mineral supplementation, taken in pharmacologic amounts, can lead to nutrient imbalances, toxicities, or interactions with drugs, especially if megadoses (10 times the RDAs) are taken.[112–114,116] High dosages can also mask symptoms of certain diseases.[46] According to the NRC[46] and various professional groups,[130] individuals should avoid taking dietary supplements in excess of the RDA in any one day, unless recommended by health professionals for specific diagnosed conditions.[38,131]

Physical Activity

The effects of inactivity mimic the effects of aging;[132] almost 50% of the functional decline attributed to aging may in fact be related to inactivity.[133] Increasing energy expenditure through exercise appears to influence mortality and morbidity through a number of complex physiologic mechanisms. Despite these benefits, there has been some reluctance in recommending fitness programs for seniors because exercising too intensely may injure muscles, provoke heart attacks and irregular heart rhythms, increase blood pressure, and increase fall-related fractures.[134] Regular eccentric training can increase protein turnover (37% higher muscle catabolism) in older people and can require a higher protein intake.[135] The inability of older individuals, in general, to maintain high-intensity training programs may explain the modest, or absence of, fat body weight reductions in some human studies.[136–139] Therefore, for older people, it has been unclear what intensity and duration of physical training are necessary to delay declines in functional capacity,[140] although recent studies suggest some answers.

Combined with a calorie-appropriate diet, regular physical activity maintains a reasonable body weight, delays loss of lean muscle mass, and promotes good physical performance. A high activity level can predict survival for both institutionalized and free-living people aged 60 to 90 years.[141,142] High-intensity training appears to decrease fat cell hypertrophy, increase production of high-density lipoproteins, decrease hypertension, increase insulin resistance, and slow the rate of decline of Vo_2max in older persons.[143–145]

Exercise programs designed for older people can reduce bone loss and strengthen skeletal muscle in both men and women of very advanced age,[143,146] thus decreasing the risk of falls and fractures.[147,148] For example, a group of sedentary men and women aged 86 to 96 years, including previous fallers, increased the strength in their knee extensors between 167% and 180% after an 8-week course of weight-lifting exercise.

Health educators should instruct individuals over age 40 years to have a thorough medical examination and discuss safe, appropriate exercise regimens before they begin physical activity. Advice should also include home safety measures that prevent falls in the elderly[149] (Figure 17-1).

Cigarette Smoking

At any age, cigarette smoking imposes higher risks of coronary heart disease, lung and mouth cancers, stroke, and osteoporosis.[150] Smoking cessation results in decline of body nicotine within 6 months, risk of sudden heart attack in 1 to 2 years, and risk of cancer in about 15 years.[151] Smoking combined with low calorie intakes can also compromise vitamin C status,[48] but the health consequences of these observations are not well established. A survey of 9000 adults in the United Kingdom found that smokers usually skipped breakfast, consumed fried foods more frequently, and ate fruit and brown bread less frequently than did non-smokers. Although the more cigarettes subjects smoked, the worse their eating habits, smokers who stopped tended to eat as much as lifetime nonsmokers.[152]

Fortunately, the smoking prevalence is decreasing across all race and gender groups of adults, as both men and women stop the smoking habit.[153] In general, men quit more easily and abstain from cigarettes longer than do women. Compared with younger adults, a lower percentage of current smokers over age 65 years use the highest-tar cigarettes (>15mg), and fewer smoke the lowest-tar cigarettes (<10mg).[154] Cigarette smoking also appears to increase the waist-hip ratios (WHR) despite a reduction in overall weight.[155] Higher WHRs are associated with an increased risk of heart disease and other chronic diseases. The best preventive message is never start smoking or stop immediately.

- Provide handy light switches and good illumination
- Consider night light
- Eliminate extension cords by installing sufficient numbers of electrical outlets
- Provide toilet facility on same floor near bedroom
- Install high toilet seat
- Install handrails for toilet, bath, and stairways
- Remove casters from furniture; if casters are essential, put furniture against wall
- Make floors, bathtub, and carpets nonslip
- If possible, have home without steps inside or out, or have stairs with small gradient
- Make last step (up and down) a different color

Figure 17-1 Recommendations for home safety measures to prevent falls in the elderly. *Source*: Reprinted from *FDA Consumer* (1988;May:22), U.S. Food and Drug Administration.

Alcohol Abuse

Like smoking, excessive alcohol intakes increase morbidity and mortality rates among individuals at any age. Besides advancing nutrient deficiencies (ie, thiamine and niacin), heavy drinking also damages organs and tissues important to nutrient absorption and utilization. High alcohol intakes also depress appetite and reduce the desire and ability to eat; poor nutritional status can result.

Older people have a lower tolerance for alcohol, because blood alcohol becomes more concentrated as total body water declines with age. Approximately 32% of those aged 65 years and over consume alcohol on a regular basis (at least one time per week). About 15% of this cohort are considered light drinkers, 11% are moderate drinkers, and 6% are heavy drinkers.[156]

Alcoholics (consuming more than 2 oz/d) are likely to suffer fractures, due to weakened bones and increased risk for falling, and other injuries.[142] Alcohol consumption is a risk factor for osteoporosis, diabetes, hypertension, cancer, and liver disease. Moderation of intake is advisable at any age. The older individual whose balance and judgment are impaired by excess alcohol is particularly vulnerable to injury and illness.

Drug Use

The high use of drugs among the aging may further compromise their health (Chapter 14). The average older person receives more than 13 prescriptions per year and may take as many as 6 drugs at a time. Cardiac drugs (eg, diuretics) are most widely used by the aging population, followed by drugs to treat arthritis, psychic disorders, and respiratory and gastrointestinal conditions. Many of these diseases are diet-related, and the use of drugs may complement, supplement, or replace diet therapy.

Long-term use of a variety of drugs, often at high doses, raises the risk of drug-nutrient interactions that can have iatrogenic consequences, often more pronounced in old age. Individuals with nutritionally inadequate intakes and impaired nutritional status are at the highest risk. To improve drug compliance, altering the drug therapy may be more appropriate than recommending dietary changes or food restrictions. Periodic assessments can identify borderline nutritional status requiring appropriate dietary recommendations, nutrient supplementation, or change in drug regimen.

Use of high-potency nutrient supplements may also affect drug efficacy. Physicians need to explain carefully the potential side effects when certain drugs and foods or supplements are taken together. The potential health threat of nutrient-drug interactions emphasizes the need for effective counseling of older people on the proper use of drugs.[157] Drugs can alter food intake through changes in appetite, taste, and smell, and adverse gastrointestinal effects.[158] Drugs may concentrate more readily in the blood of older people than in the blood of younger people because the capacity to eliminate them declines with age.[24]

Malnutrition also alters drug absorption, protein binding, drug metabolism, and drug clearance. Protein-bound drugs such as warfarin and diazepam may be more toxic in patients with hypoalbuminemia. On the other hand, some drugs decrease absorption of nutrients or cause mineral depletion. Such drugs include laxatives, antacids, anti-inflammatory agents (eg, aspirin), diuretics, antibiotics, analgesics (eg, indomethacin), and cholesterol-lowering medications (eg, cholestyramine).

Appetite generally increases with use of tricyclic antidepressants, reserpine, antihistamines, and anabolic steroids; whereas amphetamines and related drugs depress the appetite. Aging slows metabolism and can reverse these effects. Phenothiazine, a psychotropic agent that usually increases food intake, may decrease appetite in older people. Specific foods can adversely react with drugs, such as tyramine-containing foods with their life-threatening interaction with monoamine oxidase. Alcohol taken with disulfiram and hypoglycemic agents induces unpleasant results.

Food Safety

Food-borne microbial illnesses affect large numbers of Americans, ranging from 400 reported cases per year to as many as 5 million outbreaks per year reported to the Centers for Disease Control.[159] Microbiologic contamination causes great discomfort, days lost from work, and even death. Older people and the chronically ill are most susceptible to the ill effects of microbial diseases. In fact, evidence suggests that food-borne infection may trigger arthritis in genetically predisposed individuals.[160]

In a frail or malnourished elder, the subsequent diarrhea, vomiting, and anorexia related to abdominal cramps can disturb electrolyte balance, lead to nutritional losses, and quickly compromise health.[20] Immediate fluid replacement is paramount to reverse dehydration. Table 17-7 enumerates the most common types of food poisoning, the symptoms, and the means of prevention. Over 95% of all reported food-borne bacterial illness results from mishandling food in food service establishments or in the home. Proper education of food handlers is a critical prevention strategy, especially for staff in food service operations serving frail or chronically ill older people.

Health Fraud

Older people may be particularly susceptible to extravagant claims for the benefits of nutritional manipulations and supplements, as they seek the "fountain

Table 17-7 Understanding the Food Poisoners

Food poisoning, caused by harmful bacteria, normally produces intestinal flu-like symptoms lasting from a few hours to several days. In cases of botulism, or when food poisoning affects infants, the ill, or the elderly, the situation can be quite serious, even fatal. Knowing the tricks of proper food handling, however, can effectively prevent such dire consequences.

Bacteria	How It Attacks	Symptoms	Prevention
Staphylococcus (staph)	Staph spreads from someone handling food. It is found on the skin and in boils, pimples, and throat infections. At warm temperatures, staph produces a poison.	In 2–8 hours after eating you could have vomiting and diarrhea lasting a day or two	Cooking won't destroy the staph poison, so: —Wash hands and utensils before preparing food. —Don't leave food out more than 2 hours. Susceptible foods are meat, poultry, meat and poultry salads, cheese, egg products, starchy salads (potato, macaroni, and pasta), custards, cream-filled desserts.
Salmonella	You can get salmonella when infected food—meat, poultry, eggs, or fish—is eaten raw or undercooked. Other cases occur when cooked food comes in contact with infected raw food, or when an infected person contaminates food.	In 12–36 hours you could have diarrhea, fever and vomiting lasting 2–7 days	Keep raw food away from cooked food, and —Thoroughly cook meat, poultry, and fish. —Be especially careful with poultry, pork, roast beef, or hamburger. —Don't drink unpasteurized milk.
Clostridium perfringens	This 'buffet germ' grows rapidly in large portions of food that are cooling slowly. It can also grow in chafing dishes that may not keep food sufficiently hot, and even in the refrigerator if food is stored in large portions that do not cool quickly.	In 8–24 hours you could have diarrhea and gas pains, ending usually in less than a day. But older people and ulcer patients can be seriously affected.	Keep food hot (over 140°F) or cold (under 40°F), and —Divide bulk cooked foods into smaller portions for serving and cooling. —Be especially careful with poultry, gravy, stews, and casseroles.

Campylobacter jejuni	This germ spreads through drinking untreated water or unpasteurized milk, or eating raw or undercooked meat, poultry, or shellfish.	In 2–5 days you could have severe (possibly bloody) diarrhea, cramping, fever, and headache lasting 2–7 days.	Don't drink untreated water or unpasteurized milk, and —Thoroughly clean hands, utensils and surfaces that touch raw meat, poultry, and fish.
Clostridium botulinum	This organism often occurs in home-canned or any canned goods showing warning signs—clear liquids turned milky, cracked jars, loose lids, swollen or dented cans or lids. Beware of any jar or can that spurts liquid or has an off-odor when opened.	In 12–48 hours your nervous system could be affected. Symptoms include double vision, droopy eyelids, trouble speaking and swallowing, and difficult breathing.	Carefully examine home-canned goods before use, and —Don't use any canned goods showing danger signs. —If you or a family member has botulism symptoms, get medical help immediately. Untreated, botulism can be fatal.

Source: Reprinted with permission from *Environmental Nutrition* (1988;November:2), Copyright © 1988, Environmental Nutrition, Inc. Adapted from *Food News for Consumers*, United States Department of Agriculture, (1988;5:2).

of youth'' or a simple, quick solution to guarantee health and relief of pain. Sixty percent of health fraud victims are older adults. Health fraud can be hazardous, since it delays or supplants needed medical care and may cause damage through unbalanced dietary regimens. Also, the high cost of these products and regimens often robs money that could otherwise be spent on a good diet and better health care.

Food fraud, as a type of health fraud, encompasses practices ranging from advocating foods with magical powers to prescribing unneeded or harmful herbals, nostrums, teas, and food components.[49] Although useful for legitimate deficiencies, most vitamin and mineral supplements are not needed. Megadoses of several vitamins constitute a major component of orthomolecular psychiatry, although benefits of this questionable therapy are largely anecdotal. Quackery has extended to the promotion of pseudovitamins such as flavinoids, pangamic acid (vitamin B_{15}), Gerovital H3 (procaine hydrochloride), and Laetrile (vitamin B_{17}).

Professionals who interpret nutritional science provide an important service by evaluating health claims and limiting the damage resulting from quackery. Often the claims for quick or natural cures use unsubstantiated research or misrepresent scientific findings to discredit more traditional medical approaches. Broader public education on how to recognize fraudulent statements about a product and how to report food fraud may discourage some seniors from unwise expenditures. However, better ways of counseling older people on how to avoid unhealthy diets and health practices are sorely needed.

TRAINING OF HEALTH PROFESSIONALS

The great majority of Americans rely on their personal physician for advice about health matters, as well as for remedies for their ills. While many health personnel, physicians as well as nurses and pharmacists, still do not receive a solid education in nutrition, they are nonetheless better prepared than their predecessors. Because of the significantly heightened public demand for information about health, considerably expanded media coverage of nutrition-related ''news,'' and the promotion of a vast array of supposedly ''healthy'' foods and supplements, health professionals have essentially been forced to become more aware of the relationship between nutrition and health.

For elderly individuals, health professionals remain an important source of information about health and nutrition. It is incumbent that all health professionals be aware of current nutrition science, take careful histories as part of their evaluation of patients, and incorporate this information into an overall plan of care. Perhaps most important of all, health professionals must have a clear understanding of the limitations of nutritional principles as they relate to the unique problems of particular patients. Consultation with a registered dietitian or a trained nutritionist may prove helpful under these circumstances.

CONCLUSION

Disease prevention and health promotion advice for older people presents a new challenge to health professionals. Recent research has begun to document the benefits of smoking cessation, diet modifications, increased exercise, and limited intakes of alcohol and drugs for older as well as younger adults. Health promotion strategies can improve function as well as reduce the risk of morbidity and premature death.

For those over age 50 years, health promotion is less about preventing the symptoms of disease and more about preserving function and maintaining independence, productivity, and personal fulfillment.[3]

Reasons for geriatric health promotion and disease prevention activities are[3]:

- Aging is a lifelong phenomenon consisting of physiologic, psychologic, and behavioral processes.
- Aging occurs at different rates, meaning that biologic age may not be equal to chronologic age.
- Most disabilities of old age are not inevitable, universal, or irreversible.

Effective health promotion and disease prevention messages should be directed toward all older people when knowledge justifies such recommendations. Additional guidance and health interventions should be based on individual asssessments of health status for those identified as being at high risk for disease or disability.

A geriatric assessment should be included as a regular part of health monitoring of older people, in addition to chronic disease screening.[13,161] Continuous health care by a single practitioner, or health team, over time assures good preventive care.[14] Care givers can then observe subtle changes in function (eg, hearing, vision, cognition, oral health, bowel habits, and continence)[34,43] and monitor changes in biomarkers (eg, serum cholesterol and glucose levels)[10] and body composition (bone density, lean body mass, and fat distribution patterns).[10,46,154,162] Health promotion begins with believing that additional years, as well as additional years of independent living, are achievable at almost any age.

REFERENCES

1. McGinnis JM. Year 2000 health objectives for the nation. In: *Surgeon General's Workshop on Health Promotion and Aging*. Washington, DC: US Dept of Health and Human Services; 1988:20–25.

2. Walker SN. Health promotion for older adults: directions for research. *Am J Health Promotion*. Spring 1989;3(4):47–52.

3. Ory MG. Considerations in the development of age-sensitive indicators for assessing health promotion. *Health Promotion*. 1988;3(2):139–149.

4. National Institutes of Health. *Nutrition Coordinating Committee, Program in Biomedical and Behavioral Research and Training, 11th Annual Report of the National Institutes of Health.* Washington, DC: US Dept of Health and Human Services; 1987:111.

5. Koop CE. Exploring the myths and realities of aging and health. *Aging.* 1984;5(3):5–9.

6. Koop CE. Keynote Address, March 20–23, 1988. *Surgeon General's Workshop on Health Promotion and Aging.* Washington, DC: US Dept of Health and Human Services; 1988:1–4.

7. *NCHS Health Statistics on Older Persons: United States, 1986: Analytical and Epidemiological Studies.* Series 3. Washington, DC: NCHS; 1987. US Dept of Health and Human Services publication No. 25 (PHS):87–1409.

8. Roybal ER. Elderly health care costs likely to rise to one-fifth of income. *Congressional Record.* March 23, 1989:E978–E980.

9. Sundwall D. Health promotion and Surgeon General's Workshop. *Surgeon General's Workshop on Health Promotion and Aging.* Washington, DC: US Dept of Health and Human Services; March 1988.

10. Aging. In: *Surgeon General's Report on Nutrition and Health.* Washington; DC: US Public Health Service; 1988. US Dept of Health and Human Services publication 88-50210.

11. Sorenson AW, Seltser R, Sundwall D. Primary cancer prevention as an attainable objective for the elderly. In: Yancik R, ed. *Perspectives on Prevention and Treatment of Cancer in the Elderly.* New York, NY: Raven Press; 1983:24. Raven Press Aging Series.

12. Fisk CF. Address, Opening Plenary Session. *Surgeon General's Workshop on Health Promotion and Aging.* Washington, DC: US Dept of Health and Human Services; March 1988.

13. Fried LP, Bush TL. Morbidity as a focus of preventive health care in the elderly. *Epidemiol Rev.* 1988;10:48–64.

14. Macfayden D. International Geriatric Health Promotion Study/Activities. *Surgeon General's Workshop on Health Promotion and Aging.* Washington, DC: US Dept of Health and Human Services; March 1988.

15. McGinnis JM, Nestle N. The Surgeon General's report on nutrition and health: policy implications and implementation strategies. *Am J Clin Nutr.* 1989;49(1):23–28.

16. Sommers KB. Book review of Louise B. Russell: *Is Prevention Better Than Cure? J Public Health Policy.* Spring 1986:124–128.

17. Libby P, Russell RM. Hypertension in the elderly. In: Horan MJ, Blaustein M, Dunbar JB, et al, eds. *NIH Workshop on Nutrition and Hypertension.* New York, NY: Biomedical Information Corp; 1985.

18. Kaplin NM. An overview of hypertension: the clinical problem and its possible relationship to nutrition. In: Horan MJ, Blaustein M, Dunbar JB, et al, eds. *NIH Workshop on Nutrition and Hypertension.* New York, NY: Biomedical Information Corp; 1985.

19. Foster EM. Is there a food safety crisis? *Food Technol.* 1982;36(8):82–93.

20. Infections and immunity. In: *Surgeon General's Report on Nutrition and Health.* Washington, DC. US Public Health Service; 1988. US Dept of Health and Human Services publication 88-50210.

21. Joint Committee on Detection, Evaluation, and Treatment of High Blood Pressure. 1988 Report. NIH Publication No. 88-1088; 1988.

22. Maloney S. Healthy older people. In: *Surgeon General's Workshop on Health Promotion and Aging.* Washington, DC: US Dept of Health and Human Services; March 1988.

23. Munro HN. Aging and nutrition: a multifaceted problem. In: Hutchinson ML, Munro HN, eds. *Nutrition and Aging.* Orlando, Fla: Academic Press Inc, 1986.

24. Watkin DM. Preface, Nutrition in older persons. *Clin Geriatr Med.* 1987;3.

25. Obesity. *Surgeon General's Report on Nutrition and Health*. Washington, DC: US Public Health Service; 1988. US Dept of Health and Human Services publication 88-50210.

26. Muggia FM, Blum RH. Cancer treatment and age-dependent considerations. In: Yancik R, ed. *Perspectives on Prevention and Treatment of Cancer in the Elderly*. New York, NY: Raven Press; 1983.

27. Tinetti ME, Speechley M, Ginter SF. Risk factors for falls among elderly persons living in the community. *N Engl J Med*. 1988;319(26):1701–1707.

28. Isles CG, Hole DJ, Gillis CR, et al. Plasma cholesterol, coronary heart disease, and cancer in the Renfrew and Paisley survey. *Br Med J*. 1989;298(5):920–924.

29. Iso H, Jacobs DR, Wentworth D, et al. Serum cholesterol levels and six-year mortality from stroke in 350,977 men screened for the Multiple Risk Factor Intervention Trial. *N Engl J Med*. 1989;320(4):904–910.

30. Forette B, Tortrat D, Wolmark Y. Cholesterol as a risk factor for mortality in elderly women. *Lancet*. April 22, 1989;1:868–869.

31. Severe acquired hypcholesterolemia: two case reports. *Nutr Rev*. 1989;47(7):202–207.

32. Heaney RP. Prevention of age-related osteoporosis in women. In: Avioli LV, ed. *The Osteoporotic Syndrome: Detection, Prevention, and Treatment*. Orlando, Fla: Grune & Stratton Inc; 1983.

33. Pruzansky ME, Turano M, Luckey M, et al. Low body weight as a risk factor for hip fracture in both black and white women. *J Orthop Res*. 1989;7(2):192–197.

34. Rudman D, Feller AG. Protein-calorie malnutrition in the nursing home. *J Am Geriatr Soc*. 1989;37(2):173–183.

35. Rowe JW. Physiologic interface of aging and nutrition. In: Hutchinson ML, Munro HN, eds. *Nutrition and Aging*. Orlando, Fla: Academic Press Inc; 1986.

36. Nizel AE. Role of nutrition in the oral health of the aging patient. *Den Clin North Am*. 1976;20(3)569–584.

37. Wysocki CJ, Glbert AN. National Geographic smell survey: effects of age are heterogeneous. In: Murphy C, Cain WS, Hegsted DM, eds. Nutrition and the chemical senses in aging: recent advances and current research needs. *Ann N Y Acad Sci*. 1989;561:12–28.

38. Rudman D. Kidney senescence: a model for aging. *Nutr Rev*. 1988;46(6):209–214.

39. *Health Resources for Older Women*. Washington, DC: National Institute on Aging; 1987. National Institutes of Health DHHS (PHS) publication 87-2899.

40. Brody JA, Schneider EL. Diseases and disorders of aging: an hypothesis. *J Chronic Dis*. 1986;39(11):871–876.

41. Skeletal diseases. *Surgeon General's Report on Nutrition and Health*. Washington, DC: US Public Health Service; 1988. US Dept of Health and Human Services publication 88-50210.

42. O'Hanlon P, Kohrs MB, Hilderbrand E, et al. Socio-economic factors and dietary intakes of elderly Missourians. *J Am Diet Assoc*. 1983;82:646–653.

43. Bell I, Edman J, Marby D, et al. Nutritional factors in depression, cognition and hematological status of geriatric psychiatry inpatients. Presented at the 41st Annual Meeting of the Gerontological Society of America; November 1988; San Francisco, Calif.

44. Howell SC, Loeb MB. Culture, myths, and food preferences among aged. *Gerontologist*. 1969;9:31–37.

45. *Surgeon General's Report on Nutrition and Health*. Washington, DC: US Public Health Service; 1988. US Dept of Health and Human Services publication 88-50210; Government Printing Office Stock No. 017-001-00465-1.

46. Commission on Life Sciences, National Research Council. *Report on Diet and Health.* Washington, DC: National Academy Press; 1989.

47. USDHHS/USDA. *Dietary Guidelines for Americans*, 3rd ed. Washington, DC: USDA Home and Garden Bulletin No. 232; 1985.

48. Food and Nutrition Board, National Research Council. *Recommended Dietary Allowances.* 10th ed. Washington, DC: National Academy Press; 1990.

49. Dietary fads and frauds. *Surgeon General's Report on Nutrition and Health.* Washington, DC: US Public Health Service; 1988. US Dept of Health and Human Services publication 88-50210.

50. Freeland-Graves JH, Bales CW. Dietary recommendations of minerals for the elderly. In: Bales CW, ed. *Mineral Homeostasis in the Elderly.* New York, NY: Alan R Liss Inc; 1989.

51. Russell RM. Implications of gastric atrophy for vitamin and mineral nutriture. In: Hutchinson ML, Munro HN, eds. *Nutrition and Aging.* Orlando, Fla: Academic Press Inc; 1986.

52. Hollander D, Dadufalza V. Lymphatic and portal absorption of vitamin E in aging rats. *Dig Dis Sci.* 1989;34(5):768–772.

53. Krasinski SD, Russell RM, Otradovec CL, et al. Relationship of vitamin A and vitamin E intake to fasting plasma retinol, retinol-binding protein, retinyl esters, carotene, alpha-tocopherol, and cholesterol among elderly people and young adults: increased plasma esters among vitamin A-supplement users. *Am J Clin Nutr.* 1989;49:112–120.

54. Meydani SN, Meydani M, Verdon CP, et al. Vitamin E supplementation suppresses prostaglandin E synthesis and enhances the immune response of aged mice. *Mech Aging Dev.* 1986;34:191–201.

55. Garry PJ, Chumlea WC, eds. Epidemiologic and methodologic problems in determining nutritional status of older people. *Am J Clin Nutr.* 1989;50(5 suppl):1121–1235.

56. Holt PR, Rosenberg IH, Russell RM. Causes and consequences of hypochlorhydria in the elderly. *Dig Dis Sci.* 1989;34(6):933–937.

57. Davis MA, Randall E. 1981 Social change and food habits of the elderly. In: *National Institute of Aging's Social and Psychological Developments in Aging.* Washington, DC: Paper for the White House Conference on Aging; 1981.

58. Massachusetts Department of Health. Determining the needs of the elderly and chronically disabled. *N Engl J Med.* 1976;294:110–111.

59. Norton L, Wozny MC. Residential location and nutritional adequacy among elderly adults. *J Geronol.* 1984;39:592–595.

60. Akin JS, Guilkey DK, Popkin BM, et al. Cluster analysis of food consumption patterns of older Americans. *J Am Diet Assoc.* 1986;86:616–624.

61. Davis MA, Murphy SP, Neuhaus JM. Living arrangements and eating behaviors of older adults in the United States. *J Gerontol.* 1988;43(3):596–598.

62. Villers Foundation. *On the Other Side of Easy Street.* Washington, DC: Villers Foundation; 1987.

63. *Nutrient Content of the U.S. Food Supply.* Washington, DC: Human Nutrition Information Service Adm Rep No 299-21; 1988.

64. Dresser CM. Dietary status of community-based older persons. Paper Presented at the American Dietetic Association 67th Annual Meeting; October 15–18, 1984; Washington, DC.

65. Cronin FJ, Krebs-Smith SM, Wyse BW, et al. Characterizing food usage by demographic variables. *J Am Diet Assoc.* 1982;81:661–673.

66. Judge TG. The milieu interieur and aging. In: Brocklehurst JC, ed. *Textbook of Geriatric Medicine and Gerontology.* 2nd ed. Edinburgh, Scotland: Churchill Livingstone; 1978.

67. Morley JE. Nutritional status of the elderly. *Am J Med.* 1986;81:679–695.

68. Food and Nutrition Board, National Academy of Sciences. *Recommended Dietary Allowances*, 9th ed. Washington, DC: National Academy Press; 1980.

69. Chernoff R, Lipschitz DA. Aging and nutrition. *Compr Ther.* 1985;11(8):29–34.

70. Krause MV, Mahan LK. *Food, Nutrition and Diet Therapy.* 7th ed. Philadelphia, Pa: WB Saunders Co; 1984.

71. McGandy RB, Russell RM, Hartz SC, et al. Nutritional status study of healthy non-institutionalized elderly: energy and nutrient intakes from three-day diet records and diet supplements. *Nutr Res.* 1986;6:785–798.

72. Garry PJ, Rhyne RL, Halioua L, et al. Changes in dietary patterns over a six year period in an elderly population. *Ann N Y Acad Sci.* 1989;561:104–112.

73. USDA. *Nutrient Intakes: Individuals in 48 States, Year 1977-78. Nationwide Food Consumption Survey 1977-78 Report No. 1-2.* Washington, DC: USDA; 1984. Human Nutrition Information Service.

74. Chapman N, Sorenson A. Nutrition background paper. *Surgeon General's Workshop on Health Promotion and Aging.* Washington, DC: US Government Printing Office; 1988.

75. Weindruch R, Walford RL, Fligel S, et al. The retardation of aging in mice by dietary restriction: longevity, cancer, immunity and lifetime energy intake. *J Nutr.* 1986;116(4):641–654.

76. Rossman J. The anatomy of aging. In: Rossman J, ed. *Clinical Geriatrics.* 2nd ed. Philadelphia, PA: JB Lippincott Co; 1989.

77. Frisancho AR. New standards of weight and body composition by frame size and height for assessment of nutritional status of adults and the elderly. *Am J Clin Nutr.* 1984;40:808–819.

78. Master AM, Lasser RP, Bechman G. Tables of average weight and height of Americans aged 65 to 94 years. *JAMA.* 1960;172:658–662.

79. Mitchell CO, Lipschitz DA. Detection of protein-calorie malnutrition in the elderly. *Am J Clin Nutr.* 1982;35:398–406.

80. Roubenoff R, Roubenoff RA, Preto J, et al. Malnutrition among hospitalized patients: a problem of physician awareness. *Arch Intern Med.* 1987;147(8):1462–1465.

81. Bienia R, Ratcliff S, Barbour GL, et al. Malnutrition in the hospitalized geriatric patient. *J Am Geriatr Soc.* 1982;30(7):433–436.

82. Braun JV, Wykle MH, Cowling WR. Failure to thrive in older persons: a concept derived. *Gerontology.* 1988;28(6):809–812.

83. Sherman MN, Lechich A, Brickner PW, et al. Nutritional parameters in homebound persons of greatly advanced age. *J Parenter Enter Nutr.* 1983;7(4):378–380.

84. Munro HN, McGandy RB, Hartz SC, et al. Protein nutriture of a group of free-living elderly. *Am J Clin Nutr.* 1987;46(4):586–592.

85. Kidney disease. *Surgeon General's Report on Nutrition and Health.* Washington, DC: US Public Health Service; 1988. Dept of Health and Human Services publication 88-50210.

86. Bidlack WR, Kirsch A, Meskin MS. Nutritional requirements of the elderly. *Food Technol.* 1986;40(2):61–69.

87. Roe DA. *Geriatric Nutrition.* Englewood Cliffs, NJ: Prentice-Hall Inc; 1983.

88. Elahi VK, Elahi D, Andres R, et al. A longitudinal study of nutritional intake in men. *J Gerontol.* 1983;38:162–180.

89. Asciutti-Moura LS, Guilland JC, Fuchs F, et al. Fatty acid composition of serum lipids and its relation to diet in an elderly institutionalized population. *Am J Clin Nutr.* 1988;48:980–987.

90. Suter, PM, Russell RM. Vitamin requirements of the elderly. *Am J Clin Nutr*. 1987; 45:501–512.

91. Garry PJ, Hunt WC. Brandrofchak JL, et al. Vitamin A intake and plasma retinol levels in healthy elderly men and women. *Am J Clin Nutr*. 1987;46(6):989–994.

92. McCarron DA, Morris CD. Calcium and hypertension: evidence for a protective action of the cation. In: Horan MJ, Blaustein M, Dunbar JB, et al, eds. *NIH Workshop on Nutrition and Hypertension*. New York, NY: Biochemical Information Corp; 1985.

93. Torrey BB, Kinsella K, Taeuber CM. An aging world. International Population Reports Series P-95 No. 78. Washington, DC: US Department of Commerce, Bureau of the Census; 1987.

94. Sorenson AW, Slattery ML, Ford MH. Calcium and colon cancer: a review. *Nutr Cancer*. 1988;11(3):135–145.

95. Chu-Y MS, Costa FM. Studies in calcium metabolism. I. Effect of low calcium and variable protein intake on human calcium metabolism. *Am J Clin Nutr*. 1975;28:1028–1035.

96. Newcomer AD, Hodgson SF, McGill DB, et al. Lactase deficiency: prevalence in osteoporosis. *Ann Intern Med*. 1978;89:218–220.

97. Riggs BL, Melton LJ. Involutional osteoporosis. *N Engl J Med*. 1986;314(26):1676–1686.

98. Garry PJ, Goodwin JS, Hunt WC., Hopper EM, Lenard AG. Nutritional status in a healthy elderly population: dietary and supplemental intakes. *Am J Clin Nutr*. 1982;36:319–331.

99. Omdahl JL, Garry PJ, Hunsaker LA, et al. Nutritional status in a healthy elderly population: vitamin D. *Am J Clin Nutr*. 1982;36:1225–1233.

100. Melton LJ, Kan SH, Wahner HW, et al. Lifetime fracture risk: an approach to hip fracture risk assessment based on bone mineral density and age. *J Clin Epidemiol*. 1988;41(10):985–994.

101. Smith EL, Gilligan C, Smith PE, et al. Calcium supplementation and bone loss in middle-aged women. *Am J Clin Nutr*. 1989;50:833–842.

102. Osteoporosis: consensus conference statement. *JAMA*. 1984;252:799.

103. Recker RR, Saville PD, Heaney RP. Effect of oestrogens and calcium carbonate on bone loss in post-menopausal women. *Ann Intern Med*. 1977;87:649–655.

104. Riis B, Karsten T, Christiansen C. Does calcium supplementation prevent postmenopausal bone loss? *N Engl J Med*. 1987;316:173–177.

105. Davies M, Mawer EB, et al. Vitamin D prophylaxis in the elderly: a simple effective method suitable for large populations. *Age Ageing*. 1985;13:349–354.

106. Peck WA, Avioli LB. Non-estrogen prevention and treatment. In: *Osteoporosis the Silent Thief*. Washington, DC: American Association of Retired Persons; 1988.

107. MacLaughlin J, Holick MF. Aging decreases the capacity of skin to produce vitamin D_3. *J Clin Invest*. 1985;76:1536–1538.

108. Reid IR, Gallagher DJA, Bosworth J. Prophylaxis against vitamin D deficiency in the elderly by regular sunlight exposure. *Age Ageing* 1986;15:35–40.

109. DHHS/FDA. *Consumer Nutrition Knowledge Study: A Nationwide Study of Food Shopper's Knowledge, Beliefs, Attitudes, and Reported Behavior Regarding Food and Nutrition Report II, 1975*. Washington, DC. US Government Printing Office; 1976.

110. McDonald JT. Vitamin and mineral supplement use in the U.S. *Clin Nutr*. 1986;5(1):27–33.

111. Hale WE, Stewart RB, et al. Use of nutritional supplements in an ambulatory elderly population. *J Am Geriatr Soc*. 1982;30:401–403.

112. Gray A, Paganini-Hill A, Ross RK, et al. Vitamin supplement use in a Southern California retirement community. *J Am Diet Assoc*. 1986;86:800–802.

113. Guthrie HA. Supplementation: a nutritionist's view. *J Nutr Educ*. 1986;18(3):130–132.

114. Garry PJ, Goodwin JS, Hunt WC, et al. Nutritional status in a healthy elderly population: dietary and supplemental intakes. *Am J Clin Nutr*. 1982;36:319–331.

115. Stewart ML, McDonald JT, Levy AS, et al. Vitamin/mineral supplement use: a telephone survey of adults in the United States. *J Am Diet Assoc*. 1985;85(12):1585–1590.

116. Shank FR, Wilkening VL. Consideration for food fortification policy. *Cereal Foods World*. 1986;31(10):728–740.

117. Yearick ES, Want NS, Pisias SJ. Nutritional status of the elderly: dietary and biochemical findings. *J Gerontol*. 1980;35:663–671.

118. Ranno BS, Wardlaw GM, Geiger CJ. What characterizes elderly women who overuse vitamin and mineral supplements? *J Am Diet Assoc*. 1988;88:347–348.

119. Cordaro JB, Dickinson A. The nutritional supplement industry—realities and opportunities. *J Nutr Educ*. 1986;18(3):128–129.

120. Scheider CL, Nordlund DJ. Prevalence of vitamins and mineral supplement use in the elderly. *J Fam Prac* 1983;17:243–247.

121. Garry PJ, Hunt WC. Biochemical assessment of vitamin status in the elderly: effects of dietary and supplemental intakes. In: Hutchinson ML, Munro HN, eds. *Nutrition and Aging*. Orlando, Fla: Academic Press Inc; 1986.

122. Garry PJ, Goodwin JS, Hunt WC, et al. Nutritional status in a healthy elderly population: vitamin C. *Am J Clin Nutr*. 1982;36:332–339.

123. Bieri JG, Corash L, Hubbard VS. Medical uses of vitamin E. *N Engl J Med*. 1983; 308:1063–1071.

124. Sauberlich HE. Ascorbic acid. In: Olson RE, ed. *Nutrition Reviews: Present Knowledge in Nutrition*. Washington, DC: Nutrition Foundation; 1984.

125. Mann BA, Garry PJ, Hunt WC, et al. Daily multivitamin supplementation on vitamin blood levels in the elderly: a randomized, double-blind, placebo-controlled trial. *J Am Geriatr Soc*. 1987;35(4):302–306.

126. Tobin A. Fish oil supplementation. *Lancet*. 1988;1:1046–1047.

127. Enstrom JE, Pauling L. Mortality among health-conscious elderly Californians. *Proc Natl Acad Sci U S A*. 1982;79:6023–6027.

128. Haeger K, Lanner E, Magnusson PO. Oral zinc sulfate in the treatment of venous leg ulcer. In: Pories WJ, Strain WH, et al, eds. *Clinical Applications of Zinc Metabolism*. Springfield, Ill: Charles C Thomas; 1974.

129. Vitamin E may help elderly resist diseases. *J Am Diet Assoc*. 1988;88(11):1440.

130. Council on Scientific Affairs, American Medical Association. Vitamin preparations as dietary supplements and as therapeutic agents. *JAMA*. 1987;257:1929–1936.

131. Draper HH. Nutrients and nutrients as prophylactic drugs. *J Nutr*. 1988;118:1420-1421.

132. Drinkwater BL. *The Role of Nutrition and Exercise in Health*. Seattle, Wash: Continuing Dental Education, University of Washington; 1985.

133. Nieman DC. *The Sports Medicine Fitness Course*. Palo Alto, Calif: Bull Publishing Co; 1986.

134. Peck WA, Avioli LV. Physical exercise and bone health. In: *Osteoporosis the Silent Thief*. Washington, DC: American Association of Retired Persons; 1988.

135. Suominen H, Heikkinen E, Liesen H. Effect of 8 weeks endurance training on skeletal muscle metabolism in 56-70 year old men. *Eur J Appl Physiol*. 1987;37:173–180.

136. Adams GM, DeVries HA. Physiological effects of an exercise training regimen upon women aged 52 to 79. *J Gerontol.* 1973;28:50–55.

137. Pollack ML, Cureton T, Grenninger L. Effects of frequency of training on working capacity, cardiovascular function and body composition of adult men. *Med Sci Sports.* 1969;1:70–74.

138. Sidney KH, Shepard RJ, Harrison JE. Endurance training and body composition of the elderly. *Am J Clin Nutr.* 1977;30:326–333.

139. Shock NW. Physiological aspects of aging in man. *Annu Rev Physiol.* 1961;23:97–122.

140. Goldberg AP. Physical exercise. In: *Surgeon General's Workshop on Health Promotion and Aging.* Washington, DC: US Public Health Service, Dept of Health and Human Services; 1988.

141. Kaplin GA, Seeman TE, Cohen RD, et al. Mortality among the elderly in the Alameda County study: behavioral and demographic risk factors. *Am J Public Health.* 1987;77(3):307–312.

142. Stones MJ, Dornan B, Kozma A. The prediction of mortality in elderly institution residents. *J Gerontol Psychol Sci.* 1989;44(3):72–79.

143. Evans W. Exercise and muscle metabolism in the elderly. In: Hutchinson ML, Munro HN, eds. *Nutrition and Aging.* Orlando, Fla: Academic Press Inc; 1986.

144. Craig BW, Garthwaite SM, Holloszy JO. Adipocyte insulin resistance: effects of aging, obesity, exercise, and food restriction. *Am Physiol Soc.* 1987;62(1):95.

145. Wang JT, Ho LT, Tang KT, et al. Effect of habitual physical activity on age-related glucose tolerance. *J Am Geriatr Soc.* 1989;37(3):203–209.

146. Smith EL, Gilligan C, Smith PE, et al. Calcium supplementation and bone loss in middle-aged women. *Am J Clin Nutr.* 1989;50:833–842.

147. Blake AJ, Morgan K, Bendall MJ, et al. Falls by elderly people at home: prevalence and associated factors. *Age Ageing.* 1988;17(6):365–372.

148. Tinetti ME, Speechley M. Prevention of falls among the elderly. *N Engl J Med.* 1989;320(16):1055–1059.

149. Stehlin D. The silent epidemic of hip fractures. *FDA Consumer.* 1988;22:18–23.

150. Hemenway D, Coldtz GA, Willet WC, et al. Fractures and lifestyle: effects of cigarette smoking, alcohol intake, and relative weight on risk of hip fracture in middle-aged women. *Am J Public Health.* 1988;78:1554–1558.

151. *Smoking and Health: A Report of the Surgeon General.* Washington, DC: Dept of Health, Education, and Welfare; 1979. US Public Health Service, US Dept of Health, Education, and Welfare publication PHS-79-50066.

152. Wichelow JW, Golding JF, Treasure FP. Comparison of some dietary habits of smokers and non-smokers. *Br J Addict.* 1988;83:295–304.

153. Fiore MC, Novotny TE, Pierce JP, et al. Trends in cigarette smoking in the United States. *JAMA.* 1989;261:49–55.

154. *Surgeon General's Report on Smoking and Health.* Washington, DC: US Dept of Health and Human Services, US Public Health Service; 1988.

155. Shimokata H, Muller DC, Andres R. Studies in the distribution of body fat, III: effects of cigarette smoking. *JAMA.* 1989;261:1169–1173.

156. DHHS/NCHS. *Health Promotion Data for the 1990 Objectives.* Vital and Health Statistics, No. 126. Washington, DC: US Government Printing Office; September 1986.

157. Abdellah FG, Moore SR, eds. *Surgeon General's Workshop on Health Promotion and Aging.* Washington, DC: US Dept of Health and Human Services, US Public Health Service; March 1988.

158. Blumberg JB. Drug induced malnutrition in the geriatric patient. *Nutr M.D.* 1987;13(8):1–4.

159. Institute of Food Technologists Expert Panel on Food Safety and Nutrition. *Food Technol.* 1986;40:49.

160. Perspective on Food Safety Concerns. *Dairy Counc Dig.* 1987;58:1–6.

161. Ludman E, Newman JM. Frail elderly: assessment of nutrition needs. *Gerontologist.* 1986;26(2):198–202.

162. Ross Laboratories. *Nutritional Assessment: What Is It? How Is It Used?* Columbus, Ohio: Ross Laboratories; 1988.

Index

A

Absorption. *See also* Specific type
  food effects, 350–351
  nutritional status, 345–347
    drug effects, 345–347
Addison's disease, 320
Administration on Aging/Public Health
  Service Joint Initiative on Health
  Promotion for Older Americans,
  434–435
Adrenal cortex, 320–321
Adrenal hormone, 320–321
Adult day health care, 8
Aging
  anemia, 273–276
    etiology, 274–275
    hematopoiesis, 275–276
    incidence, 274
    prevalence, 273–274
  basal metabolic rate, 15–16
  body composition, 11, 12, 370
  bone
    changes at menopause, 299–300
    oral, 113–114
  calcium metabolism, 323–324

cardiovascular system, 229–248
circumoral structure, 113–119
creatinine clearance, 256–257, 258
defined, 1. *See also* Specific type
deglutination, 117
demographics, 1–9
energy requirement, 15–17
  estimation, 16–17
factors, 1, 2–4
gastrointestinal system, 183–184
gingiva, 116
glomerular filtration rate, 255–257
glomerular permeability, 261
health care system impact, 5
hematopoietic system, 271–273
homeostasis, 343
kidney, 253–266
  asymptomatic bacteriuria, 262–263
  creatinine clearance, 262
  pathophysiology, 253, 262–263
  renal clearance studies, 253
liver, 207–208
  drug hepatic biotransformation, 341
  drug renal excretion, 342
  function, 208
marrow function, 272–273

mastication, 117
maximal tubular transport capacity, 259
measurement effects, 363
mucous membrane, 116
oral musculature, 117
oral structure, 113–119
pancreas, 193–194
versus pathology, 455–457
periodontal ligament, 116
periodontium, 116–117
pharmacodynamics, 342–344
pharmacokinetics, 339–342
    absorption, 339
    disposition, 340
    excretion, 341–342
    metabolism, 341
receptor, 342–343
renal blood flow, 257–259
salivary gland, 117
skeleton, 289, 293–300, 301–302
smell, 118–119
stature, 370
taste, 118
temporomandibular joint, 115–116
tissue sensitivity, 343–344
tongue, 116–117
tooth, 114–115
    attrition, 114–115
trabecular bone, 303
weight, 370, 373–377
Alcohol, 470
    folate, 39–40
    retinol, 28
    vitamin A, 28
    vitamin B_6, 38
Aldosterone, 320
Alkalosis, hypokalemia, 63
Aluminum, 93–95
    dietary exposure, 93
    sources, 93–94
Aluminum toxicity, 94–95
    Alzheimer's disease, 95
    clinical signs, 94–95
    senile dementia, 95
Alveolar bone, 114

Alzheimer's disease, aluminum toxicity, 95
Amino acid
    protein, 14
    requirements, 13–14
Androgen, bone mass, 306
Anemia. See also Iron deficiency anemia
    aging, 273–276
        etiology, 274–275
        hematopoiesis, 275–276
        incidence, 274
        prevalence, 273–274
Angular cheilitis, 133
Anorexia of aging, 397
Anthropometric assessment, nutritional
    assessment, 369–383
Anticoagulation therapy, vitamin K, 33
Antidiuretic hormone, 54
Antigen-recall skin testing, 387
Antihypertensive therapy, 243
Antioxidant, 30
Apathetic hypothyroidism, 317
Aphthous stomatitis, 124–125
Aphthous ulcer, 124–125
Artificial saliva, 136–137
Artificial sweetener, 153
Ascites, 214–215
Ascorbic acid. See Vitamin C
Atherosclerosis, 230–234
    risk factors, 230, 234–247
Atrophic gastritis
    vitamin B_6, 38
    vitamin B_{12}, 41
Australian National Blood Pressure Study,
    242–243
Azotemia, potassium therapy, 65

B

Bacterial overgrowth, small intestine,
    203–204
Baltimore Longitudinal Study of Aging,
    1, 15
Barium, oral health effects, 150
Basal metabolic rate
    aging, 15–16

energy output, 327–328
physical activity, 16–17
sex, 15–16
Benign keratosis, 125–126
Biceps skinfold, 379
Biologic aging, 1
Biotin, 42
  deficiency, 42
Blood lipid, 234–241
  obesity, 245–246
Blood pressure, 241–244
  obesity, 245–246
Blue Cross/Blue Shield, 441–442
Body composition
  aging, 11, 12
  compartments, 371
Body weight, 370, 373, 463–464
  cardiovascular disease, 244, 245
Bombesin, energy intake, 326, 327
Bone, aging
  changes at menopause, 299–300
  oral, 113–114
Bone calcium, 67
Bone density, 68
  exercise, 302–304
  measurement, 290–293
  mechanical stress, 302–304
  peak, 300–301
  radius, 294–295
Bone hypertrophy, 293
Bone loss, 289
  onset, 295–299
Bone mass
  androgen, 306
  calcium, 304–305
    estrogen, 305
  changes with age, 293–295
  estrogen, 305
  loss, 301–302
  menopause
    calcium, 305
    parathyroid hormone, 305
  muscle strength, 302
  physical activity, 302–304
  regulation mechanisms, 302–306

reproductive endocrine status, 305–306
testosterone, 306
trabecular bone compressive strength, 301
Bone modeling, 293
Bone remodeling, 293
Bone repair, 293
Bone resorption, 120
Bone strength
  loss, 301–302
  trabecular bone compressive strength, 301
Boron, oral health effects, 150
Buccal mucosa, 109
Burst-forming unit-erythroid, 272

C

Calcium, 66–72
  bone mass, 304–305
    estrogen, 305
  measurement, 68
  megadoses, 353
  menopause, 69
  oral health effects, 150
  requirement, 68
  serum calcium concentrations, 68
  supplements, 70
Calcium absorption, vitamin D, 29
Calcium metabolism, 323–324
  aging, 323–324
  parathyroid hormone, 323–324
Campylobacter jejuni, 473
Candidiasis, 125, 129
Canker sore, 124–125
Carbohydrate, dietary requirement, 20
Carbohydrate absorption, small intestine,
  198–199
Cardiovascular disease
  body weight, 244, 245
  obesity, 244–246
Cardiovascular risk reduction, dietary
  modification, 245–246
Cardiovascular system
  aging, 229–248
  disease processes, 230–234
Cariogenicity, 152–153

Carotene, 28
Celiac disease, 202–203
Cementum, hypersensitive, 122
Cerebrovascular accident, dysphagia,
    187–190
Cheilosis, 133
Chewing, 110–111
Chlorpropamide, hypoglycemia, 314
Cholecystokinin, energy intake, 326, 327
Cholestasis, 212
Cholesterol, 18–19, 235–239, 419, 465
    dietary therapy, 237, 239–241
    recommendations, 237–238
Chromium, 88–91
    factors impairing, 88–89
    food, 88, 89
    glucose tolerance, 88, 91
Chromium absorption, 89, 90
Chromium deficiency, 90
    diabetes mellitus, 315–316
Chronic illness, 367
    competing risk factors, 454
    functional disabilities, 454
    retinol, 27
    vitamin A, 27
Chronic liver disease
    retinol, 27
    vitamin A, 27
Cigarette smoking, 468
Circumference measurement, 379–383
    average mid-upper-arm muscle, 381
    percentile norms, 382–383
Circumoral structure
    aging, 113–119
    disease, 119–137
Cirrhosis, 209, 212–213
Clostridium botulinum, 473
Clostridium perfringens, 472
Cognitive function, nutritional assessment,
    368
Colon, 215–218
Colony-forming unit-erythroid, 272
Colony-forming unit-spleen, 271–272
Commercial liquid supplement, 400–401
Compensatory renal hypertrophy, 263

Compliance, polypharmacy, 338, 339
Constipation, 216–217
Copper, 84–88
    bone metabolism, 87
    oral health effects, 150
Copper absorption, 86–87
Copper-containing enzymes, 84, 85
Copper deficiency, 85, 87
    neonatal ataxia, 87–88
Copper requirements, 85–86
Coronary heart disease, 454
    serum cholesterol, 18–19
Cortical bone, 289–290, 291
Cortical glomerulus, 254
Cortisol, 320
Creatinine clearance, aging, 256–257, 258
Critical nutrient density, 79
Crohn's disease, 204–205
Cushing's syndrome, 320

D

Day care program, 8
Death, causes, 453
Death rate, 2
Deglutination, 111
    aging, 117
Dehydration, 17–18, 59–60, 320–321, 365
    presentation, 366
    risk factors, 367
    sodium, 53–54
Dehydroepiandrosterone, 320
Dental caries, 121–122, 149–154
    dietary control, 152
Dental disease, characteristics, 119
Dentin, hypersensitive, 122
Dentition status, 155–161
Denture-related oral pathology, 128–129,
    130
Denture stomatitis, 129–130
Department of Veterans Affairs system, 442
Dermatitis, zinc deficiency, 83
Diabetes mellitus
    chromium deficiency, 315–316
    etiology, 312

long-term care, 316
  diet, 316
  weight, 316
  zinc, 316
micronutrient status, 315–316
nutrition, 311–316
reasons for control, 312, 313
sulfonylurea oral hypoglycemic agent,
  314
thiamine, 316
treatment, 312–314
vitamin B_{12} deficiency, 316
zinc deficiency, 315
Diastolic pressure, 241–242
Diet, zinc, 78–79
Diet history questionnaire, 388–389
Dietary choice, trace mineral, 78
Dietary fiber, 20–21
Dietary guidelines, 459–461
Dietary Guidelines for Americans, 459
Dietary history, 388
  24-hour recall, 389
Dietary recommendations, 418
Dietary restriction, longevity, 21
Dietary status, health promotion, 463–466
Dietary supplement, 399–400, 466–467.
  See also Nutrient supplementation
Digestion, in mouth, 111
Dilutional hyponatremia, 56–57
Disaccharidase deficiency, 201
Disease prevention, 449, 452–455
  attitude, 452
  counseling, 454
  criteria, 451–452
  planning, 454
  primary, 450
  secondary, 450
  socioeconomic determinants, 461–462
  strategies, 458–474
  tertiary, 451
  types, 450–451
Distribution, food effects, 351
Diuretic therapy, potassium therapy, 63–64
Diverticulosis, 217–218
Dopamine, energy intake, 325

Drug interaction, 338
Drug reaction, 337
Drug therapy
  effect of nutrient supplements, 352–353
  food effects on, 350–352
Drug use, 470–471
  extent, 337–339
  patterns, 337–339
Duodenum, 192–193
Dyskinesia, 134
Dysphagia, 133–134
  causes, 185
  cerebrovascular accident, 187–190
  esophageal, 190–191
  incidence, 184
  oropharyngeal, 186–190
    treatment, 187–188
  symptoms, 185

E

Eating pattern, 463
Ectopic corticotropin syndrome, 320
Edentulousness, 123
Educational level, nutritional assessment,
  369
Effective renal plasma flow, 257
Electrocardiogram
  hyperkalemia, 66
  hypokalemia, 66
Energy balance, hormonal regulation,
  324–329
  energy intake, 325–327
  energy output, 327–329
Energy intake, 463–464
  bombesin, 326, 327
  cholecystokinin, 326, 327
  decline, 15–16
  dopamine, 325
  estrogen, 327
  gastrin-releasing peptide, 327
  gastrointestinal hormone, 327
  glucagon, 327
  glucocorticoid, 326–327
  gonadal steroid, 327

growth hormone, 326
insulin, 326
monoamine, 325
naloxone, 326
neurohormone, 325
neuropeptide, 326
neuropeptide Y, 326
neurotensin, 326, 327
norepinephrine, 325
opioid, 326
serotonin, 325
somatostatin, 327
substance P, 326, 327
testosterone, 327
thyroid hormone, 327
Energy output
    basal metabolic rate, 327–328
    physical activity, 328
    thermic effect of feeding, 328–329
Energy requirement, aging, 15–17
    estimation, 16–17
Enteral feeding
    complications, 406–408
    delivery, 405–406
    enteral formula selection, 404–405
    gastric feeding, 401–403
    jejunal feeding, 403
    nutritional support, 401–408, 409
    risk factor, 406
    route selection, 401–403
Epidermal growth factor
    kidney, 265–266
    salivary gland, 266
Ergocalciferol, supplements, 70
Erythrocyte hemolysis test, 31
Esophageal dysphagia, 190–191
Esophagus, 184–191
Essential amino acid, requirements, 13–14
Estrogen
    bone mass, 305
    energy intake, 327
Excretion, nutritional status, 348
    drug effects, 348
Exercise, 467–468
    bone density, 302–304

glucose tolerance, risks, 314
Exogenous steroid use, 320–321
Extracellular fluid volume, hyponatremia
    contracted, 56
    expanded, 56–57
    normal, 57
    primary salt depletion, 56

F

Fall, prevention, 469
Fat, 18–20, 419
    calculation, 380
    dietary requirement, 18
Fat absorption, small intestine, 199
Fat–free mass, calculation, 380
Fatty liver, 210–211
Feeding, thermic effect, 328–329
Fiber, 238
    benefits, 20–21
Fluid consumption, 463
Fluorine, oral health effects, 150
Folate, 39–40
    alcohol, 39–40
    function, 39
    recommended daily allowances, 39
    sources, 39
Folate deficiency
    causes, 284
    diagnosis, 284
    megaloblastic anemia, 284
Folic acid, 283–284
    incidence, 283–284
    megadoses, 353
    oral health effects, 150
Food
    drug absorption effects, 350–351
    drug distribution effects, 351
    drug effects, 348–350
    drug metabolism effects, 351–352
    effects on drug therapy, 350–352
Food choice, 344–345
    factors, 344
Food consumption behavior, 425, 426
Food fraud, 474

Food poisoning, 471
Food-purchasing habits, 425, 426
Food record, 389
Food safety, 471, 472–473
Food services, 420–421
Food Stamp Act of 1964, 427
Food stamps, 428, 435
Food supply, 462
Framingham Diet Study, 16, 235–236
Free radical damage, 31–32
Functional limitation, sources, 455

G

Gastric feeding, 401–403
Gastric function, vitamin B_6, 38
Gastrin-releasing peptide, energy intake, 327
Gastritis, 192, 193
Gastroesophageal reflux, 190–191
Gastrointestinal blood loss, iron deficiency, 281
Gastrointestinal hormone, energy intake, 327
Gastrointestinal system, aging, 183–184
Gingiva, aging, 116
Gingivitis, 130
Glomerular filtration rate, aging, 255–257
Glomerular permeability, aging, 261
Glomerular sclerosis, 264
Glossitis, 132
Glossodynia, 132
Glossopyrosis, 132
Glucagon, energy intake, 327
Glucocorticoid, energy intake, 326–327
Glucose, 20
    hyperthyroidism, 318
Glucose tolerance, 311
    chromium, 88, 91
    exercise, risks, 314
    physical activity, 313–314
Gluten-sensitive enteropathy, 202–203
Glycemic index, 313
Gold, oral health effects, 150
Gonadal steroid, energy intake, 327
Growth hormone, 322
    energy intake, 326

H

Hairy tongue, 132–133
Hard palate, 109
Health, nutritional status, 416–417
Health and Nutrition Examination Survey, 16
Health care cost, 6–8, 451
Health fraud, 424, 450, 471–474
Health maintenance organization, Medicare, 440
Health professional training, 474
Health promotion, 449, 452–455
    attitude, 452
    counseling, 454
    criteria, 451–452
    dietary status, 463–466
    nutritional status, 463–466
    planning, 454
    socioeconomic determinants, 461–462
    strategies, 458–474
Health status, quality of life, 5–6
Healthy Older Americans, 428
Hearing, 367
Height and weight table, 375, 377
Hematocrit, 387
Hematopoiesis, 271–285
Hematopoietic system
    aging, 271–273
    pluripotent stem cell, 271–272
Hemoglobin level, 387
Hepatic encephalopathy, 213–214
Hepatitis, 209
    acute, 211–212
High-density lipoprotein, 19, 235–239
Home health agency, Medicare, 440–441
Home health care
    hospital, 7–8
    physician, 7
Home nutritional support, 410
Homeostasis, aging, 343
Hormonal regulation, energy balance, 324–329
    energy intake, 325–327
    energy output, 327–329
Hospice care, Medicare, 441

Hospital, home health care, 7–8
Hypercalcemia, 71–72
  causes, 71
  mechanisms, 71
  symptoms, 71
  therapy, 71–72
Hypercholesterolemia
  dietary control, 19
  dietary treatment, 19
Hyperfiltration, kidney, 263–266
Hyperfusion, kidney, 263–266
Hyperglycemia of aging, 312
  etiology, 312
Hyperkalemia, 64–66
  causes, 65
  clinical manifestations, 65
  electrocardiogram, 66
  kidney, 64
  therapy, 65–66
Hypermagnesemia, 74
Hypernatremia, 59–60
Hyperparathyroidism, 323–324
Hypertension, 241–244
  calorie control, 243
  dietary management, 244
  sodium restriction, 243
Hypertension Detection and Follow-up
  Program, 242–243
Hyperthyroidism
  glucose, 318
  osteopenia, 318
  weight loss, 318
Hypervitaminosis A, 27
Hypoadrenalism, 320
Hypocalcemia, 70
  causes, 70
  etiology, 70
  hypomagnesemia, 70
  treatment, 70
Hypoglycemia, chlorpropamide, 314
Hypogonadism, 322–323
Hypokalemia, 61–64
  alkalosis, 63
  causes, 62
  diuretic therapy, 62

  electrocardiogram, 66
  kidney, 62
  manifestastions, 63
  pathophysiologic mechanisms, 62
  potassium chloride, 63
Hypomagnesemia
  causes, 73
  hypocalcemia, 70
Hyponatremia, 54–57, 320–321
  dilutional, 56–57
  in elderly, 57–59
    antidiuretic hormone, 58
    cause, 58
    prevalence, 57–58
  extracellular fluid volume
    contracted, 56
    expanded, 56–57
    normal, 57
    primary salt depletion, 56
  vasopressin, 58
Hyponatremic syndrome, 55
Hypovitaminosis D, 67

I

Immune response, zinc, 84
Impotence, 322–323
  zinc, 322
Income, malnutrition, 422–423
Inflammatory bowel disease, 204–205
Insulin, energy intake, 326
Insulin growth factor, 322
Iodine, 99
  recommended daily allowances,
    99
  sources, 99
Iodine deficiency, 99
Iron, oral health effects, 150
Iron deficiency
  causes, 282
  gastrointestinal blood loss, 281
  incidence, 280–281
  iron stores, 282
  oral iron, 283
  therapy, 283

Iron deficiency anemia, 280–283
  diagnosis, 280, 281–283
Iron stores, iron deficiency, 282
Ischemic heart disease, vitamin E, 32
Isolated systolic hypertension, 242

J

Jaundice, nonhepatitis causes, 209
Jejunal feeding, 403
Juxtamedullary glomerulus, 254

K

Kidney
  aging, 253–266
    asymptomatic bacteriuria, 262–263
    creatinine clearance, 262
    pathophysiology, 253, 262–263
    renal clearance studies, 253
  compensatory renal hypertrophy, 263
  concentrating ability, 259–260
  diluting ability, 260
  epidermal growth factor, 265–266
  hyperfiltration, 263–266
  hyperfusion, 263–266
  hyperkalemia, 64
  hypokalemia, 62
  renal reserve, 263–266
  sodium, 261

L

Lactose deficiency, 400
Lead, oral health effects, 150
Leukoplakia, 125–126
Life expectancy, 2
Life span, 2
Lingual papillitis, 132
Lip, 107–108
  squamous cell carcinoma, 133
Lipid, 465
Lipid malabsorption syndrome
  retinol, 27
  vitamin A, 27

Lithium, oral health effects, 150
Liver, 207–215
  aging, 207–208
    drug hepatic biotransformation, 341
    drug renal excretion, 342
    function, 208
    fatty, 210–211
    multisystem disease influence, 208–209
    vitamin D, 30
Liver disease
  nutrition, 210–215
  vitamin B_6, 38
Long-term care, 7
  diabetes mellitus, 316
    diet, 316
    weight, 316
    zinc, 316
Longevity
  dietary restriction, 21
  nutrition, 21
Low-density lipoprotein, 19, 234–239
  free radical attack, 32

M

Macroglossia, 133
Macronutrient requirements, 11–22
Magnesium, 72–74
  oral health effects, 150
  recommended dietary allowances, 73
Magnesium deficiency, 73–74
  causes, 73
Male hypogonadism, 322–323
Malnutrition, 154. *See also* Specific type
  frailty, 423–424
  functional capacity loss, 423–424
  income, 422–423
  nutritional assessment, 363
  oral health effects, 154
  oral signs, 159
  poor nutrition knowledge, 424–425
  poverty, 422–423
  risk, 422–425
  social isolation, 423
Mandible, 108

Manganese, 96–98
    function, 97
    oral health effects, 150
    requirements, 97–98
    sources, 97
Manganese deficiency, 97, 98
Marrow function, aging, 272–273
Mastication, 110–111
    aging, 117
Maxilla, 108
Maximal tubular transport capacity, aging, 259
Meals-on-Wheels America, 428, 434
Mechanical stress, bone density, 302–304
Medicaid, 7, 427, 428, 441
Medical model adult day care, 8
Medicare, 7, 427, 428, 437–438
    ambulatory nutrition services, 440
    health maintenance organization, 440
    home health agency, 440–441
    hospice care, 441
    hospital-based care, 438–439
    post-hospital care, 439–440
Megaloblastic anemia, folate deficiency, 284
Menopause
    biochemical effects, 69
    bone mass
        calcium, 305
        parathyroid hormone, 305
    calcium, 69
Metabolism. *See also* Specific type
    food effects, 351–352
    nutritional status, 348
        drug effects, 348
Microbiologic contamination, 471, 472–473
Micronutrient absorption, small intestine, 200
Micronutrient status, diabetes mellitus, 315–316
Mineral, 465–466
Mineral requirements, 53–75
Molybdenum, 95–96
    oral health effects, 150
    sources, 96

Moniliasis, 125
Monoamine, energy intake, 325
Morbidity, sources, 455, 456
Mortality rate, 2
Motility, small intestine, 200–201
Motor skill, 368
Mucositis, 126
Mucous membrane, aging, 116
Muscle strength, bone mass, 302

N

Naloxone, energy intake, 326
National Cholesterol Education Program, 236–237
Necrotizing ulcerative gingivitis, 131
Neonatal ataxia, copper deficiency, 87–88
Neurohormone, energy intake, 325
Neuropeptide, energy intake, 326
Neuropeptide Y, energy intake, 326
Neurotensin, energy intake, 326, 327
Niacin, 37
    megadoses, 353
Nickel, 98–99
    oral health effects, 150
Nickel deficiency, 98
Nonsteroidal anti-inflammatory drug, 193
Norepinephrine, energy intake, 325
Nutrient, oral health effects, 150
Nutrient absorption, drug-induced alteration, 345–347
Nutrient deficiency, 422
    drug-induced, risk factors, 354
    oral manifestations, 156–158
Nutrient supplementation, 345.
    See also Dietary supplement
    drug therapy effects, 352–353
    high-dose vitamin, 353
Nutrition
    diabetes mellitus, 311–316
    liver disease, 210–215
    longevity, 21
    oral health status, 149–164
    periodontal disease, 154
    thyroid disease, 318–319

thyroid hormone, 319
Nutrition education, 434
Nutrition program, 428–429
  community-based, 431–436
Nutrition Program for Older Americans,
  428
Nutrition screening, 427–430
Nutrition services, 415–443
  continuum, 431, 432
  payment systems, 433, 436–437
  providing, 425–431
  recommendations, 420–421
  volunteer services, 435–436
Nutritional assessment, 420–421
  anthropometric assessment, 369–383
  biochemical measures, 383–386
  clinical assessment, 364–369
  cognitive function, 368
  dietary assessment, 387–389
  educational level, 369
  hematologic measures, 387
  immunologic measures, 386–387
  malnutrition, 363
  physical assessment, 364–366
  physical disability, 366–368
  psychologic function, 368
  social support system, 369
  socioeconomic factors, 368–369
Nutritional counseling, 420–421
Nutritional deficiency, clinical signs,
  365–366
Nutritional excess, 419–422
  factors, 419–422
Nutritional status
  absorption, 345–347
    drugs effects, 345–347
  drug effects, 345–350
  excretion, 348
    drug effects, 348
  health, 416–417
  health promotion, 463–466
  metabolism, 348
    drug effects, 348
Nutritional support, 397–411
  commercial liquid supplement, 400–401

dietary supplement, 399–400
enteral feeding, 401–408, 409
home nutritional support, 410
indications, 397–399
oral supplement, 399–401
parenteral nutrition, 408–410

O

Obesity, 369
  blood lipid, 245–246
  blood pressure, 245–246
  cardiovascular disease, 244–246
Old age
  definition, 2
  income, 3
Older Americans Act of 1965, 431
Omega-3 fatty acid, 238
Opioid, energy intake, 326
Oral cancer, 126–128, 161
  cause, 127
  warning signals, 127
Oral cavity
  anatomy, 107–110
  functions, 110–111
Oral examination, 364
Oral health, 107–164
  needs, 113
Oral health status, 111–112
  nutrition, 149–164
  surveys, 112
Oral iron, iron deficiency, 283
Oral manifestation
  drug-induced, 146–148
  systemic diseases, 138–145
Oral mucosa, 124–130
Oral musculature, aging, 117
Oral pain, 162
Oral structure
  aging, 113–119
  disease, 119–137
Oral supplement, 399–401
Oral ulceration, traumatic ulcer, 128
Oropharyngeal dysphagia, 186–190
  treatment, 187–188

Oropharyngeal function assessment, 186
Osteon, 293
Osteopenia, 120, 324
    hyperthyroidism, 318
Osteoporosis, 67–70, 120, 289
    mechanisms, 67
    pathophysiology, 69
    postmenopausal, 67, 289, 290
    senile, 67, 289, 290
    types, 289, 290
Overhydration, 54, 364

P

Pancreas, 193
    aging, 193–194
Pancreatitis
    acute, 195–196
    chronic, 196
        nutritional management, 197
    nutrition, 196
Pantothenic acid, 42
para-Aminohippuric acid clearance,
    257
Parathyroid hormone, 66
    calcium metabolism, 323–324
Parenteral nutrition
    hypertonic glucose solutions, 408
    intravenous fat emulsions, 408
    nutritional support, 408–410
Parotid gland, 109
Peptic ulcer disease, 192–193
Periodontal disease, 130–131
    nutrition, 154
Periodontal ligament, aging, 116
Periodontitis, 130
Periodontium, aging, 116–117
Pharmacodynamics, aging, 342–344
Pharmacokinetics, aging, 339–342
    absorption, 339
    disposition, 340
    excretion, 341–342
    metabolism, 341
Phosphorus, 72
    oral health effects, 150

Physical activity, 467–468
    basal metabolic rate, 16–17
    bone mass, 302–304
    energy output, 328
    glucose tolerance, 313–314
Physical disability, 366–368
Physician, home health care, 7
Plaque, 130
Plaque formation, 149
Pluripotent stem cell, hematopoietic
    system, 271–272
Polypharmacy, 327–338, 470–471
    compliance, 338, 339
Population growth
    by age, 4
    by sex, 4
Potassium, 60–66
Potassium chloride, hypokalemia, 63
Potassium therapy
    azotemia, 65
    diuretic therapy, 63–64
Poverty, 368–369
    malnutrition, 422–423
Primary biliary cirrhosis, 209
Protein, 464–465
    amino acid, 14
    biochemical measurements, 384–386
    body content, 11–12
    distribution, 11–12
    oral health effects, 150
    protein metabolism, 11–15
    quality, 14
    recommended allowance, 15
    renal function, age-related decline, 14–15
    requirements, 11–15
        daily, 12–13
        factors affecting, 14
        measurement, 12
    turnover, 11–12
    vitamin B_6, 37
Protein absorption, small intestine, 199–200
Protein energy malnutrition, 369, 398
    defined, 277
    hematologic manifestations, 276–280
    iron, 276

Pseudocheilosis, 133
Psychologic function, nutritional
    assessment, 368
Public nutrition education, 420–421
Public policy statement, 417, 418
Pyridoxal phosphate, 37

Q

Quality of life
    defined, 5
    health status, 5–6

R

Radiation enteritis, 205–207
    acute, 206–207
    chronic, 207
Receptor, aging, 342–343
Recommended dietary allowances, 459–460
Red marrow, 290
Renal blood flow, aging, 257–259
Renal function, protein, age-related
    decline, 14–15
Renal reserve, kidney, 263–266
Renin, 320
Report on Diet and Health, 459
Reproductive endocrine status, bone mass,
    305–306
Resting metabolic rate, 16
Retinol, 26–28
    absorption, 27
    alcoholism, 28
    body stores, 28
    chronic disease, 27
    chronic liver disease, 27
    functions, 26
    lipid malabsorption syndrome, 27
    plasma/serum levels, 27
    sources, 26
    toxicity, 27
Retinol-binding protein, 386
Riboflavin, 36
    deficiencies, 36
    recommended daily allowances, 36

sources, 36

S

Saliva, 162–163
Salivary gland, 109–110
    aging, 117
    epidermal growth factor, 266
    tumor, 135
Salmonella, 472
Scurvy, 33
Selenium, 91–93
    anticancer agent, 92
    oral health effects, 150
    vitamin E, 91–93
Selenium supplementation, 93
Self-written dietary food record, 389
Senile dementia, aluminum toxicity, 95
Serotonin, energy intake, 325
Serum albumin level, 384–385
Serum calcium, 67
Serum cholesterol, 235–239
    coronary heart disease, 18–19
Serum transferrin, 385
Sex, basal metabolic rate, 15–16
Sexual dysfunction, 322–323
Sialolithiasis, 134–135
Silicon, oral health effects, 150
Skeleton
    aging, 289, 293–300, 301–302
    organization, 289–290
Skinfold measure, 378–379
Small intestine, 198–201
    bacterial overgrowth, 203–204
    carbohydrate absorption, 198–199
    fat absorption, 199
    function, 198–200
    micronutrient absorption, 200
    morphology, 198
    motility, 200–201
    protein absorption, 199–200
Smell, 366–367
    aging, 118–119
Smoking, 468
    vitamin C, 34

Social day care program, 8
Social isolation, malnutrition, 423
Social support system, nutritional
    assessment, 369
Sodium, 53–60, 419
    dehydration, 53–54
    kidney, 261
    water, 53–54
Somatostatin, energy intake, 327
Speech, 111
Squamous cell carcinoma, 127
    lip, 133
Staphylococcus, 472
Stomach, 192–193
Stomatitis, 126
Stomatitis prosthetica, 129–130
Stress, vitamin C, 34
Strontium, oral health effects, 151
Sublingual gland, 110
Submaxillary gland, 109–110
Subscapular skinfold, 379
Substance P, energy intake, 326, 327
Sugar alcohol, 153–154
Sulfonylurea oral hypoglycemic agent,
    diabetes mellitus, 314
Sulfur, oral health effects, 151
Suprailiac skinfold, 379
Surgeon General's Report on Nutrition
    and Health, 459
Swallowing, 111
    oropharyngeal physiology, 186
Systolic pressure, 241–242

T

Taste, 163–164, 366–367
    aging, 118
    zinc deficiency, 83
Taste dysfunction, 137
Temporomandibular joint, 109
    aging, 115–116
    disease, 123–124
Testosterone, 323
    bone mass, 306
    energy intake, 327

Thiamine
    absorption, 35
    diabetes mellitus, 316
    recommended daily allowances, 35
Thiamine hypovitaminemia, 35
Thirst, 60
    reduced, 17–18
Thrush, 125
Thyroid, 317–319
Thyroid disease
    atypic presentations, 317–318
    nutrition, 318–319
    vitamin, 319
Thyroid hormone, 318
    energy intake, 327
    nutrition, 319
Thyrotropin, 317
Thyrotropin-releasing hormone, 317
Thyroxine-binding prealbumin, 386
Tissue sensitivity, aging, 343–344
Title IIIc Nutrition Program for Older
    Americans, 431–434
    education, 434
    evaluation, 433, 433–434
    funding, 433
alpha-Tocopherol, 31, 32
Tongue
    aging, 116–117
    fissured, 131–132
Tooth, 108–109
    abrasion, 122
    aging, 114–115
        attrition, 114–115
    components, 108–109
    erosion, 122
Tooth decay, 121–122
Tooth loss, 123
Total arm length, 372
Total lymphocyte count, 387
Toxicity, vitamin A, 27
Trabeculae, 290
Trabecular bone, 289–290, 291
    aging, 303
    architecture, 301–302
    strength, 301–302

Trace metal requirements, 77–100
Trace mineral, dietary choice, 78
Trace mineral metabolism, 77
Trench mouth, 131
Triceps skinfold, 378–379, 381
Trismus, 134
Tryptophan, 37
Tryptophan loading test, 38
Tumor, salivary gland, 135

U

Ulcerative colitis, 204–205
Ulcerative stomatitis, 124–125
Undernutrition, chronic, 399
Urine
    acidification, 260–261
    osmolality, 260

V

Vanadium, oral health effects, 151
Vasopressin, hyponatremia, 58
Vestibule, 108
Vincent infection, 131
Vision, 367
Vitamin, 465–466
    thyroid disease, 319
Vitamin A, 26–28, 28–30
    absorption, 27
    alcoholism, 28
    body stores, 28
    chronic disease, 27
    chronic liver disease, 27
    functions, 26, 28
    lipid malabsorption syndrome, 27
    oral health effects, 151
    plasma levels, 28–29
    plasma/serum levels, 27
    recommended dietary allowances, 28
    serum levels, 28–29
    sources, 26
    toxicity, 27
Vitamin B_1, 35–36
    absorption, 35

    oral health effects, 151
    recommended dietary allowances, 35
Vitamin B_1 metabolism, 35
Vitamin B_2, 36
    deficiencies, 36
    oral health effects, 151
    recommended dietary allowances, 36
    sources, 36
Vitamin B_6, 37–38
    alcohol, 38
    atrophic gastritis, 38
    gastric function, 38
    liver disease, 38
    oral health effects, 151
    plasma levels, 37
    protein, 37
    recommended dietary allowances, 37
    serum levels, 37
Vitamin B_{12}, 40–42
    absorption, 41
    atrophic gastritis, 41
    deficiency, 40–41, 41
    recommended dietary allowances, 40
Vitamin B_{12} deficiency, diabetes mellitus, 316
Vitamin B_{12} metabolism, 41
Vitamin C, 33–35
    absorption, 34
    levels, 34
    megadoses, 353
    oral health effects, 151
    recommended dietary allowances, 33–34
    smoking, 34
    stress, 34
    supplements, 34
Vitamin D
    calcium absorption, 29
    liver, 30
    megadoses, 353
    oral health effects, 151
    supplementation, 29
Vitamin D endocrine system, age-related changes, 29
Vitamin D malabsorption, 29

Vitamin E, 30–32
  absorption, 31
  ischemic heart disease, 32
  megadoses, 353
  plasma levels, 31
  recommended dietary allowances,
    30–31
  requirements, 31
  selenium, 91–93
  supplements, 31
  vitamin K, 33
Vitamin E supplementation, 93
Vitamin K, 32–33
  anticoagulation therapy, 33
  deficiency, 33
  recommended dietary allowances, 32
  sources, 33
  vitamin E, 33
Volunteer services, nutrition services,
  435–436

W

Water, sodium, 53–54
Water depletion, 54
Water intake, 17–18
Water metabolism, 320–321
Water-soluble fiber, 238
Weight, 370, 373
  average, 376
Weight for height, 370–373
Weight loss, 397–398
  hyperthyroidism, 318
White patch, 125–126

Working Group on Hypertension in the
  Elderly, 242–243
Wound healing, zinc, 83

X

Xerostomia, 135–137
  etiology, 136
  management, 136

Y

Yellow marrow, 290

Z

Zinc
  diet, 78–79
  food content, 80–81
  immune response, 84
  impotence, 322
  oral health effects, 151
  recommended dietary allowances,
    78–79
  wound healing, 83
Zinc absorption, 79
  conditioning factor, 81
Zinc deficiency, 83
  conditions predisposing, 82
  dermatitis, 83
  diabetes mellitus, 315
  symptoms, 83
  taste acuity, 83
Zinc homeostasis, 79